A PRACTICAL TREATISE ON THE OFFICE OF SHERIFF:

COMPRISING THE WHOLE OF

THE DUTIES, REMUNERATION, AND LIABILITIES OF SHERIFFS,

IN THE

EXECUTION AND RETURN OF WRITS,

AND IN

THE ELECTION OF KNIGHTS OF THE SHIRE.

SECOND EDITION.

BY WILLIAM HENRY WATSON, ESQ.
OF LINCOLN'S INN, ONE OF HER MAJESTY'S COUNSEL.

Fred B. Rothman & Co.
Littleton, Colorado
1994

Library of Congress Cataloging-in-Publication Data

Watson, William Henry, 1796-1860.
A practical treatise on the office of sheriff : comprising the whole of the duties, remuneration, and liabilities of sheriffs in the execution and return of writs and in the election of knights of the shire / by William Henry Watson. -- 2nd ed.
p. cm.
Originally published: London : S. Sweet : A. Maxwell : V. & R. Stevens & G.S. Norton, 1848.
Includes index.
ISBN 0-8377-2776-6
1. Sheriffs--Great Britain. 2. Writs--Great Britain. 3. Process--Great Britain. I. Title.
KD7312.W38 1994
347.41'016--dc20
[344.10716]
94-19792
CIP

Printed in United States of America

The paper used in this publication meets the minimum requirements of American National Standard for Information Sciences—Permanence of Paper for Printed Library Materials, ANSI Z39.48-1984.

A PRACTICAL TREATISE ON THE OFFICE OF SHERIFF:

COMPRISING THE WHOLE OF

THE DUTIES, REMUNERATION, AND LIABILITIES OF SHERIFFS,

IN THE

EXECUTION AND RETURN OF WRITS,

AND IN

THE ELECTION OF KNIGHTS OF THE SHIRE.

SECOND EDITION.

By WILLIAM HENRY WATSON, Esq.
OF LINCOLN'S INN, ONE OF HER MAJESTY'S COUNSEL.

LONDON:
S. SWEET; A. MAXWELL & SON; V. & R. STEVENS & G. S. NORTON,
Law Booksellers and Publishers:
HODGES & SMITH, GRAFTON STREET, DUBLIN.

1848.

LONDON:

PRINTED BY C. ROWORTH AND SONS,
BELL YARD, TEMPLE BAR.

ADVERTISEMENT

TO THE SECOND EDITION.

THE extensive changes that have taken place in the law relating to the execution and return of writs, and otherwise in connection with the Office and Duties of the Sheriff, since the publication of this Treatise, have rendered the preparation of a new edition almost as laborious as the original compilation of the Work, and have necessarily added greatly to its bulk. A considerable portion of the Volume was prepared for press by J. S. WILLES, Esq.; the remainder has been completed, and the whole revised, by W. N. WELSBY, Esq. The order of subjects adopted in the First Edition has been preserved, and a Chapter is added on the subject of the Writ of Trial. It is hoped that the great object of a law book—a correct statement of the law as it now exists—has been attained, without unnecessary diffuseness or iteration.

TEMPLE,
October, 1848.

PREFACE

TO THE FIRST EDITION.

THE Author feels no little anxiety in offering the present work, on the Office and Duty of Sheriff, to the Profession at large; conscious that many imperfections and inaccuracies must necessarily be found in a work of this nature.

The Author has attempted to combine the law respecting the office of Sheriff with practical directions for the guidance of Under-sheriffs. How far this has been accomplished the Author leaves to the Profession. The division adopted in the present work differs from that of any other publication on the same subject. In the first three chapters the nature of the office, and the oaths and ceremonies necessary on the first appointment of the Sheriff, are noticed; the fourth chapter treats of the duties of bailiffs of franchises; the fifth chapter enters fully into the duties and powers of the Sheriff in the execution and return of writs in general; and the subsequent chapters embrace the Sheriff's duty on particular writs, classing under the head of each the manner in which it is to be executed; how returned; the fees payable in respect thereof; and the proceedings against the Sheriff for not, or for improperly, executing or returning the writ. Thus, by reference to each head, the manner in which a writ is to be executed and returned will be easily found. In Chap. II., Sect. 2, the Sheriff will find in what manner the office is to be transferred; in Chap. III., Sect. 1, he will find what deputies and officers should be appointed on his entrance into office, and when and in what manner the appointments should be made. The Forms of Warrants and Returns are collected in the Appendix; in the corresponding chapter of which are arranged all the forms belonging to each chapter of the book. Those forms the Author has obtained from gentlemen who have served the office of Under-sheriff, and they have been carefully compared with analogous forms in other works. To the gentlemen who have furnished him with these forms, and with practical information on this subject, the Author acknowledges his obligations.

2, Lamb's Buildings, Temple,
February 1, 1827.

TABLE OF CONTENTS.

CHAP. I.

OF THE OFFICE AND MODE OF ELECTING SHERIFFS.

CHAP. II.

OF THE WARRANT OF APPOINTMENT AND OATHS OF THE NEW SHERIFF; AND THE TRANSFER OF THE OFFICE.

CHAP. III.

OF THE SHERIFF'S OFFICERS; THEIR APPOINTMENT, POWER, AND DUTIES.

CHAP. IV.

OF BAILIFFS OF FRANCHISES.

CHAP. V.

OF THE EXECUTION AND RETURN OF WRITS IN GENERAL.

CHAP. VI.

OF THE SHERIFF'S DUTY ON A BAILABLE CAPIAS.

CHAP. VII.

CAPIAS AD SATISFACIENDUM.

CHAP. VIII.

THE SHERIFF'S DUTY IN THE EXECUTION AND RETURN OF PROCESS OF OUTLAWRY.

CHAP. IX.

HABEAS CORPUS.

CHAP. X.

FIERI FACIAS.

CHAP. XI.

ELEGIT.

CHAP. XII.

HABERE FACIAS POSSESSIONEM.

CHAP. XIII.

WRIT OF INQUIRY.

CHAP. XIV.

WRIT OF TRIAL.

CHAP. XV.

OF THE EXECUTION OF PROCESS IN REAL ACTIONS.

CHAP. XVI.

OF THE EXCHEQUER WRITS.

CHAP. XVII.

OF JURIES, AND OF THE SHERIFF'S DUTY AT SESSIONS AND ASSIZES.

CHAP. XVIII.

OF THE SHERIFF'S COURTS, AND PROCEEDINGS THEREIN.

CHAP. XIX.

OF THE SHERIFF'S DUTY IN THE ELECTION OF MEMBERS OF PARLIAMENT.

CHAP. XX.

CHAP. XXI.

APPENDIX.

THE

OFFICE AND DUTIES OF SHERIFFS.

CHAPTER I.

OF THE OFFICE AND MODE OF ELECTING SHERIFFS.

SECTION I.

Of the Antiquity and Dignity of the Office of Sheriff.

THE sheriff is an officer of great antiquity in this kingdom, his name being derived from two Saxon words, *seyre*, that is, a shire or county, and *reve*, keeper, bailiff, or guardian. And it is said by Camden (*a*), that sheriffs were first appointed by king Alfred, on his division of England into counties. But Lord Coke seems to think that the office is of still greater antiquity, indeed that the sheriffs, shires, and counties, existed in the time of the Romans in this country, and before, and that under the Romans the sheriff was the officer of the consul, and the Romans called that *consulatum*, which we call *comitatum* (*b*). He is certainly

The antiquity of the office.

(*a*) Page 156.

(*b*) Co. Litt. 168 a; Dalt. Sheriff, 5.

CHAP. I. SECT. I.

styled in Latin *vice comes;* as being the deputy of the earl, or *comes;* to whom the custody of the shire is said to have been committed, at the first division of this kingdom into counties. And it seems that earls, by reason of their high employments, and attendance upon the king, being unable to follow all the business of the county, were delivered of all that burthen, and only enjoyed the honour as they now do, and that the labour devolved upon the sheriff; "so that now the sheriff doth all the king's business in the county; and although the sheriff is still called *vice comes,* yet all he doth and all his authority is immediately from and under the king, and not from and under the earl (*c*)."

The dignity and duties of the office.

At this day the sheriff has all the authority, for the administration and execution of justice (excepting so far as it has been abridged by statutes since that time), which the earl or *comes* had; the queen committing to the sheriff the charge or custody of the county; *commisimus vobis custodiam comitatûs nostri de,* &c. (*d*). His office is fourfold. 1st, He is the keeper of the queen's peace within the county, both by the common law and by special commission; and as such he is the first man in the county, and superior to any nobleman therein, during his office(*e*). He may apprehend, and commit to prison, all persons who break the peace, or attempt to break it; and may bind any one in a recognizance to keep the queen's peace. He may, and is bound, *ex officio,* to pursue and take all traitors, murderers, felons, and rioters; he hath also the custody and safe-keeping of the county gaol; he is to defend the same against rioters, and for this purpose, as well as for taking rioters and others breaking the peace, and also for attending the queen to the war when enemies come; he may command all the people of his county to attend him, which is called the *posse comitatus,* or power of the county, and this summons every person above fifteen years old, and under the degree of a peer, is bound to attend upon warning, under pain of fine and imprisonment(*f*).

Conservator of the peace.

(*c*) Dalt. 2; Co. Litt. 168 a.

(*d*) Co. Litt. 168; 9 Rep. 49; Dalt. 2; 1 Bl. Com. 339. This charge is said by Lord Coke to be threefold. 1st. *Vitæ justitiæ;* for no suit begins, and no process is served, but by the sheriff; also he is to return indifferent juries for the trial of men's lives, liberties, lands, goods, &c. 2ndly. *Vitæ legis;* he is, after long suits, chargeable to make execution, which is the life and fruit of the law. 3rdly. *Vitæ reipublicæ;* he is *principalis conservator pacis* within the countie, which is the life of the commonwealth, *vita reipublicæ pax.*

(*e*) 1 Roll. Rep. 337.

(*f*) Stat. 2 Hen. 5, c. 8.

CHAP. I. SECT. I.

The ministerial duty of the sheriff in executing writs.

2dly, In his ministerial capacity, the sheriff is bound to execute within his county or bailiwick, all process issuing from the queen's superior courts of justice. On bailable process, he is to execute the writ, to arrest, and to take bail; when the cause comes to trial, he must summon and return the jury; and when it is determined, he must execute the judgment of the court. In criminal matters, he also arrests and imprisons; he returns the jury; he has the custody of the delinquent, and he executes the sentence of the court, though it extend to death itself (*g*).

The sheriff is also bound to execute the precepts of commissioners of sewers, of coroners, and verderers, and, as will be more fully detailed hereafter, to attend the judges of the superior courts of law on their circuits, and execute all their lawful commands.

The custody of gaols.

He has also the custody of the gaol of his county, and this duty cannot be transferred by the crown to any other officer (*h*).

To collect the queen's revenues, &c.

3dly, As the queen's bailiff, he must seize into the queen's hands all lands devolved to the crown by attainder or escheat; must levy all fines and forfeitures; must seize and keep all waifs, wrecks, estrays, and the like, unless they be granted to some subject; and must also collect the queen's rents within his bailiwick, if commanded by process out of the Exchequer (*i*).

His judicial capacity; county courts: election of members of parliament.

4thly, In his judicial capacity he is to hear and determine all causes of 40*s*. value and under by plaint, or to any amount by *writ of justicies*, in his county court; and also to make, to hear, and determine replevins, and other suits in his county court. Also, in the course of the suit it may become his duty to preside as judge at the execution of writs of trial, or of inquiry of damages. He formerly held pleas of the crown in his torne; but by *Magna Charta*, he, together with the constable, coroner, and certain other officers of the crown, are forbidden to hold any pleas of the crown. He is likewise to decide the elections of knights of the shire (subject to the control of the House of Commons), of coroners, and of verderers; and to return such as he shall determine to be elected.

Authority co-extensive of his county.

The sheriff hath no power or authority out of his county (*k*);

(*g*) 1 Bla. Com. 444; see R. *v*. Antrobus, 2 Ad. & El. 788.

(*h*) Mytton's case, 4 Rep. 32 b.

(*i*) Dalt. c. 9, c. 5.

(*k*) Le Count de Northumberland *v*. Le Count de Devon, 2 Roll. Rep. 163; Plowd. 37 a.

CHAP. I. SECT. I.

excepting where he is commanded by a writ of *habeas corpus* to convey a prisoner out of his county: and then, if the sheriff convey his prisoner through several counties, yet the prisoner is in the custody of the sheriff in every one of those counties (*m*); and excepting also, where a prisoner of his own wrong, without the consent of the sheriff or gaoler, make an escape, and fly into another county, the sheriff or his officers, upon fresh pursuit, may take him again in another county (*n*). The sheriff, however, may do mere ministerial acts out of his county, as making a panel or any return (*o*), or assigning a bail bond (*p*); but it is said, that if the sheriff make a panel or a return when he is out of England, it is void; for he is an officer only in England (*q*).

Qualification for the office of sheriff.

Because the office of sheriff is of high trust and confidence, "it is meet," says Dalton, "that such persons as be chosen thereunto be men of good sufficiency, and such as may attend it, lest otherwise the king be much indamaged, and his people be disinherited and oppressed; and for that purpose, the statutes made 9 Edw. 2, *de vice comitibus;* 2 Edw. 3, c. 4; 4 Edw. 3, c. 9; and 5 Edw. 3, c. 4, have ordained, that no man shall be sheriff in any county except he have sufficient lands within the same county where he shall be sheriff, whereof to answer the king and his people, in case any man shall complain against him." At the present day the most opulent and respectable commoners in each county fill the office of sheriff (*r*). By stat. 9 Edw. 2, Lincoln, it is enacted "that no steward or bailiff to any great lord be made sheriff, (except he be put forth of service), but such persons only shall be appointed as may wholly attend to the king and his people."

Who are exempt or disqualified from serving the office.

By the stat. 1 Rich. 2, c. 11, (which does not extend to the sheriffs of a town corporate, although a county in itself (*s*),) it is ordained, that none that hath been sheriff of any county by an whole year, shall be within three years next ensuing chosen

(*m*) Plowd. 37 a.

(*n*) Dalt. 23; Plowd. 37 a.

(*o*) Dalt. 22.

(*p*) Gregson *v.* Heather, 2 Lord Raym. 1455; 2 Stra. 727, S. C.

(*q*) 9 Hen. 4, 1; Bro. Officer, 7; Dalt. 22.

(*r*) "In ancient times this office was frequently executed by the nobility, and persons of the highest rank in the kingdom. *Eligebantur olim ad hoc officium potentissimi sæpenumero totius regni proceres, barones, comites, duces, interdum et regum filii.*—Spel. Glos. *Vicecom.* Bishops also were not unfrequently sheriffs. Richard, Duke of Gloucester (afterwards Richard 3) was sheriff of Cumberland five years together." 1 Bla. Com. 346, note, Christian's edition.

(*s*) R. *v.* Haythorne, 5 B. & C. 529, n.

again, or put in the same office of sheriff, if there be other sufficient in the said county of possessions and goods to answer to the king and to his people" (*t*); and by the stat. 23 Hen. 6, c. 8, whosoever shall take upon him to have or occupy the office of sheriff by any grant or patent thereafter to be made for years, life, in fee, or in tail, shall stand for ever and at all times disabled to be or bear the office of sheriff within any county of England, and liable to forfeit 200*l*. As the queen has an interest in every subject, and a right to his service, it is a general rule that no man can be exempt from the office of sheriff but by act of parliament, or letters patent (*u*): but if a man is disabled by judgment or process of law, as imprisonment for debt, to bear an office, he is excused, *nam judicium redditur in invitum* (*x*); yet where he may remove the disability, as in case of excommunication, he shall take no advantage of his disability (*y*). Another exception exists in the case of practising barristers and attornies, who are exempt by reason of the incompatibility of the office with their professional duties (*z*). And the same it would seem in the case of members of parliament (*a*). By 2 Geo. 2, c. 20, a militia officer while on service is exempt.

The question formerly agitated, whether or not persons elected sheriffs in corporate towns were exempt from serving the office of sheriff by reason of their being dissenters, or of not having taken the sacrament as required by the stat. 13 Car. 2, c. 2, s. 1 (*b*), and for many years settled by a decision of the House of Lords, where it was decided that a dissenter, or person not complying with the provisions of the 13 Car. 2, was wholly disabled from serving the office (*c*), was finally set at rest by the statute of 9 Geo. 4, c. 17, (explained by 5 & 6 Will. 4, c. 28,)

(*t*) By the stat. 9 Geo. 1, c. 3, s. 9, the sheriff of Norwich, on payment of a fine of 300*l*., is exempted from serving the office: but by paying the fine it was held that he was only exempt for one year; Rex *v.* Woodrow, 2 T. R. 731. See also Rex *v.* Bower, 2 Dowl. & Ry. 842; 1 Bar. & Cress. 585, S. C.

(*u*) Earl of Shrewsbury's case, 9 Rep. 46; Moore, 111; Pelham's case, Saville, 43.

(*x*) Rex *v.* Larwood, 1 Salk. 169; 1 Ld. Raym. 29; 4 Mod. 273, S. C.

(*y*) The Attorney-General *v.* Read, 2 Mod. 299.

(*z*) Mayor of Norwich *v.* Berry, 4 Burr. 2114.

(*a*) Resolution of the House of Commons, 7th January, 1689; 1 Roe on Elections, 161.

(*b*) Rex *v.* Larwood, 1 Salk. 167; Lord Raym. 29, S. C.; 4 Mod. 269; Eyre, J. *dissentiente*, with whom the Lord Keeper is said to have coincided in opinion; Mayor, &c. of Guildford, *v.* Clarke, 2 Vent. 247.

(*c*) Harrison *v.* Evans, 2 Burn's Ecc. L. 185; 6 Bro. P. C. 181; cit. in Cowp. 535, *ib.* 393 n.; Bac. Abr. Sheriff (B.)

CHAP. I. SECT. I.

which makes dissenters eligible to the office. And since 5 & 6 Will. 4, c. 28, a Jew has been one of the sheriffs of London.

How punished for refusing the office.

If a person refused to take upon him the office of sheriff, when appointed, it was usual to punish him in the Star Chamber; but now he may be proceeded against by indictment or information in the Queen's Bench (*d*). Also, if he refuse to take the oaths enjoined him, or officiate in his office before he is thus qualified, that court, which hath a general superintendency over all officers and ministers of justice, will grant an information against him. It has been held, that a refusal to take the oaths amounts to a refusal of the office (*e*). By particular statutes, or the bye laws of cities and towns, (which, being counties, have sheriffs,) certain pecuniary penalties are inflicted upon persons refusing to take upon them the office when elected, and those penalties are recoverable by action (*f*).

He need not reside in his county.

By the statute of 4 Hen. 4, c. 7, it was ordained, "that every sheriff of England shall abide in proper person within his bailiwick for the time that he should be such officer;" and this formed part of the oath of both the sheriffs of England and Wales. But it would appear that this statute is repealed in this respect by the statute of 3 Geo. 1, c. 15, ss. 18, 20; for by the oath of office directed by that act to be taken, it is not required of either the sheriffs of England or Wales to swear that they will be resident in their counties.

He cannot be a magistrate or a member for the county.

By the statute of 1 Mary, st. 2, c. 8, s. 2, sheriffs are disqualified from acting as justices of the peace during the continuance of their office, and all acts done by them as justices of the peace are void. And it is holden, that the sheriff cannot be elected a knight of the shire for the county of which he is sheriff (*g*).

Not to serve the office above one year.

In former times, the sheriffs held their offices for a term of years, of the king's grant, and great oppressions having resulted therefrom, it was ordained and established, by divers acts of parliament, "that no sheriff (*h*), under-sheriff (*i*), or sheriff's clerk, shall tarry or abide in his office, or shall occupy the said office above one year, upon pain of forfeiting 200*l*. yearly as

(*d*) Dalt. 15; Rex *v*. Woodrow, 2 T. R. 731.

(*e*) Starr *v*. The Mayor of Exeter, 3 Lev. 116; 2 Show. 158, S. C.; Carth. 307.

(*f*) See *post*, tit. Sheriffs of London, &c.

(*g*) 4 Inst. 48; Litt. Rep. 326.

(*h*) 14 Edw. 3, stat. 1, c. 7; 28 Edw. 3, c. 7.

(*i*) 42 Edw. 3, c. 9; 23 Hen. 6, c. 8.

long as he occupieth the office:" and every pardon made for such offence, occupation, or forfeiture shall be void; and all letters patent (*k*) made to occupy such office for term of years, for term of life, in fee simple or in fee tail, shall be void, any words or clause of *non obstante* put into such patent notwithstanding, and whosoever shall presume to take upon him to occupy the office of sheriff above one year, by virtue of such grant or patent, shall be disabled for ever after to be sheriff within any county of England; and any man, who will, may sue for the said sum of 200*l.* so forfeited against such sheriff, under-sheriff, or sheriff's clerk, in any action of debt, in his own name, and the king shall have the one moiety of all that which is recovered, and he that sueth shall have the other moiety (*l*). By the statute of the 6 Hen. 8, c. 18, all persons inheritable to the office of sheriff in any county, and the sheriff, under-sheriff, and other officers in London and Bristol, are excepted out of these statutes. And by other statutes (*m*) it is enacted, that every old sheriff of every county shall have full power, and may occupy his office, as also do and execute every other thing to his office of a sheriff appertaining, during the terms of St. Michael and Hilary, (after the year that their office is ended,) unless before the same time he be lawfully discharged.

Office when and how determined.

The sheriff holds his office only during the queen's pleasure, although he cannot remain therein above one year; and therefore, during his year, his office may be determined by the crown (*n*). The office is not determined by the sheriff becoming a peer, but he continues sheriff notwithstanding (*o*). But the office of sheriff cannot be determined, nor any part thereof, by the crown, until a new sheriff is appointed. Although the queen may determine the office at her pleasure, yet she cannot determine it in part, as for one town or one hundred,

(*k*) It is clear that the king might have dispensed with these statutes; but by the Bill of Rights, in this respect the prerogative was abrogated. Mr. Justice Blackstone, in his Commentaries, vol. i. p. 342, says, that it seems that the sheriff may be appointed *durante bene placito*; and so was the form of the royal writ, as given in Dalton, and of the warrant of appointment under 3 & 4 Will. 4, c. 99, Schedule, *post*, p. 16; and see 4 Rep. 32. It is apprehended that a sheriff could not be continued in office for more than one year at this day; indeed, a few lines before Mr. Justice Blackstone had shown how the prerogative had been abridged by the Bill of Rights. 2 Hawk. P. C. c. 37.

(*l*) 23 Hen. 6, c. 8; 6 Hen. 6, c. 18.

(*m*) 12 Edw. 4, c. 1; 17 Edw. 4, c. 6; Cromp. 208 b.

(*n*) Finch, 11.

(*o*) Sir Lewis Mordaunt's case, Cro. Eliz. 12.

CHAP. I. SECT. I.

or any other part; neither can she abridge the sheriff of any thing incident or belonging to his office, for the office is entire and indivisible (*p*). The office formerly determined by the death of the king or queen, but now, by the stat. 1 Anne, s. 1, c. 8, all officers appointed by the preceding king or queen may hold their offices for six months, unless sooner displaced by the successor. And also by the death of the sheriff himself the office is determined; and, formerly, between the death of the old sheriff and the appointment of the new, the prisoners were in the custody of the law, and not of the under-sheriff; and the party had no remedy for an escape of a prisoner during that time (*q*); but now, by the stat. of 3 Geo. 1, c. 15, s. 8, where the sheriff dies before the determination of his office, it is enacted, "that the under-sheriff, or deputy sheriff, by him appointed, shall, nevertheless, continue in his office, and shall execute the same, and all things belonging thereunto, in the name of the deceased sheriff, until another sheriff be appointed for the said county, and sworn as directed; and the said under-sheriff, or deputy-sheriff, shall be answerable for the execution of the said office in all things, and to all respects, intents and purposes whatsoever, during such interval as the high sheriff so deceased would by law have been, if he had been living; and the security given to the high sheriff so deceased, by the said under-sheriff, and his pledges, shall stand and remain, and be a security to the king, his heirs and successors, and to all persons whatsoever, for such under-sheriff's due performance of his office during such interval."

When sheriff's power ceases on discharge.

Before the 3 & 4 Will. 4, c. 99, it was held, that until the writ of discharge was delivered to the sheriff, he might lawfully exercise the duties of his office (*r*). But if, after he had notice of his discharge, he made his warrant or precept to any of his late bailiffs or officers to arrest another, and the officer by force thereof arrested the party, an action of false imprisonment would lie against both the sheriff and the officer (*s*). The same law would probably now be held applicable, after the lapse of a rea-

(*p*) Dalt. Sheriff, 6; Mitton's case, 4 Rep. 33; Norton *v.* Simmes, Hob. 13.

(*q*) Westby's case, 3 Rep. 72; Cro. Eliz. 366, S.C. See also 1 Mod. 14.

(*r*) St. John's case, Moor. 186, 364; Fitz's case, Cro. Eliz. 12; Boucher *v.* Wiseman, Cro. Eliz. 440; Dyer, 355, in marg.; Dalt. 18. See also 12 Edw. 4, c. 1; 17 Edw. 4, c. 6.

(*s*) Dyer, 41, 355, in marg.; Dalt. 18.

sonable time for completing the transfer under 3 & 4 Will. 4, c. 99, s. 7.

Transfer of writs, &c.

The law relative to the transfer of process and prisoners by the old to the new sheriff, and consequent discharge of the responsibility of the former, will be found in a subsequent chapter.

Section II.

Sheriffs, how and when elected.

How and when elected.

Sheriffs were formerly chosen by the inhabitants of their respective counties; in confirmation of which it was ordained by the statute of 28 Edw. 1, c. 8 and 13, that "the people should have the election of sheriffs in every shire, when the shrievalty is not of inheritance." For anciently, in some counties, the office of sheriff was hereditary; as, at this day, the shrievalty of the county of Westmoreland is hereditary in the Earl of Thanet; and also as the shrievalty of the county of Middlesex is vested in the city of London by charter (*t*). But, by the statute of the 9th of Edw. 2, s. 2, this popular mode of election was done away; for by that statute it was enacted, that "the sheriffs should thenceforth be chosen or assigned yearly by the chancellor, treasurer, and the judges;" and the election is required to be annually, on the morrow of All Souls, in the Exchequer (*u*). The statute of Cambridge, 12 Rich. 2, c. 2, ordains, that the chancellor, treasurer, keeper of the privy seal, steward of the king's house, the king's chamberlain, clerk of the rolls, the justices of one bench and the other, the barons of the exchequer, and all other that shall be called to ordain, name, or

(*t*) Mr. Justice Blackstone, in his Commentaries, vol. i. p. 340, makes the following observation on this ancient mode of election:—"The reason of these popular elections is assigned in the same statute, c. 13, 'that the commons might choose such as would not be a burden to them.' And herein appears plainly a strong trace of the democratical part of our constitution; in which form of government it is an indispensable requisite that the people should choose their own magistrates. This election was in all probability not absolutely vested in the commons, but required the royal approbation. For in the Gothic constitution the judges of the county courts (which office is executed by the sheriff) were elected by the people, but confirmed by the king; and the form of the election was thus managed: the people, or *incolæ territorii*, chose *twelve* electors, and they nominated three persons, *ex quibus rex unum confirmabat*." *Stiernh. de Jure Goth.* l. 1, c. 3.

(*u*) 9 Edw. 2, s. 2; 14 Edw. 3, c. 17; 23 Hen. 6, c. 8.

CHAP. I. SECT. II.

make justices of the peace, *sheriffs*, and other officers of the king, shall be sworn to act indifferently, and to appoint no man that sueth, either privately or openly, to be put in office, but such only as they shall judge most sufficient (*x*). And the custom now is (and has been, at least ever since the time of Fortescue, who was chief justice and chancellor to Henry the Sixth), that all the judges, together with the other great officers and privy councillors, meet in the Exchequer on the morrow of All Souls, yearly (which day is now altered to the morrow of St. Martin, by the last act for abbreviating Michaelmas term), and then and there the judges propose three persons, to be reported (if approved of) to the queen, who afterwards appoints one of them sheriff (*y*).

This mode of nominating *three* persons, from whom the queen is to choose one, is supposed by Blackstone to have originated in some statute which cannot now be found; and he draws the conclusion, which is a very just one, from the entry in the council book, 3d March, 34 Hen. 6, which Lord Coke (*z*) says he copied from the council book with his own hand. The case was, that the king had, of his own authority, appointed a man sheriff of Lincolnshire, which office he refused to take upon him; whereupon the opinions of the judges were taken, what should be done in this behalf. And the two chief justices, Sir John Fortescue and Sir John Prisot, delivered the unanimous opinion of them all: "that the king did an error when he made a person sheriff that was not chosen and presented to him according to the *statute;* that the person refusing was liable to no fine for disobedience, as if he had been *one of the three* chosen according to the tenor of the *statute;* that they would advise the king to have recourse to the *three* persons that were chosen according to the *statute;* or that some other thrifty man be intreated to occupy the office for this year; and that the next year, in eschewing such inconveniences, the order of the *statute* in this behalf made be observed."

The king has no power to make a compulsory appointment.

This extract proves one thing, which the stat. 34 & 35 Hen. 8, c. 26, s. 61, expressly recognizes, that the king has no power to name any person to be sheriff whom he pleases, unless such person is nominated in the usual way. But as long as the king was held to have (or rather before he was deprived of) the dis-

(*x*) See also 5 & 6 Edw. 6, c. 16.
(*y*) 1 Bla. Com. 340; 24 Geo. 2, c. 48, c. 12.
(*z*) 2 Inst. 559.

pensing power, he was supposed to possess the prerogative of naming whom he pleased to be sheriff. Although the practice of naming pocket-sheriffs has existed since the Revolution, yet no case of a compulsory appointment has occurred.

Sheriff of Durham.

The sheriff of Durham, previously to the 6 & 7 Will. 4, c. 19, (by which the palatinate jurisdiction was transferred to the crown,) used to be appointed by the bishop during his pleasure. But since the passing of that act he is appointed by the crown.

Sheriffs of Wales.

Formerly, the sheriffs of Welch counties were nominated yearly by the lord president, council, and justices of Wales, the names of persons were certified by those officers, and one person was afterwards chosen and elected by the king, as other sheriffs; but by the stat. of 1 W. & M. c. 27, s. 4, the nomination of three proper persons to be sheriff of each of the Welch counties was vested in the justices of the great sessions, who were to certify the names of such persons to the privy council, *crastino animarum*, that the king might appoint out of them; and by the 19th section of 11 Geo. 4 & 1 Will. 4, c. 70, (which abolishes the courts of great session,) this power has been vested in the judges of assize.

By the stat. 34 Hen. 8, c. 26, the sheriffs of Wales shall have full power within their sheriffwick to do as the sheriffs of England; and shall accomplish and execute all the lawful commandments and precepts of the justices, &c., and of coroners, in all things appertaining to their offices and authorities.

Sheriff of Westmoreland.

The shrievalty of Westmoreland is hereditary in the family of the Earl of Thanet, and descends as well to females as to males, for Ann Countess of Pembroke exercised the office in person (*a*).

Sheriffs of cities and towns corporate.

There are also many cities and towns which by charter are counties of themselves, and had sheriffs even before the Municipal Corporation Act (5 & 6 Will. 4, c. 76). Thus the cities of London (which is exempt from the operation of that act), York, Bristol, Coventry, Chester, Gloucester, Lincoln and Norwich are counties, and even before the Municipal Corporation Act had each two sheriffs; and the cities of Canterbury, Exeter, Lichfield and Worcester, and the towns of Southampton, Kingston-upon-Hull, Nottingham, Poole, Newcastle-upon-Tyne, Carmarthen and Haverfordwest, are counties, and even before that

(*a*) Harg. Co. Litt. 326. Cumberland is also said to be hereditary by a charter of King John; Impey.

CHAP. I. SECT. II.

act had each one sheriff. Since the Municipal Corporation Act the cities of Oxford and Berwick-upon-Tweed, as well as the above-named cities and towns, have been empowered by the 61st section to elect sheriffs, through the municipal council, on the 1st of November in each year. But the sheriffs elected in pursuance of that act in places where previously there was no officer on whom the duty of sheriff devolved, have not, like the sheriffs of those cities and towns which formerly were and still are *counties* corporate, the execution of process, that duty still rests on the same shoulders as before the act passed (*b*). Within the limits of the counties corporate already enumerated, the duties of the shrievalty must be performed by their own sheriffs.

Of the sheriffs of London and Middlesex.

The city of London claims by prescription the right to elect *two* sheriffs for the city (*c*). These are two officers, and are styled the *sheriffs* of London. And by a charter of Hen. 1, confirmed by King John, the shrievalty of Middlesex was granted to the citizens of London, with all customs belonging both within the city and without. The sheriffs of London are always sheriff of Middlesex; but in Middlesex the two persons are styled *sheriff;* and although the same persons are *sheriff of Middlesex* and *sheriffs of London*, yet as sheriffs of London, on a writ directed to them, they have no authority to execute it in Middlesex, and so *è converso* (*d*).

How elected.

The qualifications for, and the exemptions from, the offices of sheriff of London and Middlesex, and also the mode of their election, are regulated by bye laws of the city. By one of which bye laws, an act of council, 7th of April, 1748, it is enacted that from thenceforth the right of election to the shrievalties of London and Middlesex shall be vested in the liverymen of the several companies of the city, assembled in the Guildhall for that purpose; the election to take place annually on the 24th day of June, unless that day be a Sunday, and then the day after; and in case of vacancy, the lord mayor may

(*b*) Granger *v.* Taunton, 3 Bing. N. C. 64; 5 Dowl. 190, S. C.

(*c*) London had no sheriffs in the 13 Edw. 1; 1 Leon. 284. In Nicol *v.* Boyne, 2 Dowl. 761; 3 M. & S. 812; 10 Bing. 339, S. C., Tindal, C. J., said, that London has two sheriffs *by a grant of King John—quære.*

(*d*) See Hammond *v.* Taylor, 3 Bar. & Ald. 408. And a person in Newgate, in custody of the sheriff of London, cannot be detained on a writ directed and delivered to the sheriff of Middlesex, for the prisons are several and distinct. 1 Roll. Abr. 894. As to improper direction of writs to these officers, see *post*, chap. 5, s. 1.

appoint a day of election; the new sheriffs are to take upon them the office on the vigil of St. Michael, and to hold it until that time in the ensuing year.

By whom nominated. The lord mayor may nominate to the court of aldermen, between the 14th of April and the 14th of June in every year, one or more fit persons, (not exceeding nine,) being free of the city, to be publicly put in nomination; also any two or more liverymen at the day of election may nominate any freeman of the city as a proper person to be elected.

Fine for being excused the office. Any person nominated by the lord mayor may discharge himself from such nomination, and the serving of the office of sheriff for ever, unless he become an alderman, by paying, after six days' notice, 400*l.* and twenty marks to the chamberlain, for certain purposes by that act of council declared; and by another act of council, 11th of June, 1799, any person either elected or nominated may be discharged from such nomination or election, by making affidavit before the court of aldermen that he is not worth 20,000*l.* in lands, goods, and separate debts, supported also by the oaths of six other citizens and freemen of the city that they believe his affidavit to be true.

Sheriffs elect are to appear on the 14th of September after their election, before the court of aldermen, to enter into an obligation in the penal sum of 1000*l.* to the chamberlain of the city, conditioned to appear on Michaelmas day at the Guildhall, and to take upon them the oath (*e*) usually taken by the sheriffs

(*e*) The oath to be taken by the sheriffs of London and Middlesex at Guildhall on Michaelmas day is as follows: " Ye shall swear, that ye shall be good and true unto our sovereign lady the queen of *England*, and unto her heirs and successors; and the franchise of the city of London, within and without, ye shall save and maintain to your power; and ye shall well and lawfully keep the shires of *London* and *Middlesex*; and the offices that to the same shires appertain to be done, well and lawfully ye shall do after your wit and power; and right ye shall do, as well to poor as rich, and good custom ye shall not break, no evil custom arrere, and the assize bread, all and all other victuals within the franchise of this city, and without, well and lawfully ye shall keep and do to be kept, and the judgments and executions of your court ye shall not tarry without cause reasonable; ne right shall you none disturb. The writs that to you come touching the state and franchise of this city, you shall not return, till you have showed them to the mayor and the council of this city for the time being, and of them had advisement, and ready you shall be at reasonable warning of the mayor, for keeping of the peace, and maintaining the state of this city; and all other things that longen to your office, and the keeping of the said shires, lawfully you shall do, by you and yours; and the city you shall keep from harm after your power, and the shire of Middlesex; ne the gaol

CHAP. I. SECT. II.

of London and Middlesex. And in case such sheriffs, elected at the general election day, do not appear on the 14th of September to take the oath; or, if elected between the 14th and 22nd of September, do not take the oath on Michaelmas day; or, if elected at any other period, do not within six days after notice of election take the oath, they are subject to a penalty, if an alderman of the city, or a commoner nominated by the lord mayor, of 600*l.*; or if any other freeman, of 400*l.*

Persons disqualified.

Any person who has paid the fine, unless he afterwards become an alderman, is exempt from serving the office; and no person who has once served the office of sheriff of London, or sheriff of Middlesex, is again eligible.

of Newgate you shall not let to farm. *As help you God.*

Addition.

Ye shall also swear that ye shall freely give all such rooms and offices of serjeants and yeomen, as shall happen to become void during the time of ye shall remain in the office of sheriffalty, to such apt and able person and persons, as shall be by you nominated to the lord mayor and court of aldermen, and by them admitted, without any money or other reward to be had, taken or hoped for in respect thereof, according to the act of council made and provided in that behalf, the nine-and-twentieth day of April, in the six-and-twentieth year of the reign of our sovereign lady Queen Elizabeth, &c. *As help you God.*" The next day the sheriffs attend at the Exchequer before the cursitor baron, to be sworn, and to pay the fees, &c.

CHAPTER II.

OF THE WARRANT OF APPOINTMENT AND OATHS OF THE NEW SHERIFF; AND THE TRANSFER OF THE OFFICE.

SECT. I.—*The Sheriff's Warrant of Appointment.*

II.—*The Sheriff's Oath of Office, how and before whom taken.—The Declaration and Oaths at Sessions, when and how to be taken.*

III.—*Of the Transfer of the Office.—Of the Assignment of Writs; of Prisoners.—When the Authority of the Sheriff ceases.—Of the Liabilities of the old Sheriff after expiration of his office.—Apportionment of Fees between the old and the new Sheriff on a* Levari Facias.

SECTION I.

The Sheriff's Warrant of Appointment.

CHAP. II. SECT. I.

FORMERLY sheriffs were appointed by patent, but their appointment is now governed by the act of 3 & 4 Will. 4, c. 99 (*a*), which, after reciting, *inter alia,* that the appointment of sheriffs is attended with unnecessary expense, delay, and trouble, and partly repealing the acts of 3 Geo. 1, c. 15 and 16, proceeds to enact by the second section,

Sheriffs not to sue out patent or pass accounts in Exchequer.

" That from and after the passing of this act it shall not be " necessary for any sheriff or sheriffs of any county, city, or " town in England or Wales to sue out any patent or writ of " assistance, or to make or pay proffers, nor shall any bailiff or " bailiffs of liberties in England or Wales be required to make " or pay any proffers, nor shall he or they have any day of pre- " fixion, or be apposed, or take any oath or oaths before the " cursitor baron to account, or account or be cast out of court,

(*a*) See Appendix.

CHAP. II. SECT. I.

"as now or heretofore in use in his majesty's Court of Exchequer, any law, statute, or usage to the contrary notwithstanding."

Appointment of sheriff.

And the third section enacts, "that whenever any person "shall be duly pricked or nominated by his majesty for and to "be sheriff of any county in England or Wales, except the "county palatine of Lancaster, the same shall be forthwith notified in the London Gazette, and a warrant in the form set forth "in the schedule to this act shall be forthwith made out and "signed by the clerk of the privy council, and transmitted by "him to the person so nominated and appointed sheriff as aforesaid; and the appointment of sheriff thereby made shall be "as good, valid, and effectual in the law, to all intents and purposes whatsoever, as if the same had been made by patent "under the great seal of Great Britain, or by any ways and "means heretofore in use; and the sheriff and sheriffs so appointed as aforesaid shall thereupon, and upon taking the oath "of office hereafter mentioned, have and exercise all powers, "privileges, and authorities whatsoever usually exercised and "enjoyed by sheriffs of counties in England and Wales, without "any patent, writ of assistance, or other writ whatsoever, or "entering into any recognizance by himself or sureties, and "without payment of or being liable to pay any fees whatsoever "for the same."

Clerk of peace to enrol duplicate.

And the fourth section enacts, "that a duplicate of the said "warrant shall, within ten days next after the date of the same "warrant, be transmitted by the said clerk of the privy council "to the clerk of the peace of the county for which such person "shall be nominated and appointed sheriff, to be by the said "clerk of the peace enrolled, and which he is hereby required "to enrol and keep without fee or reward."

The form of the warrant is given by the schedule of the act, and is as follows:—

"*At the Court at , the Day of . Present, the Queen's most Excellent Majesty in Council.*

"*To A. B. of, &c.*

"*Whereas her majesty was this day pleased, by and with the advice of her privy council, to nominate and appoint you for and to be sheriff of the county of during her majesty's pleasure: These are therefore to require you to take the custody and charge of the said county, and duly to perform the duties of sheriff thereof during her majesty's pleasure; and whereof you are duly to answer according to law.*

"*Dated this day of .*

"*By her majesty's command.*
"*C. D.*"

Section II.

Of the Oaths of Office.

The oaths to be taken by sheriffs.

The 3 & 4 Will. 4, c. 99, s. 6, enacts, "that each and every person so appointed sheriff and under-sheriff as aforesaid, except the sheriffs of London and Middlesex and their under-sheriffs, shall before he enter upon the execution of his office take the *oath of office* heretofore and now required by law, which oath shall be fairly written on parchment (without being subject to any stamp duty) and signed by him, and shall and may be sworn before the barons of his majesty's Exchequer or any of them, or any one of his majesty's justices of the peace for the county of which he shall be appointed sheriff or under-sheriff; and the same shall be thereupon transmitted to the clerk of the peace for the same county, who is hereby required to file the same among the records of his office, and for which he shall be entitled to demand and have from such sheriff or under-sheriff the sum of five shillings and no more."

The oaths required are in general the oaths of allegiance, supremacy, and abjuration (*b*), or in case of a Roman Catholic, the oath prescribed by 10 Geo. 4, c. 7, which is substituted for the oaths of allegiance, supremacy, and abjuration, and in all cases the "oath of office" prescribed by the statute 3 Geo. 1, c. 15, s. 18, which is as follows:—'I, A. B., do swear that I will well and truly 'serve the queen's majesty in the office of sheriff of the county 'of N., and promote her majesty's profit in all things that be'long to my office as far as I legally can or may; I will truly 'preserve the queen's rights, and all that belongeth to the crown;

(*b*) 13 & 14 Will. 3, c. 6; 1 Ann. stat. 1, c. 22; 4 Ann. c. 8; 1 Geo. 1, stat. 2, c. 13, s. 2.

CHAP. II. SECT. II.

'I will not assent to decrease, lessen or conceal the queen's 'rights, or the rights of her franchises; and whensoever I shall 'have knowledge that the rights of the crown are concealed or 'withdrawn, be it in lands, rents or franchises, suits or ser-'vices, or in any other matter or thing, I will do my utmost to 'make them be restored to the crown again; and if I may not 'do it myself, I will certify and inform the queen thereof, or 'some of her judges; I will not respite or delay to levy the 'queen's debts for any gift, promise, reward or favour, where I 'may raise the same without great grievance to the debtors; 'I will do right as well to poor as to rich in all things belonging 'to my office; I will do no wrong to any man, for any gift, 'reward or promise, nor for favour or hatred; I will disturb 'no man's right, and will truly and faithfully acquit at the Ex-'chequer all those of whom I shall receive any debts or duties 'belonging to the crown; I will take nothing whereby the queen 'may lose, or whereby her right may be disturbed, injured or 'delayed; I will truly return and truly serve all the queen's 'writs, according to the best of my skill and knowledge; I will 'take no bailiffs into my service but such as I will answer for, 'and I will cause each of them to take such oaths as I do, 'in what belongeth to their business and occupation; I will 'truly set and return reasonable and due issues of them that 'be within my bailiwick, according to their estates and circum-'stances, and make due panels of persons able and sufficient 'and not suspected or procured, as is appointed by the statutes 'of this realm; I have not sold or let to farm, or contracted 'for, nor have I granted or promised for reward or benefit, 'nor will I sell or let to farm, nor contract for or grant for 'reward or benefit, by myself or any other person for me or 'for my use, directly or indirectly, my sheriffwick or any baili-'wick thereof, or any office belonging thereunto, or the profits 'of the same, to any person or persons whatsoever; I will 'truly and diligently execute the good laws and statutes of this 'realm, and in all things well and truly behave myself in my 'office for the honour of the queen and the good of her subjects, 'and discharge the same according to the best of my skill and 'power.—*So help me God.*"

Oaths taken by the sheriffs of Wales;

The sheriffs of *Wales* and *Chester* do not take the above-men-tioned oath, but take the accustomed oath which they formerly did, except the following words, "Ye shall be dwelling in your own proper person within your bailiwick, for the time ye shall continue in the same office, except ye be otherwise licensed by the queen," which words are now left out (*c*).

by the sheriffs of London, Durham and Westmoreland.

The sheriffs of *London* and *Middlesex*, the county palatine of *Durham*, the county of *Westmoreland*, and the sheriffs of *cities* and *towns* being *counties of themselves*, are to take the same oath before their entrance on the duties of their office, as the sheriffs of English counties, except that part that relates to the placing in or disposing of any of the offices of their under-sheriffs, county clerks, bailiffs, or other officers, or their continuance therein (*d*).

Before whom the oaths are to be taken.

The sheriff may take the "oath of office" before the Court of Exchequer, or before a single baron of that court, or before any justice of the peace for the county (*e*). This oath should be taken by the sheriff as soon as he receives his warrant, for until he be sworn he may not intermeddle, nor take upon him to use or exercise his office (*e*). And if he do so his acts as sheriff, (though perhaps not void as to third persons), would most probably be held unauthorized and unjustifiable so far as regards his own protection, unless indeed they fall within the protection of an indemnity act (*f*).

Oath of allegiance, &c.

The oaths of allegiance, supremacy, and adjuration must be taken, made, and subscribed in one of the courts at Westminster, or a court of quarter sessions for the county, and between nine and twelve in the forenoon, within six calendar months after appointment, under a penalty of 500*l.* and certain disabilities (*g*). In the case of a Roman Catholic, the oath prescribed by the 10 Geo. 4, c. 7, s. 6, is to be taken instead of the oaths of allegiance, supremacy and adjuration. That oath is as follows:

'I, A. B., do sincerely promise and swear that I will be 'faithful and bear true allegiance to her Majesty Queen Vic-'toria, and will defend her to the utmost of my power against

(*c*) 3 Geo. 1, c. 15, s. 20. See this oath, Appendix.

(*d*) 3 Geo. 1, c. 15, s. 21.

(*e*) 3 & 4 Will. 4, c. 99, s. 6.

(*f*) R. *v.* Parry, 14 East, 550; Re Steavenson, 2 B. & C. 34.

(*g*) 1 Geo. 4, stat. 2, c. 13, s. 2; 2 Geo. 2, c. 31, ss. 3, 4, 9; 9 Geo. 2, c. 26, s. 3; 16 Geo. 2, c. 30, s. 3. The clerk of the peace administers the oath, and has them with the declaration ready ingrossed on a parchment roll, for which the clerk of the peace is entitled to a fee; in some counties this fee is 2*s*.

CHAP. II. SECT. II.

'all conspiracies and attempts whatever which shall be made 'against her person, crown or dignity, and I will do my utmost 'endeavours to declare and make known to her majesty, her 'heirs and successors, all treasons and traitorous conspiracies 'which may be formed against her or them: And I do faith-'fully promise to maintain, support and defend to the utmost 'of my power the succession of the crown, which succession, 'by an act intituled 'An Act for the further Limitation of the 'Crown, and better securing the Rights and Liberties of the 'Subject,' is and stands limited to the Princess Sophia, Elec-'tress of Hanover, and the heirs of her body being Protestants, 'hereby utterly renouncing and abjuring any obedience or alle-'giance unto any other person claiming or pretending a right to 'the crown of this realm. And I do further declare, that it is 'not an article of my faith, and that I do renounce, reject and 'abjure the opinion that princes excommunicated or deprived 'by the Pope, or any other authority of the see of Rome, may 'be deposed or murdered by their subjects, or by any person 'whatsoever: And I do declare, that I do not believe that the 'Pope of Rome, or any other foreign prince, prelate, person, 'state, or potentate, hath or ought to have any temporal or civil 'jurisdiction, power, superiority or pre-eminence, directly or 'indirectly, within this realm; I do swear that I will defend 'to the utmost of my power the settlement of property within 'this realm, as established by the laws: And I do hereby dis-'claim, disavow and solemnly deny any intention to subvert the 'present Church Establishment as settled by law within this 'realm: And I do solemnly swear that I never will exercise 'any privilege to which I am or may become entitled, to dis-'turb or weaken the Protestant religion or Protestant govern-'ment in the united kingdom: And I do solemnly in the 'presence of God profess, testify and declare, that I do make 'this declaration, and every part thereof, in the plain and ordi-'nary sense of the words of this oath, without any evasion, 'equivocation or mental reservation whatsoever.—*So help me 'God.*'

Declaration instead of sacrament.

The sheriff of a county at large must also, within six months after his admittance into office (instead of taking the sacrament, which was formerly requisite (*i*)), make and subscribe in the

(*i*) 25 Car. 2, c. 2, ss. 2, 3, 9.

Court of Chancery, Queen's Bench, or Quarter Sessions of the county or place of his residence, the declaration required by 9 Geo. 4, c. 17, s. 5, which is as follows:

'I, A. B., do solemnly and sincerely, in the presence of God, 'profess, testify, and declare, upon the true faith of a Christian, 'that I will never exercise any power, authority, or influence 'which I may possess by virtue of the office of sheriff of ——, 'to injure or weaken the Protestant Church as it is by law 'established in England, or to disturb the said Church, or the 'bishops and clergy of the said Church, in the possession of any 'rights or privileges to which such Church, or the said bishops 'and clergy, are or may be by law entitled.'

No declaration in county of city or town.

But this declaration is not necessary in the case of a sheriff of a city or town being a county of itself (*j*). And indeed there seems to be nothing now to prevent a member of any or no religious persuasion from holding the office of sheriff in a city or town being a county of itself.

Section III.

Of the Transfer of the Office from the old to the new Sheriff.

Before the 3 & 4 Will. 4, c. 99, the old sheriff, to exonerate himself from charge, was required, (by the statute 20 Geo. 2, c. 37,) "at the expiration of his office, to turn over to the succeeding sheriff, by indenture and schedule, all such writs and process as remained in his hands unexecuted, who should duly execute and return the same." Also, after the new sheriff had taken the necessary oaths, and the writ of discharge (now abolished) had been delivered to the old sheriff, the new sheriff was to take an assignment from the old sheriff of all his prisoners which were in the gaol, by their names, by view and by indenture, to be made between the old and the new sheriff (*k*).

So that, before the 3 & 4 Will. 4, c. 99, the old sheriff was

(*j*) 5 & 6 Will. 4, c. 28.

(*k*) Dalt. 15. In the Register, 295, there is a writ commanding the old sheriff to deliver to the new sheriff the gaol, &c. by indenture. The Court of Exchequer granted an injunction to the coroner to put the sheriff in possession of the county gaol, after hearing divers counsel. May 25, 29, and July 1, 11, 1696. Sheriff of Worcester.

CHAP. II. SECT. III.

not discharged from liability, nor was any liability imposed upon the new sheriff, until the former had received his writ of discharge, and had assigned over the process in his hands unexecuted, and prisoners in his custody, by indenture to the latter (*l*). Since the 3 & 4 Will. 4, c. 99, the writ of discharge and indenture of assignment are altogether unnecessary; and the seventh section of that act enacts,

Prisoners and writs to be turned over at expiration of office to incoming sheriff.

"That every sheriff of any county, city, liberty, division, town corporate, or place, shall at the expiration of his office make out and deliver to the new or incoming sheriff a true and correct list and account under his hand of all prisoners in his custody, and of all writs and other process in his hands not wholly executed by him, with all such particulars as shall be necessary to explain to the said incoming sheriff the several matters intended to be transferred to him, and shall thereupon turn over and transfer to the care and custody of the said incoming sheriff all such prisoners, writs, and process, and all records, books, and matters appertaining to the said office of sheriff; and the said incoming sheriff shall thereupon sign and give a duplicate of such list and account to the sheriff going out of office, to whom the same shall be a good and sufficient discharge of and from all the prisoners therein mentioned and transferred to the said incoming sheriff, and the further charge of the execution of the writs, process, and other matters therein contained, without any writ of discharge, or other writ whatsoever; and the said incoming sheriff shall thereupon stand and be charged with the said prisoners, and also with the execution and care of the said writs, process, and other matters, contained in the said list and account, as fully and effectually as if the same writs and process had been turned over by indenture and schedule; and in case any sheriff shall refuse or neglect at the expiration of his office to make out, sign and deliver such list and account as aforesaid, and to turn over the process aforesaid in manner aforesaid, every such sheriff so neglecting or refusing shall be liable to make such satisfaction by damages and costs to the party aggrieved as he, she, or they shall sustain by such neglect or refusal."

This section, it is to be observed, only alters the mode in which the transfer is to be made by the old to the new sheriff. Under the former system, the old sheriff was discharged on

(*l*) Davidson *v.* Seymour, Moo. & M. 34.

receiving the writ of discharge, and executing the assignment required by the 20 Geo. 2, c. 37. Under the present system, he is discharged on receiving from the new sheriff the duplicate list above mentioned. The law applicable to the former mode of discharge seems in most respects also applicable to the mode prescribed by 3 & 4 Will. 4, c. 99.

CHAP. II. SECT. III.

Transfer and receipt of prisoners and process.

As to the transfer of prisoners and process, the high sheriff under the law as it stood previous to 3 & 4 Will. 4, c. 99, did not in general receive the prisoners himself, but executed a letter of attorney, duly stamped, empowering the under sheriff, and others therein named, or any one of them, to receive the gaol, and execute a counterpart of the indenture of assignment, in which indenture there must have been specified, and distinctly set forth, all the detainers lodged against each prisoner. In case any cause was omitted, for such cause the prisoner was confined at the peril of the old sheriff (*n*). And if the old sheriff failed to mention in the assignment one of the prisoners, or omitted to mention one of several detainers against a prisoner, and the prisoner escaped, the old sheriff was liable to an action for an escape at the suit of the person whose suit was omitted (*o*). And on the same principle, the old sheriff would now be liable for omitting or insufficiently describing any prisoner or unexecuted writ in the list prescribed by the 3 & 4 Will. 4, c. 99, s. 7. It would seem that the doctrine formerly laid down in some cases, that if the old sheriff gave notice of the prisoners, and the causes of detention, by parol or by writing under his hand or under the hand of the under-sheriff, and not by indenture, it was sufficient provided the new sheriff did not object (*p*), (if it was ever good law, which there is strong reason to doubt (*q*),) is at all events not applicable at the present day, and that, unless by adopting the mode pointed out by 3 & 4 Will. 4, c. 99, s. 7, the old sheriff cannot transfer his liability to his successor (*r*). It may be doubted whether in order to discharge the old sheriff, the dupli-

(*n*) Westby's case, 3 Rep. 72, S.C.; Cro. Eliz. 365; Poph. 85. See also Chandler *v.* Thompson, Hob. 266; Egerton *v.* Morgan, 1 Bulstr. 70; Hanmer *v.* Winmer, 1 Sid. 335, S.C.; 2 Keb. 2224; 2 Leon. 54; Noy, 51.

(*o*) See cases *ante*, n. (*n*). And see 20 Geo. 2, c. 37.

(*p*) Dalt. 16; Poulter *v.* Greenwood, Barnes, 367; Sir Thomas Read's case, 2 Roll. Rep. 146.

(*q*) Davidson *v.* Seymour, Moo. & M. 34, and the learned note of the reporter.

(*r*) See Thomas *v.* Newnam, 2 Dowl. N. S. 33.

cate list should not be signed by the new sheriff himself (*s*), and not merely by the under-sheriff or other agent.

Prisoners where to be transferred.

The new sheriff before 3 & 4 Will. 4, c. 99, was only bound to receive the prisoners from the old sheriff at the county gaol, and in no other place (*t*); yet, if the old sheriff delivered, and his successor received the prisoners out of the gaol, the old sheriff was discharged by that delivery (*t*); and under the 3 & 4 Will. 4, c. 99, s. 7, it would seem that the old sheriff is by the signature of the duplicate list discharged from future responsibility for prisoners in any place of lawful custody properly described in the list.

Transfer in case of death.

In case of the death of a sheriff, it is said that the new sheriff is bound at his peril, as soon as he is sworn into office, without any delivery or notice, to take notice of the prisoners in the gaol, and of the causes of their commitment (*u*). In the meantime the under-sheriff of the former sheriff is responsible (*x*), and it may be doubted whether that responsibility does not continue until the prisoners have been duly transferred to the new sheriff.

Transfer of process partly executed.

Questions sometimes arise as to the stages at which process may be transferred to the new sheriff, and at which the old sheriff is bound to complete its execution. With reference to this question it is observable, that the words of the act now in force, 3 & 4 Will. 4, c. 99, s. 7, are somewhat different from those of the former act, 20 Geo. 2, c. 37, s. 1. The 20 Geo. 2 directs the sheriffs, at the expiration of their office, "to turn over to the succeeding sheriffs all such writs and process as shall remain in their hands *unexecuted*, who shall duly execute and return the same." The words of 3 & 4 Will. 4, are, "all writs and other process in his hands *not wholly executed*." While the former act was in force, the construction put upon the word "unexecuted" seems to have been "*wholly* unexecuted;" and therefore before 3 & 4 Will. 4, c. 99, if a sheriff had commenced the execution of a writ, as of a *fieri facias* by seizure, he was bound to complete it, and might have proceeded to sell the goods

(*s*) See Hyde *v*. Johnson, 2 Bing. N. C. 776, on the construction of a statute similarly worded.

(*t*) Dalt. 16, cit. 11 Rich. 2; Fitz. Attorney, 61.

(*u*) Westby's case, 3 Rep. 72 b, S. C.; Cro. Eliz. 366; Dalt. 17.

(*x*) 3 Geo. 1, c. 15, s. 8.

without waiting for a *venditioni exponas* (*y*), and might be compelled to sell them by a *distringas nuper vicecomitem* (*z*). The present act, on the first impression, seems hardly susceptible of this construction, though there is a dictum attributed to Parke, B., in one rèport of Yaroth *v.* Hopkins (*a*), "that if the old sheriff had seized he must have gone on with the execution." And where the sheriff has seized *and sold* under a *fi. fa.*, and nothing remains to be done but to hand over the proceeds to the execution creditor, the writ must be considered as wholly executed, and ought not to be transferred to the incoming sheriff (*b*). Nor can any liability be imposed upon the new sheriff by the attempted transfer of such a writ, even though he employ the same under-sheriff (*b*).

Of the liability of the old sheriff to return process after expiration of office.

All writs not executed by the old sheriff, and not returnable, it is of course the duty of the new sheriff to execute. And if a *capias* be returned *non est inventus* by both sheriffs for different portions of time, if the new sheriff has been guilty of negligence in the execution of the writ, he alone is liable to an action (*c*). To all writs executed by the *late* sheriff, he is the proper person to make the return (*d*); and a return by the new sheriff of *cepi corpus* of a defendant who has never been in his custody, to a writ executed by the old sheriff, is bad (*e*). The courts will order the old sheriff to amend his return if it be erroneous (*f*). The old sheriff when he goes out of office should hand over the writs executed by him to the new sheriff, who should return the writ with the old sheriff's return thereon, and that he received the writ as above endorsed from his predecessor (*g*). The old sheriff may be ruled to return any writ executed by him when in office, and would be liable to an attachment for not complying with the rule (*h*). But the sheriff is not in general liable to be

(*y*) Ayre *v.* Aden, Cro. Jac. 73; 1 Roll. Abr. 893; Doe dem. Stevens *v.* Donston, 1 Bar. & Ald. 230; Yelv. 44, *contrà*.

(*z*) Clerk *v.* Withers, 6 Mod. 299; 2 Lord Raym. 1074, S. C. And see *post*, chap. 11, s. 4.

(*a*) 3 Dowl. 711. The report of the same case, under the name of Yrath *v.* Hopkins, 2 C. M. & R. 250, gives the supposed dictum merely in the shape of a question thrown out by the learned judge during the argument.

(*b*) Harrison *v.* Paynter, 6 M. & W. 387.

(*c*) See Fonseck *v.* Magnay, 6 Taunt. 231; 1 Marsh, 554, S.C.

(*d*) Westby's case, 3 Rep. 72.

(*e*) Rex *v.* Sheriff of Middlesex, 4 East, 604.

(*f*) Dalt. 19.

(*g*) 2 Roll. Abr. 457; Dalt. 516; 1 Bulstr. 70.

(*h*) Rex *v.* Adderley, Doug. 464. See also Rex *v.* Sheriff of Middlesex, 4 East, 604.

CHAP. II. SECT. III.

called on to return any writ executed by him, unless ruled within six lunar (*i*) months from the expiration of his office (*k*); and although it has been intimated that a sheriff might be called upon to return the writ after that time under peculiar circumstances (*l*), yet it will be found difficult to carry out such intimation without overruling the statute of 20 Geo. 2, c. 37.

Apportionment of fees on Exchequer writs.

By the statute 3 Geo. 1, c. 15, s. 9, it is enacted, that when any sheriff shall, by process out of the Exchequer, seize or extend any goods, chattels or personal estate, into the hands of his majesty, &c. for any debts or duties due to the crown, and shall die or be superseded before a *venditioni exponas* be awarded for sale, or before he has made any actual sale thereof, and a writ shall afterwards be awarded to a subsequent sheriff, who shall make sale of such goods, &c., the barons of the Exchequer, if sitting, or if not sitting, they or any one of them of the degree of the coif, shall settle the fees or poundage for such seizure or sale between such preceding and subsequent sheriff, with regard to the trouble each sheriff had in the execution of such process.

(*i*) Rex *v.* Adderley, Doug. 463, note.

(*k*) 20 Geo. 2, c. 37. He must be ruled within six months; to be requested within that time is not sufficient, Rex *v.* Jones, 2 T. R. 1.

(*l*) Wilton *v.* Chambers, 3 Dowl. 333.

CHAPTER III.

OF THE SHERIFF'S OFFICERS, THEIR APPOINTMENT, POWER, AND DUTIES.

SECTION I.

Of the Sheriff's Officers.—Appointments in General.—Replevin Clerks, &c.

BY 4 Hen. 4, c. 5, and 23 Hen. 6, c. 9, it is enacted, " that no sheriff shall let to farm in any manner his county, nor any of his bailiwicks, hundreds, or wapentakes (*a*); and it has been resolved, that a lease thereof, though no rent was reserved, is within the

The sheriff is not to let his bailiwick to farm;

(*a*) In Ellis *v.* Nelson, 3 Keb. 678, this statute was held to be a private act; but in more recent cases, upon other provisions of the statute, it has been decided to be a public statute. Samuel *v.* Evans, 2 T. R. 569.

CHAP. III. SECT. I.

statute, the intent being that the sheriffs should keep their counties in their own hands (*b*).

but may appoint deputies and officers: when to be appointed.

This statute does not prevent the sheriff from employing deputies in the execution of the duties of his office; indeed, by several statutes, the sheriff is required to appoint an under-sheriff, and at least four replevin clerks. At the time the sheriff takes his oath of office, and thereby fully enters upon the duties thereof, he should execute the appointments of his officers; and they, on the other hand, at the same time should be required to give security for the due and faithful execution of the duties of their respective offices. The under-sheriff should therefore have the appointments and the securities of himself, and of the other officers of the sheriff, ready to be executed when the oaths are taken; the officers of the sheriff are his under-sheriff (*c*), bailiffs (*d*), gaoler (*e*), replevin clerks (*f*), county clerks, and deputies, whose duties, appointments and liabilities will be treated of in this chapter.

Offices under the sheriff are not to be bought or sold.

By the statute 3 Geo. 1, c. 15, s. 10, it is enacted, "that it shall not be lawful to or for any person whatsoever to buy, sell, let, or take to farm, the office of under-sheriff, or deputy sheriff, seal keeper, county clerk, shire clerk, gaoler, bailiff, or any other person pertaining to the office of high sheriff *of any county of England and Wales*, or to contract, promise, or grant for money, or other reward or benefit, the said offices, or any of them; nor to give, take, promise, or receive, any other consideration whatsoever for the said offices, or any of them, directly or indirectly, by themselves, or any person in trust for them, or for their use, on a penalty of 500*l*., one half to the king, the other half to the informer; the action for the same to be brought within two years. Provided that nothing in this act shall hinder any high sheriff from constituting and appointing an under-sheriff or deputy sheriff, as by law he may *and ought to do;* nor to hinder the under-sheriff, in case of the high sheriff's death, when he acts as high sheriff, from constituting a deputy, which he is thereby empowered to do; nor to hinder,

(*b*) 20 Hen. 7; 13 Dalt. 23; 21 Hen. 7, 36. See also Plowd. 87; Stockwith *v.* Northy, Moor, 781.

(*c*) For the nature and duties of the office of under-sheriff, see the 2nd section of this chapter.

(*d*) For the nature and duties of the office of bailiff, see the 3rd section of this chapter.

(*e*) See the 4th section of this chapter.

(*f*) For the duties, &c., of these officers, see the latter part of this section.

prevent, or abridge such sheriff or under-sheriff, from demanding, taking, or receiving the lawful fees and perquisites of his office, or any place or appointment pertaining thereunto; or for taking security for the due answering the same; nor to hinder such under-sheriff, deputy sheriff, county clerk, &c., or any person executing any office under the sheriff, from accounting to the high-sheriff for all such lawful fees as shall be by them taken or received in their offices, &c., nor for giving security so to do; nor to hinder the high-sheriff from allowing such salary or recompence to his under-sheriff, county clerk, &c., or other officer, for the execution of the said offices, places, or employments, or any of them, as to him shall seem meet; nor to hinder or prevent the under-sheriff, &c., from taking or receiving such salary or recompence for his or their pains or services therein." But the sheriffs of *London* and *Middlesex*, and of *Durham* and *Westmoreland*, and of towns and cities being counties of themselves, may notwithstanding this act dispose of the offices of under-sheriff, county clerk, bailiff, or other officer (*g*). If the sheriff take a bond of his bailiff to pay 20*d*. for every defendant's name in every warrant on *mesne process*, it is not letting his sheriffwick to farm (*h*).

Replevin clerks.

By the statute 1 & 2 Phil. & Mary, c. 12, s. 3, it is enacted, "that every sheriff of shires, not being cities or towns made shires, shall at his first county day, or within two months next after he hath received his patent of his office of sheriff, depute, appoint, and proclaim, in the shire town within his bailiwick, *four deputies at the least*, dwelling not above twelve miles distant from one another, which said deputies, so appointed and proclaimed, shall have authority, in the sheriff's name, to make replevin and deliverance of such distresses, in such manner and form as the sheriff may and ought to do, upon pain that every sheriff, for every month he shall be without such deputy, shall forfeit 5*l*., one half to the king, and the other to the informer." It is usual to appoint more than four replevin clerks; the appointment is given to attorneys in each of the places of any size in the county, and is usually made by letter of attorney under seal (*i*). There must be some act of appointment; for

(*g*) 3 Geo. 1, c. 15, s. 21.

(*h*) Ballantime *v.* Irwin, Fortes. 368.

(*i*) See form, Append. It would be sufficient however to make the appointment of the replevin clerk by a minute in the county court book, at the first county court; but the other mode of appointment by letter of attorney is the best. If the appointment be by entry in the county court book, it is as follows:—"The sheriff, by

CHAP. III. SECT. I.

where (*k*) a replevin was granted by a person who had acted for many years as clerk of replevins to several sheriffs, and had been recognized by the then sheriff as such, but without any appointment in writing, the court granted a prohibition to restrain the sheriff from proceeding in a suit granted by that person, he not being appointed to the office within the meaning of the above statute. The mode of granting replevins will be treated of in the chapter on the county court. A replevin clerk is not bound to make personal inquiries as to the responsibility of the sureties on granting a replevin; if they be apparently responsible at the time it is sufficient, for he will not be liable to an action at the suit of the sheriff, although they afterwards turn out to have been insolvent (*l*). But it seems, that, although the replevin clerk is not bound to go out of his office to make personal inquiries, still he is bound to exercise a reasonable discretion, and if the sureties be unknown to him he ought not to be satisfied with their own statements as to their solvency (*m*). He, as well as the sheriff, is answerable to the defendant for the sufficiency of all and each of the pledges (*n*).

The county clerk.

The office of county clerk, or clerk of the county court, is in the appointment of the sheriff; it is not usual to appoint this officer (who is generally an attorney, residing at the county town) by letter of attorney, but by entry or minute on the proceedings of the county court. In Mitton's case (*o*), it was resolved, that a grant by Queen Elizabeth of the office of county clerk during the vacancy of the office of sheriff was void, for the appointment belongs to the sheriff, the county court being the court of the sheriff. Indeed it is optional in the sheriff whether he will appoint a county clerk or not (*o*).

A person to hold the county court.

If the under-sheriff reside at a distance from the town where the county court is held, the sheriff should depute some attorney of respectability at that place to hold the court for him, by letter of attorney under the official seal (*p*).

virtue of the statute in that behalf, did appoint A. B. of, &c., C. D. of, &c., E. F. of, &c., G. H. of, &c., I. K. of, &c., to be his deputies for granting replevins within the said county."

(*k*) Griffiths *v.* Stephens, 1 Chit. Rep. 196; see Brandon *v.* Hubbard, 2 Brod. & Bing. 11.

(*l*) Sutton *v.* Waite, 8 Moore, 27. See also Hindle *v.* Blades, 1 Marsh. 27; S. C. 5 Taunt. 225.

(*m*) Jefferies *v.* Bastard, 4 Ad. & Ell. 813; 6 Nev. & M. 303, S. C.

(*n*) Page *v.* Eamer, 1 B. & P. 378; Scott *v.* Waithman, 3 Stark. 168.

(*o*) 4 Rep. 33. See 9 & 10 Vict. c. 95, ss. 24 et seq., as to the appointment and duties of clerks to the county courts established under that act.

(*p*) See 9 & 10 Vict. c. 95, s. 9, et seq. as to the appointment, duties, &c. of judges of the county courts established under that act.

By the statute 23 Hen. 6, c. 9, it is enacted, "that every sheriff shall make yearly a deputy in the king's courts of his Chancery, King's Bench, Common Pleas, or Exchequer of Record, before they shall return any writs, to receive all manner of writs and warrants to be delivered to them;" and if any such sheriff shall do the contrary, he shall forfeit 40*l.* (to the king and informer) for every such default, and treble damages to the party grieved. And by 1 Edw. 6, c. 10, 5 Edw. 6, c. 26, and 31 Eliz. c. 9, similar provisions were made as to the twelve counties of Wales, and the counties palatine of Lancaster, Chester, and city of Chester. And by rules of the Court of King's Bench, Hil. 23 Car. 1, and E. 15 Car. 2, the sheriffs are enjoined to comply with the statute 23 Hen. 6, above mentioned; and by the last of these rules, the sheriff's deputies are required "to give their personal attendance daily in Westminster Hall in term time, that so they may, with the more convenience, dispatch those services which appertain to their offices respectively" (*q*). And by the rule of the Court of Common Pleas, each deputy, before Hilary term, shall have his name and place of residence, in London and Westminster, set and continued up in tables in the office of the prothonotary (*r*). By an order of the Court of Exchequer, the sheriff is to assign his attorney or deputy, and on giving his recognizance shall deliver to the clerk in the remembrancer's office, the name of the attorney or deputy so assigned (*s*).

Sheriff's deputies in the courts at Westminster.

And now the 3 & 4 Will. 4, c. 42, s. 20, enacts, that "from and after the 1st day of June, 1833, the sheriff of each county in England and Wales shall severally name a sufficient deputy, who shall be resident or have an office within one mile from the Inner Temple Hall, for the receipt of writs, granting warrants thereon, making returns thereto, and accepting of all rules and orders to be made on or touching the execution of any process or writ to be directed to such sheriff."

3 & 4 W. 4, c. 42, s. 20.

Under the former enactments and rules it was usual to nominate the under-sheriff as the sheriff's deputy, and the under-sheriff then appointed his agent in town, who performed the du-

Deputy identified with sheriff.

(*q*) I do not find that this rule has been altered, but it appears to be a dead letter.

(*r*) R. M. 1654, C. P.

(*s*) Ord. & R. Exchequer. As to the force of orders of the Court of Exchequer decreeing penalties, see 3 Geo. 1, c. 15, s. 15.

CHAP. III. SECT. I.

ties. And the sheriff was held liable upon engagements made by an agent so appointed in the course of the office. But it was considered that he was not such a deputy as that notice served on him of a defendant being in the county into which the writ is issued, would be sufficient to fix the under-sheriff with knowledge of that fact (*t*). Since the 3 & 4 Will. 4, c. 42, s. 20, it seems to be considered that the deputy is identified with the sheriff, and it has since that act been repeatedly held that a delivery of process to the deputy is equivalent to a delivery to the sheriff himself, so as to be binding from the moment of delivery (*u*).

SECTION II.

Of the Under-sheriff.

Of the antiquity and appointment of the under-sheriff.

But, although by the statute 23 Hen. 6, c. 9, s. 1, the sheriff is prohibited from assigning or letting to farm his bailiwick, we have seen he is not compelled to perform the duty of his office in person. From the earliest time, the sheriff has always appointed a deputy; this deputy was formerly called the *sub-vicecomes,* seneschalus *vice-comitis;* and in the statute of Westminster 2, c. 39, he is first called under-sheriff, by which name he is now styled (*x*). Before 3 & 4 Will. 4, c. 99, the appointment was usually made by deed, under the seal of office; though an appointment by parol was sufficient (*y*). The fifth section of that act directs, that every sheriff "shall within one calendar month after the notification of his appointment in the London Gazette, by *writing under his hand,* nominate and appoint some fit and proper person to be his under-sheriff."

The same section directs the sheriff to transmit to the clerk of the peace for the county, a duplicate of the appointment, which he is to file amongst the records of his office, on payment of a fee of five shillings.

(*t*) Gibbon *v.* Coggon, 2 Camp. 188.

(*u*) Woodland *v.* Fuller, 11 Ad. & El. 859; Harris *v.* Lloyd, 5 M. & W. 432; Williams *v.* Waring, 4 Dowl. 200.

(*x*) In 9 Rep. 40, Lord Coke says, that he was formerly called *shire clerk,* but it is apprehended that this is, properly speaking, clerk of the County Court, which offices, although generally filled by the same person, are not the same.

(*y*) Dalton, 457; 22 Hen. 7, 6, 7.

No stamp is required on either the appointment or the duplicate (*z*).

Whether the under-sheriff may be an attorney.

There does not seem to be any particular qualification required for the office of under-sheriff; in each county, at this day, it is filled by some attorney of respectability. And the statute of 1 Hen. 5, c. 4, that "no under-sheriff or sheriff's officer shall practise as an attorney during the time he continues in office," has been repealed by 7 Will. 4 & 1 Vict. c. 55. It is however provided by a rule of Q. B. 1654, s. 1, "no under-sheriff, or bailiff of sheriffs or liberties, be admitted, during such their employment, to practise as attornies, under pain of expulsion from the employment of an attorney, and not to be re-admitted." But inasmuch as that rule was made while the statute of 1 Hen. 5, c. 4, was in force, it is probable that it was founded on a desire to carry out that statute, since the repeal of which, therefore, it may be doubted whether the rule is in force or whether at this day there is any legal objection to the filling the office of under-sheriff by an attorney (*a*).

Practising at quarter sessions.

By the statute 22 Geo. 2, c. 46, s. 14, "no under-sheriff, or his deputy, shall act as a solicitor, attorney or agent, or sue out any process, *at any general or quarter sessions of the peace* to be held for any place where he shall execute his office, upon pain of forfeiture of 50*l.*"; and this enactment remains unrepealed (*b*).

May be in office more than a year.

Formerly by several statutes (*c*), no under-sheriff, or sheriff's clerk, should abide or tarry in his office above one year, upon pain to forfeit 200*l.* yearly, so long as such person should occupy such office contrary to the effect of those statutes, and every man that would, might sue for the same" (*d*). But the under-sheriff, and all other officers in the city of London and Bristol, *and of all other counties in which any persons were inheritable at the time of making the statute* (*e*), were excepted out of

(*z*) 3 & 4 Will. 4, c. 99, s. 5.

(*a*) See Cox *v.* Balne, 2 Dowl. & L. 720.

(*b*) See Faulkner *v.* Chevell, 5 A. & E. 213; Briggs *v.* Sowton, 9 Dowl. 105.

(*c*) 42 Edw. 3, c. 9; 23 Hen. 6, c. 8; 6 Hen. 8, c. 18; Dalton (p. 454) says, "that under-sheriffs and sheriffs' clerks, in many places, also, do continue in their said offices many years together, interchanging from one into the other; by reason of which continual being and continuing in the said offices, the under-sheriffs and sheriffs' clerks, and bailiffs, have grown so cunning in their several places, as that they are able to deceive, and may well be feared that many of them do deceive, both the king, their sheriff, and county."

(*d*) See Barrett *v.* Johnson, 2 Jones Rep. Exch. Ir. 297.

(*e*) 23 Hen. 6, c. 3. These are Middlesex, Durham, and Westmoreland.

CHAP. III. SECT. II.

the statute. And now, since 7 Will. 4 & 1 Vict. c. 55, s. 1, has repealed so much of the 42 Edw. 3, c. 9, "as relates to the time during which under-sheriffs and sheriffs' clerks may abide in their respective offices," it seems there is no limit to the time for which the office may be held.

Oaths to be taken by under-sheriffs.

Before the statute 27 Eliz. c. 2, the under-sheriff did not take any oath. But by that statute an under-sheriff is subjected to the penalty of 40*l*., (one half to the queen, the other half to the informer,) for executing the duties of his office without taking the oath of supremacy; and by subsequent statutes, the under-sheriff was directed to take the oaths of allegiance, supremacy, and abjuration, and receive the sacrament and subscribe the declaration against transubstantiation, within the same time, in the same manner as the sheriff. But, as before observed in treating of the oaths of the sheriff himself, a declaration has, by 9 Geo. 4, c. 17, been substituted for taking the sacrament; and by 10 Geo. 4, c. 7, declarations against transubstantiation were abolished. So that the only oath now required, in additon to those of allegiance, supremacy, and abjuration, or that substituted in case of Roman Catholics by 10 Geo. 4, c. 7, is that prescribed by the statute 3 Geo. 1, c. 15, s. 19, which enacts that the under-sheriff of all counties of South Britain, except the counties of Wales and Chester, shall take the following oath (at the same time, and before the same persons, as the sheriff) (*f*); viz.:

'I, A. B., do swear, that I will well and truly serve the queen's 'majesty in the office of under-sheriff in the county of N., and 'promote her majesty's profit in all things that belong to the 'said office, as far as I legally can or may; I will preserve the 'queen's rights, and all that belongeth to the crown; I will not 'assent to decrease, lessen, or conceal the queen's rights, or the 'rights of her franchises; and whensoever I shall have know-'ledge that the rights of the crown are concealed or withdrawn, 'be it in lands, rents, franchises, suits or services, or in any 'other matter or thing, I will do my utmost to make them be 'restored to the crown again; and if I may not do it of myself, 'I will certify and inform some of her majesty's judges thereof: 'I will not respite or delay to levy the queen's debts for any 'gift, promise, reward, or favour, when I may raise the same 'without great grievance to the debtors; I will do right as well

(*f*) For the mode of administering the oaths, see *ante*, p. 19.

'to poor as to rich, in all things belonging to my office; I will 'do no wrong to any man for any gift, reward, or promise, nor 'for favour or hatred; I will disturb no man's right, and will 'truly and faithfully acquit at the Exchequer all those of whom 'I shall receive any debt, duties, or sums of money belonging 'to the crown; I will take nothing whereby the queen may lose, 'or whereby her rights may be disturbed, injured, or delayed; 'I will truly return, and truly serve, all the queen's writs, to the 'best of my skill and knowledge; I will truly set and return 'reasonable and due issues of them that be within my bailiwick, 'according to their estates and circumstances, and make due 'panels of persons able and sufficient, and not suspected, or 'procured, as is appointed by the statutes of this realm; *I have 'not bought, purchased, or taken to farm, or contracted for, nor 'have I given or promised any consideration, nor will I buy, pur- 'chase, or take to farm, or contract for, promise, or give any con- 'sideration whatsoever, by myself or any other person for me, or 'for my use, directly or indirectly, or any person or persons what- 'soever, for the office of the under-sheriff of the county of N., which 'I am now to enter upon and enjoy, nor for the profits of the same, 'nor for any bailiwick thereof, or any other place or office belong- 'ing thereunto; I have not sold nor contracted for, or let to farm, 'nor have I granted or promised, for reward or benefit, by myself 'or any other person for me, or for my use, directly or indirectly, 'any bailiwick thereof, or any other place or office belonging there- 'unto* (*g*); I will truly and diligently execute the good laws and 'statutes of this realm, and in all things well and truly behave 'myself in my said office for her majesty's advantage, and for 'the good of her subjects, and discharge my whole duty to the 'best of my skill and power. So help me God.'

There is an indemnity act passed annually to protect persons who have omitted to take the oaths of allegiance, &c., and it has been lately determined (*h*), that this indemnity act extends as well to those persons who have made default in not taking the oath, although not at that time liable to the penalties, as to those who have incurred the penalty for not taking the oaths.

(*g*) These words in italics are omitted in the oath of the under-sheriffs of London and Middlesex, Durham, and Westmoreland, and of all cities and towns being counties of themselves; 3 Geo. 1, c. 15, s. 21.

(*h*) In the matter of Stevenson and others, 2 Bar. & Cres. 34.

CHAP. III. SECT. II.

The power and duty of the under-sheriff.

The sheriff, in *making an under-sheriff*, does implicitly give him power to execute the ordinary and ministerial offices of the sheriff himself that may be transferred by law; as serving of process and executions, making returns, and the like (*i*); but the judicial acts of the sheriff cannot be delegated to the under-sheriff; as to deal in writ of redisseisin, for in that the sheriff is judge (*j*); nor in the case of a writ of inquiry of waste, where the sheriff is commanded to go to the place wasted, because it is personal unto the sheriff himself (*k*). So in a writ of partition, the sheriff must execute it in person, and cannot delegate it to the under-sheriff (*l*). So in a writ of advancement of dower or pasture, unless they are removed into C. B., the sheriff cannot delegate his authority (*m*). And although the sheriff may do the whole duty of his office in person, yet he cannot make an under-sheriff for executing *part* of the duty of the office, and reserve the residue to himself (*n*). Therefore it was decided, that a covenant by the under-sheriff that he would not make executions above 20*l.*, before he had first made known the nature and quality of the writ to the sheriff, and without the special warrant of the sheriff, was void and illegal; and in an action against the under-sheriff on this obligation, notwithstanding such proviso, the under-sheriff was held to be liable thereon, for allowing a prisoner, arrested on a writ above 40*l.*, to escape (*o*). Where the sheriff appointed two under-sheriffs extraordinary to hold an inquest, the court, for that reason, set the inquisition aside, as the under-sheriff was the proper person to hold the inquest (*p*).

Acts to be in the name of the sheriff.

At this day, all the office and duty of sheriff is transacted by

(*i*) Norton *v.* Simes, Hob. 13; 9 Edw. 4, c. 31, 32; Levett *v.* Farrar, Cro. Eliz. 294. See also 1 Roll Rep. 274.

(*j*) 11 Hen. 4, c. 7; 6 Rep. 12; Norton *v.* Simes, Hob. 13. And see of the writ *de nativo habendo*, Fitz. *Retorn*, 32; Bro. Offices, 36. These cases are retained as illustrations, notwithstanding the abolition of real actions by 3 & 4 Will. 4, c. 27, s. 36. There are however cases in which real actions may still be brought; see Doe *d.* Gilbert *v.* Ross, 7 M. & W. 102.

(*k*) Norton *v.* Simes, Hob. 13; Cro. Eliz. 10, *dub.*; Darell *v.* Waburne, Dyer, 204 a: Warneford *v.* Haddock, Cro. Eliz. 290, *contrà*--for it is only form. In the cases where the sheriff ought to execute his duty in person, if the sheriff in such writ returneth that he was there in proper person, and this return be received, and the writ filed, then the court cannot examine it; for the return is good, and the party can have no averment against the return, nor can he have error; Clay's case, Cro. Eliz c. 10; Dalt. 34.

(*l*) Clay's case, Cro. Eliz. 10.

(*m*) F. N. B. 148; Dalt. 34; Noy, 21.

(*n*) Boucher *v.* Wiseman, Cro. Eliz. 440; see also 2 Brownl. 281.

(*o*) Norton *v.* Simes, Hob. 13; Boucher *v.* Wiseman, Cro. Eliz. 440; Chamberlain *v.* Goldsmith, 2 Brownl. 280. See also 12 Mod. 468; Moore, 85, pl. 175; Noy, 51; Holt, 157.

(*p*) Denny *v.* Trapnell, 2 Wils. 378.

the under-sheriff, who, however, is only a deputy, and therefore all his acts must be done in the name of the sheriff; as is said in the Year Book, 20 Hen. 7, 12 *b*, that the under-sheriff is one that occupieth the place or office in the right of the high sheriff, and doth all things in the name of the high sheriff. And upon every writ or process delivered to the under-sheriff, he, as well as the high sheriff, may, by warrant in writing, command the bailiffs to execute such writ or process; but it must be done in the high sheriff's name (*q*). The under-sheriff, without express authority from the high sheriff, may raise the *posse comitatus* (*r*). So a return made by the under-sheriff cannot be disavowed by the high sheriff, if he have made him his under-sheriff (*s*). And in a recent case, on proving a deed under the official seal of the sheriff, executed by the under-sheriff, it was held not to be necessary to prove the authority of the under-sheriff so to do; proof that he acted as under-sheriff was sufficient; for the under-sheriff, *virtute officii*, has authority to do all official acts (*t*). It was formerly held, that although the acts of the under-sheriff were binding on the sheriff, and valid; yet that the assignment of bail bonds, or the like, by the clerk employed in the sheriff's office, was not sufficient (*u*); but it is now holden, that an assignment of a bail bond or return made in the sheriff's name, by a person generally employed in the sheriff's office, is valid and binding on the sheriff (*v*). The under-sheriff, however, cannot appoint a deputy to execute a writ of trial (*w*).

How the office of under-sheriff may be determined.

The under-sheriff has no estate or interest in his office (*x*); for the sheriff can only appoint the under-sheriff at will, as the under-sheriff is in effect but the sheriff's *deputy;* and, therefore, according to the nature of a deputation, must be removable, as an attorney is; so that if the sheriff should express that the appointment should be irrevocable, yet he may remove him; for it is said to be necessary, both for the public service and for the indemnity of the sheriff, that he be removable (*y*). Of course the under-sheriff's power and authority determine on the sheriff's discharge. Formerly by the death of the sheriff

(*q*) Dalt. 103.

(*r*) Dalt. 104.

(*s*) 16 Hen. 4, 7, 6; 9 Rep. 3.

(*t*) Doe *d.* James *v.* Brawn, 5 Bar. & Ald. 243.

(*u*) Kidson *v.* Fagg, 1 Str. 60; S. C. 10 Mod. 288.

(*v*) Francis *v.* Neave, 6 J. B. Moore, 120; S. C. 3 Brod. & Bing. 26; Bac. Abr. tit. *Sheriff* (H.) 3.

(*w*) Jones *v.* Williams, 7 Dowl. 938.

(*x*) Parker *v.* Kett, Salk. 95.

(*y*) Norton *v.* Simes, Hob. 13.

CHAP. III. SECT. II.

during his shrievalty, the authority of the under-sheriff was determined; but, by the statute 3 Geo. 1, c. 15, s. 8, it was enacted, "that if any sheriff shall die before the expiration of his year, or before he be superseded, the under-sheriff, or deputy sheriff, shall nevertheless continue in his office, and execute the same in the name of the deceased sheriff, till another sheriff be appointed and sworn; and the under-sheriff shall be answerable for the execution of the office during such interval, as the high sheriff would have been; and the security given by the sheriff and his pledges shall stand a security to the king, and all persons whatsoever, for the due performance of his office during such interval." The courts will not grant a rule absolute for an attachment for not bringing in the body, in the first instance, against an under-sheriff, where the sheriff has died during the year (*y*); nor does it appear to be settled, whether or not the under-sheriff would be liable to be attached for not bringing in the body after the death of the sheriff, where the sheriff in his lifetime had returned *cepi corpus* (*z*).

Sheriff's liability for his acts.

If the return to a writ be false, or there be any neglect of duty by the under-sheriff or bailiffs, the sheriff is alone responsible to the party injured; attachments are always granted against the sheriff, and not against the under-sheriff; so no action will lie against the under-sheriff for any default in him, but the sheriff is answerable, and the default is a matter to be settled between the sheriff and under-sheriff (*a*). But the sheriff is not answerable criminally for the acts of the under-sheriff unsanctioned by him (*b*).

The security given by the under-sheriff, and acts he must do, on his appointment.

Dalton recommended sheriffs to keep their office in their own houses, in order to prevent themselves from being injured by their under-sheriffs, which recommendation has been long unattended to; the sheriff, however, should take security from the under-sheriff to save himself harmless. It seems extraordinary that it should for a long time be made a question, whether or not covenants from the under-sheriff to the sheriff for duly executing the office were void by the statute of 23 Hen. 6, c. 9:

(*y*) Anon. 2 Chit. Rep. 389.

(*z*) *Id. ibid.*

(*a*) Cameron *v.* Reynolds, Cowp. Rep. 406. See also 2 Bla. Rep. 832; 3 Wils. 314; Dougl. 40. *Sed vide* Cas. in B. R. 454, cited in Bac. Abr. *Sheriff* (H.) 3. And *quære*, whether an action for a *false* return may not be brought against the under-sheriff. In Ireland all actions may, by express enactment, 57 Geo. 3, c. 68, s. 3, be brought against the under-sheriff, unless for the immediate act of the sheriff.

(*b*). Latch. 187.

the legality of such securities is now clearly established (*c*). But any covenant, or proviso, excepting or reserving any part of the office, in the security from the under-sheriff to the sheriff, is void and contrary to law; though such exception does not make the security void *in toto* (*d*). The under-sheriff frequently finds sureties to join with him in indemnifying the sheriff, but it is optional with the sheriff whether he will take the security of the under-sheriff alone or not. The form and extent of the terms of the under-sheriff's bond are nearly the same in all counties, the under-sheriff covenanting for the performance of all the duties of the office; a form thereof will be found in the Appendix. The under-sheriff should have his security ready, and execute it, with his sureties, if any, at the time that he and the sheriff take the oaths of office, at which time it is usual for the sheriff to execute the appointment of the under-sheriff (*e*).

Section III.

Of the Bailiffs.

Perpetual bailiffs.

The sheriff's officers, called bailiffs, are of three kinds. The first, perpetual bailiffs, or bailiffs in fee, who have by charter or prescription the execution of writs within the guildable (*f*). These bailiffs are different from bailiffs of franchises, for perpetual bailiffs of the guildable have not the return of writs, but the sheriff must make the return of a writ executed by such bailiffs (*g*).

Bound bailiffs.

Secondly, common bailiffs, (called, in the old books, bailiffs errant), who are also called bound bailiffs. These are the ordinary officers of the sheriff, and are bound in an obligation with sureties for the faithful discharge of the duties which they are appointed to perform (*h*). In Cumberland (*i*) and in Corn-

(*c*) Cartwright *v.* Dalesworth, Moor, 542. See also Norton *v.* Simes, Hob. 13; Bac. Abr. *Sheriff* (H.) 2.

(*d*) Sir Daniel Norton *v.* Simes, Hob. 13; Boucher *v.* Wiseman, Cro. Eliz. 440.

(*e*) *Ante*, 32.

(*f*) Dalton distinguishes the *guildable* from a *franchise* thus, "*tiel part del county que est contributary inter eux mesmes, a payer tribute ou common charges, est appel le guildable; et si ascun special liberty la soit, ceo est appel le franchise.*" "*Et ceo parol guilde, est un brotherhood, society, ou company incorporate.*"

(*g*) Dalt. 185, 187.

(*h*) See form of a bailiff's obligation, *post*, Append.

(*i*) 2 Bla. Rep. 952; Taylor *v.* Richardson, 8 T. R. 505. In Higgins *v.* M'Adam, 3 Y. & J. 3, it is said

CHAP. III. SECT. III.

wall (*k*) it would appear there are no bound bailiffs. In observing upon the sheriff of Cumberland having no bound bailiffs, Lord Kenyon, C. J., is reported to have said, "What protection the sheriff of Cumberland has in cases of this kind that other sheriffs have not, it is not necessary to inquire in this case; but, though he may not have bound bailiffs, he may perhaps learn, whenever the question arises, that he is bound, like all other sheriffs, either to execute the writ personally, or to procure it to be executed by some other person for whom he is responsible" (*l*).

Special bailiffs.

Thirdly, special bailiffs: these are officers appointed by the sheriff merely for the execution of a particular writ at the instance of the plaintiff (*m*).

Questions have often been raised as to what is sufficient evidence of the appointment of a special bailiff. It has been held, that a mere request to a sheriff to deliver his warrant to a particular officer did not amount to such an appointment, because "in point of practice particular bailiffs are employed by certain attornies to perform all the duties of their office" (*n*). But the following letter from the plaintiff has been held to amount to such an appointment,—"Myself against D. I enclose you a writ herein, and shall feel obliged by your granting a warrant hereon, directed to Mr. M. and Mr. B. I shall write to Mr. B. in a day or two" (*o*). So, where the plaintiff's attorney requested that the warrant on a *ca. sa.* might be addressed to a particular officer, himself delivered the warrant to that officer, took him in his carriage to the place of arrest, and overruled doubts which he entertained as to the legality of the arrest; it was held, that the officer must be considered as a special bailiff (*p*).

Liability for acts of special bailiff.

Where a special bailiff has been appointed at the instance of the plaintiff, the sheriff is not in general liable to be ruled by the plaintiff to return the writ (*q*). But under special circum-

that in Cumberland there are bound bailiffs, but each warrant is made out and delivered to a special bailiff appointed by the party on an indemnity given to sheriff.

(*k*) 1 Dowl. & Ry. 309.

(*l*) Taylor *v.* Richardson, 8 T. R. 505.

(*m*) It is usual and advisable, in all cases when a special bailiff is appointed, to take an indemnity, a form whereof will be found, *post*, Append.

(*n*) Balson *v.* Meggatt, 4 Dowl. 558; Corbet *v.* Brown, 6 Dowl. 794; Alderson *v.* Davenport, 13 M. & W. 42.

(*o*) Ford *v.* Leche, 6 Ad. & El. 699; 1 N. & P. 737, S. C.; *sed quære*, see Alderson *v.* Davenport, *ubi sup.*

(*p*) Doe *v.* Trye, 5 N. C. 573; 7 Scott, 704, S. C.

(*q*) De Moranda *v.* Dunkin, 4 T. R. 119; Hamilton *v.* Dalziel, 2 Blac. Rep. 952; and if such a rule be obtained, the Court will discharge it on motion, where a special bailiff has been appointed.

stances (of which notice should be given him and an indemnity offered) he may be so ruled. For instance, where a *fi. fa.*, after seizure, has by reason of an adverse claim turned out abortive, and the plaintiff requires a return of *nulla bona* to enable him safely to sue out a *ca. sa.* (*r*). The appointment of a special bailiff also frees the sheriff from liability to any action or suit of the plaintiff for irregularity of the bailiff in the execution of the process (*s*). And no liability in such case accrues to the sheriff until the duty of the special bailiff is exhausted; for instance in case of arrest on a *ca. sa.*, not until the party is arrested and delivered into the actual custody of the sheriff (*t*). Therefore, where a sheriff, holding a *capias* at suit of R. against D., received from F. a *capias* at suit of F. against D., together with an appointment by F. of M. and B. as special bailiffs, and then issued a warrant to M. on the writ at the suit of R., whereupon D. was arrested, gave a bail-bond, and was thereupon allowed to go at large by all who at the time had not received any warrant at suit of F.; it was held, that although the actual arrest at suit of R. was a constructive arrest at suit of F., yet that the agency of M. and B. did not cease when the arrest was made, and that the sheriff was not liable (*u*). But in such a case the sheriff would be liable after the duty of the special bailiff is performed, *e. g.*, the arrest made and the prisoner delivered into the actual custody of the sheriff (*v*). These questions obviously can only arise between the person who has appointed the special bailiff and the sheriff. To all other persons the sheriff (as well as the plaintiff) must answer for the acts of the officer who holds his warrant, whether under a special or common appointment. A special bailiff is subject to the same liabilities for extortion and other misconduct as an ordinary bailiff (*w*).

Qualifications for the office.

By the sheriff's oath he swears, that "he will take no bailiffs into his service but such as he will answer for, and shall cause them to take such oaths as he himself does, in what belongeth to their business and occupation." And there is a statute, neglected in practice, which directs that sheriffs shall put in such bailiffs

(*r*) Harding *v.* Holder, 9 Dowl. 659; 2 Man. & Gr. 914; 3 Scott, N. R. 293, S. C. See Bradley *v.* Carr, Scott, N. R. 523.

(*s*) Pallister *v.* Pallister, 1 Chit. R. 614; Porter *v.* Viner, ib. 613 a; Ford *v.* Leche, 6 Ad. & El. 699; 1 N. & P. 737, S. C.; Doe *v.* Trye, 5 N. C. 573; 7 Scott, 704, S. C.

(*t*) Ford *v.* Leche, *ubi supra.*

(*u*) *Ibid.*

(*v*) Taylor *v.* Richardson, 8 T. R. 505.

(*w*) See Plevin *v.* Prince, 10 Ad. & El. 494; and as to liability of bailiffs, *post*, 44, 45.

CHAP. III. SECT. III.

and hundredors having land within the said bailiwicks and hundreds for whom they will answer (*x*). It seems that inasmuch as the office of bailiff is one of responsibility and trust, it cannot properly be intrusted to an infant (*y*).

Disqualifications by reason of the office.

By rule of the court of K. B. 1654, a sheriff's officer was prohibited from being an attorney, and until lately there was a statutory prohibition to the same effect in 1 Hen. 5, c. 4; but since the repeal of that statute by 7 Will. 4 & 1 Vict. c. 55 (*z*), it may be doubted whether the prohibition by the rule of 1654 is any longer in force. By rule of court, C. B., M., 14 Geo. 2, no sheriff's officer, bailiff, or other person, concerned in the execution of process, shall be bail in any action; which rule prevails in practice in Q. B. and Exchequer (*a*).

The bailiff's authority, how derived.

When the sheriff appoints a bailiff, he cannot abridge him of his power (*b*). The bailiff is not, however, the general recognized officer of the sheriff, like the under-sheriff (*c*); it is from the warrant, and not from his appointment as a sheriff's officer, that the bailiff derives his authority to execute the writ; therefore the act of a regular sheriff's bailiff in the execution of process, is not sufficient to fix the sheriff with a liability for such act, without proving the warrant (*d*); therefore, if a bailiff make an arrest before a warrant is delivered to him, he is a trespasser, nor will a warrant subsequently sealed and delivered to him legalize the arrest (*e*). If the warrant be directed to one bailiff and he adds the name of another bailiff (*f*), or if the warrant be issued in blank and the bailiff's name be afterwards inserted (*g*), the persons whose names are so added or inserted would be trespassers for taking the defendant or his goods under such an authority. But it seems sufficient, if the bailiff's name be inserted before the warrant is given out of the sheriff's office, though after the sealing (*h*). And a mere verbal mistake does not vitiate the

(*x*) 14 Ed. 3, s. 1, c. 9.

(*y*) Cuckson *v*. Winter, 2 Man. & Ry. 313.

(*z*) Overlooked, as it seems, in framing the 2nd sched. to 6 & 7 Vict. c. 73.

(*a*) *Ante*, 33. See Doldern *v*. Feast, Stra. 890. A person employed by the sheriff in warning juries is within this rule. Bolland *v*. Pritchard, 2 Bla. Rep. 799. And this applies to officers of the palace-court being bail in the superior courts, Barnes' Supp. 9. 10.

(*b*) 2 Brownl. 283.

(*c*) Drake *v*. Sykes, 7 T. R. 113.

(*d*) *Id. ibid.* And see 3 Stark. Ev. 1337.

(*e*) Hall *v*. Roche, 8 T. R. 187. See Plomer *v*. Bull, 5 Ad. & El. 823. The defendant may be arrested again on a proper warrant.

(*f*) Houssin *v*. Barrow, 6 T. R. 122.

(*g*) Burslem *v*. Fern, 2 Wils. 47,

(*h*) Rex *v*. Harris, 1 Russell on Crimes, 513; 1 East, P. C. Add. 18; 2 Leach, C. C. 920; Rex *v*. Stockley, 1 East, P. C. 310; Foster, 312; Stevenson's case, 19 State Trials.

CHAP. III. SECT. III.

warrant (*i*). The authority given by the warrant, being for the administration of justice, is not to be strictly construed; therefore, on a warrant to four bailiffs, *jointly and severally*, two may execute it (*k*); but if the warrant be to several *jointly but not severally*, they must all be acting in the execution of it (*l*). As to when a warrant to the bailiff of a liberty may be acted on as an ordinary warrant to the sheriff's bailiff, and when not, see *post*, Chapter 4 (*m*).

His duty in executing writs.

The mode and time in which the bailiff must execute his duty on writs directed to him, will be the subject of several of the following chapters of this work. It has been said, that in executing a writ it is not necessary for the known officer of the sheriff to show his warrant, although the party demands it (*n*); nor is any other bailiff bound to produce his warrant without a demand of it (*o*). But it has been doubted whether or not every officer is not bound to produce his warrant, on making an arrest, if it be demanded (*p*). When an officer makes an arrest, or the like, he ought to show at whose suit, out of what court, and for what cause he makes the arrest (*q*).

Promises to bailiffs.

An undertaking made to the bailiff to put in good bail, in consideration of his discharging a person arrested by him on mesne process, is void by the statute 23 Hen. 6, c. 9 (*r*). So a promise to pay the bailiff a sum of money for admitting to bail a defendant in his custody on mesne process, is void; for, by 23 Hen. 6, it is his duty to admit such persons to bail, and a promise made in consideration of the bailiff's doing his duty is *nudum pactum* (*s*). But in one case, a promise made to a bailiff, on the behalf of the plaintiff, in consideration of allowing a prisoner to remain in the house of a third person all night, was held good (*t*).

(*i*) Williams *v.* Lewis, 1 Chit. 611.

(*k*) White *v.* Wiltshire, Palm. 52; Lashbroke's case, Hut. 127; Rex *v.* Hobbs, Cro. Eliz. 913; S. C. Yelv. 25.

(*l*) Boyd *v.* Durant, 2 Taunt. 161.

(*m*) And see Jackson *v.* Hill, 10 A. & El. 477.

(*n*) Macalley's case, 9 Rep. 69, 6th Resolution. Lord Coke there says, "Where the books speak of a known bailiff, it is not requisite that he be known to the party who is to be arrested, but if he be commonly known it is sufficient."

(*o*) *Id. ibid.*

(*p*) Hall *v.* Roche, 8 T. R. 188. "It is very important that in all cases where an arrest is made by virtue of a warrant, the warrant, if demanded at least, should be produced."—Per Lord Kenyon.

(*q*) Macalley's case, 9 Rep. 69; The Duchess of Rutland's case, 6 Rep. 54 a.

(*r*) Rogers *v.* Reeves, 1 T. R. 418.

(*s*) Stotesbury *v.* Smith, 2 Burr. 924.

(*t*) Benskin *v.* French, 1 Sid. 132; S. C. 1 Lev. 98, recog. T. Jones, 139; and per Buller, J., 1 T. R. 422.

CHAP. III. SECT. III.

Responsibility of sheriff and bailiff for acts done by the bailiff.

The sheriff is responsible for all the acts of his bailiff done in the execution of writs (*u*), directed to the sheriff in his ministerial capacity (*v*); but he is not liable to be indicted for the acts of his officer (*x*). "It is a general rule that the law looks to the sheriff, and to him alone. He is responsible even for the bailiff's *wilful misconduct* or *deliberate fraud*. 'He is identified with his officers in every case, except where, as in Crowder *v.* Long (*y*), the party opposed to the sheriff is colluding with the officer (*z*).'" And his civil responsibility is not confined to the improper manner of executing what is commanded by his warrant, but extends to all acts, however wrongful, provided they be done under colour of the writ (*a*); even though against the sheriff's express instructions (*b*). Thus the sheriff is liable where his officer, in executing a writ against the goods of A., takes the goods of B. (*c*), or takes the person instead of the goods of the debtor, under a *fi. fa.* (*d*), or receives the debt and costs when he ought to have arrested (*e*). So where a bailiff in possession of goods under a distress received a *fi. fa.* from the sheriff, and sold the goods under it, the sheriff was held liable for poundbreach and rescue at the suit of the landlord (*f*). And the sheriff, though morally innocent, is liable to the consequences of a fraud perpetrated by his officer, *e. g.* in procuring an indemnity bond (*g*). Also for the extortion of his officer (*h*), and to a penal action on the 32 Geo. 3, c. 28, for an offence of his officer under that act (*i*). And so it was held, that a *qui tam* action would lie against the sheriff on the statute 44 Geo. 3, c. 13, s. 1,

(*u*) Saunderson *v.* Baker, 2 Bla. Rep. 832; S. C. 3 Wils. 309. See also 2 Keb. 352.

(*v*) Not in case of writs issuing out of county court, in which he exercises a *judicial* capacity. Tunno *v.* Morris, 4 Dowl. 225; 2 C. M. & R. 298, S. C.

(*x*) Laycock's case, Latch, 187; S. C. Noy, 90, per Gould, J.; 3 Wils. 316. See R. *v.* Huggins, 2 Lord Raym. 1880.

(*y*) 8 B. & C. 598; 3 Man. & Ry. 17, S. C. See Cook *v.* Palmer, 6 B. & C. 739; 9 Dow. & Ry. 723, S. C.

(*z*) J. W. Smith's Mercantile Law, 129 (*w*), referring to Raphael *v.* Goodman, 8 Ad. & El. 565; Smart *v.* Hutton, ibid. 568, n.

(*a*) *Secus*, if not under colour of the writ. See Cook *v.* Palmer, 6 B. & C. 739; 9 Dowl. & R. 723, S. C.; Tomkinson *v.* Russell, 9 Price, 287; Bowden *v.* Waithman, 5 Moore, 183; Stuart *v.* Whitaker, 1 Ry. & M. 310.

(*b*) Scarfe *v.* Halifax, 7 M. & W. 288.

(*c*) Saunderson *v.* Baker, 3 Wils. 309; S. C. 2 Bla. Rep. 832; Ackworth *v.* Kempe, Doug. 40.

(*d*) Smart *v.* Hutton, 8 A. & E. 568, n.

(*e*) Woodman *v.* Gist, 8 C. & P. 213, Littledale, J.

(*f*) Reddell *v.* Stowey, 2 M. & Rob. 358.

(*g*) Raphael *v.* Goodman, 8 Ad. & El. 565.

(*h*) Woodgate *v.* Knatchbull, 2 T. R. 148.

(*i*) Pechell *v.* Layton, *id.* 712, 512. See Plevin *v.* Prince, 10 Ad. & El. 494; Barsham *v.* Bullock, 10 Ad. & El. 23, and *post*.

where the bailiff had discharged a seaman in his custody on giving a bail-bond, instead of delivering him to the commander of one of her majesty's ships, as required by that statute (*j*). In that case it was urged in argument, that the bailiff who discharged the seaman at all events was liable to the penalties of that act; to which Lord Ellenborough, C. J., replied, "That is not so clear; for if the sheriff were made responsible for the acts of his own officers, I am not prepared to say that any of his bailiffs would be liable to the penalty." Whether or not the bailiff himself be liable to penalties under similar acts of parliament, where bailiffs are not expressly mentioned (*k*), may be questionable, but it seems that the court would not allow penalties to be recovered against both the sheriff and his officer (*l*). The bailiff is liable to an action if he commit a trespass in the execution of the writ, although the sheriff is also responsible. But for negligence or misfeasance, or nonfeasance in executing a writ, to an action by the person at whose suit such writ issued, the sheriff is alone responsible (*m*). Where an action is brought against a bailiff for what he might lawfully do in the execution of the writ, he shall not be prejudiced by the sheriff's return (*n*). The liability of the sheriff for the acts of *special* bailiffs has been already discussed (*o*).

Liability for process of county court. What has been said above as to the liability of the sheriff refers to cases where he is a ministerial officer, and the process is directed to him; but he is not liable, merely as sheriff, for the wrongful acts of his bailiffs in executing other process. For instance, he is not in ordinary cases liable for the wrongful act of a bailiff to whom process out of the county court (of which the sheriff is a component part though not judge) (*p*) is directed (*q*). But he would be liable even on such process if he directed it to a special bailiff, taking an indemnity (*r*).

How punished for misbehaviour. Bailiffs in some cases have been punished summarily by the

(*j*) Sturmy, q. t. *v.* Smith, 11 East, 25. See also Stanway, q. t. *v.* Perry, 2 Bos. & Pul. 157.

(*k*) See where they are, Plevin *v.* Prince, 10 Ad. & El. 494.

(*l*) Pechell *v.* Layton, 2 T. R. 712.

(*m*) Cameron *v.* Reynolds, Cowp. 403.

(*n*) Parkes *v.* Mosse, Cro. Eliz. 181. And see Shaw *v.* Simpson, 1 Lord Raym. 184.

(*o*) *Ante*, 40, 41.

(*p*) Jones *v.* Jones, 5 M. & W. 523.

(*q*) Tinsley *v.* Nassau, M. & M. 52; 2 C. & P. 582, S. C.; Tunno *v.* Morris, 4 Dowl. 224; 2 C. M. & R. 298, S. C.; Pitcher *v.* King, 9 Ad. & El. 288; 1 Per. & Dav. 297, S. C.; where a false return was alleged to have been made by the sheriff's direction.

(*r*) See Bradley *v.* Carr, 3 Scott, N. R. 523.

CHAP. III. SECT. III.

courts. The courts are empowered by statute in some cases which will be mentioned in their proper places to redress offences of bailiffs on petition; and also, if bailiffs, in executing the process of a court, behave themselves illegally or oppressively, it has been said that the court would punish them on motion (r). Where a sheriff's officer had been guilty of outrageous conduct in arresting a defendant, the plaintiff not being cognizant of such conduct, the court, on discharging the defendant, ordered the officer to pay the costs (s). But a sheriff's bailiff cannot be considered, like an attorney or the sheriff himself, as an officer of the superior courts, and therefore the courts have no power summarily to compel a bailiff to fulfil an undertaking (t).

Sheriff's remedy against bailiff's sureties.

If the sheriff be damnified by the act or negligence of his officer, he has his remedy over on the bailiff's bond. It is essential to aver, in an action by the sheriff against the surety of a bailiff, for a default by him in executing a writ, that the warrant was *delivered* to the bailiff, and it seems to be necessary to aver also that the warrant was *directed* to the bailiff (u). And where a gaoler was under covenant to perform duties relative to removal of prisoners, and had given a bond with sureties for due performance of his covenants, and the sheriff directed a warrant for removal to the gaoler and J. S. "by him, the sheriff for that time only, thereto especially appointed," and J. S. permitted an escape, it was held, that, as the sheriff had specially appointed J. S., the sureties were not liable (v). The sureties are liable only for the due performance of acts within the scope of the officer's duty; therefore they have been held not liable for money received under an agreement entered into by the officer on the sale of goods taken in execution, in entering into which he had exceeded his authority (w).

An action may be maintained by the sheriff against the sureties on covenant to indemnify from the costs, &c. touching or concerning any matter whereby the bailiff should act as bailiff, and to indemnify him from all damages, losses, costs, &c. by reason

(r) Park and Percival v. Evans, Hob. 62. See *ib.* 263, 264.

(s) Taylor v. Evans, 1 Bing. 367; S. C. 8 Moore, 398.

(t) Brown v. Gerard, 1 C. M. & R. 595; S. C. 3 Dowl. 217.

(u) Desanges v. Priestley, 3 Moore, 246. And see Horton v. Day, Sty. 18, cit. 2 Saund. 414.

(v) Ryland v. Lavender, 9 Moore, 71.

(w) Cooke v. Palmer, 6 B. & C. 739; 9 D. & R. 723 See Webb v. James, 7 M. & W. 279, and cases there cited by E. V. Williams, *arguendo*.

of any return, &c. where costs or loss have been incurred by him in defending an action, if he has been damnified in consequence of any act done by the bailiff, although the bailiff may not have done any thing wrong in the matter wherein he acted, in respect of which the action had been brought against the sheriff, or the loss had been sustained (*x*). Thus where the bailiff dictates a return of *nulla bona*, being a correct return, and the sheriff is sued on it as a false return, and is put to expense in defending the action, he may recover his expenses against the bailiff, or his sureties, under the general clause of the covenant to indemnify, there being nothing put on the record impugning either the act or mode of defending the action (*y*). In averring the damages sustained and the costs the sheriff has been put to, it is not necessary to allege that they were necessarily sustained, if the averment, pursuing the terms of the covenant, have no such qualification; nor is it necessary to aver the misconduct of the bailiff, if the covenant apply to the acts of the bailiff generally (*z*). And if a sheriff defend an action for a false return as well as he can, he may recover his costs from the sureties, though he has a verdict against him on the ground that evidence was not produced, which in another and subsequent suit between the same parties, involving the same question, was obtained (*a*). If in such an action, after he has obtained a rule nisi for a new trial, he compromises the suit with the assent of some of the sureties, by paying a less sum for damages than would be recoverable, and a less sum for costs than were incurred, he may recover his own costs against a surety who did not assent, if it appear that the compromise was under such circumstances reasonable (*b*). In such a case the words "costs of any application to the court touching or concerning any matter wherein the bailiff should act or assume to act as bailiff," comprise the costs of an application to the court to set aside the judgment on which the execution was founded, the return to which gave rise to the action against the sheriff (*c*). A surety cannot discharge himself of his obligation within the year, without the consent of the sheriff (*d*).

(*x*) Fairbrother *v.* Worsley, 1 Price, P. C. 65; 1 Tyr. 424; 1 C. & J. 549; 5 C. & P. 102.

(*y*) *Ibid.*

(*z*) *Ibid.*

(*a*) *Ibid.*

(*b*) *Ibid.*

(*c*) *Ibid.*

(*d*) Martin *v.* Wenman, Lofft, 225.

CHAP. III.
SECT. IV.

Section IV.

Of the Gaoler (*e*).

Of the jurisdiction of the sheriffs over gaols.

Every county has two kinds of gaol; viz. one for debtors, which the sheriff may appoint in any house within his county that he pleases; and the other gaol for breakers of the peace, and matters of the crown, which is the county gaol (*f*). And although all gaols and prisons regularly belong to the king, yet the sheriff, or the lord of a franchise, shall have the custody and keeping of all persons taken by virtue of any precept or authority to him directed, notwithstanding any grant by the king of the custody of prisoners to another person (*g*). By

(*e*) It would be altogether out of place to introduce in this work even an outline of the various statutory regulations by which gaols and gaolers are governed. These subjects will be found fully treated of in Chit. Burn's Justice (29th edit.) tit. *Gaols*: and see 4 Geo. 4, c. 64; 5 Geo. 4, c. 84, 85; 6 Geo. 4, c. 40; 7 Geo. 4, c. 18; 9 Geo. 4, c. 31; 5 & 6 Will. 4, c. 38, 76; 5 & 6 Will. 4, c. 53, 98; 2 & 3 Vict. c. 56; 5 & 6 Vict. c. 98. This section will be confined to a general statement of the law affecting the relation of sheriff and gaoler.

(*f*) Anon. Latch, 16; Vin. Abr. tit. *Gaols* (A).

(*g*) Mitton's case, 4 Rep. 44; T. Raym. 423. In Bac. Abr. 6th edit. tit. *Gaols and Gaoler* (B), an opinion of the Attorney and Solicitor Generals, De Grey and Willes, is quoted, which was presented to the king, 21 Jan. 1767, touching a dispute between the Bishop of Ely on the one hand, and the inhabitants of that liberty on the other, as to the obligation to repair the gaol; the passage cited is as follows: "Although all gaols, whether in counties at large, or in particular franchises, are deemed to belong to the crown, as far as the public administration of justice is concerned, and it is but the custody of them which is placed in the hands of the sheriff, or the lords of the franchise; yet we are not able, in a matter which lies buried in much obscurity, and has scarcely ever been called into discussion in modern times, to find upon what authority a great writer in our law has inferred from the position, 'that all prisons belong to the crown, they are, therefore, to be repaired at the common charge.' Nor does it appear by whom, and from what persons, and in what manner, this charge could have been raised. It seems to us more probable, that from the time the public gaols were re-joined to the counties, and committed to the sole custody of sheriffs, the charge of keeping and preserving them in a proper condition lay, in the first instance, on the sheriffs, and it is probable that the sheriffs might have had an allowance for extraordinary expenses of that sort in the Exchequer: and we observe, that in the stat. 23 Hen. 8, for building new gaols in several counties particularly mentioned, at the charge of the respective counties, provision is made that the sheriffs shall be allowed what they shall expend in the future necessary reparations of such new-built gaols, in their accounts in the Exchequer. In the same manner, it should seem, that lords of franchises who have the custody of public gaols in their respective jurisdictions committed to them, and are thereby responsible to the public for their prisoners, should be bound to find good and sufficient gaols as incidental to their public trust; and they having no accounts with the Exchequer, can have no such allowance made to them, but may well be supposed to submit to

the statute 14 Edw. 3, c. 10, it is enacted, that "gaols which were wont to be in the sheriff's custody shall be again rejoined to their bailiwicks, and they shall put in such keepers for whom they will answer." And by the 13 Rich. 2, c. 15, "the king's castles and gaols, which were wont to be joined to the bodies of the counties, and are now severed, shall be re-joined to the same." And by the statute 19 Hen. 7, c. 10, it is provided, that "the sheriff of every county shall have the keeping of the common gaol there, except such as are held by inheritance or succession. And all letters patent, or the keeping of gaols for life or years are annulled and void; howbeit, that neither the King's Bench nor Marshalsea shall be in the custody of any sheriff; and the patents of Edward Courtney, Earl of Devonshire, and John Morgan, for keeping prisons, are excepted." And by 11 & 12 Will. 3, c. 19, s. 3, "all murderers and felons shall be imprisoned in the common gaol, and the sheriff shall have the keeping of the said gaol."

It has been said that a sheriff may move the gaol from one place to another within the county, but he must keep his prisoners within it, and not suffer them to go out though he himself attends them (*h*).

Who may be a gaoler.

It is enacted by 4 Geo. 4, c. 64, s. 10, "that no keeper of any such prison (all county gaols and some borough gaols) shall be an under-sheriff or bailiff, nor shall be concerned in any occupation or trade whatsoever."

The sheriff's liability for default of gaoler.

The gaoler, it is said, is the sheriff's servant, whom he may discharge at pleasure (*i*). The duty of the gaoler is the safe custody of all persons committed to his charge: in this he is but the sheriff's deputy; and if the gaoler permit a debtor to escape from the gaol, the sheriff is liable to an action for an escape. As, where a court, not having jurisdiction in the par-

such charge in consideration of the honourable exemption of their franchise." For those reasons those two great lawyers were of opinion, that the Bishop of Ely was liable to repair the gaol of his franchise. Orders were given to institute a suit at the expense of the crown to try the question; but Dr. Mawson, who then filled that see, submitted, and repaired the gaol at his own expense. In Rex *v.* The Earl of Exeter, 6 T. R. 373, it was held, that a lord of a franchise could only be charged for the repair of a gaol within the franchise by immemorial usage. As to the constable of the castle of Chester, see Rex *v.* Antrobus, 2 A. & E. 791.

(*h*) Hob. 292; Latch, 16; Sid. 318; Williams *v.* Mostyn, 4 M. & W. 145.

(*i*) Bac. Abr. tit. *Sheriff* (H), 5. *Sed vide* 24 Geo. 3, sess 2, c. 54; 31 Geo. 3, c. 46; 34 Geo. 3, c. 84.

CHAP. III. SECT. IV.

ticular case, ordered the discharge of a prisoner in the county gaol for debt, the sheriff was held liable to an action for this as an escape (*k*). In the case of Plummer *v.* Whitchcott (*l*), it was held, that where the warden of the Fleet in fee grants the office for life to A., who suffered a prisoner in execution to escape, and was not of ability to answer for the escape, that the warden himself was liable. By the statute 8 & 9 Will. 3, c. 27, s. 1, "prisoners upon contempt or mense process, or in execution, committed to the custody of the marshal of the King's Bench, or warden of the Fleet (*m*), shall be detained within the said prison, or the rules thereof, until discharged by due course of law; and if the marshal, or warden, or keeper of any prison, shall suffer any prisoner committed to their custody, either in mesne process or in execution, to go or be at large out of the rules of the prison, (except by virtue of some writ of *habeas corpus*, or rule of court, to be granted only upon motion made or petition read in open court,) such going, or being at large, shall be deemed an escape;" and by sect. 8, "if the keeper of any prison, after one day's notice in writing, refuse to show any prisoner *committed in execution* to the creditor, or his attorney, such refusal shall be deemed an escape;" and by sect. 9, "if any person, desiring to charge another with any action or execution, shall desire to be informed by the keeper of the prison, whether such person be a prisoner or not, the keeper shall give a note in writing thereof, to such person upon demand, at his office for that purpose, upon pain of forfeiting 50*l.*, and such note shall be sufficient evidence that such person was at that time a prisoner in actual custody;" and by statute 8 & 9 Will. 3, c. 26, "the keeper of a prison, for taking bribes for conniving at or permitting an escape, is subject to a penalty of 500*l.*, and to be for ever incapable of executing his office;" and by statute 6 Geo. 4, c. 16, s. 38, "the gaoler to whose custody a bankrupt is committed, suffering him to escape, is liable to a penalty of 500*l.*" But where the gaoler permits a prisoner committed to his charge on a criminal account to escape, the gaoler, and not the sheriff, is answerable; for the sheriff is liable to an action,

(*k*) Brown *v.* Compton, 8 T. R. 424.

(*l*) 2 Lev. 159; S. C., T. Jon. 60; 1 Vent. 314. See also Wainwright *v.* Griffith, Hard. 29.

(*m*) See now as to Queen's Prison, 5 & 6 Vict. c. 22.

but not to an indictment, for the default of his officer in suffering a voluntary escape (*n*). By statute 19 Hen. 7, c. 10, a fine for a negligent escape of any person indicted for high treason shall be one hundred marks at least; if committed for suspicion of high treason, forty pounds; if indicted for murder or petty treason, twenty pounds; if for suspicion of these, or indicted for other felony, ten pounds; if not indicted, five pounds: and if the gaoler be not sufficient, the sheriff shall answer for his neglect.

Security from the gaoler to the sheriff.

As the sheriff is liable for the escapes of prisoners confined in the county gaol for debt, he should require from the gaoler a bond, with sufficient sureties for the due performance of the duties of his office (*o*). In an action on a bond given by a gaoler to the sheriff, the condition of which was, to indemnify the sheriff against escapes, and to attend at sessions and assizes, and "also when any writ of *habeas corpus* for the removal of any prisoner should be served on the sheriff, under-sheriff, or deputy, or on the gaoler, to convey, by the commandment or appointment of the said sheriff, his under-sheriff, or deputy, safely and without delay, all prisoners to and from the gaol of the county to such court or place as the writ should direct," it appeared that the sheriff had directed a warrant on a *habeas corpus* to the gaoler, and to W. W., "for this time only specially appointed;" the prisoner escaped from W. W. whilst conveying him to London, the gaoler at that time attending sessions, it was held that the gaoler was not liable on his bond for this escape (*p*).

Liability of gaoler.

It seems to have been considered by the court of King's Bench in Brandling *v.* Kent (*q*), that a gaoler would not be liable for any irregularity in the arrest of a prisoner committed to his charge, but that the sheriff alone would be answerable, and that it was the duty of the gaoler to receive a person tendered to him

(*n*) 1 Hale's P. C. 597. But see R. *v.* Fell, 1 Ld. Raym. 424; 1 Salk. 272; see also 2 Hawk. P. C. 135, 136, 139. A gaoler *de facto* is liable to be indicted for suffering a criminal to escape, Vin. Abr. Gaoler (C).

(*o*) For the form of the condition of the gaoler's bond see Append. The under-sheriff should, from time to time, compare his indent book with the gaoler's, and mark all the discharges, &c., in the margin. The gaoler should be enjoined, that as soon as he receives a prisoner he must inform the under-sheriff, that a charge may be sent upon the receipt of any other process against such prisoner, otherwise an escape might easily happen.

(*p*) Ryland *v.* Lavender, 2 Bing. 65.

(*q*) 1 T. R. 60. See per Buller, J. and Ollier *v.* Bessey, T. Jones, 214.

CHAP. III. SECT. IV.

by the sheriff, whether the arrest was legal or not. That doctrine, however, was unnecessary to the decision of the case, in which it was only held that the mere fact of the prisoner being tendered to the gaoler after the return of the writ did not excuse him. And it has been ruled by Lord Ellenborough that a gaoler though acting bonâ fide, and without the means of ascertaining the identity of the person imprisoned, is liable to an action if by mistake of the sheriff's officer the warrant was executed against a wrong person (*r*). But a gaoler receiving a prisoner under a magistrate's warrant is protected by 24 Geo. 2, c. 44, s. 6 (*s*).

Regulation of gaols.

There are several statutes which provide for the regulation of gaols, and for the punishment of gaolers who have been guilty of extortion or oppression of criminals committed to their charge, which it would be tedious and out of place to embody in this work (*t*).

The gaoler may use force, but not cruelty.

The gaoler is bound to have sufficient force to prevent a breach of the prison; for nothing but the act of God or the king's enemies will excuse an escape; even breaking the prison by mobs or rebels is not an answer to an action for an escape (*u*). On the other hand the gaoler must not be guilty of cruelty, or of putting debtors in irons, without a good cause (*x*). Where felons in a gaol were breaking their fetters, and the gaoler went to them with a hatchet, and they assaulted and beat him, the gaoler killed two of them with the hatchet—resolved by all the council that it was well done (*y*). Lord Holt ruled, that if a prisoner be imprisoned in a room by the gaoler where a person is ill of the small-pox, to which he objects, and catches the small-pox and dies, it is murder in the gaoler (*z*).

Bond given to a gaoler by a prisoner.

Bonds given by a prisoner to a gaoler for ease and favour are

(*r*) Aaron *v*. Alexander, 3 Camp. 35; see White *v*. Taylor, 4 Esp. 80.

(*s*) Bute *v*. Newman, 1 Gow, N. P. 97.

(*t*) See T. Chitty's Burn's Justice, 29th edit., tit. Gaols; and Bac. Abr. tit. Gaol and Gaoler, where the provisions of the legislature will be found.

(*u*) Elliott *v*. the Duke of Norfolk, 4 T. R. 789; Southcote's case, 4 Rep. 84; Crompton *v*. Ward, Stra. 429; O'Neil *v*. Marson, 5 Burr. 2812; Roll. Abr. Escape (D), 7. See the Indemnity Acts passed after Lord George Gordon's riots.

(*x*) 2 Inst. 38; Fleta, l. 1, c. 26; 3 Inst. 34. By the stat. 32 Geo. 2, c. 28, s. 11, the judges or a judge of assize have the power of redressing and making orders upon complaints made to them of the oppression of a gaoler, &c.

(*y*) Jenk. 23, pl. 42.

(*z*) Castel *v*. Bambridge, 2 Stra. 856. See R. *v*. Huggins, 2 Ld Raym. 1574.

void, by the statute 23 Hen. 6, c. 10 (*a*). So a bond to indemnify the gaoler from the consequences of allowing his prisoner to go at large is void (*b*); however, a bond given to a gaoler by a prisoner to be and continue a true prisoner, if not for ease or favour, is good (*c*); but a bond given to a gaoler for his fees or diet is void (*d*).

Fees.

We have seen how the fees payable by prisoners are regulated (*e*). Formerly the gaoler, and from him the under-sheriff, received a fee, generally 2*s.* 6*d.*, on a *liberate* granted to a debtor on his discharge; but now, by the statute 55 Geo. 3, c. 50, s. 10, it is enacted, "that such *liberate* shall be granted to such debtor, free of all expenses;" and the court of quarter sessions, subject to the approbation of the judges of assize, are empowered to make compensation to the sheriff, or under-sheriff, as they think fit (*f*). And by the 13th section of the same act, "any gaoler who shall, after the 1st of October, 1815, exact from any prisoner any fee or gratuity for or on account of the entrance, commitment, or discharge of such prisoner, or who shall detain any prisoner in custody for non-payment of any fee or gratuity, shall be rendered incapable of holding his office, be guilty of a misdemeanor, and be punished by fine and imprisonment." Where a writ of *habeas corpus* is delivered to the gaoler to bring up a prisoner in his custody for debt, he is bound to obey it, and cannot detain the defendant for his fees (*g*). The court, however, will order that the fees be paid before he is turned over (*h*). An action for money had and received is maintainable against a gaoler who takes more than the rates settled by regulation of magistrates, for lodging &c. within the gaol, though he has paid over the money to the magistrates (*i*).

(*a*) Oaks *v.* Cell, 3 Keb. 320, 361; Mosdell *v.* Middleton, 1 Vent. 237; S. C. T. Raym. 222; 3 Keb. 133; in that case, Twisden, J. held, that if the bond be also given for a just debt, it is void *in toto*. Hale, C. J., *contra*.

(*b*) Hob. 14; 1 Vent. 237. And see the opinions of Holt and Treby, chief justices, and of Powel, J.; 1 Ld. Raym. 278, 279; Plowd. 60.

(*c*) Oaks *v.* Cell, 3 Keb. 361; Lenthal *v.* Cooke, 1 Saund. 160.

(*d*) *Id. Ibid.*; Atkinson *v.* Hobbs, 1 Rol. Rep. 338.

(*e*) *Ante*, p. 42, 43.

(*f*) This extends to Middlesex, R. *v.* Justices of Middlesex, 3 B. & Adol. 100.

(*g*) Hopman *v.* Barber, Stra. 814; White *v.* Haugh, *ib.* 1262; Vin. Abr. tit. *Gaoler* (D).

(*h*) Per Foster, J., Stra. 1262; Rex *v.* Greenway, 2 Show. 172.

(*i*) Miller *v.* Aris, 3 Esp. 231.

CHAPTER IV.

OF BAILIFFS OF FRANCHISES.

Of the Nature of a Liberty.—What Writs the Bailiff may execute in his Liberty.—Bailiff's Qualification.—To keep a Gaol, attend Assizes, &c.—Of the Sheriff's Mandate.—The Bailiff's Power and Duties.—His Liabilities.

Of the origin and nature of a franchise with return of writs.

FRANCHISES or liberties, in which the bailiff or officer hath the return of writs and the ordinary jurisdiction of the sheriff, exist in various parts of England, and are of great antiquity (*a*). It would appear that after the Conquest, the lords, to maintain their authority, purchased the bailiwicks of hundreds, sometimes for years, for life, or in fee, and for this they had courts leet and return of writs (*b*). Their franchises are derived from the Crown, and exist either by grant or prescription (*c*). They are of two kinds, either a grant to a person and his heirs, or to a body politic, for their successors to have the franchise of the return of writs within a particular district, or a grant to the *lord* of a franchise to appoint a bailiff who is to have the return of writs within the district or liberty (*d*). In the former case the grantee, his *heirs* or *successors*, is the officer or bailiff of the liberty, and has the return of writs therein, and is responsible for the due execution of the duties incident thereto (*e*). In the latter case the duty of the grantee or lord of the franchise is to appoint a bailiff, who is the person who has the benefit and obligation of return of writs (*f*). And this distinction is to be attended to, for the lord of the franchise in the latter case is bound to appoint a sufficient

(*a*) It would appear that there was a roll of Liberties, Stat. West. 2, c. 39. This roll seems to have been lost. Ritson's Bailiff of a Liberty, pp. 3, 4.

(*b*) Gilb. History of C. B., 25, 26. 3rd edit.; Vin. Abr. tit. *Return*, 206.

(*c*) Hardr. 422.

(*d*) Dalton, Sheriff, 459; Newland *v.* Cliffe, 3 Bar. & Adol. 636.

(*e*) See judgment of the Court in Newland *v.* Cliffe, 3 Bar. & Ad. 648. And see Entries, 538 b. and 552 a. there cited.

(*f*) Dalton, 459.

bailiff of the liberty, and a writ shall go to compel him to choose another (*g*), or he may lose his franchise by his default. But in case of the death of the bailiff before return made, or in case of the default of the bailiff, in that case the lord of the franchise is not responsible (*h*). And where a grant was made to the earl of W., his heirs and assigns, by his bailiff or bailiffs for that purpose, by the said earl &c. from time to time to be deputed, shall and may have the full return of writs &c., it was held that the bailiff appointed by the lord of the franchise, and not the lord himself, was the person to make the return (*i*). When the bailiff dies, the successor and not the lord of the franchise is the proper person to make a return (*k*).

Where the bailiff of a franchise has the return of all writs within his liberty, he also has execution of such writs as are incident thereto (*l*). Lord Coke says, that a grant of the return of writs for a county at large is void, for in effect it taketh away the office of sheriff (*m*). But the statute 2 Edw. 3, c. 12, has taken away from the crown the power of granting franchises of *retorna brevium* at this day; however, it would appear to be the better opinion, that re-grant of such a franchise that had fallen to the crown by escheat, is not prohibited by that statute (*n*). The bailiffs of franchises may execute the duties of the office by deputy, but the returns must be made in the name of the chief bailiff (*o*).

What writs the bailiff of a liberty has power to execute.

Although the franchise of *retorna brevium* within a liberty is generally claimed to be a return of all writs, precepts, and processes whatsoever, yet it is quite clear that there are many writs, of which the bailiff has not the execution in his franchise; as where the Queen is a party, the sheriff is bound to execute the writ within all liberties in his county (*p*). So the sheriff, and

(*g*) Dalton, 461; Fitz. Nat. Brev. 164 b.

(*h*) Year Book, 14 Ed. 4, fo. 1, 6. Vin. Abr. *Return*, p. 213; Bro. Abr. *Retorne de Briefe*, pl. 99.

(*i*) Newland *v.* Cliffe, 3 B. & Ad. 630.

(*k*) See cases in the two last notes.

(*l*) Per Hale, C. B., 1 Ventris, 412. Lord Hale, in that case, complains that these franchises are great evils, and that their destruction "would avoid a great delay of justice, many suits and vexations, grievous wrongs and oppressions, and would do more good to the kingdom than all the liberties of *retorna brevium* have been worth these 100 years; they are a feather in his cap that hath them, but they are a thorn in the foot of every one that hath to do with them."

(*m*) 2 Inst. 452, per Lord Hale; 1 Ventr. 405; 2 H. 4, pl. 12.

(*n*) Atkyns *v.* Clare, 1 Ventr. 399; 4 Inst. 267.

(*o*) Cro. Jac. 242.

(*p*) 38 Ass. 19; Bro. Chal. 129; Plowd. 216, 243; 5 Rep. 91 b, 92.

CHAP. IV.

not the bailiff, has the return and execution within the liberty, of all writs of *quo minus* (q), of writs of inquiry of waste (r), of redisseisin (s), of writs of inquiry (t), or of *distringas juratores* (u), or of writs where the bailiff is a party (x), or wherever the sheriff is judge; where the sheriff is to take pledges, he ought to take them, although the execution of the writ belongs to the bailiff of a franchise (y). But the execution of all other writs within a liberty belongs to the bailiff of the liberty; thus it has been determined, that the bailiff of a liberty has the right to make inquisition and extent upon an *elegit*, by virtue of a warrant of the sheriff directed to him (z). Where a writ is to be executed in two liberties, viz. partly in one liberty, and partly in another, the sheriff should send a mandate to each (a). And where the writ is to be executed partly in the liberty, and partly in the county at large, the sheriff should direct a mandate to the bailiff of the liberty, to do execution for the part within his franchise, and should as to the residue do execution by his own officers (b). The duty of summoning jurors within the liberty, it would appear, belongs to the officer of the franchise having the execution and return of writs (c).

He is a trespasser for executing a writ immediately directed to him.

Under a grant of a return of writs within a certain district, the bailiff of such liberty has no power to execute process immediately directed to him, for he is not the known officer of the court, like a sheriff; and if a writ be directed to the bailiff of such liberty either against the body, or the goods of a party, by so doing the bailiff becomes a trespasser (d). And if the bailiff of a franchise, on a writ of mesne process directed to him, arrest the defendant, the courts will discharge him out of custody on filing common bail (e).

(q) 1 Ventr. 399, 406.

(r) By stat. West. 1, c. 17; Gilb. Hist. C. B. 28; T. 11 Hen. 4, (81).

(s) *Ibid.*

(t) Com. Dig. Ret. D. 4; Wirely v. Gunstone, 2 Rol. Abr.; S. C. Hob. 83.

(u) 19 H. 6, 67 a.

(x) By analogy to the case of sheriffs, Dalt. 463, citing 7 Edw. 3, 56; Fitz. Chall. 2.

(y) Bro. Ret. 61; 14 Hen. 6, 3; 21 Hen. 7, 14.

(z) Sparrow v. Matersock and others, Cro. Car. 319.

(a) See 5 Rep. 92.

(b) 14 Hen. 6, 48, 67; Bro. Abr. *Retorne de Briefe*, 50.

(c) Rex v. Jaram, 4 Bar. & Cres. 692; S. C. 7 Dow. & Ryl.

(d) Grant v. Bagge, 3 East, 128. But the sheriff of a county palatine is not a trespasser for executing a writ, directed to him in the first instance, Jackson v. Hunter, 6 T. R. 71.

(e) Bowring v. Pritchard, 14 East, 289; Bracebridge v. Johnson, 1 Brod. & Bing. 12.

By the statute 4 Hen. 4, c. 19, "no steward or bailiff, nor minister of a franchise, which have return of writs, shall be attorney in any plea within the franchise or bailiwick, whereof he is or shall be officer or minister in any time to come." And also, by rule of K. B., 1654, s. 1, "no bailiffs of liberties shall be admitted, during their employment, to practise as attorneys, under pain of expulsion from an attorney, and not to be re-admitted." And, by the statute 4 Edw. 3, c. 9, and by 5 Edw. 3, c. 4, "no bailiffs of franchises, &c., shall henceforth be, except he have lands sufficient in the same county, whereof to answer the king and his people, if any will complain (*f*)."

Not to be an attorney.

The bailiff of a liberty should have a gaol situated within the franchise. It has been considered, that the bailiff of a franchise was liable to repair the gaol of the franchise at his own expense (*g*); but it is now held, that he is only subject to such obligation by immemorial usage (*h*). If the bailiff of a liberty arrest a person on a mandate directed to him, and he convey such person to the county gaol, situate *out of* the liberty, it is an escape (*i*). Bailiffs of franchises, having the power of keeping gaols in their liberty, shall certify the names of the prisoners in their keeping at the next general gaol delivery in the county or franchise (*k*). "Bailiffs and officers of liberties, which in times past have been accustomed to attend justices of assize, shall attend upon the justices of assize, justices of gaol delivery, and justices of the peace for the same shire wherein such franchises and liberties be (*l*), and make due execution of all process to them to be directed for ministration of justice within such liberties or franchises; and that also all such bailiffs, or their deputies or deputy, shall give their attendance and assistance upon the sheriff, together with the sheriff's bailiffs, at all courts of gaol delivery, from time to time, for execution of prisoners according to justice." Where it appeared that King Charles II., by charter, (reciting

To have a gaol within his liberty, to attend assizes, &c.

(*f*) See Fitz. N. B. 164.

(*g*) Bac. Abr. tit. *Gaol and Gaolers*, (B).

(*h*) Rex *v*. Earl of Exeter, 6 T. R. 373.

(*i*) Boothman *v*. Earl of Surry, 2 T. R. 5. See Jackson *v*. Hill, 10 Adol. & Ellis, 491; 2 P. & D. 455, S.C.

(*k*) 3 Hen. 6, c. 3. As to receiving criminals, see 4 Edw. 3, c. 10; 5 Edw. 4, c. 14; and 27 Hen. 8, c. 24. See also Rex *v*. Jaram, 4 Bar. & Cres. 692; S. C. 7 Dow. & Ryl.

(*l*) 27 Hen. 8. c. 24, s. 7. It would appear, that before this statute, bailiffs of franchises were bound to give their attendance on the justices of assize, on pain of forfeiture for neglecting so to do, Bro. Forf. pl. 115, cit. 20 Edw. 4, fol. 6.

CHAP. IV.

former grants of the franchise, by Philip and Mary, and by Charles I.,) granted the execution of all writs to Viscount Dunbar, his heirs and assigns, in the liberty of Holderness, and it appeared that the officer had, since 1787, been in the habit of summoning jurors within the liberty to attend the quarter sessions, it was held that this evidence raised a presumption that this was a franchise existing at the time of passing the statute 27 Hen. 8, there being no evidence to the contrary: and that it was the bailiff's duty, on receiving the sheriff's mandate, to summons a sessions jury (*m*).

Of the sheriff's mandate, and where he may enter a liberty to execute a writ.

Where a writ (without a *non-omittas* clause) can only be executed within a liberty, the sheriff should make his mandate to the bailiff of the liberty to execute the writ (*n*).

Some nice distinctions have been raised in very recent cases in construing warrants, how far they can be treated as mandates to the bailiff of a liberty, or as the ordinary warrants to a sheriff's officer. In Platel *v.* Dowse (*o*) an ordinary warrant directed to the deputy bailiff of a liberty having been acted upon as a mandate, it was held that the chief bailiff could not refuse to return the mandate, on the ground that the document was a sheriff's warrant. But in a more recent case (*p*), where a warrant of the sheriff of Yorkshire was addressed to the keeper of the county gaol, "*and also to the chief bailiff of the liberty of Pickering Lythe, his deputies, and John Doe, my bailiffs,*" he directed them to take the defendants, if they should be found in the *sheriff's* bailiwick. In an action against the chief bailiff of Pickering Lythe, for an escape, it was held that this was a warrant, and not a mandate. Indeed, Mr. Justice Patteson said, "I think that where the bailiff of a franchise is addressed as an officer or bailiff of the sheriff, he may waive his franchise, and act upon the warrant, as an ordinary sheriff's officer."

By the statute 13 Geo. 2, c. 18, s. 6, "the sheriff, at the request and costs of the lord of a franchise having return of writs, shall appoint a deputy to reside in or near the same, who, on receipt of process, shall, under the seal of the sheriff, issue

(*m*) Rex *v.* Jaram, 4 Bar. & Cres. 692; 7 Dowl. & Ryl. S. C. 549, S. C.

(*n*) See form, Append. c. 4.

(*o*) 4 Bing. N. C. 204; 5 Scott,

(*p*) Jackson *v.* Hill, 10 Adol. & Ellis, 491; S. C. 2 Per. & Dav. 455.

his warrant to the lord of the franchise to execute the process." The statute of West. 2, c. 29, in affirmance of the common law, provides, that if such bailiff give no answer to the sheriffs, the court may grant a special warrant, with a *non-omittas* (q). And where there are two liberties in a county, and the sheriff makes his mandate to the bailiff of one of them, who gives him no answer, he may, upon a *non-omittas*, arrest the defendant in either liberty (r). Now, however, in practice, it is not unusual to issue a *non-omittas* writ, in the first instance, without default being made by the bailiff (s). As the practice of thus suing out a *non-omittas* writ, in the first instance, to be executed in a liberty with return of writs, has grown into general use, it was decided that a party was not liable to an action, at the suit of the bailiff of the liberty, for so doing, although it was alleged that the *non-omittas* writ was sued out to deprive the bailiff of his fees (t). Although a sheriff is liable to an action, at the suit of the owner of the franchise, for executing a writ without a *non-omittas* clause, within a liberty having the return of writs (u), yet the execution, in such case, is good, and therefore the sheriff is not a trespasser for executing such a writ within a liberty within the limits of his county (x); so, on the other hand, if the sheriff arrest a person within such liberty, and suffer him to escape, he is liable to an action; for although he was liable to an action at the suit of the owner of the franchise, for an infringement of it, yet the arrest was good (y). Indeed, it appears that the bailiff of a liberty may waive his franchise; thus, where he has the option of acting as bailiff of the liberty, or as the sheriff's bailiff, he may waive the former, and elect to act as sheriff's officer (z).

Power to replevy.

As regards granting replevins, where the bailiff of the liberty

(q) 2 Inst. 453.

(r) 5 Rep. 92 a; 9 East, 335, 340.

(s) Carrett *v.* Smallpage, 9 East, 330.

(t) *Ibid.*

(u) Villa de Darby *v.* Foxley, 1 Roll. Rep. 118; 1 Ventr. 406; Show. 18; 5 Rep. 92; Fitz. N. B. 98.

(x) Spinks *v.* Spinks, 7 Taunt. 311; Fitzpatrick *v.* Kelly, cit. in Rex *v.* Stubbs, 3 Term Rep. 740; 5 Rep. 92.

(y) Piggott *v.* Wilkes, 3 Bar. & Ald. 502. But in the case of Rex *v.* Mead and another, 2 Starkie, 207; S. C. Holt's N. P. C. 593, Wood, B., ruled, that a common bailiff of the sheriff executing a writ within a liberty, was a trespasser, and that a defendant who resisted the bailiff, and cut him with an axe, was not guilty of maliciously cutting under Lord Ellenborough's act.

(z) Jackson *v.* Hill, 10 Adol. & Ellis, 477; S. C. 2 Per. & Dav. 455; Munday *v.* Froggate, 2 Kel. 71, 117, 125; and see also Marsh. 25.

CHAP. IV.

has the power of granting replevins, the sheriff cannot enter the liberty and grant replevins and make deliverance, unless there has been a default in the bailiff of the liberty (*a*) Before the statute of Marlbridge, 52 Hen. 3, the sheriff could only grant replevin upon a writ of replevin issuing out of Chancery (*b*). The power of granting replevins is conferred by the 21st chapter of that statute.

The bailiff's power and duties within his liberty.

After the bailiff of a liberty has received the sheriff's mandate, he is to execute the same within his liberty, in the same manner as the sheriff is bound to execute it in the county at large. By the statute 27 Hen. 8, c. 24, s. 14, "all other statutes made before the 4th February, in that year, against sheriffs, or their under-sheriffs, bailiffs, or other ministers (*for making or returning any juries, serving of any writs, taking of fees, for extortions, or for any thing concerning their offices*) ; and all pains and penalties in every such statute contained, shall be in force against and extend to all stewards, bailiffs, and other ministers and officers of liberties and franchises having returns of writs and executions thereof, in like manner as they extend to sheriffs, under-sheriffs, &c. ; as if the said stewards, &c. had been particularly named therein," saving that the said stewards and bailiffs of franchises, their deputies or clerks, may occupy their offices above one year, viz., for so long time as they be given to them. Since that act, usually all the acts of parliament and rules of court, regulating the manner in which writs are to be executed, or the fees to be taken thereon, in terms extend to bailiffs of franchises. If the bailiff of a liberty arrest a person, he should imprison him within the liberty, for if he convey a prisoner to the county gaol, situated out of the liberty, it is an escape (*c*); and if the bailiff take a bail-bond from a person in his custody on mesne process, the bail-bond should be given to the bailiff, and not to the sheriff (*d*).

Return of writs by and liability of.

By stat. 27 Hen. 8, c. 24, s. 9, "The amercement for insufficient returns made by stewards and bailiffs of franchises shall be set on the head of such bailiffs and stewards, and not on the sheriffs." The responsibility of the sheriff in executing a writ

(*a*) Mounsy *v.* Dawson, 6 Ad. & Ellis, 752 ; 1 Nev. & Per. 763, S. C.

(*b*) 2 Inst. 139, 140, 194 ; Gilb. Replevin, 81, 85 b.

(*c*) Boothman *v.* Earl of Surry, 2 T. R. 5.

(*d*) Keld *v.* Harding, Com. Rep. 378 ; per Buller, J., 1 T. R. 4. *Sed vide* Dalt. 460.

ceases on making his mandate to the bailiff; and his return *mandavi ballivo* with the bailiff's return, or by stating that the bailiff hath made no return, is sufficient to discharge the sheriff. But it is said, that if the sheriff return *mandavi ballivo*, who answered some matter which is insufficient as a return, the sheriff shall be amerced, for the bailiff's return, in such case, is no return, and the sheriff should have returned *nullum dedit responsum* (*e*). It is said, that if the sheriff return *mandavi ballivo* to a writ, which he should execute within the liberty himself, as a writ of inquiry in waste, the sheriff shall be amerced (*f*).

And if the sheriff return that he has made his mandate to the bailiff of a liberty, when in fact there is no such liberty, he is amenable to the party and to the queen (*g*).

The sheriff's mandate always requires that the bailiff shall make his return to the sheriff; but in practice, the bailiffs make their returns directly to the court. The bailiff should put his name to the return (*h*).

And when the bailiff's return is made to the court, the bailiff is alone responsible; thus, when he returns *cepi corpus*, to a writ of mesne process, he shall be immediately ruled to bring in the body, and on failing so to do, the bailiff, and not the sheriff, shall be attached (*i*). Where the sheriff issues his mandate to the bailiff of a liberty, to summon a jury to attend the quarter sessions, the sessions has the power of fining the acting bailiff for not complying with the mandate (*k*). If the sheriff return the answer of the bailiff which is false, an action lies against the bailiff for the false return, but not against the sheriff (*l*). But if the sheriff alter the return of the bailiff of a franchise, he shall answer to the queen and to the bailiff of the franchise (*m*). If, after the delivery of the mandate to the bailiff of a franchise, he die or be removed, and a new bailiff succeeds before the return, the new bailiff should make the return (*n*), and where, under those circumstances, the sheriff returned the answer of an old bailiff,

(*e*) Roll. Abr. tit. *Retorn* (M), 1, 2, 3, 4, 5; 3 Hen. 7; 12 Bro. *Retorn*, 87.

(*f*) Fitz. *Retorn*, 53.

(*g*) See stat. West. 2, s. 39.

(*h*) 12 Edw. 2, c. 5.

(*i*) See 2 T. R. 5; T. Raym. 193.

(*k*) Rex *v.* Jaram, 4 Bar. & Cres. 692; S. C. 7 Dowl. & Ryl.

(*l*) Jackson *v.* Hill, 10 Adol. & Ellis, 477; 2 Per. & D. 455, S. C.; 2 Roll. Abr. 461, l. 35; 1 Roll. Abr. 98, l. 37; *Ib.* 99, l. 30.

(*m*) 2 Roll. Abr. 563, l. 25; Dalt. 461.

(*n*) 14 Edw. 4, fol. 1 b; 6 Vin. Abr. *Return*, 213; Bro. Abr. *Retorne de Briefe*, 99.

which was false, it was holden that no action lay against the old bailiff for such answer, for it was the return of a mere stranger (*n*). The bailiff is, of course, liable to an action on the case (*o*) for the escape of a prisoner out of his custody (*p*). The removal of a prisoner out of the liberty, we have seen, even to the county goal, without a *habeas corpus*, is an escape (*q*). If the sheriff return the bailiff's answer falsely, the bailiff is responsible, and must seek his remedy over against the sheriff (*r*).

The sheriff's return does not conclude a party in an action against the bailiff of a liberty. Thus, if the bailiff be guilty of an escape, a return of *cepi corpus* by the sheriff is no bar to an action against the bailiff of the liberty for an escape; for the return does not operate as an *estoppel* in such action (*s*).

Fees and poundage.

As to the fees and poundage to which the bailiff of a franchise in entitled, see *post*, chapter 5, section 5.

(*n*) Palmer *v.* Marsh, 1 Roll. Abr. 99, l. 35. It is there said, that an action would have lain against the sheriff for making such a return.

(*o*) See 5 & 6 Vict. c. 98, s. 31.

(*p*) Boothman *v.* Earl of Surry, 2 T. R. 5.

(*q*) Boothman *v.* Earl of Surry, 2 T. R. 5.

(*r*) Shaw *v.* Simpson, 1 L. Raym. 184.

(*s*) Jackson *v.* Hill, 10 Adol. & Ellis, 488; S. C. 2 Per. & Dav. 455.

CHAPTER V.

OF THE EXECUTION AND RETURN OF WRITS IN GENERAL.

SECTION I.

Writs, to whom Directed.

ALL mesne and judicial writs are directed to the sheriff of the county in which they are to be executed; or, in certain excepted **Writs, to whom directed.**

CHAP. V. SECT. I.

cases, which shall presently be mentioned, to some officer on whom the performance of the duties of sheriff for the particular place is imposed by law. And, as a general rule, the writ should be directed to the person or persons who are bound to execute it, and not in the alternative, "To A. *or* B." (*a*). If the sheriff be a party, the writ should (except in the case of mere serviceable process (*b*)) be directed to the coroner (*c*), in which case the officer executing the writ is the servant of the coroner, not of the sheriff (*d*). If there be two sheriffs, and one of them be a party to, or interested in, the suit, the writ should be directed to the other, and not to the coroner (*e*). But it is otherwise where one of two sheriffs dies; for in that case it is said, that the writ should not be awarded to the survivor (*f*). If the coroner also be a party, then the writ should be directed to elisors, named for that purpose by the Master (*g*). When there are more than one sheriff, as in the county of Middlesex, they should be addressed by the writ in the plural number; and a direction to the "sheriff," instead of "sheriffs," would be faulty (*h*). And *vice versâ*, where two or more persons constitute but one officer, as in the city of London, the writ should address them in the singular number, and it would be incorrect to style them "sheriffs," instead of "sheriff" (*i*); though there is a case in which the Court of Exchequer refused to set aside a writ so directed (*k*). The county should be correctly stated; but such a trifling error as "Middesex" for "Midd*l*esex," does not, it seems, vitiate the writ (*l*).

In a liberty.

In the execution of writs, the sheriff is the known, public, and

(*a*) See R. *v.* Fowler, 1 Ld. Raym. 586.

(*b*) Mayor of Kingston *v.* Bubb, 1 Dowl. 151.

(*c*) Western *v.* Coulson, 1 Black. Rep. 506. And if directed to the sheriff, the court will set aside the writ, on affidavit that he is interested.

(*d*) Sarjeant *v.* Cowan, 1 C. & M. 491.

(*e*) Letsom *v.* Bickley and others, 5 Maule & Sel. 144; Rex *v.* Warrington, Salk. 152; S. C. 4 Mod. 65; 12 Mod. 22; Carth. 214; Comb. 191; 1 Show. 327; Rich *v.* Player, 2 Show. 262, 286.

(*f*) 4 Mod. 65; Curle's case, 11 Rep. 4; *sed quære*.

(*g*) Andrews *v.* Sharp, 2 Blac. Rep. 911; see Mayor of Norwich *v.* Gill, 1 Dowl. 246; 1 M. & Scott, 91; 8 Bing. 27, S. C.

(*h*) Jackson *v.* Jackson, 3 Dowl. 182; 1 C. M. & R. 438, S. C.

(*i*) Nicol *v.* Boyne, 2 Dowl. 761; 3 M. & Scott, 812; 10 Bing. 387, S. C.; Barker *v.* Weedon, 2 Dowl. 767; Ulugh *v.* Kingswood, 1 Lord Ken. 287.

(*k*) Clutterbuck *v.* Wiseman, 2 C. & J. 213; and see Anon. 1 Tidd, 149.

(*l*) Colston *v.* Berens, 1 C. M. & R. 833; 3 Dowl. 253, S. C. overruling Hodgkinson *v.* Hodgkinson, 2 Dowl. 535.

responsible officer of the court, whose process he is bound to execute, and is justified in the execution of. A bailiff of a liberty, we have seen, does not derive his authority to execute a writ within his liberty immediately from the court, for he is not the officer of the court; therefore if the bailiff of a liberty, who hath execution and return of all writs therein, arrest a defendant on process immediately directed to him, he will be a trespasser (*m*). The writ should, in such a case, be directed to the sheriff of the county, who provides for its execution in the manner already pointed out in the fourth chapter. For instance, in the Isle of Ely the writ is directed to the sheriff of Cambridgeshire (*n*), and in the borough of Southwark to the sheriff of Surrey (*o*).

In the counties palatine.

Writs, either on mesne process or in execution, should not be directed to the sheriff *of a county palatine* immediately; but in the county palatine of Lancaster to the chancellor of the county palatine, or his deputy there, commanding him, by writ under the seal of the county palatine, to command the sheriff of such county palatine to execute the writ (*p*). And the same in the county palatine of Durham, since the act of 6 & 7 Will. 4, c. 19, by which the palatinate of Durham has been transferred from the bishop to the crown, as a separate franchise and royalty (*p*). As to the county palatine of Chester, however, the writ is now directed to the sheriff of the county in the first instance, the act of 11 Geo. 4, c. 70, s. 14, having abolished the jurisdiction of the chamberlain, to whom writs were formerly directed (*q*). The chancellor should not be directed to execute the writ himself, but only to command the sheriff to execute it; a writ commanding the chancellor to execute it himself would be a nullity (*r*). And as it is irregular to direct a writ in the first instance to the sheriff of a county palatine, the court, on motion, will set aside a writ so directed, and all proceedings thereon (*s*); but the sheriff of a county palatine is not a trespasser for executing a writ immediately directed to him; and it

(*m*) Grant *v.* Bagge and others, 3 East, 128. Or the Court will set aside the writ on motion, Bowring *v.* Pritchard, 14 East, 289.

(*n*) Grant *v.* Bagge, 3 East, 128.

(*o*) Bowring *v.* Pritchard, 14 East, 289.

(*p*) See 1 & 2 Vict. c. 110, s. 3.

(*q*) See stat. 9 & 10 Vict. c. 44.

(*r*) Branbridge *v.* Johnson, 3 Moore, 237; 1 Brod. & B. 12, S. C.

(*s*) Bradshaw *v.* Davis, 1 Chit. R. 374.

CHAP. V. SECT. I.

has been holden, that a bail-bond given by a defendant, arrested by the sheriff of Durham by virtue of a writ directed to him, was good (*t*).

In the Cinque Ports, Berwick, &c.

Writs to be executed in the Cinque Ports should be directed to the constable of Dover Castle, his deputy, or lieutenant (*u*); in Berwick-upon-Tweed, to the mayor and bailiffs of that borough (unless where the process is merely serviceable) (*v*); for the Cinque Ports do not form part of the bailiwick of the sheriff of Kent (*x*), and Berwick was never annexed to any county (*y*).

In counties of cities and boroughs.

In cities and towns which are counties in themselves the writs should be directed to the sheriff or sheriffs, as the case may be, of the city or town. But in those which are not counties in themselves, the writ should be directed in the same way as in other parts of the county in which they are situate. And the Municipal Corporation Act (5 & 6 Will. 4, c. 76,) has made no difference in this respect; for instance, in Oxford the writs must still be directed to the sheriff of Oxfordshire (*z*), and the same in other cities and boroughs not counties in themselves; thus we have seen that even in the borough of Southwark, though a liberty, and having a bailiff, writs must be directed to the sheriff of Surrey (*a*).

In places surrounded by another county.

In "districts and places parcel of some one county, but wholly situate within and surrounded by some other county," much inconvenience and delay formerly occurred in the service and execution of process; to remedy which it has been enacted by 2 Will. 4, c. 29, s. 30, "that every such district and place shall and may, for the purpose of the service and execution of every

(*t*) Jackson *v.* Hunter, 6 T. R. 71; Needham *v.* Bennet, Sir T. Raym. 171; 3 East, 134; Chapman *v.* Maddison, 2 Str. 1089; And. 198, S. C.; R. T. 21 Car. 1.

(*u*) Williams *v.* Gregg, 2 Marsh. 550; S. C. 7 Taunt. 233, in which case interlocutory judgment and all proceedings were set aside, on the ground that the writ, which was served in Deal, within the Cinque Ports, was directed to the sheriff of Kent. A direction "To the Constable of the Castle of Dover," instead of "Dover Castle," is not irregular. Frank *v.* James, 5 Dowl. 723.

(*v*) See 2 Burr. 855. In a case where the mayor, &c. of Berwick were the plaintiffs, the Court of Common Pleas refused to set aside the *service* of a *capias ad respondendum*, on application being made on the ground that the writ should have been directed to elisors. Mayor of Berwick *v.* Williams, 10 Moore, 266.

(*x*) See Williams *v.* Gregg, 2 Marsh. Rep. 550; S. C. 7 Taunt. 233.

(*y*) See 2 Burr. 850 *et seq.*

(*z*) Granger *v.* Taunton, 5 Dowl. 190; 3 Bing. N. C. 64, S. C.

(*a*) Bowring *v.* Pritchard, 14 East, 289.

writ and process (whether mesne or judicial) issued out of either of the superior courts at Westminster, be deemed and taken to be part as well of the county wherein such district or place is so situate as aforesaid, as of the county whereof the same is parcel; and every such writ and process may be directed accordingly and executed in either of such counties." But this enactment does not apply where the place so surrounded is a county of itself; for instance, in the case of a county of a borough which is a county in itself, the writs must be directed to the sheriff of the borough, not the sheriff of the surrounding county (*b*).

What writ the sheriff is bound to execute, and in what cases protected.

When a writ is delivered to the sheriff, he is *bound* to execute it, according to the exigency thereof, without inquiring into the regularity of the proceeding whereon the writ is grounded; and it will be found, by a variety of cases, that although the process, under which the sheriff takes the person or goods of the defendant, be voidable (*c*), or erroneous, and of which the defendant might have availed himself in the original action, yet such writ is a sufficient justification (*d*) for the sheriff in an action of trespass brought against him, for the sheriff is a ministerial officer in the execution of writs, and is not to examine their legality. So, on the other hand, in an action for an escape, or for a false return, brought against a sheriff, he cannot show that the process under which he acted was erroneously awarded (*e*). But this position is not universally true; for if a sheriff pays over money levied under a *fi. fa.*, with notice that the judgment on which the *fi. fa.* issued was *fraudulent*, he will be liable to a subsequent execution creditor for the amount (*f*). And a distinction prevails between cases where the court acts *inverso ordine*, by issuing irregular process, or the like, and where there is a total want of jurisdiction in the court; for the sheriff, in executing the process of a court not having jurisdiction over the cause, would be a trespasser (*f*). Upon the rule, that the sheriff is justified in the execution of erroneous process, it was held, that if a *capias* be awarded against a duke, earl, or other person having privilege of peerage,

(*b*) Davis *v.* Sherlock, 7 Dowl. 530.

(*c*) Parsons *v.* Lloyd, 3 Wills. 345; 2 Keb. 705.

(*d*) Cro. Jac. 280, 289; 2 Saund. 100; Cro. Eliz. 271; *ib.* 466, *contra.*

(*e*) Case of the Marshalsea, 10 Rep. 76; Bowsar *v.* Collins, 22 E. 4, 33 b, there cited, Poph. 203; Smith *v.* Bouchier, Str. 993; Odes *v.* Clarke, 1 L. Raym. 397; S. C. 5 Mod. 413; Brown *v.* Compton, 8 T. R. 424; Thomas *v.* Hudson, 14 M. & W. 364.

(*f*) Warmoll *v.* Young, 5 B. & C. 663; Imray *v.* Magnay, 11 M. & W. 267.

CHAP. V. SECT. I.

against whom a *capias*, by the law, doth not lie, notwithstanding, as the court hath jurisdiction of the cause, the sheriff is excused (*g*). So if a sheriff arrest a person upon *ca. sa.*, in which a whole term intervenes between the teste and the return; yet this writ is a justification to the sheriff (*h*). So the sheriff is justified in arresting a person upon a writ tested out of term. So if a *ca. sa.* be taken out after the year without a *sci. fa.*, and the defendant be arrested thereupon, and after suffered to escape, an action lies for this escape, though the process was erroneous; for the sheriff was bound to execute the writ, and therefore cannot let him at large (*i*). And so in an action for rescuing a debtor in custody upon mesne process sued out of the palace court, it was decided that it was not a sufficient ground to arrest the judgment, that it was not alleged that the cause of action in the inferior court arose within the jurisdiction, or, that it was not alleged that the party below did not appear on the return of the writ (*k*). The distinction between the erroneous judgment of a court having jurisdiction, and the want of jurisdiction, is thus illustrated by Dalton: "If the justices of peace arraign a person of treason in their sessions, who is convicted and executed, this is felony as well in the justices as in the sheriffs or officer who executed the sentence; but if he had been indicted of a trespass, found guilty, and hanged, though this had been felony in the justices, yet it would not be so in the sheriff; because a matter in which the justices had jurisdiction, and which they only were to blame in exceeding their authority" (*l*). And where, in debt against a sheriff for the escape of one in execution, the declaration very unnecessarily stated, that A. obtained

(*g*) Isabel Countess of Rutland's case, 6 Rep. 54. See also 10 Rep. 76.

(*h*) Parsons *v.* Lloyd, 3 Wils. 341; S. C. 2 Blac. Rep. 845; Plucknet *v.* Grenes, 2 Keb. 705; Shirley *v.* Wright, Lord Raym. 775; S. C. 2 Salk. 700; Nector *v.* Gennett, Cro. Eliz. 466; Wooden *v.* Moxon, 6 Taunt. 490; S. C. 2 Marsh. 186. *Qu.* in case of mesne process, see Willet *v.* Archer, 1 Man. & Ry. 317.

(*i*) Bush's case, Cro. Eliz. 188. See also Ognell *v.* Paston, Cro. Eliz. 165; Keiser *v.* Tyrrel, 2 Bulstr. 256; 1 Salk. 273.

(*k*) Bentley *v.* Donelly, 8 T. R. 127. See also Bull *v.* Steward, 1 Wils. 255; Luttin *v.* Bennin, 11 Mod. 50; Salk. 201; 1 Roll. Abr. 809; Squibb *v.* Hole, 2 Mod. 29; Higginson *v.* Martin, 2 Mod. 195; see 1 Vent. 369; 2 Lutw. 1569. From these cases it is to be collected, that if it appeared in the declaration that the original cause of action did not arise within the jurisdiction, then the sheriff would not be liable for the escape.

(*l*) Dalton's Sheriff, 197. And if the Q. B. issues process in a real action, the sheriff should not execute it, for there is a want of jurisdiction. 2 Bulstr. 64; Dalt. 105.

judgment in K. B. against B., who afterwards died intestate, and the plaintiff took out administration by an inferior ordinary, namely, the archdeacon of B. and brought a *scire facias* upon that judgment, to which he had judgment to have execution, and thereupon a *ca. sa.* issued against B., upon which he was taken, and in custody of the defendant, who was sheriff, &c., and afterwards escaped; and upon *nihil debet* pleaded, and a verdict for the plaintiff, it was moved in arrest of judgment that it appeared in the declaration, upon the plaintiff's own showing, that the administration was granted by a peculiar jurisdiction, whereas it likewise appeared that the intestate had *bona notabilia* in another diocese, namely, the judgment at Westminster; for which reason the administration granted by a peculiar jurisdiction by the archdeacon, was merely void; and then an action of escape would not lie against the sheriff, for the escape of a prisoner taken upon a void judgment; for if there were no judgment against B., there was no cause to detain him in prison. To which it was answered, and so resolved, that it was only error, of which the sheriff could not take advantage in an action for an escape brought against him; and the difference was where the judgment was merely void, or where it was only erroneous; and that depended on another distinction, namely, where the court in which the judgment was obtained had cognizance of the cause and where not; for, in the first case, if the plaintiff obtain a judgment, and by his own showing had no cause of action, yet because the court had jurisdiction of the cause, this is only an erroneous and not a void judgment; but it is otherwise where the court had no jurisdiction of the cause; but in the present case the court had cognizance of the cause, and therefore the matter was only error (*m*). But it does not follow that the sheriff is *bound* to detain a person in his custody, in every case where he would be *justified* in so doing; thus, where the defendant is privileged from arrest, the sheriff would not be liable to an action for discharging him, although he would be justified in detaining him (*n*). So if a person was arrested by the sheriff on the old process of *latitat,* in which a term intervened between the *teste* and return, and was discharged, the sheriff was not liable to an action of escape, notwithstanding he

(*m*) Gold *v.* Strode, 3 Mod. 324; S. C. Carth. 148.

(*n*) See next chap. *post.*

CHAP. V. SECT. I.

would be justified in executing such process (*o*). If the sheriff be ordered to return *non est inventus* to a *ca. sa.*, and in the meantime the defendant surrenders, he is bound to take him (*p*).

Where the defendant is misnamed.

Whenever a writ of *mesne process* is delivered to a sheriff, wherein the defendant is sued by a wrong name, the sheriff should not execute it, for in such case, even if the defendant was known by that name, or had assumed it in the particular case, so as to afford a sufficient justification to the sheriff in acting under it, yet he would not be liable to an action for not executing it (*q*). Whereas on the other hand, unless the defendant was as commonly known by the name by which he was sued as his real name, the sheriff would be liable to an action of trespass for taking the defendant or his goods under it (*r*). But the sheriff is bound to execute a *ca. sa.* in which the defendant is misnamed, for the defendant should have pleaded in abatement, and by not doing so he has admitted the name by which he is sued to be his real name (*s*).

Section II.

How, where, and when the Sheriff may execute a Writ.

By whom executed.

When the writ is delivered to the sheriff, or at the under-sheriff's office, the sheriff may personally execute the writ (*t*). So the under-sheriff, without a warrant, may execute the writ in person, for he is the known and responsible officer of the sheriff, and by his appointment clothed with all the powers of a

(*o*) Shirley *v.* Wright, Lord Raym. 775; S. C. 2 Salk. 790; Nector *v.* Gennet, Cro. Eliz. 476. See also Eden *v.* Lloyd, Cro. Eliz. 877. *Quære* as to the justification, Willet *v.* Arthur, 1 Man. & Ry. 317.

(*p*) Magnay *v.* Mongor, 1 Dav. & M. 24; 4 Q. B. 847, S. C.

(*q*) Morgans *v.* Bridges, 1 Bar. & Ald. 647; and see Keisar *v.* Tyrrell, 2 Bulstr. 256.

(*r*) Cole *v.* Hindson, 6 T. R. 234; Shadgett *v.* Clipson, 8 East, 328; Price *v.* Harwood, 2 Camp. 108; Scondover *v.* Warne, 2 Camp. 270; Finch *v.* Cocken, 2 C. M. & R. 196; Hoye *v.* Bush, 2 Scott, N. R. 86; Brunskill *v.* Robertson, 9 Ad. & El. 840; 2 Per. & D. 269, S. C. See Jarmain *v.* Hooper, 6 Man. & Gr. 827.

(*s*) Crawford *v.* Satchwell, Stra. 1218; Smith *v.* Patten, 6 Taunt. 115; 1 Marsh. 474, S. C.; Reeves *v.* Slatter, 7 B. & C. 486; Fisher *v.* Magnay, 1 Dowl. & L. 48.

(*t*) See per Littledale, J., Rose *v.* Tomblinson, 3 Dowl. 49, where the warrant varied from the writ, and Littledale, J., expressed an opinion that the sheriff might justify under the writ, though the warrant were wrong. And see R. *v.* Fowler, 1 Lord Raym. 586.

general deputy (*u*). And it is laid down in Dalton (*x*), that the sheriff may command his servant by word only (without precept in writing) to serve or execute any process, and it is good, and any stranger may justify by command of the sheriff any seizure of any goods or the taking of the defendant's person, without a warrant; but it is conceived that this only applies where the sheriff is himself acting personally in the execution of the process (*y*), and then, certainly, any person at his request may assist him without a warrant (*z*). But where a warrant is directed to a bailiff to execute a writ, the bailiff cannot depute the execution of it to another person (*a*); yet it is not necessary that his should be the hand that executes the writ; it is sufficient if he be near, and *acting* in the execution of such writ (*b*).

Of the warrant to the officer.

As soon as the writ is delivered at the sheriff's office, the under-sheriff makes out a warrant to one or more bailiffs for the execution of the writ, *in the name and under the seal of the sheriff*. The warrant must be according to the nature of the writ, commanding the officer to obey the mandatory part of the writ: but if there be a recital in the writ, it need not be inserted in the warrant (*c*). It need not specify the court out of which the writ issued (*d*). By the stat. 6 Geo. 1, c. 21, s. 53, no high sheriff, under-sheriff, their deputies or agents, shall make out any warrants before they have in custody the writs upon which such warrants ought to issue, on forfeiture of 10*l.*; and by s. 54 of the same act, (after reciting the stat. 5 & 6 W. & M. c. 21, s. 4; 9 & 10 Will. 3, c. 25, s. 42, which require the time of signing any writ on mesne process to be indorsed thereon by the clerk who signs the same,) every warrant upon any writ *before judgment to arrest any person* shall have the same day and year set down thereon as shall be set down on the writ itself, under forfeiture of 10*l.*, to be paid by the person who shall fill up or deliver out such warrant. If the warrant be directed to two or

(*u*) Dalt. 103. See *ante*, p. 35 *et seq.*

(*x*) Page 103, citing Bro. *Faux Imprisonment*, 43, *Tresp.* 339.

(*y*) But see per Littledale, J., Rose *v.* Tomblinson, *ubi supra*; and see Hamor *v.* Lord Jermyn, 1 Ld. Raym. 190.

(*z*) Drake *v.* Sykes, 7 T. R. 113.

(*a*) Lamb. 91; Dalt. 103; and see Robinson *v.* Yewens, 5 M. & W. 149; Pearson *v.* Yewens, 5 Bing. N. C. 489; Collins *v.* Yewens, 10 Ad. & El. 570.

(*b*) Blatch *v.* Archer, Cowp. 63.

(*c*) Dalt. 117. For different forms see Append. Blank printed forms of warrants may be had at all the law stationers.

(*d*) Astley *v.* Goodyer, 2 Dowl. 619; 2 C. & M. 682; 4 Tyr. 414.

CHAP. V. SECT. II.

more *jointly and severally*, it may be executed by any one or more of them, for as it is for the administration of justice, and for the public good, that execution be made, the authority need not be strictly pursued (*e*). But if the warrant be directed to several bailiffs *jointly, but not severally*, all must be acting in the execution of the writ, and if executed by one, his acts are illegal (*f*). If the bailiff make an arrest or execute a writ before the warrant is issued, he is a trespasser, and a warrant subsequently directed and delivered to him will not legalize his acts (*g*). A bailiff is not bound to receive a warrant sent him by post in a letter, the postage of which is unpaid (*h*). If the warrant be directed to one person, and he inserts the name of another bailiff, or if the place for the name be left blank, and the name inserted after it is issued (*i*), the person whose name was so substituted would be a trespasser for taking the defendant or his goods under such a warrant (*j*). And by the stat. 9 Geo. 2, c. 23, s. 22, "every warrant that shall be made out upon any writ, process, or execution, shall, before the service or execution thereof, be subscribed or indorsed with the name of the *attorney, clerk in court, or solicitor*, by whom such process, &c. shall be sued forth." But the not subscribing or indorsing the name on any warrant, &c. shall not vitiate the same; but such writ shall be valid and effectual, provided the writ whereon such warrant is made out be regularly subscribed or indorsed; and every sheriff or other officer, who shall make out any warrant upon any writ, process, or execution, and shall not subscribe or indorse thereon the name of the attorney, clerk in court, or solicitor, who sued out the same, shall forfeit 5*l.*, to be assessed as a fine by the court out of which such writ, &c. shall issue; one moiety to his majesty and the other to the person aggrieved (*k*). The fees allowed for making out warrants will be found in a subsequent section (*l*).

(*e*) White *v.* Wiltshire, Palm. 52; S. C. 2 Roll. Rep. 137; Dalt. 351; Lasbroke's case, Hutt, 127; Rex *v.* Hobbs, Yelv. 25; S. C. Cro. Eliz. 913; Co. Litt. 181 b.

(*f*) Boyd *v.* Durand, 2 Taunt. 161.

(*g*) Greene *v.* Jones, 1 Saund, 295, n. 5; Hall *v.* Roche, 8 T. R. 187.

(*h*) Hart *v.* Weatherby, 4 Dowl. 171.

(*i*) Housin *v.* Barrow, 6 T. R. 122.

(*j*) Burslem *v.* Fern, 2 Wils. 47; see Robinson *v.* Yewens, 5 M. & W. 149; Pearson *v.* Yewens, 5 Bing. N. C. 489; Collins *v.* Yewens, 10 Ad. & El. 570.

(*k*) 12 Geo. 2, c. 13, s. 4.

(*l*) Page 103. See Dew *v.* Parsons, 2 Bar. & Ald. 562; S. C. 1 Chit. Rep. 295.

CHAP. V. SECT. II.

If a sheriff, having a good writ, make an ill warrant, it seems he may justify under the writ, but not the bailiff (*m*).

Erroneous warrant. Showing warrant.

It is said, that in executing a writ, a sworn and known officer, be he sheriff, under-sheriff, bailiff, or serjeant, need not show his warrant or writ when he cometh to serve it upon any man's person or goods, although the party demandeth it (*n*); but that a special bailiff must show his warrant, if the party demands it, otherwise he need not obey it. And it is not clear but that *every* bailiff must do so (*o*). And even a known officer, upon the arrest, ought to declare the contents of his warrant; at whose suit he makes the arrest; out of what court; when returnable; to the end that, if it be upon an execution, he may pay the money, and so free his person; or if on mesne process, that he may put in bail, or agree with his adversary (*p*). And if a bailiff make an arrest before the writ comes to the sheriff's hand, or before the warrant is made upon it, the bailiff is a trespasser (*q*).

Of raising the *posse comitatus*.

Before the statute of Westminster, the sheriff or his officers might have raised the *posse comitatus* to execute the process issuing from the king's courts, and by that statute (West. 2nd, cap. 39) it is provided: "That the sheriff, as soon as his bailiffs do testifie that they found such resistance, forthwith all things set apart (taking with him the power of the shire) he shall go in proper person to do execution." This statute only applies to writs of execution, and therefore in executing *mesne process*, although the sheriff may, yet he is not compelled to raise the *posse comitatus* (*r*). In raising the *posse comitatus* the sheriff may command every one above the age of fifteen, and below the rank of a peer, to assist him; and persons acting, when the sheriff raises the *posse* on writs of execution, are justified, although there was no absolute necessity for raising it (*s*). But the sheriff should not raise the *posse comitatus* unless resistance is first shown (*t*). When the sheriff raises the *posse*, he is to

(*m*) Rex *v.* Fowler, 1 Lord Raym. 586; Rose *v.* Tomblinson, 3 Dowl. 49; Williams *v.* Lewis, 1 Chit. R. 611.

(*n*) Mackalley's case, 9 Rep. 69, 6*th Resolution*; Dalt. 109, 110, 111.

(*o*) Hall *v.* Roche, 8 T. R. 188; and see Robins *v.* Hender, 3 Dowl. 543.

(*p*) Mackalley's case, 9 Rep. 68; the Countess of Rutland's case, 6 Rep. 54 a.

(*q*) Greene *v.* Jones, 1 Saund. 299, note 5.

(*r*) Noy, 40; 1 Stra. 432; Cro. Jac. 419; 1 Roll. Rep. 440.

(*s*) Dalt. 355; 5 Hen. 7, 4, 5.

(*t*) 2 Inst. 454; Hob. 62, 264. It would appear that a warrant to execute a writ is a sufficient authority to the sheriff's officers to raise the *posse comitatus*, if necessary, Dalt. 355, 356.

CHAP. V. SECT. II.

judge of the force requisite, and for that reason the court, in one case, would not declare three hundred men to be excessive (*u*). There are several particular statutes respecting the sheriff quelling riots in some bad parts of the metropolis, but by the change of times these have become obsolete (*v*). At this day, when the sheriff raises the *posse* in his county to execute a writ, he incurs considerable expense, yet there does not seem any means by which the sheriff can be remunerated for such expense; on the other hand, the law has imposed the obligation upon every one to attend the sheriff when required, without prescribing any reward, therefore all sums paid by the sheriff to the *posse* are gratuitous on his part.

Where. In what county.

The authority of the sheriff is confined to the county whereof he is sheriff; if the sheriff therefore execute a writ out of his county, he is a trespasser: but on a writ of *habeas corpus*, the sheriff has power to carry a prisoner in his custody through other counties (*x*); and on fresh pursuit, the sheriff may, in another county, retake a person who has escaped from his custody (*y*). Thus, if the sheriffs of London, on a writ directed to them, make an arrest in the county of Middlesex, or *vice versâ*, the arrest is void (*z*), and will be set aside on motion, or summons at chambers, provided it sufficiently appear on affidavit that the arrest took place in the wrong county, and that there is no dispute as to the boundaries (*a*).

Places surrounded by other county.

The 2 Will. 4, c. 39, s. 20, after reciting that there are "certain districts and places parcel of some one county, but wholly situate within and surrounded by some other county," enacts, "that every such district and place shall and may, for the purpose of the service and execution of every writ and process, whether mesne or judicial, issued out of either of the said courts, be deemed and taken to be parts as well of the county within which such district or place is so situated as aforesaid as of the county whereof the same is parcel, and every such writ and process may be directed accordingly, and executed in either of such counties (*b*)."

(*u*) Dalt. 355; see also 1 Keb. 99.

(*v*) 8 & 9 Will. 3, c. 27; 9 Geo 1, c. 21.

(*x*) 2 Roll. Rep. 163; Plowd. 37 a.

(*y*) Dalt. 23.

(*z*) Hammond *v.* Taylor, 3 Bar. & Ald. 408; see Chase *v.* Joyce, 4 M. & Sel. 414.

(*a*) Webber *v.* Manning, 1 Dowl. 24; Lloyd *v.* Smith, 1 Dowl. 372; Storer *v.* Rayson, 4 D. & R. 739.

(*b*) See also 2 & 3 Vict. c. 82, and 7 & 8 Vict. c. 62.

Palaces.

It is not lawful for the sheriff to make an arrest or execute a writ in the queen's presence, or in a court of justice, whilst the justices are sitting, or in any of the royal palaces (*c*), or their verge, unless by leave of the board of green cloth (*d*), or in the Tower (*e*). In such cases, however, the execution is not void, but only a contempt, and it will not be set aside on motion (*f*).

Tower.

Franchise.

If the sheriff enter a franchise, the owner of which has the execution and return of writs, and execute a writ without a *non omittas* clause therein, the execution is good (*g*), although the sheriff may be liable to an action at the suit of the owner of the franchise, for an infringement thereof (*h*).

When the officer may enter houses and break open doors, &c.

To execute a writ at the suit of the king, as an extent or the like, the sheriff may (after signifying the cause of his coming and demanding admission) (*i*) break open the outer door of a house wherein the defendant or his goods may be (*j*); so in executing a *capias utlagatum*, the sheriff may break open the outer door of a house (*k*). The sheriff or his officer may also break open an outer door in executing a writ of seisin or *habere facias possessionem* (*l*); but to execute any other writ or process in civil actions, whether on mesne process or in execution, the sheriff cannot break open the outer door of the defendant's dwelling-house (*m*), for it is said every man's house is his castle and fortress, as well for defence against injury and violence, as for his repose (*n*). A distinction has been supposed to exist in this respect between the outer door of the defendant's own house and that of a third person in which the defendant or his goods are concealed. The words of Lord Coke, from which that doctrine has been drawn, are as follows (*o*): " It was resolved, that

(*c*) Winter *v.* Miles, 10 East, 578; 1 Camp. 475; Gilb. C. P. 27; Bell *v.* Jacobs, 1 Moo. & P. 309; 4 Bing. 523, S. C.

(*d*) Rex *v.* Stobbs, 3 T. R. 735; see Winter *v.* Miles, 1 Camp. 475; 10 East, 578, S. C.

(*e*) See Batson *v.* M'Clean, 2 Chit. Rep. 51; Bell *v.* Jacobs, 1 Moo. & P. 309.

(*f*) Sparks *v.* Spinks, 7 Taunt. 311.

(*g*) Piggott *v.* Wilkes, 3 B. & Ald. 502; Sparks *v.* Spinks, 7 Taunt. 311.

(*h*) See Carrett *v.* Smallpage, 9 East, 330.

(*i*) Launock *v.* Brown, 2 Barn. & Ald. 592.

(*j*) Semayne's case, 5 Rep. 92; S. C. Cro. Eliz. 908; 4 Leon. 4; Fitz. *Trespass*, 232; Bro. *Trespass*, 248; Burdett *v.* Abbott, 14 East, 157; Lanock *v.* Brown, 2 Barn. & Ald. 592.

(*k*) 2 Hale's P. C. 202; Semayne's case, 5 Rep. 92; Rex *v.* Bird, 2 Show. 87.

(*l*) Semayne's case, 5 Rep. 92, 1*st Resolution*.

(*m*) Semayne's case, 5 Rep. 90; S. C. Cro. Eliz. 908; 4 Leon. 4; Cooke's case, Cro. Car. 537; S. C. Sir W. Jones, 429; Foster *v.* Hill, 1 Bulstr. 146.

(*n*) *Id. ibid.*

(*o*) See 5 Rep. 93, 5*th Resolution*; Foster, 309.

CHAP. V. SECT. II.

the house of any one is not a castle or privilege but for himself, and shall not extend to protect any person who flies to his house, or the goods of any other, which are brought and conveyed into his house, to prevent a lawful execution, and to escape the ordinary process of the law, for the privilege of his house extends only to him and his family, and to his own proper goods, or to those which are lawfully *and without fraud and covin there.*" This has been construed to mean that the outer door of the house of a stranger, in which a defendant or his goods are, may be broken open to execute a writ: but it seems evident that Lord Coke only means to refer to cases of fraudulent concealment of goods, or the retaking a prisoner who has escaped, on fresh pursuit, or on an escape-warrant (*p*); in which latter case of retaking a prisoner who has escaped, on fresh pursuit, any outer door may, after request, be broken open, just as in the case of the crown (*q*). It is laid down as the result of the cases, in a very able work (*r*), that, although the sheriff may (after request made) justify breaking open the outer door of a third person's house, in order to execute process of the law upon the defendant or his property removed thither in order to avoid an execution, still he does so at his peril, for if it turn out that the defendant was not in the house or had no property there, he is a trespasser (*s*). It has also been considered that the sheriff cannot, even though he may have grounds for suspicion, justify entering the dwelling-house of a third person, although he breaks no door, unless it prove in the event that the defendant or his goods were actually therein (*t*). The author above referred to however goes on to say (*u*), that circumstances may exist under which the sheriff would be justified in entering the house of a stranger on suspicion, even though the defendant were not actu-

(*p*) Per Best, C. J., in Rex *v.* Conolly, Hertford Spring Assizes, 1824; see also Hutchinson *v.* Birch, 4 Taunt. 619; Johnson *v.* Leigh, 6 Taunt. 248; Cooke *v.* Birt, 5 Taunt. 765.

(*q*) R. *v.* Gansel, Lofft, 380; see Genner *v.* Sparkes, 1 Salk. 79; 6 Mod. 173; White *v.* Wiltshire, 2 Rol. Rep. 138; Lloyd *v.* Sandilands, 8 Taunt. 280.

(*r*) John William Smith's Leading Cases, 44, n.

(*s*) Johnson *v.* Leigh, 1 Marsh. 565; 6 Taunt. 248; Ratcliffe *v.* Burton, 3 B. & R. 229, explained in Hutchinson *v.* Birch, 4 Taunt. 627; Com. Dig. *Execution*, C 5; see White *v.* Wiltshire, Palm. 52; 2 Rol. Rep. 138; Biscop *v.* White, Cro. Eliz. 759; judgment in Cooke *v.* Birt, 5 Taunt. 769; Morrish *v.* Murrey, 13 M. & W. 52.

(*t*) Cooke *v.* Birt, 5 Taunt. 765, per Gibbs, C. J. and Dallas, J.; Johnson *v.* Leigh, 6 Taunt. 248, per Gibbs, C. J.; Morrish *v.* Murrey, 13 M. & W. 52.

(*u*) John William Smith's Leading Cases, 45.

ally there. And he instances the case of the defendant being on a visit with a third person, where the house of the third person would be *pro tempore* the defendant's dwelling-house (*x*), so that the outer door could not be broken open even after demand and refusal; and also the case where fraud is used to inveigle the sheriff into a belief that the defendant is in the house. The right of the sheriff to enter the defendant's own house does not depend upon the contingency of the defendant being there, for that is the most natural place for the defendant or his goods to be. And on the same principle, where there is a judgment against an administratrix *de bonis testatoris*, and she marries, the sheriff may enter her husband's house to search for the goods of the testator (*y*).

If the officer gain admittance at the outer door of a house, he may break open the inner doors or chests to do execution (*z*), even without first demanding that such doors should be opened (*a*). And in like manner, the sheriff may break open the door of a barn detached from a dwelling-house and not within the same curtilage, to do execution, although the door may be locked (*b*). Also, if, after a peaceable entrance at the outer door of a house, the sheriff or officer be locked in, he may justify breaking open the outer door to get out, and the court would probably grant an attachment against the defendant (*c*). And it is said that goods may be taken through a window, if open (*d*). If the sheriff break open an outer door when he is not justified in so doing, this, it is said, does not vitiate the execution, but merely renders the sheriff liable to an action of trespass (*e*). In practice, however, the courts will discharge a defendant out of custody when so arrested, or order goods so seized to be restored.

At what time the sheriff may and should execute the writ.

The sheriff is, in general, bound to set about executing all writs delivered to him within a reasonable time after he receives them for execution, and if he omit doing so, and any damage

(*x*) See Shears *v.* Brooks, 2 H. Bl. 129.

(*y*) Cooke *v.* Birt, 5 Taunt. 771.

(*z*) Sir Thomas Kemp and Windsor's case; Lee *v.* Gansel, Cowp. 1; Lloyd *v.* Sandilands, 8 Taunt. 250; S. C. 2 J. B. Moore, 207; see also 5 Rep. 92.

(*a*) Hutchinson *v.* Birch, 4 Taunt. 619; Ratcliffe *v.* Burton, 3 Bos. & Pul. 223.

(*b*) Penton *v.* Browne, 1 Sid. 186; S. C. 1 Keb. 698; Bac. Ab. tit. *Sheriff*, (N. 3).

(*c*) White *v.* Wiltshire, Cro. Jac. 555; S. C. 2 Rol. Rep. 137; Palm. 52; Pugh *v.* Griffith, 7 Ad. & El. 827; 3 N. & P. 189, S. C.

(*d*) 1 Rol. Abr. 671, pl. 7; see Doe *v.* Trye, 5 Bing. N. C. 573.

(*e*) Semayne's case, 5 Rep. 93 a. But see Bac. Abr. *Execution*, (N.)

arise from such omission, he is answerable for it (*f*). His power to execute the writ continues from the time it is delivered to him until the expiration of the return day of the writ, if returnable on a particular day (*g*). The sheriff could not execute process between the return day and the *quarto die post* (*h*), and for so doing he would be a trespasser, as the four days between the return day and the *quarto die post* were merely *ex gratiâ* (*i*). But where the sheriff held an inquest on the return day of the writ, but the jury did not give their verdict for two or three days afterwards, the writ was held to be well executed (*k*). So, where a writ of trial under 3 & 4 Will. 4, c. 42, was returnable on the 27th July, and the trial commenced on that day, but the verdict was not delivered till the 28th, an objection by the unsuccessful party, on motion for a new trial, that the sheriff had no power to receive and enter the verdict, was not entertained (*l*). If the trial have not *commenced* before the writ is returnable, the proper course would seem to be to apply to a judge to have the time extended (*m*); although it has been said that even in such case the court would amend the record on motion (*n*). Where no particular return day is mentioned, but the writ is returnable "immediately after execution," the power of the sheriff (while in office) to execute the writ continues until the writ is actually executed or returned, even though it be a writ of execution, and more than a year has elapsed from the time of the judgment (*o*). If, however, the execution of it be in the mean time countermanded by the execution creditor, the sheriff is a trespasser if he proceed to execute it notwithstanding (*p*). In the case of

(*f*) Brown *v.* Jarvis, 1 M. & W. 704; 5 Dowl. 285, S. C.; see Jacobs *v.* Humphries, 2 C. & M. 13; Bates *v.* Wingfield, 2 N. & M. 831; Aireton *v.* Davis, 9 Bing. 740; 3 M. & Scott, 138, S. C.; Doker *v.* Hasler, 2 Bing. 479; 10 Moore, 210, S. C.; Randell *v.* Wheble, 10 Ad. & El. 719; Mason *v.* Paynter, 1 Gale & D. 386; Clifton *v.* Hooper, 6 Q. B. 468.

(*g*) Bugberd's case, Cro. Eliz. 180; Gaven *v.* Ludlow, *ib.* 468; Wolley *v* Moseley, *ib.* 761; S. C. Moor, 711; Anon. 3 Salk. 51; 2 Roll. Abr. 278; Parlims *v.* Wollaston, 6 Mod. 130. Even after the rising of the court on that day, Maud *v.* Barnard, 2 Burr. 812; Dyke *v.* Blakston, 2 Lord Raym. 1449; Towne *v.* Crowder, 2 C. & P. 355.

(*h*) 2 Roll. Abr. 278, pl. 10, cit. 33 Hen. 6, 45, 46; Ellis *v.* Jackson, 1 Lev. 143; S. C. 1 Sid. 229; 1 Keb. 718, 805; see Loveridge *v.* Plaistow, 2 H. Bl. 29.

(*i*) See Coulson *v.* Hammon, 2 Bar. & Cres. 626; S. C. 4 D. & R. 160.

(*k*) 2 Rol. Abr. 278, pl. 5; Dyke *v.* Blakston, 2 Lord Raym. 1449.

(*l*) Pinkney *v.* Booth, 1 Dowl. N. S. 421.

(*m*) Mortimer *v.* Preedy, 3 M. & W. 602.

(*n*) Sherman *v.* Tinsley, 4 Scott, 286.

(*o*) Simpson *v.* Heath, 5 M. & W. 631; Greenshields *v.* Harris, 9 M. & W. 774; Thomas *v.* Harris, 1 Dowl. N. S. 793.

(*p*) Hunt *v.* Hooper, 12 M. & W. 664.

some writs a certain time is prescribed by statute within which the writ is to be executed; *e. g.* the *capias* under 1 & 2 Vict. c. 110, s. 3, must be executed within a month.

After year of office.

Before the 3 & 4 Will. 4, c. 99, if the sheriff levied goods on a *fi. fa.* and went out of office, he might still have proceeded to sell the goods, even without a *venditioni exponas*, for the same sheriff that began must have finished the execution (*q*). Whether the 7th section of that statute makes any difference in this respect has been already considered (*r*).

The sheriff cannot execute a writ on a Sunday.

By the statute 29 Car. 2, c. 7, s. 6, it is enacted, "That no person upon the *Lord's day* shall serve or execute, or cause to be served or executed, any writ, process, warrant, order, judgment, or decree (except in cases of treason, felony, or breach of the peace), but that the service of every such writ, process, warrant, order, judgment or decree shall be void to all intents and purposes whatsoever, and the person or persons so serving or executing the same shall be liable to the suit of the party grieved, and to answer damages to him for doing thereof, as if he or they had done the same without any writ, process, warrant, order, judgment, or decree at all." It has been holden that, under the provisions of this statute, the execution of a writ of inquiry on a Sunday is bad (*s*); and that the statute extends to render void the mere service of process on a Sunday. Thus, the service on a Sunday of a Master's order (*t*), or of an award (*u*) to ground an attachment, has been held void; for neither of these is in the nature of a criminal proceeding, but of a civil execution. So on this statute it has been held, that an arrest on Sunday upon a *capias utlagatum* (*x*), or for non-payment of a penalty upon conviction (*y*), is void; but after a *negligent* escape the defendant may be retaken on Sunday, either upon fresh pursuit or upon an escape warrant, for this is not an original taking (*z*). And it would seem that bail may take their principal on Sunday, in order to surrender him, for he is considered to be always in

(*q*) Ayre *v.* Aden, Cro. Jac. 73; 1 Salk. 323; 1 Ves. 196.

(*r*) *Ante*, pp. 24, 25.

(*s*) Hoyle *v.* Lord Cornwallis, 1 Stra. 387.

(*t*) M'Ileham *v.* Smith, 8 T. R. 86.

(*u*) Rex *v.* Myers, 1 T. R. 266; and it has been holden that notice of plea served on a Sunday is void by this statute, Roberts *v.* Monkhouse, 8 East, 547.

(*x*) Barnes, 319.

(*y*) Rex *v.* Myers, 1 T. R. 265.

(*z*) Parker *v.* Sir W. Moore, 6 Mod. 95; S. C. 2 Lord Raym. 1028; 2 Salk. 626.

CHAP. V. SECT. II.

their custody; and this case does not fall within the statute, inasmuch as this is not by virtue of any process at all (*a*). But the sheriff cannot retake a party on Sunday after a *voluntary* escape (*b*). It would appear that a citation out of the spiritual court might be served on a Sunday (*c*); or an attachment for a rescue (*d*); or a person may be arrested on a Sunday on the Lord Chancellor's warrant, on an order of commitment for contempt (*e*). And a person may voluntarily surrender himself to prison on a Sunday if he will (*f*). As, after a voluntary escape, a party cannot be retaken on a Sunday, so where A. was arrested at the suit of B., and discharged, the sheriff not knowing that there also was a detainer in his office at the suit of C., and on the Sunday following he was arrested at C.'s suit, the court held this arrest void (*g*). But where a defendant, in custody in the county gaol on a *ca. sa.*, received on a Saturday an order from the creditor for his discharge, which was on the same day forwarded by the gaoler to the under-sheriff, who lived at another town in the county, and on the Sunday a warrant of detainer on another *ca. sa.*, which had been received by the sheriff on the Saturday, was forwarded to the gaoler, who thereupon detained the defendant, it was held that he had no right to his discharge; for the sheriff was entitled to a reasonable time to search his office for other writs against the defendant, which time would not elapse till the Monday (*h*).

Where a person has been arrested, or served with a process on a Sunday, the arrest or service is wholly void, so much so, that no waiver by the party can cure the irregularity (*i*). And if the defendant or his goods be in the custody of the sheriff, the court will set the execution aside, or discharge the defendant out of custody, on motion (*j*). And it seems quite clear, from the words of the statute, that an action of trespass would lie against the sheriff, if he took either the defendant or his goods

(*a*) Anon. 6 Mod. 231; 1 Atk. 239. *Sed vide* Brookes *v.* Warren, 2 Blac. Rep. 1273, *contra*.

(*b*) Featherstonhaugh *v.* Atkinson, Barnes, 273; Atkinson *v.* Jameson, 5 T. R. 25. He cannot retake him on any day.

(*c*) Alanson *v.* Brookbank, 5 Mod. 449; Carth. 504; Walgrave *v.* Taylor, 1 Lord Raym. 706; 12 Mod. 606.

(*d*) Anon. Willes, 459.

(*e*) *Semb.* 1 Atk. 55.

(*f*) *Ibid.*

(*g*) Atkinson *v.* Jameson, 5 T. R. 25.

(*h*) Samuel *v.* Buller, 1 Exch. R. 439.

(*i*) Taylor *v.* Phillips, 3 East, 155.

(*j*) 5 T. R. 25; see also 6 Mod. 95.

by virtue of any civil process on Sunday (*k*). And as all arrests are unlawful which are made on a Sunday, it would appear to be the better opinion, that if a sheriff's bailiff attempt to arrest a person on a Sunday, and that person resists and slays the bailiff, this is not murder (*l*).

SECTION III.

Of the Rule or Order to return the Writ.

When it is necessary to return the writ.

Regularly, the sheriff should make his return to every writ (*m*): but it is not usual for sheriffs to do so, unless ruled for that purpose. The writ of *elegit*, however, is an exception to this; for if lands be extended on it, it is absolutely essential that it should be returned (*n*). And it has been doubted whether the sheriff ought not to return writs returnable immediatley after execution, without waiting for a rule (*o*). The writ is no justification to the sheriff for arresting a person upon mesne process, unless it be shown that it is returned (*p*); otherwise of writs of execution (*q*).

Who may rule sheriff to return, and when.

The party whose writ it is may rule the sheriff to return it at any time. The party against whom it issued may rule the sheriff to return it after the object of the writ has been effected (*r*). But it seems that this could not be done by such party before that time, except on special grounds (*s*). And a side-bar rule obtained for such a purpose was discharged by the Court of C. P. (*t*). If it could be done before, it would be in the power of any person against whom a writ returnable "immediately after execution" issues, to defeat the writ, by ruling the sheriff to return it as soon as he knows of its existence, and before it is executed (*u*). It may sometimes be advisable for the person

(*k*) Wilson *v.* Guttery, 5 Mod. 95; S. C. Salk. 78, *nomine* Wilson *v.* Tucker; and see 6 Mod. 95.

(*l*) Hawk. P. C. c. 32, s. 58.

(*m*) See Woodman *v.* Gist, 8 C. & P. 213.

(*n*) Hoe's case, 5 Rep. 90; Garraway *v.* Harrington, Cro. Jac. 569.

(*o*) Woodman *v.* Gist, 8 C. & P. 213. It is not easy to see the distinction.

(*p*) Britton *v.* Cole, Salk. 409; Freeman *v.* Blewett, 12 Mod. 394; S. C. Salk. 410; Lord Raym. 632.

(*q*) Cheasley *v.* Barnes, 10 East, 73; Rowland *v.* Veale, Cowp. 18.

(*r*) See Edmunds *v.* Watson, 7 Taunt. 5; 2 Marsh. 333, S. C.; France *v.* Clarkson, 2 Dowl. 532.

(*s*) Daniels *v.* Gompertz, 2 Gale & D. 751.

(*t*) Williams *v.* Webb, 2 Dowl. N. S. 904.

(*u*) See Daniels *v.* Gompertz, 2 Gale & D. 751.

CHAP. V. SECT. III.

against whom the writ issues to rule the sheriff to return it, in order to prevent improper conduct in the officer. The court will not however, at the instance of the party against whom a writ of *fi. fa.* issued, order the sheriff to make a specific return of the goods sold and their proceeds, on the ground that the officer has wasted the property seized (*x*).

May be ruled in term or vacation.

By the common law, the rule could only have been obtained in term time. But by 2 Will. 4, c. 39, s. 15, "It shall be lawful in term time for the court out of which any writ issues *by authority of this act*, or any writ of *capias ad satisfaciendum, fieri facias*, [including the ancillary process of *venditioni exponas* (*y*)], or *elegit*, shall have issued, to make rules, and also for any judge of either of the said courts, in vacation, to make orders for the return of any such writ, and every such order shall be of the same force and effect as a rule of court made for the like purpose; provided always, that no attachment shall issue for disobedience thereof until the same shall have been made a rule of court (*z*)."

When the old sheriff may be ruled to return.

If the sheriff execute a writ, and go out of office, as in strictness he ought to have returned the writ before he was out of office, he is still liable to be ruled to return the writ, and to an attachment for not returning it, for the contempt was actually committed whilst he was a servant of the court (*a*). It is, however, enacted by the statute 20 Geo. 2, c. 37, "That no sheriff shall be liable to be called upon to make a return of any writ or process, unless he be *required* so to do within six months after the expiration of his said office." The word *required*, means ruled to return; therefore the sheriff is not liable to an attachment for not returning a writ if not ruled, although requested so to do, within that time (*b*). The months mentioned in this statute have been construed to mean lunar months (*c*). And according to R. *v.* Adderley (*d*), the day on which he goes out of office is to be reckoned in the six months, but it may be doubted how far that case is consistent with more modern decisions (*e*). It is reported to have been decided in one case

(*x*) Willett *v.* Sparrow, 2 Marsh. 293; 6 Taunt. 576, S. C.

(*y*) Hughes *v.* Rees, 4 M. & W. 468; 7 Dowl. 56, S.C.; Reg. *v.* Berles, 6 Dowl. P. C. 97.

(*z*) See *post*, 85.

(*a*) Rex *v.* Adderley, Doug. 464; and see Rex *v.* Sheriff of Middlesex, 4 East, 604.

(*b*) Rex *v.* Jones, 2 T. R 1.; Doug. 463, n.; see Garth *v.* Hopkins, 3 Dowl. 711.

(*c*) Rex *v.* Adderley, Doug. 463.

(*d*) Doug. 463.

(*e*) See Webb *v.* Fairmaner, 3 M. & W. 473, where the cases are col-

that a sheriff, under special circumstances, might be compelled to return a writ, though he had been *more than three years* out of office (*f*). But the statute 20 Geo. 2, c. 37, was not adverted to. The subject of the transfer of unexecuted writs to the incoming sheriff has been already discussed (*g*).

Cases where the sheriff cannot be ruled to return the writ.

If the plaintiff has taken an assignment of the bail bond, he has determined his election, and is not at liberty afterwards to rule the sheriff to return the writ of capias (*h*). If however the bond be void, as being executed after the return of the writ, or the like, the sheriff may be ruled to return the writ, notwithstanding an assignment of the bail bond (*i*).

It has been holden that the sheriff cannot be ruled by the plaintiff to return the writ, where it has been executed by a *special bailiff*, appointed by the plaintiff or his agent (*k*). But it seems that if in such a case it becomes essential, with a view to further proceedings, that a return should be made, *e. g.* where after a *fi. fa.*, under which an unproductive seizure has been made, the plaintiff wishes to issue a *ca. sa.*, the plaintiff, after informing the sheriff of the purpose for which the return is desired and offering an indemnity, may, in case of refusal, rule him to return the writ (*l*). Where the plaintiff takes from the defendant a *cognovit*, conditioned to pay the debt and costs by instalments (*m*), or where the parties, either with or without their attorney's consent, compromise, so that the sheriff cannot complete the execution, and the return would be useless (*n*), or there is any collusion between the officer and the plaintiff or his attorney (*o*), or the plaintiff (or his assignees, if he has become bankrupt or insolvent) has made an arrangement with the

lected. Rex *v.* Adderley may perhaps be supported on the ground there suggested by Parke, B.

(*f*) Wilton *v.* Chambers, 3 Dowl. 338.

(*g*) *Ante*, p. 24, 25.

(*h*) Etherick *v.* Cowper, 1 Salk. 99; Lord Brooke *v.* Stone, 1 Wils. 223.

(*i*) *Id. ibid.*

(*k*) Hamilton *v.* Dalziel, 2 Blac. Rep. 952; De Moranda *v.* Dunkin, 4 T. R. 119. See also Porter *v.* Viner, 1 Chit. Rep. 613, n.; Palister *v.* Palister, *ib.* 614, n. See fully *ante*, p. 40, 41, as to the liability of the sheriff where a special bailiff has been appointed.

(*l*) Harding *v.* Holder, 3 Scott, N. R. 293; 2 Man. & Gr. 914; 9 Dowl. 659, S. C.

(*m*) Rex *v.* Sheriff of Surrey, 1 Taunt. 159; Farmer *v.* Thorley, 4 Bar. & Ald. 91; and see Rex *v.* The late Sheriff of Middlesex, 2 Bing. 366.

(*n*) Alchin *v.* Wells, 5 T. R. 470; Hodges *v.* Jordan, 5 Dowl. 6; see Edmunds *v.* Watson, 2 Marsh. 333; 7 Taunt. 5, S. C.; Balson *v.* Meggatt, 4 Dowl. 558.

(*o*) Ruston *v.* Hatfield, 3 B. & Ald. 204; 1 Chit. R. 613, S. C.

CHAP. V. SECT. III.

sheriff as to the disposal of the goods (*p*), or the defendant against whom a *ca. sa.* issues has become an insolvent or a bankrupt, and the plaintiff has accepted the office of assignee (*q*), or indeed in any case where the party seeking to compel a return has by his conduct placed the sheriff in any difficulty as to the return (*r*), the sheriff cannot be ruled to return the writ; and if a rule be obtained, the court on motion will discharge it (*s*). The new sheriff cannot be compelled to return writs not regularly transferred to him by the old sheriff (*t*).

No estoppel. No estoppel as to the validity of a writ is created by ruling the sheriff to return it, and the filing that return of record (*v*).

The rule or order. We have seen that the proceeding to compel a return is in term time by rule, and in vacation by a judge's order. The rule is a side-bar rule, and may be obtained, like other side-bar rules, at the master's office on any day of the term, even the last (*u*). The order may be obtained in vacation at judge's chambers as a matter of course, without any affidavit (*x*).

To whom directed. It is directed in ordinary cases to the sheriff or "*late* sheriff," who should be so designated in rules addressed to him (*y*).

Where the writ is issued to a county palatine, the rule should not be made on the chancellor, but on the sheriff of the county (*z*). So where the writ is executed within a liberty by the bailiff, he may be ruled to return the writ either in the first instance, or after the sheriff has returned *mandavi ballivo*. In either court the rule or order expires in *four* days after service in London and Middlesex, and eight days after service in any other county or city (*a*).

Service of. Formerly, in every county except London and Middlesex, the rule must have been served on the sheriff or under-sheriff (*b*),

(*p*) Gilbert *v.* Whalley, 2 C. M. & R. 722.

(*q*) Hepworth *v.* Sanderson, 8 Bing. 19.

(*r*) See Hook *v.* Weatherby, 4 Dowl. 171.

(*s*) See De Moranda *v.* Dunkin, 4 T. R. 119; Hamilton *v.* Dalziel, 2 B. & C. 952; 1 Chit. Rep. 614, n.; Hodges *v.* Jordan, 5 Dowl. 6.

(*t*) Thomas *v.* Newman, 2 Dowl. N. S. 33.

(*v*) Jones *v.* Williams, 8 M. & W. 349; 9 Dowl. 302, S. C.

(*u*) R. H. 2 Will. 4, r. 96.

(*x*) Reg. Gen. H. T. 1 Vict.

(*y*) See R. *v.* Sheriff of Cornwall, 7 Dowl. 600.

(*z*) Chitty's Arch. 7th ed. 550.

(*a*) Reg. Gen. M. T. 7 W. 4. This rule no doubt includes orders, though it specifies only rules. See Chitty's Archbold, 7th ed. 550.

(*b*) Rex *v.* Coles, Doug. 420. Where the under-sheriff shut himself up to avoid the service of the rule to return the writ, the court directed that leaving a copy at his house should be good service; Richardson *v.* Baily, Barnes, 35.

CHAP. V. SECT. III.

now, by the effect of 3 & 4 Will. 4, c. 42, s. 20, service on the sheriff's deputy in town will suffice.

A copy of the rule (with the name of the officer by whom the defendant was arrested indorsed on it) must be served personally on the under-sheriff or deputy (*c*), and the original rule shown at the same time (*d*). At the time of serving the rule, the party making the service should make a memorandum of the person on whom he served it, that it may be inserted in the affidavit.

At what time the rule or order should be complied with, and attachment for neglect or delay.

If the rule expire in term time, the sheriff should return the writ *on or before* the day on which the rule expires, otherwise the plaintiff may move for an attachment on the day following (*e*); or if the rule expire on the last day of term, the plaintiff may move for an attachment at the rising of the court on that day, if the writ be not then returned (*f*). If the rule be obtained in term, and expires in vacation, then by Reg. Gen. H. T. 2 Will. 4, rule 11, "the sheriff shall file the writ at the expiration of the rule, or as soon after as the office shall be open." And by r. 12, "the officer with whom it is filed shall indorse the day and hour when it was filed." And by R. T. 7 Will. 4, Q. B., assimilating the practice of the three courts, it was ordered that sheriffs may file their returns to writs in vacation, and searches may be made in vacation for writs and returns filed, without payment of the extra fee hitherto charged. If he fail to return the writ in vacation, on the expiration of the rule, an attachment may be obtained on the first day of the next term (*g*).

In case of orders made in vacation, pursuant to 2 Will. 4, c. 39, s. 15, it is provided by Reg. Gen. M. 3 Will. 4, r. 13, "that in case a judge shall have made an order in vacation for the return of any writ issued by authority of the said act, or any writ of *ca. sa.*, *fi. fa.* (including *venditioni exponas* (*h*)), or *elegit*, on any day in the vacation, and such order shall have been duly served, but obedience shall not have been paid thereto, and the same shall have been made a rule of court in the term then next following,

(*c*) Barnes, 30, 35; 3 & 4 Will. 4, c. 42, s. 20.

(*d*) Barnard *v.* Berger, 1 N. R. 121; Rex *v.* Smithies, 3 T. R. 351.

(*e*) R. M. 30 Geo. 3, 4 T. R. 496.

(*f*) Rex *v.* Sheriff of Surrey, 11 East, 591.

(*g*) Rex *v.* Sheriff of Middlesex, 1 Marsh. 270; S. C. 5 Taunt. 647; Smith *v.* Blyth, 9 Price, 255.

(*h*) Hughes *v.* Rees, 4 M. & W. 648; 7 Dowl. 56; Reg. *v.* Berles, 6 Dowl. 97.

CHAP. V. SECT. III.

it shall not be necessary to serve such rule of court or to make any fresh demand of performance thereon, but an attachment shall issue forthwith for disobedience of such order, whether the thing required by such order shall or shall not have been done in the meantime." This rule, be it observed, is strictly confined to the cases mentioned in it, namely, *orders* made *and* returnable in vacation. It does not apply to *rules* of court (*i*), nor to orders, unless they expire *in vacation*, and therefore, except in the case of an order expiring in vacation, an attachment will not be allowed to stand, if a return be made before the rule for an attachment has been obtained (*k*). But if the sheriff return the writ after the rule for an attachment is obtained, though before it is actually served, yet the contempt is not thereby purged (*l*). It is no waiver of an attachment for not returning a writ of *fi. fa.* to direct the sheriff, after the order to return has expired, to proceed with the execution (*m*).

Where the sheriff, on being ruled to return a writ, gave notice to the plaintiff that the writ was lost, and that the defendant was in custody on other process, the court set aside an attachment obtained against the sheriff for not returning the writ, as irregular under those circumstances (*n*).

Motion for attachment.

Affidavit necessary to ground an attachment.

The rule for an attachment, which is absolute in the first instance (*o*), is moved for upon an affidavit, stating a personal service of a copy of the rule, and that the original rule was at the same time shown to the person served (*p*).

The attachment against a sheriff is directed to the coroner, or if he be interested, then to elisors in the first instance (*q*).

Setting aside attachment on terms.

When an attachment has been irregularly obtained, it will of course be set aside. And even where the attachment is regular, yet where the omission or delay of the sheriff has caused no loss to the party who ruled him, the attachment will be set aside on

(*i*) As to rules or orders for returning a bailable writ of capias, which expire in vacation, and to which *cepi corpus* is returned, see Reg. Gen. H. 3 Will. 4, *post*, chap. 6.

(*k*) Williamson *v.* Harrison, 9 M. & W. 225; 1 Dowl. N. S. 664, S. C.

(*l*) See Rex *v.* Sheriff of Surrey, 11 East, 591.

(*m*) Howitt *v.* Rickaby, 9 M. & W. 52; 1 Dowl. N. S. 389, S. C.

(*n*) Rex *v.* Sheriff of Kent, 1 Marsh. 289. Gibbs, C. J., said, that the plaintiff might have proceeded as if the sheriff had returned *cepi corpus, and had actually brought in the body.*"

(*o*) 2 Chitty's Archb. 1263.

(*p*) Barnard *v.* Berger, 1 N. R. 121; Rex *v.* Smithies, 3 T. R. 351.

(*q*) Reg. *v.* Sheriff of Glamorganshire, 1 Dowl. N. S. 308.

payment of costs only (*r*). And the sheriff will not be compelled to make good more than the loss actually occasioned by his omission or delay (*s*).

Section IV.

Returns in general (*t*).

The return.

Returns are nothing else but the sheriffs' answers, touching that which they are commanded to do by the king's writ, and are but to ascertain the court of the truth of the matter; and yet this is one of the most difficult things belonging to the office: for, as Dalton says (*u*), if he be not circumspect in making his returns, "he shall not only endanger himself to be amerced, or sued for the same; but also he shall indamage the parties, and may hazard the cause or suit itself; for you shall find that judgments have been often stayed for faults apparent in the sheriff's return, yea, and that judgments have been often reversed by writs of error for this cause."

By whom made.

The return is made by the under-sheriff in the name of the high sheriff, as the high sheriff is the person to make the return. But if a writ be directed to the sheriff to be executed, and afterwards a new sheriff is elected, the successor (if the writ be transferred to him) ought to return the writ with the old sheriff's return thereon, and that he received the writ as above indorsed from his predecessor (*x*). Now it is the practice for the late sheriff to make his return (*y*). If the sheriff die during his year of office, the under-sheriff, before the appointment of a new sheriff, should make the return in the name of the *deceased sheriff* (*z*). Where the sheriff has sent his mandate to the bailiff of a liberty to execute a writ, it is, strictly speaking, the duty of the bailiff to make his return to the sheriff, who returns *mandavi ballivo*, with the bailiff's return; but it is now usual to rule the bailiff himself

(*r*) R. *v.* Sheriff of Essex, 8 Dowl. 5; Dorrien *v.* Sheridan, 6 Bing. N.C. 150; 8 Scott, 363, S. C.

(*s*) Reg. *v.* Sheriff of Herts, Dod *v.* Coleman, 9 Dowl. 916; see R. *v.* Sheriff of Kent, Potter *v.* Simpson, 2 M. & W. 316. As to enforcing the return of a *fi. fa.* out of the Court of Chancery, see Evans *v.* Davies, 7 Beav. 81.

(*t*) The returns to particular writs will be discussed in the chapters relating to such writs respectively.

(*u*) P. 182.

(*x*) 2 Roll. Abr. 457; 1 Bulst. 70; Gibbons *v.* Roberts, 1 Salk. 266; R. *v.* Sheriff of Middlesex, 4 East, 604.

(*y*) *Per* Lord Ellenborough, C. J., 4 East, 606.

(*z*) 3 Geo. 1, c. 15, s. 8.

CHAP. V. SECT. IV.

after a return of *nullum dedit responsam*, in which case the bailiff makes his return directly to the court (*a*).

The sheriff of a county palatine, having execution of a writ out of one of the superior courts at Westminster, may either return the writ to the chancellor, to be returned by him to the superior court, or may at once return it to the superior court himself (*b*).

The form of the return.

The forms of returns used at this day are the same as when Dalton wrote, excepting that now they are in English instead of in Latin. The return is made on the back (*c*) of the writ itself; and if long, a schedule is annexed to the writ, and referred to in an indorsement on the writ. Where the return is made on the back of the writ it may be in this form, viz. "By virtue of this writ, to me directed and delivered, I have [*here state what has been done under the writ,*] as by the said writ I am directed and commanded; A. B. esq., sheriff." The writ and return should be filed in the office of the court, before or on the day on which the rule or order to return the writ expires (*d*). And to ensure punctuality, it is ordered (*e*) that "the officer with whom it is filed shall indorse the day and hour when it was filed." Formerly, it was held that any formal defects, as the want of words of reference, vitiated a return, but the addition of *modo et forma quod breve exigit et requirit,* cured any defects in the formal parts of the return (*f*). Where the sheriff returned that he had taken the body of C. D., without saying the *within-named*, it was held that the return was bad, for C. D. might be a stranger (*g*); but such an objection would not avail at this day (*h*). When the return is long, as where the inquisition as taken by a jury is set out, as on a return to an elegit, or a writ of inquiry, the return is made in this form (*i*): "The execution of this writ appears in a certain schedule hereto annexed; A. B. esq., sheriff:" and

(*a*) Boothman *v.* Earl of Surrey, 2 T. R. 5; T. Raym. 193. See Jackson *v.* Taylor, 5 Dowl. 140.

(*b*) R. *v.* Sheriff of Lancaster, 7 Dowl. 765.

(*c*) This is the universal practice; but semble, a return on the face of the writ would be good; Dalton, 189.

(*d*) See *ante*, p. 85.

(*e*) Reg. Gen. H. 2 W. 4, r. 12.

(*f*) Fitz. *Retorn*, 44; 2 Hen. 4, 13; Bro. *Expos.* 34; 1 Hen. 6, 6.

(*g*) Bro. *Amendment*, 64; 12 Hen. 6, 19; 11 Hen. 7, 28.

(*h*) And see Fitz. *Retorn*, 2, 44; Bro. *Retorne de Briefe*, 28, 64; Com. Dig. *Pleader*.

(*i*) It was determined that a return was vicious where it was stated that "the residue of this writ appears," &c. instead of the "residue of the *execution*," &c. Fitz. *Retorn*, 14; 19 Hen. 6.

a separate piece of parchment containing the inquisition is annexed to the writ. By stat. 12 Edw. 2, c. 5, it was provided, "That from thenceforth sheriffs and other bailiffs that receive the king's writs returnable in his court shall put their names with the returns, so that the court may know of whom they took such return, if need be. And if any sheriff or other bailiff leave out his name in his return, he shall be grievously amerced to the king's use." The sheriff ought to put his christian name and surname to the return (*k*); where there are two sheriffs, they both ought to put their names; and a return in the name of one is not aided, for it is no return at all (*l*). It seems, howeve, that a return is not bad for the sheriff's omitting his name, although he is liable to be amerced (*m*). Where a new sheriff makes a return to a writ which has been executed by his predecessor, the new sheriff returns the writ with his predecessor's return; in which case the old sheriff's subscription of "A. B. esq., *late sheriff*," is sufficient, for the statutes only require the name, and the words "late sheriff" are surplusage (*n*); but the new sheriff should return the writ as executed by his predecessor, and not as executed by himself (*o*). Formerly, the want of the sheriff's name to a *venire facias* was error, but this omission is cured by the statute of *jeofails*, 21 Jac. 1, c. 13, s. 2; 4 & 5 Ann. c. 16, s. 1; and by 16 & 17 Car. 2, s. 8, the want of the sheriff's name being returned on the original writ is cured.

The return must be certain and direct.

The return ought to be certain (*p*). But it seems that inasmuch as it is only to ascertain the court of the truth of the matter, it requireth not such precise certainty as is required in pleading (*q*). It must be certain in time, place, and all other material circumstances (*r*). Therefore, where the sheriff returns that the defendant had no goods, or that the defendant *non est inventus prout ei constare poterit*, the return is bad, for the sheriff

(*k*) Dive *v.* Maningham, Plowd. 63, a; Fitz. *Retorn*, 8; 8 Hen. 6, 27; Carth. 56; and see Ingoldsby *v.* Martin, Strange, 316, where a return in the name of *George* instead of *Henry*, Earl of Lichfield, was held well enough.

(*l*) See 11 Rep. 4; Lamb *v.* Wiseman, Hob. 70; 39 Hen. 6, 41.

(*m*) Dalston *v.* Thorp, Cro. Eliz. 767; 1 Leon. 139, *tamen quære.* And see 1 Bulstr. 73; 3 Bulstr. 78; Vin. Abr. *Retorn*, C.; 1 Chit. Arch. 7th ed. 413.

(*n*) Bethyll *v.* Parry, Cro Car. 189, 570.

(*o*) Rex *v.* Sheriff of Middlesex, 4 East, 604.

(*p*) Dalt. 168.

(*q*) *Ibid.*

(*r*) *Ibid.*

CHAP. V. SECT. IV.

should have said directly *nulla bona* or *non est inventus* (*s*). Upon a *habere facias seisinam*, the sheriff returned that the party *non prosecutus est breve*, this return is bad for uncertainty (*t*). In a replevin, if the sheriff return that he could not deliver the goods *quia visum inde habere non potuit*, it is bad, because he does not say that he came to the place (*u*). So to a *fi. fa.*, a return that the premises of the defendant are so barricadoed that the sheriff cannot ascertain whether there are goods on which a levy can be made or not, is bad, for he ought to give a direct answer either that there are no goods which can be levied upon, or that there are, and that he has levied (*x*). So a return that the sheriff has caused to be seized divers goods of A. B., the value whereof is to him unknown, which remain in his hands for want of buyers, is irregular; some value must be stated (*y*). But a return stating, "I have caused to be made of the goods of A. B. &c., *22l. 2s.*, out of which I have paid 11*l.* 5*s.* for *rent due* for the premises wherein the said goods were taken," &c., was held sufficient, on the ground that it must be reasonably intended to refer to rent due to the landlord at the time of the seizure (*z*). An argumentative return subjects the sheriff to an attachment, unless the court give leave to amend (*a*).

The return must be a full answer.

The return must answer the whole writ up to the time of making the return; therefore the return of a panel with nine or less names than twelve is void (*b*). So a return upon a grand cape, *cepi manus*, &c., if it say nothing as to the summons of the tenant, it is void (*c*). *Scire facias* against the heir and terre-tenants, if the return say nothing as to the heir, it is void (*d*). A sheriff's return upon an *extendi facias*, that he has delivered such land, without saying that there is no other land, is void (*e*). Upon a *petit cape*, where the count was for a house and stable, the return was *cepi* as to the house, but said nothing as to the

(*s*) Bro. *Retorne de Briefe*, pl. 8; Roll. Abr. *Return* (L), 1; 9 Hen. 6, 557.

(*t*) Roll. Abr. *Return* (L), 2, 3, 4.

(*u*) *Ibid.* (L), 5.

(*x*) Munk *v.* Cass, 9 Dowl. 332.

(*y*) Barton *v.* Gill, 12 M. & W. 315.

(*z*) Reynolds *v.* Barford, 7 Man. & Gr. 449; 8 Scott, N. R. 237, S. C.

(*a*) See Master *v.* Cooper, 1 Price, P. C. 8.

(*b*) Roll. Abr. *Return* (M), 2; Bro. *Retorne de Briefe*, 47, 48.

(*c*) Roll. Abr. *Return* (M), 2.

(*d*) Eyres *v.* Taunton, Cro. Car. 295; but this was held to be cured by appearance, Cro. Car. 313; Eyres *v.* Cowley, Sir W. Jones, 319.

(*e*) 1 Brownl. 37; see Eldrin *v.* Hopkins, 7 Dowl. 146.

stable; it was held, for this omission, void (*f*). So to a *fi. fa.* returnable *Oct. Mich.*, a return that the defendant had no goods at *Mich.* is bad, for perhaps the defendant had some before *Oct. Mich.* (*g*); so, a return to a *latitat*, that the bailiff found the defendant insane, and so ill that he could not be moved, is defective, for not saying that he continued so until the return of the writ (*h*); so where a *venditioni exponas* to sell goods levied as to part of the debt, and a *fieri facias* as to the residue were included in the same writ, the sheriffs made a return to the *venditioni exponas*, without making any return as to the *fi. fa.*, it was held bad for this omission (*i*).

Must be in usual form.

The return ought to follow the usual precedents,—even a slight departure in this respect is prohibited. Thus a return of "not *to be* found" instead of "not found" (the usual form of return *non est inventus*) has been holden bad (*k*).

The return must not falsify the writ, record, or a former return.

The return of the sheriff must not falsify the writ or the record (*l*), or be contrary to a former return of the sheriff (*m*), or of his predecessor (*n*); it must not be against the admittance of the party (*o*). These rules are so easy in application, that it will not be necessary, excepting by reference to the cases upon the subject, (which are not in themselves of much practical use at this day,) to enter into further detail on the subject.

Return, how aided.

The insufficiency of a return is cured by appearance; as where the sheriff omits the names of the manucaptors on the return to the *distringas juratores*, this is cured by the appearance of the jurors; so a return of *scire feci per visum A. et B.*, instead of *scire feci per A. et B.*, is cured by appearance (*p*). And where in debt for an escape it was objected that the sheriff's return on the original writ was void, the objection was held immaterial;

(*f*) Taste *v.* Haynes, Sir W. Jones, 357.

(*g*) Palmer *v.* Potter, Cro. Eliz. 512.

(*h*) Cavenagh *v.* Collett, 4 Bar. & Ald. 279; Baker *v.* Davenport, 8 D. & R. 606; Perkins *v.* Meacher, 1 Dowl. 21.

(*i*) Rex *v.* Sheriff of Middlesex, 1 Marsh. 344.

(*k*) Rex *v.* Sheriff of Kent, 2 M. & W. 316; 5 Dowl. 451, S. C.

(*l*) Com. Dig. *Retorn* (E), 4; Moor *v.* Watts, Salk. 581; S. C. 1 Lord Raym. 613; 12 Mod. 424; see also Doyley *v.* White, Cro. Jac. 323; S. C. 2 Bulstr. 80. Return to a writ of *pone*, "I could not execute this writ, the cause therein alleged for the execution thereof not being true," is bad for this reason. Greenshaw *v.* Emerson, 1 Dowl. 337.

(*m*) Roll. Abr. *Return* (E); Vin. Abr. *Return* (E).

(*n*) Roll. Abr. *Return* (F); Vin. Abr. *Return* (F).

(*o*) Roll. Abr. *Return* (G); Vin. Abr. *Return* (G).

(*p*) Vin. Abr. *Return* (W).

CHAP. V. SECT. IV.

for after appearance and pleading, no advantage shall be taken of such misprision nor of misawarding of mesne process (*q*). So the insufficiency of a return in matters of form may, according to a decision of Coleridge, J., be aided by lapse of time. In that case a sheriff, on the 6th March, returned to a *fi. fa.* "goods in hand for want of buyers," omitting to state their value; and an application on the 24th April to quash the return for this defect was held to be too late (*r*). But this doctrine (which seems novel as applied to acts of the sheriff) can only apply to returns defective in point of form, for a void return cannot be "aided." For instance, if a writ be directed to two sheriffs of a town corporate, and one make the return without his fellow, this is bad, and not aided as an insufficient return, for this is no return at all (*s*).

When amended.

Where the return is defective, it may be amended, even although the return was made in the time of the former sheriff (*t*); and even after the death of the sheriff, the court will allow an amendment by the under-sheriff (*u*). Thus, where the sheriff returned too small issues, and prayed to amend, it was granted (*x*). And where the sheriff by negligence omits any of the jurors in the *distringas* which were in the *venire facias*, or returns T. B. for A. B., or returns *octo tales* for *decem tales*, these shall be amended by the sheriff upon his examination in court (*y*). So where the sheriff returned that the defendant was insane, and unable to be removed at the time that the officer went to take him, the court allowed him to amend his return, by stating that the defendant continued so until the return day of the writ, on supporting it by an affidavit (*z*). Where the sheriff returned to a writ of *venditioni exponas*, as to goods taken in execution sufficient to satisfy part of the debt, with a *fieri facias* for the residue, that he had sold the goods already taken, but made no return to the *fieri facias*, the court, on an affidavit by the under-sheriff's clerk that it was a mere mistake, allowed the return to be amended (*a*). Where the

(*q*) Dalston *v.* Thorp, Cro. Eliz. 767.

(*r*) Chambers *v.* Coleman, 9 Dowl. 588.

(*s*) Lambe *v.* Wiseman, Hob. 70; see also 11 Rep. 4.

(*t*) Dalton, 189.

(*u*) Fitz. *Amendment*, 40, cit. 33 Hen. 6, 47.

(*x*) Bro. *Issues*, 1.

(*y*) Dalton, 189.

(*z*) Cavenagh *v.* Collett, 4 Bar. & Ald. 279.

(*a*) Rex *v.* Sheriff of Monmouth, 1 Marsh. 344.

sheriff returned *cepi corpus* to a writ of mesne process, the court, after an attachment granted against the sheriff for not bringing in the body, allowed the sheriff to amend his return according to the fact, by stating that the defendant was in prison in the custody of the sheriff (*b*). And the same where the sheriff had returned "is not *to be* found" instead of "is not found (*c*)." So where, to a writ of extent, the sheriff returned that he had seized money into the hands of her Majesty, which money was in the hands of the accountant-general in bankruptcy, and the Court of Review declined to order the accountant-general to pay over the money to the sheriff (*d*), the Court of Exchequer made absolute a rule for discharging one which required the sheriff to pay the money to the crown, and for amending the return (*e*). But the sheriff ought to apply promptly for such indulgence, for he will not be permitted to amend where he has been guilty of laches. For instance, where the sheriff falsely returned to a *fieri facias* "goods in hand for want of buyers," and upon an action for a false return being brought, obtained time to plead on the usual terms, an application to amend the return to *nulla bona* was held to be too late (*f*). Where the sheriff, under a *fi. fa.* and a writ of extent, seized not only the defendant's goods, but also goods belonging to a stranger which were on the premises, and the sheriff returned to both writs, that he had seized goods to the amount, but that they remained in his hands for want of buyers; the sheriff being obliged afterwards, by order of the Court of Exchequer, to levy the amount of the extent upon the defendant's goods, and not upon the goods of the stranger, and having no longer goods of the defendant to satisfy the *fi. fa.*, applied to the court for leave to amend his return to the latter writ; the court however refused to allow the amendment, saying, that as he had seized sufficient property of the defendant under this writ, he must be accountable to the plaintiff for it; had he, as soon as he received the order of the Court of Exchequer, stated the facts of the case to that court,

(*b*) Rex *v.* Sheriff of Wilts, 8 Moore, 518.

(*c*) Rex *v.* Sheriff of Kent, in Potter *v.* Simpson, 2 M. & W. 316; 5 Dowl. 451.

(*d*) See Ex parte Magnay, 2 Mont. D. & D. 671.

(*e*) Rex *v.* Austin, 10 M. & W. 691; 2 Dowl. N. S. 468, S. C.

(*f*) Wylie *v.* Pearson, 1 Dowl. N. S. 807.

CHAP. V. SECT. IV.

they would have relieved him from his embarrassment (*g*). Unnecessary amendments will not be allowed; thus where the sheriff returned to a *capias*, "I have taken the body of the defendant, whose body remains in the prison of our lord the king, under my custody," and the defendant after this return escaped from the sheriff on bringing him up to London on a *habeas corpus* in another suit, the sheriff, being ruled to bring in the body, prayed leave to amend his return by stating that the defendant had been in custody at the suit of other persons as well as the plaintiff; but the court refused, as the return was substantially correct (*h*).

Amendment on motion of any person interested.

The amendment may be applied for by any person interested, and even, it would seem, without making the sheriff a party to the rule, if his conduct be not impeached. Where the plaintiff's attorney became the defendant's attorney, and improperly procured a return to a *fi. fa.* of a sum having been levied greater than what was actually levied, an amendment was ordered (*i*).

Return, how far conclusive.

Credence is given to the return of the sheriff: so much so, that, as a general rule, there can be no averment against the sheriff's return in the same action (*k*); although a party in any other action, or in an action against the sheriff, may show that such return is false (*l*), and *in favorem vitæ* a party is not concluded by the sheriff's return (*m*). But the sheriff's return of a *devastavit* is not conclusive against an executor (*n*). And where the sheriff returns that the defendant is dead, the plaintiff may be received against this return, otherwise the suit would abate (*o*). And although the party cannot aver against the sheriff's return, yet he may show that the person making the return is not sheriff (*p*). Even in another action, the sheriff's return is *primâ facie* evidence of the facts contained in it; as in an action for maliciously suing out a *fi. fa.* after a sufficient levy,

(*g*) 1 Chitty's Archbold, 7th ed. 414; see Saunders *v.* Bridges, 3 Bar. & Ald. 95; but see Tomlinson *v.* Shynn, 4 Moore, 505; 2 B. & B. 77, S. C.

(*h*) Ibbotson *v.* Tindal, 1 Bing. 156; 7 Moore, 552, S. C.

(*i*) Green *v.* Glassbrook, 2 Bing. N. C. 143; 2 Scott, 261, S. C.

(*k*) Dalton, 189, 190, 191; Roll. Abr. *Return* (O).

(*l*) Dalton, 190; Vin. Abr. *Return* (O).

(*m*) Dalton, 191, 192.

(*n*) Gibson *v.* Brooke, Cro. Eliz. 859; Mounson *v.* Bourne, Sir W. Jones, 418; S. C. Cro. Car. 519, 528.

(*o*) Vin. Abr. *Return* (O), 22.

(*p*) Arundell *v.* Arundell, Yelv. 34.

the sheriff having returned that he had forborne to sell under the first writ, and had sold under the second writ, at the instance and with the consent of the then plaintiff, it was held that these returns were *primâ facie* evidence of such consent (*q*). The court will not try the truth or falsehood of a return or affidavit, but will leave parties injured by a false return to their remedy by action (*r*).

When the sheriff and his officers are concluded by a return.

The sheriff, generally speaking, is concluded by his own return; and so the bailiff of a liberty, it would appear, is concluded by the sheriff's return, although false, and his remedy is over against the sheriff (*s*). Where a sheriff having levied under a *fi. fa.*, after notice that defendant had petitioned the Insolvent Court, returned *fieri feci*, he was held bound by that return, and compelled to pay over the amount to the plaintiff, though the defendant was afterwards discharged under the insolvent act (*t*). He ought to have applied to the court in the first instance, to relieve him from his embarrassment. But where the sheriff returned to a *fi. fa.* that he had levied goods, and a commission of bankruptcy issued against the defendant on an act of bankruptcy committed before the delivery of the writ to the sheriff, which goods the sheriff gave up to the assignees, it was held that he was not bound by his return, but might show those facts in an action brought against him for not selling the goods under a *venditioni exponas* (*u*).

The sheriff's officer, for the purposes of his own justification, is not concluded by a false return of the sheriff (*x*).

Excuses for return.

If the sheriff hath any *valid excuse* for not executing a writ, he may state such matter of excuse in his return, as that the defendant is privileged (*y*); although it is quite clear that, excepting in the case of peers and members of parliament, he is not *bound* to take notice of privilege (*z*).

Tardè.

Upon a *capias ad respondendum*, it is said that a return of *tardè*

(*q*) Gyfford *v.* Woodgate, 11 East, 297. See Leonard *v.* Simpson, 2 Bing. N. C. 176; 2 Scott. 835.

(*r*) Goubot *v.* De Crouy, 2 Dowl. 86; see Barber *v.* Mitchell, 2 Dowl. 574; Anon. Lofft, 371.

(*s*) Shaw *v.* Simpson, 1 Lord Raym. 184.

(*t*) Field *v.* Smith, 2 M. & W. 388; 5 Dowl. 735, S. C.; see Wylie, *v.* Pearson, 1 Dowl. N. S. 807.

(*u*) Brydges *v.* Walford, 6 M. & Sel. 42; see also Clutterbuck *v.* Jones, 15 East, 78.

(*x*) Parker *v.* Mosse, Cro. Eliz. 181.

(*y*) See Bro. *Retorne de Briefe*, pl. 46.

(*z*) See *post*, chap. 6, sec. 1.

is bad, for the manifold mischiefs which might follow thereon; and it was formerly the practice to amerce the sheriff if he returned *tardè* (*a*). But if a writ come so late that it cannot be executed, there does not seem to be any sound reason why this should not be a good return.

Languidus.

A return that a defendant is so sick that he cannot be removed without danger of his life, or remains so sick in prison, is a good return (*b*); but in such return it must be shown that the defendant continued so ill until the return of the writ that he could not be moved (*c*). A return that the sheriff has relinquished the custody of the defendant because he could not be removed without danger to his life, has been held bad (*d*). But the court will, in such a case, enlarge the time for making the return (*e*). If the sheriff discharge a defendant arrested on mesne process, on giving a bail-bond, he will not be liable to an action for returning *languidus;* for that is only an excuse that he had not the body: and he is only fineable by the court if he bring not in the body, and the party shall not have any remedy against him (*f*).

Rescue. Remedy against rescuers.

To a writ of mesne process, a return that the defendant was rescued (*g*) out of the custody of the sheriff, or that the defendant overpowered the officer and rescued himself (*h*), is good. So a sheriff's return of the answer of the bailiff of a liberty, that the defendant was rescued out of the bailiff's custody on mesne process, is good (*i*); *that is, that the defendant was rescued before he was conveyed to prison;* for a return to a writ of mesne process that the defendant was rescued out of prison, is bad (*k*).

(*a*) Fitz. *Retorne*, 37, 42; Com. Dig. *Retorne* (D), 1. Such a return was holden good on a *capias*, on an appeal of murder. Bro. *Retorne de Briefe*, 34; 8 Hen. 4, 21.

(*b*) Bro. *Retorne de Briefe*, 100, 102; Fitz. *Retorne*, 94, 105, 122; Dalt. 213.

(*c*) Cavenagh *v.* Collett, 4 Bar. & Ald. 280; Perkins *v.* Meacher, 1 Dowl. 21.

(*d*) Baker *v.* Davenport, 8 D. & R. 606.

(*e*) Jones *v.* Robinson, 11 M.& W. 758.

(*f*) Boles *v.* Lassels, Cro. Eliz. 852.

(*g*) May *v.* Proby, Cro. Jac. 419; S.C. 1 Roll. Rep. 388, 440; 3 Bulstr. 198; Hill *v.* Montague, 2 Lev. 144; Lord Gorges *v.* Gore, 3 Lev. 46.

(*h*) Fermor *v.* Phillips, Holt's N. P. C. 537; Rex *v.* Sheriff of Middlesex, 1 Bar. & Ald. 190; Com. Dig. *Rescue* (D), 4.

(*i*) Lady Russel and Wood's case, Cro. Eliz. 781.

(*k*) Crompton *v.* Ward, Stra. 435. See this distinction in May *v.* Probie, 1 Roll. Rep. 440; S.C. Cro. Jac. 419; O'Neil *v.* Marson, 5 Burr. 2812; Roll. Abr. *Escape* (D), 1, 2, 3:—*unless* the prison was broken by the king's enemies, although he is liable if broken by traitors or rebels. Morse *v.* Shee, 1 Vent. 239; Southcote's case, 4 Rep. 84.

But to writs of execution, whether to a *ca. sa.* (*l*) or *fi. fa.* (*m*), it is not a good return, that the defendant or his goods were rescued from the sheriff; for in executing such writs, the sheriff is ordered by the statute West. 2, to raise the *posse comitatus;* and herein rests the distinction between rescue on mesne and final process; for in the former the sheriff *may*, although he is not, as in executing final process he is, compelled to, raise the *posse comitatus* (*n*). When the sheriff may return a rescue, it is necessary to state in the return a legal arrest; therefore a return of rescue, which did not state that the defendant was *arrested* within the county, was held bad (*o*). In some cases it has been holden good to return that the defendant was rescued out of the custody of the *sheriff's bailiff* (*p*); whereas in other cases similar returns have been held to be bad, for not alleging that the defendant was rescued out of the custody of the sheriff (*q*). But it would appear that a return either way is good; for a person in the custody of the sheriff's officer is in the custody of the sheriff (*r*). But a return was held bad which stated that the defendant was taken by the bailiffs, and *habuerunt in custodiâ meâ quousque* such persons rescued him out of the custody of the bailiffs (*s*). It appears necessary to state, in a return of rescue, the time (*t*) and place (*u*) where the rescue was made; but it is not necessary to state the day of the caption (*x*). Although it seems to have been deemed requisite to state the names of the rescuers, yet it is conceived that a return would be sufficient without stating their names; for how are the sheriff and his officers to

(*l*) May *v.* Probie, Cro. Jac. 419; S. C. 1 Roll. Rep. 388, 440; 3 Bulstr. 198; either on a *ca. sa.*, or *capias utlagatum* after judgment, Dyer, 241 *a.*

(*m*) Rex *v.* Baldwin, Barnes, 430; Slie *v.* Finch, 2 Roll. Rep. 57; S. C. Cro. Jac. 514; Sheriff of Surry *v.* Udderton, Holt, 145.

(*n*) Noy, 40; 1 Stra. 432.

(*o*) Rex *v.* Sheriff of Middlesex, 1 Bar. & Ald. 190; see 2 Roll. Rep. 255.

(*p*) Dyer, 241 a, n.; Webb *v.* Withers, 2 Roll. Rep. 255.

(*q*) Dyer, 241 a. *Per* Buller, J., 2 T. R. 156; 1 Sid. 332; 2 Roll. Rep. 263. For the distinction of a return of rescue out of the custody of a sheriff's bailiff and the bailiff of a liberty, see Cro. Jac. 241, and 2 Keb. 217.

(*r*) Rex *v.* Sims, 1 Lev. 214; S.C. Raym. 161. *Per* Holt, C. J., Salk. 586; Penfold's case, Sir T. Jones, 197; Rex *v.* Clapham, 2 Lev. 28. *Sed vide* the report of Rex *v.* Sims, 2 Keb. 217.

(*s*) Salk. 586.

(*t*) Bro. *Retorne de Briefe*, 27; Fitz. *Coron.* 45, *Attachment* 1; see also 2 Bulstr. 137.

(*u*) Anon. Moore, 422, pl. 585; Wolfreston's case, Yelv. 51; see also 2 Bulstr. 137.

(*x*) Palm. 532.

CHAP. V. SECT. IV.

know the names of persons composing a mob (*y*)? The return of a rescue is in the nature of a conviction, and the courts will grant an attachment thereon in the first instance, the return of a rescue not being traversable (*z*). For a rescue on mesne process the plaintiff may bring an action against the rescuers (*a*); but where the rescue is in execution, either the sheriff or plaintiff may bring the action (*b*): in such action he must state and prove the judgment, and that the taking *was lawful* (*c*).

Mandavi ballivo.

If the bailiff of a liberty have the execution and return of the writ, by reason of the defendant or his goods being within the liberty, it is a good return for the sheriff to say that he commanded the bailiff to do execution of the writ; if the bailiff of the franchise has not made a return, the sheriff should return accordingly (*d*); or if he have made a return, then the sheriff should return *mandavi ballivo,* with the answer of the bailiff (*e*). But if a bailiff answers some matter which is insufficient as a return, the sheriff should return *nullum dedit responsum,* for an insufficient answer is no answer at all (*f*). If the sheriff return *mandavi ballivo* where he ought to have entered the liberty, the return is void, and the sheriff may be attached (*g*). It would appear, that a return by the sheriff, that he had commanded the bailiff of the liberty to whom the execution of the writ belonged, is sufficient, without mentioning the name of the place whereof he was bailiff (*h*). A return to a writ of inquiry by the sheriff, that he had commanded the bailiff of a liberty to execute it, is bad, for it is the sheriff's duty to execute it (*i*). Where the sheriff and bailiff of a franchise had both obtained time to return a writ, and the sheriff afterwards returned it, the court refused to compel the high bailiff to return the mandate (*k*).

(*y*) See Sir W. Jones, 201; Cro. Jac. 419; 1 Bar. & Ald. 190.

(*z*) Rex *v.* Pember, Rep. temp. Hard. 112; Faucet *v.* Catten, T. Jones, 39; Anon. Salk. 586; 2 Vent. 175; Rex *v.* Thomas Elkins, 4 Burr. 2129; Rex *v.* Phillips, Barnes, 429. Although it was formerly held to be traversable, Dyer, 212 a; T. Jones, 39; the only remedy the rescuer has, if the return be false, is by action against the sheriff. See Rex *v.* Horsley, 3 T. R. 562,

(*a*) Kent *v.* Elwis, Cro. Jac. 241.

(*b*) Myric *v.* Coughton, Cro. Car. 109.

(*c*) Earl of Bristol *v.* Wilsmore, 2 Dowl. & Ry. 755; S. C. 1 B. & C. 514.

(*d*) See Forms, Append.

(*e*) *Id. ibid.*

(*f*) Roll. Abr. *Return* (M), 2, 3; Bro. *Retorne de Briefe*, 47.

(*g*) Fitz. *Retorn*, 53.

(*h*) Roll. Abr. *Return* (N), 1.

(*i*) Virely *v.* Gumstone, Hob. 83; Roll. Abr. *Return* (N), 2.

(*k*) Jackson *v.* Taylor, 5 Dowl. 140.

An insufficient return is as no return, and therefore the courts will grant an attachment against the sheriff if he make an insufficient return; or on a bailable *capias*, he may be ruled to bring in the body (*l*); indeed, if he return the insufficient answer of the bailiff of a liberty, it would seem that he would be liable to an attachment (*m*).

Liable to an attachment, if the return be insufficient.

The various forms of returns to different writs will be more conveniently treated of hereafter, under the head of each particular writ.

Different forms of return.

Section V.

Of the Remuneration to Sheriffs for executing and returning Writs.

By the common law, it was the duty of the sheriff to do execution of all the king's writs without any fee, remuneration, or reward; nor is the sheriff entitled at this day to any remuneration for executing a writ, excepting by the provisions of particular statutes. Thus the sheriff, before 1 Vict. c. 55, was not entitled to any fee for executing an attachment (*n*), or a writ of *capias utlagatum* against the goods of the defendant (*o*). In affirmance of the common law, it was provided by the statute of Westminster 1, c. 26, "That no sheriff shall take any reward to do his office; but shall be paid of that which they hold of the king, and he that so doth shall yield twice as much, and be punished at the king's pleasure" (*p*).

At the common law the sheriff was not entitled to fees.

It was in the course of time, however, considered just and politic to allow the sheriff a remuneration for his trouble, and several statutes have from time to time been passed for the purpose of carrying out this principle. The principal statutes now in force, are 28 Eliz. c. 4 (*poundage*); 3 Geo. 1, c. 15 (*crown debts, elegit, habere facias possessionem*); 8 Geo. 1, c. 25 (*extent and liberates*); 43 Geo. 3, c. 46, s. 5 (*allowing plaintiff to levy poundage and expenses of execution in certain cases*); and 7 Will. 4 & 1 Vict. c. 55 (*fees payable to sheriffs upon the execution of civil process*).

(*l*) Rex *v.* Sheriff of Middlesex, 1 Bar. & Ald. 190.

(*m*) Roll. Abr. *Return* (M), 1, 2.

(*n*) Rex *v.* Palmer, 2 East, 411.

(*o*) Graham *v.* Grill, 2 M. & S. 294.

(*p*) See 2 Inst. 210, for Lord Coke's commentary on this statute.

The general provisions of the statutes, with the decisions upon them, will first be stated, and then the provisions as to particular writs.

Poundage on writs of execution.

By the statute 28th Elizabeth, c. 4 (*q*), it is enacted, "That it shall not be lawful to or for any sheriff, under-sheriff, bailiff of franchises (*r*), or liberties, nor for any of their or either of their officers, ministers, servants, bailiffs, or deputies, nor for any of them, by reason or colour of their or either of their office or offices, to have, receive, or take of any person or persons whatsoever, directly or indirectly, for the serving and executing of any extent or execution upon the body (*s*), lands (*t*), goods or chattels of any person or persons whatsoever, more or other consideration or recompense than in this present act is and shall be limited and appointed, which shall be lawful to be had, received, and taken; that is to say, twelve pence of and for every twenty shillings, where the sum exceedeth not one hundred pounds; and sixpence of and for every twenty shillings, being over and above the said sum of one hundred pounds, that he or they shall so levy or extend, and deliver in execution, or take the body in execution for, by virtue and force of any such extent or execution whatsoever; upon pain and penalty that all and every sheriff, under-sheriff, bailiff of franchises and liberties, their and every of their ministers, servants, officers, bailiffs, or deputies, which at any time shall directly or indirectly do the contrary, shall lose and forfeit to the party grieved his treble damages, and shall forfeit the sum of forty pounds for every time that he, they, or any of them shall do the contrary; the one moiety thereof to be to our sovereign lady the queen, her heirs and successors, and the other moiety thereof to the party or parties that will sue for the same by any plaint, action, suit, bill, or information, wherein no essoign, wager of law, or protection shall be allowed."

(*q*) This statute has been improperly cited as the 29th Eliz. See Rumsey *v.* Tuffnell, 2 Bing. 255; Savage, q. t. *v.* Smith, 2 Bla. Rep. 1101, where the statement of this act as of the 29th Eliz. was held fatal. See also Brockwell *v.* Lock, Salk. 331. It has not been repealed by 1 Vict. c. 55; Davies *v.* Griffiths, 4 M. & W. 377; 7 Dowl. 204, S. C.; Pilkington *v.* Cooke, 16 M. & W. 615.

(*r*) Where a writ is executed within a liberty by the bailiff of that liberty, he, and not the sheriff, is entitled to the fees under this statute. See Latch, 52; Salk. 331.

(*s*) See now as to *ca. sa.* 5 & 6 Vict. c. 98, s. 31, *post*.

(*t*) See now as to *habere facias* and *elegit*, 3 Geo. 1, c. 15, s. 16; Nash *v.* Allen, 1 Dav. & M. 16.

CHAP. V. SECT. V.

"Provided always, that this act or any thing therein contained, shall not extend to any fees to be taken or had for any execution within any city or town corporate." This proviso has been construed to mean, that if the sheriff, bailiff of a franchise, or other officer, execute any execution on a judgment given in the courts at Westminster, within a city or town corporate, he is not to be deprived of the fee given by the statute; but if the bailiff or other officer execute process on a judgment given in a court of a corporation or liberty, he is within the proviso, and not entitled to fees within the statute (*u*).

In cities or towns corporate.

The amount of the fee to be taken is not expressed in very clear words in the statute 28 Eliz. c. 4; but it has been decided in a variety of cases, that the sheriff is entitled under that statute to one shilling in the pound for the first 100*l.*, and sixpence in the pound for every pound above 100*l.* (*x*).

Amount to be taken under 28 Eliz. c. 4.

This statute, 28 Eliz. c. 4, regulates the fees to be taken on a *fi. fa.* (*y*), but does not apply to an attachment (*z*), a writ of *capias utlagatum* (*a*), a writ of *habere facias possessionem* or *seisinam* (*b*), the seizure of land under a writ of *elegit* (*c*), a writ of *levari facias* for a crown debt (*d*); a writ of *ca. sa.* since 1 May, 1843 (*e*); or money taken on a bailable *capias*, and paid into court by the sheriff, under 13 Geo. 3, c. 46, s. 2, or 7 & 8 Geo. 4, c. 71 (*f*); or an execution upon a judgment of *non pros.* (*g*).

To what writs the statute 28 Eliz. c. 4, extends.

The statute 1 Vict. c. 55, intituled *An Act for better regulating the Fees payable to Sheriffs upon the Execution of Civil Process*, after reciting that 'it is expedient to amend the laws relating to 'the fees payable to sheriffs, under-sheriffs, deputy sheriffs, she-

(*u*) Brockwell *v.* Lock, Salk. 331; S. C. 5 Mod. 97; Jesson, Sheriff of Coventry, *v.* Wesley, cited in Cro. Car. 287; Latch, 18, 52; Poph. 173; Palm. 399; *sed vide* The Sheriff of Gloucester's case, Cro. Eliz. 264.

(*x*) Lyster *v.* Bromley, Cro. Car. 286; S. C. Sir W. Jones, 307.

(*y*) Tyson *v.* Paske, 2 Lord Raym. 1212; S. C. Salk. 333; Jayson *v.* Rash, Salk. 209. As to the amount, see Price *v.* Hollis, 1 M. & Sel. 105; Nash *v* Allen, 1 Dav. & M. 16.

(*z*) Rex *v.* Palmer, 2 East, 411; Rex *v.* Sheriff of Devon, 3 Dowl. 10.

(*a*) Graham *v.* Grill, 2 M. & S. 294.

(*b*) Peacock *v.* Harris, Salk. 331; 2 Sid. 155; 1 Vent. 351.

(*c*) Nash *v.* Allen, 1 Dav. & M. 16.

(*d*) Stephens *v.* Rothwell, 6 Moore, 338; S. C. 3 Brod & Bing. 143: see Lake *v.* Turner, 4 Burr. 1981, where the suit was for the benefit of the crown.

(*e*) 5 & 6 Vict. c. 98, s. 31. *Quære*, whether this enactment applies to writs tested but not executed before 1 May, 1843.

(*f*) Stewart *v.* Bracebridge, 2 B. & Ald. 770; 1 Chit. R. 529, S. C.; Haines *v.* Nairn, 2 Dowl. 43; Hume *v.* Bruce, 6 Moore, 124.

(*g*) Anon., 2 Chit. Rep. 353.

CHAP. V. SECT. V.

'riffs' agents, bailiffs, and others the officers or ministers of 'sheriffs in England and Wales, and to give the Courts of Record 'at Westminster Hall a due control over such fees; and also 'to provide a summary remedy against such officers and others 'as shall extort or receive other or greater fees than by law 'they shall be entitled to: and whereas divers enactments 'touching the said officers, contained in certain ancient statutes, 'have become inconvenient, and ought to be repealed; be it 'therefore enacted by the Queen's most excellent majesty, by 'and with the advice and consent of the lords spiritual and tem-'poral, and commons, in this present parliament assembled, and 'by the authority of the same, that so much of an act passed in 'the forty-second year of his late majesty King Edward the 'Third, intituled *Estreats shall be shewed to the party indebted, 'and that which is paid shall be totted: no sheriff &c. shall con-'tinue in Office above a Year*, as relates to the time during which 'under-sheriffs and sheriffs' clerks may abide in their respective 'offices; and also an act passed in the first year of the reign of 'his late majesty King Henry the Fifth, intituled *Sheriffs' Bai-'liffs shall not be in the same Office in Three Years after: Sheriffs' 'Officers shall not be Attornies*: and also so much of an act 'passed in the twenty-third year of the reign of his late majesty 'King Henry the Sixth, intituled *No Sheriff shall let to farm his 'County or any Bailiwick: the Sheriffs' and Bailiffs' Fees and 'Duties in many Cases*, as relates to the fees to be taken by she-'riffs, under-sheriffs, sheriffs' clerks, and other officers and 'ministers of sheriffs, be and the same are hereby repealed.'

Part of 42 Ed. 3, c. 9, the act 1 Hen. 5, c. 4, and part of 23 Hen. 6, c. 9, repealed.

Fees to be allowed by taxing officer of Courts at Westminster.

2. 'And be it enacted, that from and after the passing of this 'act it shall be lawful for sheriffs, or their officers concerned in 'the execution of process directed to sheriffs, to demand, take, 'and receive such fees, and no more, as shall from time to time 'be allowed by any officer of the several courts of law at West-'minster charged with the duty of taxing costs in such courts, 'under the sanction and authority of the judges of the said 'courts respectively.'

Fees to the sheriffs of Lancashire and Durham.

5. 'And be it enacted, that from and after the passing of this 'act, the sheriffs of Lancashire and Durham, and their officers, 'shall have and be entitled to the like fees, and no more, upon 'process issuing out of the Court of Common Pleas at Lancaster 'and out of the Court of Pleas at Durham respectively, as from

'time to time shall be allowed under the authority of this act to 'sheriffs upon process issuing from the superior courts at West- 'minster; and that the said Court of Common Pleas at Lan- 'caster and Court of Pleas at Durham respectively, or any judge 'thereof respectively, being also judge of one of the superior 'courts at Westminster, shall have the same powers in every 'particular, with respect to offences against this act upon process 'issuing out of the said Court of Common Pleas at Lancaster 'and Court of Pleas at Durham respectively, as are hereinbefore 'given to the courts at Westminster respectively in respect of 'process issuing from those courts.' CHAP. V. SECT. V.

The following is the list of fees prepared pursuant to the 2nd section of the act, and sanctioned by the judges. Table of fees.

TABLE OF FEES.

A Table of Fees to be taken by the Sheriffs, Under-Sheriffs, Deputy-Sheriffs, Sheriffs' Agents, Bailiffs, and others the Officers or Ministers of Sheriffs in England and Wales, pursuant to the Statute of 1 *Vict. c.* 55.

For every Warrant which shall be granted by the Sheriff to his Officers upon any Writ or Process:—[*See* post, 108, *as to the charge where there are several defendants.*] On warrants and arrests.

	£	s.	d.
In London and Middlesex	0	2	6
And on crown (*h*) and outlawry process, an additional	0	2	6
In all other counties, where the most distant part of the county shall not exceed 100 miles from London	0	5	0
Not exceeding 200 miles	0	6	0
Exceeding 200 miles	0	7	0
For an arrest in London	0	10	6
In Middlesex, not exceeding a mile from the General Post Office	0	10	6
Not exceeding seven miles from same place	1	1	0

(*h*) But by Reg. Gen. M. 10 Vict. (16 Nov. 1846) so much of this table of fees as relates to process at the suit of the crown is annulled.

CHAP. V.
SECT. V.

	£	s.	d.
In other counties, not exceeding a mile from officer's residence	0	10	6
Not exceeding seven miles	1	1	0
Exceeding seven miles	1	11	6
For conveying the defendant to gaol from the place of arrest (*i*) ... *per mile*	0	1	0
For an undertaking to give a bail bond	0	10	6

For a Bail Bond.

	£	s.	d.
If the debt shall not exceed £50	0	10	6
Ditto £100	1	1	0
Ditto £150	1	11	6
Ditto £300	2	2	0
Ditto £400	3	3	0
Ditto £500	4	4	0
If it shall exceed £500	5	5	0
For receiving money under the statute upon deposit for arrest, and paying the same into court, if in London or Middlesex	0	6	8
If in any other county	0	10	0

For Filing the Bail Bond.

	£	s.	d.
If the arrest be made in London or Middlesex	0	2	0
If in any other county	0	4	0

Assignment of Bail or other Bond.

	£	s.	d.
If in London or Middlesex	0	5	0
If in any other county, including postage	0	7	6
(Return to habeas corpus.) For the return to any writ of habeas corpus, if one action	0	12	0
And for each action after the first	0	2	6
(For taking prisoner to gaol.) For the bailiff to conduct prisoner to gaol .. *per diem*	0	10	0
And travelling expenses ... *per mile*	0	1	0
(Search for detainers.) For searching offices for detainers	0	1	0
Bailiff's messenger for that purpose	0	2	6

For execution of certain writs.

To the bailiffs, for executing warrants on extent, capias utlagatum, levari facias, fieri facias, ca. sa., ne exeat, attachment, elegit, writ of possession, for-

(*i*) See for bailiff's fee, *post*.

CHAP. V. SECT. V.

	£	s.	d.
feited recognizance, process from pipe office, and other like matters, for each, if the distance from the sheriff's office or the bailiff's residence do not exceed five miles	1	1	0
If beyond that distance *per mile*	0	0	6
On distringas, in London	0	5	0
In Middlesex, not exceeding five miles from General Post Office	0	5	0
Exceeding five miles	0	10	0
In other counties, not exceeding five miles from officer's residence	0	5	0
Exceeding five miles	0	10	0
For each man left in possession (*k*), when absolutely necessary— (Man in possession.)			
If boarded *per diem*	0	3	6
If not boarded *per diem*	0	5	0
For every sale by auction (*l*), notwithstanding the defendant should become bankrupt or insolvent, where the property sold does not produce more than 300*l*., 5 per cent.—480*l*., 4 per cent.—500*l*., 3 per cent.—and where it exceeds 500*l*., 2½ per cent. (Sale by auction.)			
For the certificate of sale to save auction duty	0	2	6
Bond of indemnity, besides stamps (Indemnity.)	1	10	0
Certificate of execution having issued for record (Certificate of execution.)	0	5	0

On Writs of Trial and Inquiry.

	£	s.	d.
For a deputation	1	1	0
On lodging writ for entering cause and warrant for summoning jury, which fee shall be forfeited in case of countermand of trial	0	4	0

On Trial or Inquisition.

	£	s.	d.
Sheriff for presiding	1	1	0

(*k*) The term "possession-money" does not include the expense of the keep of cattle seized by the sheriff. Gaskell *v.* Sefton, 14 M. & W. 802.

(*l*) No fee for *appraisement* on any other kind of sale; Phillips *v.* Viscount Canterbury, 11 M. & W. 619. So, if the execution creditor pays the expenses of a sale by appraisement, he cannot set it off against the sheriff's poundage. Marshall *v.* Hicks, 16 Law J., Q. B. 134.

	£	s.	d.
Bailiff for summoning jury, and attendance in court	0	4	0
And if held at the office of the under-sheriff—			
For hire of room, if actually paid, not exceeding....	0	10	0
For travelling expenses of under-sheriff from his office to place where trial or inquisition held....*per mile*	0	1	0
To the bailiff, from his residence ....*per mile*	0	0	6
In all cases in which it shall appear to the master that a saving of expense has accrued to the parties by reason of a writ of trial having been executed by deputation, the fee for such deputation shall be allowed.			
On writs of extent, elegit, capias utlagatum, and others of the like nature; for summoning the jury, use of room, presiding at the inquisition, &c.	2	2	0
Jury	0	12	0
For travelling expenses of under-sheriff from his office to the place of inquisition ....*per mile*	0	1	0
For drawing and ingrossing the inquisition, *per folio*	0	1	6
For a summons for the attendance of a witness.....	0	5	0

[*As to the apportionment of the travelling expenses of the under-sheriff and bailiff, see* post, 108.]

Replevin.

In Replevin.

[*Bond, see* post, 108.]

	£	s.	d.
Precept to bailiff..............................	0	2	6
Notice for service on defendant..................	0	2	6
Broker, where the sum demanded and due shall exceed 20*l.*, and shall not exceed 50*l.*, for appraisement and affidavit of value..................	0	10	6
Where it shall exceed 50*l.*......................	1	1	0
And his travelling expenses from his residence to the place where the goods are.............*per mile*	0	0	6
Bailiff for summoning parties and delivering goods to tenant	1	1	0
And his travelling expenses same as broker.			
For the warrant, record, and return of a re. fa. lo., accedas ad curiam, pone, or writ of false judgment	0	16	6

	£	s.	d.	
For writ retorno habendo	0	4	6	
For each summons on a writ of sci. fa., or for the service of writ of capias where no arrest	0	5	0	Summons on sci. fa.
And mileage ... per mile	0	1	0	
For recording each demand or proclamation under writs of outlawry	0	2	0	Proclamation of outlawry.
For bailiff for making each demand or proclamation on writs of outlawry in London and Middlesex	0	2	6	
In other counties	0	5	0	
And travelling expenses, if the distance shall exceed five miles, then for every mile beyond that distance	0	0	6	
For any supersedeas, writ of error, order, liberate, or discharge to any writ or process, or for the release of any defendant in custody (unless in the prison of the county), or of goods taken in execution	0	4	6	Supersedeas, discharge, &c. of person or goods.
For the return of any writ or process, and filing same, exclusive of the fee paid on filing	0	1	0	Return.

Jury Process (*m*).

	£	s.	d.
For return to common venire	0	3	6
The like to special	0	5	0
The like on distringas or habeas corpus for common jury	0	12	0
The like for special jury	0	14	0
The like with a view	1	0	0
The like to a traverse venire	0	14	6
For attendance naming special jury	2	2	0
Twenty-four warrants to summon special jury	1	4	0
For bailiff for summoning each special juror	0	2	0
Sheriff attending in court	1	1	0

For attending a view, the fees as allowed by rule of court, Trinity Term, 7 Geo. 4, 1826.

For any duty not herein provided for, such sum as one of the masters of the Courts of King's Bench or Exchequer, or one of the

(*m*) No greater fees, it seems, when jurors reside at a distance, Lane *v.* Sewell, 1 Chit. R. 175. Nor extra expenses of summoning knights in a real action, *ibid.*

CHAP. V. SECT. V.

	£	s.	d.
Prothonotaries of the Court of Common Pleas, may upon special application allow.			

[*Signed by all the Judges.*]

SHERIFFS' FEES—ADDENDA.

Bond in Replevin.

	£	s.	d.
Instead of the allowance of the fees upon the same scale as the bail-bond, the fee of one pound one shilling only is allowed, whatever be the amount, if above 20*l.*	1	1	0

Fees on Writs of Trial and Inquisition.

The travelling expenses of the under-sheriff from his office, and of the bailiff from his residence, to the place where the trial or inquisition is held, are to be apportioned rateably to the parties, if more than one trial or inquisition be held at the same time and place.

[*Signed by all the Judges.*]

Where there are several defendants in a writ of capias, and warrants are issued thereon by the under-sheriff against more than one defendant, no more shall be charged in any case for each warrant, after the first, than two shillings and sixpence.

[*Signed by eight of the Judges.*]

Amount of expenses, &c. recoverable.

The above statute of 1 Vict. c. 55, has not repealed any statutes except those expressly mentioned in the recital (*n*).

Before the passing of 1 Vict. c. 55, there was much confusion as to the remuneration of sheriffs. The Court of Common Pleas seem to have been of opinion, that where the sheriff did any thing beyond his official duty, as in allowing time for dividing the property seized into lots, for the benefit of selling them to more advantage, at the instance of the defendant, the officer was entitled to some remuneration beyond poundage (*o*). But the

(*n*) Davies *v.* Griffiths, 4 M. & W. 377; 7 Dowl. 204, S. C.; Pilkington *v.* Cook, 16 M. & W. 615.

(*o*) Stephens *v.* Rothwell, 6 Moore, 338; S. C. 3 Brod. & Bing. 143. *Sed vide* 3 Campb. 374.

sheriff could not then charge the expenses of selling the goods *by auction*, because he was bound to sell the goods himself: yet if the auction were at the request of the plaintiff or defendant, the party so requesting must have paid the expenses of it (*p*). And it was held that the sheriff could not legally retain out of the sum levied on a *fi. fa.* the expenses of keeping possession of the goods pending an injunction out of Chancery, and for so doing he was adjudged to be guilty of extortion (*q*). At the present day, these and similar questions may be answered by reference to the table of fees prepared pursuant to 1 Vict. c. 55; the general effect of which act is to restrict the sheriff to the fees mentioned in that table and poundage (when allowed by other statutes), no matter how great may be the expenses incurred in the performance of his duty (*r*). There is, however, a provision in the table of fees, that for any duty *not therein provided for* the sheriff is to be allowed such sum as one of the Masters of the several courts of common law may *upon special application* allow. It may be doubted how far this sweeping clause is consistent with the 1 Vict. c. 55, s. 2, which requires the sanction and authority of the *judges*. It has been laid down in a recent case, that the sheriff, on making a levy under an execution, is entitled, under this table of fees, to a per-centage on the whole proceeds of the sale, including a year's rent paid by him to the landlord; but not to an allowance of such extra expenses, incurred by him respecting the levy, as are not included in the table of fees (*s*).

Poundage and expenses where judgment or execution irregular.

It is said in an Anonymous case (*t*), "a sheriff shall not be entitled to poundage if judgment irregular." This dictum, however, in its generality, seems equally opposed to justice and to later authorities. In a case where the sheriff had levied the amount and his poundage under a *fi. fa.*, and the writ was afterwards set aside for irregularity, and the plaintiff compelled to refund the whole amount to the defendant, it was held that the

(*p*) *Per* Buller, J., Woodgate *v.* Knatchbull, 2 T. R. 157; Bilke *v.* Havelock, 3 Campb. 374; Stephens *v.* Rothwell, 6 Moore, 338; S. C. 3 Brod. & Bing. 143.

(*q*) Buckle *v.* Bewes, 5 Dowl. & Ry. 495; S. C. 3 Bar. & Cres. 688.

(*r*) Slater *v.* Hames, 7 M. & W. 413; 9 Dowl. 221, S. C. See Buckle *v.* Bewes, 3 B. & C. 688; 5 D. & R. 595, S. C.; Stephens *v.* Rothwell, 6 Moore, 338; 3 Brod. & B. 143, S. C.

(*s*) Davies *v.* Edmonds, 12 M. & W. 31.

(*t*) Lofft, 253.

CHAP. V. SECT. V.

sheriff was entitled to retain his poundage (*u*). And in a later case, where the sheriff, having levied under a *fi. fa.*, on the judgment and execution being set aside for irregularity, with the plaintiff's assent, restored the amount of the levy to the defendant, it was held that he might sue the plaintiff for his poundage (*x*). The principle of these decisions will probably be held applicable to the fees which the sheriff is entitled to receive under 1 Vict. c. 55. Cases have occurred in practice, in which the plaintiff and defendant, on a compromise, have, with a view to defraud the sheriff of his fees and poundage, procured the judgment and execution to be set aside for irregularity by consent. It is hardly necessary to observe, that in such a case, independently of any summary remedy which the Court might apply, the sheriff's right of action against the plaintiff would not be affected.

Poundage and expenses of fi. fa.

On a writ of *fi. fa.*, besides the expenses allowed under the schedule of fees pursuant to 1 Vict. c. 55 (*ante*, p. 103), the sheriff is also entitled to poundage under the 28 Eliz. c. 4 (*ante*, 100). In order to entitle the sheriff to poundage under that statute, there must be an actual levy; and the sheriff is not entitled to poundage if the money is paid to him without any levy (*y*). Consequently a defendant, against whom a *fi. fa.* is issued, may stop its execution by tendering to the sheriff the amount and expenses without poundage: and if the sheriff proceeds to levy for it after such tender, the Court will compel him to refund (*z*). Nor is the sheriff entitled to poundage on more than the sum he actually receives under the execution, though the amount claimed or seized be greater (*a*). It is even stated (*b*), that "it seems, on inquiry into the practice, the sheriff cannot have poundage until the goods are *sold*." This proposition, however, if correct, does not apply to a case where after the seizure of the goods the parties enter into a compromise before the sheriff sells them. In such case the sheriff

(*u*) Bullen *v.* Ansley, 6 Esp. 111. See Earle *v.* Plummer, Salk. 332.

(*x*) Rawstorne *v.* Wilkinson, 4 M. & Sel. 256.

(*y*) Graham *v.* Grill, 2 M. & Sel. 296.

(*z*) Colls *v.* Coates, 11 Ad. & El. 826; 3 Per. & D. 511, S. C.; Brine *v.* Hutchinson, 2 Dowl. & L. 43.

(*a*) Rex *v.* Robinson, 2 C. M. & R. 334; 4 Dowl. 447, S. C.

(*b*) Anon. Lofft, 433 (H. T. 14 Geo. 3, K. B.) See *per* Lord Ellenborough, Bilke *v.* Havelock, 3 Campb. 374.

has been held to be entitled to his poundage (*d*). It is observable that the words of the statute are "levy or extend *and deliver in execution.*" Therefore the sheriff is not entitled to poundage on a sum of money paid over to a landlord under 8 Anne, c. 14 (*e*). An action is not maintainable on an implied promise to pay a sheriff the expenses of seizing and keeping possession under a *fi. fa.*, which was ultimately abandoned on account of the refusal of an indemnity, even after the claim has been recognized by payment of money on account (*f*). Under a *fi. fa.* against a defendant, the poundage and expenses may be levied, even, it seems, though there be no indorsement to that effect (*g*). As to levying the amount of poundage and expenses, see further, page 114.

Poundage and expenses of *ca. sa.*

With respect to poundage and fees on a *ca. sa.*, it is enacted by 5 & 6 Vict. c. 98, s. 31, "that after the 1st day of March, 1843 (*h*), no poundage shall be payable to sheriffs and others for taking the body of any person in execution, but there shall be payable to the sheriff or other person having the return of writs, upon every such execution against the body, such fees only as shall be allowed to be taken by sheriffs or other officers concerned in the execution of process under the sanction and authority of the judges of the courts of common law at Westminster, pursuant to 1 Vict. c. 55." The law applicable to a *ca. sa.* previous to that day will be found in the note (*i*). The

(*d*) Alchin *v.* Wells, 5 T. R. 470.

(*e*) Gore *v.* Gofton, Str. 653.

(*f*) Bilke *v.* Havelock, 3 Campb. 374; Lane *v.* Sewell, 1 Chit. 175. See Maybery *v.* Mansfield, 16 Law J. Q. B. 102.

(*g*) Curtis *v.* Mayne, 2 Dowl. N. S. 37.

(*h*) It seems the statute does not apply where the party was taken on the *ca. sa.* before that day. Bunbury *v.* Matthews, 1 Car. & Kir. 380.

(*i*) On a *ca. sa.* the sheriff, before 5 & 6 Vict. c. 98, s. 31, was entitled to the poundage allowed by the statute 28 Eliz.; but where the *ca. sa.* issued only for a part of the sum recovered, it was provided by statute 3 Geo. 1, c. 15, s. 17, that the sheriff should not demand or take poundage for any greater sum than the debt *bonâ fide* due to the plaintiff; which sum the plaintiff is obliged to mark on the writ before it is delivered to the sheriff. And by the same statute it is declared to be extortion to offend against that act, and subjects the party to the penalty of double the sum extorted, and treble damages. And if a mistake was made in the indorsement, and the sum was reduced by judge's order to the correct amount, the sheriff was held entitled to poundage on the reduced amount only. Evans *v.* Manero, 7 M. & W. 463; 9 Dowl. 256, S. C. The sheriff was entitled to poundage on a *ca. sa.*, although the defendant went to prison without paying the debt; Lake *v.* Turner, 4 Burr. 1981; or although the defendant was already in custody of the sheriff when the *ca. sa.* was delivered to him; Tayler *v.* Ward, Tidd's Prac. 1084, 8th ed.

CHAP. V. SECT. V.

plaintiff cannot levy under a *ca. sa.* the expenses of the execution above the sum recovered by the judgment, unless by express authority from the defendant (*k*). It seems that there is no remedy for extra costs incurred in consequence of the defendant's being too ill to be removed (*l*).

Poundage and expenses on crown writs.

The sheriff is not entitled to poundage on process at the suit of the crown under the provisions of the 28 Eliz.; his claim for poundage on such writs is regulated by the statute 3 Geo. 1, c. 15, s. 13, 14, which will be treated of in the chapter on Extents (*m*). For other expenses, see the table of fees, p. 105.

Poundage and expenses on an *elegit*, *habere facias possessionem* or *seisinam.*

It has been stated, that the sheriff was not entitled to poundage under the 28 Eliz. for executing a *habere facias seisinam*, or *possessionem*, or an *elegit* against land. By the statute 3 Geo. 1, c. 15, s. 16, for ascertaining fees for executing writs of *elegit* and of *habere facias seisinam* or *possessionem*, it is enacted, that "no sheriff, bailiff of liberty, &c. shall take, demand, or receive, by colour of their office, for executing a writ of *habere facias seisinam* or *possessionem*, any greater fee than 1*s*. for every pound of the yearly value of any manor, messuage, lands, tenements, and hereditaments, whereof possession or seisin shall be by them or any of them given, where the whole exceedeth not the yearly value of 100*l*., and the sum of 6*d*. only for every 1*l*. *per annum* over and above the yearly value of 100*l*." Although this section of the statute professes to have been passed for the purpose of ascertaining the fees upon an *elegit*, yet there is no mention whatsoever made of *elegits* in the enacting part of the statute. Nevertheless the sheriff, for executing an *elegit*, is not entitled to poundage upon the whole debt, but only on the value of the lands extended (*n*). Where goods are taken under an *elegit*, it seems the sheriff is entitled to poundage on their value, just as he would under a *fi. fa.*

Who to pay poundage and expenses.

In general the party at whose suit the writ is issued must bear the expenses of execution, and has no remedy against his debtor, except by express agreement, as usual in a judge's order, warrant of attorney or cognovit.

(*k*) See Hayley *v.* Racket, 5 M. & W. 620.

(*l*) Jones *v.* Robinson, 11 M. & W. 758.

(*m*) *Post*, chap. xvi.

(*n*) Nash *v.* Allen, 1 Dav. & M. 16; 1 Chitty's Archbold, 7th edit. 416. See Price *v.* Hollis, 1 M. & S. 105; Tyson *v.* Paske, 2 Ld. Raym. 1212; S.C. Salk. 333. That the sheriff is entitled to poundage on the debt, see Peacock *v.* Harris, Salk. 331. But that case was cited without avail in Nash *v.* Allen.

CHAP. V. SECT. V.

43 Geo. 3, c. 46, s. 5.

But the 43 Geo. 3, c. 46, s. 5, enacts, that "in every action in which the plaintiff or plaintiffs shall be entitled to levy under an execution against the *goods* of any *defendant*, such plaintiff or plaintiffs may also levy the poundage fees and expenses of the execution, over and above the sum recovered by the judgment." It is observable that this act extends only to executions against *defendants*, and does not enable a *defendant* to levy poundage, &c. on an execution against the *plaintiff* for the costs of the action (*o*). Nor does it apply to crown process (*p*). Also that it applies to executions against *goods*, and not to executions against the person (*q*) or land. The words "expenses of the execution," do not mean only the costs of the writ (*r*); they include such expenses as the sheriff, &c. is put to in keeping possession of the goods, selling, &c. which the plaintiff would have to pay to the sheriff if there was no such statute. But they do not include expenses *dehors* the execution, such as the costs of an interpleader rule (*s*). And where a judge's order directed execution to issue for debt and costs, sheriff's poundage, officer's fees, "and all other incidental expenses," it was held that the sheriff could not levy, nor was the defendant liable to pay, as "incidental expenses," the costs of rules to return the writ (*t*). The plaintiff, when he includes in the writ a sum to be levied for expenses, must take care to levy only such sum as will afterwards be allowed on taxation; for if he levy more, the court will order him to restore the excess with costs (*u*). It seems the sheriff may, in cases within 43 Geo. 3, c. 46, levy for his fees under 1 Vict. c. 55, though there be no indorsement to that effect on the writ, and he need not particularize their respective amounts in his return (*x*).

Rule of court.

A question may perhaps arise whether executions on rules of court are within the above statute; and whether, inasmuch as 1 & 2 Vict. c. 110, s. 18, gives them to some extent the effect of judgments, the person to whom the money is payable thereby

(*o*) Baker *v.* Lyder, 7 Taunt. 179; Anon. 2 Chit. 353. See Woodgate *v.* Knatchbull, 2 T. R. 158.

(*p*) See R. *v.* Miles, 7 T. R. 367; West, 238.

(*q*) Hayley *v.* Racket, 5 M. & W. 620.

(*r*) Per Best, C. J., Rumsey *v.* Tuffnell, 1 Bing. 256.

(*s*) Hammond *v.* Nairn, 1 Dowl. N. S. 351; 9 M. & W. 221, S. C.

(*t*) Hutchinson *v.* Humbert, 1 Dowl. N. S. 78; 8 M. & W. 638, S. C.

(*u*) Benwell *v.* Oakley, 2 Taunt. 174.

(*x*) Curtis *v.* Mayne, 2 Dowl. N. S. 37.

CHAP. V. SECT. V.

may not be considered as a plaintiff for the purpose of the statute (43 Geo. 3, c. 46). But the point has not been decided.

Poundage and expenses, how recovered by the sheriff.

The sheriff may retain his poundage out of the sum levied, or he may maintain an action of debt on the statute for his poundage against the person who issued the writ (*y*); nor has the statute of the 43 Geo. 3, c. 46, s. 5, taken away the sheriff's right of action against the plaintiff for his poundage on a *fi. fa.* (*z*). So it seems the sheriff may sue for the expenses allowed him by 1 Vict. c. 55 (*a*). Or in cases within 43 Geo. 3, c. 46, s. 5, he may levy for them even although there be no indorsement to that effect on the writ (*b*). A question may arise, when the parties compromise after the sheriff has seized and before he has sold under a *fi. fa.*, whether the sheriff, on notice from the plaintiff, is bound to withdraw, and trust to his action against the plaintiff for his poundage, or whether he may, notwithstanding the compromise, proceed to sell enough to cover his poundage? In favour of his right to sell, the course pursued in Alchin *v.* Wells (*c*), and the observations of Wightman, J., in Curtis *v.* Mayne (*d*), may be referred to. On the other hand, it must not be forgotten that 43 Geo. 3, c. 46, s. 5, which alone empowers the sheriff to *levy* for poundage and expenses, was passed in favour of the *plaintiff*, not the sheriff; and therefore, if the ordinary rule applies, the benefit of it may be waived by the plaintiff. A strong case may be put, where the defendant in the compromise has settled for the poundage *eo nomine;* and the case of an *elegit*, where the sheriff can only deliver the goods in execution and not sell, furnishes an argument. The sheriff cannot refuse to execute the writ until his fees are paid (*e*);

(*y*) Lister *v.* Bromley, Sir W. Jones, 307; S. C. Cro. Car. 286; Tyson *v.* Paske, 2 Lord Raym. 1212; S. C. Salk. 333.

(*z*) Rawstorne *v.* Wilkinson, 4 M. & Sel. 256.

(*a*) The general rule is, that for a pecuniary duty created by statute, debt is maintainable. See Com. Dig. Debt, A. 1; Tilson *v.* Warwick Gas Light Company, 4 B. & C. 962; Carden *v.* General Cemetery Company, 5 Bing. N. C. 253. It has been doubted whether actions for the fees allowed by the table (*ante*, 101) to bailiffs, should be brought in the name of the sheriff or of the bailiff. Such actions have been brought in the name of the bailiff, but the point is not decided. See Foster *v.* Blakelock, 3 B. & Ald. 47.

(*b*) Curtis *v.* Mayne, 2 Dowl. N. S. 37.

(*c*) 5 T. R. 470. This point passed unnoticed there.

(*d*) 2 Dowl. N. S. 37.

(*e*) Hescot's case, 1 Salk. 330; Anon. 1 Salk. 331. See also Hopman *v.* Barber, Stra. 814; White *v.* Haugh, *ib.* 1262.

and it seems a bond (*f*), or a promise (*g*), to pay the sheriff his fees that he will be entitled to for executing a writ, is void. CHAP. V. SECT. V.

The *attorney* of the execution plaintiff is not liable to the sheriff for the fees due on the execution of a *ca. sa.* or other writ (*h*).

Extortion.

The taking more fees than is by law allowed is extortion, which is punishable at the common law by indictment (*i*). But indictments can only be maintained against the person actually guilty of the offence, and when the officer of the sheriff takes more than he is entitled to for poundage, the sheriff is liable to an action (*k*), but not to an indictment for the offence of his officer (*l*).

The person from whom the money has been extorted may apply summarily to the Court for restitution (*m*), or bring an action for money had and received, or resort to the remedies furnished by the following statutes, where they are respectively applicable.

28 Eliz c. 4.

By the statute 28 Eliz. c. 4, (*ante*, 100), sheriffs, &c. offending against that act, are subject to pay treble damages to the party aggrieved, and a penalty of 40*l.*, one half to the crown and the other half to the party suing for the same. The treble damages on this statute are calculated as three times the amount of the damages found by the jury (*n*); the damages are in general the sum overcharged (*o*). An action cannot be maintained on the 28th Eliz. for extortion against a sheriff, for taking more fees than he is entitled to in executing a *levari facias* at the suit of the crown; for the sheriff is not entitled to poundage on such a writ *under that statute* (*p*). Nor, it would seem, will an action lie for taking excessive fees, other than poundage, upon the con-

(*f*) Raym. 62; Hutt. 52.

(*g*) Bridge *v.* Cage, Cro. Jac. 103; see Bilke *v.* Havelock, 3 Camp. 374.

(*h*) Maybery *v.* Mansfield, 16 Law J. Q. B. 102; Dew *v.* Parsons, 2 B. & Ald. 562, *semb. contra.* See Bilke *v.* Havelock, 3 Campb. 374.

(*i*) Smith *v.* Mall, 2 Rolle's Rep. 263; S. C. Palm. 318; "extortio est crimen quando quis colore officii extorquet quod non est debitum, vel quod supra debitum, vel ante tempus quod est debitum." See 1 Inst. 368; 2 Inst. 206; 10 Rep. 102; 2 Salk. 680.

(*k*) Woodgate *v.* Knatchbull, 2 T. R. 148.

(*l*) *Per* Gould, J., in Saunderson *v.* Baker, 3 Wils. 316.

(*m*) See Phillips *v.* Viscount Canterbury, 11 M. & W. 619.

(*n*) Woodgate *v.* Knatchbull, 2 T. R. 159; Buckle *v.* Bewes, 6 Dowl. & R. 1; 4 B. & C. 154, S. C.

(*o*) Woodgate *v.* Knatchbull, *ubi sup.* See Buckle *v.* Bewes, 5 D. & R. 495, 3 B. & C. 688, S. C.

(*p*) Stephens *v.* Rothwell, 6 Moore, 338; 3 Bro. & B. 143, S. C.

CHAP. V. SECT. V.

joint operation of the statute 28 Eliz. c. 4, and 1 Vict. c. 55 (*q*). In order to raise that question, the declaration ought to aver that a table of fees has been prepared and sanctioned by the judges under 1 Vict. c. 55, s. 2, and specify in respect of what items the defendant has taken more than that table allows (*r*). It seems that, in a declaration for extortion, the declaration ought to state the amount actually taken, and that it is not sufficient to allege that the sheriff took "£ more than by law is allowed (*s*)."

32 Geo. 2, c. 28, s. 12.

The statute 32 Geo. 2, c. 28, s. 12, giving a penalty of 50*l.* in certain cases of improper conduct of sheriffs in the execution of mesne process, and which has been supposed to extend to extortion of greater fees than are allowed by other statutes upon the execution of mesne process, will be found in the chapter on Bailable Capias (*t*).

1 Vict. c. 55, s. 3. To prevent officers taking fees not allowed or greater fees than are allowed,

The third section of 1 Vict. c. 55, enacts, 'that any sheriff, 'officer or minister acting in the execution of process directed 'to any sheriff or sheriffs, or engaged or concerned therein, who 'shall extort, demand, take, accept or receive from any person 'or persons any fee or fees, gratuity, or reward not allowed as 'aforesaid, or greater in amount than as allowed as aforesaid, 'such sheriff, or other his officer or minister, upon complaint 'thereof made against him to any of the said courts, and on 'proof being made thereof upon oath, either by the examination 'of witnesses *vivâ voce*, or on affidavits, or on interrogatories, to 'the satisfaction of the court to which the said complaint shall be 'made, that such sheriff, officer, or minister, as the case may be, 'hath offended therein as aforesaid, then and in such case every 'such sheriff, officer, or minister, as the case may be, shall be 'adjudged guilty of a contempt of such court, and punished by 'such court accordingly; and if any person, not being such 'officer or minister as aforesaid, shall assume or pretend to act 'as such, and shall extort, demand, take, accept, or receive any 'fee or fees, gratuity, or reward under colour or pretext of 'such office, he shall, on like complaint and proof, be in that 'respect dealt with by the court in like manner.'

and other persons from taking any fees.

(*q*) Usher *v.* Walters, 4 Q. B. 553; 3 G. & D. 594, S. C.; Pilkington *v.* Cooke, 16 M. & W. 617.

(*r*) *Ibid.*

(*s*) Ashby *v.* Harris, 2 M. & W 673; see Pilkington *v.* Cooke, *ubi sup.*

(*t*) *Post*, p. 125.

Sect. 4. 'And be it enacted, that in all cases of summary complaints as aforesaid the court before which such complaint shall be preferred may at its discretion award the costs of or occasioned by such complaint to be paid by either party to the other; such costs to be taxed by the master of such court: Court may award costs.

'Provided always, that no such complaint shall be entertained unless made before the last day of term then next following the act whereof complaint is made.' Complaint under 1 Vict. c. 55, when to be made.

The provisions of the 28th Eliz. c. 4, are not repealed by this statute (*u*).

Section VI.

Actions against the Sheriff in general.

The actions that the sheriff is subject to in discharge of his duty in the execution and return of writs may be classed under two heads: 1st, Actions against the sheriff by the party suing out the writ; 2dly, Those at the suit of the person whose person or goods the sheriff has taken. We have already seen that *civiliter* the sheriff is answerable for the acts of his bailiff, but not *criminaliter;* and therefore for all acts of irregularity, misfeasance, or non-feasance, in executing writs, committed by the officer, the sheriff may be sued (*a*). Actions against the sheriff.

1. As regards the actions to which the sheriff is subject at the suit of the person suing out the process. If the sheriff make a false return, he will be liable to an action; as if he return *nulla bona* to a writ of *fieri facias,* when he had an opportunity of making a levy (*b*); or if he neglects or refuses to execute any writ when he has the opportunity and is required so to do (*c*). Thus where a writ of *hab. fac. poss.* had been delivered to the sheriff, but the writ nevertheless was not executed by reason of the delay of the sheriff, and the judgment was afterwards set aside on payment of costs by the landlord, who was let in to defend by a judge's order, the sheriff was held liable to an action at the suit of the lessor of the plaintiff, for recovery of the expenses he had incurred in trying to have the writ exe- At the suit of the person suing out the writ.

(*u*) Pilkington *v.* Cooke, 16 M. & W. 617.

(*a*) See *ante*, p. 44.

(*b*) See *post*, the chapter on *Fi. fa.*

(*c*) Brown *v.* Jarvis, 1 M. & W. 704; Randell *v.* Wheble, 10 A. & E. 719; Mason *v.* Paynter, 1 Q. B. 974.

CHAP. V. SECT. VI.

cuted (*d*). So also, an action will lie against the sheriff for discharging a person arrested on a bailable writ of *capias* without taking sufficient bail, if he have him not at the return of the writ (*e*).

But an action will not lie for omitting to execute a writ of mesne process before the eight days, unless some actual damage is alleged and proved (*f*). The sheriff is liable to an action for a neglect of duty in omitting to arrest a debtor on a *ca. sa.* *without* proof of actual damage; but if the jury negative actual damage, the plaintiff is only entitled to a verdict with nominal damages (*g*). So in an action against the sheriff for negligence in executing a *fi. fa.*, the plaintiff cannot recover *more* than nominal damages, unless he prove actual damage; and it was doubted whether without such proof even nominal damages could be recovered (*h*).

If the sheriff discharge a defendant on taking a bail-bond on an arrest on mesne process, and return *non est inventus*, he would be liable to an action for a false return (*i*). But the sheriff is not liable to an *action* at the suit of the plaintiff for not returning the writ (*k*). If a person in the sheriff's custody in execution be rescued, or escape out of custody, or be discharged by the sheriff, even on payment to him of the debt and costs, the sheriff is liable to an action for an escape (*l*). Or if the sheriff, on request, refuse to assign to the plaintiff a bail-bond taken by him on an arrest on mesne process, the sheriff is liable to an action; but for such a refusal it seems that there is no other remedy (*m*). For money levied by the sheriff on a *fi. fa.* an action will lie by the plaintiff against the sheriff (*n*). It has been doubted whether an action will lie against the sheriff at the suit of a party issuing an attachment out of the Court of Chancery for arresting the defendant while privileged, so that the plaintiff was obliged to issue a fresh attachment (*o*).

(*d*) Mason *v.* Paynter, 1 Q. B. 974.

(*e*) Brunskill *v.* Robertson, 9 A. & E. 840.

(*f*) Williams *v.* Mostyn, 4 M. & W. 145; Brown *v.* Jarvis, *supra*; Randle *v.* Wheble, *supra*.

(*g*) Clifton *v.* Hooper, 6 Q. B. 468.

(*h*) Bates *v.* Wingfield, 4 Q. B. 580, n.; 2 Nev. & M. 831, S. C.

(*i*) See *post*, chap. 6.

(*k*) 2 Inst. 452.

(*l*) See *post*, chap. on *Ca. sa.*

(*m*) Stamper *v.* Milbourne, 7 T. R. 122. And see Mendez *v.* Bridges, 5 Taunt. 325.

(*n*) See *post*, chapter on *Fi. fa.*

(*o*) See Lloyd *v.* Wood, 5 Ad. &. E. 228, *per* Patteson, J.

CHAP. V. SECT. VI.

At the suit of the person whose goods, &c. are taken.

2. If the defendant be styled by a wrong name in a writ of mesne process, either against his goods or his person, the sheriff is liable to an action of trespass for executing such writ (*m*), unless the name be *idem sonans* (*n*), or unless the defendant be known by one name as well as the other (*o*), or has assumed in the particular instance the name by which he is sued (*p*). And where the defendant is styled by a wrong name in a writ of mesne process, in a plea of justification it must be alleged that the defendant was known by one name as well as the other (*q*). And the 3 & 4 Will. 4, c. 42, s. 11, which takes away the right of a defendant to plead in abatement for a misnomer, does not in any way affect the law in this respect (*r*).

Although the sheriff will be justified in arresting a defendant wrongly named in the writ where he is as well known by the wrong name, still he is not bound to do so; and even after actual arrest under such circumstances, he is not, it seems, liable to all the consequences which attach to an arrest under ordinary circumstances, unless he has *notice* that the defendant was as well known by one name as the other (*s*).

If on a writ against A. the sheriff arrest B., although B. says that he is A., yet it has been said that the sheriff is liable to an action for false imprisonment (*t*). But it may be doubted, notwithstanding such dicta, whether any action would lie against a sheriff for a mistake induced by the misrepresentation of the complainant (*u*).

For executing a writ of final process against a defendant wrongly named in the writ no action will lie against the sheriff, provided that the person upon whose body or goods the writ is

(*m*) Cole *v.* Hindson, 6 T. R. 234; Shadgett *v.* Clipson, 8 East, 328; Price *v.* Harwood, 3 Camp. 108; Scandover *v.* Warne, 2 Camp. 270. See Thurbane *et al.* Hard. 323; Rex *v.* Sheriff of Surrey, 1 Marsh. 75; Rex *v.* Sheriff of Middlesex, 2 Chit. Rep. 357. It is otherwise in writs of execution, if the judgment were against the defendant by a wrong name; Crawford *v.* Satchwell, Stra. 1218.

(*n*) See Abithol *v.* Beniditto, 2 Taunt. 401.

(*o*) See the cases in the two last notes; also Fisher *v.* Magnay, 1 Dowl. & Low. 40.

(*p*) Price *v.* Harwood, 3 Camp. 108; Morgan *v.* Bridges, 1 Bar. & Ald. 647; Crawford *v.* Satchwell, 2 Stra. 1218.

(*q*) See the cases cited *supra*; also Fisher *v.* Magnay, 1 Dowl. & L. 45, *per* Tindal, C. J.

(*r*) Finch *v.* Cocken, 3 Dowl. 678; 2 C. M. & R. 196, S. C.

(*s*) Brunskill *v.* Robertson, 9 A. & E. 840; Morgan *v.* Bridges, 1 B. & Ald. 647.

(*t*) Moor, 457; Hard. 323.

(*u*) See *per* Lord Ellenborough, C. J., 1 B. & Ald. 650; Smith's Leading Cases, 44, n.; *ante*, p. 76.

CHAP. V. SECT. VI.

executed be *in fact* the person against whom the judgment was entered up and the writ issued; and it is quite immaterial whether he be generally known as well by one name as another. Indeed the sheriff would be bound to execute such a writ (*x*).

If the officer on a writ against A. take the goods of B., the sheriff is liable to an action of trespass or trover for the act of his officer (*y*). Even if there are two persons of the same name and address, and a writ issues against one of them, and the sheriff through inadvertence or mistake executes the writ against the wrong person, he is liable to an action. For instance, where a father and son both bore the name of "Joseph Jarmain," and judgment was recovered and a *fi. fa.* issued against the son by that name, not adding "the younger," the sheriff was held liable in trespass for levying on the goods of the father (*z*). In such cases, if the goods have been sold and the price of them received by the sheriff, the owner may waive the tort and bring an action for money had and received against the sheriff to recover the proceeds (*a*); but in such an action the plaintiff will be entitled to the amount only which has been actually realized by the sale; whereas in an action *ex delicto* he might recover the *value* of the goods seized without reference to the price for which they were sold, and also compensation for the inconvenience, &c. occasioned by the seizure (*b*).

Where the sheriff under a *fi. fa.* seizes goods in the possession of the defendant, to which the defendant has but a defeasible title, and such title is afterwards defeated by events having a retrospective effect, as frequently happens in cases of bankruptcy, the sheriff generally becomes liable to an action of trover (*c*), but not of *trespass*, because he cannot be made a trespasser by relation (*d*).

(*x*) Reeves *v.* Slater, 7 B. & C. 486; Fisher *v.* Magnay, 1 Dowl. & L. 40; 6 Man. & G. 827, S. C.; *ante*, p. 70.

(*y*) Ackworth *v.* Kempe, Dougl. 40. See also Oughton *v.* Seppings, 1 B. & Ad. 241; Glasspoole *v.* Young, 9 B. & C. 696.

(*z*) Jarmain *v.* Hooper, 1 Dowl. & L. 769; 6 Man. & G. 827, S. C.

(*a*) Feltham *v.* Terry, cit. Cowp. 419. See also Notley *v.* Buck, 8 B. & C. 160; 2 Man. & R. 68, S. C.; Oughton *v.* Seppings, 1 B. & Adol. 241.

(*b*) Glasspoole *v.* Young, 9 B. & C. 696. See also Vaughan *v.* Wilkins, 1 B. & Ad. 370. *Quære*, whether such special damage could be recovered in trover; Brewer *v.* Dew, 11 M. & W. 625.

(*c*) Cooper *v.* Chitty, 1 Burr. 20; Smith *v.* Miles, 1 T. R. 475; Balme *v.* Hutton, 9 Bing. 471; Groves *v.* Cowham, 10 Bing. 5; Garland *v.* Carlisle, 4 Bing. N. C. 7; Whitmore *v.* Greene, 12 M. & W. 184.

(*d*) See cases in last note.

Thus, if a sheriff, having seized goods under a *fi. fa.* issued on a judgment founded on a warrant of attorney, sells after the issuing of the fiat, he will be liable to an action of trover at the suit of the assignees, for such an execution is defeated, and the property in the goods transferred to the assignees, after issuing of the fiat before sale (*e*); or if the sheriff has received the proceeds, he may be sued for money had and received (*f*). Where there is any abuse in the execution of process, trespass will lie against the sheriff and his officer; as if the officer arrests a person on a writ of *fi. fa.* (*g*), or take the defendant out of the sheriff's bailiwick (*h*); or after the return day of the writ (*i*); or if he break open an outer door (*j*), or execute a writ of execution after notice of the allowance of a writ of error (*k*); or if he execute a writ against the person or goods of a defendant, after a direction from the plaintiff not to do so, or after notice from the plaintiff that he has released the debt (*l*); or if, after seizure and sale of chattels real under a *fi. fa.*, he remain in possession for an unreasonable time for the further execution of the writ (*m*); or if he be guilty of any other excess (*n*), even though such excess or abuse be committed by the officer contrary to the express orders given him by the under-sheriff (*o*), or contrary to the express terms of the writ (*p*).

Unlawful detainer after rightful arrest.

If the sheriff, having lawfully arrested a party, detains him after such detainer ceases to be *lawful* and notice thereof, he will be liable in *trespass*; and if, in an action for false imprisonment under such circumstances, the sheriff justify under the process, the plaintiff may new assign the unlawful detainer (*q*). But it seems that a sheriff cannot be sued in any form of action for detaining a prisoner, who having been un-

(*e*) Cheston *v.* Gibbs, 1 Dowl. & L. 420; S. C. 12 M. & W. 111.

(*f*) Notley *v.* Buck, 8 B. & C. 160.

(*g*) Smart *v.* Hutton, 8 Ad. & E. 568, n.

(*h*) See Holliet *v.* Bessey, Sir T. Jones, 214.

(*i*) 2 Esp. Rep. 585.

(*j*) Lee *v.* Gansel, Cowp. 1.

(*k*) Belshaw *v.* Marshall, 4 B. & Ad. 336.

(*l*) Barker *v.* St. Quintin, 12 M. & W. 441.

(*m*) Playfair *v.* Musgrove, 13 M. & W. 239.

(*n*) Ratcliffe *v.* Burton, 1 Bos. & Pul. 223.

(*o*) Scarfe *v.* Hallifax, 7 M. & W. 288; also *per* Patteson, J. in Balme *v.* Hutton, 9 Bing. 474.

(*p*) Smart *v.* Hutton, 8 Ad. & E. 568, n. See further as to liability for acts of bailiffs, *ante*, 44.

(*q*) Magnay *v.* Burt, 5 Q. B. 381; 1 Dav. & M. 652, Exchequer Chamber in error, reversing the judgment of the Queen's Bench. See also Smith *v.* Egginton, 7 Ad. & Ell. 167.

lawfully in custody, has become entitled to his discharge, unless the sheriff has notice of the facts which entitle him to his discharge, and a request to be discharged is not tantamount to such notice (*r*).

Not entitled to notice of action.

The sheriff is not in any case entitled to notice of action for any thing done by him in executing the process of the court (*s*). Where an act of parliament gave a power to the sheriff to levy debts due in respect of taxes, when recorded in the Exchequer, it was held that the sheriff was not such a collector as is entitled to a month's notice of action, under the 43 Geo. 3, c. 99, s. 33 (*t*).

Justification by the sheriff.

It is not necessary for the sheriff to show the judgment in justifying under a writ of execution; it is enough to show the writ only (*u*). The sheriff is justified in executing a *fi. fa.* issued after the defendant has been discharged by the Insolvent Debtors' Court, and no action will lie against him for so doing (*v*). But where the sheriff or his officer justifies under any writ or warrant, it is necessary for him to set it forth in his plea; for it is not sufficient to allege *generally* that he committed the act complained of by virtue of a certain writ or warrant to him directed (*x*). The defendant should also show that he has substantially pursued his authority (*y*), and that the acts complained of were all done under the writ; for it is not sufficient to justify the sheriff, that a writ has been delivered to him, under which he *might, had he chosen, have committed the acts,* unless in fact he did commit them under such writ (*z*); and therefore, where in trespass for breaking and entering the plaintiff's house, the defendants (the sheriff and his bailiff) justified under a *fi. fa.* and warrant of execution against the goods of B., alleging that the warrant was delivered to one of the defendants, a bailiff, to be executed; that goods of B. were in the house, and that by virtue of the writ and warrant, defendants, being sheriff and bailiff, broke and entered, &c.; to which the plaintiff, admitting the issuing and delivery of the writ to

(*r*) Smith *v.* Egginton, 7 Ad. & Ell. 167.

(*s*) See *per* Park, J., 1 Bing. 373.

(*t*) Copland *v.* Powell, 1 Bing. 369; S. C. 8 Moore, 400.

(*u*) Cotes *v.* Michell, 3 Lev. 20; Moravia *v.* Sloper, Willes, 30, 34; Andrews *v.* Marris, 1 Q. B. 17, *per* Lord Denman, C. J.

(*v*) Whitworth *v.* Clifton, 1 M. & Rob. 531.

(*x*) 1 Saund. 298, n. (1).

(*y*) *Id.*

(*z*) See Lucas *v.* Nockells, 10 Bing. 157; Carnaby *v.* Welby, 8 Ad. & E. 872.

the sheriff, and the making and delivery of the warrant to the bailiff, replied that the defendants of their own wrong, *and without the residue of the cause in their plea alleged, committed the trespasses:* it was held, that, in order to justify the defendants, it should have been shown by evidence that the entry and seizure were *under the writ and warrant*—that upon the record no other facts were admitted than those admitted in terms by the replication, and that the plaintiff was at liberty to show that the seizure was a mere colourable one, and not under the writ (*a*). Yet if the officer has a legal warrant at the time of seizing the defendant's goods, although he declared he entered for a different purpose, this is a good justification for the officer (*b*). We have seen, that if the court out of which the writ issues has jurisdiction over the cause, although the proceedings whereon the writ is grounded be erroneous, or even the writ itself be irregular, yet the writ is sufficient for the sheriff's justification (*c*); even if the writ be set aside for *irregularity*, after it is executed by the sheriff, yet it is sufficient to justify his acts (*d*). But the sheriff would not be justified in executing a writ which, upon the face of it, appeared to be a nullity and unauthorized by law (*e*); nor in executing a writ, after notice that it has been superseded, as if he executes a *fi. fa.* after notice of the allowance of a writ of error (*f*); nor in executing it after notice from the plaintiff not to execute it without further order (*g*). In justifying under a writ of mesne process, it is necessary for the sheriff to show the writ returned (*h*); but it is not necessary in a plea of justification by a sheriff's bailiff (*i*); and the sheriff may justify acting under a *ca. sa.* or *fi. fa.* without having returned them (*j*). It is always ad-

(*a*) Carnaby *v.* Welby, *supra.*

(*b*) Crowther *v.* Ramsbottom, 7 T. R. 654. *Per* Holt, C. J. in Grenville *v.* The College of Physicians, 12 Mod. 387. See Baillie *v.* Kell, 4 N. C. 638.

(*c*) *Ante*, p. 67; Andrews *v.* Marris, 1 Q. B. 3; Carratt *v.* Morley, *ib.* 18.

(*d*) Turner *v.* Felgate, 2 Sid. 125; S. C. 1 Lev. 95. See also In the matter of the Glatton Land Tax, 4 M. & W. 570, *per* Parke, B.

(*e*) See Carratt *v.* Morley, 1 Q. B. 18.

(*f*) Belshaw *v.* Marshall, 4 B. & Ad. 336.

(*g*) Hunt *v.* Hooper, 12 M. & W. 664.

(*h*) Britton *v.* Cole, 1 Salk. 509; Freeman *v.* Blewitt, *id. ibid.*; S. C. 12 Mod. 394; 1 Ld. Raym. 632.

(*i*) Girling's case, Cro. Car. 446; S. C. Sir W. Jones, 378. And see cases in last note, and Cro. Eliz. 181.

(*j*) Rowland *v.* Veale, Cowp. 18; Cheasley *v.* Barnes, 10 East, 82; Mountney *v.* Andrews, Cro. Eliz. 237; Hoe's case, 5 Rep. 90.

visable, where an action of trespass is brought against the sheriff or his officer, jointly with the plaintiff or his attorney, for the sheriff to justify separately; for if the justification be joint, and it be bad for the plaintiff, it will be bad for the sheriff or his officer also; and there are many cases in which the sheriff is justified, but not the party or his attorney (*k*). For instance, if the officer and party justify under a *ca. sa.* together, they are bound to show a regular judgment; whereas it is a sufficient justification for the sheriff to show the writ without the judgment (*l*). Where a *stranger* brings an action of trover against the sheriff, or against a person claiming under a bill of sale of goods from the sheriff, for goods seized and sold under a *fi. fa.*, it is said to be necessary to prove the judgment as well as the writ (*m*); but it is not necessary to prove the judgment where the action is by the defendant himself (*n*), or by his assignees if he has become a bankrupt, for they stand precisely in the same situation as the defendant would do (*o*).

Proof of judgment, when necessary in trover.

When the action lies against the old, and when against the new sheriff.

As between the *old* and *new* sheriff, we have seen that the new sheriff is not chargeable with such things which are wholly executed before they are delivered over to him by the old sheriff (*p*); for if the old sheriff take a man in execution, and afterwards a new sheriff be made, and before the old sheriff deliver his prisoner to the new sheriff the prisoner escape, the old sheriff only is chargeable for the escape; for the new sheriff shall not be chargeable for any other prisoners than what are legally delivered over to him (*q*).

The law relative to actions against the sheriff, in respect of the execution of process, will be found more particularly noticed in the chapters relating to each process.

(*k*) Phillips *v.* Biron, Stra. 509; Smith *v.* Bouchier, Stra. 993; Middleton *v.* Price, Stra. 1184; Andrews *v.* Marris, 1 Q. B. 17; Samuel *v.* Duke, 9 M. & W. 622.

(*l*) See cases in last note; Cotes *v.* Michell, 3 Lev. 20.

(*m*) Martin *v.* Podger, 5 Burr. 2631; S. C. 2 Bla. Rep. 701; Lake *v.* Billers, 1 Ld. Raym. 733.

(*n*) Lake *v.* Billers, 1 Ld. Raym, 733; Doe *v.* Murless, 6 M. & Sel. 110.

(*o*) Glasier *v.* Eve, 1 Bing. 209; S. C. 8 Moore, 46.

(*p*) Westby *v.* Skinner, Cro. Eliz. 365; S. C. 3 Rep. 71.

(*q*) See judgment of Lord Ellenborough, 4 East, 606; Thomas *v.* Newnam, 2 Dowl. N. S. 33. See *ante*, p. 21, *et seq.*

CHAPTER VI.

OF THE SHERIFF'S DUTY ON A BAILABLE CAPIAS (*a*).

SECT. I.—*Of the Arrest; when, where, how made.—Detainer.—Sheriff's Fees on an Arrest.—Privilege from Arrest, when to be allowed by the Sheriff.—Peers, Ambassadors, Attornies, Witnesses, &c., Bankrupts, Seamen and Soldiers.*

II.—*Sheriff's Duty after the Arrest.—How the Defendant should be treated after the Arrest.—Deposit in lieu of Bail.—The Bail Bond; Sheriff obliged to discharge Defendant on giving a Bail-Bond; In what Form, to whom, for what amount to be made;—When the Sheriff must discharge the Defendant.*

III.—*Proceedings on the Bail-Bond.—Assignment of the Bail-Bond; where, by whom, and how made.—Action on the Bail-bond; in what Court to be brought; when Proceedings may be stayed on the Bail-Bond.*

IV.—*Proceedings against the Sheriff.—Rule to return the Writ.—Return.—Rule to bring in the Body; Object thereof, at what time obtained, how complied with.—Attachment for not bringing in the Body, how obtained, when set aside for irregularity; regular, on what Terms set aside; to what Extent the Sheriff is liable on the Attachment; his Remedy over.*

V.—*Actions for Escape, &c.—In what Cases maintainable.—The Declaration.—Evidence.—Damages.*

SECTION I.

Bailable Capias.—Arrest; when and how made.

A WARRANT must be made out to a bailiff as soon as the writ comes to the under-sheriff's office, if he knows where the de-

(*a*) This writ, since 1 & 2 Vict. c. 110, can no longer properly be called a *capias ad respondendum*. All the proceedings *ad respondendum* are had under the writ of summons. The *capias* is only a collateral process to enforce security in case the debtor is about to quit England.

CHAP. VI. SECT. I.

fendant lives (*b*); on which point he is, it seems, bound to make reasonable inquiry, as the plaintiff is not bound to identify and point out the defendant as a condition precedent to the sheriff's being bound to arrest him (*c*). The form of the warrant, and the indorsements requisite thereon, and when it must be jointly executed, have been already considered (*d*). The name of the attorney suing out the writ (*e*), and the day and year indorsed on the writ (*f*), must be indorsed on the warrant. But an omission in this respect only subjects the sheriff to a penalty, and does not vitiate the warrant (*g*).

In cases of misnomer.

If the defendant be sued by a wrong name, the sheriff would be a trespasser for arresting the defendant on mesne process, unless the defendant were known as well by the name mentioned in the writ as by his real name (*h*). And even although the defendant should be known by both names, or had used the name in the writ in the particular transaction, the sheriff, although he would be *justified* in making the arrest if he thought fit so to do, would not, at least without notice of the circumstances, be liable to an action for not executing the writ, or for an escape (*i*).

At what time the arrest ought to be made.

If the bailiff make the arrest before the writ is delivered to the sheriff, or before he has received his warrant, he will be subject to an action for false imprisonment (*k*). But after the writ is delivered to the sheriff, and after the warrant is delivered to the officer, the arrest may be made, according to the memorandum subscribed (*l*) to it (according to 1 & 2 Vict. c. 110, sched.), within one calendar month from the date thereof, including the day of such date, and not afterwards. It may be made at any hour of the day or night (*m*). An arrest on such process upon a Sunday, we have seen, is illegal by the statute 29 Car. 2, c. 7, s. 6 (*n*).

It has also been noticed that the sheriff must execute the

(*b*) See form, Appendix.
(*c*) Dyke *v.* Duke, 4 Bing. N.C. 197.
(*d*) See *ante*, p. 71, *et seq.*
(*e*) 2 Geo. 2, c. 23, s. 22; 12 Geo. 2, c. 13, s. 4; see 2 W. 4, c. 39, s. 12.
(*f*) 6 Geo. 1, c. 21, s. 54; see *ante*, p. 71.
(*g*) *Ante*, 71; 1 Chit. Archb. 525.
(*h*) *Ante*, pp. 70 and 120.
(*i*) Morgan *v.* Bridges, 1 Bar. & Ald. 647; Brunskill *v.* Robertson, 9 A. & E. 840.
(*k*) 1 Saund. 298; Hall *v.* Roche, 8 T. R. 187; Astley *v.* Goodjer, 2 Dowl. 619.
(*l*) See *ante*, p. 78.
(*m*) Macally's case, 9 Co. 66; Anon. 1 Chit. 357.
(*n*) *Ante*, p. 79. Wilson *v.* Tucker, 1 Salk. 78; Loveridge *v.* Plaistow, 2 Hen. Blac. 29; Taylor *v.* Phillips, 3 East, 155. It is said in the case in

process within a reasonable time, and if he neglects to do so will subject himself to an action for recovery of any damage sustained by reason of his neglect (*o*). In an action for default made before the writ has become returnable, special damage must be alleged and proved (*p*). Mere delay in the execution of the writ is no ground for an *attachment* against the sheriff (*q*).

Where made. The sheriff or his officer may arrest the defendant at any place within his county; but the sheriffs of London, on a writ directed to them, cannot make an arrest in Middlesex, or *vice versâ*. If the officer arrest a person out of the county to which a writ is directed, he will be liable to an action for false imprisonment, and the Court (on a speedy application, but not after considerable delay) (*r*) will discharge the defendant out of custody, or order a bail-bond, if taken on such arrest, to be cancelled (*s*); but the Court, to interfere summarily in such case, will require an affidavit that there is no dispute as to the boundary (*t*). An arrest cannot be legally made in the king's presence, nor in any of his royal palaces (*u*); nor in the Tower of London (*x*), nor in a Court of justice whilst the justices are sitting (*y*); but it seems the Court would not summarily discharge a defendant out of custody if so arrested (*z*), though it would be punishable as a contempt. If the writ do not contain a *non omittas* clause, we have seen that the sheriff should issue his mandate to the bailiff of a liberty to arrest the defendant, if he reside within a liberty (*a*). And although a sheriff is liable to an action at the suit of the owner of the franchise for executing a writ without a *non omittas* clause within a liberty (*b*), yet an arrest there made by the sheriff is good; he is not therefore liable to an action of trespass; nor will the Courts discharge a defendant so arrested out of custody, although such arrest be

Salk. that the party arrested on a Sunday may have an action for false imprisonment.

(*o*) *Ante*, 78; Randell *v.* Wheble, 10 Ad. & El. 719.

(*p*) *Ib.*

(*q*) Rex *v.* Sheriff of Kent, 2 M. & W. 316.

(*r*) Greenshield *v.* Pritchard, 8 M. & W. 148; Fownes *v.* Stokes, 4 Dowl. 125.

(*s*) Hammond *v.* Taylor, 3 Bar. & Ald. 408.

(*t*) *Id. ibid.* Storer *v.* Rayson, 4 Dowl. & Ry. 739; S. C. 3 Bar. & Cres. 158; —— *v.* Walters, 1 Chit. Rep. 14, 15, n. (*d*); *ante*, 74.

(*u*) Winter *v.* Miles, 10 East, 578; 1 Camp. 475; *ante*, 75.

(*x*) Batson *v.* M'Lean, 2 Chit. Rep. 51; *ante*, 74.

(*y*) *Ante*, 75.

(*z*) Spinks *v.* Spinks, 7 Taunt. 311.

(*a*) 5 Geo. 2, c. 27, s. 3.

(*b*) See Carrett *v.* Smallpage, 9 East, 330.

CHAP. VI. SECT. I.

made within the verge of the palace (*c*). So, on the other hand, if the sheriff enter a franchise without a *non omittas*, and arrest a defendant, he will be liable to an action for allowing the defendant to escape out of his custody (*d*). It is no objection to an arrest that it was made in a gaol, the defendant being there for his own purposes (*e*).

How made—may not break open an outer door.

The officer cannot legally break open the outer door or window of the house, either of the defendant or of a stranger, to make an arrest (*f*); but having once gained peaceable admission to the house, the officer may break open an inner door, even if it be the door of a lodger (*g*). It has indeed been laid down, that although the sheriff cannot break open the outer door of the house of the defendant to arrest him, yet he may break open the outer door of the house of a stranger for that purpose (*h*). This, however, it is submitted, is not correct; in neither case can he break open the outer door, excepting when he has already arrested the defendant, who escapes; then, on fresh pursuit, the sheriff may break open the outer door of any house to retake the defendant (*i*). There is also this diversity between the house of the defendant and a stranger; the house of the former the plaintiff is justified in entering, without forcing the door, to seek for the defendant, even if he should happen not to be there (*k*); but the sheriff is only justified in entering the house of a stranger if the defendant be *actually therein;* for it is no justification if the defendant be not there, even if he has resided there immediately before the entry, and the officer had probable cause to suppose that the defendant was there at the time of the entry (*l*).

What amounts to an arrest.

In making the arrest, the sheriff should actually seize or touch the defendant's body (*m*); a touch, however slight, will constitute an arrest (*n*). Thus where the sheriff's officer went

(*c*) Spinks *v.* Spinks, 7 Taunt. 311.

(*d*) Piggott *v.* Wilkes, 3 Bar. & Ald. 502.

(*e*) Lovet *v.* Hill, 4 Dowl. 579.

(*f*) *Ante*, 75; see Doe *v.* Trye, 5 Bing. N. C. 573, where the officer unjustifiably thrust his hand through some paper which supplied the place of a broken pane, and took out a key with which to open the outer door.

(*g*) Lee *v.* Gansell, Cowp. 1; and see *ante*, 75.

(*h*) Foster, 319.

(*i*) *Per* Best, C. J., Rex *v.* Conolly, Hertford Spring Assizes, 1824.

(*k*) Ratcliffe *v.* Burton, 3 Bos. & Pul. 223; and see Hutchinson *v.* Birch, 4 Taunt. 619.

(*l*) Johnson *v.* Leigh, 6 Taunt. 246; Cooke *v.* Birch, 5 Taunt. 765; see also 4 Taunt. 619; Morrish *v.* Murrey, 13 M. & W. 52.

(*m*) Genner *v.* Sparkes, 1 Salk. 79; S. C. 6 Mod. 173.

(*n*) W. Fish's case, cited 2 Roll. Rep. 138; Palmer, 53; Nicholl *v.* Darley, 2 Y. & J. 399.

to the defendant's house to arrest him on a *ca. sa.*, and read the warrant over to him, whereupon the defendant rushed out against the officer, who seized him round the waist, but was unable to hold him, it was held that this amounted to an arrest (*o*). Mere words, as "I arrest you," will not, however, of themselves constitute an arrest (*p*). So where the officer, without producing the warrant to the defendant, or threatening to arrest him, sent a message asking him to fix a time and call and give bail, and the defendant accordingly fixed a time, called, and gave bail; such proceeding was held no arrest (*q*). And where the officer called with the warrant on the defendant's attorney, and required bail to the sheriff, which was afterwards given, it was held no arrest (*r*). But if the officer, being in a position to arrest the defendant, uses such words as "I arrest you," and the defendant acquiesces, and goes with the officer, it will be a good arrest (*s*). So it will in general be an arrest, if the defendant does any act under the immediate compulsion of the process, though the officer does not actually touch him. It was so held, where the defendant was offered the alternative of being arrested and giving bail, or giving up property in his possession, and he chose to give up the property (*t*). And if a bailiff comes into a room and tells the defendant he arrests him, and locks the door, that is an arrest, for the defendant is then in custody of the officer (*u*).

In order to constitute an arrest under such circumstances, it seems the warrant ought to be produced, or at least the defendant made aware that the officer has it, and is in a position actually to arrest him in case of resistance (*x*). It is not necessary that the officer to whom the warrant is directed should be the hand that arrests, nor that he should be in the presence of the person arrested, nor actually in sight, nor is any exact distance prescribed; it is sufficient if he be near, and acting in the arrest (*y*).

(*o*) Nicholl *v.* Darley, 2 Y. & J. 399.

(*p*) Russen *v.* Lucas, 1 Car. & P. 153; see also 1 Salk. 79; 6 Mod. 173.

(*q*) Berry *v.* Adamson, 6 B. & C. 528.

(*r*) James *v.* Askew, 8 A. & E. 351.

(*s*) Homer *v.* Battyn and others, Bull. N. P. 62. Per Abbott, C. J., 1 C. & P. 153.

(*t*) Grainger *v.* Hill, 4 N. C. 212.

(*u*) Williams *v.* Jones, Rep. temp. Hard. 301. See also Arrowsmith *v.* Le Mesurier, 2 New Rep. 211, 212, and *quære*.

(*x*) Robins *v.* Hender, 3 Dowl. 542, Williams, J. See also Barratt *v.* Price, 9 Bing. 566; 1 Dowl. 725; 2 M. & Scott, 339, S. C.

(*y*) Blatch *v.* Archer, Cowp. 63.

CHAP. VI. SECT. I.

Detainer.

If, whilst the defendant is in the legal custody of the sheriff, any other writ be delivered to him, or at the under-sheriff's or deputy's office, at the suit of the same or of any other plaintiff, the defendant is, by virtue of such delivery, in custody as well under such other writ as the writ upon which he is arrested (*z*). So also, if a defendant be legally arrested by the sheriff in one action, such arrest will operate as an arrest in all actions in which the sheriff holds writs against him at the time (*a*), and the sheriff would in such case be justified in detaining the defendant upon such other writs, even though the defendant subsequently obtained an order for his discharge from custody in the action upon which he was arrested (*b*). And therefore if the defendant should be ordered to be discharged in the action in which he is arrested, the officer should always search the sheriff's office, to see if there be any other process lodged against the defendant, before he discharges him. But if the first arrest be void as made without any process (*c*), or after it is returnable (*d*), or if it be made under process which is afterwards set aside for irregularity (*e*), or if it be made by means of any trickery of the plaintiff or his attorney or agent (*f*), the defendant cannot be detained by subsequent process, at suit of the same plaintiff.

And where an arrest is effected by a wrongful act of the sheriff, or of another person, afterwards adopted by the sheriff, such arrest will not operate as an arrest, even upon valid writs previously lodged; nor, whilst the defendant is in custody upon such illegal

See Cuckson *v.* Winter, 2 Man. & R. 315, n.; Barratt *v.* Price, *ubi sup.* Fownes *v.* Stokes, 4 Dowl. 125; 1 Chit. Arch. 530.

(*z*) Frost's case, 5 Rep. 89; Wright *v.* Stanford, 1 Dowl. N. S. 272. It is said that if a person be in the custody of the sheriff of Northumberland in that county, and another writ against the same person be delivered personally to the sheriff in London, the prisoner is thereby immediately in custody in that suit; Salk. 274. *Sed quære.*

(*a*) Barratt *v.* Price, 9 Bing. 570, Tindal, C. J.; Collins *v.* Yewens, 10 A. & E. 570; Ford *v.* Leche, 6 A. & E. 707, Patteson, J.; Barrack *v.* Newton, 1 Q. B. 525.

(*b*) Ex parte Coggs, 6 Dowl. 461; Barrack *v.* Newton, 1 Q. B. 525. See also Watson *v.* Carroll, 4 M. & W. 592; Barclay *v.* Faber, 2 B. & A. 743; S. C. 1 Chit. Rep. 579. And see note to 1 Chit. 579, 580; Davis *v.* Chippendale, 2 Bos. & Pul. 282; Howson *v.* Walker, 2 Bla. Rep. 823. White *v.* Gompertz, 5 Bar. & Ald. 905.

(*c*) Loveridge *v.* Plaistow, 2 Hen. Bla. 29.

(*d*) Barlow *v.* Hall, 2 Anstr. 461; Birch *v.* Podger, 1 N. R. 135.

(*e*) Hall *v.* Hawkins, 4 M. & W. 591; 7 Dowl. 200, S. C.

(*f*) Barratt *v.* Price, 9 Bing. 566; 1 Dowl. 725, S. C. See Jacobs *v.* Jacobs, 3 Dowl. 677; Goodwin *v.* London, 1 A. & E. 378; Mackie *v.* Warren, 2 Moo. & P. 279; 5 Bing. 176, S. C.

arrest, can he be detained upon valid writs subsequently lodged (*g*), unless upon a fresh arrest. And such fresh arrest cannot, it seems, be made whilst he is in or returning from the illegal custody (*h*); certainly not before the rule for his discharge has been served on the person in whose custody he is (*i*). But where an authorized person, even a bailiff, without the sanction of or collusion with the sheriff or any authorized person, arrests the defendant without a warrant, either he or any other bailiff, who obtains a legal warrant, may arrest pending such illegal custody (*k*). To entitle a prisoner to his discharge under such circumstances, the first wrongful arrest must have been either the act of or ratified by the plaintiff or the sheriff. Where several processes are lodged, and one is irregular, the question under which the defendant was first arrested is not concluded by the marshal's return (*l*).

If the defendant be privileged from arrest at the time of the caption, he cannot be detained at the suit of the same or any other plaintiff; for if he could, his privilege would be illusory (*m*). The order for discharge in such a case should be headed in all the causes under which the prisoner is detained, as he is only entitled to be discharged from those mentioned therein (*n*).

It is only, however, in cases where the first arrest is void or illegal by reason of privilege or of the wrongful act of the sheriff, that third parties other than and not connected with him, under whose process the first arrest took place, can be affected by the impropriety of the first arrest. If the defendant has been arrested upon irregular process, which is afterwards set aside, he is not entitled to be discharged from the process of another plaintiff, unless there be some collusion (*o*).

(*g*) Barratt *v.* Price, 9 Bing. 566; Collins *v.* Yewens, 10 A. & E. 570; Humphrey *v.* Mitchell, 2 Bing. N. C. 619; Pearson *v.* Yewens, 5 Bing. N. C. 489.

(*h*) R. M. 15 Car. 2, s. 2. And see Farmer *v.* Jenkinson, Cook, 34; Webb *v.* Dorwell, Barnes, 400; 1 Chit. Arch. 479.

(*i*) Pearson *v.* Yewens, 5 N. C. 567.

(*k*) Collins *v.* Yewens, 10 A. & E. 570; Robinson *v.* Yewens, 5 M. & W. 149. See also Goodwin *v.* Lordon, 1 A. & E. 378

(*l*) Wright *v.* Stanford, 1 Dowl. N. S. 272.

(*m*) Spence *v.* Stuart, 3 East, 89.

(*n*) Watson *v.* Carroll, 4 M. & W. 592.

(*o*) Ex parte Cogg, 6 Dowl. 461; Barrack *v.* Newton, 1 Q. B. 525; Barclay *v.* Faber, 2 B. & Ald. 743; S. C. 1 Chit. Rep. 579. And see note to 1 Chit. 579, 580; Davis *v.* Chippendale, 2 Bos. & Pul. 282; Howson *v.* Walker, 2 Bla. Rep. 823; and see White *v.* Gompertz, 5 Bar. & Ald. 905.

CHAP. VI. SECT. I.

Where a defendant, on a *capias* since 1 & 2 Vict. c. 110, is in the custody of an officer to whom process can be directed, he can of course be detained under similar process directed to the same officer; but when he is in custody of an officer, such as the marshal of the Queen's prison, to whom such process cannot be directed, there is no direct mode of detaining him, and resort must be had to the expedient of procuring a warrant from the sheriff, directed to one of the turnkeys, so as at once to arrest the defendant in case of his discharge from the first custody (*p*).

Fees payable to the sheriff and bailiff on the arrest.

The fees payable to the sheriff and bailiff on the arrest will be found in the section on the remuneration of sheriffs (*q*).

When the sheriff must allow the defendant's privilege.

Of the privilege from arrest, little is required in this place; for there are very few cases in which the sheriff is bound to take notice of the defendant's privilege. If the sheriff, on a bailable writ, were to arrest a peer, or a member of the House of Commons, he would render himself liable to be committed for a breach of privilege (*r*), although he would not be liable to an action for false imprisonment at the suit of the party arrested (*s*). And by the statute 7 Anne, c. 12, s. 4, the sheriff, or his officer, would be subject to fine and imprisonment, and corporal punishment, for arresting on civil process an ambassador or his servant, provided the name of such servant had been registered according to the provisions of that act. But in all other cases of privilege the sheriff may arrest the defendant, and no action for false imprisonment can be maintained against him for so doing (*t*). Nor will any action on the case lie for arresting, even after notice, a privileged person, when the privilege, as in the case of a witness, is the privilege of the court (*u*). It *may* be otherwise where the arrest is mali-

(*p*) See Edwards *v.* Robertson, 5 M. & W. 520.

(*q*) *Ante*, p. 99, *et seq*. See as to the previous practice, Martin *v.* Slade, 2 N. R. 59; Martin *v.* Bell, 6 M. & Sel. 220; Dew *v.* Parsons, 2 B. & Ald. 562; Plevin *v.* Prince, 10 Ad. & E. 498.

(*r*) Bac. Ab. Privilege (C) 6; see 1 Keble, 845; 4 Moore, 34; see also Stockdale *v.* Hansard, 11 A. & E. 253.

(*s*) The Countess of Rutland's case, 6 Rep. 53. *Per* Buller, J., Doug. 677.

(*t*) Tarlton *v.* Fisher, Doug. 672; Crossley *v.* Shaw, 2 Bla. Rep. 1085; Cameron *v.* Lightfoot, *ibid.* 1190; see also Parsons *v.* Lloyd, 3 Wils. 341; Walter *v.* Rees, 4 Moore, 34; Stokes *v.* White, 1 C. M. & R. 223; Magnay *v.* Burt, 5 Q. B. 381, in error.

(*u*) Magnay *v.* Burt, Exchequer Chamber, in error from Queen's Bench, 5 Q. B. 381; and see Newton *v.* Constable, 2 Q. B. 157.

ciously made after notice of a *personal* privilege (*x*). The proper remedy for a privileged person who is arrested, is by moving the Court, out of which the process issued, to be discharged. For if the sheriff were obliged to allow the defendant's privilege, it would impose upon him the responsibility of deciding and acting upon questions of great difficulty. If, after the sheriff has received an order for the discharge of a person from custody on the ground of privilege, he unlawfully detains him, the proper remedy is an action of trespass, not case (*y*).

However, the sheriff may, if he pleases, allow the defendant's privilege, and return it to the court (*z*); but he must determine it at his own peril, for if the party be not in fact privileged, the sheriff will be liable to an action (*a*).

It will be merely necessary to notice generally the different grounds on which persons are privileged from arrest.

The privilege from arrest is either *permanent*, *temporary*, or *local*. Local privileges have been mentioned in another place (*b*).

The royal family and the servants of the queen.

The persons permanently privileged from arrest are, the king or queen regnant, the queen consort, and the royal family. The *servants in ordinary*, or menial servants, of the king or queen regnant (*c*); who even for a debt contracted in trade carried on by them (*d*), are not liable to be arrested, even upon a *ca. sa.*, without leave obtained from the lord chamberlain of the royal household (*e*). Thus a chaplain in ordinary (*f*), a lord of the bed chamber (*g*), a page of the presence (*h*), a herald at arms (*i*), a clerk of the kitchen (*k*), a candle and fire lighter to the yeomen of the guard (*l*), are privileged. But when a gentleman of the privy chamber was arrested, the Court of King's Bench refused

(*x*) See Watson *v.* Carroll, 4 M. & W. 598, *per* Parke, B.

(*y*) Magnay *v.* Burt, in error, reversing the judgment of the Queen's Bench, 5 Q. B. 381.

(*z*) Inge *v.* Herrick, B. R., M. 22 Geo. 3, cit. Doug. 675.

(*a*) Delvalle *v.* Plomer, 3 Camp. 47; see also 1 Wils. 20; 4 Taunt. 631; and *per cur.*, Watson *v.* Carroll, 4 M. & W. 592.

(*b*) *Ante*, p. 75.

(*c*) Bartlett *v.* Hebbes, 5 T. R. 686; Forster *v.* Hopkins, 2 Chit. Rep. 46; see 1 Dowl. & Ry. 127.

(*d*) Rex *v.* Forter, 2 Taunt. 167.

(*e*) Rex *v.* Moulton, 2 Keb. 3; T. Raym. 152; Winter *v.* Dibdin, 13 M. & W. 25; Dyer *v.* Disney, 16 M. & W. 312.

(*f*) Byrn *v.* Dibdin, 3 Dowl. 448; Winter *v.* Dibdin, 13 M. & W. 25.

(*g*) Aldridge *v.* Barry, 3 Dowl. 450, n.

(*h*) Reynolds *v.* Pocock, 7 Dowl. 4.

(*i*) Dyer *v.* Disney, 16 M. & W. 312.

(*k*) Bartlett *v.* Hebbes, 5 T. R. 686.

(*l*) Hatton *v.* Hopkins, 6 M. & S. 271.

CHAP. VI. SECT. I.

to discharge him on motion, leaving him to his writ of privilege, as it appeared by the affidavits that the attendance of the gentleman of the privy chamber was very rarely required (*m*). And the same in the case of the fort major or deputy governor (*n*), or wardens (*o*) of the Tower. And it seems that the servants of a queen consort, or dowager, have no such privilege (*p*).

Peers.

Peers of the realm are privileged from arrest both upon mesne process and in execution (*q*). Peeresses are also entitled to the same privilege, whether they are peeresses by birth, by creation, or by marriage (*r*). This privilege, by the Act of Union with Scotland (5 Anne, c. 8, art. 38), is extended to Scotch peers and peeresses, whether chosen to sit in parliament or not (*s*). So in like manner, by the stat. 39 & 40 Geo. 3, c. 67, art. 4, the Irish peers and peeresses are privileged from arrest (*t*). But if it be a disputed peerage, and the defendant has not been summoned to the House of Peers (if an English peer), the Court will not try the question upon motion (*u*). But this privilege does not protect peers from being attached for contempt of the process of the Court (*x*), although they cannot be taken on an attachment for the non-performance of an award (*y*).

(*m*) Luntley *v*. Battine, 2 Bar. & Ald. 234; Tapley *v*. Battine, 1 Dowl. & Ry. 79; see also Rex *v*. Frampton, 2 Keb. 485; and 2 Dowl. & Ry. 250; S. C. 1 B. & C. 139. But see Dyer *v*. Disney, *ubi supra*. As to the writ of privilege, see Magnay *v*. Burt, 5 Q. B. 381.

(*n*) Batson *v*. M'Lean, 2 Chit. R. 48; Sand *v*. Forest, 1 B. & C. 189; 2 D. & R. 250, S. C. But it seems he could not be arrested within the Tower, except by leave of the governor: *ante*, 75.

(*o*) Bidgood *v*. Davies, 6 B. & C. 84; see last note.

(*p*) Starkie's case, 1 Keb. 842; King and Capell *v*. Band and Segrave, 1 Keb. 877.

(*q*) 6 Rep. 53; 9 Rep. 49 a, 68 a; Sty. Rep. 222; 2 Salk. 512; 2 H. Bla. 272; 3 East, 127.

(*r*) 1 Vent. 298; 6 Rep. 53, *sed vide* Sty. Rep. 252; 2 Chan. Cas. 224; see also 7 B. & C. 389, note to Coates *v*. Lord Hawarden. And a peeress in her own right, although she marry a commoner; it is otherwise in the case of a peeress by marriage, if after the death of her husband she marry a commoner; Co. Litt. 16 b; 2 Inst. 50.

(*s*) Fortescue, 165; see Digby *v*. The Earl of Sterling, 8 Bing. 55; S. C. 1 Dowl. 248. Where the defendant having voted in the character of a Scotch peer on three occasions, the Court held him entitled to his privilege without strict proof of his title.

(*t*) Coates *v*. Lord Hawarden, 7 B. & C. 388.

(*u*) Lord Banbury's case, 2 Salk. 152; Chester *v*. Upsdale, 1 Wils. 278; S. C. 2 Lord Raym. 1247. In the case of a disputed peerage before the House of Lords, the application for discharge should be made to that house, if sitting; Smart *v*. Johnson, 6 Dowl. 90.

(*x*) 1 Wils. 332; 1 Burr. 631.

(*y*) Walker *v*. The Earl of Grosvenor, 7 T. R. 171.

The servants of peers were formerly privileged from arrest, but this privilege is now taken away, by the stat. 10 Geo. 3, c. 50, s. 10. The Courts will, on motion, discharge a peer who is arrested (*z*); but the sheriff is not a trespasser for arresting a peer (*a*), although he might be committed for a contempt of the House of Peers (*b*).

Members of the House of Commons.

Members of the House of Commons are privileged from arrest to the same extent as peers. The limit of their privilege when parliament is not sitting has never been very strictly defined (*c*); but it seems now to be admitted law that the privilege extends to forty days after every prorogation or dissolution, and forty days before the day appointed for the next meeting of parliament (*d*). It seems that candidates and voters are not privileged (*e*). The Courts, on motion, will discharge a member of the House of Commons who has been arrested on civil process (*f*). If an unprivileged person, whilst in custody on civil process, is elected a member of parliament, he thereby becomes entitled to his discharge (*g*). In case of a conflict between the Court and the House, on a question of privilege, the sheriff's duty is to obey the Court, not the House (*h*); but it seems the House, if he does so, will, notwithstanding such duty, commit the sheriff, and not the Court (*i*); and the Court cannot help him.

Clergy and members of the convocation.

Clergymen going to and returning from church, and whilst performing divine service, are privileged from arrest (*k*), but not if they stay in church to avoid process (*l*). Members of the convocation, when sitting, it seems, enjoy the same privilege as members of the House of Commons (*m*).

(*z*) Stra. 990. And the Court will set aside proceedings; 4 Taunt. 668.

(*a*) Countess of Rutland's case, 6 Rep. 53.

(*b*) Bac. Abr. Privilege (C) 6; see Stockdale *v.* Hansard, 9 Ad. & El. 1; 11 Ad. & El. 253, 297.

(*c*) See Bac. Abr. Privilege (C) 4; Scobell, 109, 110.

(*d*) Holiday *v.* Pitt, Rep. temp. Hard. 28, 37; S. C. 2 Stra. 985; Comyns' Rep. 444; Goudy *v.* Duncombe, 1 Exch. R. 430.

(*e*) London case, 2 Peckw. 288; 1 Chit. Arch. 466.

(*f*) See Cassidy *v.* Steuart, 2 Man.& G. 437; Goudy *v.* Duncombe, *ubi. sup.*

(*g*) Phillips *v.* Wellesley, 1 Dowl. 9.

(*h*) Stockdale *v.* Hansard, 11 Ad. & El. 253.

(*i*) See Case of the Sheriffs of Middlesex, 11 Ad. & El. 273.

(*k*) 50 Edw. 3, c. 5; 1 Rich. 2, c. 15; and see 1 Mar. sess. 2, c. 3; see also 12 Rep. 100; and Goddard *v.* Harris, 7 Bing. 320; and see 9 Geo. 4, c. 31, s. 23.

(*l*) 8 Hen. 6, c. 1; 1 Eq. Cas. Abr. 349.

(*m*) 12 Rep. 100; 3 Wils. 341; 2 Bla. Rep. 1087, 1190; 1 Eq. Cas. Abr. 349.

CHAP. VI. SECT. I.

Ambassadors and their servants.

By the statute 7 Anne, c. 12, (which is merely declaratory of the law of nations (*o*)), "All writs and processes that should at any time thereafter be sued forth or prosecuted, whereby the person of any ambassador, or other public minister of any foreign prince or state, authorized and received as such by her majesty, her heirs or successors, or the domestic, or domestic servant of any such ambassador or other public minister, might be arrested or imprisoned, or his or their goods and chattels might be distrained, seized, or attached, should be deemed and adjudged to be utterly null and void, to all intents, constructions, and purposes whatsoever." Consuls are not public ministers within the meaning of this act, and neither they nor their servants are thereby privileged from arrest (*p*). And in order that a minister should entitle himself to the privilege conferred by this act, he must be accredited by our court (*q*). By the 5th section of the above statute, such of the domestic servants of an ambassador, &c., as are subject to the bankrupt laws, are deprived of this privilege (*r*). And it has been adjudged (*s*) that a person claiming this privilege as the servant of an ambassador, must be really and *bonâ fide* his servant at the time of the arrest (*t*). For, by the law of nations, a public minister cannot protect a person who is not his *bonâ fide* servant. And a person cannot be considered a *bonâ fide* servant of a minister, if he holds a situation incompatible with his duties as such servant (*u*). But this privilege does not merely extend to *servants* strictly speaking, but a secretary to an ambassador has been holden to be privileged from arrest under this act (*x*). However, it is not necessary that the servant should reside in the ambassador's house (*y*). Nor is it material whether the servant be a foreigner or a subject of this country (*z*). The servant of an ambassador is entitled to this

(*o*) *Per* Lord Mansfield, C. J., 4 Burr. 2016; Triquet *v.* Bath, 3 Burr. 1478.

(*p*) Viveash *v.* Becker, 3 Maule & Sel. 284; Barbuit's case, Rep. temp. Talbot, 281.

(*q*) *Per* Lord Mansfield, 4 Burr. 2016.

(*r*) Fontainier *v.* Heyl, 3 Burr. 1731.

(*s*) Lockwood *v.* Dr. Coysgarne, 3 Burr. 1676; see also 3 Camp. 47; 1 Wils. 20; Novello *v.* Toogood, 2 Dowl. & Ry. 833; S. C. 1 Bar. & Cress. 554.

(*t*) Heathfield *v.* Chilton, 4 Burr. 2015.

(*u*) Masters *v.* Manby, 1 Burr. 401; Darling *v.* Atkins, 3 Wils. 33.

(*x*) Triquet *v.* Bath, 3 Burr. 1478; Hopkins *v.* De Roberts, 3 T. R. 79.

(*y*) Evans *v.* Hicks, 2 Lord Raym. 1524; S. C. 2 Stra. 797.

(*z*) Triquet *v.* Bath, 3 Burr. 1438; Lockwood *v.* Coysgarne, *ibid.* 1676; Heathfield *v.* Chilton, 4 Burr. 2015.

privilege, although his name be not registered under the 5th section of the act (*a*). This privilege, however, is the privilege of the ambassador and not of the servant, and a clear case of service must be made out before the court will interfere to discharge the defendant on motion (*b*).

Punishment upon persons arresting ambassadors or their servants.

By section 4 of the statute of 7 Anne, c. 12, every person presuming to sue forth or *prosecute* any writ, &c. against any foreign minister or his servant, are to suffer such penalties and corporal punishment, as the Lord Chancellor, the five Chief Justices, or any two of them, may judge fit to be inflicted; provided the name of such servant has been registered at the office of the secretary of state, and transmitted to the office of the sheriff of London and Middlesex (*c*). But although the name be registered as the act directs, if the person be not *bonâ fide* the servant of the ambassador, and the sheriff refuse to execute the process, the plaintiff may maintain an action against him (*d*), or rule him to return the writ (*e*), and in either case the question of the defendant's privilege will be raised before the court (*f*).

Attornies.

Attornies and other officers of the courts were, before the stat. 1 & 2 Vict. c. 110, privileged from arrest upon mesne process. But an attorney who had ceased to practise (*g*), or had neglected to take out his certificate for one whole year, was not privileged from arrest (*h*). Therefore it was held, that an attorney who had not practised for several years might be arrested, though after suing out the writ, and before the arrest, he had recommenced his practice and taken out his certificate (*i*). The sheriff, however, could not take notice of the privilege of an attorney; nor was he bound to discharge him, even upon producing his writ of privilege (*k*), except where the arrest was by

(*a*) 4 Burr. 2017; 3 T. R. 79.

(*b*) Fisher *v.* Begrez, 2 Dowl. 279; see also S. C. 1 Dowl. 588; Novello *v.* Toogood, 1 B. & C. 554; S. C. 2 D. & R. 833; Heathfield *v.* Chilton, 4 Burr. 2015.

(*c*) Section 5.

(*d*) Delvalle *v.* Plomer, 3 Camp. 41. "This is one among many other questions which sheriffs, in the execution of process, must determine at their peril. In cases of real difficulty, they may call for an indemnity, and the court will enlarge the time for making their return till an indemnity is given." *Per* Lord Ellenborough, C. J. *Id. ibid.*

(*e*) Seacomb *v.* Bowlney, 1 Wils. 20.

(*f*) Redman's case, 1 Mod. 10; 2 Salk. 544; 1 Wils. 298; 2 Keb. 555.

(*g*) Brooke *v.* Bryant, 7 T. R. 25; 1 Bos. & Pul. 4.

(*h*) Skirrow *v.* Tagg, 5 M. & Sel. 281.

(*i*) Brooke *v.* Bryant, 7 T. R. 25.

(*k*) Crosley *v.* Shaw, 2 Bla. Rep. 1085.

CHAP. VI. SECT. I.

process issuing out of an inferior court, in which case it is said that the officer should allow the writ of privilege *instanter* (*l*). And now it seems that an attorney about to quit England may, under 1 & 2 Vict. c. 110, be arrested under a judge's order like any other person (*m*).

Witnesses, &c. attending the court.

The parties to a suit, and their witnesses, are, for the sake of public justice, protected from arrest in coming to, attending upon, and returning from courts of justice (*n*); or, as it is usually termed, *eundo, morando, et redeundo:* and this privilege has been holden to extend to all persons who have any relation to a cause, and who attend in the course of that cause, though not compelled by process; such as bail (*o*), barristers on the circuit (*p*), (but not when attending at petty sessions, or, as it seems, at the quarter sessions, without a previous retainer (*q*),) attorneys also on their way to, from, and during their attendance in a cause in court (*r*), or before an arbitrator (*s*), witnesses attending before an arbitrator under a reference at *nisi prius* (*t*), before commissioners of bankrupt (*u*), before the court of insolvent debtors (*x*), all of whom have been holden to be privileged from arrest. Witnesses attending a cause in inferior courts are in like manner privileged (*y*); and by the Mutiny Act, the like privilege is given to witnesses attending courts martial. This privilege is the privilege of the court in which the cause is pending, and on application to such court, the defendant will be discharged, although he may have been arrested on process out of another court (*z*). But the sheriff is not bound to notice this privilege, and therefore may, on a claim of such privilege, keep the defendant in safe custody

(*l*) 2 Bla. Rep. 1087.

(*m*) Thompson *v.* Moore, 1 Dowl. N. S. 283; Flight *v.* Cook, 1 Dowl. & L. 714.

(*n*) Lightfoot *v.* Cameron, 2 Bla. Rep. 1113; 1 Vent. 11; 2 Rol. Abr. 272; 1 H. Bla. 636; 1 Campb. 229; and see 11 East, 439; 3 Bar. & Ald. 252.

(*o*) Meekins *v.* Smith, 1 H. B. 636; Rimmer *v.* Green, 1 M. & Sel. 638; 2 Rose, 23.

(*p*) 1 H. Bla. 637; see also Newton *v.* Constable, 2 Q. B. 167, *per* Lord Denman, C. J.

(*q*) Newton *v.* Constable, *ubi supra.*

(*r*) See Williams *v.* Webb, 2 Dowl. N. S. 660.

(*s*) Webb *v.* Taylor, 1 Dowl. & L. 676.

(*t*) Spence *v.* Stewart, 3 East, 89. See also 3 Bar. & Ald. 252; S. C. 1 Chit. Rep. 679. And see Watson on Awards, 78.

(*u*) Selby *v.* Hills, 1 Dowl. 257; S. C. 8 Bing. 166; 7 Ves. 316; 1 Rose, 265, n.

(*x*) Wittingham *v.* Matthews, 6 Taunt. 356.

(*y*) Com. Dig. Privilege (A); 2 Rol. Abr. 272; Walters *v.* Rees, 4 Moore, 34.

(*z*) Walters *v.* Rees, 4 Moore, 34; Walker *v.* Webb, 3 Anstr. 941.

until he is ordered to be discharged by the court(*a*). A person is not however privileged during his return home from lawful custody (*b*). The privilege, in general, enures *eundo*, *morando*, *et redeundo*, and it is not essential that the party in going or returning should go at full speed, or by the nearest way possible (*c*); thus, where a defendant, after the rising of the court, went with his attorney and witnesses to dine at a tavern in Palace Yard, and was arrested whilst at dinner, it was held that his privilege *redeundo* had not expired (*d*). So where the plaintiff, after a motion in the cause, in his way home first called at his office to refresh himself and sort his papers, and after a lapse of two hours left the office to proceed home, but on the way went into a tailor's shop, where he was arrested, his privilege was allowed (*e*). If, however, there is any substantial deviation (*f*) or unreasonable delay, even for want of means (*g*), the privilege ceases. A man who has been in custody on a criminal charge, and who is acquitted and discharged, has, it seems, no privilege from arrest *redeundo* (*h*).

Bankrupts.

By the Bankrupt Act, 5 & 6 Vict. c. 122, s. 23, it is enacted, that any person adjudged bankrupt "shall be free from arrest or imprisonment by any creditor in coming to surrender, and after such surrender during the time by this act limited for such surrender, and such further time as shall be allowed him for finishing his examination, and for such time after finishing his examination until his certificate be allowed and confirmed, as the court authorized to act in the prosecution of the fiat shall from time to time, by indorsement upon the summons of such bankrupt, think fit to appoint, provided he was not in custody at the time of such surrender; and if such bankrupt shall be arrested for debt or on any escape warrant in coming to surrender, or shall after his surrender be so arrested within the time aforesaid, he shall, on producing his summons signed as

(*a*) Walters *v.* Rees, 4 Moore, 34; Watson *v.* Carroll, 4 M. & W. 592.

(*b*) Anon. 1 Dowl. 157; Goodwin *v.* Lordon, 1 A. & E. 378.

(*c*) See *per* Lord Abinger, C. B. in Strong *v.* Dickenson, 1 M. & W. 491.

(*d*) Lightfoot *v.* Cameron, 2 W. B. 1113.

(*e*) Pitt *v.* Coombs, 5 B. & Adol. 1078. See also Williams *v.* Webb, 2 Dowl. N. S. 660; Luntley *v.* Nathaniel, 2 Dowl. 51; Phillips *v.* Price, 1 D. & L. 110.

(*f*) Smith *v.* Dickenson, 1 M. & W. 488.

(*g*) Spencer *v.* Newton, 1 N. & P. 818; 6 A. & E. 623, S. C.

(*h*) Goodwin *v.* Lordon, 1 Ad. & El. 378.

CHAP. VI. SECT. I.

required by this act to the officer who shall arrest him, and giving such officer a copy thereof, be immediately discharged; and if any officer shall detain any such bankrupt after he shall have shown such summons to him, such officer shall forfeit to such bankrupt, for his own use, the sum of 5*l.* for every day he shall detain such bankrupt, to be recovered by action of debt in any court of record at Westminster, in the name of such bankrupt, with full costs of suit (*i*); and it shall be lawful for the court, at the time appointed for the last examination of the bankrupt, or any enlargement or adjournment thereof, to adjourn such examination *sine die*, and in such case he shall be free from arrest for such time, not exceeding three months, as such court shall from time to time by indorsement upon the summons of such bankrupt appoint, with like penalty upon any officer detaining such bankrupt after having been shown such summons." And by the 42d section of the same act, a certificated bankrupt is privileged from arrest for any debt, claim, or demand which was proveable under the fiat, and shall be discharged on entering an appearance, and may plead in general that the cause of action accrued before he became bankrupt. The decisions on the above sections would be out of place here, as they do not affect the sheriff, and are to be found in the treatises on bankrupt law (*k*). Nor does it belong to a treatise on the duty of the sheriff, to enter upon the question what things are and what are not proveable under the fiat, as it is not for the sheriff to decide whether or not the defendant is privileged from arrest, the sheriff being protected if he arrest the bankrupt. A certificated bankrupt, or discharged insolvent, however, it has been held, is not liable to be arrested on a subsequent promise to pay a debt discharged by his bankruptcy or insolvency (*l*).

Besides and independently of the privilege conferred on the bankrupt by statute, he has been held privileged (in the same manner as parties, witnesses, &c. attending a cause) during

(*i*) It may be questionable whether this action should be brought against the sheriff or the bailiff; from the wording of the act it would appear the latter. See Sturney *q. t. v.* Sheriff of Middlesex, 11 East, 25.

(*k*) Archbold's Bankrupt Law, by Flather, 10th edit. 318.

(*l*) Peers *v.* Gadderer, 2 Dow. & Ry. 240; S. C. 1 Bar. & Cres. 116; Wilson *v.* Kemp, 3 M. & Sel. 595. See also 6 Taunt. 563; 2 Burr. 736; By the 5 & 6 Vict. c. 122, s. 43, a bankrupt is not liable on a subsequent promise to pay a debt barred by his certificate, unless the promise is in writing.

attendance on proceedings before the commissioners, *e. g.* in returning from the hearing of a petition for leave to surrender (*m*), and in going to, staying at, and returning from a meeting to declare a dividend which he attended at the verbal request of the commissioners (*n*).

Insolvents. In like manner, by the Insolvent Debtors' Act, 1 & 2 Vict. c. 110, s. 90, an insolvent discharged under that act is protected from arrest under the judgment entered up in pursuance of the act, and also for any debt, money, or costs in respect of which he is entitled to the benefit of the act, or any judgment, decree, or order for payment of the same; and a judge may, on application, order the discharge of a prisoner arrested for such debt, and with such costs as he shall think fit.

And by 5 & 6 Vict. c. 116, and 7 & 8 Vict. c. 96, protection may be granted by the Court of Bankruptcy to persons who petition under the provisions of those acts.

Provisions to a similar effect are contained in the 7 & 8 Vict. c. 90, for facilitating arrangements between debtors and creditors.

The sheriff, notwithstanding the defendant claims privilege from arrest by his bankruptcy and certificate, or under a discharge as an insolvent debtor, should not discharge him without an indemnity, or by order of the Court, for otherwise he might be driven to litigate with the plaintiff the question of the defendant's privilege; for the Court will not stay proceedings in the event of an action brought against a sheriff for discharging a certificated bankrupt arrested by him, without an order of a judge (*o*).

Seamen and soldiers. No petty officer or seaman, marine or non-commissioned officer of marines, on board of any of his majesty's vessels, and no soldiers (*p*), shall be holden to bail, or arrested on any

(*m*) Exp. Jackson, 15 Ves. 116.

(*n*) Arding *v.* Flower, 3 Esp. 117; 8 T. R. 534. See Selby *v.* Hills, 8 Bing. 166; 1 M. & Scott, 253, S. C.; Willingham *v.* Matthews, 2 Marsh. 57.

(*o*) Sherwood *v.* Benson, 4 Taunt. 631; see Tarlton *v.* Fisher, 2 Doug. 671; Whitworth *v.* Clifton, 1 M. & Rob. 531.

(*p*) By the Annual Mutiny Act. These acts have been construed to extend not merely to common soldiers and troopers in the life guards, &c., Bayley *v.* Jenner, 1 Stra. 2, but also to non-commissioned and warrant officers, as gunners, Johnson *v.* Lowth, 1 Stra. 7; serjeants and drummers, Lloyd *v.* Woodall, 1 Wils. 216. For a serjeant is a soldier with a halbert, and a drummer a soldier with a drum; Lloyd *v.* Woodall, 1 Bla. Rep. 30. These acts do not, however, extend to

CHAP. VI. SECT. I.

process or execution whatsoever, contracted subsequently to his having entered the service; nor for any debt under 30*l.* previously to his having so entered; and in case of any of the above-mentioned persons being arrested, any of the judges of the Court out of which the process or execution issued is empowered to discharge him.

And by the 44 Geo. 3, c. 13, ss. 1, 4, if any petty officer or seaman pay the debt for which he has been arrested, give a bail bond, or be otherwise entitled to be discharged out of the custody, the sheriff or other officer in whose custody he shall be, instead of discharging him, shall, under the penalty of 100*l.*, have him conveyed to the commander of one of his majesty's ships, or some authorized commissioned officer, in order that he may be kept to serve on board the fleet as before. On this statute it was held, where a bailiff, having arrested a seaman, discharged him on giving a bail-bond, that the sheriff was liable to a *qui tam* action for this penalty (*r*).

Writ of protection.

The last privilege necessary to be noticed is, that the queen may privilege, by her writ of protection, any person in her service from arrest, during a year and a day (*s*). But these writs are never granted at this day; even in Lord Coke's (*t*) time they were almost totally disused.

Executors, &c.

Besides the privilege from arrest which the persons above-mentioned have, there are many persons who by the practice of the Courts, and by particular statutes, are not allowed to be holden to bail, as executors and administrators for debts due in their representative capacity, assignees of bankrupts, hundredors, corporators, for demands on them in their representative character; the consideration of this subject, however, belongs not to the duty of the office of sheriff, for he would not be punishable for making the arrest, if commanded so to do; and it is his duty to obey the writ, as he is protected in so doing. Who may or may not be holden to bail will be found discussed at length in Mr. Tidd's and Mr. Archbold's books of Practice; it

commissioned officers; Tidd's Prac. 202, 9th edit.; Chit. Arch. 475. See further Flanders *v.* Nicholls, Barnes, 432; Bowler *v.* Owen, 2 T. R. 270; R. *v.* Archer, 1 Burr. 636, 637, 446; Rickman *v.* Studwick, 8 East, 105; Lord Raym. 1246; Bryan *v.* Woodward, 4 Taunt. 557.

(*r*) Sturney *v.* Smith, 11 East, 25.

(*s*) Burrodale *v.* Lord Cutts, 3 Lev. 332; Finch, L. 454. And see Sir T. Shirley's case, Hob. 115.

(*t*) 1 Inst. 131.

is hoped that all that is necessarily connected on that head with the duty of sheriff will have been found in the foregoing pages.

Copy of writ to be delivered to defendant on arrest.

The stat. 2 Will. 4, c. 39, s. 4, requires that so many copies of the *capias*, together with every memorandum or notice subscribed thereto, and all indorsements thereon, as there may be persons intended to be arrested thereon, shall be delivered to the sheriff or other officer or person to whom the same may be directed, or who may have the execution and return thereof, and who shall upon or forthwith after the execution of such process cause one such copy to be delivered to every person upon whom such process shall be executed by him, and shall indorse on such writ the true day of the execution thereof. And a similar provision is introduced in the form of *capias* given by the stat. 1 & 2 Vict. c. 110. Where the arrest took place at nine o'clock in the morning, and the copy of the writ was not delivered to the defendant until seven in the evening, it was held that the statute had not been complied with (*u*). The copy delivered must be a correct copy, and any variance by which the meaning of the writ is altered will be fatal, and will invalidate the arrest; as if the form of action (*x*) or the date of the writ be omitted (*y*), or if the copy of a writ be addressed to the sheriff instead of the sheriffs of London (*z*); but a mere literal variance, not in any way affecting the sense of the writ, would be immaterial; as if the copy was "if *se* shall be found, &c.," instead of "if *she* shall be found, &c." (*a*). The omission to serve a true copy of the writ does not render the arrest void, but merely irregular, and such irregularity may be waived by the defendant's omitting to take advantage of it within a reasonable time (*b*). If a defective copy of a *capias* is delivered to the defendant, the court will presume that a defective copy was delivered to the sheriff; it will not presume that

(*u*) Shearman *v.* M'Knight, 5 Dowl. 572.

(*x*) Copley *v.* Medeiros, 7 Man. & G. 426.

(*y*) Smart *v.* Johnstone, 3 M. & W. 69.

(*z*) Nicol *v.* Boyne, 2 Dowl. 761; Moore *v.* Magan, 16 M. & W. 95. See also other instances of variances which have been held material, Smith *v.* Pennell, 2 Dowl. 654; Street *v.* Carter, *ib.* 671; Smith *v.* Crump, 1 Dowl. 319; Cooke *v.* Vaughan, 4 M. & W. 69.

(*a*) Sutton *v.* Burgess, 3 Dowl. 489. See also other instances of variances from the writ which have been held immaterial, Pocock *v.* Mason, 1 Bing. N. C. 245; Colston *v.* Berens, 3 Dowl. 253; Cooper *v.* Wheale, 4 Dowl. 281; Macdonald *v.* Mortlock, 2 Dowl. & L. 963.

(*b*) Brashour *v.* Russell, 6 Dowl. 185.

CHAP. VI. SECT. I.

the sheriff was wrong by receiving a correct copy from the plaintiff, and serving a defective one (*c*). The court will not permit an amendment in the copy served (*d*).

Day of arrest to be indorsed on the writ.

The 2 Will. 4, c. 39, s. 4, also requires the sheriff to indorse on the writ the true day of the execution thereof; and by Reg. Gen. M. T. 3 Will. 4, r. 4, it is ordered, that such indorsement shall be made within six days at the latest after the execution thereof, and that in default thereof the sheriff or other officer, &c. shall be liable in a summary way to make such compensation for any damage which may result from his neglect, as the court or a judge shall direct. And the day of the execution ought to appear in the return. But an omission of it would not, it seems, be ground for an attachment (*e*). The consequence of the omission is, that the plaintiff may apply to the court to compel the sheriff to amend his return, and pay such damages as the plaintiff has sustained by the omission. The stat. 1 & 2 Vict. c. 110, does not in terms require this indorsement to be made on a *capias* issued under the authority of that act, but it seems to be necessary (*f*). And the *capias* commands the sheriff to state the day of its execution in the return.

Section II.

Proceedings after the Arrest.

Sheriff's duty when a person is in his custody on a bailable capias.

When a defendant is arrested, or in the custody of the sheriff, on *mesne process*, the sheriff must take care that he have him at the return of the writ, and should keep him in close custody, unless he deposit money in lieu of bail, or give a bail-bond with sufficient sureties, or the plaintiff consent to his discharge. The sheriff's duties and liabilities on these heads will be the subject of this section.

Within what time after the arrest the defendant must be conveyed to prison.

The defendant being in the custody of the sheriff on a bailable *capias*, the sheriff is liable to a penalty of 50*l.* if he carry him to any tavern or other house without his consent, or to prison

(*c*) Hodd *v.* Langridge, 5 Dowl. 721.

(*d*) Byfield *v.* Street, 10 Bing. 27; 2 Dowl. 739, S. C.; Rennie *v.* Bruce, 2 Dowl. & L. 963; Moore *v.* Magan, 16 M. & W. 95.

(*e*) 1 Chit. Arch. 534, &c.; Ridley *v.* Watson, 2 M. & Scott, 724.

(*f*) See Jervis's New Rules, 95.

within twenty-four hours, unless he refuse to be carried in the meantime to some safe and convenient dwelling-house, to be named by him, not being his own house (*a*). And it is the duty of the officer making the arrest, and in whose custody the defendant is, to ask him to nominate some safe and convenient dwelling-house to which he may be carried; and the taking of him to prison within twenty-four hours cannot be justified, unless he has *refused* to nominate such house; and evidence that the defendant did not *express any objection* to being carried

(*a*) 32 Geo. 2, c. 28. I subjoin the act itself, as it may be desirable for the purpose of reference:—"No sheriff, under-sheriff, bailiff, serjeant at mace, or other officer or minister, shall convey, or carry, or cause to be conveyed or carried, any person or persons by him or them arrested, or being in his or their custody, by virtue or colour of any action, suit, process, or attachment, to any tavern, ale-house, or other public victualling or drinking house, or to the private house of any such officer or minister, or of any tenant or relation of his, without the free and voluntary consent of the person so arrested, or in custody; nor charge any such person or persons with any sum of money for any wine, beer, ale, victuals, tobacco, or any other liquor or things whatsoever, save what he shall call for of his own free accord; nor shall cause or procure him to call or pay for any such liquor or things, except what he shall particularly and freely ask for; nor shall demand, take, or receive, or cause to be demanded, taken, or received, directly or indirectly, any other or greater sum or sums of money than is or shall be by law allowed to be taken or demanded for any arrest or taking, or for detaining or waiting till the person or persons so arrested or in custody shall have given an appearance or bail, as the case shall require, or agreed with the person or persons at whose suit or prosecution he shall be taken or arrested, or until he shall be sent to some proper gaol belonging to the county, riding, division, city, town, or place where such arrest or taking shall be; nor shall exact or take any reward, gratuity, or money, for keeping the person or persons so arrested or in custody out of gaol or prison."

Sect. 2. "No sheriff, &c. shall carry any such person to any gaol or prison within twenty-four hours from the time of such arrest, unless such person or persons so arrested shall refuse to be carried to some safe and convenient dwelling-house of his own nomination or appointment, within a city, borough, corporation, or market town, in case such person or persons shall be there arrested, or within three miles from the place where such arrest shall be made, if the same shall be made out of any city, borough, corporation, or market town, so as such dwelling-house be not the house of the person so arrested, and be within the city, &c. in which the person under arrest was arrested; and then and in any such case, it shall be lawful to and for any such sheriff, or other officer or minister, to convey or carry the person or persons so arrested, and refusing to be carried to such safe and convenient dwelling-house as aforesaid, to such gaol or prison as he may be sent to by virtue of the action, writ, or process against him; and that no sheriff, &c. shall take or receive any other or greater sum or sums for one or more night's lodging, or for a day's diet, or other expenses, of any person or persons under arrest on any writ, action, attachment, or process, other than what shall be allowed as reasonable in such cases by some order or orders made by justices of the peace in pursuance of the said act."

CHAP. VI. SECT. II.

to prison will not alone be sufficient evidence of his consent (*b*). The sheriff has a right to make any reasonable objection to the house nominated by the defendant, if he thinks it is not a safe and convenient house; and on this ground he may reasonably object to his being carried to his attorney's house (*c*). A request to be taken to the house of a person, merely for the purpose of consulting him, is not a nomination of a house within the meaning of the statute; for the sheriff is not bound to take a prisoner to any house he may desire to go to for any purpose whatever, but only to some safe and convenient dwelling-house for the purpose of his remaining there the twenty-four hours (*d*). Where the defendant, while the officer was conveying him to gaol illegally, within twenty-four hours after the arrest, consented to go to a tavern to execute an agreement with his creditor to obtain his discharge, it was held that this was not a consent to be carried there within the meaning of the statute (*e*). Generally speaking, where the defendant does not give a bail-bond, it is the duty of the sheriff to lodge the defendant in the county gaol on the return of the writ; but he cannot be taken there until the twenty-four hours have expired; and if the defendant be kept in a lock-up house or other place, the sheriff keeps him at his peril; but the sheriff is not liable to an action on the case as for an escape, for keeping a defendant arrested by him in custody after the return of the writ, without taking him to the county gaol, unless the jury find that the plaintiff has been delayed or prejudiced in his suit (*f*); and of course it can be no escape to keep the defendant in a lock-up house from the arrest until the return of the writ (*g*).

Where defendant is too ill to be removed.

If the defendant is ill, and unable to be removed, the sheriff should nevertheless arrest him, and detain him in custody; and if he continues in the same state up to the time of the return of the writ, the sheriff should return "*languidus*," which would be a sufficient excuse for not having him in court (*h*).

(*b*) Dewhirst *v.* Pearson, 1 Dowl. 664; Simpson *v.* Renton, 5 B. & Adol. 35.

(*c*) Silk *v.* Humphery, 4 A. & E. 959.

(*d*) *Ibid.*

(*e*) Barsham *v.* Bullock, 10 Ad. & E. 23.

(*f*) Planck *v.* Anderson, 5 T. R. 37; see also Houlditch *v.* Birch, 4 Taunt. 608; Brandling *v.* Kent, 1 T. R. 60; Williams *v.* Mostyn, 4 M. & W. 145.

(*g*) Houlditch *v.* Birch, 4 Taunt. 608.

(*h*) See Perkins *v.* Meacher, 1 Dowl. 21; Cavenagh *v.* Collett, 4 B. & Ald. 27; Baker *v.* Davenport, 8 Dowl. & R. 606; Stevens *v.* Jackson, 6 Taunt. 106.

Regulations respecting the treatment of persons arrested by the sheriff.

Whilst the defendant is in custody, he should be allowed, at his free will and pleasure, to send for and have at all seasonable times any beer, ale, or other food, bedding, linen, or other necessary things, without paying anything therefor to the sheriff, &c., in whose custody he is (*i*); and also, to prevent extortion, the gaolers are not allowed to take any greater fees than are settled, enrolled, and registered (*k*), according to the directions of that act. And the court out of which the process issues, in term, or a judge in vacation, or at the assizes, have full power to hear, examine, and redress any abuses in any gaol or prison, whereof any prisoner shall present his complaint (*l*). The statute also enacts, "that if any sheriff, under-sheriff, bailiff of any liberty, bailiff, serjeant at mace, gaoler, and other officer and person as aforesaid, shall offend in anywise against the said act, he shall for every such offence (over and above such other penalties or punishments as he may be liable to) forfeit and pay to the party thereby grieved the sum of 50*l.*, to be recovered with treble costs of suit, by action of debt, bill, plaint, or information, in any of his majesty's courts of record at Westminster (*m*)." In order to recover against a sheriff on this statute, it is incumbent on the plaintiff to prove the table regulating the fees to be allowed, for this statute superseded the stat. 23 Hen. 6, c. 9, as to fees to be allowed on arrests on *mesne process* (*n*). It was ruled at nisi prius, by Lord Kenyon, that a sheriff was not liable to an action for extortion committed by an *officer not named in the warrant*, to whose lock-up house the defendant had been brought on being arrested (*o*).

Deposit of money with the sheriff in lieu of bail, and payment thereof into court.

At common law, the sheriff was not justified in discharging a defendant arrested by him on *mesne process*, even upon receiving from him the sum sworn to and costs (*p*); and as it often happened that persons, who were able to deposit a sum of money equal to the sum sworn to and costs, were not able to find bail for their appearance, for this reason it was first provided by the stat. 43 Geo. 3, c. 46, s. 2, that any persons arrested upon

(*i*) 32 Geo. 2, c. 28, s. 4.

(*k*) *Ibid.* s. 12.

(*l*) *Ibid.* s. 11; Ex parte Evans, 3 Bos. & Pul. 88.

(*m*) *Ibid.* s. 12.

(*n*) Martin *v.* Slade, 2 N. R. 59; Jaques *v.* Whitcomb, 1 Esp. 361. The 23 Hen. 6, c. 9, is now repealed by 1 Vict. c. 55. As to recovering on the count for money had and received, see Lovell *v.* Simpson, 3 Esp. 153; 2 N. R. 60.

(*o*) George *v.* Perring, 4 Esp. 63.

(*p*) Slackford *v.* Austen, 14 East, 468; see also Wooden *v.* Moxon, 6 Taunt. 490.

CHAP. VI. SECT. II.

mesne process, within England and Ireland, in lieu of giving a bail-bond, may deposit with the sheriff, under-sheriff, or other officers, the sum indorsed upon the writ, together with 10*l.* to ensure the costs which may have accrued to the time of the return of the writ, and also such sum as may have been paid for the king's fine, where the action is by original, and thereupon he shall be discharged; and that the sheriff shall, at or before the return of the writ, pay into court the sum so deposited with him; and if bail be afterwards duly put in and perfected, the defendant may obtain the money out upon motion. By a subsequent act, 7 & 8 Geo. 4, c. 71, s. 2, after reciting the 43 Geo. 3, c. 46, s. 2, and that it was expedient to extend its provisions, it was enacted, "that in all cases in which any defendant shall have been discharged from arrest upon making such deposit as is required by the said recited act, and the sum so deposited shall have been paid into court, it shall be lawful for such defendant, instead of putting in and perfecting special bail in the action according to the course and practice of the court, to allow the sum so deposited with the sheriff, and by him paid into court as aforesaid, together with the additional sum of 10*l.*, to be paid into court by such defendant as a further security for the costs of the action, to remain in the court to abide the event of the suit; and in all cases where the defendant shall have been arrested, and shall have given bail to the sheriff, or shall have been arrested and remain in custody, it shall be lawful for such last-mentioned defendant, instead of putting in and perfecting special bail, to deposit and pay into the said court the sum indorsed upon the writ, together with the amount of the king's fine, if any, upon the original writ, and the further sum of 20*l.* as a security for the costs of the action, there to remain to abide the event of the suit; and thereupon the said defendant may and he is hereby required to enter a common appearance, or file common bail in the action, within such time as he would have been required to have put in and perfected special bail in the action according to the course of the said court, or in default thereof the plaintiff in the action is hereby empowered to enter such common appearance or file common bail for the said defendant, and the cause may proceed as if the defendant had put in and perfected special bail; and in case judgment in the said action shall be given for the plaintiff, he shall be entitled, by order of the court, upon motion made for that purpose, to receive the money so remaining in, or so deposited or paid into the court as aforesaid, or so much thereof as will be sufficient to satisfy the sum recovered by the judgment, and the costs of the application; and if judgment be given in the said action for the defendant, or the plaintiff discontinue his suit, or be otherwise barred, the said money so deposited and paid into court, or so much thereof as shall remain, shall, by order of the court, upon motion to be made for that purpose, be repaid to such defendant." Section 3 of the same act enacted, "that it shall and may be lawful for the said defendant who hath made his election to make such deposit and payment as aforesaid, at any time in the progress of the cause, before issue joined in law or fact, or final or interlocutory judgment signed, to receive the same out of court, by order of the said court, upon putting in and perfecting special bail in the cause, and payment of such costs to the plaintiff as the said court shall direct." And section 4 provides also, "that it shall and may be lawful for any defendant who shall have put in and perfected special bail in any cause, upon motion to the court in which the action is brought, if the court shall so think fit, to deposit and pay into court the sum which would have been deposited and paid in case the defendant had originally elected to do so, together with such further sum to answer the costs as the court may direct, to abide the event of the said suit, and to be disposed of in manner aforesaid, and thereupon it shall be lawful for the court to direct a common appearance to be entered, or common bail to be filed, for the defendant, and an exoneretur to be entered upon the bail-piece in the said cause."

Finally, when the stat. 1 & 2 Vict. c. 110, abolished the general power of arrest on mesne process, but gave the collateral power of arrest in certain cases, under a judge's order made upon affidavit that the defendant was about to quit England, it provided, by sect. 4, "that such defendant, when so arrested, shall remain in custody until he shall have given a bail-bond to the sheriff, or shall have made deposit of the sum indorsed on such writ of capias, together with 10*l.* for costs, according to the present practice of the said superior courts; and all proceedings as to the putting in and perfecting special bail, or making deposit and payment of money into court instead of putting in and

CHAP. VI. SECT. II. perfecting special bail, shall be according to the like practice of the said superior courts, or as near thereto as the circumstances of the case will permit (*r*)."

Money paid to an officer on an arrest is presumed to have been paid in lieu of bail under the authority of these statutes, unless a discharge, or an acknowledgment in writing for the debt and costs be given to the defendant (*s*). The sheriff is not entitled to any poundage or fees deducted from money so deposited with him, or paid by him into court (*t*).

Where the sheriff pays into court, in pursuance of the statute, the money deposited with him in lieu of bail, the defendant may afterwards, on putting in and perfecting bail in due time (*u*), or on rendering in discharge of his bail (*x*), obtain the money out of court upon motion, whether deposited by himself, or by a friend on his behalf (*y*). On the other hand, if bail be not duly put in and perfected, and the defendant be not rendered, then, by order of the court, upon motion, the money so deposited and paid into court may be taken out by the plaintiff, and that, since 1 & 2 Vict. c. 110, without waiting for the final determination of the suit (*z*). Where, however, a defendant who was arrested by a wrong name deposited money in lieu of bail, without prejudice, the court refused to allow the plaintiff to take it out on the defendant's failing to perfect bail (*a*). And where, the defendant having paid the debt and 10*l*. for costs to the sheriff on his arrest, a *bonâ fide* correspondence commenced for the purpose of settling the action, which did not terminate until after the day for perfecting special bail, and on its termination the defendant

(*r*) See Scherwinski *v*. Peronnet, 6 M. & W. 90; 8 Dowl. 229, S. C.

(*s*) Wain *v*. Bradbury, 1 Smith's Rep. 127.

(*t*) Stewart *v*. Bracebridge, 2 B. & Ald. 770; 1 Chit. Rep. 529, S. C.; Haines *v*. Nairn, 2 Dowl. 43.

(*u*) Green *v*. Glasscock, 1 Bing. N. C. 516; 1 Scott, 402, S. C.; Young *v*. Maltby, 3 Dowl. 604; Geach *v*. Coppin, *id*. 74; see Newman *v*. Hodgson, 1 B. & Adol. 422; Stultz *v*. Heneage, 4 M. & Scott, 472; Ball *v*. Stafford, 2 Scott, 426.

(*x*) Chadwick *v*. Battye, 3 M. & Sel. 283; Harford *v*. Harris, 4 Taunt. 669. See also Gould *v*. Berry, 1 Chit. Rep. 143; Hill *v*. Ching, 7 Moore, 432; 1 Bing. 103, S. C.

(*y*) See Nunn *v*. Powell, 1 Smith's Rep. 13; Edelsten *v*. Adams, 2 Moore, 610; 8 Taunt. 557, S. C.; Bull *v*. Turner, 1 M. & W. 47; Douglass *v*. Stanbrough, 3 Ad. & Ell. 316.

(*z*) Tuton *v*. Gale, 1 Dowl. N. S. 383; see Rowe *v*. Softly, 6 Bing. 634; 4 Moo. & P. 464, S. C.; Johnson *v*. Wall, 4 Dowl. 315; Hews *v*. Pyke, 2 C. & J. 359; Hubbard *v*. Wilkinson, 8 B. & C. 496; Reynolds *v*. Wedd, 6 Dowl. 728.

(*a*) Cadby *v*. Parsons, 5 Taunt. 623.

paid in the additional 10*l.* required by the 7 & 8 Geo. 4, c. 71, the plaintiff was not allowed to take the money out of court (*b*).

It is not necessary, for the purposes of this work, to enter minutely into the details of the practice relating to the putting in and perfecting bail, and the payment out of court of money deposited in lieu of bail; it is fully stated in the books of practice, and in the authorities referred to in the preceding notes.

Bail-bond.

Before the statute of 23 Hen. 6, c. 9, the sheriff was only obliged to bail a defendant in his custody on *mesne process*, when he sued out a writ of mainprize; though the sheriff might take a security for releasing a defendant out of his custody if he pleased (*c*). To remedy the extortion and oppression necessarily consequent on such discretion, that statute was passed, the enactment whereof is twofold; *first*, as to the *persons* to be let to bail, with respect to whom it is enacted, that "sheriffs, &c., shall let out of prison all manner of persons by them arrested, or being in their custody, by force of any writ, bill, or warrant, in any action personal, or by cause of indictment of trespass, upon reasonable sureties of sufficient persons having sufficient within the counties where such persons be so let to bail or mainprize, to keep their days in such place as the said writs, bills, or warrants shall require; persons being in their ward by condemnation, execution, *capias utlagatum*, surety of the peace, or by special commandment of any justice, and vagabonds refusing to serve according to the statute of labourers, only excepted (*d*)."

In what cases the sheriff is obliged to discharge a defendant on a bail-bond.

This part of the statute is obligatory upon the sheriff. And therefore if a bail-bond be tendered to under-sheriff or bailiff,

(*b*) Strafford .Love, 3 Dowl. 593.

(*c*) Bac. Abr. tit. Sheriff (O); Dalt. Sher. 356; Fitz. N. B. 251; Plowd. 67.

(*d*) This was long considered to be a private, or as said by Montague (in Plowden, 67) a *private general* act, but it is now holden to be a public act, and need not be specially pleaded; Samuel *v.* Evans, 2 T. R. 569. See also 15 East, 323. A sheriff has no authority, either under this statute or at common law, to take a bond for the appearance of persons arrested by him under process issuing upon an indictment at the quarter sessions for a misdemeanor; but can only take a recognizance for their appearance; Bengough *v.* Rossiter, 4 T. R. 505, in K. B.; affirmed in Exchequer Chamber, 2 H. Bl. 418. The sheriff is not liable to an action for not taking a bail-bond on an attachment out of Chancery; Studd *v.* Acton, 1 H. Bl. 468. Nor is the sheriff prohibited from so doing by the statute; but a bail-bond taken on an attachment is good at the common law; Morris *v.* Hayward, 2 Marsh. 280; 6 Taunt. 569, S. C.; Rex *v.* Dawes, 1 Lord Raym. 722; 2 Salk. 608, S. C.; Lewis *v.* Morland, 2 Bar. & Ald. 56; *Sed vide* 4 Price, 23; Com. Rep. 264; 2 Blac. Rep. 955; 2 Vent. 234, 238; 2 Str. 479; Cro. Car. 309; 3 Leon. 208.

CHAP. VI. SECT. II.

with sufficient sureties, and the under-sheriff refuse to discharge the defendant out of his custody, he is liable to an action on the case (*e*). For a refusal by the bailiff to discharge a defendant out of custody, on a tender to him of a bail-bond with sufficient sureties, the sheriff, and not the bailiff, is liable to an action (*f*). But in order to maintain such action, it must be alleged and proved that the sureties offered had sufficient *within the county* where the arrest was made (*g*); thus a declaration against the sheriffs of London for not discharging the defendant on bail, in which it was alleged that the sureties tendered had sufficient "within the city of London and county of Middlesex," was held bad on demurrer, for it should have been alleged that they had sufficient in the city of London (*h*). But the statute neither prescribes any particular number of sureties, nor that each should be worth any particular sum (*i*); and therefore where a bond was tendered with five sureties, three of whom were proved to be worth more than the penalty in the bond, it was held that the sheriff was liable to an action for not discharging the defendant out of his custody (*k*), for if three were sufficient, it was quite immaterial what the others had. Although a sheriff is not obliged to take a bond with less than two sureties, yet a bond taken with only one surety is good (*l*); for this clause, which requires reasonable sureties, was introduced for the benefit of the sheriff; for the same reason it was resolved, that the bond was good, although the sureties had not sufficient, or did not reside within the county (*m*), as the number or suffi-

(*e*) Salmon *v.* Percival, Cro. Car. 196; Sir W. Jones, 226, S. C.; Smith *v.* Hall, 2 Mod. 31; 2 Vent. 96.

(*f*) *Per* North, C. J., 2 Mod. 32.

(*g*) Lovell *v.* Sheriffs of London, 15 East, 320. And in such action the plaintiff is entitled to costs, under the Statute of Gloster; Cresswell *v.* Houghton, 6 T. R. 355.

(*h*) *Id. ibid.*

(*i*) Cro. Jac. 286.

(*k*) Matson *v.* Booth, 5 Maule & Sel. 223. *Quære*, would the sheriff be liable if the aggregate amount of the property of the whole was sufficient?

(*l*) Clyfton *v.* Web, Cro. Eliz. 808; Cotton *v.* Wale, *ib.* 862; Sir W. Drury's case, cit. 10 Rep. 100 b; but where the sheriff has taken only one surety, the court will not set aside an attachment regularly obtained against the sheriff for not bringing in the body; Rex *v.* Sheriffs of London, 2 Bing. 227; 9 Moore, 422, S. C.; Reg. *v.* Sheriff of Middlesex, 7 Dowl. 313. But it will be otherwise if the application is made at the instance of the bail, R. *v.* Sheriff of Middlesex, 2 Dowl. 140; or if the attachment has been obtained for not returning the writ, R. *v.* Sheriff of Surrey, 2 C. M. & R. 698.

(*m*) Cotton *v.* Wale, Cro. Eliz. 862; Blackburn *v.* Michelbourn, Cro. Eliz. 852.

ciency of the bail is not traversable in an action on a bail-bond (*n*).

When to be executed.

The sheriff may take a bail-bond from the defendant without arresting him, for the words in the statute are sufficiently comprehensive to apply to persons who have not been arrested, and it would be attended with mischievous consequences to hold bail-bonds to be illegal, taken civilly, without exposing the party to an arrest (*o*). Indeed, it has been holden that a bail-bond taken after the writ was issued, but before the delivery thereof to the sheriff, was good (*p*). A bail-bond taken after the time limited for putting in special bail is bad (*q*), for the condition can only be for the defendant to put in bail according to the exigency of the writ; consequently the bond should always be executed before or on the day limited for putting in special bail (*r*). A bail-bond executed in blank, before the condition is filled up, is void (*s*).

The form of the security.

By the second branch of this statute, which prescribes the nature and form of the security to be taken, it is enacted, "that no sheriff, &c., shall take any obligation for any cause aforesaid, or by colour of their office, but only to themselves, of any person, nor by any person, who shall be in their ward in course of law, but by name of their office, and upon condition written, that the prisoners shall appear at the day and place contained in the writ, bill, or warrant; and if any sheriff, &c. take any obligation in other form, by colour of their office, it shall be void."

The security must be by *bond or obligation* under seal (*t*); therefore an agreement in writing, made by a third person with the sheriff's officer, to put in good bail for the defendant at the return of the writ, or surrender his body to the officer, or pay the debt and costs (*u*), has been holden void by the statute above mentioned, and an action will not lie on such agreement. And the courts will not grant an attachment against an attorney, on

(*n*) Bentley *v.* Hore, 1 Lev. 86; 1 Sid. 96, S. C.

(*o*) Watkins *v.* Parry, Str. 444; Haley *v.* Fitzgerald, *ib.* 643. See Taylor *v.* Clow, 1 B. & Adol. 223. *Sed vide* Noy. 43.

(*p*) Say. Rep. 116; Bramfield *v.* Penhay, 1 Keb. 554; 1 Sid. 151. But see Hall *v.* Roche, 8 T. R. 187.

(*q*) Pullien *v.* Benson, 1 Lord Raym. 349; Samuel *v.* Evans, 2 T. R. 569; Thompson *v.* Rock, 4 M. & Sel. 338; Courtney *v.* Phillips, 1 Sid. 300.

(*r*) Call *v.* Thelwell, 1 C. M. & R. 780; 3 Dowl. 443.

(*s*) Powell *v.* Duff, 3 Camp. 181; see also Holden *v.* Raphael, 4 Ad. & E. 228; 5 N. & M. 655, S. C.

(*t*) 10 Rep. 101.

(*u*) Roger *v.* Reeves, 1 T. R. 418; Lewis *v.* Knight, 8 Bing. 271; 1 M. & Scott, 353, S. C.

CHAP. VI. SECT. II.

his undertaking to the officer to give a bail-bond to the sheriff in due time(x), or for the appearance of the defendant(y). But the statute only makes void securities to *the sheriff or his officers* in other form than that prescribed by the statute, but does not render void agreements or undertakings to *the party* himself, for the appearance of the defendant(z).

Stamp.

The bail-bond was formerly required to be on a half-crown stamp, but now a bail-bond no longer requires to be stamped (a).

The amount for which the bond should be taken.

By the statute of 12 Geo. 1, c. 29, s. 2, it is enacted, "that the sheriff or other officer to whom the writ or process is directed shall take bail for no more than the sum indorsed on the back of such writ." Notwithstanding this statute, it is usual always to take the bond in double the sum indorsed on the back of the writ. The statute of 12 Geo. 1, c. 20, s. 2, is only directory, and a bail-bond taken for more than the sum indorsed on the writ, or taken where there is no affidavit of debt, is not therefore void (b). If the bail-bond be taken for a larger sum than the sum indorsed on the writ, the bail are liable to satisfy the whole debt due to the plaintiff, not exceeding the penalty of the bond(c). And where a bail-bond was taken for a larger amount than the sum sworn to, it was ordered to be set aside (d).

To whom made; form of the condition.

With regard to the form of the bond, in the first place, it is required that it *be made to the sheriff by his name of office*. And if, therefore, the bail-bond be made to the sheriff's officer (e), or to the sheriff, but not by his name of office (f), it is void. In the next place, the condition of the bond must be for the defendant to put in special bail according to the exigency of the writ, and for no other purpose; therefore, if the bond be single without any condition at all, or with an impossible condition, or the condition be not for the defendant's appearance, or be for

(x) Sedgworth *v.* Spicer, 4 East, 568; Lewis *v.* Knight, *sup.*

(y) Fuller *v.* Prest, 7 T. R. 109.

(z) Hall *v.* Carter, 2 Mod. 304; Milward *v.* Clerk, Cro. Eliz. 190; Benson *v.* French, 1 Lev. 98; 1 Sid. 132, S. C. *Per* Buller, J., 1 T. R. 422. And see Rushant *v.* Wate, T. Jones, 139.

(a) 5 Geo. 4, c. 41.

(b) Whiskard *v.* Wilder, 1 Burr. 331; Norden *v.* Horsley, 2 Wils. 69; Cooke's Cas. Prac. 43; Fortes. 336; Prac. Reg. C. B. 67; Walker *v.* Carter, 2 Bla. Rep. 816.

(c) Mitchell *v.* Gibbons, 1 H. Bla. 76.

(d) Cock *v.* Cooper, 7 Ad. & E. 605.

(e) Rogers *v.* Reeves, 1 T. R. 418; Sedgworth *v.* Spicer, 4 East, 568.

(f) Guybon *v.* Whitetost, Cro. Eliz. 800; Kikebridge *v.* Wilson, 2 Lev. 123; Cudwell *v.* Dunkin, T. Jones, 137; Dyer, 119 a, 119 b, 120 a; Symes *v.* Oakes, 2 Stra. 893.

that and some thing else, it is void by the statute (*g*). But if the bond comply with these requisite formalities, the courts will not avoid it for any informality in the descripton of the court, or cause of action, provided they are described with common certainty (*h*). Thus, where (before the 2 Will. 4, c. 39) the writ was for the defendant to appear, &c. "wheresoever our lord the king shall then be in England," a bail-bond conditioned to appear at Westminster was holden good; and in a similar case, where the condition of the bond omitted the words "wheresoever, &c." the bond was holden good (*i*); and a bond conditioned to appear "in the office of Pleas in the Court of Exchequer," was held sufficient, although the writ was to appear before the "Barons," &c. (*k*). So where the bail-bond did not follow the writ in stating that the defendant was to appear "according to the custom of the court," the bond was held good (*l*). But a bail-bond taken on a *capias* out of C. P. was held bad, where the condition was to appear before "*the king at Westminster* (*m*)," for that must be intended the Court of King's Bench; a bail-bond, taken on process out of K. B., conditioned to appear in *his majesty's Court of the Bench at Westminster* (*n*), was held bad, for that must be intended the Court of Common Pleas. A bond conditioned for the appearance of the defendant in eight days after the date, the arrest having been made on the same day, was held sufficient (*o*). As to the description of the cause of action, the following points have been determined. Where the writ was to answer the plaintiff in a plea of debt for *three hundred and twenty pounds*, or in a plea of trespass, with an *ac etiam* in debt, and the condition was to answer the plaintiff in

(*g*) Graham *v.* Crashaw, 3 Lev. 74; Dyer, 119, 120; 2 Saund. 59 b, n. If the objection to the bail bond appear on the face of the declaration, or upon oyer, the defendant may demur, but otherwise he should plead such facts as show the bond to be void under the statute; and when, by pleading or otherwise, this appears on any part of the record, the defendant may move in arrest of judgment; Samuel *v.* Evan, 2 T. R. 569; 2 Saund. 59.

(*h*) See Large *v.* Atwood, 1 Dowl. & Ry. 551; Atkinson *v.* Saunderson, 4 Dougl. 254.

(*i*) Jones *v.* Sturdy, 9 East, 55. And see Kirkebridge *v.* Curwen, T. Jones, 46; 2 Lev. 180, S. C.; Lawson *v.* Haddock, 2 Vent. 237.

(*k*) Shuttleworth *v.* Pilkington, 2 Stra. 1155.

(*l*) Case cit. *id. ibid.*

(*m*) Renalds *v.* Smith, 6 Taunt. 551; 2 Marsh. 258, S. C.

(*n*) Impey *v.* Taylor, 3 M. & Sel. 166; see also Mill *v.* Pollon, 1 Moore, 19; 7 Taunt. 271, S. C.

(*o*) Evans *v.* Mosely, 2 C. & M. 490; 2 Dowl. 364, S. C.

CHAP. VI. SECT. II.

a plea of *debt generally* (*p*), or without mentioning the plea at all, the variances were holden immaterial (*q*). And so where the writ was to answer the plaintiff in "*a plea of trespass on the case upon promises,* to the damage, &c." and the condition of the bond was to answer the plaintiff in a "*plea of trespass,* &c.," the court held the bail-bond good, for the statute does not require that the bond should disclose the nature of the action (*r*). The omission of the defendant's name in the recital and operative part of the condition was held to vitiate the bond (*s*).

How prepared, fee, &c.

The sheriff's officer, in whose custody the defendant is, or by whom he has been arrested, upon being furnished with the names of the defendant's sureties, and having satisfied himself of their sufficiency, will prepare the bond immediately. It is the sheriff's duty to prepare it; and therefore, to an action for refusing to take bail, it would be no answer for the sheriff to say that the party did not tender a bail-bond (*t*). It seems, however, that the sheriff is entitled to be paid for such bond by the party arrested (*u*). As to the amount which he is entitled to charge, see *ante*, pp. 100, 102.

When the sheriff should discharge the defendant.

When the bail-bond is executed, or a deposit duly made in lieu of bail, or the sheriff's officer in whose custody the defendant is has received a written authority from the plaintiff to discharge him (*x*), search having been first made at the sheriff's office to see that there are no detainers against the defendant, he should be discharged out of custody upon payment of his fees, the costs of the bail-bond, &c. So also the defendant is entitled to his discharge when the debt and costs in the action have been paid to the plaintiff, no matter by whom (*y*). The sheriff is allowed a reasonable time to search for detainers (*z*);

(*p*) Villiers *v.* Hastings, Cro. Jac. 286; Kirkebridge *v.* Wilson, 2 Lev. 123.

(*q*) Gardiner *v.* Dudgate, 2 Show. 51; Cudwell *v.* Dunkin, T. Jones, 137; Grovenor *v.* Soame, 6 Mod. 122.

(*r*) Owen *v.* Nail, 6 T. R. 702. In the case of Rench *v.* Britton, 10 Mod. 327, Parker, C. J., is reported to have said, "that the statute only requires that the sheriff should take a bond conditioned for the appearance of the party on such a day at Westminster; it does not say even to answer the plaintiff." And see Huckett *v.* Plummer, 5 Moore, 538, *acc.*

(*s*) Holden *v.* Raphael, 4 Ad. & E. 228; 5 N. & M. 655, S. C.

(*t*) Milne *v.* Wood, 5 C. & P. 587.

(*u*) *Ibid.*

(*x*) Martin *v.* Francis, 2 B. & Ald. 402.

(*y*) Rimmer *v.* Turner, 3 Dowl. 601.

(*z*) Taylor *v.* Brander, 1 Esp. 45; see Samuel *v.* Buller, 1 Exch. R.

and he is not obliged to discharge a defendant on giving a bail-bond, without being paid his fees (*a*). Although, however, the sheriff may detain the defendant for his fees, the plaintiff's attorney has no lien on the body of a defendant for his costs; and therefore a sheriff was held justified in discharging a defendant out of his custody upon the authority of the plaintiff, although his attorney had given him notice not to discharge him until he was satisfied his costs (*b*).

SECTION III.

Of the Assignment of the Bail-Bond.

Sheriff obliged to assign the bail-bond.

The sheriff, before the statute of 4 Anne, c. 16, was not compellable to assign a bail-bond (*c*) taken by him on an arrest, although for refusing to assign it the courts would have amerced the sheriff (*d*); and according to the old practice, the bail-bond was never assigned until the sheriff had been ruled to bring in the body (*e*). And even after the sheriff had assigned the bond, the action still must have been brought in the name of the sheriff, and of course the sheriff might have released the action. But those inconveniences were remedied by the 20th section of the statute 4 Anne, c. 16, s. 20 (*f*), whereby it is enacted, that

(*a*) Chit. Archb. 543, 7th ed.; Milne *v.* Wood, *ubi sup.*

(*b*) Martin *v.* Francis, 2 Bar. & Ald. 402.

(*c*) 1 Mod. 288.

(*d*) 2 Mod. 84.

(*e*) Etherick *v.* Cowper, 1 Salk. 99.

(*f*) The act provides, "that if any person shall be arrested by any writ, bill, or process, issuing out of any of the courts of record at Westminster at the suit of any common person, and the sheriff or other officer taketh bail from such person against whom such writ, bill, or process is taken out, the sheriff or other officer, at the request and costs of the plaintiff in such action or suit, or his lawful attorney, shall assign to the plaintiff in such action the bail-bond, or other security, taken from such bail, by indorsing the same, and attesting it under his hand and seal, in the presence of two or more credible witnesses, which may be done without any stamp, provided the assignment so indorsed be duly stamped before any action be brought thereon; and if the said bail-bond of assignment, or other security taken for bail, be forfeited, the plaintiff in such action, after such assignment made, may bring an action and suit thereupon in his own name, and the court where the action is brought may by rule or rules of the same court give such relief to the plaintiff and defendant in the original action, and to the bail upon the said bond or other security taken from such bail, as is agreeable to justice and reason, and that such rule or rules of the said court shall have the nature and effect of a defeazance to such bail bond or other security for bail." This statute does not authorize the assignment of a bail-bond given by a party attached for contempt for not putting in an answer in chancery; Meller *v.* Palfreyman, 4 B. & Ad. 146.

CHAP. VI. SECT. III.

where a defendant shall be arrested, and the sheriff takes a bail-bond, the sheriff shall, at the request and costs of the plaintiff or his attorney, assign to the plaintiff such bail-bond, by indorsing the same, and attesting it under his hand and seal, in the presence of two or more credible witnesses, which may be done without any stamp, provided such assignment be afterwards duly stamped before any action be brought thereon. If, upon request of the plaintiff, the sheriff refuse to assign the bail-bond, he is liable to an action on the case (*g*).

At what time the plaintiff may take the assignment.

The plaintiff cannot take an assignment of the bail-bond after service of the rule of allowance of bail (*h*). Nor could he formerly have taken an assignment of the bail-bond, if the defendant had rendered before the return of the writ (*i*); but since the Uniformity of Process Act, 2 Will. 4, c. 39, it is otherwise, unless the defendant has put in special bail according to the exigency of the writ, *i. e.* within eight days after the arrest (*k*). If the plaintiff elect first to proceed against the sheriff, he cannot afterwards bring an action on the bond, pending the rule to bring in the body (*l*).

Properly speaking, the plaintiff cannot take an assignment of the bail-bond before it is forfeited (*m*), viz., if the defendant do not put in bail in due time, and perfect them if excepted to, or do not perfect bail if put in after the time appointed; although it has been said that the plaintiff may take an assignment before it is forfeited (*n*). The assignment must be made whilst the original cause is pending in court (*o*). By Reg. Gen. Hil. 2

(*g*) Stamper *v.* Milbourne, 7 T. R. 122; Mendez *v.* Bridges, 5 Taunt. 325.

(*h*) 1 Esp. 87; Short *v.* Doyle, 4 Dowl. 202. But until the service of the rule for the allowance of bail, the plaintiff is entitled to take an assignment of the bail-bond; Holland *v.* White, 2 Bos. & Pul. 341; Rex *v.* Sheriff of Middlesex, 4 T. R. 493. See also 1 Taunt. 119; Ellis *v.* Bates, 2 C. & M. 143.

(*i*) Jones *v.* Lander, 6 T. R. 753; Stamper *v.* Milbourne, 7 T. R. 122; Hyde *v.* Whiskard, 8 T. R. 456; Plimpton *v.* Howell, 10 East, 100; And see Lewis *v.* Davis, 5 Moore, 267; Maddocks *v.* Bullock, 1 Bos. & Pul. 325.

(*k*) Hodgson *v.* Mee, 3 Ad. & E. 765; 5 N. & M. 302, S. C.

(*l*) Reg. Gen. H. 2 W. 4, r. 23. See Whittle *v.* Oldacre, 7 B. & C. 478; Blackford *v.* Hawkins, 1 Bing. 181.

(*m*) Dent *v.* Weston, 8 T. R. 4.

(*n*) Barnes, 77.

(*o*) Sparrow *v.* Naylor, 2 Black. Rep. 876. The plaintiff may commence his action on the bail-bond at any time *after* the cause is out of court, provided the bond was assigned in time; Pigott *v.* Truste, 3 Bos. & Pul. 221; Collett *v.* Bland, 4 Taunt. 715. If there has been laches on the part of the plaintiff, the court, in the exercise of its equitable jurisdiction, will grant relief; 3 Bos. & Pul. 222.

Will. 4, r. 35, the plaintiff is out of court, unless he declare within one year after the process is returnable, which would now be construed to mean after the service or execution of the process.

By whom and how made.

The assignment may be made by the high sheriff, or by the under-sheriff (*p*), or his clerk (*q*), in the high sheriff's name. The assignment must be made by indorsement on the back of the bond, under the hand and seal of the sheriff, and made in the presence of two or more credible witnesses (*r*). *Credible* here means *disinterested;* therefore an attestation by the plaintiff in the action and another person renders the assignment invalid (*s*). The bail-bond may be assigned, and an action brought on it in any county (*t*). The usual fee paid to the under-sheriff for assigning a bail-bond in London and Middlesex is 5*s.*; in any other county 6*s.* 8*d.* (*u*).

The effect of the assignment.

By taking an assignment of a valid bail-bond, the sheriff is discharged, for the plaintiff cannot, after taking an assignment of the bail-bond, rule the sheriff to return the writ (*x*); but if the bail-bond be not valid, the plaintiff may still proceed against the sheriff (*y*). Formerly, in the Queen's Bench, after taking an assignment of the bail-bond, if the bail to the sheriff become bail above, the plaintiff could not except to them, for the acceptance of the assignment was an admission of the sufficiency of the bail (*z*); but the bail must justify, if they were excepted to *before* the plaintiff took the assignment (*a*). But in the Common Pleas, if the bail to the sheriff became bail to the

(*p*) Kitson *v.* Fagg, 1 Stra. 60; 10 Mod. 288, S. C.

(*q*) Doe *v.* Brawn, 5 Bar. & Ald. 243; Middleton *v.* Sandford, 4 Camp. 36; Harris *v.* Ashly, Sit. Midd. in 30 Geo. 2; French *v.* Arnold, T. 5 Geo. 3, cit. Tidd's Prac. 301, 8th edit.

(*r*) See stat. 4 Ann. c. 16, s. 20. The witnesses need not subscribe their names in the presence of the officer assigning; Phillips *v.* Barlow, 1 Bing. N. C. 433; 1 Scott, 322, S. C.

(*s*) White *v.* Barrack, 2 M. & W. 425.

(*t*) Gregson *v.* Heather, Stra. 727; 2 Lord Raym. 1455, S. C. If the bail-bond be taken in Middlesex, application should be made at the sheriff's office in Red Lion Square; if in London, at the secondary's office, 28, Coleman Street; or if in any other county, at the office of the under-sheriff, or of his agent in town, and the bond, with an assignment to the plaintiff indorsed on it, will be given to the plaintiff; Chit. Archbold's Prac. 559, 7th edit.

(*u*) Chit. Archb. 559, 7th edit.

(*x*) Etherick *v.* Cooper, 1 Salk. 99; Lord Brooke *v.* Stone, 1 Wils. 223.

(*y*) *Id. ibid.*

(*z*) Anon. 1 Salk. 97; Fish *v.* Horner, 7 Mod. 62; How *v.* Granville, 7 Mod. 117; Grovenor *v.* Soame, 6 Mod. 122.

(*a*) Hill *v.* Jones, 11 East, 321; Edmond *v.* Ross, 9 Price, 5.

CHAP. VI. SECT. III.

action, the plaintiff might except to them, notwithstanding he had taken an assignment of the bail-bond (*b*). And now, by Reg. Gen. Hil. 2 Will. 4, r. 15, the latter practice is extended to all the courts. Before the 1 & 2 Vict. c. 110, the plaintiff was not at liberty to proceed in the original action so long as he retained his right to sue on the bail-bond (*c*); but now, the *capias* being wholly collateral, the taking an assignment of the bail-bond no longer affects the right of the plaintiff to proceed in the original action (*d*).

Action on the bail-bond, by whom and when brought.

The sheriff, if he has been obliged to pay the debt and costs upon an attachment, may put the bond in force to reimburse himself; and the plaintiff also, after an assignment made to him, if the defendant has not complied with the condition of the bond, may bring his action thereon (*e*); and this, though he have become bankrupt (*f*). The plaintiff cannot, however, in any case sue on the bond before forfeiture; if he does, it will be a good ground for setting aside the writ in the action on the bond, or the nonforfeiture may be pleaded in bar (*g*). Before the rules of Hil. T. 2 Will. 4, in the Queen's Bench, the action could not be commenced until four days after the return of the writ, if the arrest were in London or Middlesex, or until six days if in any other county, the fourth and sixth day being reckoned exclusive (*h*). In the Common Pleas, a bail-bond taken in London or Middlesex, on process returnable on the first return of any term, could not be put in suit until the fifth day in term, and in any other county until the ninth day in full term; and on process returnable on any other return day but the first, if the arrest were in London or Middlesex, the bail-bond could not be put in suit until four days exclusive, if in any other county until eight days exclusive, after the return day of the process (*i*). But by Reg. Gen. Hil. 2 Will. 4, c. 24, it was ordered that no bail-bond taken in London or Middlesex should be put in suit until after the expiration of four days, nor if taken elsewhere till after the expiration of eight days exclusive, from the ap-

(*b*) R. M. 6 Geo. 2, C. P., Boughton *v.* Chaffey, 2 Wils. 6.

(*c*) Collet *v.* Bland, 4 Taunt. 715; Pigott *v.* Truste, 3 Bos. & Pul. 221.

(*d*) Betts *v.* Smyth, 2 Q. B. 113; 2 G. & D. 113, S. C.; Reg. *v.* Sheriff of Montgomeryshire, 9 M. & W. 448; Ede *v.* Collingridge, 11 M. & W. 61.

(*e*) 4 Ann. c. 16, s. 20.

(*f*) Anon. T. T. 1831, K. B., Chit. Archb 560, 7th ed.

(*g*) Edwards *v.* Danks, 4 Dowl. 357.

(*h*) R. M. 8 Ann. s. 6, K. B.

(*i*) R. T. 30 Geo. 3, C. P., 1 H. Black. 525, 526. See a former rule, 2 Blac. Rep. 1009.

pearance day of the process. This rule, however, was superseded by the Uniformity of Process Act, 2 Will. 4, c. 39, the schedule to which gave the form of the writ of *capias*, in which the defendant was required to take notice "that within eight days after execution thereof on him, inclusive of the day of such execution, he shall cause special bail to be put in for him to the action, and that in default of his so doing, such proceedings might be had and taken as are mentioned in the warning hereunder written;" and the warning states that "if the defendant, having given bail on the arrest, shall omit to put in special bail as required, the plaintiff may proceed against the sheriff as on the bail-bond (*j*)." And inasmuch as the form of the *capias* given by the 1 & 2 Vict. c. 110, is in this respect the same, and the same warning is to be subscribed to it, it follows that if a defendant held to bail on a *capias* under that statute do not put in special bail within eight days after execution of the process upon him, including the day of such execution, the plaintiff, immediately on the expiration of that time, may put the bail-bond in suit; even though the defendant, after the expiration of the eight days, renders himself to the sheriff (*k*).

The plaintiff may proceed on the bail-bond, unless the bail be justified, although not excepted to, if the bail have not been put in in time (*l*). The plaintiff may treat bail to the action, who are insufficient by the practice of the court, as a nullity, and proceed on the bail-bond as soon as the time for putting in bail has expired, unless good bail be duly put in in the meantime (*m*). Where the plaintiff, with the consent of the bail to the sheriff, took from the defendant a *cognovit* with a stay of execution for a month, it was held that, although the bail continued liable notwithstanding the *cognovit*, they could not be sued on the bail-bond until they received notice that the *cognovit* was unsatisfied (*n*).

(*j*) Hillary *v.* Rowles, 5 B. & Ad. 460.

(*k*) See Hodgson *v.* Mee, 3 Ad. & E. 765; 5 N. & M. 302, S. C.

(*l*) Turner *v.* Cary, 7 East, 607.

(*m*) Reg. Gen. Hil. 2 Will. 4, r. 13. Before this rule, in K. B., the plaintiff could not treat such bail as a nullity, but was bound to except to them as if regular; Rex *v.* Sheriff of Surry, 2 East, 180; Thomson *v.* Roubell, Doug. 466, n. (1). The practice was otherwise in C. P.; Fenton *v.* Ruggles, 1 Bos. & Pul. 356; Wallace *v.* Arrowsmith, 2 Bos. & Pul. 49.

(*n*) Clift *v.* Gye, 9 B. & C. 422; see also Woosnam *v.* Price, 1 C. & M. 352; Surman *v.* Bruce, 10 Bing. 444; 4 M. & Scott, 184.

CHAP. VI. SECT. III.

In what court an action on a bail-bond may be brought.

Where the action is by the plaintiff as assignee of the sheriff, by the practice of all the courts, it must be brought in the *same* court where the original action was brought; otherwise the parties could not have the relief intended by the statute (*o*). In the Courts of Common Pleas (*p*) and Exchequer (*q*), where the action on the bail-bond is brought by the sheriff, the sheriff has been allowed to bring actions on bail-bonds taken on process issuing out of another court. In the Queen's Bench the sheriff could not sue on a bail-bond taken on process issuing out of another court (*r*). But now, when brought by the sheriff, the action may be in any court (*s*). The bringing an action in a different court from that in which the original action was commenced is only an irregularity, of which advantage must be taken by special application to the court where the action on the bail-bond is pending; but this irregularity is no objection on the plea of *non est factum* (*t*). The venue in an action on a bail-bond may be laid in any county (*u*).

Parties cannot be holden to bail in an action on a bail-bond.

In an action on the bail-bond, whether brought by the sheriff or by his assignee, neither the defendant nor his sureties could ever be holden to bail (*x*). But if either the sheriff or his assignee recover judgment on the bail-bond, the defendants may be holden to bail on that judgment (*y*).

The declaration.

Where the action is by the sheriff himself, the bond is usually declared on as a common money bond, without setting out the condition. Where the action is by the assignee, it is not necessary to make profert of the assignment (*z*); it is sufficient to allege that the sheriff assigned the bond according to the form of the statute, and it need not be stated that the assignment was under his hand and seal (*a*). Neither need the names of the attesting witnesses be stated, nor need it even be alleged that the assignment was made in the presence of two witnesses, as

(*o*) Mellor *v.* Palfreyman, 1 N. & M. 696.

(*p*) Morris *v.* Rees, 3 Wils. 348; 2 Blac. Rep. 838, S. C.; Chesterton *v.* Middlehurst, 1 Burr. 642; Walton *v.* Bent, 3 Burr. 1923; Newman *v.* Faucitt, 1 H. Blac. 631.

(*q*) Yorke *v.* Ogden, 8 Price, 174.

(*r*) Donatty *v.* Barclay, 8 T. R. 152.

(*s*) Reg. Gen. Hil. 2 Will. 4, r. 28.

(*t*) Wright *v.* Walmsley, 2 Camp. 396; Reg. Gen. H. T. 4 Will. 4.

(*u*) Gregson *v.* Heather, Stra. 727; 2 Lord Raym. 1455, S. C.

(*x*) Brander *v.* Robson, 6 T. R. 336; Mellish and another *v.* Petherick, 8 T. R. 450.

(*y*) Prendergast *v.* Davis, 8 T. R. 85.

(*z*) Leafe *v.* Box, 1 Wils. 121.

(*a*) Dawes *v.* Papworth, Willes, 458.

required by the statute (*b*): though the declaration would be bad, if on the face of it it appeared that the assignment was *not* according to the statute (*c*). Neither is it necessary to aver in the declaration, that the defendant in the original action was arrested, and such an averment, if made, would not be traversable (*d*). Neither need it be averred that the writ was issued on an affidavit of debt, and indorsed with the sum sworn to (*e*).

Pleadings.

If the defendant do not justify his bail in due time, and *comperuit ad diem* be pleaded to a declaration on the bail-bond, the court will order the appearance of the defendant to be recorded as of the day on which the bail justified (*f*). And if bail above be justified before the expiration of the rule to bring in the body, the bail below might, before the abolition of the doctrine of relation to the first day of term, in an action on the bond, plead *comperuit ad diem*, and that plea was satisfied by the production of the recognizance roll, containing an entry of the defendant's appearance generally; and such roll might be made up at any day before the day given for producing it (*g*); or, instead of so pleading, the defendant in the action on the bond might, it would seem, apply to the court or a judge to stay the proceedings on it. But now, perhaps, as the doctrine of relation is abolished, and the recognizance roll does not enter the appearance generally, this plea could not be successfully adopted, though the defendant may still obtain a stay of the proceedings (*h*).

Extent of liability on the bail-bond.

The bail to the sheriff are liable to satisfy the whole debt due to the plaintiff, to the full extent of the penalty of the bond, though beyond the sum sworn to, and costs (*i*). Where several actions were brought on a bail-bond against the defendant and

(*b*) Robinson *v.* Taylor, Fortesc. 366; Leafe *v.* Box, 1 Wils. 121; Lewis *v.* Parkes, 3 M. & W. 133; 6 Dowl. 93, S. C., nom. Lewis *v.* Parker.

(*c*) Neott *v.* Mills, Fortesc. 371.

(*d*) Taylor *v.* Clow, 1 B. & Adol. 223. See also Call *v.* Thelwell, 3 Dowl. 443; Watkins *v.* Parry, Stra. 444; Haley *v.* Fitzgerald, *ib.* 643; *ante*, p. 153.

(*e*) Sharpe *v.* Abbey, 5 Bing. 193. See Hume *v.* Liversedge, 1 C. & M. 332; 1 Dowl. 660, S. C.; Knowles *v.* Stevens, 1 C. M. & R. 26.

(*f*) Ladd *v.* Arnaboldi, 1 C. & J. 97.

(*g*) Whittle v. Oldaker, 7 B. & C. 478; 1 M. & R. 298, S. C.

(*h*) Chit. Archb. 561, 7th edit.

(*i*) Stevenson *v.* Cameron, 8 T. R. 29; Mitchel *v.* Gibbons, 1 H. Bla. 76; Orton *v.* Vincent, Cowp. 71; Miffin *v.* Morgan, 2 Ld. Raym. 1564; and see 7 T. R. 370; 3 East, 604.

CHAP. VI. SECT. III.

his sureties, the court stayed the proceedings on the payment of the costs of one action only, the bringing several actions being considered oppressive (*d*). And now, by Reg. Gen. Hil. 2 Will. 4, r. 30, proceedings on the bail-bond may be stayed on payment of costs in one action, unless sufficient reason be shown for proceeding in more. But such an application must be made promptly, and is too late after the several actions have proceeded to verdict (*e*). Unless, however, all the obligors in the bail-bond are sued jointly, they, or such of them as the plaintiff chooses to sue, should be sued separately; for if two out of three were to be sued jointly, although it would not be any *irregularity* (*f*), still it would be ground for a plea in abatement for nonjoinder.

When and on what terms proceedings on the bail-bond will be stayed.

The courts will in many cases, where the justice of the case requires it, set aside proceedings on the bail-bond. Thus, if the *plaintiff* die after the arrest and before the return of the writ, the court will set aside proceedings (*g*). And where the *defendant* dies before the plaintiff could have had judgment against him, if there had been no delay in putting in and perfecting bail, the court will stay proceedings on the bail-bond, upon payment of costs only (*h*); but where the plaintiff might have had judgment against the defendant, if bail above had been put in and perfected in time, the bail to the sheriff are liable for the whole debt and costs, and the court will not relieve them (*i*). Where the defendant becomes *bankrupt* after he has given a bail-bond, the bail may be relieved on motion, if the defendant has obtained his certificate before they are fixed (*k*); but if he do not obtain his certificate until *afterwards*, they remain liable (*l*). Where a bankrupt obtained his certificate under a third commission, the Court refused to cancel a bail-bond given upon arrest for a debt proveable under that commission, he not having paid fifteen shillings in the pound under either of the former commissions (*m*).

(*d*) Key *v.* Hill, 2 B. & Ald. 598; 1 Chit. Rep. 337, S. C., Abbott, C. J., *dissentiente.*

(*e*) Johnson *v.* Macdonald, 2 Dowl. 44.

(*f*) Knowles *v.* Johnson, 2 Dowl. 653.

(*g*) Hutchinson *v.* Smith, 8 Mod. 240; Chit. Archb. 568, 7th edit.

(*h*) Castell *v.* Grave, Barnes, 99.

(*i*) Orton *v.* Vincent, Cowp. 71; Evening *v.* Spearman, Barnes, 99; Morly *v.* Carr, Barnes, 112.

(*k*) Sanders *v.* Spincks, Barnes, 105.

(*l*) Wolley *v.* Cobbe, 1 Burr. 244; 1 Ld. Ken. 504, S. C.; Cockerill *v.* Owston, *ib.* 436; see also Coulson *v.* Hammond, 4 Dowl. & Ry. 160; 2 Bar. & Cress. 626, S. C.; Streeter *v.* Scott, 2 Dowl. 362.

(*m*) Summers *v.* Jones, 6 Dowl. 139.

If the plaintiff has been guilty of laches (*n*), or has taken a *cognovit* for the debt unknown to the sureties (*o*), the court will stay proceedings on the bail-bond. And where the plaintiff, with the consent of the bail, took a *cognovit* with a stay of execution for a month, it was held that although, the debt being unpaid, the bail continued liable, yet the plaintiff could not proceed against them without first giving them notice that the *cognovit* was unsatisfied (*p*).

But after the bond has been forfeited and assigned, the bail will not be discharged by time being given to their principal, even without their consent (*q*). If one of the bail to the sheriff consents to time being given to the principal, such consent is binding upon both (*r*).

If proceedings are taken on the bail-bond contrary to good faith, they will be set aside with costs (*s*). So where the proceedings in the action are irregular, or where the defendant ought not to have been holden to bail (*t*), or the defendant has been misnamed in the writ (*u*), the court will set aside the bail-bond, although in the last case the defendant has signed the bail-bond with his initials, which correspond with the name in the writ (*x*). The affidavit in support of a rule to set aside a bail-bond for this defect must be intituled with the right name of the party, and not with the name by which he was arrested (*y*). Formerly, also, before the Uniformity of Process Act, if, on or before the return day of the writ, the defendant had rendered himself to the sheriff, or had put in bail and rendered in dis-

(*n*) Pigott *v.* Truste, 3 B. & P. 221; Merryman *v.* Carpenter, 2 Stra. 1262; Hutchinson *v.* Hardcastle, Barnes, 103.

(*o*) Farmer *v.* Thorley, 4 Bar. & Ald. 91; otherwise, if at the instance of one of the bail, Rex *v.* Sheriff of Middlesex, 1 Dowl. & Ry. 388.

(*p*) Clift *v.* Gye, 9 B. & C. 422; 4 M. & Sc. 184; 2 Dowl. 777, S. C.; and see also Surman *v.* Bruce, 10 Bing. 434; Charelton *v.* Morris, 6 Bing. 427.

(*q*) Woosnam *v.* Price, 1 C. & M. 852.

(*r*) Howard *v.* Bradberry, 3 Dowl. 92. See also Rex *v.* The Sheriff of Middlesex, 1 Dowl. & R. 388.

(*s*) Sweeting *v.* Weaver, 11 Price, 734; Yeates *v.* Chapman, 3 Bing. N. C. 264, Tindal, C. J.

(*t*) 1 Stra. 399. See Yeates *v.* Chapman, 3 Bing. N. C. 262.

(*u*) See Finch *v.* Cocker, 3 Dowl. 678.

(*x*) Coles *v.* Gunn, 1 Bing. 424; Johnson *v.* Cooper, 5 Moore, 472; Smith *v.* Innes, 4 M. & Sel. 360; Taylor *v.* Butternam, 6 Moore, 264. But the court of C. P. have declared that they will not for the future set aside bail-bonds, where the defendant is sued by the initials of his Christian name only; Lake *v.* Silk, 3 Bing. 296; Kitching *v.* Alder, 1 Chit. Rep. 282.

(*y*) Finch *v.* Cocker, 2 Dowl. 383.

CHAP. VI. SECT. III.

charge, the court would stay proceedings on the bail-bond (z). But since that act, a render to the sheriff would not be a ground for staying the proceedings, unless the defendant has put in special bail according to the exigency of the writ (a). If the defendant render himself, or is rendered in discharge of his bail, *after* the return of the writ, or even after the time for justification of the bail has expired, the court will stay proceedings on the bail-bond on payment of costs (b). By Reg. Gen. H. T. 2 Will. 4, r. 23, a plaintiff shall not be at liberty to proceed on the bail-bond pending a rule to bring in the body.

Moreover, if the proceedings be regular, the court will, on the defendant's justifying bail above, stay proceedings on the bail-bond, either on the application of the defendant or of his bail (c). By a rule in the Queen's Bench, "no rule shall be drawn up to stay proceedings regularly commenced on the assignment of a bail-bond, unless application for such rule shall, if made on the part of the defendant, be grounded on an affidavit of *merits;* or if made on the part of the bail, at their own expense, and for their own indemnity, and without collusion with the defendant (d)." A similar rule now exists in the Exchequer (e), and it is adopted also in the Common Pleas (f). The courts, however, impose terms upon the defendant or his bail, in setting aside proceedings. The terms used to be these; if the plaintiff had not lost a trial, the proceedings were stayed on payment of costs incurred upon the bail-bond, perfecting bail in the original action, and if necessary, that the defendant should receive a declaration, plead issuably, and take short notice of trial; but if the plaintiff had lost a trial, the bail-bond should

(z) Jones *v.* Lander, 6 T. R. 753; Stamper *v.* Milbourne, 7 T. R. 122; Harding *v.* Hennem, 3 Bos. & Pul. 232; Hyde *v.* Whiskard, 8 T. R. 456; Pimpton *v.* Howell, 10 East, 100; Hamilton *v.* Wilson, 1 East, 383; Maddocks *v.* Bullock, 1 Bos. & Pul. 325; Lewis *v.* Davis, 5 Moore, 267.

(a) Hodgson *v.* Mee, 3 Ad. & E. 765; 5 Nev. & M. 302, S. C.

(b) Rex *v.* Sheriff of Middlesex, 7 T. R. 529; Edwin *v.* Allen, 5 T. R. 401; Meysey *v.* Carnell, *ib.* 534; Seaver *v.* Spraggon, 2 N. R. 85.

(c) 1 Chit. Archb. Prac. 569, 7th edit.

(d) Reg. Gen. K. B., M. T. 59 Geo. 3, 2 B. & Ald. 240; 1 Chit. Rep. 127, n. (a). See Grottick *v.* Bailey, 5 Bar. & Ald. 703; for the practice in C. P. see 1 N. R. 123; in Exchequer, see 1 M'Cleland, 44; 2 C. & J. 671.

(e) Reg. Gen. H. T. 7 Will. 4, 5 Dowl. 446. See Call *v.* Thelwell, 3 Dowl. 444; R. *v.* Sheriff of Surrey, *id.* 174.

(f) Rex *v.* Sheriffs of London, 1 M. & P. 177; 4 Bing. 427, S. C.; Chit. Arch. 570, 7th ed.

then remain as a security for the debt and costs in the original action, if the plaintiff should have a verdict (*g*). And by Reg. Gen. H. T. 2 Will. 4, r. 29, in all cases where the bail-bond was directed to stand as a security, the plaintiff might sign judgment upon it.

Since the 1 & 2 Vict. c. 110, the *capias* being a mere collateral proceeding, it seems that the court will in all cases stay the proceedings on putting in and perfecting bail, or payment into court in lieu of bail, or render and payment of costs (*h*); for since that statute there is no impediment to the plaintiff's proceeding against the defendant, whether bail above be put in or not (*i*). Where the application is by the bail, no terms can be imposed on the defendant (*k*).

Proceedings may be stayed, either for *irregularity*, or by putting in bail where the proceedings are *regular*, by application to the court in term time, or to a judge in vacation (*l*). The affidavits, summons, and orders must be intituled in the original action (*m*), excepting where the irregularity is in the process in the action on the bail-bond, and then it should be intituled in the action on the bail-bond, and not in the original action (*n*).

Section IV.

Rule to return the Writ.

Rule to return the writ.

Where the plaintiff is dissatisfied with the bail to the sheriff, he can only proceed against the sheriff, if the defendant do not put in bail, or render himself in due time. The object of ruling the sheriff to return the writ is either to compel the defendant to put in bail, or, if bail be already put in, to compel them to justify at the same time as the plaintiff excepts to the bail, and gives notice of exception. The plaintiff should not be guilty

(*g*) 1 Archbold's Prac. 100, 2d ed. And see *post*, as to setting aside an attachment obtained against the sheriff.

(*h*) Chit. Arch. 569, 7th ed.

(*i*) Betts *v.* Smyth, 2 Q. B. 113. See also Reg. *v.* Sheriff of Montgomeryshire, 1 Dowl. N. S. 388; Ede *v.* Collingridge, 11 M. & W. 61.

(*k*) Call *v.* Thelwell, 3 Dowl. 445; 1 C. M. & R. 780, S. C.

(*l*) Chit. Archb. 565, 7th ed.

(*m*) 4 T. R. 688; 8 T. R. 456; 3 Bos. & Pul. 118.

(*n*) Willes, 461; 1 Bos. & Pul. 337; Stride *v.* Hill, 1 M. & W. 37, *per* Parke, B.

CHAP. VI. SECT. IV.

of any delay in ruling the sheriff to return the writ; for if the party has been guilty of any laches, the court will not interfere to compel the sheriff to put in bail, particularly if by such delay the sheriff would be placed in a worse situation than he would have been if he had been ruled to return the writ in the first instance.

When the sheriff may be ruled to return the writ, and when not, and when and how the courts will grant an attachment against him for not returning the writ, has been fully considered in a former part of this work (*o*).

By Reg. Gen. M. 7 Will. 4, all rules upon sheriffs, other than the sheriffs of London and Middlesex, to return writs, whether of mesne or final process, and rules to bring in the bodies of defendants, are to be eight day rules instead of six day rules (*p*).

Non est inventus.

The sheriff's return to a bailable writ of *capias*, that the defendant is *not found* in his bailiwick, is proper only in case he had no opportunity of arresting the defendant; for where the sheriff has or might have taken the defendant, he is liable for a false return, if he return *non est inventus* (*q*). But the court will not set aside the return (*r*). A return that "the defendant is not *to be* found in my bailiwick" would be bad (*s*). It is said that if a sheriff takes one by force of a *capias*, he does well, but if he returns *non est inventus*, he shall be a trespasser *ab initio* (*t*).

Cepi corpus.

But where the defendant has been arrested, and discharged on giving a bail-bond, the sheriff should return *cepi corpus et paratum habeo* (*u*), for it was his duty to take bail; for this, which was the ancient return, is not altered by the statute of the 23d Hen. 6, c. 9 (*x*); and if bail be not duly put in and perfected, the mode of proceeding against the sheriff is by attachment for not bringing in the body (*y*). If the defendant has been discharged, on being arrested, without giving a bail-bond,

(*o*) See *ante*, from p. 81 to p. 87.

(*p*) Jervis's Rules, 152.

(*q*) Hawkins *v.* Mildmay, Cro. Eliz. 729; 12 Mod. 311; 2 Keb. 291; Beckford *v.* Montague, 2 Esp. 475.

(*r*) Goubot *v.* De Crouy, 1 C. & M. 772; 2 Dowl. 86, S. C.

(*s*) Rex *v.* Sheriff of Kent, 2 M. & W. 316; 5 Dowl. 451, S. C.

(*t*) See Plowd. 16. *Quære.*

(*u*) See this return, Append. c. 6, s. 4.

(*x*) Cro. Eliz. 624, 808, 852; Noy, 39; 1 Sid. 22, 439; 1 Vent, 55, 85; 2 Saund. 60, 154; 1 Mod. 33, 57, 227; 2 Mod. 83, 177; 3 Salk. 314.

(*y*) See *post*, 173; also Neck *v.* Humphery, 3 Ad. & E. 131, *per cur.*; 4 N. & M. 738, S. C.

and does not appear at the return of the writ, the sheriff will be liable to an action; but in such case it is usual to return *cepi corpus et paratum habeo*, in order to give the defendant an opportunity of putting in bail; for it does not necessarily follow, when the sheriff returns *cepi corpus et paratum habeo*, that he has taken a bail-bond; he may have allowed the defendant to be at large, intending to put in bail when required, *if he can* do so (*z*). If the defendant be in the county gaol, the sheriff should mention this in his return, and not say *paratum habeo* (*a*). And generally, if the fact be that the defendant is in custody, the sheriff should return that fact (*b*). If the sheriff has discharged the defendant, or delivered him over to another custody, by direction of the plaintiff, or by order of the court, or on depositing in the sheriff's hands the sum sworn to, and 10*l*. for costs, these should be mentioned in the return (*c*). When the sheriff may return that the defendant was rescued out of his custody, or that the defendant remains sick in prison, and where *mandavi ballivo* is a good return, have already been noticed (*d*); and for the returns in general, see *ante*, from page 87 to 99.

The object and time for ruling the sheriff to bring in the body.

The sheriff, having arrested the party, must, we have seen, return *cepi corpus et paratum habeo*. After such return, if the defendant be at large and no bail put in, or if bail be put in but not justified, the sheriff may be ruled, or in vacation may be ordered (*e*), to bring in the body. If the sheriff return some excuse which is not sufficient, as an *insufficient* return of rescue or *languidus*, he may, notwithstanding, be ruled to bring in the body (*f*). The intent of the rule, where the defendant is not in custody, is to compel the sheriff to put in and perfect bail (*g*). If bail be put in, and notice of justification be given, yet unless the plaintiff except to the bail, he cannot rule the sheriff to bring in the body (*h*). This rule cannot in general be taken

(*z*) See 4 Nev. & M. 738, *per* Patteson, J.

(*a*) Rex *v.* Sheriff of Wilts, 8 Moore, 518.

(*b*) 4 Nev. & M. 708, *per* Littledale, J.

(*c*) See each of these returns, Append. c. 6, s. 4.

(*d*) *Ante*, p. 96 to 99.

(*e*) Reg. Gen. H. T. 3 Will. 4, Archb. 553, 7th ed.

(*f*) Rex *v.* Sheriff of Middlesex, 1 Bar. & Ald. 190; Cavenagh *v.* Collett, 4 Bar. & Ald. 279.

(*g*) Wolfe *v.* Collingwood, 1 Wils. 262.

(*h*) Rex *v.* Sheriff of Middlesex, 8 T. R. 258; Rogers *v.* Mapleback, 1 H. Blac. 107. See also Bond *v.* Evans, 4 Bar. & Cr. 864.

CHAP. VI. SECT. IV.

out until the time for putting in bail has expired (*i*): for it is necessary that the proceedings against the sheriff should keep pace with the times allowed for putting in and perfecting bail; otherwise it might happen that the defendant might justify bail after the sheriff is fixed with the debt and costs, whereby the sheriff would be without remedy, for if he brings an action on the bail-bond against the defendant, or his bail, they may plead *comperuit ad diem*, and so defeat the action (*k*). If the time for putting in bail has not expired, the rule to bring in the body must not be taken out until the *day after* the expiration of the rule to return the writ. In such case, if the rule to bring in the body be taken out on the day on which the rule to return the writ expires, an attachment for non-compliance therewith will be set aside for irregularity (*l*). But it is the settled practice, where the time for putting in bail has expired, that the plaintiff may rule the sheriff to bring in the body on *the same day* that he returns *cepi corpus* (*m*). Where there has been *laches* on the part of the plaintiff in ruling the sheriff to bring in the body, the court will set aside an attachment for not bringing in the body; as where the sheriff returned *cepi corpus*, in *Hilary* term, and the plaintiff did not rule him to bring in the body until Michaelmas term, the court set aside an attachment for not doing it (*n*).

When the sheriff cannot be ruled to bring in the body.

Where the plaintiff, on the return of *cepi corpus*, has recovered damages in an action of escape against the sheriff, he cannot rule him afterwards to bring in the body, for he cannot proceed against the sheriff as if the defendant was not in his custody, and then as if the return were true (*o*). Nor can the plaintiff rule

(*i*) Rolfe *v.* Steel, 2 H. Blac. 276; Rex *v.* Sheriff of Middlesex, 8 East, 464.

(*k*) 2 Saund. 61 e. But if bail has been put in but not justified, and the sheriff obliged to put the bail-bond in force for his indemnity, to which action the defendants plead *comperuit ad diem*, the court will not order the recognizance of bail to be struck off the file; Leigh *v.* Bertles, 1 Marsh. 520; 6 Taunt. 167, S. C. And the court will order the *date* of appearance to be entered in the filacer's book on motion, where issue is joined in a plea of *comperuit ad diem* to an action on a bail-bond; Austen *v.* Fenton, 1 Taunt. 23.

(*l*) Hutchins *v.* Hird, 5 T. R. 479; Rex *v.* Sheriff of London, 2 East, 241.

(*m*) Rex *v.* Sheriff of Middlesex, 4 Maule & Sel. 427.

(*n*) Rex *v.* Sheriff of Surrey, 7 T. R. 452; Rex *v.* Sheriff of London, 1 Taunt. 111. And also where there are laches in moving for an attachment; Rex *v.* Perring, 3 Bos. & Pul. 151; Rex *v.* Sheriff of Surrey, 9 East, 467; Rex *v.* Sheriff of Middlesex, 1 Dowl. 53.

(*o*) Borwick *v.* Walton, 2 Bar. & Ald. 623; 1 Chit. Rep. 993, S. C.

the sheriff to bring in the body after he has taken a *cognovit* from the defendant, for the defendant appears in court on the giving the *cognovit*, and the sheriff has done his duty (*p*).

Late sheriff may be ruled to bring in the body.

It was formerly usual, in the Queen's Bench, to proceed against the *late* sheriff for not bringing in the body by *distringas*. But now by rule of that court, "where any sheriff, before his going out of office, shall arrest any defendant, and a *cepi corpus* shall afterwards be returned, he shall and may, within the time allowed by law, be called upon to bring in the body, by a rule for that purpose, notwithstanding he may be out of office before such rule granted (*q*)." If the old sheriff be ruled to return the writ, and the new sheriff make a return of *cepi corpus*, the old sheriff cannot be ruled to bring in the body, for he has made no return (*r*). A similar practice has also obtained in C. P. (*s*), and in that court, a sheriff who is ruled on the last day of the term, but goes out of office before the next term, is liable for an attachment for not bringing in the body (*t*).

In the counties palatine.

In the counties palatine, the attachment, or other process of contempt (*u*), issues against the party who is in default; as against the Chancellor of Lancaster, Bishop of Durham (*x*), or the Chamberlains of Chester or their officers, if they refuse to make a mandate to the sheriff, or to return the writ into court after he has made his return to them; or against the sheriff if he will not return the mandate, or bring in the body of the defendant, pursuant to his return of *cepi corpus*, &c., for though the sheriff is not the immediate *officer* of the court above, yet he is answerable to it for contempts.

How served.

As the object of the rule to bring in the body is to bring the sheriff into contempt, it must be served in the same manner as the rule to return the writ (*y*).

How complied with.

This rule, like the rule to return the writ, is a four-day rule

(*p*) Rex *v.* Sheriff of Surrey, 1 Taunt. 159. So if the surrender of the defendant be dispensed with by the plaintiff. See West *v.* Ashdown, 1 Bing. 164; 7 Moore, 566, S. C. See also Bowsfield *v.* Tower, 4 Taunt. 456; Crofts *v.* Johnson, 1 Marsh. 59; 5 Taunt. 319, S. C.

(*q*) R. T. 31 Geo. 3, K. B. 4 T. R. 379. And see 1 Bulstrode, 70.

(*r*) Rex *v.* Sheriff of Middlesex, 4 East, 604.

(*s*) Price *v.* Street, Barnes, 102.

(*t*) Meekins *v.* Smith, 1 H. Blac. 629.

(*u*) Flight *v.* Stanley, Tidd's Prac. 8th edit. where a *distringas* issued against the Bishop of Durham, being a peer.

(*x*) —— *v.* The Mayor of Wigan, 1 Sid. 92.

(*y*) See *ante*, 84.

in London and Middlesex (*z*), and an eight-day rule in every other county (*a*). The only mode of complying with the rule, is either by bringing the defendant into court, or putting in and perfecting bail. If the defendant is not in custody, or special bail put in and perfected, the sheriff is liable to be attached for not bringing in the body. The sheriff has the whole of the day on which the rule expires to bring in the body; therefore an attachment cannot be moved for until the day after; or if the rule expire on the last day of the term, not until the second day of the next term.

And now, by R. G., H. T. 1 Vict., it is ordered that in all cases special bail may be justified before a judge at chambers, both in term and vacation (*b*).

Where two days' (*c*) time was given to justify, and bail was not justified on the last of those two days, an attachment was allowed to issue on that day. If the sheriff show that the defendant has been rendered in discharge of his bail, and is then in custody, this is a sufficient compliance with the rule (*d*). Even if the defendant be not in custody at the return of the writ, the sheriff may put in bail for the defendant, and those bail may take and render him without justifying (*e*), but they must not take him before the time for putting in bail has expired (*f*).

If the time limited has expired, and the rule or order has not been obeyed, the contempt is not purged by rendering the defendant, or by putting in and perfecting bail on a subsequent day, although before the attachment is moved for (*g*). If *cepi corpus* is returned to a writ of capias, without either a rule or an order to return the writ, the sheriff may still be ruled or ordered to bring in the body, and may be attached for dis-

(*z*) R. T. 6 Geo. 3, K. B.; R. H. 7 Geo. 3, C. P.

(*a*) R. G., M. T. 7 Will. 4, *ante*, p. 84. Formerly it was a six day rule in every other county; R. G. 5 & 6 Geo. 3, K. B.

(*b*) R. H. T. 2 Will. 4, r. 17, was annulled by this rule.

(*c*) 1 Chit. Rep. 356. Where bail were rejected after time given to inquire into their sufficiency, and the defendant was rendered on the same day, but before notice of render an attachment was moved for and granted, the attachment was held to be regular; Rex *v.* Sheriff of Middlesex, 2 Dowl. & Ry. 225. And see Rex *v.* Sheriff of London, 1 Chit. Rep. 567.

(*d*) Rex *v.* Sheriff of Middlesex, 8 T. R. 464; 2 M. & S. 562.

(*e*) Berchere *v.* Colson, Stra. 876; Rex *v.* Butcher, Peake's N. P. C. 169; 7 T. R. 527; Evans *v.* Swete, 2 Bing. 271.

(*f*) Taylor *v.* Evans, 1 Bing. 367; 8 Moore, 398, S. C.

(*g*) R. G., H. T. 3 Will. 4; Smith *v.* Andrews, 2 M. & W. 536; R. *v.* Sheriff of Middlesex, 2 Dowl. 432; R. *v.* Sheriff of Middlesex, 3 Dowl. 186.

obedience under the R. H. T. 3 Will. 4, just as though the return had been made under a rule or order (*h*).

Where the rule to bring in the body expires in vacation, or on the last day in term, the sheriff has all the first day of the next term to comply with the rule, and an attachment granted on that day is irregular (*i*); and although a sheriff may be in contempt, yet it appears to be the practice of the Courts of Queen's Bench and Common Pleas, that if the defendant be rendered, and notice thereof be given, or bail be justified before the attachment is moved for, the sheriff is not liable to an attachment (*j*). The Court of Common Pleas have refused to allow any advantage to be taken of the priority of motion on the same day; therefore, if bail be brought up on the same day on which an attachment has been obtained against the sheriff, that court will permit them to justify and set the attachment aside (*k*). But where the defendant died before an attachment issued, but after the sheriff was in contempt, the attachment was held regular (*l*). The sheriff should, as soon as he is served with the rule to bring in the body, give notice thereof to the bail and the defendant, in order that bail may be put in and perfected, or the defendant be rendered in discharge of his bail, which being done the rule is complied with. Where the sheriff is ruled to bring in the body, he is bound to obey the rule, even though the plaintiff's proceedings have been stayed by injunction (*m*).

Of the attachment, when and how granted.

If on the expiration of the rule to bring in the body, bail above be not put in and perfected, or the defendant be not in custody, the court on motion will grant an attachment against the sheriff (*n*). Or formerly, before the Uniformity of Process Act, if the process were by original, and bail were put in with the filacer of a wrong county, this being held no bail, the court

(*h*) Bertram *v.* Davis, 6 Dowl. 180.

(*i*) Rex *v.* Sheriff of Middlesex, 8 T. R. 464.

(*j*) Thorold *v.* Fisher, 1 H. Blac. 9; Turner *v.* Bristow, 2 Bos. & Pul. 38; Weddall *v.* Berger, 1 Bos. & Pul. 325; Rex *v.* Sheriff of Middlesex, 2 Maule & Sel. 562; *sed vide* Anon. 1 Chit. Rep. 567.

(*k*) Turner *v.* Bristow, 2 Bos. & Pul. 38. In such case the plaintiff is entitled to his costs in moving for the attachment; *id. ibid.*; Jarrat *v.* Creasy, 3 Bos. & Pul. 603. The costs of instructing to move for the attachment where the bail justify before the motion for the attachment is made; Rex *v.* Sheriff of Middlesex, 1 Taunt. 56.

(*l*) Rex *v.* Sheriff of Middlesex, 3 T. R. 133; *sed vide* cases last note.

(*m*) Rex *v.* Sheriff of Middlesex, 1 Dowl. 454.

(*n*) 2 Saund. 61, that is if the rule expire in term on the day after the expiration of the rule, if on the last day in term on that day, 11 East, 191; if in vacation, on the second day of the next term, 8 T. R. 464.

CHAP. VI. SECT. IV.

would grant an attachment (*o*). The attachment is a criminal process, directed to the coroner, when it issues against the present sheriff, or to the present sheriff when it issues against the late sheriff (*p*). Where the coroner is the defendant in the cause, the attachment against the sheriff must issue to elisors in the first instance (*q*). Until the attachment is granted, it is on the plea side of the Court of Queen's Bench; but as soon as the attachment is granted, the proceedings are on the crown side of that court (*r*). The motion for the attachment must be grounded on an affidavit of the service of a copy of the rule, and that the original was shown at the same time; and also that no bail has been put in, or that bail has been put in but not justified. And in the case of a judge's order to bring in the body, the affidavit should also state that the order was made a rule of court in the term next following the order. In the Queen's Bench and Exchequer, it seems that the judge's order may be made a rule of court, and an attachment for not obeying it obtained in one motion, but it seems otherwise in the Common Pleas; and in the Queen's Bench it seems to be necessary to have two *rules* (*s*). Where there are two defendants in one writ, and separate rules have been given to bring in the body of each defendant, it is proper to issue two attachments against the sheriff for not obeying those rules (*t*).

Attachment will be set aside for irregularity.

If any of the proceedings against the sheriff be irregular, the court will set aside the attachment; so if any of the proceedings on the part of the plaintiff relative to bail be irregular, the court will set aside an attachment granted against the sheriff. But the sheriff cannot be relieved on account of the defendant's death after the contempt incurred, but before the attachment issued (*u*).

Or for *laches* on the part of the plaintiff.

If the plaintiff has not moved for his attachment within a reasonable time, the court will set it aside, for by such delay

(*o*) Rex *v.* Sheriff of Middlesex, 1 Chit. Rep. 237; Smith *v.* Miller, 7 T. R. 96; Harris *v.* Calvert, 1 East, 603; *sed vide* Rex *v.* Sheriff of Middlesex, 3 Maule & Sel. 532.

(*p*) Tidd's Prac. 314, 8th edit.; Chit. Archb. Prac. 556, 7th edit.

(*q*) Reg. *v.* Sheriff of Glamorganshire, 1 Dowl. N. S. 308.

(*r*) 1 Tidd's Prac. 314, 8th edit.

(*s*) Barnard *v.* Berger, 1 N. R. 121; Rex *v.* Smithies, 3 T. R. 351. In this last case, the court allowed the plaintiff to make a supplemental affidavit; Arch. 556, 7th edit. See form Append. to chap.

(*t*) Constable *v.* Bristow, 8 Moore, 162.

(*u*) 5 T. R. 134; *sed vide* 2 Maule & Sel. 562.

the sheriff may be deprived of his remedy against the party. Thus where, an attachment having been obtained on the 19th November, at the desire of the sheriff's officer the attachment was not then sued out, nor was it sued out and served on the sheriff until the 19th of March following, the court set aside the attachment as irregular (*x*). So where an attachment was granted against the sheriff for not bringing in the body on the 11th of February, returnable on the 4th of May, and *was not issued till the day* before; in the mean time, on the 19th of March, the defendant became bankrupt; the court set aside the attachment on account of the *laches* of the plaintiff (*y*). Lord Ellenborough, in giving his opinion, said, "there is no occasion to lay down any general rule with respect to the lapse of time which shall be deemed sufficient to discharge the sheriff from the attachment in these cases; but certainly eighty days exclusive is a long time to lay by after the party is armed with the process of the court against the sheriff: and here, in the mean time, an important change of circumstances has taken place by the bankruptcy of the defendant." For the same reason, it is holden that a *cognovit* taken for payment of the debt and costs by instalments discharges the sheriff, although it was agreed that the right of moving for an attachment against him should remain with the plaintiff as a security, in case any of the instalments should not be paid (*z*). But where the plaintiff, at the desire of the sheriff's officer, forbore to enforce an attachment, and two days afterwards applied to the sheriff for the debt and costs, the Court of Common Pleas held that the sheriff was not discharged by the indulgence given to the officer, it not appearing that the sheriff was prejudiced by the delay (*a*). Where the plaintiff had agreed to delay proceedings for a month, at the instance of one of the bail, on payment of debt and costs; the action not being settled, an attachment was obtained against the sheriff, which the court refused to set aside on the application of the bail (*b*). Where the rule to bring in the body

(*x*) Rex *v.* Perring, 3 Bos. & Pul. 151.

(*y*) Rex *v.* Sheriff of Surrey, 9 East, 467; and see Rex *v.* Sheriffs of London, 2 Chit. Rep. 58; Rex *v.* Sheriffs of London, 1 Dowl. & Ry. 163.

(*z*) Rex *v.* Sheriff of Surrey, 1 Taunt. 159; see also West *v.* Ashdown, 1 Bing. 164; 7 Moore, 566, S. C.; Bousfield *v.* Tower, 4 Taunt. 456, Crofts *v.* Johnson, 1 Marsh. 59; 5 Taunt. 319, S. C.

(*a*) Rex *v.* Sheriffs of London, 1 Taunt. 489.

(*b*) Rex *v.* Sheriff of Middlesex, 1 Dowl. & Ry. 388.

CHAP. VI. SECT. IV.

expired on the second day of Michaelmas term, during the vacation after the service of the rule, a judge's order was obtained by consent to stay proceedings, on payment of debt and costs within a month: on a motion to discharge an attachment for not bringing in the body, the Court of Common Pleas was equally divided in opinion, whether the sheriff was discharged or not (c). Where defendant obtained a summons for payment of debt and costs, returnable on the same day as the day on which the defendant should have justified bail, which summons the plaintiff's attorney failed to attend, the summons was renewed for the next day, on which an attachment was obtained against the sheriff, which was set aside for irregularity (d). Since the stat. 1 & 2 Vict. c. 110, the plaintiff does not waive his right to an attachment by declaring in chief (e). And the capias being now a mere collateral proceeding, it seems that the court would in all cases set aside the attachment on putting in and perfecting bail, or payment into court in lieu of bail, or render and payment of costs (f).

Regular attachment, on what terms set aside.

Also, where the attachment is *regular*, it may be stayed or set aside by the favour and indulgence of the court, in order to let in a trial of the merits, or for the benefit of the sheriff, or of the defendant, or his bail (g). Formerly, if the plaintiff had not lost a trial, the court would set aside a regular attachment upon putting in and perfecting bail above, on payment of costs (h). But if a trial had been lost, the court would further require that the attachment should remain in the office, and stand as a security to the plaintiff for the sum recovered (i). And it seems that the attachment would stand as a security as

(c) Rex *v.* The late Sheriff of Middlesex, 2 Bing. 366.

(d) Rex *v.* Sheriff of Middlesex, 5 Bar. & Ald. 746.

(e) Reg. *v.* Sheriff of Montgomeryshire, 1 Dowl. N. S. 388; 9 M. & W. 448, S. C.

(f) *Ante*, p. 167; Chit. Archb. 569, 7th edit.

(g) See Stride *v.* Hill, 1 M. & W. 37.

(h) Hill *v.* Bolt, 4 T. R. 352; Callan *v.* Tye, 2 H. Blac. 235.

(i) Phillips *v.* Whithead, 1 Chit. Rep. 270. The technical term, "lost a trial," signified that by the neglect of the defendant to perfect bail in due time, the plaintiff had been prevented from trying his cause in, and obtaining judgment of, the term in which the writ was returnable. According to the practice of the Courts of Queen's Bench and Common Pleas, a trial was not considered to be lost unless the plaintiff had declared *de bene esse*; 5 Taunt. 608. So decided in K. B., Hil. 5 & 6 Geo. 4. Now, however, (since the 2 Will. 4, c. 39,) there can be no declaration *de bene esse*; and the plaintiff, moreover, cannot be prevented from proceeding to trial by the default of the bail to the sheriff, or of the sheriff, because the original action, being commenced by writ of summons, may go on, though the sheriff do not bring in the body, *i. e.* put in bail above, or the bail to the sheriff do not put in and perfect special bail. *Ante*, p. 167.

well as the bail-bond, where a trial had been lost, although the defendant had been surrendered in discharge of his bail (*j*). The Court of King's Bench refused to discharge so much of a rule to set aside an attachment as required it to stand as a security, at the instance of the sheriff, on the ground of his being no party to the rule in the ensuing term, the application being too late (*k*). But when the sheriff has been guilty of a breach of duty, in discharging the defendant out of custody without the plaintiff's assent, and without taking a bail-bond (*l*); or where he has taken a bail-bond with one surety only (*m*), or an undertaking for the appearance of defendant (*n*), the courts will not set aside a regular attachment. But where by affidavits it appeared that the omission to take a bail-bond was by mistake, on an application by the defendant the court set aside the attachment, on the terms of its remaining in the office as a security (*o*).

Affidavit required in moving to set aside a regular attachment.

By a rule of the Court of King's Bench (*p*), and by a similar rule in the Exchequer (*q*), "No rule shall be drawn up for setting aside an attachment regularly obtained against a sheriff for not bringing in the body, or for staying proceedings regularly commenced on the assignment of any bail-bond, unless the application for such rule shall (if made on the part of the original defendant) be grounded upon an affidavit of merits, or (if made on the part of the sheriff, or bail, or any officer of the sheriff) be grounded upon an affidavit showing that such application is really and truly made on the part of the sheriff, or bail, or officer of the court, (as the case may be), at his or their own expense, and for his or their indemnity only, and without collusion with the original defendant:" and such affidavits are necessary also by the practice of the Court of Common Pleas (*r*). In swearing to merits, an affidavit that the

(*j*) 1 Chit. Rep. 270, n.

(*k*) Lee *v.* Cary, 1 Chit. Rep. 180.

(*l*) Vanderhaden *v.* Britten, 4 Dow. & Ry. 155; Rex *v.* Sheriff of Surry, 7 T. R. 239; Collins *v.* Snuggs, 6 Moore, 111; Rex *v.* Sheriffs of London, 2 B. & Ald. 354; 1 Chit. Rep. 68, S. C.; Rex *v.* Sheriffs of London, *ibid.* 567; Ibbotson *v.* Tindal, 1 Bing. 156; 7 Moore, 552, S. C. And see 1 Bos. & Pul. 225; 2 Bos. & Pul. 35, 246; 1 Esp. 87; 7 East, 606; 1 Taunt. 119; 6 Taunt. 554; 2 Marsh. 261, S. C.

(*m*) Rex *v.* Sheriffs of London, 2 Bing. 227.

(*n*) Fuller *v.* Prest, 7 T. R. 109.

(*o*) Turnbull *v.* Moreton, 1 Chit. Rep. 721.

(*p*) Reg. Gen. M. T. 59 Geo. 3, 2 B. & Ald. 240; 1 Chit. Rep. 348, n. (*a*).

(*q*) H. T. 7 W. 4, 2 M. & W. 219.

(*r*) Hardisty *v.* Storer, 1 N. R. 123.

CHAP. VI. SECT. IV.

defendant has a *good defence* to the action is not sufficient, it must state a *good defence on the merits* (s). An affidavit of merits must be made by the defendant himself (t), or by his attorney or agent, and if the affidavit be made by the attorney, it must show that he is the attorney for the defendant (u); and when such an affidavit is made, it is not necessary to state in the affidavit on whose behalf the application is made (x).

The application may be made by one of the bail on his own affidavit, without an affidavit from the other bail (y). Where, in an affidavit on behalf of the sheriff, the word "*protection*" was used for "indemnity," the affidavit was held to be insufficient (z). And where the affidavit on behalf of bail stated that the application was made their "only indemnity," instead of for their "indemnity only," it was held insufficient (a). On an application by an officer, he need not deny collusion with the bail (b). If the affidavit be defective, the court may allow it to be amended (c).

Extent of the sheriff's liability on the attachment.

If the court will not set the attachment aside, the sheriff is liable to the extent of the sum really due from the defendant to the plaintiff, although it be beyond the sum sworn to, and costs (d); but where a bail-bond has been taken, the sheriff is not liable beyond the penalty of the bond (e) and the costs of the attachment (f). And where several actions were brought at the same time against the acceptor, drawer, and indorser of a bill of exchange; in the action against the acceptor, the sheriff was attached for not bringing in the body, but the court relieved

(s) Grottick *v.* Bailey, 5 Bar. & Ald. 703; 1 D. & R. 155, S. C.; see also Rex *v.* Sheriff of Middlesex, 1 Dowl. 398; Lane *v.* Isaacs, 3 Dowl. 652; Tate *v.* Bodfield, *ibid.* 218; Page *v.* South, 7 Dowl. 412; Bower *v.* King, 1 Dowl. 282; Hallett *v.* Aubrey, *ibid.* 688; Crossby *v.* Innes, 5 Dowl. 566; Scholefield *v.* Huggins, 3 Dowl. 427; Bromley *v.* Gerish, 1 Dowl. & L. 768.

(t) Rex *v.* Sheriff of Middlesex, 1 Chit. Rep. 347.

(u) Bormefor *v.* Russell, 5 Dowl. 546.

(x) Bell *v.* Taylor, 1 Chit. Rep. 572.

(y) Rex *v.* Sheriff of Middlesex, 3 Dowl. 186.

(z) Reg. *v.* Sheriff of Middlesex, 8 A. & E. 938.

(a) Reg. *v.* Sheriff of Cheshire, 6 Dowl. 709; 3 M. & W. 605, S. C.

(b) Rex *v.* Sheriff of Middlesex, 3 Dowl. 194.

(c) Reg. *v.* Sheriff of Cheshire, *supra*; Call *v.* Thelwell, 3 Dowl. 444; 1 C. M. & R. 780, S. C.

(d) Heppel *v.* King, 7 T. R. 370; Stevenson *v.* Cameron, 8 T. R. 29; Fowlds *v.* Mackintosh, 1 H. Blac. 233; see also Rex *v.* Sheriff of Middlesex, *ibid.* 543.

(e) Rex *v.* Sheriff of Middlesex, 3 East, 604; and see the cases cited in the last note.

(f) Rex *v.* Sheriff of Devon, 1 B. & Adol. 159.

the sheriff on payment of the sum due on the bill, and the costs in *that action only* (*g*). The statute of 43 Geo. 3, c. 46, s. 2, made no difference in the extent of the liability of the sheriff, where he has not taken money on the arrest under that act; in such case, now, as before that act, he can only relieve himself on payment of debt and costs (*h*).

What remedy the sheriff has after being obliged to pay the debt and costs on the attachment.

If the sheriff has taken a bail-bond, and is obliged to pay the debt and costs by reason of the defendant's nonappearance, he may reimburse himself by bringing an action on the bail-bond (*i*); but if the sheriff has not taken a bail-bond on the arrest, he cannot maintain an action for the money paid by him under the attachment (*k*), nor can he detain the defendant in custody for it (*l*). Where the defendant has put in but not justified bail, and to an action on the bail-bond pleads *comperuit ad diem*, the court will order the recognizance to be struck off the file (*m*). The Court of Common Pleas, in one case, on motion, ordered the date of the defendant's appearance to be entered in the filacer's book, after issue joined on the plea of *comperuit ad diem* in an action on a bail-bond (*n*).

SECTION V.

Actions against the Sheriff for Escape, &c.

What shall be an escape.

If the sheriff arrest the defendant, and discharge him without taking a bail-bond, but have him not at the return of the writ, it is an escape (*o*); and if the defendant be in the sheriff's custody at the return of the writ, but be afterwards allowed to go at large without the consent, or without the order of a court of competent jurisdiction, or if the defendant be rescued from the county gaol (*p*), or if, being in custody in the county gaol

(*g*) Rex *v.* Sheriffs of London, 2 Bar. & Ald. 192.

(*h*) Rex *v.* Sheriffs of London, 9 East, 316.

(*i*) The money is generally paid by the officer on the attachment, who brings the action on the bail-bond in the name of the sheriff.

(*k*) Pitcher *v.* Bailey, 8 East, 171.

(*l*) Rimmer *v.* Turner, 3 Dowl. 601.

(*m*) Leigh *v.* Bertles, 1 Marsh. 520; 6 Taunt. 167, S. C.

(*n*) Austen *v.* Fenton, 1 Taunt. 23.

(*o*) See Bac. Abr. Escape (D); Com. Dig. Escape (B); Cro. Jac. 419; S. C. 1 Roll. Rep. 388, 440.

(*p*) See *ibid.*; Stra. 435.

CHAP. VI. SECT. V.

after the writ is returnable, he be taken from the gaol to another place in the same county, even in the gaoler's custody (*q*), it is an escape, although for such escape no action will lie against the sheriff, unless the plaintiff has sustained some actual damage, either from having been delayed in his suit or otherwise (*r*).

Re-caption.

Before the Uniformity of Process Act, if the sheriff allowed a person arrested by him on *mesne process* to go at large, he might retake him at any time before the return of the writ (*s*); but since the Uniformity of Process Act, the day of the execution of the writ being the return day of it, it seems that the recapture ought to be on that day (*t*); and even afterwards the sheriff may put in bail at the return of the writ, which bail may take and render the defendant (*u*); or if the defendant escape out of custody, without the privity of the sheriff or his officer, he may be retaken either before or after the return of the writ on fresh pursuit (*x*), even on a Sunday (*y*), or although he has been declared a bankrupt after his escape, and at the time of the retaking had the protection from arrest giving him by the commissioners (*z*); but after the sheriff has discharged the defendant with the consent of the plaintiff, he cannot retake him for his fees (*a*). If a person obstructs the sheriff from retaking a person after his escape, the court will grant an attachment for such obstruction (*b*).

Escape-warrant.

It may not be an improper place to introduce here the provisions of the statute of 1 Anne, c. 6, respecting escape-warrants. By that statute it is provided, that if any person in the King's Bench or Fleet Prisons, in execution or on mesne process, or upon contempt for not performing orders or decrees (*c*), shall escape from such prisons, a judge of the court from which he

(*q*) Williams *v.* Mostyn, 4 M. & W. 145.

(*r*) *Ibid.*; Planck *v.* Anderson, 5 T. R. 37; Randell *v.* Wheble, 10 A. & E. 719; Brown *v.* Jarvis, 1 M. & W. 704; see also Wylie *v.* Birch, 4 Q. B. 566; 3 G. & D. 629, S. C.

(*s*) Atkinson *v.* Matteson, 3 T. R. 172; see also Fuller *v.* Prest, 7 T. R. 109.

(*t*) Chit. Arch. 543, 7th edit.

(*u*) Rex *v.* Butcher and others, Peake, N. P. C. 169; Evans *v.* Swete, 2 Bing. 271; Berchere *v.* Colson, Stra. 876; see also 7 T. R. 572; Taylor *v.* Evans, 1 Bing. 367; 8 Moore, 398, S. C.

(*x*) Com. Dig. Escape (E).

(*y*) Anon. 6 Mod. 231, 95.

(*z*) Anderson *v.* Hampton, 1 B. & Ald. 308.

(*a*) Willing *v.* Goad, Stra. 909.

(*b*) See Miller *v.* Knox, 4 Bing. N. C. 574; Arch. 545, 7th edit.

(*c*) On an attachment against A., B. opposes the execution, and is committed for contempt: this is not a contempt within this act; Hinchliffe *v.* Payne, Stra. 99.

was committed (*d*), on the oath of one or more credible witnessses (*e*), may grant an escape-warrant, on the application of any person whatsoever who may demand the same, which warrant is to have effect all over England; and every sheriff in his respective county has power to execute it in his county, and to commit him to the county gaol, to be kept without bail or mainprize (*f*), until judgment be satisfied or reversed, or the contempt, whereon he was committed, purged, or until he have verdict in his favour (*g*), if committed on *mesne process*.

Where the plaintiff proceeds against the sheriff by action, it is usual to insert three counts in the declaration: 1st, for an escape; 2dly, for not arresting the defendant; 3dly, for not assigning the bail-bond on request.

For what default the sheriff is liable to an action.

Where the defendant has been arrested, and has given a bail-bond for his appearance at the return of the writ, and does not appear, the sheriff is not liable to an action for an escape, for he was obliged by the statute to take bail (*h*). The only mode of proceeding in such case against the sheriff is by attachment. And where the plaintiff was told by a clerk, on application at the sheriff's office, that no bail-bond had been taken, and brought an action for an escape against the sheriff, but had no count in his declaration for not assigning the bail-bond, and it appeared in evidence that a bond had been taken, the plaintiff was nonsuited, which nonsuit the court refused to set aside (*i*). But if the defendant have not given a bond, and bail be not put in and perfected in due time, or the defendant be not in custody at the return of the writ, the sheriff is liable to an action for an es-

(*d*) If the defendant has been turned over from the King's Bench to the Fleet by the Court of Common Pleas, a judge of either court may grant the warrant; Rex *v.* Dunbar, 10 Geo. 1, 8 Mod. 240.

(*e*) The oath may be taken before a commissioner in the country; 5 Ann. c. 9, s. 2.

(*f*) Nor can he be discharged on bringing the money into court, Hothershell *v.* Bows, 6 Mod. 21; nor shall he be allowed a day-rule, Cotton *v.* Martin, 6 Mod. 63.

(*g*) Where, by the practice of the court, the defendant was supersedable at the time of his escape, the court will supersede an escape-warrant obtained thereon; Webb *v.* Thompson, 1 Stra. 401.

(*h*) Posterne *v.* Hanson, 2 Saund. 61; Benson *v.* Welby, *ib.* 154; Anon. 1 Vent. 55; Parker *v.* Welby, *ib.* 85; Ellis *v.* Yarborough, 1 Mod. 227; 2 Mod. 177, S. C.; Grovenor *v.* Soame, 6 Mod. 122; Kitton *v.* Fag, 10 Mod. 288; Page *v.* Tulse, 2 Mod. 83; 1 Mod. 240, 244, S.C.; Bentley *v.* Hoare, 1 Lev. 86; Allen *v.* Robinson, 1 Sid. 22; Barton *v.* Aldeworth, Cro. Eliz. 624.

(*i*) Mendez *v.* Bridges, 5 Taunt. 325.

CHAP. VI. SECT. V.

cape (*k*). And if the sheriff has taken a bail-bond on the arrest, but the defendant do not appear at the return of the writ, an action on the case will lie against the sheriff if he refuse to assign the bail-bond *on request* (*l*). Also, if the officer will not arrest the defendant when he has notice of his being in the county, and he might have arrested him, the sheriff is liable to an action on the case, provided the defendant do not appear at the return of the writ, and provided also that the plaintiff has sustained any damage by reason of the sheriff's neglect (*m*). The plaintiff is not, however, bound to give information to the sheriff so as to enable him to arrest and identify the defendant, for the sheriff himself is bound to make due inquiries after the defendant for the purpose of finding him (*n*). But the sheriff is not liable to an action for an escape for discharging a defendant out of custody who was misnamed in the writ, although he had assumed the name by which he was sued in the particular transaction out of which the action arose (*o*). As the duty of the sheriff is merely to have the defendant at the return of the writ, an action against the sheriff will be defeated if bail be put in before the expiration of the rule to bring in the body, although after an action for an escape commenced (*p*). And after an action commenced against the sheriff, the putting in and perfecting bail of the term in which the writ is returnable is an answer to such action (*q*); but bail put in of a subsequent term would be no answer to such action (*r*). And where bail is put in to defeat an action commenced against the sheriff, the plaintiff should oppose the justification (*s*); or if the bail have been allowed to justify without opposition, the court, on

(*k*) Fuller *v.* Prest, 7 T. R. 109; Webb *v.* Matthews, 1 Bos. & Pul. 225; Atkinson *v.* Matteson, 2 T. R. 176, 177.

(*l*) Stamper *v.* Milborne, 7 T. R. 122. It is always advisable to demand an assignment of the bail-bond before commencing an action against the sheriff; see Mendez *v.* Bridges, 5 Taunt. 325.

(*m*) Brown *v.* Jarvis, 1 M. & W. 704; 5 Dowl. 285, S. C.; Williams *v.* Mostyn, 4 M. & W. 145.

(*n*) Dyke *v.* Duke, 4 Bing. 197.

(*o*) Morgan *v.* Bridges, 1 Bar. & Ald. 647; *ante*, p. 70.

(*p*) Pariente *v.* Plumbtree, 2 Bos. & Pul. 36; Murray *v.* Durand, 1 Esp. 87.

(*q*) Allingham *v.* Flower, 2 Bos. & Pul. 246; but the bail must be *perfected*, 7 East, 607. *Sed vide* Webb *v.* Matthew, 1 Bos. & Pul. 225, and the judgment of Gibbs, C. J., in Birn *v.* Bond, 6 Taunt. 554; 2 Marsh. 261, S. C.

(*r*) Moses *v.* Norris, 4 M. & Sel. 397.

(*s*) Fuller *v.* Prest, 7 T. R. 109; Webb *v.* Matthew, 1 Bos. & Pul. 225. See also Birn *v.* Bond, 6 Taunt. 554; 2 Marsh. 261, S. C.

motion, will set aside the allowance of bail on payment of the costs of justification (*t*). But where the defendant was rendered on the day of the expiration of the rule to bring in the body, the Court of Exchequer refused to set aside the allowance of bail obtained after an action commenced against the sheriff for an escape, though no bail-bond had been taken, nor bail above put in in due time (*u*).

The venue in an action on the case for an escape is transitory (*v*).

The declaration.

In a declaration in an action against a sheriff for not performing his duty, framed in either of the three ways above mentioned, it must be alleged that the plaintiff had a cause of action against the defendant in the original action, otherwise the declaration is bad on demurrer (*x*). But it seems to be sufficient to allege generally that the plaintiff had a cause of action, without minutely stating the cause of action with the same precision as in an action against the defendant himself (*y*). The declaration must allege the issuing of the process and the delivery to the sheriff within one month after such issuing, or it will, it seems, be bad on special demurrer (*z*). A variance in the description of the process in the declaration, in an action for not arresting the defendant, or for escape on *mesne process*, or in any other action against the sheriff for misconduct or negligence in executing such process, is fatal (unless amended under 3 & 4 Will. 4, c. 42, s. 23); thus (when such writs were in use) where a *latitat* in trespass, with an *ac etiam*, was stated to be a *latitat* in a plea of trespass, the variance was held fatal (*a*). And where in the declaration it was alleged that the party was arrested under a writ indorsed for bail by virtue of an affidavit *now*

(*t*) How *v*. Lacey, 1 Taunt. 119; Bosanquet *v*. Simpson, Tidd's Practice, 235, 8th edit. And see Leigh *v*. Bertles, 1 Marsh. 520.

(*u*) Morley *v*. Cole, 1 Price, 103.

(*v*) Griffith *v*. Walker, 1 Wils. 336; Gawdy's case, Dyer, 278 b; Anon. 2 Salk. 669, 670.

(*x*) Gunter *v*. Cleyton, 2 Lev. 85; Alexander *v*. Macauley, 4 T. R. 611; 2 Saund. 150 a, n. 1.

(*y*) Com. Dig. Pleader (E) 18, 2 P. 1; Lutw. 110. See the precedents, 2 Chitty's Pleading, 552, 7th edit.; 2 Saund. 150; 8 Went. Ind. xxxiii. It is not necessary to state the precise sum due, 2 Lev. 85; if the declaration state the debt to be for goods sold, it must be so proved, 2 Esp. 476; a declaration stating the debt to be for goods sold, &c., proof of goods sold on credit was held to be a fatal variance, 5 Esp. 102.

(*z*) 1 & 2 Vict. c. 110, s. 3; Randell *v*. Wheble, 10 A. & E. 719; 2 P. & D. 602, S. C.

(*a*) Gunter *v*. Cleyton, 2 Lev. 85; Bull. N. P. 66.

CHAP. VI. SECT. V.

on record, but no affidavit was produced upon the trial, the Court of Common Pleas held that the plaintiff had been properly nonsuited (*b*). It is sufficient to allege that the writ was duly indorsed for "bail," without adding "by virtue of an affidavit made and filed of record(*c*)." But in an action for an escape, where a *latitat* against *Douner* and two others, was stated as a *latitat* against *Douner* and *J. Doe*, this was ruled to be no variance (*d*). Where the declaration stated a writ "of the king," and on the trial a writ was produced, properly tested as to the date and the name of the chief justice, but a mistake was made of George the *Third* instead of George the *Fourth*, it was held no variance (*e*).

The declaration should also specially allege that the plaintiff has sustained damage by reason of the sheriff's default (*f*), and that eight days have elapsed since such default (*g*).

Declaration in an action for an escape.

In the action for an escape of a debtor on *mesne process*, it must be alleged in the declaration that the debtor was arrested, and that the sheriff without the leave of the plaintiff allowed him to go at large. Under an allegation that the sheriff *voluntarily* permitted the debtor to escape, a negligent escape may be given in evidence, and *vice versâ* (*h*).

The precedents of declarations in actions for escapes usually aver that the defendant in the original action did not appear or put in special bail according to the exigency of the writ (*i*); but it is sufficient to state that the sheriff had not the body of the defendant in court at the return of the writ (*k*). If the sheriff has returned the writ, it is usual to state the return,

(*b*) Webb *v.* Herne, 1 Bos. & Pul. 281. *Sed quære*, see Williams *v.* The Sheriff of Middlesex, Guildhall, 25th July, 1817, before Abbott, J., note to 2 Chit. Pleading, p. 205, 3d edit. In an action for escape, the declaration stated the writ to have been indorsed for 24*l.*, but the writ when produced was 24*l.* and upwards, besides, &c., this was held no variance. And see Wigley *v.* Jones, 5 East, 440; Stark. on Evid. part 4, p. 1336, n. (*o*). The allegation that the debt was sworn to is unnecessary; Whiskard *v.* Wilder, 1 Burr. 330.

(*c*) Nightingale *v.* Wilcoxon, 10 B. & C. 202; 4 Bing. 510, S. C., in error.

(*d*) Hendray *v.* Spencer, cited in Rex *v.* Pippott, 1 T. R. 238.

(*e*) Elvin *v.* Drummond, 4 Bing. 278; 1 M. & P. 88, S. C.

(*f*) Randell *v.* Wheble, 10 Ad. & Ell. 719; 2 P. & D. 602 S. C.; Brown *v.* Jarvis, 1 M. & W. 704; Williams *v.* Mostyn, 4 M. & W. 145.

(*g*) Randell *v.* Wheble, *supra*.

(*h*) Sir Ralph Bovey's case, 1 Vent. 217; 3 Keb. 55, S. C.; Bonafons *v.* Walker, 2 T. R. 126; O'Neil *v.* Marson, 5 Burr. 2812.

(*i*) See precedents, 3 Went. 456, 482; 2 Chitt. Plead. 554, 7th edit.

(*k*) Appleton *v.* Burr, Cro. Eliz. 289; Stovin *v.* Perring, 2 Bos. & Pul. 561.

but this seems to be unnecessary, as the escape is the gist of the action (*l*).

In an action for not arresting the defendant.

In an action against a sheriff for not arresting the debtor when he had an opportunity, it should be alleged that the debtor was within the sheriff's bailiwick, and might have been arrested if the sheriff had chosen so to do, yet the sheriff would not, although often requested, arrest the defendant (*m*). In such action it is not necessary to allege that the sheriff had notice that the defendant was in his bailiwick (*n*).

Pleas.

The plea of not guilty, in an action for an escape on a bailable capias, will operate as a denial of the neglect or default of the sheriff or his officers, but not of the debt or preliminary proceedings; and in an action for not arresting, or for not assigning the bail-bond, the plea of not guilty will operate as a denial only of the breach of duty or wrongful act alleged to have been committed by the defendant, and not of the facts stated in the inducement (*o*). If any of those facts, therefore, e. g. the issuing of the writ, the delivery thereof to the sheriff, the arrest, or the taking of the bail-bond, are denied, they must be specially traversed.

Evidence in such actions.

In an action against a sheriff for an *escape* on *mesne process* the plaintiff must (if called upon to do so by the pleadings) prove the cause of action in the original suit, the issuing and delivery of the writ to the sheriff within a month after the date thereof (*p*), the arrest and the escape. In the action for *not arresting a debtor*, he must in like manner prove the original debt for which the process issued, the writ and delivery to the sheriff, notice to the officer that the debtor was in his bailiwick, and that he refused to arrest him. In the action for not assigning the bail-bond, the same evidence of the debt, and of the issuing and delivery of the writ to the sheriff, is necessary as in the two preceding actions; and the arrest and the giving of the bail-bond, with the demand and refusal to assign the bond, are also, if traversed, necessary to be proved in order to support such action.

The plaintiff must prove his cause of action against the

(*l*) 2 Saund. 155, n. (5).

(*m*) See precedents, 2 Chitt. Plead. 340, 3d edit.; 8 Went. 487, 501.

(*n*) Dean and Chapter of Hereford *v*. Macnamara, 5 Dowl. & Ry. 95.

(*o*) Reg. Gen. H. T. 4 W. 4.

(*p*) Randell *v*. Wheble, 10 Ad. & Ell. 719; 2 P. & D. 602, S. C.

CHAP. VI. SECT. V.

Proof of the original cause of action.

debtor in the original action (*q*); and any evidence which would be admissible against the defendant in the original action will be evidence in the action against the sheriff (*r*); even an admission of the debtor as to the existence and amount of the debt, made previously to the default, is evidence for this purpose; thus, where the debtor was sued as the drawer of a bill of exchange, proof of the acknowledgment by him that he received notice of the dishonour, is evidence of that fact in an action of escape against the sheriff (*s*). So also, an acknowledgment of the debt made after the arrest and before the escape would be evidence against the sheriff (*t*).

Proof of the issuing of the writ.

If the process has been returned and filed, an examined copy of the writ and return will be sufficient evidence of the issuing and delivery of the writ (*u*). If the writ has not been returned, as regularly it ought to be, the plaintiff will have to establish that fact by proof of the requisite search at the treasury; and after proving the delivery of the writ to the under-sheriff, or to his deputy in London (*x*), or at the sheriff's office, and a notice to produce the original, secondary evidence of the process will be admitted (*y*).

The indorsement by the sheriff of *non est inventus* is sufficient evidence of the delivery of the writ to him (*z*).

Proof to connect the sheriff with the officer.

In order to prove the default in the sheriff, he must be connected with the officer who suffered the debtor to escape, or who refused to arrest him, by proving the issuing of a warrant from the sheriff's office to arrest the defendant.

Proof of the escape.

In an action for an escape, direct evidence that the debtor was in the custody of the sheriff or his officer, and by him suffered to escape, must be given. The proof, however, of the

(*q*) Alexander *v.* Macauley, 4 T. R. 611; Parker *v.* Fenn, 2 Esp. N. P. C. 476, n. As to what has been held a variance between the proof and the statement of the debt, see *ante*, 183, n. (*y*). 2 Lev. 85; Bull. N. P. 66; 5 Esp. N. P. C. 162.

(*r*) Gibbon *v.* Coggon, 2 Camp. 188; Sloman *v.* Herne, 2 Esp. N. P. C. 695.

(*s*) Williams *v.* Bridges, 2 Stark. 42.

(*t*) Rogers *v.* Jones, 7 B. & C. 89, Bayley, J.

(*u*) Blatch *v.* Archer, Cowp. 63; Tildar *v.* Sutton, Bull. N. P. 66; M'Neil *v.* Richard, 1 Esp. N. P. C. 269; Jones *v.* Wood. 3 Camp. 229; Fairlie *v.* Birch, 3 Camp. 397.

(*x*) Woodland *v.* Fuller, 11 Ad. & Ell. 859.

(*y*) 2 Phill. Evid. 222. See also Stark. Evid. part 4, 1335. As to what shall be a variance between the allegation and proof of the process, see *ante*, 183.

(*z*) Blatch *v.* Archer, Cowp. 63; See also Cook *v.* Round, 1 M. & Rob. 512, Tindal, C. J.

sheriff's return of *cepi corpus,* and that the party neither put in bail above, nor was in the sheriff's custody at the return of the writ, will dispense with such evidence (*b*).

The arrest may be proved by producing the sheriff's return of *cepi corpus et paratum habeo,* and the latter words of the return will not preclude the plaintiff from proving that the prisoner was at large after the return, and no bail-bond lodged with the sheriff (*c*). It is no answer to a voluntary escape on a bailable capias to say that the debtor was arrested by the plaintiff on a second capias directed to another sheriff, and that he authorized his discharge from such second capias without a bail-bond or deposit of the debt and costs (*d*).

Proof of failing to arrest defendant.

Proof that the officer had an opportunity to arrest the debtor and neglected so to do, is necessary in the action for not arresting. It is the officer's duty to search and make the arrest, therefore if the debtor follows his daily occupation and does not abscond, the sheriff is responsible; the sheriff, or under-sheriff, or bailiff, who has the execution of the writ, must however be aware of the fact that the defendant is within the county (*e*). The evidence in such action generally is, that the bailiff was informed where the debtor was to be found; notice to the under-sheriff's agent in town will not be sufficient notice to the sheriff (*f*).

The writ being, since the Uniformity of Process Act, returnable immediately, the sheriff has not, as of course, the whole of the month from the issuing to execute it, but he must arrest as soon as he reasonably can (*g*). Where the declaration was for an escape, and the evidence was of a neglect to arrest, the judge at nisi prius refused to allow an amendment under 3 & 4 Will. 4, c. 42, s. 23, but allowed the case of negligent omission to arrest to be proved, which was done, and the finding of the jury, with 30*l.* damages, was specially indorsed on the record under sect. 24, and the court afterwards gave judgment for the plaintiff according to the right of the case, the variance being immaterial, and the defendant not being prejudiced in his defence (*h*).

(*b*) Fairlie *v.* Birch, 3 Camp. 397; but a return of *non est inventus* is only evidence of the delivery of the writ to the sheriff; Cowp. 65. See Adey *v.* Bridges, 2 Starkie, 189.

(*c*) Neck *v.* Humphrey, 3 Ad. & Ell. 130.

(*d*) Woodman *v.* Gist, 2 Jur. 942.

(*e*) 2 Phil. Evid. 222, 1st edit.; Stark. on Evid. part 4, 1339.

(*f*) Gibbon *v.* Coggon, 2 Camp. 189.

(*g*) Brown *v.* Jarvis, 1 M. & W. 704.

(*h*) Guest *v.* Elwes, 5 A. & E. 118.

Evidence of not assigning the bail bond.

In the action for not assigning the bail-bond, the fact that the debtor gave a bail-bond should be regularly proved. Notice to produce the bond should be given; and the request to assign it made at the under-sheriff's office, with the refusal, should be proved.

Admissions of the under-sheriff.

The admissions of an escape by the under-sheriff are evidence in an action against the sheriff for an escape (*i*); but a mere assertion at the under-sheriff's office that no bail-bond had been taken is not conclusive evidence of that fact in an action against the sheriff (*k*). The admissions of a sheriff's bound bailiff are no evidence in an action against the sheriff, until the connection between the sheriff and the bailiff be proved (*l*). But when once the bailiff is identified with the sheriff by evidence, then whatever the bailiff had admitted in evidence against the sheriff, as admissions of the bailiff when asked by the plaintiff's attorney why he did not execute the writ, are evidence against the sheriff (*m*): so declarations made by the bailiff whilst he has the debtor in his custody, are evidence in an action against the sheriff (*n*).

Proof on the part of the defendant.

It is competent for the defendant (the sheriff), the facts being properly pleaded to enable him to do so, to show that bail above were put in of the term in which the writ was returnable, or that the defendant was rendered in due time (*o*). If the action be brought for not arresting the debtor, or for an escape, the sheriff may defeat the action by showing that he took a bail-bond on the arrest (*p*). But in such case he must prove that he took a valid bail bond (*q*).

Damages.

As the plaintiff, in an action for an escape, is only entitled to recover what damages the jury choose to give him, he must prove any damnification that he has sustained by the sheriff's default (*r*). And he must prove some damnification, to enable him to recover at all (*s*).

(*i*) Yabsley *v.* Doble, 1 Ld. Raym. 190; 2 Phill. Evid. 218, 1st edit.
(*k*) Mendez *v.* Bridges, 5 Taunt. 325.
(*l*) Drake *v.* Sykes, 7 T. R. 113.
(*m*) North *v.* Miles, 1 Camp. 389.
(*n*) Bowsher *v.* Calley, 1 Camp. 391, n.
(*o*) Allingham *v.* Flower, 2 Bos. & Pul. 246.
(*p*) Mendez *v.* Bridges, 5 Taunt. 325.
(*q*) Holden *v.* Raphael, 4 A. & E. 228.
(*r*) Barker *v.* Green, 2 Bing. 317.
(*s*) Williams *v.* Mostyn, 4 M. & W. 145.

CHAPTER VII.

CAPIAS AD SATISFACIENDUM.

SECT. I.—*In what Cases it lies—The Arrest—The Sheriff's Duty after the Arrest.—Poundage.—Return.—Prisoner, how discharged.*

SECT. II.—*Escape.—What shall be said to be an Escape.—When the Sheriff shall be excused.—Voluntary and negligent.—Of the Action for Escape; by whom, against whom, it lies.—Declaration.—Pleas.—Evidence.—Action over, by the Sheriff for his Indemnity, where the Defendant has escaped.*

SECTION I.

Ca. Sa. how executed.

Of the nature of the writ.

THE writ of *capias ad satisfaciendum* is a writ of execution directed to the sheriff, commanding him to take the body of the defendant, and him safely keep, so that he may have his body in court immediately after the execution thereof, or on a return day named in the writ, to satisfy the plaintiff.

When it lies.

The writ lies in all cases within a year from the time of the judgment where a *capias ad respondendum* would have lain before the passing of the 1 & 2 Vict. c. 110; and in several cases where a *capias ad respondendum* would not lie before the passing of that statute (*a*). Thus a *ca. sa.* always lies against an attorney, although before the passing of the 1 & 2 Vict. c. 110, an attorney could not be holden to bail (*b*). An infant (*c*) or a *feme covert* (*d*) is liable to be taken on a *ca. sa.*; but if the judgment

(*a*) For the authority by which the *capias* in the several actions is given, see Chitty's Archbold's Prac. 448, 7th ed. And see Bac. Abr. Execution (C) 3. A *ca. sa.* does not lie in an execution of damages in dower; Tidd's Prac. 1066, 8th edit.; 3 Salk. 286.

(*b*) Chit. Archb. Practice, 7th ed. 449.

(*c*) Gardiner *v.* Holt, 2 Stra. 1217; Madox *v.* Eden, 1 Bos. & Pul. 480; see also Finlay *v.* Jowle, 13 East, 6; Dow *v.* Clark, 2 Dowl. 302.

(*d*) Tidd's Pr. 1066, 1067, 8th ed.

CHAP. VII. SECT. I.

was obtained against the husband and wife (*e*), the courts will, in their discretion, discharge the wife if she be taken on a *ca. sa.*, unless she has separate property out of which the demand can be satisfied; but before she will be entitled to her discharge it must appear that she has no such separate property, or that there is fraud and collusion between the plaintiff and her husband to keep her in prison (*f*). Where grounds are shown for supposing that the wife has separate property, the onus of proving that she has none is thrown upon her, and she must in her affidavit swear not only that she is not entitled, but also that no person is entitled in trust for her (*g*). So also bail may be taken in execution on a *ca. sa.* (*h*). So may executors or administrators, if a devastavit has been returned (*i*), but not otherwise (*j*).

When it does not lie.

The 7 & 8 Vict. c. 96, s. 57, enacts, "that from and after the passing of this act, no person shall be taken or charged in execution upon any judgment obtained in any of her majesty's superior courts, or in any county court, court of requests, or other inferior court, in any action for the recovery of any debt wherein the sum recovered shall not exceed the sum of twenty pounds, exclusive of the costs recovered by such judgment (*k*)." And sect. 59 enacts, "that if at any time it shall appear to the judge who shall try such cause, being either a judge of one of the superior courts, or a barrister or attorney at law, that the defendant, in incurring the debt or liability which may be the subject of demand, has obtained credit from the plaintiff under false pretences, or with a fraudulent intent, or has wilfully contracted such debt or liability without having at the same time a reasonable assurance of being able to pay or discharge the same, or shall have made, or caused to be made, any gift, delivery, or

Where sum recovered is under 20*l.*

(*e*) *Secus*, where the action was commenced against the wife when sole, and judgment is, after her marriage, obtained against her in her name when sole; Beynon *v.* Jones, 15 M. & W. 566.

(*f*) See Chalk *v.* Deacon, 6 B. M. 128; Sparkes *v.* Bell, 8 B. & C. 3; Bayley, J., Hoad *v.* Matthews, 2 Dowl. 149; Chit. Arch. Pr. 7th ed. 449.

(*g*) Ferguson *v.* Clayworth, 6 Q.B. 269.

(*h*) Goodchild *v.* Chaworth, 2 Str. 822; 3 Salk. 286; Troughton & Clark, 2 Taunt. 113, and see 2 Marsh. 187, n.

(*i*) Chit. Arch. Pr. 7th ed. 882.

(*j*) *Ibid.*; Ward *v.* Thomas, 2 Dowl. 87.

(*k*) If the plaintiff sue upon the judgment for debt and costs, and in that action recover to the amount of 20*l.*, the defendant may be taken in execution on the judgment in that action; Hopkins *v.* Freeman, 13 M. & W. 372; Joseph *v.* Buxton, 1 C. B. 221; Mason *v.* Nicholls, 14 M. & W. 118.

transfer of any personal property, or shall have removed or concealed the same with an intent to defraud his creditors, or any of them, it shall be lawful for such judge, if he shall think fit, to order that such defendant may be taken and detained in execution upon such judgment in like manner and for such time as he might have been if this act had not been passed, or for any time not exceeding six calendar months in any case in which the time for which a person taken in execution under process issuing out of any such court could lawfully be detained in custody, according to the constitution of the said court, before the passing of this act, in less than six calendar months, whether or not execution against the goods and chattels of such defendant shall have issued as hereinafter provided (*l*)."

Against privileged persons.

But a *ca. sa.* does not lie against members of the royal family, or their servants, against peers or peeresses, or members of the House of Commons during the time of privilege (*m*); and a *ca. sa.* issued against a member of the House of Commons, in an action of assumpsit, is irregular, even although it is issued in order to ground proceedings to outlawry, and is delivered to the sheriff with that view, and with a direction to be returned *non est inventus* (*n*). Neither will a *ca. sa.* lie against ambassadors or their servants (*o*); or against corporators or hundredors (*p*); or against executors or administrators, for debts of their testators or intestates, unless a *devastavit* be returned (*q*); or against an heir for a debt to be levied of the lands descended (*r*); or against seamen or soldiers in her majesty's service, unless in actions for debts for *30l.* or upwards, contracted before they entered the service (*s*); or against bankrupts who have obtained their certificates for any debt which might have been proved under their commission (*t*); or against persons discharged under the insolvent

(*l*) See 8 & 9 Vict. c. 127, and 9 & 10 Vict. c. 95.

(*m*) *Ante*, p. 134, 135. See 1 Leon. 173; Bartlett *v.* Hebbes, 5 T. R. 686.

(*n*) Cassidy *v.* Steuart, 2 Man. & G. 437; see also Butcher *v.* Steuart, 1 Dowl. N. S. 620. But where judgment of respondeas ouster was given on a plea of peerage, and judgment was afterwards obtained for the plaintiff, the court refused to set aside a *ca. sa.* which was issued against the defendant on an affidavit of peerage; Digby *v.* Alexander, 9 Bing. 412.

(*o*) See *ante*, p. 136.

(*p*) Chit. Arch. Pr. 7th ed. 449, 473; Tidd's Prac. 1066, 8th ed.

(*q*) Brooke's Abr. Execution, 12; Tidd's Prac. 1066, 8th edit.; Chit. Arch. Pr. 882, 7th ed.; Ward *v.* Thomas, 2 Dowl. 87.

(*r*) 2 Saund. 7, n. (4).

(*s*) See the statutes and cases collected, Chit. Arch. Pr. 7th ed. 474, 475.

(*t*) 5 & 6 Vict. c. 122, s. 42.

CHAP. VII. SECT. I.

act (u), for debts contracted before such discharge; or against an insolvent under the judgment entered up on the warrant of attorney executed by him on obtaining his discharge (x); or against any person who has obtained an interim order of protection under the provisions of the statute 5 & 6 Vict. c. 116, s. 13, during the time mentioned in the order (y).

If any person privileged from arrest (excepting members of parliament and ambassadors) be arrested on a *ca. sa.*, it is not advisable to discharge such person, unless under the order of the court or a judge, for the sheriff does it on his own responsibility (z).

A writ of *ca. sa.* issued before the return of a *fi. fa.*, which has been executed on the defendant's goods, is irregular (a), even though the whole amount levied under the *fi. fa.* has been swallowed up in discharging the landlord's claim for rent, and in part payment of the expenses of the execution (b). But if no levy at all has been made on the defendant's goods—thus if the sheriff seizes under the *fi. fa.* goods already *in custodia legis*, or assigned under a bill of sale (c); or goods which the defendant declares "he has sold to cheat the plaintiff," and so induces the sheriff to withdraw from possession (d); in such case the *ca. sa.* may be executed before the return of the *fi. fa.* (e). But a *ca. sa.* may issue before the return of, or even at the same time as a *fi. fa.*, although they cannot both be executed (f). A defendant arrested on a *ca. sa.*, and discharged on account of irregularity, may be taken on a second *ca. sa.* on the same judgment (g). A *ca. sa.* cannot issue after an elegit, if lands have been taken under such writ (h). But the sheriff

(u) 1 & 2 Vict. c. 110, s. 90.

(x) See Rivett *v.* Lark, 3 Dowl. 62.

(y) See Marsh *v.* Woolley, 1 Dowl. & L. 84.

(z) Sherwood *v.* Benson, 4 Taunt. 631; see also *per cur.* in Watson *v.* Carroll, 4 M. & W. 592.

(a) Miller *v.* Parnell, 6 Taunt. 370; 2 Marsh. 78, S. C.; Chapman *v.* Bowlby, 8 M. & W. 249.

(b) Hodgkinson *v.* Whalley, 2 C. & J. 86; 1 Dowl. 298, S.C.; Lawes *v.* Codrington, 1 Dowl. 30.

(c) Dicas *v.* Warne, 2 Dowl. 762; 11 Bing. 341, S.C.; Edmond *v.* Ross, 9 Price, 512.

(d) Knight *v.* Coleby, 5 M. & W. 274. This case was decided upon the ground that the defendant, having once denied the goods to be his, could not afterwards set up the *fraudulent* sale to show that they were liable to seizure.

(e) See the cases above cited; also 2 Man. & G. 914, note (c).

(f) Primrose *v.* Gibson, 2 Dowl. & Ry. 193.

(g) Merchant *v.* Frankis, 3 Q. B. 1.

(h) Bac. Abr. Execution (D); otherwise if the sheriff return *nihil* as to the lands, see 1 Archbold's Prac. 446, 7th edit.

may justify arresting a defendant under an irregular *ca. sa.*, for he is bound to execute the process of the court without inquiring into its regularity (*i*).

When to be executed.

The writ of *ca. sa.* runs until it is executed, and therefore an arrest may be made upon it even although more than a year has elapsed since its date (*k*).

The arrest on a *ca. sa.* may be made at the same time, in the same places, and in the same manner, as an arrest on *mesne* process, and the sheriff's duty in either case is the same (*l*). In an action for negligently omitting to arrest a debtor on a *ca. sa.*, the plaintiff will be entitled to nominal damages, even though he has sustained no actual damage, if the jury find that the sheriff has been guilty of a default (*m*).

A writ of *ca. sa.*, issued in the lifetime of the judgment creditor, may be executed after his death, for no judicial writ after judgment is abateable by the death of him who sues it (*n*).

Where a writ of *ca. sa.* is delivered to the sheriff with an indorsement "to be returned *non est inventus*," the sheriff is, notwithstanding such indorsement, bound to arrest and detain the party, if he either render himself or is rendered by his bail; the meaning of such an indorsement being only that the sheriff is not to look for the party (*o*). The sheriff has no right to execute a *ca. sa.* after direction from the plaintiff not to do so (*p*).

Where a defendant is in the custody of the sheriff under a writ, the delivery to the sheriff of a *ca. sa.* against the defendant in another suit is quite sufficient to complete the execution on such *ca. sa.* against such defendant, without any admission or acknowledgment on the part of the sheriff (*q*)

The sheriff, in executing a *ca. sa.*, as we have seen, is bound, if necessary, to take the *posse comitatus*, and therefore if the defendant be rescued out of the sheriff's custody, it is an

(*i*) See 2 Tidd's Prac. 1072, 8th edit.

(*k*) Simpson *v.* Heath, 5 M. & W. 631; Greenshields *v.* Harris, 9 M. & W. 774; Thomas *v.* Harris, 1 Dowl. N. C. 793.

(*l*) See *ante*, 125, *et seq.*

(*m*) Clifton *v.* Hooper, 6 Q. B. 468.

(*n*) Thorogood's case, Noy, 73; Cleve *v.* Veer, Cro. Car. 459; Ellis *v.* Griffith, 16 M. & W. 106; see also Fothergill *v.* Walton, 4 Bing. 711.

(*o*) Magnay *v.* Monger, 4 Q. B. 817.

(*p*) Barker *v.* St. Quintin, 12 M. & W. 441. See also Howard *v.* Cauty, 2 Dowl. & L. 115.

(*q*) Owen *v.* Owen, 2 B. & Ad. 805.

CHAP. VII. SECT. I.

escape (*r*). If the defendant be sued to judgment by a wrong name, and the *ca. sa.* be also against him by such wrong name, the sheriff is compelled to arrest the defendant, for by not pleading in abatement the defendant has admitted that to be his name (*s*). If the sheriff arrests the wrong party under a writ in consequence of a false representation made to him that he was the right party, no action will lie against the person making that representation, unless at the time of making it he knew it to be false, or made it fraudulently (*t*).

The sheriff's duty after the arrest.

It is the sheriff's duty to keep every person taken by him by virtue of a writ of execution *in salvâ et arctâ custodiâ;* for if the sheriff allow a defendant, arrested by him on a *capias ad satisfaciendum*, to go at large for the shortest time, either before or after the return-day of the writ, without the consent of the plaintiff, it is an escape, for which the sheriff is answerable (*u*). If the sheriff let a defendant arrested by him on a *ca. sa.* go at large on bail or baston (*v*), or even on payment of debt and costs to himself, (the sheriff) (*x*), it is an escape. The officer may carry a person arrested on a *ca. sa.* to the county gaol *immediately* after the arrest, for the statute 32 Geo. 2, c. 28, only applies to persons arrested on mesne process (*y*). If the sheriff carry a defendant in his custody out of the county, excepting in conveying him by the most convenient route to the county gaol, he will be guilty of an escape (*z*), and likewise liable to an action for false imprisonment (*a*). So if the bailiff of a liberty convey a defendant arrested by him out of his liberty to the county gaol, it is an escape (*b*). It is an escape to allow a defendant arrested on a *ca. sa.* to go about his affairs, even, as it would seem, in the custody of an officer (*c*). But the sheriff is not *bound* to take a person arrested on a *ca. sa.* to the county

(*r*) *Ante*, 73.

(*s*) Crawford *v.* Satchwell, Stra. 1218; Reeves *v.* Slater, 7 B. & C. 486; Fisher *v.* Magnay, 1 Dowl. & L. 40.

(*t*) Collins *v.* Evans, 5 Q B. 820.

(*u*) Doctor & Stud. 18; Bro. Abr. Escape; Rol. Abr. Escape (C); Boyton's case, 3 Rep. 44; stat. West. 2, c. 11.

(*v*) Rol. Abr. Escape (A), 3, 4, (D) 9.

(*x*) Slackford *v.* Austin, 14 East, 468. See also Crozier *v.* Pilling, 4 Barn. & Cr. 26; 6 D. & R. 129, S. C.; Wooden *v.* Moxon, 6 Taunt. 490; 2 Marsh. 186, S. C.

(*y*) Evans *v.* Atkins, 4 T. R. 555.

(*z*) Boyton's case, 3 Rep. 44.

(*a*) Bro. Escape, 11,—*per* Choke and Billing.

(*b*) Boothman *v.* The Earl of Surry, 2 T. R. 5.

(*c*) Benton *v.* Sutton, 1 Bos. & Pul. 24; Balden *v.* Temple, Hob. 202; Platt *v.* Locke, Plowd. 35; Hawkins *v.* Plomer, 2 Bla. Rep. 1048.

gaol immediately; he may confine him in a lock-up house until the return of the writ, without being liable to an action for an escape, although such lock-up house is not the house of the officer to whom the warrant is directed (*d*). Whenever the sheriff or his officer receives an order for the discharge of the defendant, search should be made in the sheriff's office to ascertain whether or not there be any other writs lodged against the defendant; for a person in custody at the suit of one plaintiff is in custody at the suit of any other person who delivers a writ to the sheriff before the discharge of the defendant (*e*). And the sheriff has a reasonable time for the purpose of making such search: therefore, where an order for the defendant's discharge was received at the gaol where he was confined on a Saturday, and forwarded to the under-sheriff, who lived at some distance; and on the *Sunday* the latter sent to the gaoler a warrant of detainer against the defendant under another writ of *ca. sa.* issued on the Saturday; it was held that he was not entitled to be discharged on the ground that the service of the warrant on a Sunday was void (*f*).

Poundage and fees.

The amount to which the sheriff is entitled for executing a writ of *ca. sa.* has been already shown (*g*); but although a writ of *ca. sa.* be improperly indorsed to levy "sheriff's poundage and officer's fees," the defendant will not be discharged out of custody unless he has paid or tendered the proper amount (*h*). If the plaintiff's attorney employ the officer to make the caption, and it is usual for him to pay him under the circumstances, the officer may maintain an action against the attorney for his caption fees and conduct money (*i*). But in general, and without such proof of employment of the officer, the client, not the attorney, is the person liable for the sheriff's fees on the execution of a *ca. sa.* (*k*).

The sheriff does not in general return a writ of *ca. sa.* with-

(*d*) Houlditch *v.* Birch, 4 Taunt. 608.

(*e*) *Ante*, 130. Frost's case, 5 Rep. 89; Benton *v.* Sutton, 1 Bos. & Pul. 24. See also Watson *v.* Carroll, 4 M. & W. 592.

(*f*) Samuel *v.* Buller, 1 Exch. R. 439.

(*g*) *Ante*, 111.

(*h*) Pitcher *v.* Roberts, 2 Dowl. N. S. 394.

(*i*) Newton *v.* Chambers, 1 Dowl. & L. 869. See also Foster *v.* Blakelock, 5 B. & C. 328; Townshend *v.* Carpenter, Ry. & M. 314; 2 C. & P. 118, S. C.; Walbank *v.* Quarterman, 3 C. B. 94.

(*k*) Maybery *v.* Mansfield, 16 Law. J. Q.B. 102; *ante*, 115.

CHAP. VII. SECT. I.

out being ruled so to do, for the writ is a sufficient justification for acts done under it, although it be never returned (*l*). A rule may be obtained at any time within six months after the expiration of the office of the sheriff, for him to return the writ; and if the sheriff do dot comply with the rule, he is liable to an attachment (*m*); but the court will not assent to an application on the part of the *defendant* against the sheriff to return a *ca. sa.*, unless special grounds be shown for the application (*n*).

When the sheriff is obliged to return a *ca. sa.*

Cepi corpus.

If the sheriff has taken the body of the defendant, he should return *cepi corpus* (*o*), for which return, if untrue, the sheriff will be liable for an escape, as the return is conclusive evidence of the arrest (*p*). If the sheriff had not an opportunity of arresting the defendant, he should return *non est inventus* (*q*). If the defendant has been taken under the writ, but at the return of the writ is too ill to be removed, we have already seen (*r*) that the sheriff should return "*languidus*," and such return should show that the sickness continued up to and at the time of the return (*s*). The court has no power to allow the sheriff any extra costs incurred by him in keeping in custody a person, arrested by him on a *ca. sa.*, who is too ill to be removed (*t*).

Privilege.

If the defendant were privileged from arrest on a *ca. sa.*, a return of such privilege would be good (*u*), although it leaves the sheriff to the risk of contesting with the plaintiff the truth of such return (*v*); therefore, excepting in cases of members of the royal family, peers, members of the House of Commons, ambassadors, or their servants (*w*), it is not advisable for the sheriff to take notice of the privilege, but to arrest the defendant,

(*l*) Hoe's case, 5 Rep. 90; Doiley *v.* Joliffe, Lane, 52; Rowland *v.* Veale, Cowp. 18; 10 East, 82; Cro. Eliz. 237.

(*m*) As to the rule to return the writ, and the granting the attachment, and as to returns in general, see *ante*, p. 81, *et seq.*

(*n*) Williams *v.* Webb, 2 Dowl. N. S. 904; Daniels *v.* Gompertz, 2 Gale & D. 751; 3 Q. B. 322, S. C.

(*o*) See form of return, *post*, Append.

(*p*) Stark. Evid. part iv. 1346. See also 3 Camp. 397.

(*q*) This form of return should be strictly adhered to. A return that the defendant "is not *to be* found in my bailiwick," is irregular; Rex *v.* The Sheriff of Kent, 2 M. & W. 316. See also 2 Man. & G. 439, note (*e*).

(*r*) *Ante*, 96.

(*s*) *Ibid.* See also Jones *v.* Robinson, 2 Dowl. N. S. 1044; 11 M. & W. 758, S. C.

(*t*) Jones *v.* Robinson, *supra.*

(*u*) Inge *v.* Herrick, cit. Doug. 675.

(*v*) Sherwood *v.* Benson, 4 Taunt. 631. For the court will not stay proceedings in an action of escape brought against the sheriff in such case; *id. ibid.*

(*w*) For in such case the sheriff is punishable if he arrest them on a *ca. sa.* See *ante*, 134.

and leave him to apply to the court to be discharged if he be entitled to it (*x*); and he may apply for such discharge even though he has been guilty of laches (*y*).

If the *ca. sa.* do not contain a *non omittas* clause, and the sheriff has sent his mandate thereon to the bailiff of a liberty to be executed, the proper return will be a return of *mandavi ballivo*, with the answer of the bailiff if he have made any; if not, with *nullum dedit responsum* (*z*). So also if the bailiff makes an insufficient return, the sheriff should return *nullum dedit responsum* (*a*). But if the sheriff might himself have entered the liberty under the writ, the return of *mandavi ballivo* would be insufficient (*b*).

The return to a *ca. sa.* that the defendant was rescued, either before or after he was conveyed to prison, is bad, for the sheriff is obliged to be provided with sufficient force (*c*). Therefore, if the sheriff make such return, he is liable to an action for an escape (*d*).

When to be discharged.

After being arrested on a *ca. sa.*, it is the sheriff's duty to keep the defendant in close custody until the plaintiff authorizes his discharge, or the prisoner is removed by *habeas corpus*, or is discharged by other lawful means; but if the plaintiff authorize the discharge of the defendant, and there be no detainers against him, the sheriff is bound to discharge him. The attorney for the plaintiff has not, however, any right to authorize the sheriff to discharge the defendant (*e*), for the attorney's duty ends when judgment is signed (*f*). In a case where a person delivered a discharge to the warden of the Fleet, which the plaintiff before the discharge of the defendant informed the warden had been obtained from him by fraud and countermanded the discharge, the warden notwithstanding released the prisoner; the court decided, that as the discharge was fraudulently obtained, which the warden knew, that it was an escape; the abstract question was also argued, but not determined, how far

(*x*) See 4 Taunt. 631.

(*y*) Webb *v.* Taylor, 1 Dowl. & Low. 676.

(*z*) See forms of returns, Append. c. 7. And see *ante*, p. 98.

(*a*) *Ante*, 99.

(*b*) Fitz. Retorn, 53.

(*c*) May *v.* Proby, Cro. Jac. 419; Com. Dig. Rescous (D) 7; Bac. Abr. Rescue (E) 1.

(*d*) O'Neil *v.* Marson, 5 Burr. 2812; Elliot *v.* Duke of Norfolk, 4 T. R. 789; Roll. Abr. Escape (D) 3. See also *ante*, 95.

(*e*) Savory *v.* Chapman, 11 Ad. & Ell. 829. See also Davis *v.* Jones, 5 Dowl. 504, Tindal, C. J.

(*f*) 5 Dowl. 504, Tindal, C. J.

CHAP. VII. SECT. I.

the authority of the plaintiff for the discharge of the prisoner was countermandable before it was executed (*g*).

Where a defendant, being in the custody of the marshal, was brought up by *habeas corpus cum causâ* before the Central Criminal Court to plead to an indictment, and was committed to Newgate and afterwards bailed, and the keeper of Newgate then, without any fresh warrant, redelivered him to the marshal, who received him into his custody, from which custody he escaped; it was held that the marshal was not liable to an escape, for his custody was at an end when the defendant's body was given up under the *habeas corpus*, and he could not lawfully receive him again without a fresh commitment (*h*).

With regard to prisoners in custody, who have obtained protection from process by a final order, it is by 7 & 8 Vict. c. 96, s. 23, enacted, "that if any such petitioner, being a prisoner in execution at the time of filing his petition, shall be detained in prison for any debt or claim in respect of which he is protected from process by his final order, it shall be lawful for the commissioner to order any officer who shall have such petitioner in custody by virtue of such execution to discharge such petitioner without exacting any fee; and such officer shall be hereby indemnified for so doing."

With regard to persons in execution upon judgments for sums under 20*l*., the 7 & 8 Vict. c. 96, s. 58, enacts, "that all persons in execution, at the time of passing this act, upon any judgment obtained in any of the courts aforesaid in any action for the recovery of any debt wherein the sum recovered shall not exceed the sum of twenty pounds, exclusive of the costs recovered by such judgment, shall and may, upon the application of every such person or persons for that purpose, made at any time after the passing of this act, to a judge of one of her majesty's superior courts of law at Westminster, or to the court in which such judgment shall have been obtained, to the satisfaction of such judge or court, be forthwith discharged out of custody as to such execution by an order of such judge or court: provided always, that if it shall happen that any such discharge shall have been unduly or fraudulently obtained upon any false allegation of

(*g*) Holland *v.* Eyles, M. 28 Geo. 3, reported in Bac. Abr. Escape (E) 3, 6th edit. See also *per* Lord Denman, C. J., 11 Ad. & El. 836.

(*h*) Coutant *v.* Chapman, 2 Q. B. 771.

circumstances, which, if true, might have entitled the prisoner to be discharged by virtue of this act, such prisoner shall, upon the same being made to appear to the satisfaction of the judge or court by whose order such prisoner shall have been so discharged, be liable to be again taken in execution, and remanded to his former custody by an order of such judge or court: provided also, that no sheriff, gaoler, or other person whatsoever, shall be liable as for the escape of any such prisoner in respect of his enlargement during such time as he shall have been at large by means of such his undue discharge as aforesaid: provided also, that for and notwithstanding the discharge of any debtor or debtors by an order of any such judge or court in manner aforesaid, the judgment whereupon any such debtor or debtors was or were taken or charged in execution shall nevertheless remain and continue in full force, to the intent and purpose that the judgment creditor or creditors may have and take remedy and execution upon every such judgment against the property and effects of any such debtor or debtors, in such manner and form as such creditor or creditors otherwise could or might have done in case such debtor or debtors had never been taken or charged in execution upon such judgment, and it shall be lawful for such creditor or creditors to have and take such remedy and execution (*i*)."

The effect of an order of the Insolvent Court for the discharge of a defendant from custody as to the detainer of the plaintiff at the expiration of a certain period, is to authorize the defendant's discharge when that period arrives; but it does not take away the power of the plaintiff to release him previously, if he thinks fit (*j*). The discharge of one of two defendants under the Insolvent Act, does not operate as a discharge also of the other (*k*).

If a defendant dies in custody, the sheriff has no power to detain his dead body until any other claims are satisfied; and if the dead body be not delivered up to his executors on request, a peremptory *mandamus* will be granted in the first instance (*l*).

(*i*) See also 8 & 9 Vict. c. 127; 9 & 10 Vict. c. 95; Ex parte Foulkes, 15 M. & W. 612; Fitzball *v.* Brooke, 6 Q. B. 873.

(*j*) *Ibid.*, *per* Lord Denman, C. J., p. 783.

(*k*) Nadin *v.* Battie, 5 East, 147; see also Raynes *v.* Jones, 1 Dowl. N. S. 373; 9 M. & W. 104, S. C.

(*l*) Reg. *v.* Fox, 2 Q. B. 246; Reg. *v.* Scott, *ib.* 248.

CHAP. VII.
SECT. II.

Section II.

Escape.

What is an escape of a prisoner in execution.

If the sheriff take a prisoner arrested on a *ca. sa.* out of his county, excepting in necessarily conveying him to the proper gaol, or if the sheriff or gaoler allow a prisoner to go at large, at any time after an arrest, out of the prison, (except upon a *habeas corpus,*) either before or after the return of the writ, it is an escape (*m*). Thus. where the defendant, after having been conveyed to the county gaol, was seen at large, this was holden to be an escape (*n*). And where the defendant was arrested, and was afterwards seen riding with an officer of the sheriff, (not the officer who made the arrest,) this was holden to be an escape (*o*). So where the defendant was taken from the county gaol, in custody of the gaoler, to another place in the same county, in order to give evidence before a revising barrister, and was returned into gaol on the same evening, this was holden to be an escape (*p*). So the bailiff of a liberty, who has the return and execution of writs, is liable to an action for an escape if he remove a prisoner taken in execution to the county gaol, situate out of the liberty, and there deliver him to the sheriff (*q*). But it is not an escape in the sheriff confining the defendant in the lock-up house of an officer (although not the officer to whom the warrant was directed) for ten days before the return-day of the writ (*r*). Neither is it an escape if the defendant was, at the time of his going at large, unlawfully in custody of the sheriff. Thus, where a defendant in execution of the marshal on a *ca. sa.* was brought up under a *habeas corpus cum causâ* before the Central Criminal Court, and committed to Newgate, and afterwards bailed, and the keeper of Newgate then, without any fresh warrant, re-delivered him to the marshal, who received him into his custody, and afterwards suffered him to go at large, it was held that the marshal was not liable to an action for an escape, the defendant, for want of a fresh warrant, not being legally in his custody at the time it took place; and it was also held that

(*m*) 8 & 9 Will. 3, c. 27, s. 1. Stat. 5 & 6 Vict. c. 22, s. 12, abolishes the liberty of the rules.

(*n*) Balden *v.* Temple, Hob. 202; Hawkins *v.* Plomer, 2 Bla. Rep. 1048; Platt *v.* Locke, Plowd. 35.

(*o*) Benton *v.* Suton, 1 Bos. & Pul. 24.

(*p*) Williams *v.* Mostyn, 4 M. & W. 145.

(*q*) Boothman *v.* Earl of Surrey, 2 T. R. 5; Hepworth *v.* Sanderson, 1 M. & Sc. 64; 8 Bing. 19, S. C.

(*r*) Houlditch *v.* Birch, 4 Taunt. 608; see also Hard. 31.

the fact of the marshal having received the defendant into his custody did not estop him from denying the legality of it (*s*). Even if the sheriff discharge the defendant on payment of debt and costs to him, without the assent of the plaintiff, it is an escape (*t*); but if the sheriff had received the money, and paid it over to the plaintiff, it would appear however that the plaintiff could not bring an action for an escape against the sheriff (*u*).

The plaintiff's attorney has no authority, without the plaintiff's consent, to give a discharge from custody; and therefore if, on the bare authority of the plaintiff's attorney, the sheriff were to discharge a defendant from custody before the plaintiff had been satisfied his judgment, he would be liable for an escape (*v*). But if the judgment has been in fact satisfied, either by payment to the plaintiff, or to his attorney on the record, the defendant may be released (*x*).

If the keeper of a prison, after one day's notice in writing, refuse to show any prisoner committed in execution to the creditor at whose suit he was committed or charged, or to his attorney, such refusal shall be deemed an escape (*y*). It is said, that if a sheriff marry a woman in execution in his custody, it will be deemed an escape in law (*z*). If a man have judgment against two persons, and both are taken in execution, if the sheriff suffer one of them to escape, he shall be answerable for the whole debt, though he has the other still in his custody (*a*).

If the sheriff permit a prisoner to escape out of execution, he is liable to an action for an escape, although the judgment on which the *ca. sa.* issued is erroneous (*b*); or if the *ca. sa.* itself be erroneous, the sheriff is liable to an action for allowing a person arrested thereon to go at large (*c*). As if the chancellor of

(*s*) Coutant *v.* Chapman, 2 Q. B. 771.

(*t*) Slackford *v.* Austen, 14 East, 468.

(*u*) *Id. ibid.*

(*v*) Savory *v.* Chapman, 11 A. & E. 827.

(*x*) See Crozier *v.* Pilling, 4 B. & C. 26.

(*y*) Stat. 8 & 9 Will. 3, c. 27, s. 8.

(*z*) Bac. Abr. Escape (B) 3, citing Plowd. 17, but nothing to that point can be found in that reference.

(*a*) Roll. Abr. Escape (F) 4. So where baron and feme were in custody in execution, and the feme escaped, it was held that the sheriff was liable to an action for allowing her to escape; *ibid.* (F) 5; Whiting *v.* Reynell, Cro. Jac. 657; Sukliff *v.* Reynell, 2 Bulstr. 320. Since the 5 & 6 Vict. c. 98, s. 31, the sheriff would, under the circumstances stated in the text, be liable only for such damages as the plaintiff might recover in an action on the case.

(*b*) Gold *v.* Strode, Carth. 148; 3 Mod. 324, S. C.; otherwise, where the judgment is reversed, then the sheriff is not liable for an escape, Dr. Drury's case, 8 Rep. 284; Dalt. 563.

(*c*) Burton *v.* Eyre, Cro. Jac. 289; Weaver *v.* Clifford, Cro. Jac. 3; Yelv.

the duchy of Lancaster, on a writ directed to him, make his warrant to the sheriff to have the body before the justices, instead of before the chancellor, that he might have the body before the justices (*d*); or if a *capias* be issued on a recognizance, where by the practice of the court it does not lie (*e*); or where, after a year from the time of signing judgment, a *ca. sa.* issues without a *sci. fa.* to revive the judgment (*f*); or (before the 3 & 4 Will. 4, c. 67,) if a term intervened between the *teste* and return of a *ca. sa.* (*g*); in any of these cases the process would be erroneous, but not void, and the sheriff would be guilty of an escape for suffering a defendant arrested thereon to go at large. So also it is no defence in an action for an escape to say that the judgment on which the *ca. sa.* was issued was obtained by the plaintiff as indorsee of a bill of exchange given for money won at play (*h*). But where the process is absolutely *void*, there, if the sheriff arrest the defendant and suffer him to escape, he will not be liable to an action (*i*); as if the court out of which the execution issued had no jurisdiction over the cause, this is no escape (*k*). And although in some cases the sheriff is justified in executing a writ, yet he may not be guilty of an escape for discharging the defendant in his custody on such writ; as if a writ of execution (before the 3 & 4 Will. 4, c. 67) bore *teste* out of term, the sheriff was justifiable, and yet he was not liable to an action of escape, for it was a void writ (*l*).

So we have seen that a sheriff may justify arresting a party privileged under a writ; and yet he would not be liable for an escape, if, after making the arrest, he allowed such privilege and

42, S. C.; 2 Bulstr. 62; Ognel *v.* Paston, Cro. Eliz. 165; see also *per* Lord Denman, in Coutant *v.* Chapman, 2 Q. B. 785.

(*d*) Burton *v.* Eyre, Cro. Jac. 288, 289. As if the writ were directed immediately to the sheriff of a county palatine, and the sheriff arrested the defendant, and afterwards discharged him, it would appear that he would be liable to an action for an escape, as the writ is erroneous but not void; *Id. ibid.*; Jackon *v.* Hunter, 6 T. R. 81.

(*e*) See cases last note but one, Moore, 174; Cro. Eliz. 271; 2 Saund. 100.

(*f*) Bushe's case, Cro. Eliz. 188; and see Keisar *v.* Tyrrell, 2 Bulstr. 256.

(*g*) Shirley *v.* Wright, 2 Ld. Raym. 775; 1 Salk. 273, S. C.

(*h*) Lane *v.* Chapman, 11 A. & E. 966.

(*i*) Nector *v.* Gennett, Cro. Eliz. 466; 21 Hen. 7, 16, pl. 27; Marshalsea case, 10 Rep. 76 a.

(*k*) See *ante*, 67 *et seq.* And if the sheriff were to make arrest under a writ which disclosed a want of jurisdiction, he could not justify under such writ; see Carratt *v.* Morley, 1 Q. B. 18.

(*l*) *Per* Holt, C. J., Salk. 700; 2 Lord Raym. 775; *sed quære.*

suffered the defendant to go at large. Where a sheriff within a liberty arrested a defendant on a *ca. sa.* without a *non omittas*, and suffered him to escape, the sheriff was held liable to an action for so doing, for the arrest was good (*m*); and the only effect of its having been made within the liberty was to expose the sheriff to an action at the suit of the lord of the liberty (*n*).

If the plaintiff appoints a special bailiff to make the arrest, and he does so, the sheriff is not liable for an escape from the custody of such bailiff before the defendant has been given into the actual custody of the sheriff (*o*). When the sheriff is ordered by a writ of *habeas corpus* to bring up the body of a person in his custody in execution, it is his duty to convey him by the shortest and most convenient road to the court at Westminster. If he deviate from such direct road, or let the defendant go about his affairs, although he has him at the return of the *habeas corpus*, it is an escape (*p*). And if a *habeas corpus* issue in one term to the sheriff to bring up a prisoner in his custody in execution on the ensuing term, if he let him go at large in the mean-time, it is an escape (*q*).

The sheriff is allowed a reasonable time to bring up a prisoner on a *habeas corpus*, of which the court will judge (*r*). It is laid down by Lord Coke, that if a sheriff, in taking a prisoner in execution from his county gaol to Westminster on a *habeas corpus*, lodge him in an inn on the direct road, and the defendant of his own head goes at large, but the sheriff has him at Westminster on the return day of the *habeas corpus*, this is no escape (*s*).

So, a sheriff is allowed a reasonable time to bring and keep a prisoner beyond the limits of his county, in obedience to the

(*m*) Piggott *v.* Wilkes, 3 Bar. & Ald. 502.

(*n*) Villa de Darby *v.* Foxley, 1 Roll. Rep. 119; see also Jackson *v.* Hill, 10 A. & E. 493, Patteson, J.

(*o*) See *ante*, 40, 41; Pascoe *v.* Vyvyan, 1 Dowl. N. S. 939. See also Alderson *v.* Davenport, 13 M. & W. 42, *ante*, 40, that merely requesting the under-sheriff to forward the warrant to a particular officer of the sheriff, and instructing that officer by letter as to where the defendant is likely to be found, does not constitute such officer a special bailiff. See also Brown *v.* Copley, 8 Scott, N. R. 332; 7 Man. & G. 558, S. C.; Botten *v.* Tomlinson, 16 Law J. (C. P.) 138; Seale *v.* Hudson, 11 Jurist, 610.

(*p*) See Roll. Abr. Escape (D) 9; Cro. Car. 14, 466; Hard. 476; 1 Mod. 116. See 1 Sid. 13; Bull. N. P. 67, as to *habeas corpus ad testificandum*.

(*q*) Hard. 476; Roll. Abr. Escape (D) 9; 1 Lord Raym. 241; 1 Mod. 116.

(*r*) Holdroid *v.* Liddell, 1 Ld. Raym. 241.

(*s*) Boyton's case, 3 Rep. 44; Moore, 257.

warrant of a commissioner of bankrupts for examination before him; and it is sufficient if during such time the prisoner be accompanied and carefully watched by the officer, and it is no escape that he is allowed to go about with the officer to different places, and to dine and sleep at an inn (*t*).

Discharging a defendant by order of a court without jurisdiction is an escape.

In all the cases where the sheriff is ordered to discharge a prisoner in his custody in execution, the sheriff is bound to see that the court has jurisdiction to make such order, for he is liable to an action for an escape if the court should not have jurisdiction; as where a gaoler, by the command of the lord chancellor and treasurer, allowed a prisoner in his custody in execution to go at large to collect money to pay the king, this was holden to be an escape, for the lord chancellor and treasurer had no authority to grant such a license (*u*). So where, by an act of parliament for the relief of insolvent debtors, the justices in sessions were enabled to discharge certain prisoners, and made an order on the gaoler to discharge a person that did not come within the description of the act, whom he allowed to go at large, the sheriff was held to be liable for an escape (*v*). But the sheriff would be justified in obeying an order of the Insolvent Court for the discharge of a prisoner, without inquiring into all the circumstances to see if the defendant was entitled to such order, provided that the order itself was good upon the face of it (*x*).

Escape by act of God, or by the king's enemies.

The sheriff is, however, excused if the escape be occasioned *by the act of God, or by the queen's enemies.* Thus, it is laid down, that if prisoners escape from prison by *sudden fire*, no action lies against the sheriff, for this is the act of God (*y*). It has been supposed that the sheriff is only excused where the prison is burned by *fire by lightning* (*z*). And it has been decided that the decay of the prison for want of repair is not an excuse for an

(*t*) Nias *v.* Davis, 2 Carr. & K. 280.

(*u*) Roll. Abr. Escape (D) 8; Dyer, 162, 297; Cromp. Courts, 106; Dalt. Sheriff, 142; Colston *v.* Ross, Cro. Eliz. 893. Nor even can a gaoler allow his prisoners to go at large when the plague is raging in the prison. See also Roll. Abr. Escape (D) 10; Cro. Car. 466.

(*v*) Brown *v.* Compton, 8 T. R. 424; Anon., Salk. 273. The case of Orby *v.* Hales, 1 Ld. Raym. 3; 4 Mod. 353, S. C., *contrà*, is not law.

(*x*) 1 & 2 Vict. c. 110, s. 110; Saffery *v.* Jones, 2 B. & Adol. 598; see also Marsh *v.* Woolley, 1 Dowl. & L. 84.

(*y*) Roll. Abr. Escape (D) 6; Dyer, 66.

(*z*) *Per* Eyre, C. J., 2 H. Blac. 113. See also 1 T. R. 27.

escape (*a*). So if any *foreign enemies* of the king break open the prison and release the prisoners, the sheriff and gaoler are excused; but if traitors and rebels (*b*), or if a large and irresistible mob (*c*), break open a prison and set the prisoners at large, the sheriff is liable to an action for an escape.

Escape by the contrivance of plaintiff.

So also, the sheriff will be excused if the escape be occasioned by the fraud and covin of the plaintiff, or the party really interested in the judgment (*d*). Thus where the party enticed the defendant out of the rules, it was held that the marshal, in whose custody he was, could not be charged with his escape (*e*). So where a prisoner, being in custody in execution at the suit of the plaintiff, and having escaped beyond the rules, was, by the contrivance and with the privity of the plaintiff, arrested on a writ of mesne process at the suit of a third person, and detained out of the rules, in order to prevent him from returning into custody, as he otherwise would have done, and in order to deprive the marshal of the defence which such return would have afforded him, it was held that he could not sue the marshal for an escape occasioned by the detainer which he had so contrived (*f*).

Distinction between voluntary and negligent escapes: herein of recaption.

Escapes are of two kinds, either *voluntary* or *negligent*. In the case of a *voluntary* escape, the sheriff can never afterwards retake the defendant, but is liable to an action of false imprisonment if he do (*g*); even although such voluntary escape were occasioned through a mere mistake. Thus, where a person, being in custody at the suit of A., a *ca. sa.* was afterwards, and whilst he was so in custody, lodged against him at the suit of B., and the

(*a*) Alsept *v.* Eyles, 2 H. Blac. 108.

(*b*) Roll. Abr. Escape (D) 7, referring to 3 E. 6, 66, 15; Southcot's case, 4 Rep. 84; Dyer, 66 b.

(*c*) O'Neil *v.* Marson, 5 Burr. 2812; Elliott *v.* Duke of Norfolk, 4 T. R. 789; Roll. Abr. Escape (D) 3.

(*d*) Hiscocks *v.* Jones, Moo. & Mal. 269; Merry *v.* Chapman, 10 Ad. & Ell. 516.

(*e*) Hiscocks *v.* Jones, *supra*.

(*f*) Merry *v.* Chapman, 10 A. & E. 516.

(*g*) Featherstonehaugh *v.* Atkinson, Barnes, 373; Atkinson *v.* Jameson, 5 T. R. 25; 1 Show. 174; 1 Sid. 330; Whiting *v.* Reynell, Cro. Jac. 657; also *per* Lord Denman, C. J., in Coutant *v.* Chapman, 2 Q. B. 788. By the stat. 8 & 9 Will. 3, c. 27, s. 4, it is enacted, "that if any marshal or warden, or their respective deputy or deputies, or any keeper of any other prison within this kingdom, shall take any sum of money, reward, or gratuity whatsoever, or security for the same, to procure, assist, connive at, or permit any such escape, and shall be thereof lawfully convicted, the said marshal or warden, or their respective deputy or deputies, or such other keeper of any prisons as aforesaid, shall for every such offence forfeit the sum of 500*l.* and his said office, and be for ever after incapable of executing any such office."

CHAP. VII. SECT. II.

writ at the suit of A. having been withdrawn, the defendant was discharged out of prison, without any notice being taken of B.'s writ (that writ having by mistake been omitted to be entered in a book in which detainers were generally entered), it was held that the escape was clearly voluntary, and, being so, the sheriff could not retake the defendant on B.'s writ (*h*). If, however, the escape be without the consent of the plaintiff, the plaintiff may retake him on a fresh *ca. sa.* (*i*); but where, after a voluntary escape, the plaintiff recovered against the sheriff for an escape, it was held that a fresh *ca. sa.* could not be sued out in the plaintiff's name, with a view to the indemnification of the sheriff (*k*), and it seems that for executing such a writ the sheriff would be liable to an action at the suit of the defendant (*l*); but if the defendant, after a *voluntary* escape, return to prison, the plaintiff may treat him as in execution (*m*); but it seems he would thereby waive his action for the escape (*n*). After a *negligent* escape, the sheriff may on fresh pursuit retake the defendant; and if on such fresh pursuit he be retaken (*o*), or voluntarily (*p*) return into the sheriff's custody before action brought, it is a good defence if pleaded to the action for the escape; but if before the defendant has been retaken the plaintiff has commenced his action against the sheriff, the sheriff is still liable (*q*). So also the sheriff would be liable, if at any time between the escape and the return to custody he knew where to find the defendant, but omitted to retake him, or to take any

(*h*) Filewood *v.* Clement, 6 Dowl. 508.

(*i*) See 8 & 9 Will. 3, c. 27, s. 7. And see 1 Sid. 330; 1 Vent. 4, 69; 1 Lev. 211; 2 Mod. 136; Cro. Car. 255; 2 Sir T. Jones, 21; Cro. Eliz. 555. But if the plaintiff consent to the discharge of the defendant, he cannot retake him on a fresh *ca. sa.*, for it is considered satisfaction, 2 East, 243; 1 Bos. & Pul. 242; 6 T. R. 525; 1 T. R. 557; 4 Burr. 2482; nor sue out a *fi. fa.*; nor can he set off the judgment in another action whilst the defendant is in custody in execution, Taylor *v.* Waters, 5 M. & Sel. 103.

(*k*) Gilbert *v.* Aston, 2 Dowl. N. S. 413.

(*l*) *Ibid.*

(*m*) Lenthall *v.* Lenthall, 2 Lev. 109; James *v.* Peirce, 1 Vent. 269; S. C. 2 Lev. 132; 3 Keb. 453, 463; see also *ib.* 487; Dyer, 275; Hob. 202, *contrà*, denied to be law.

(*n*) See cases in last note: Roll. Abr. Execution (U) 8; 1 Ld. Raym. 399; 1 Salk. 271; Stra. 423; Grant *v.* Southern, 6 Mod. 183. But see Ravenscroft *v.* Eyles, 2 Wils. 294.

(*o*) Ridgway's case, 3 Rep. 52 b; Moore, 660, S. C.; Harvey *v.* Rennell, Sir W. Jones, 145; Roll. Abr. Escape (E), 1, 3.

(*p*) Chambers *v.* Gambier, Com. 544; Bonafous *v.* Walker, 2 T. R. 129. See also 2 Blac. 1050; 11 East, 406; 1 Bos. & Pul. 413.

(*q*) Roll. Abr. Escape (E), 2, 4; Whiting *v.* Rennell, Cro. Jac. 657; 3 Rep. 52; Stonehouse *v.* Mullins, Stra. 873.

steps towards his recapture (*r*). We have, however, already seen (*s*) that the sheriff will not be liable for a negligent escape occasioned by the fraud of the plaintiff. The sheriff may retake a prisoner who has escaped out of his custody without his privity in any county (*t*), on fresh pursuit; and to do so he may break open an outer door (*u*), and he may retake the defendant on a Sunday (*x*). Fresh pursuit means pursuit made as soon as the sheriff has notice of the escape (*y*). It was held that the marshal of the King's Bench might retake a prisoner who had escaped from his custody, notwithstanding the prisoner had obtained his protection from the commissioners of bankrupt after the escape but before the recaption, inasmuch as such protection only applies to an original taking (*z*). And it appears to be law that the sheriff, although fresh pursuit have not been made, and although the plaintiff have brought an action against the sheriff, may retake the defendant until he is satisfied by the defendant for the escape (*a*), if the plaintiff have recovered against the sheriff for a negligent escape.

The sheriff's remedy for the escape.

The sheriff, after a retaking of the defendant, may detain him until he is satisfied for the damage sustained by reason of the escape (*b*); or he may bring an action against the defendant to recover damages for the costs sustained by him.

Of the action for an escape of a prisoner in execution.

The only action which lies against the sheriff for an escape of a debtor in execution, since the passing of the 5 & 6 Vict. c. 98 (10th August, 1842), is an action *upon the case* for such damage as the plaintiff at whose suit he was imprisoned may have sustained by reason of such escape (*c*). The action on the case was the only action which lay against the sheriff at common law for an escape, in which action the plaintiff is only entitled to such damages as the jury will give (*d*); but by several statutes (stat. of Westminster 2nd, 13 Edw. 1, c. 11; 1 Rich. 2, c. 12; 1 Ann. stat. 2, c. 6, s. 2), an action of *debt* was also given, in

(*r*) Davis *v.* Chapman, 5 Bing. N. C. 453.

(*s*) *Ante*, 201.

(*t*) Dalt. Sheriff, 139. And see Roll. Abr. Execution (U) 9; Ridgway's case, 3 Rep. 52.

(*u*) See *ante*, 128; 5 Rep. 93.

(*x*) Sir W. Moore's case, 2 Lord Raym. 1028; see also Atkinson *v.* Jameson, 5 T. R. 25. See *ante*, 80.

(*y*) Roll. Abr. Escape (E) 3. See also tit. Execution (U) 5.

(*z*) Anderson *v.* Hampton, 1 Bar. & Ald. 309.

(*a*) Dalt. Sheriff, 139; Ridgway's case, 3 Rep. 52.

(*b*) *Id. ibid.*

(*c*) 5 & 6 Vict. c. 98, s. 31.

(*d*) Bonafous *v.* Walker, 2 T. R. 132. See also Gabel *v.* Perchard, 2 Anst. 522.

CHAP. VII. SECT. II.

which action the plaintiff might recover the whole debt for which the defendant was in execution (*e*). This action of debt is now, however, expressly taken away by the 31st section of 5 & 6 Vict. c. 98, which enacts, "that if any debtor in execution shall escape out of legal custody, the sheriff, bailiff, or other person having the custody of such debtor, shall be liable to an action upon the case for damages sustained by the person or persons at whose suit such debtor was taken or imprisoned, and shall not be liable to any action of debt in consequence of such escape."

Who may maintain an action for an escape.

If, whilst the defendant be in custody of the sheriff in an action at the suit of A., a writ be lodged in the office of the sheriff at the suit of B., and the defendant escape, B. as well as A. may have an action against the sheriff for the escape, for the delivery of the writ is an arrest in law (*f*). An action will lie by an executor for an escape out of execution in the time of his testator (*g*). Where a judgment was obtained by the plaintiff as administratrix, it was held that she might bring an action for the escape without suing as administratrix (*h*). Where the plaintiff is nonsuited in an action against a hundred, who take him in execution for the costs of the nonsuit, and the sheriff allows him to escape, the hundred may sue the sheriff for an escape (*i*). Where a defendant in execution in an action of trespass for mesne profits, brought in the name of the nominal plaintiff, escape, an action for the escape may be brought in the name of the nominal plaintiff (*k*). The action may be brought by the plaintiff, for an escape on a *capias utlagatum*, in his own right; for it was reported by the prothonotaries that the precedents were in that way as well as *qui tam* (*l*).

Neither the heir nor the executor of the sheriff is liable for an escape, because it is a personal tort, which dies with the person of the sheriff (*m*). But where there are two sheriffs who

(*e*) Hawkins *v.* Plomer, 2 Blac. Rep. 1048; Alsept *v.* Eyles, 2 H. Blac. 113. See also 2 T. R. 129.

(*f*) Benton *v.* Sutton, 1 Bos. & Pul. 24; Jackson *v.* Humphreys, Salk. 273; Frost's case, 5 Rep. 89; see also *ante*, 130, and Filewood *v.* Clement, 6 Dowl. 508.

(*g*) *Per* Holt, C. J., in Berwick *v.* Andrews, Lord Raym. 973; S. C. 6 Mod. 125; Dyer, 322 a, note; W. Jones, 173; 1 Vent. 31.

(*h*) Bonafous *v.* Walker, 2 T. R. 126.

(*i*) Fitzg. 296.

(*k*) Doe *v.* Jones, 2 M. & Sel. 473.

(*l*) Moore *v.* Reynolds, Cro. Jac. 619, recog. in Throgmorton *v.* Church, Dom. Proc., 1 P. Williams, 693.

(*m*) Dyer, 271, 322 a; Dalt. Sher. 517; see also 6 Mod. 125; 1 Lord Raym. 399.

suffer an escape, and one dies, the action lies against the survivor, or if pending the action one dies, the action survives (*n*). The old sheriff, at the expiration of his office, should regularly turn over all the prisoners to the new sheriff, in the manner hereinbefore pointed out (*o*); and if he omit any, it is an escape (*p*). If the sheriff died, the new sheriff was (before 3 Geo. 1, c. 15,) bound to take notice of all the prisoners, and the actions with which they were charged (*q*). And where a prisoner had escaped from prison by the assent of the gaoler, and returned to prison, and afterwards a new sheriff was appointed, during whose shrievalty the defendant again escaped, the new sheriff was held to be liable to an action for this escape; for it was optional for the defendant to proceed against the old sheriff, or hold the defendant in execution (*r*). Between the death of the old sheriff and the appointment of his successor, formerly there was no officer that was responsible for the safe custody of prisoners; but by the statute 3 Geo. 1, c. 15, s. 8, "in case of the death of the high sheriff, the under-sheriff shall execute his office until another sheriff be appointed, and shall be answerable for the execution of the office in all things during that interval as the high sheriff would have been if living (*s*)."

Declaration.

The *venue* in this action is transitory (*t*). In a declaration for an escape of a prisoner in execution, it is necessary to state that the plaintiff recovered a judgment against the debtor,—that the *ca. sa.* was issued and delivered to the defendant,—the arrest under it,—and that the debtor afterwards escaped; as, however, the judgment is only inducement to the action, the allegation "*quod cum recuperasset*" is sufficient (*u*). If it be alleged that the plaintiff recovered a judgment in a particular term, as it appears by record, and on the evidence it appears that the judgment is of a different term from that stated in the declaration, the variance is not material; for the term is not material,

(*n*) Bennion *v.* Watson, Cro. Eliz. 625; see also stat. 8 & 9 Will. 3, c. 11, s. 7.

(*o*) *Ante*, 22.

(*p*) Westby's case, 3 Rep. 71 b.

(*q*) *Ibid.*; Cro. Eliz. 366.

(*r*) Lenthall *v.* Lenthall, 2 Lev. 109; James *v.* Pearse, 1 Vent. 269; 2 Lev. 132, S. C.; 3 Keb. 453, 463; Dyer, 275; Roll. Abr. Execution (U) 8; Langdon *v.* Wallis, 1 Ld. Raym. 399; 1 Salk. 271.

(*s*) *Ante*, 24.

(*t*) 1 Wils. 336; Plowd. 35; Dyer, 278 b; Bac. Abr. Escape (F).

(*u*) Eden *v.* Lloyd, Cro. Eliz. 877; Waites *v.* Briggs, 2 Salk. 565; 1 Saund. 38 b, note (4).

CHAP. VII. SECT. II.

and the *prout patet per recordum* may be rejected as surplusage (*x*). And where the declaration in an action for an escape stated a judgment, and also an award of execution against the prisoner for the damages recovered, and that thereupon the prisoner was committed, &c., it was held that the allegation that a *sci. fa.* had been sued out was immaterial, and that it need not be proved, proof of the judgment being sufficient (*y*). But the judgment must correspond substantially with the declaration; for where, in an action for a false return to a *fi. fa.*, the declaration stated that the plaintiffs, *by the judgment of the court, recovered* against the bail, and the evidence adduced was the *sci. fa.* roll, which concluded in the common form, that the *plaintiffs should have execution* against the bail, the variance was held to be fatal (*z*). And where, in a declaration in an action for an escape, it was stated the bail was put in before a *judge in chambers, prout patet per recordum*, who had rendered the defendant, and on the entry of the bail being produced, it appeared to have been taken *before the court at Westminster*, this was held to be a fatal variance (*a*).

A *negligent* escape may be given in evidence under a count for a voluntary escape (*b*). Before the passing of the 5 & 6 Vict. c. 22, if a prisoner was brought up by *habeas corpus*, and committed to the custody of the marshal of the Queen's Bench, or the warden of the Fleet, in an action against the marshal or warden for an escape, it must have been alleged in the declaration that the commitment was of record; for the prisoner was not in point of law in the marshal's custody until the commitment was entered of record (*c*); and the law would seem to be the same since the passing of the 5 & 6 Vict. c. 22, in the case

(*x*) Stoddart *v.* Palmer, 4 Dowl. & Ry. 624; 3 Bar. & Cress. 2, S. C.; Purcell *v.* Macnamara, 9 East, 157; Phillips *v.* Shaw, 4 Bar. & Ald. 435; 5 Bar. & Ald. 964; Bennett *v.* Isaac, 10 Price, 154; see also Cocks *v.* Brewer, 2 Dowl. N. S. 759; Lewis *v.* Alcock, 6 Dowl. 78.

(*y*) Bromfield *v.* Jones, 6 Dowl. & Ry. 500; 4 Bar. & Cress. 380, S. C.

(*z*) Phillipson *v.* Mangles, 11 East, 516.

(*a*) Bevan *v.* Jones, 6 Dowl. & Ry. 483; 4 Bar. & Cress. 403, S. C. As to the power of amendment, see now stat. 3 & 4 Will. 4, c. 42, s. 23.

(*b*) Bonafous *v.* Walker, 2 T. R. 131; Sir Ralph Bovey's case, 1 Vent. 211, 217; 1 Saund 35, n. 1.

(*c*) Wightman *v.* Mullins, 2 Stra. 1226; Barnes *v.* Eyles, 2 Moore, 561; 8 Taunt. 512, S. C.; see also Turner *v.* Eyles, 3 Bos. & Pul. 456; Wigley *v.* Jones, 5 East, 440; Reg. Gen. 41 Geo. 3, K. B., 1 East, 410; Purdom *v.* Brockridge, 3 Dowl. & Ry. 597; 2 B. & C. 342, S. C.

of persons committed to the custody of the keeper of the Queen's prison.

CHAP. VII. SECT. II.

A count for neglecting to arrest the debtor may be joined with a count for an escape in the same declaration (*d*); and in an action against a sheriff for not arresting the defendant, it is not necessary to aver in the declaration that the sheriff had notice of the defendant being in his bailiwick (*e*).

Particulars of escape.

In an action for an escape, the plaintiff may be ordered to give a particular of the alleged escape, specifying the time and place (*f*).

Pleas.

In an action on the case for an escape, the plea of not guilty (except in cases otherwise provided for by particular statutes) operates as a denial of the neglect or default of the sheriff or his officers, but not of the debt, judgment, or preliminary proceedings (*g*); if the defendant wishes to dispute the existence or validity of the debt, judgment, or any other proceedings, or the fact of the arrest having been made by himself or his officers, he must plead specially; so must he also, if, admitting the fact of the escape, he wishes to set up any matter of excuse, as, for instance, a recaption before action, in the case of a negligent escape.

We have seen (*h*) that under a count for a voluntary escape the plaintiff may give evidence of a negligent escape. To a count for a voluntary escape, therefore, the defendant need not traverse that the escape was voluntary, but may plead that it was negligent (*i*), and that the defendant was retaken on fresh pursuit, or that he voluntarily returned into custody before the commencement of the action; and if the plaintiff relies on a voluntary escape, he may show it in his replication (*j*), It was, even before the new rules of H. T. 4 W. 4, necessary that the defence of recaption or voluntary return into custody should be specially pleaded (*k*); such a plea, however, must be verified by affidavit, for by the statute of 8 & 9 Will. 3, c. 27, s. 6, "no retaking on fresh pursuit shall be given in evidence, on

(*d*) Raymond *v.* Bridges, Lofft, 59.

(*e*) Dean, &c. of Hereford, *v.* Macnamara, 5 Dowl. & Ry. 95; Duke *v.* Duke, 4 Bing. N. C. 197.

(*f*) Webster *v.* Jones, 7 D. & R. 774; Davis *v.* Chapman, 6 A. & E. 767.

(*g*) Reg. Gen. H. T. W. 4, r. 4.

(*h*) *Supra.*

(*i*) See Davis *v.* Chapman, 5 Bing. N. C. 453.

(*j*) Sir Ralph Bovey's case, 1 Vent. 211, 217; S. C. 3 Keb. 55; 1 Saund. 35, n. (1). See also 2 T. R. 131; *sed vide* Whiting *v.* Reynell, Cro. Jac. 657.

(*k*) See 8 & 9 Will. 3, c. 27, s. 6; Bonafous *v.* Walker, 2 T. R. 131.

CHAP. VII. SECT. II.

the trial of any issue in any action of escape, unless the same be specially pleaded; nor shall any special plea be taken, received, or allowed, unless an oath be first made by the marshal or keeper of the prison, and filed in the office of the respective courts, that the prisoner escaped without his knowledge." It is necessary, as well in a plea of recaption as of voluntary return of the defendant to custody, to allege that such recaption or return was before action brought(*l*), and also that the defendant was detained in prison from the time of such recaption or return to the commencement of the action against the sheriff(*m*), or until the defendant's legal discharge(*n*); and also that the defendant did not know where the prisoner was during any period of his absence (*o*).

In a plea of recaption, or of voluntary return into custody, it is sufficient to show a detention of the prisoner from the time of such recaption or return, *up to the time of action brought;* and therefore where a plea of a voluntary return alleged that after such return the defendant did therefore keep and detain, *and always from thence hitherto hath kept and detained, and still doth keep and detain,* the prisoner in the custody, &c., to which the plaintiff replied de injuriâ; it was held that the plea was supported by proof of a detention up to the time of the commencement of the suit, and that the allegation that the defendant thence *hitherto* kept and *still* doth *keep,* &c., was superfluous and immaterial, and was not put in issue by the replication de injuriâ, because that replication only puts in issue the material allegations of the plea (*p*). If the judgment upon which the ca. sa. was issued is *absolutely void* between the parties, it seems that that circumstance would afford a good defence to an action for an escape. It would, of course, be necessary to plead that defence specially, and the plea should set forth all the circumstances to show why and how the judgment was void(*q*). If the defence be that the prisoner was discharged by the plaintiff, or by the order of a court having jurisdiction to make such order, such discharge should be specially pleaded. A plea that

(*l*) Stonehouse *v.* Mullins, Stra. 873.

(*m*) Chambers *v.* Jones, 11 East, 406; Meriton *v.* Briggs, 1 Ld. Raym. 39; explained in 11 East, 410; see also Griffiths *v.* Eyles, 1 Bos. & Pul. 413.

(*n*) Willis *v.* Gambier, Prac. Reg. 199.

(*o*) Davis *v.* Chapman, 5 Bing. N. C. 453; see also S. C. 2 Man. & G. 921.

(*p*) Davis *v.* Chapman, 2 Man. & G. 921.

(*q*) See Lane *v.* Chapman, 11 A. & E. 966.

the attorney for the plaintiff authorized the discharge would be bad, unless it contained an averment, either that the amount for which the execution issued had been paid, or that the discharge was authorized by the plaintiff (*r*). The defence that the prisoner was discharged by the order of the Insolvent Court, may be given in evidence under the general issue (*s*), or it may be specially pleaded; and in such special plea it will be sufficient to set out the order of the court, and it need not be shown that all the proceedings upon which the order was grounded were properly taken (*t*).

We have seen (*u*) that the sheriff may defend himself by showing that the arrest was made by, and the escape from, a special bailiff appointed by the plaintiff himself; and this defence appears to have been pleaded specially in one case (*v*) without objection; but, on special demurrer, it may be doubted whether such a plea would not be held to amount to an argumentative traverse of the arrest *by the defendant.* We have also seen (*w*) that the sheriff may defend himself by showing that the escape was occasioned through the fraud and covin of the plaintiff himself; but to an action for a negligent escape, a plea that the plaintiff or others by his contrivance fraudulently detained the debtor out of his custody, *while he was intending and about to return,* should allege not only that the debtor *could,* but also that he *would,* but for such fraudulent detainer, *have returned into custody before the commencement of the action* (*x*). To a declaration against the bailiff of a liberty for an escape after an arrest under a mandate, it would be no defence against the further maintenance of the action to plead, by way of estoppel, that, after the commencement of the suit, the sheriff returned *cepi corpus* (*y*).

Replications.

To any plea setting up matter of excuse for the wrongful act complained of, the plaintiff may reply de injuriâ; and this replication will put in issue all the material allegations in the plea,

(*r*) Savory *v.* Chapman, 11 A. & E. 829.

(*s*) 1 & 2 Vict. c. 110, s. 110. If the general issue by statute be relied on, the words "By Statute" must be inserted in the margin of the plea; Reg. Gen. T. T. 1 Vict.

(*t*) Saffery *v.* Jones, 2 B. & Adol. 598.

(*u*) *Ante,* 199.

(*v*) Pascoe *v.* Vyvyan, 1 Dowl. N. S. 939.

(*w*) *Ante,* 201.

(*x*) Merry *v.* Chapman, 10 A. & E. 516.

(*y*) Jackson *v.* Hill, 10 A. & E. 477.

but not such as are superfluous or immaterial (*z*). To a plea setting up as a defence a recaption or a voluntary return, the plaintiff may reply, by way of new assignment, that, after such recaption or return to custody, the prisoner again escaped, which escape is the one complained of in the declaration (*a*). This replication by way of new assignment, however, is not necessary, for under a replication traversing that the debtor was detained in custody up to the time of the commencement of the suit, the same evidence may be given (*b*).

Evidence in an action for an escape.

The plea of not guilty puts in issue only the neglect or default of the sheriff or his officers (*c*); and the plaintiff need not, unless they are expressly denied, prove either the judgment, the issuing or delivery of the writ to the sheriff, or the arrest.

Under not guilty.

Where the plea of not guilty, therefore, is pleaded alone, the plaintiff need only prove the neglect or default of the sheriff, which is the escape, and the damages sustained in consequence. In order to show the escape, the plaintiff must prove that the debtor was at large after the arrest, either before or after the return of the writ, for the shortest time; even if he be accompanied by a sheriff's officer, it is an escape (*d*). And by the statute 8 & 9 Will. 3, c. 27, s. 8, "If any marshal or warden, or their deputies, or the keeper of any prison, after one day's notice in writing, given for that purpose, shall refuse to show a prisoner committed in execution to the creditor at whose suit such prisoner was committed, or his attorney, such refusal shall be adjudged to be an escape." As to the admissions of the under-sheriff, or the bailiff who made the arrest, and as to the manner of connecting the sheriff with the officer, the observations already made on the evidence in an action for an escape on mesne process (*e*) apply equally to an action for an escape of a prisoner in execution. If the old sheriff do not assign over all the prisoners to the new sheriff, this is an escape; but if it be shown that there was an assignment by parol, to which the new sheriff assented, the sheriff is not liable for an escape (*f*).

Denial of the judgment.

The judgment on which the *ca. sa.* issued may be proved by giving in evidence an examined copy of the record. What is

(*z*) Davis *v.* Chapman, 2 Man. & G. 921.

(*a*) See 1 Bos. & P. 414.

(*b*) See 1 Bos. & P. 417.

(*c*) Reg. Gen. H. T. 4 Will. 4.

(*d*) And as to what is an escape, see *ante*, 200, *et seq.*

(*e*) *Ante*, 188.

(*f*) Poulter *v.* Greenwood, Barnes, 367, 4to.

and what is not a fatal variance in the statement of the judgment has already been considered (*g*). It is competent for the defendant to show that the judgment is wholly void, as that there was a want of jurisdiction in the court wherein it was given (*h*), but he cannot show that the judgment is erroneous (*i*).

Denial of the issuing and delivery of the writ.

The issuing and delivery of the writ to the sheriff may be proved as follows: if the sheriff has returned the writ, an examined copy thereof, and of the sheriff's return indorsed on it, will be conclusive evidence against the sheriff (*j*); if the sheriff has not made his return, notice to produce the writ having been duly served on the sheriff's attorney, and search having been made at the Treasury (*k*), parol evidence of its contents may be given; and proof should also be given of its delivery to the sheriff. A delivery to the sheriff's deputy in London is a delivery to the sheriff (*l*). Where the old and new sheriff return a writ *non est inventus*, in an action against the old sheriff for not arresting the defendant, it was was held that as the return related to the day of quitting office, that, to make the sheriff liable for the default of the officer employed, it is not enough to show that the officer's name is on the writ, but it is necessary to prove that the neglect of the officer was committed whilst the defendant was in office (*m*).

Denial of the arrest.

The arrest may be proved in the same manner as an arrest on *mesne* process (*n*). The arrest proved must be a legal one (*o*). By the statute 8 & 9 Will. 3, c. 27, s. 9, it is enacted, "that if any person, desiring to charge another with any action or execution, shall desire to be informed by the marshal of the King's Bench, or the warden of the Common Pleas, or their respective deputy, or by any other keeper or keepers of any other prison, whether such person be a prisoner in his custody or not, every the said marshal, warden, or such keeper, &c., shall give a true note in writing thereof to the person requesting the same, or his attorney, upon demand at his office for that purpose; and if such marshal, warden, deputy, or keeper shall give a note in writing that such person is an actual prisoner in his custody, every such

(*g*) See *ante*, 206.
(*h*) See *ante*, 199.
(*i*) *Ibid.*
(*j*) 2 Phill. Evid. 231, 1st edit.; Starkie's Evid. part 4, 1346; Bul. N. P. 66.
(*k*) Rosc. N. P. Ev. 610, last edit.
(*l*) Woodland *v.* Fuller, 11 A. & E. 859.
(*m*) Fonsec *v.* Magnay, 6 Taunt. 231; 1 Marsh. 554, S. C.
(*n*) See *ante*, 184.
(*o*) Coutant *v.* Chapman, 2 Q. B. 771.

CHAP. VII. SECT. II.

note shall be taken as sufficient evidence of the fact (*p*)." Where the writ has been returned, the sheriff is bound by his return both as to the fact and the time of the arrest (*q*); but if the writ has not been returned, then some evidence should be given to connect the bailiff and the sheriff (*r*).

Evidence for the defendant.

Under the plea of *nil debet*, the defendant was entitled to go into evidence of any thing which was an excuse for him, excepting recaption on fresh pursuit, or the voluntary return of the defendant to custody (*s*). On the issue, that the sheriff did not detain the creditor after the recaption, or the voluntary return, *modo et formâ*, if it appear in evidence that the defendant was at large after the return, and died out of custody, the plaintiff is entitled to a verdict (*t*). Indeed, it seems to have been the opinion of Eyre, C. J. (*u*), that on a replication that the defendant had not kept the prisoner in custody from the time of the return, proof of an escape after the first return would have entitled the plaintiff to a verdict.

Damages.

In an action on the case for an escape, the sheriff will be liable to the amount of such damages as a jury may consider that the plaintiff at whose suit he was imprisoned may have sustained by reason of the escape (*x*); and even when debt was allowed for an escape, Lord Abinger seemed to think that the sheriff stood in the same situation as the defendant in the action, and might show the real merits of the case, and to what extent the defendant was liable (*y*). If the escape was *voluntary*, the sheriff has no mode of reimbursing himself, for a bond taken by the sheriff to suffer a prisoner in his custody to go at large is void (*z*); nor can the sheriff maintain an action against the defendant to recover the money he was obliged to pay in

(*p*) In practice, when a prisoner in custody of the marshal is to be charged with a King's Bench execution, a rule is obtained from the marshal to acklowledge the defendant to be in custody. Such an acknowledgment is of course evidence to prove the fact. When a prisoner is in custody of the warden of the Fleet, and is charged with a Common Pleas or Exchequer writ, a *habeas corpus* is obtained, the return to which proves the fact of his being in custody; Stark. on Evid. part. 4, 1347.

(*q*) Cook *v.* Round, 1 M. & Rob. 512.

(*r*) Rosc. N. P. Ev. 611.

(*s*) See *ante*, 208.

(*t*) Chambers *v.* Jones, 11 East, 406.

(*u*) Griffiths *v.* Eyles, 1 Bos. & Pul. 413. *Per* Lord Ellenborough, C. J., 11 East, 409.

(*x*) 5 & 6 Vict. c. 98, s. 31. See also Bonafous *v.* Walker, 2 T. R. 126.

(*y*) Evans *v.* Manero, 9 Dowl. 265.

(*z*) See 1 Sid. 132; and see *ante*.

consequence of *voluntarily* permitting him to escape (*a*). If the escape be *negligent*, the sheriff may maintain an action against the defendant for escaping, although the sheriff has not been sued for the escape (*b*); or, as we have seen, the sheriff may retake the defendant after a negligent escape, which will be a good defence to an action commenced after such recaption (*c*); or, if the defendant be retaken when an action has already been brought against the sheriff, he may be detained until he satisfy the sheriff the damages sustained by reason of the escape (*d*).

Staying proceedings.

The court will not stay proceedings in an action commenced against a sheriff, on payment of costs, where the defendant was privileged from arrest: thus, where the defendant was arrested on a *ca. sa.*, and the defendant, on producing his certificate under a commission of bankruptcy, was discharged out of custody by the officer, the court refused to grant a rule *nisi* to stay proceedings in an action commenced for an escape, saying that they would not try the merits of the action on affidavits (*e*). But where a sheriff had arrested the defendant on a *ca. sa.*, issued *erroneously* on a recognizance of bail taken in C. P., and discharged him out of custody on payment of debt and costs, which money the sheriff refused to pay over, in consequence of having received a notice that the money belonged to the assignees of the defendant, who had become bankrupt; the Court of Common Pleas relieved the sheriff from an action commenced against him for an escape, allowing the plaintiff to litigate his right to the money on the money counts (*f*).

(*a*) Pitcher *v*. Bailey, 8 East, 171; Eyles *v*. Faikney, Peake's N. P. C. 144, n.; Barnes, 373; Dalt. 138. See also Dyer, 275; Plowd. 36 a.

(*b*) Sheriffs of Norwich *v*. Bradshaw, Cro. Eliz. 53.

(*c*) See *ante*, 203.

(*d*) Dalt. 139; Ridgway's case, 3 Rep. 52.

(*e*) Sherwood *v*. Benson, 4 Taunt. 631.

(*f*) Wooden *v*. Moxon, 6 Taunt. 490; 2 Marsh. 186, S. C.

CHAPTER VIII.

THE SHERIFF'S DUTY IN THE EXECUTION AND RETURN OF PROCESS OF OUTLAWRY.

SECT. I.—*Of the Exigent and Writ of Proclamations.—In what Cases and in what Manner a Party may proceed to Outlawry.—Exigent, how executed.—Return, how made.— Writ of Proclamations, on Outlawry in Civil Actions; on Indictments; when required, how made.—Sheriff's Return, form of; into what Office made.—Fees thereon.*

II.—*Of the general and special Writs of Capias Utlagatum; how executed.—Bail, how taken on.—Special Capias Utlagatum, how executed.—Form of the Inquisition.—Sheriff's Return.—Preference between several Writs of Capias Utlagatum; Fees thereon. —Actions against the Sheriff.—Restitution.*

SECTION I.

Of the Exigent and Writ of Proclamations.

In what cases process of outlawry lies.

AT the common law, wherever a *capias* lay, a person might be outlawed, but not otherwise (*a*); indeed, for some time after the Conquest, so penal were the consequences of outlawry (the punishment whereof was death), that no man could have been outlawed except for felony (*b*). In early times, however, persons were outlawed on all indictments for offences at the common law, as well for misdemeanors (*c*) as for treason or felony; but it seems that a person cannot be outlawed in an action, or indictment on a statute, unless it be given expressly by such statute, as in the case of *præmunire;* or impliedly, as in cases made treason or felony by statute; or where a recovery is given by an action in which such process lay before, as in the case of

(*a*) Bac. Abr. Outlawry (A); Co. Litt. 128.

(*b*) Bracton, lib. 5, p. 425; Co. Litt. 128.

(*c*) Rex *v.* Wilkes, 4 Burr. 2557, 8; Co. Litt. 128.

a forcible entry (*d*). At the common law, in civil actions where a *capias* lay in process, as in trespass *vi et armis*, a process of outlawry lay also (*e*). And by several statutes (*f*) (which introduced the *capias*) process of outlawry lies, as in the actions of account, debt, *detinue*, replevin (*g*), actions on the case (*h*), and several other actions. Outlawry is either on mesne process before, or on final process after, judgment. Formerly, in the Queen's Bench, a person could not be outlawed either before (*i*) or after (*k*) judgment, except the proceedings were by *original*. In the Common Pleas, a person might be outlawed either on a common *quare clausum fregit* (*l*), or on a special original. But in the Exchequer a person could not be outlawed, as the plaintiff could not proceed there by original (*m*). An inferior court could not in any case, for the same reason, award process of outlawry (*n*). At the present day, the writ of capias being no longer the commencement of an action, but all actions being commenced by writ of summons, the mode of proceeding to outlawry in a civil action before judgment is regulated by the Uniformity of Process Act, 2 Will. 4, c. 39; the third section of which enacts, that "in case it shall be made appear by affidavit, to the satisfaction of the court out of which the process issued, or, in vacation, of any judge of either of the said courts, ('his majesty's superior courts of law at Westminster,' sect. 1), that any defendant has not been personally served with any such writ of summons as hereinbefore mentioned, and has not, according to the exigency thereof, appeared to the action, and cannot be compelled to do so without some more efficacious process, then and in any such case it shall be lawful for such court or judge to order a writ of *distringas* to be issued, directed to the sheriff of the county wherein the dwelling-house or place of abode of such defendant shall be situate, or to the sheriff of any other county, or to any other officer to be named by such

Mode of proceeding to outlawry.

(*d*) Bac. Abr. Outlawry (A).

(*e*) 35 Hen. 6, 66; 22 Hen. 6, 13; Rast. Ent. 293; 10 Rep. 72.

(*f*) Co. Litt. 128; Bac. Abr. Outlawry (A); 25 Edw. 3, c. 17.

(*g*) 25 Edw. 3, c. 17; Earl of Banbury *v.* Wood, 2 Ld. Raym. 987; Salk. 5, S. C.; 6 Mod. 84.

(*h*) 19 Hen. 7, c. 9.

(*i*) See Davis *v.* Isaac, 1 Sid. 159.

(*k*) Crews *v.* Bayles, Cro. Eliz. 215; 1 Leon. 329.

(*l*) Barnes, 324.

(*m*) Horton *v.* Peake, 1 Price, 306.

(*n*) See Ward *v.* Elleyn, Cro. Jac. 251; 1 Sid. 248; 1 Keb. 890, 908; Doug. 62. See also Williams *v.* Lord Bagot, 3 Barn. & Cress. 772; 5 Dowl. & Ry. 719, S. C.

CHAP. VIII. SECT. I.

court or judge, in order to compel the appearance of such defendant; which writ of *distringas* shall be in the form, and with the notice subscribed thereto, mentioned in the schedule to this act, marked No. 3; which writ of *distringas* and notice, or a copy thereof, shall be served on such defendant, if he can be met with, or, if not, shall be left at the place where such *distringas* shall be executed; and a true copy of every such writ and notice shall be delivered together therewith to the sheriff or other officer to whom such writ shall be directed; and every such writ shall be made returnable on some day in term, not being less than fifteen days after the teste thereof, and shall bear teste on the day of the issuing thereof, whether in term or in vacation; and if such writ of *distringas* shall be returned *non est inventus* and *nulla bona*, and the party suing out such writ shall not intend to proceed to outlawry or waiver, according to the authority hereinafter given, and any defendant against whom any such writ of *distringas* issued shall not appear at or within eight days inclusive after the return thereof, and it shall be made appear by affidavit to the satisfaction of the court out of which such writ of *distringas* issued, or, in vacation, of any judge of either of the said courts, that due and proper means were taken and used to serve and execute such writ of *distringas*, it shall be lawful for such court or judge to authorize the party suing out such writ to enter an appearance for such defendant, and to proceed thereon to judgment and execution."

The 5th section of the same act enacts, "that upon the return of *non est inventus* and *nulla bona* as to any defendant against whom such writ of *distringas* as hereinbefore mentioned shall have issued, whether such writ of *distringas* shall have issued against such defendant only, or against such defendant and any other person or persons, it shall be lawful, until otherwise provided for, to proceed to outlaw or waive such defendant by writs of *exigi facias* and proclamation, and otherwise, in such and the same manner as may now be lawfully done upon the return of *non est inventus* to a pluries writ of *capias ad respondendum* issued after an original writ: provided always, that every such writ of *exigent*, proclamation, and other writ, subsequent to the writ of *distringas*, shall be made returnable on a day certain in term; and every such first writ of *exigent* and proclamation shall bear teste on the day of the return of the writ of *distringas*, whether such writ be returned in term or in vacation;

and every subsequent writ of *exigent* and proclamation shall bear teste on the day of the return of the next preceding writ; and no such writ of *distringas* shall be sufficient for the purpose of outlawry or waiver, if the same be returned within less than fifteen days (*o*) after the delivery thereof to the sheriff or other officer to whom the same shall be directed (*p*).

The 6th section provides, "that, *after judgment* given in any action commenced by writ of summons under the authority of this act, proceedings to outlawry or waiver may be had and taken, and judgment of outlawry or waiver given, in such manner and in such cases as may now be lawfully done after judgment in an action commenced by original writ; provided always, that every outlawry or waiver had under the authority of this act may be vacated or set aside by writ of error or motion, in like manner as outlawry or waiver founded on an original writ may now be vacated or set aside."

The effect of this statute and of the 11 Geo. 4 & 1 Will. 4, c. 70, s. 14, is, that a defendant may now be outlawed in the Exchequer as in any other of the superior courts (*q*); but the writ of *capias utlagatum* and inquisition are returned into the office of the queen's remembrancer; and on an application to traverse the inquisition, the affidavit must be intituled in that office, and the counsel must be instructed by a sworn clerk (*r*).

Justices of oyer and terminer, and justices of the peace in their sessions, have power to award process of outlawry upon indictments found before them (*s*).

A peer, or a member of the House of Commons, cannot be outlawed, excepting on an indictment; but upon an indictment

(*o*) There must be fifteen *clear* days between the delivery and the return of the writ; Chambers *v.* Smith, 12 M. & W. 2. If made returnable on a Sunday, it is a nullity; Morrison *v.* Mauley, 1 Dowl. N. S. 773.

(*p*) As to the cases in which a *distringas* will be granted for the purpose of proceeding to outlawry, the requisites of the writ, &c. see Hewitt *v.* Melton, 3 Tyrw. 822; Fraser *v.* Case, 9 Bing. 464; 4 M. & Scott, 720, S. C.; Jones *v.* Price, 2 Dowl. 42; Reay *v.* Youde, 2 M. & W. 188; Vere *v.* Gowar, 3 Bing. N. C. 503; 4 Scott, 287, S. C.; Lewis *v.* Davison, 1 C. M. & R. 655; 3 Dowl. 272, S.C.; Partridge *v.* Wallbank, 2 M. & W. 893; Simpson *v.* Lord Graves, 2 Dowl. 10; Nugee *v.* Swinford, 9 Dowl. 1038; Round *v.* Brown, 1 Dowl. N. S. 860.

(*q*) 2 Dowl. 42. See 2 Will. 4, c. 39, s. 7, whereby the Lord Chief Baron is required to appoint a fit person, holding some other office in the Court of Exchequer, to execute the duties of a filacer, exigenter, and clerk of the outlawries in that court.

(*r*) 5 M. & W. 278.

(*s*) Bac. Abr. Outlawry (B). But they cannot issue a *capias utlagatum*; the record of outlawry must be returned into the Queen's Bench and thence a *capias utlagatum* issues; Dalt. 406. A *capias* must issue before the *exigent*; 6 Hen. 6, c. 1; 8 Hen. 6, c. 10; 10 Hen. 6, c. 6.

CHAP. VIII. SECT. I.

for a *misdemeanor*, as for a libel, riot, or the like, process of outlawry will lie against a peer (*t*). A person outlawed was supposed to be put out of the law; but women are not said to be outlawed, but *waived;* for as women were not sworn to the law by taking the oath of allegiance, (as men anciently were, when of the age of twelve years or upwards,) therefore a woman cannot be outlawed (*u*); and, for the same reason, an infant under the age of twelve years cannot be outlawed (*x*).

Of the writ of *exigent*.

The writ of *exigi facias* is the first proceeding after the return of *non est inventus* and *nulla bona* to the *distringas* (*y*). It must be tested on the day of the return of the *distringas;* but it is not necessary that it should be actually sued out on that day (*z*). After judgment, it may be issued on the return of *non est inventus* to the *capias*, without an *alias* or *pluries* (*a*); but for this purpose the *capias* must have a fixed return, and the *exigi facias* cannot be grounded upon a *capias* returnable immediately after execution, under 3 & 4 Will. 4, c. 67 (*b*). The writ of *exigi facias* is directed to the sheriff of the county where the venue in the action is laid, or where the indictment is found, commanding him to cause the defendant to be *required* from county court to county court, or from husting to husting, if in London. And if there be not *five* county courts between the teste and return of the writ of *exigi facias*, there issues upon the sheriff's return thereto an *exigent de novo*, with a clause directing the sheriff to *allow* the several county courts at which the defendant has been already required, thence called the *allocatur exigent*.

Exigent, how to be executed.

The mode in which the sheriff should execute the writ of *exigent* is by calling upon the defendant, at each county court after the receipt of the writ, to appear; and the sheriff must not omit any county court, for if a county court intervene between any of the exactions without the defendant being demanded there, it is error (*c*). On mesne process, if the defendant

(*t*) 2 Hal. P. C. 199, 200; Bac. Abr. Outlawry (C). The court will not, therefore, grant a *distringas* to proceed to outlawry against a peer; Taylor *v.* Lord Stuart de Rothsay, 2 Dowl. N. S. 121.

(*u*) Co. Litt. 122 b; Litt. 186; Middleton's case, Cro. Jac. 358; Haiman's case, 1 Roll. Rep. 407.

(*x*) Co. Litt. 128 a; 2 Roll. Abr. 805; Fitz. Outlawry, 11.

(*y*) Bac. Abr. Outlawry (B).

(*z*) Lewis *v.* Davison, 1 C. M. & R. 655; Vere *v.* Gowar, 3 Bing. N. C. 503; 4 Scott, 287, S. C.

(*a*) Tidd's Prac. 128, 8th edit. See Reg. Gen. H. 2 Will. 4, r. 94.

(*b*) Lewis *v.* Holmes, 16 Law J, 430, Q. B.

(*c*) Plowd. 371. And it would appear that if there be five county courts between the teste and the return of the *exigent*, although only one or two after the receipt of the writ;

appear on the exigent, the sheriff may take bail from him as in ordinary cases (*c*). But after judgment, if the defendant appear or be taken on the *exigent*, the sheriff must keep him in close custody, as on a *ca. sa.* In criminal proceedings, where the defendant is not bailable, as in treason or felony, it is clear that the sheriff should keep the defendant in custody; but before judgment, if the defendant appear upon the *exigent*, issued on an indictment for a misdemeanor, it is apprehended that the sheriff might take a recognizance for his appearance (*d*); but after judgment it is clear that he could not, but that he should keep him in safe custody (*e*). After being five times demanded, if proclamations have been duly made, the defendant is declared to be outlawed by the coroner of the county in the county court (*f*). The judgment of outlawry is not complete unless it has been entered on the rolls, and it is not sufficient to state simply that the writ of *exigent* was duly returned by the sheriff (*g*).

Return, how made.

Great particularity is required in the return to the *exigent*, for as the consequences of outlawry are considered so penal, any irregularity will be fatal. As if an *exigent* issue against several persons, one of whom is a woman, and the return be that they were *quinto exacti* and outlawed, it is bad, for it should have been that the woman was waived (*h*). The sheriff must return that the defendant was demanded at his county court, and must show that the county court was holden *in and for* the county whereof he is sheriff, otherwise it is bad: therefore, a return stating that the defendant was demanded at my county court holden at S., in the county of N., without saying for the county of N., was holden to be bad (*i*). The return must particularly specify the days, by naming the day and year of each

yet if the sheriff return that the defendant has been demanded at the five county courts, this is regular. See Taylor *v.* Waters, 3 Dowl. & Ry. 575; 2 Bar. & C. 353, S. C. *Sed vide* Volet *v.* Waters, 3 D. & R. 55.

(*c*) See Tidd's Prac. 130, 8th edit.

(*d*) Dalton, 26. And see Bengough *v.* Rossiter, 4 T. R. 505; S. C. in error, 2 H. Blac. 418, where it was decided that the sheriff could not take a bail-bond from a person arrested by him on a *capias* issuing from the quarter sessions on an indictment.

(*e*) 4 Burr. 2537.

(*f*) Dalt. 240. And if the outlawry be on the day that the *allocatur exigent* bears teste, it is bad; Archer *v.* Archer, Cro. Jac. 660; Palm. 280, S. C.

(*g*) Attorney-General *v.* Rickards, 14 Law J., Chan., 363.

(*h*) Middleton's case, Cro. Jac. 358. See also 1 Rol. Rep. 407.

(*i*) Rex *v.* Wilkes, 4 Burr. 2563. And see Whiting's case, 2 Roll. Abr. 802, and other cases cited in Burr. 2563.

CHAP. VIII. SECT. I.

occasion on which the defendant was demanded (*j*); and if the year be not added to the day on which the demand is alleged to be made, the return will be bad (*k*). It is said to be necessary to state the year as the year of the king's or queen's reign (*l*). If the sheriff return that the defendant was demanded on five several county courts between the teste and return of the writ or writs of *exigent*, the proceedings are regular, although some of those days of exactions were *before* the delivery of the writ or writs of *exigent* to the sheriff (*m*). The name of the coroner by whom outlawry was pronounced must be inserted in the return of *quinto exactus*, and he must be stated to be coroner, but the coroner need not sign the return (*n*). Where there are not five county courts between the teste and the return of the *exigent*, the sheriff should return this, in order that the plaintiff may issue an *allocatur exigent* (*o*). It is said that it is not a good return to say that the defendant is dead, as an excuse for the sheriff not executing the *exigent*, for it is the sheriff's duty to call the defendant at all events (*p*). If the defendant be in the sheriff's custody at the time of the delivery of the writ of *exigent* to the sheriff, or before the *quinto exactus*, the sheriff should return this (*q*). If a supersedeas have been delivered to the sheriff before the return-day of the *exigent*, this should be returned by the sheriff (*r*).

Of the proclamations in civil proceedings.

In addition to the *exigent*, a writ of proclamation was introduced by the statute 6 Hen. 8, c. 4, which requires it to be directed to the sheriff of the county of which the defendant is called or described in the original, for there he was supposed to dwell. But the writ of proclamation in civil proceedings is now governed by the statute 31 Eliz. c. 3, s. 1, which enacts, that " in every action personal, wherein any writ of *exigent* shall be awarded out of any court, one writ of proclamation shall be awarded and made out of the same court, having the day of

(*j*) Rex *v.* Almon, 5 T. R. 202.

(*k*) *Id. ibid.*; 2 Roll. Abr. 802, pl. 8.

(*l*) *Per* Buller, J., 5 T. R. 205. But see Crosse's case, Hardr. 6, *contra*.

(*m*) Taylor *v.* Waters, 3 Dowl. & Ry. 575; 2 B. & C. 353, S. C. But see Volet *v.* Waters, 3 Dowl. & Ry. 55.

(*n*) Rex *v.* Yandell, 4 T. R. 533.

(*o*) See return, *post*, Append. c. 8, s. 1.

(*p*) Dalt. 239: *sed quære.* It is questioned by Dalton (239), whether or not the sheriff should proceed in case of the death of the king, but it appears that he should.

(*q*) Dalt. 239. See form, *post*, Append. c. 8, s. 1.

(*r*) See form, *post*, Append. c. 8, s. 1.

teste and return, as the said writ of *exigent* shall have directed and delivered of record to the sheriff of the county where the defendant *at the time of the exigent so awarded shall be dwelling*, which writ of proclamation shall contain the effect of the same action; and the sheriff of the county, unto whom any such writ of proclamation shall be delivered, shall make three proclamations, *one in the open county court*, *another at the general quarter sessions of the peace*, in those parts where the defendant at the time of the *exigent* awarded shall be dwelling, *and the third one month at the least before the quinto exactus*, by virtue of the said writ of *exigent*, at or near to the most usual door of the church or chapel of that town or parish where the defendant shall be dwelling at the time of the *exigent* awarded; and if the defendant shall be dwelling out of any parish, then in such place as aforesaid of the next adjoining parish in the same county next adjoining to the place of the defendant's dwelling; and upon a Sunday immediately after divine service (*s*); and that all outlawries had and pronounced, whereupon no writs of proclamation shall be awarded and returned according to the form of this statute, shall be utterly void and of none effect."

Writ of proclamation on indictments.

By the statute 4 & 5 Will. & Mary, c. 22, s. 4, made perpetual by 7 & 8 Will. 3, c. 36, s. 4, it is enacted, "that upon the issuing of any *exigent* out of any of their majesties' courts against any person or persons for any *criminal matter*, *before* judgment or conviction, there shall issue out a writ of proclamation, bearing the same teste and return, to the sheriff or sheriffs of the county, city or town corporate, where the person or persons in the record of the said proceedings is or are mentioned to be or inhabit, according to the form of the statute made in the one-

(*s*) But by the statute 1 Vict. c. 45, all proclamations theretofore made in churches or chapels during or after divine service are to be reduced into writing, and copies thereof, either in writing or in print, or partly in writing and partly in print, shall, previously to the commencement of divine service on the several days on which such proclamations had thertofore been made in the church or chapel of any parish or place, or at the door of any church or chapel, be affixed on or near to the doors of all the churches or chapels within such parish or place; and such notices, when so affixed, shall be in lieu of and as a substitution for the several proclamations and notices so theretofore made as aforesaid, and shall be good, valid and effectual to all intents and purposes. Affixing the notice on the *principal* door of each church or chapel of the Establishment is sufficient; Ormerod *v.* Chadwick, 16 M. & W. 367.

CHAP. VIII. SECT. I.

and-thirtieth year of the reign of Queen Elizabeth, which writ of proclamation shall be delivered to the said sheriff or sheriffs three months before the return of the same."

In what cases required.

This last statute only extends the provisions of the statute of Elizabeth to criminal cases *before* judgment, but leaves untouched cases of outlawry in criminal matters *after conviction;* in such case no proclamation is required (*t*). The writ of proclamations should have the same teste and return as the *exigent.* The writ, when issued into a different county from that into which the *exigent* issued, is called a foreign proclamation.

How made.

The sheriff makes his warrant to his bailiff, authorizing him to make proclamations according to the exigency of the writ. In making the proclamations, the order prescribed by the statute must be followed, first, at the county court, next at the sessions, and, last, by affixing notice on the church door on a Sunday, before divine service. If the first Sunday next after the quarter sessions happen to be the return day of the writ, the proclamation may be made on that day, and so stated in the return. The proclamation must be affixed to the door of the parish church of the last residence of the defendant in the county; if it be the church door of the parish whereof the defendant was styled in the writ, and where he lived when he gave a bond, the foundation of the action, that parish not being his residence at the time of proclamation made, the proclamation is void (*u*). This last proclamation on the church door must be made at least *one month* before the *quinto exactus* (*x*).

Sheriff's return.

The sheriff should return to the writ of proclamations, that he has caused the defendant to be proclaimed, either generally, according to the form of the statute (*y*), or specially, setting forth the times and places when and where the proclamations were made (*z*). If there be not a Sunday after the sessions and before the return-day of the writ, the return must allege that proclamations were made at the county court and at the sessions,

(*t*) Rex *v.* Wilkes, 4 Burr. 2559.

(*u*) Rayer *v.* Cooke, 3 Bar. & Cress. 529; 5 Dowl. & Ry. 392, S. C.

(*x*) Taylor *v.* Waters, 2 Bar. & Cress. 353; 3 Dowl. & Ry. 575, S. C. As to a return of proclamation made before the writ was in the sheriff's hands, see Volet *v.* Waters, 3 Dowl. & Ry. 55.

(*y*) Tidd's Prac. 8th ed. 130, 139. It may be questionable whether this return would not be too general; Rex *v.* Wilkes, 4 Burr. 2559.

(*z*) See form, Append. c. 8, s. 1.

but, because there was no Sunday after the sessions, the third proclamation could not be made; so if only one proclamation were made, as if there were no quarter sessions between the teste and return of the writ of proclamation, the return must agree with the fact (*a*). The sheriff should also return, that the defendant was outlawed by the coroner; but the sheriff may return (if the fact be so) that the coroners were absent, or that only one coroner was there, who refused to pronounce the outlawry (*b*).

Into what office returned. When the *exigent* and writ of proclamation are returned, they should be taken to the *filacer* in the Queen's Bench; but in the Common Pleas the *exigent* is taken to the clerk of the outlawries, and the writ of proclamation filed with the *exigenter* (*c*).

Fees thereon. The sheriff is not entitled to any fee for making the proclamations at the county court or at the sessions; but by the 31 Eliz. c. 3, he is entitled to a fee of one shilling for the proclamation at the church door (*d*). As to the fee for the warrant, see *ante*, p. 103.

Reversal of outlawry for want of proclamations. Formerly no averment could be made against the sheriff's return to the writs of *exigent* or proclamations, but if the defendant were outlawed without proclamations, his only remedy was by action on the case against the sheriff (*e*). But now, by the 31 Eliz. c. 3, the outlawry may be reversed for want of proclamations as prescribed by that statute.

Section II.

Capias Utlagatum.

Of the general and special writs of *capias utlagatum*. On the return of the *exigent*, the next process is the writ of *capias utlagatum*; of this there are two kinds, the *general* and the

(*a*) Where the proclamation is bad, so as it is considered as no proclamation, the bail, by the 31 Eliz. c. 3, s. 3, on reversing the outlawry, must be given to answer the condemnation money; Rayer *v.* Cooke, 3 Bar. & C. 529; 5 Dowl. & Ry. 302, S. C. Where there is only an irregularity in making the proclamations, it is optional how the court will order bail to be given, but in general in such case it is required in the alternative; Waters *v.* Taylor, 2 B. & C. 353; 3 Dowl. & Ry. 575, S. C.

(*b*) Dalt. 240.

(*c*) Tidd's Prac. 130, 8th edit.

(*d*) The sheriff is also entitled to one shilling for his return.

(*e*) Bro. Action sur le case, 122.

CHAP. VIII. SECT. II.

special capias utlagatum. The general writ commands the sheriff not to omit by reason of any liberty, but that he take the defendant and have him in court on the return day, to do and receive what the court shall consider of him in that behalf (*f*). The *special* writ of *capias utlagatum* commands the sheriff to take the defendant in the same manner as the general writ, and also "to inquire by the oath of honest and lawful men of his county what goods and chattels, lands and tenements he hath, or had on the day of his outlawry, or at any time afterwards; and by their oath to extend and appraise the same according to their true value; and to take them into the king's hands, and safely keep them, so that he may answer to the king for their true value and issues of the same, making known what he shall do thereupon to the court on the return day (*g*)."

How executed.

In executing a *capias utlagatum*, even on civil process, it appears that the officer may break open the outer door of a house to take the defendant or his goods (*h*). The writ is a *non omittas*, and therefore the sheriff may execute the writ within a liberty without sending his mandate to the bailiff of the liberty; a *capias utlagatum* in civil suits cannot be executed on a Sunday (*i*). The death of the defendant in a civil suit determines the outlawry (*j*). But in criminal cases, outlawry works an entire forfeiture of the outlaw's estate, both real and personal. Where the outlaw dies after the teste of the special *capias utlagatum*, it would appear that the sheriff still should proceed and hold the inquisition, and leave the representatives of the outlaw to obtain restitution in the Court of Exchequer, for the personal chattels are forfeited by the outlawry (*k*). If a *feme sole* be *waived*, and she marry after the *exigent*, but before the outlawry, she may nevertheless be taken on a *capias utlagatum* (*l*). And if the defendant has become bankrupt, and obtained his certificate, by which the cause of action would be barred, yet the sheriff must take him on the *capias utlagatum;* nor will the

(*f*) See Forms, Reg. Brev. 138; Tidd's Forms, 51, 5th edit.; Archbold's Forms, 523, 524.

(*g*) Tidd's Forms, 51, 52; Archbold's Forms, 524.

(*h*) Rex *v.* Bird, 2 Show. 87. *Sed vide* Golds. 179; 4 Leon. 41; Moore, 609; Cro. Eliz. 908; Yelv. 28.

(*i*) Osborne *v.* Carter, Barnes, 319.

(*j*) See 1 Tidd's Prac. 141, 8th ed.

(*k*) Salk. 395; Bac. Abr. Outlawry (D) 2.

(*l*) White *v.* Dunster, Barnes, 321; see Briscoe *v.* Kennedy, 2 Wils. 127.

courts discharge him excepting on putting in special bail (*m*). But a bankrupt cannot be arrested on a *capias utlagatum* during the period of protection given him by the Bankrupt Act (*ante*, p. 139); and if he be, the Court of Bankruptcy will discharge him (*n*).

In what cases the sheriff may take bail on a *capias utlagatum*.

At the common law, the sheriff could not have taken bail and discharged the defendant, arrested by him on a *capias utlagatum;* this case is particularly excepted out of the 23 Hen. 6, c. 9; and by the stat. 13 Car. 2, stat. 2, c. 2, s. 4, it is expressly enacted "that no sheriff, &c. shall discharge any person or persons taken upon any writ of *capias utlagatum* out of custody, without a lawful *supersedeas* first had and received for the same." But by the statute 4 & 5 Will. & Mary, c. 18, s. 4, "If any person outlawed in the Court of King's Bench, other than for treason and felony, shall be taken and arrested upon any *capias utlagatum* out of the said court, the sheriff making the arrest may, *in all cases where special bail is not required by the said court*, take an attorney's engagement under his hand to appear for the defendant, and reverse the outlawry, and may therefore discharge the defendant from such arrest. And in those cases where special bail is required by the said court (*o*), the sheriff shall and may take security by bond, with one or more sufficient surety or sureties, in the penalty of double the sum for which special bail is required, and no more, for his appearance by attorney, in court at the return of the writ, and to do and perform such things as shall be required by the same court, and, after such bond taken, may discharge the defendant from the said arrest." And by section 5 of the same statute, in case the defendant shall not be able to give security as aforesaid, *before the return* of the writ, in cases where special bail is required, he shall and may be discharged whenever he shall find security to the sheriff for his appearance, by attorney, in the said court, at some return in the ensuing term, to reverse the outlawry, and to do and perform such other thing and things as shall be required by the said court. This statute only in terms

(*m*) See Beauchamp *v.* Tomkins, 3 Taunt. 141; Summerville *v.* Watkins, 14 East, 536; Absthorpe *v.* Fiske, 8 Dowl. 68.

(*n*) Ex parte Hemsley, 1 Deac. & Ch. 16.

(*o*) The attorney's engagement would now be sufficient in all cases, special bail being no longer necessary except in the case provided for by 1 & 2 Vict. c. 110, s. 4.

CHAP. VIII. SECT. II.

applies to writs of *capias utlagatum* issuing out of the *Court of Queen's Bench*, but it has been the practice to take bail as prescribed by this act on such writs issuing out of the Common Pleas (*p*). It would appear that the sheriff has not power to bail a defendant under this statute in any *criminal* case; but it is worthy of observation, that although treason and felony are expressly, yet that misdemeanors are not, excepted out of the operation of the act; and it appears to be doubtful whether the act is or is not confined to civil actions only (*q*). However, it has been decided that a defendant is not bailable on a *capias utlagatum* upon an indictment for a misdemeanor *after conviction* (*r*).

Special *capias utlagatum*, how executed.

The sheriff, on the *special capias utlagatum*, is first required to take the defendant, which if done, and he appear to the original action, it is said not to be usual to extend the goods, and to impanel a jury. But if the defendant be not taken, it is the sheriff's duty to impanel a jury, who are to inquire of the goods and chattels (*s*) of the defendant, including his debts (*t*) and choses in action, and also of his leasehold and freehold lands and tenements; and to appraise the goods, and to extend the value of the lands, &c. (*u*). But the sheriff cannot extend copyhold lands (*x*), or trust property (*y*), on a *capias utlagatum*. Witnesses should be summoned to attend the execution of the inquiry; and when the inquest is made, the sheriff is to take possession of the goods and chattels found by the inquest to belong to the defendant at the time of the outlawry (*z*), or pur-

(*p*) Sell. Prac. 398. See observations of Chambre, J., 3 Taunt. 144.

(*q*) It seems to have been the opinion of some of the judges in Rex *v.* Wilkes (4 Burr. 2540), that the statute only applied to civil actions.

(*r*) Rex *v.* Wilkes, 4 Burr. 2539.

(*s*) As to what may be taken as the goods and chattels of the defendant, see *post*, chap. 11.

(*t*) Bullock *v.* Dodds, 2 B. & Ald. 276; Bro. Forfeiture, 107; see also Slade's case, 4 Rep. 95; Lane, 23; Lutw. 329, 1513; Dalt. 83. The cases in 2 Rol. Abr. 452, 806; Cro. Eliz. 575, 851, *contrà*, are denied to be law both in Bullock *v.* Dodds and in Slade's case.

(*u*) See Bank of England *v.* Reid, 8 Dowl. 851.

(*x*) Rex *v.* Budd, Parker, 190.

(*y*) It seems that the statute 29 Car. 2, c. 3, s. 10, does not apply to this case; Tidd's Prac. 134, 8th edit. *Sed vide* 2 Rol. Abr. 807, l. 12.

(*z*) But goods which the outlaw hath in *autre droit*, as executor or administrator, cannot be taken, 11 Hen. 6, 17, 37; Cro. Eliz. 575, 851; 2 Rol. Abr. 806; nor a term of years which the outlaw hath as executor, 2 Leon. 5, 6; Ander. 19; Moore, 100; Dyer, 309; or if a feme covert be waived, the term she had shall not be forfeited, for that belongs to her husband, Dalt. 83, cit. 9 Hen. 6, fol. 52.

chased between the outlawry and the time of taking the inquisition (*b*); and also the sheriff may extend and take possession of the leasehold tenements in the occupation of the defendant. But it is otherwise in the case of the freehold lands of the defendant; for although the king is entitled to take the profits of the freehold lands on an outlawry in a civil suit, yet the defendant cannot be disturbed in the occupation. The sheriff, upon a *levari facias* in an outlawry, in taking for the king all the profits of the lands, may mow or sever and take all the corn and grass growing on the land, and may take the feed and herbage arising on the grounds, &c., and the rents of the farmers, as the party might; but he cannot plough, sow, or grant the same, or cut or crop the trees growing, or take fixtures, for they are part of the freehold (*c*). If the outlaw, after the outlawry and before the inquisition, make a lease of or alien his freehold land (*d*), the profits of such land cannot be extended on a *capias utlagatum* in a civil action; it is, however, otherwise as to the personal chattels of the outlaw, for immediately by the outlawry they are forfeited; but the profits of the land or chattels real are not forfeited until inquisition taken (*e*). Cattle levant and couchant on the land may be extended on a *capias utlagatum*, as the issues and profits of the land (*f*). If a defendant, who is outlawed in a personal action, have an advowson of a church, which becomes void during the time the outlawry is in force, the queen shall present to the church (*g*).

Form of the inquisition.

The inquisition should set forth, with convenient certainty, the appraised value of the goods, the particulars of the debts,

(*b*) Carth. 442.

(*c*) Dalt. 82, 83; Rockley *v.* Wilkinson, T. Jones, 100; Windsor *v.* Saywell, 1 Lev. 33; Plowd. 541; Hard. 106. Indeed it is said that the corn on the ground cannot be taken, but only the rent; 2 Rol. Abr. 807. Arrearages of rent, reserved on lease for life, are not forfeited by outlawry, for they are real; otherwise if upon a lease for years; Hetl. 164. There is a distinction between outlawry in criminal and in civil cases; outlawry on an indictment for treason or felony corrupts the blood, and causes an absolute forfeiture of the party's estate, both real and personal, viz. in case of outlawry of treason his lands are forfeited to the queen, of whomsoever they are holden; and in case of outlawry of felony to the lord by escheat of whom they are immediately holden. See Bac. Abr. Outlawry (D) 1.

(*d*) Windsor *v.* Saywell, 1 Lev. 33; 1 Keb. 57, 74, 76, S. C.; see Hamond's case, Hard. 176.

(*e*) Britton *v.* Cole, 1 Ld. Raym. 305; Salk. 395, S. C.; Carth. 441; 5 Mod. 112. Deer in a park cannot be extended on a *capias utlagatum*; 10 Hen. 7, 7 a.

(*f*) Britton *v.* Cole, 1 Ld. Raym. 305; Salk. 395, S. C.

(*g*) 2 Rol. Abr. 807; and see Beverly *v.* Cornwall, Cro. Eliz. 44; Andr. 148.

CHAP. VIII. SECT. II.

of what *lands*, &c. the defendant is seised or possessed, the different parcels, in whose *tenure*, and their annual value beyond reprises (*h*). The sheriff is only to take the profits on a *levari facias* according to the extended value of the lands; if they are undervalued, the plaintiff should apply to the court to grant a *melius inquirendum* (*i*).

The sheriff must take into his possession the goods, &c. found.

Whatever goods and chattels the jury find to belong to the defendant, the sheriff should seize and keep them safely until ordered to sell them by a writ of *venditioni exponas*, but he cannot sell them before he receives such writ (*k*); nor does he take into his hands the debts of the defendant, or the profits of his freehold estate, until he is ordered so to do by the Court of Exchequer. After the return to the *capias utlagatum*, a writ of *venditioni exponas* issues, to sell the goods, a *scire facias* to collect the debts, and a *levari facias* to levy the issues and profits of the lands. In levying the issues and profits of the lands, the sheriff, we have seen, may take cattle *levant and couchant* thereon (*l*); he may mow and sever the corn and grass, and take the rents as the party himself might do, but he cannot sow the ground or cut trees (*m*).

Return.

The sheriff makes his return, when ruled, according to the fact; if the defendant is not to be found, he returns *non est inventus*, or if he has taken the defendant and has him in custody, or has discharged him on giving bail, he returns *cepi corpus*; if either goods or the profits of lands have been found by the inquisition on a *special capias utlagatum*, the sheriff should return the inquisition (*n*); if the jury find that the defendant has no goods, &c., the sheriff should not return the inquisition, but at once return that the defendant had no goods, &c. in his bailiwick (*o*). It seems to be questionable whether or not the return of a rescue to a writ of *capias utlagatum* be good (*p*). If the sheriff return that the defendant has no lay fee, but is rector of a rectory, the court will award a sequestration to the bishop (*q*).

(*h*) The inquisition is similar to the inquisition on an extent, see more of that, *post*, and forms, Appendix to the chap. on Extents.

(*i*) Master *v.* Whitefield, Hard. 106.

(*k*) Stringfellow *v.* Brownesoppe, Dyer, 67; Proctor's case, Dyer, 223; Dr. Drury's case, 8 Rep. 284; Rex *v.* Capel, 2 Show. 481.

(*l*) Britton *v.* Cole, 1 Ld. Raym. 305. See *ante*, 232, n. (*c*).

(*m*) 2 Rol. Abr. 807.

(*n*) See forms of returns, *post*, Append. chap. 8, s. 2.

(*o*) See returns and mode of making them, *post*, chap. 11, and forms, Append. thereto.

(*p*) Dalt. 217; Fitz. Retorne, 110.

(*q*) Rex *v.* Hind, 1 C. & J. 389; Rex *v.* Armstrong, 2 C. M. & R. 205.

In such case the return ought to state the name and situation of the benefice (*r*). If the sheriff is bound to take the *posse comitatus*, he cannot excuse himself, although the defendant or the goods were rescued: as the statute of Westminster 2, by which the sheriff is *compelled* to raise the *posse comitatus*, has been held to apply to writs of execution only and not to mesne process (*s*), perhaps it may be held that rescue would be a good return to *capias utlagatum*, where the outlawry was on mesne process, but not where the outlawry was after judgment (*t*). When the *capias utlagatum* is returned, it should be filed, with the inquition annexed, with the filazer, as clerk of the *exigents* and outlawries in the Queen's Bench (*u*), or with the clerk of the outlawries in the Common Pleas, and should afterwards be carried into the office of the *custos brevium* (*x*); from whence a transcript is sent to the Exchequer (*y*).

Preference in case of several outlawries. The following rules were laid down (*z*) to be the law respecting the preference between several outlawries:—First, where there are two outlawries at different times, the first inquisition shall prevail; secondly, where there are two outlawries on one day, the first inquisition shall be preferred; thirdly, where there are two inquisitions in one day, the first outlawry shall be preferred; fourthly, where there are two outlawries on one day, and both inquisitions on one day, there the first lease shall be preferred.

Fees for executing a *capias utlagatum*. As to the fees on the execution of process in outlawry, see the table of fees, *ante*, 103. The sheriff is not entitled to poundage until the execution of a *venditioni exponas* (*a*). **Landlord's claim for rent.** The special *capias utlagatum* in a civil action is considered so far in the nature of a private execution, that the landlord is entitled, under the stat. 8 Anne, c. 14, to be satisfied his year's rent out of the money in the sheriff's hands (*b*).

Actions against the sheriff. If the sheriff discharge a defendant arrested by him on a *capias utlagatum* issued upon an outlawry upon *mesne process*, without taking an undertaking or bond as prescribed by the statute of William and Mary, he is liable to an action on the

(*r*) Rex *v.* Powell, 1 M. & W. 321.

(*s*) See *ante*, 73, 96, and Cro. Jac. 419; 1 Rol. Rep. 388, 440; Cro. Eliz. 868; 2 Lev. 144; 3 Lev. 46.

(*t*) But see Bunb. 194.

(*u*) Reynolds *v.* Adams, 3 T. R. 578.

(*x*) *Id. ibid.*

(*y*) 1 Tidd's Prac. 134, 8th edit.

(*z*) In Rex *v.* Willes, Parker, 90.

(*a*) Graham *v.* Grill, 2 Maule & Sel. 294.

(*b*) Graves *v.* d'Acastro, Bunb. 194. See also St. John's College, Oxford, *v.* Murcott, 7 T. R. 259.

CHAP. VIII. SECT. II.

case (*c*); but allowing the defendant to go at large at all would be an escape if the outlawry were after judgment, for which escape an action would lie (*d*). In either case, it appears that the action may either be by the plaintiff in his own right (*e*), or *qui tam pro dominâ reginâ quam pro seipso* (*f*). But it has been determined that an action on the case will not lie against the sheriff for neglecting to extend or seize the goods and lands of a person outlawed on a *capias utlagatum*, because it was to the king's loss; and the court said that the benefit to be derived by the plaintiff from the seizure of the goods, in compelling the defendant to appear, was so very remote as not to be considered as a ground to support an action; but if it had been shown that the sheriff might have had the body, and had neglected to do it, there might have been more reason to support the action (*g*).

Restitution.

Where the outlawry is reversed before a sale under a *venditione exponas*, the defendant shall have a writ of restitution to the sheriff, whereby the defendant shall be restored to his goods or terms seized by the sheriff under the *capias utlagatum*, and not to the mere value of them as on a *fieri facias*, for we have seen that without a *venditioni exponas* the sheriff has no authority to sell goods taken by him on a *capias utlagatum* (*h*).

(*c*) Bonner *v.* Stokeley, Cro. Eliz. 652; Cooke *v.* Champness, Fitzg. 265.

(*d*) Wolf *v.* Davison, Salk. 319.

(*e*) Moor *v.* Sir Geo. Reignalls, Cro. Jac. 620; Leighton *v.* Garnons, Cro. Eliz. 706; 1 P. Wms. 693.

(*f*) Barrett *v.* Winchcomb, Cro. Jac. 360; 1 Roll. Rep. 78, S. C.; Parkhurst *v.* Powell, Cro. Jac. 532.

(*g*) Dawson *v.* The Sheriffs of London, 2 Vent. 89.

(*h*) Proctor's case, Dyer, 223 b; Hoe's case, 5 Rep. 91; 1 Roll. Abr. 778, S. C.; Eyre *v.* Woodfine, Cro. Eliz. 278. Where a termor outlawed for felony granted his term to the plaintiff, and the outlawry was reversed by writ of error, it was held that the plaintiff might maintain trespass for the profits between the reversal and the assignment; for the outlawry when reversed was as if no outlawry had taken place; Ognel's case, Cro. Eliz. 270.

CHAPTER IX.

THE SHERIFF'S DUTY IN THE EXECUTION AND RETURN OF THE WRIT OF HABEAS CORPUS.

In what Cases it lies.—How executed.—Return thereto.—Penalty for not obeying the Writ.—Actions for false Return to, Escape, &c.—Sheriff's Fees on.

THE writ of *habeas corpus* lies in civil as well as criminal cases. In *criminal* cases the writ and proceedings depend on the statute 31 Car. 2, c. 2 (*a*). The writ of *habeas corpus*, in civil cases, is a judicial writ commanding the sheriff, or other officer to whom it is directed, to have the body of the defendant, together with the day and cause of taking and detaining him, before the court or a judge, on a day *certain* in term time, or *immediate*, to *answer* or *satisfy* the plaintiff, or generally to *do* and *receive* what the court or judge shall consider of him. Hence it is called, according to the subject-matter, a writ of *habeas corpus ad respondendum, ad satisfaciendum,* or *ad faciendum, subjiciendum, et recipiendum,* though the latter is usually called a *habeas corpus cum causâ* (*b*). There is also another writ of *habeas corpus, ad testificandum,* to bring up a prisoner who is a material witness to give his testimony. By the 44 Geo. 3, c. 102, it is declared to be lawful for any of the judges

Of the writ of *habeas corpus*, and in what cases it lies.

(*a*) The provisions of this statute are extended by the statute 56 Geo. 3, c. 100, "for more effectually securing the liberty of the subject." The court will not grant, as a matter of course, a writ of *habeas corpus*, but only upon special circumstances laid before them, Hobhouse's case, 3 Bar. & Ald. 420; Chit. Rep. 207, S. C.; and even a judge in vacation, under 31 Car. 2, c. 2, is not bound to grant the writ only upon view of the warrant of commitment. *Id. ibid.* See Ex parte Boothroyd, 15 M. & W. 1. Since 1 & 2 Vict. c. 45, s. 1, a judge of any of the superior courts has power to issue a *habeas corpus ad subjiciendum* under the seal of and returnable in any other of those courts; In re Wilson, 14 Law J., Q. B. 105. If granted by a judge of the Queen's Bench, it must issue from the crown side of the court; Easton's case, 12 Ad. & E. 645. The superior courts have also, it seems, a common law power to discharge a person from illegal imprisonment for a criminal matter; Ex parte Besset, 6 Q. B. 481.

(*b*) Tidd's Prac. 349, 350, 8th edit. It is grantable either in vacation or in term.

CHAP. IX.

of the courts of King's Bench, Common Pleas, or Exchequer, in England or Ireland, to award a writ of *habeas corpus* for bringing any prisoner detained in any prison to give evidence before any of the said courts, or any sitting at *Nisi Prius*, or before any other court of record in the said parts of the united kingdom (*c*). The writ of *habeas corpus cum causâ* lies for the defendant to remove himself, or for the plaintiff to remove him, from the custody of the sheriff or other officer in whose custody he is, into the custody of the marshal of the Queen's Prison. This writ also lies for the *bail* of the defendant to bring him up, and surrender him in their discharge to the custody of the marshal, and that whether the defendant be in custody in a civil suit or on a criminal account (*d*). By the statute 1 & 2 Philip & Mary, c. 13, s. 7, it is required that every writ of *habeas corpus* shall be signed with the proper hand of the chief justice, or, in his absence, of one of the justices of the court, out of which the writ issued. The sheriff is not obliged to execute a writ of *habeas corpus* unless it be so signed (*e*).

How executed.

The writ of *habeas corpus cum causâ* is returnable immediately (*f*). A warrant is directed and delivered to an officer, generally the gaoler, or one of the turnkeys of the county gaol, directing him to convey the defendant before the judge in London, according to the exigency of the writ. The officer should bring him to the judge's chambers in due and convenient time(*g*) without permitting him to wander under pretence of such writ(*h*).

(*c*) This application ought to be made to a judge at chambers; Brown *v.* Gisborne, 2 Dowl. N. S. 963. See also 43 Geo. 3, c. 140, as to the power of granting a *habeas corpus* to convey a prisoner before commissioners of bankrupts and courts martial. Archbold's Bankrupt Laws, 176.

(*d*) Sharp *v.* Sheriff, 7 T. R. 226; Daniel *v.* Thompson, 15 East, 78; Taylor's case, 3 East, 232; Brandon *v.* Davis, 9 East, 154. But they cannot obtain this rule until the bail have justified; *id. ibid.* This writ does not lie in C. P. to remove a defendant from criminal custody to be charged in that court with a civil action. See 1 Marsh. 166; 3 Moore, 259; 1 Brod. & Bing. 23, S. C.; 2 N. R. 245; 1 Bing. 221.

(*e*) Rex *v.* Roddam, Cowp. 672. By the stat. 31 Car. 2, c. 2, s. 3, writs of *habeas corpus* under that statute are required to be marked "*per statutum tricesimo primo Caroli Secundi regis.*"

(*f*) Bettesworth *v.* Bell, 3 Burr. 1875. The rule M. 1654, sec. 7, K. B., in this respect, was held to have fallen into desuetude.

(*g*) See *id. ibid.*

(*h*) Reg. Gen. M. 1654, s. 7, K. B.; R. M. 1654, s. 10, C. P.

The officer should not deviate from the direct road, nor allow the defendant to go at liberty in conveying him to the judge's chambers, for if he do, it would be an escape (*i*); he must also take force sufficient to prevent the defendant from being rescued, as a rescue of the defendant would make the sheriff liable to an action for an escape (*k*). By the preamble of the 31 Car. 2, c. 2, it is stated, "that great delays had been used by sheriffs, &c., to whose custody the king's subjects had been committed for criminal or supposed criminal matters, in making returns of writs of *habeas corpus* to them directed, by standing out an *alias* and *pluries*," &c.; and it is enacted, that whensoever *any person* shall bring any *habeas corpus* (*l*) directed unto any sheriff, &c., for any person in his custody, and the writ shall be served upon such officer, or left at the gaol with the under officer, the said officer shall bring the prisoner up to the court or judge, and certify his *cause* of detention within three days after such service thereof, (if within the distance of twenty miles, or if beyond twenty and within one hundred miles within ten days; and if above one hundred miles within the space of twenty days,) unless the commitment were for treason or felony, upon payment or tender of charges of bringing the prisoner, to be ascertained by the judge or court that awarded the same, and indorsed on the writ, not exceeding 1*s.* per mile, and on security given by his own bond to pay the charges of carrying him back if remanded, and that he will not make any escape by the way.

The sheriff's return.

The sheriff should return to the writ of *habeas corpus* the cause of the arrest, and of the detention of the defendant (*m*). A return, that he the sheriff had no such person in his custody, nor had he on the day of issuing the (*pluries*) writ, or afterwards, was holden bad, for he might have had him on the day of issuing the first writ of *habeas corpus* (*n*). A return, that before the delivery of the writ of *habeas corpus*, he had delivered

(*i*) Roll. Abr. Escape (D) 9; Cro. Car. 14, 466; Balden *v.* Temple, Hob. 202.

(*k*) Compton *v.* Ward, Stra. 429.

(*l*) In Huntley *v.* Luscomb, 2 Bos. & Pul. 530, it was made a question whether this section, and the 5th section of the act, were confined to writs of *habeas corpus* in criminal matters, or extended to all writs of *habeas corpus*: the court gave no opinion on that point. It would seem from the preamble, and the other parts of the act, that it was meant to apply to writs of *habeas corpus* in criminal matters only. See 2 Bos. & Pul. 531.

(*m*) See several returns, *post*, Append. c. 9.

(*n*) Rex *v.* Sir R. Viner, 2 Lev. 128, 129.

the woman to her husband, and knows not where she is, nor would he produce her, is good (*o*). A return, that the defendant was not in the sheriff's custody at the coming of the writ is good (*p*); and for the purpose of filing the writ, it is good to return that before the coming of the writ, the defendant was discharged out of his custody by an order of sessions, without saying what sessions, what order, or that he was discharged by due course of law (*q*). A return, that he the gaoler had not, at the time of receiving the writ, nor had he since had, the body of the within named M. G. detained in his custody, so that he could not have her before, &c., as he is commanded, was held bad, because it did not show that M. G. was not under the gaoler's control (*r*). A return, that the defendant is sick in prison, or a lunatic, is good; but if the sheriff go out of office, and a new sheriff be appointed before the return, the return should be made in the name of both, by the old sheriff that he delivered the body to the new sheriff, by the new sheriff *languidus* (*s*). The sheriff should state fully and correctly in his return the causes or warrant of commitment, upon which the prisoner is committed or detained, that the court may judge whether the prisoner be lawfully committed or not: and if by the return it appear that he is detained without a sufficient cause, the court will order his discharge (*t*). A reasonable degree of certainty, however, is all that is required; the court will not regard the return with the same strictness as a pleading (*u*); and if the sheriff's return be informal, the court will allow it to be amended according to the fact (*x*), before or after it is filed (*y*), and although the amendment be not assented to on behalf of the prisoner (*z*).

(*o*) Rex *v.* Wright, Stra. 915.

(*p*) Rex *v.* Bethuen, Andr. 281.

(*q*) *Id. ibid.*

(*r*) Rex *v.* Winton, 5 T. R. 89.

(*s*) Bac. Abr. Habeas Corpus (B) 7; Rex *v.* Clarke, 3 Burr. 1362. Upon the return of *languidus* there issues a *habeas corpus licet languidus*; see forms, Tidd's Forms, 145, 5th edit.

(*t*) See the various returns in Com. Dig. tit. Hab. Corp. (E) 2 3; and the precedents in Hobhouse's case, 2 Chit. Rep. 207; Canadian Prisoners' case, 5 M. & W. 34; Watson's case, 9 Ad. & E. 731; Reg. *v.* Evans, 8 Dowl. 451; Reg. *v.* Dunn, 12 Ad. & E. 599; Easton's case, *id.* 648; In re Brenan, 16 Law Journ. Q. B. 289; In re Fell, 3 Dowl. & L. 384. See Rex *v.* Dugger, 1 Dowl. & Ry. 460; 5 B. & Ald. 791, S. C., as to commitment by an ecclesiastical court for contumacy; see also Burdett *v.* Abbott, 5 Dow, 199,

(*u*) In re Fell, 3 Dowl. & L. 384.

(*x*) Chambers's case, Cro. Car. 133; per Hale, C. J. 1 Mod. 103.

(*y*) Watson's case, 9 Ad. & E. 731.

(*z*) In re Clark, 2 Q. B. 619; 2 G. & D. 780, S. C.; Ex parte Lord, 16 M. & W. 462.

The sheriffs return is *primâ facie* taken to be true, and need not be supported by affidavit, until impeached. It may be impeached, and the truth inquired into, but whether upon affidavit or by pleading does not seem to be fully settled (*a*).

How far conclusive.

If the sheriff do not obey the writ of *habeas corpus*, he will be liable to an attachment in the first instance, without the issuing of an *alias*. Thus, where the return made is insufficient, as stating an insufficient reason for not bringing the defendant up upon the *habeas corpus*, the court will grant an attachment immediately on the return (*b*). By the stat. 31 Car. 2, c. 2, s. 4, if the officer refuse to bring up the body of the prisoner (*c*), or to make a return; or on demand by prisoner, or by some person on his behalf, shall refuse, within six hours after demand, to deliver a true copy of the commitment (*d*), the head gaoler, or other officer in whose custody the prisoner is, shall forfeit to the party grieved 100*l*. for the first offence, and for the second offence 200*l*., and be incapable of holding or executing that office.

Proceedings for not obeying writ.

For a false return to a writ of *habeas corpus*, an action on the case is the only remedy for the party grieved; and an information or indictment at the suit of the king (*e*). If the officer, in conveying the defendant to the judge's chambers, suffer him to go at large, and have him not at the return of the writ, it is an escape; and when the sheriff is ordered to bring up the body of a defendant by *habeas corpus*, as it is his duty to convey him by the shortest and most convenient road to the court at Westminster, if he deviates from such direct road, or lets the defendant go about his affairs, although he has him at the return of the writ, it is an escape (*f*). And if a *habeas corpus* issue in one

Action against the sheriff for false return, escape, &c.

(*a*) See Hawk. P. C. c. 2; Ex parte Beeching, 4 B. & C. 136; Watson's case, 9 Ad. & E. 731; Reg. *v*. Dunn, 12 Ad. & E. 599; In re Wilson, 14 Law J., Q. B., 105.

(*b*) Rex *v*. Winton, 5 T. R. 89; Com. Dig. Hab. Corp. (E) 3. And if the officer refuse to remove the prisoner on account of his fees not being paid, the court will grant an attachment; T. Jones, 178; Rex *v*. Armigers, 1 Keb. 272, 280. It would appear that before the court will grant an attachment for nor making a return to the *hab. cor.*, there should be a rule to return the writ; Rex *v*. Wright, Stra. 915.

(*c*) See *ante*, p. 237, n. (*l*), to what cases this section extends.

(*d*) In Huntley *v*. Luscombe, 2 Bos. & Pul. 530, it was held that a demand upon the under turnkey of the prison for a copy of the warrant of commitment was not a sufficient demand to make the head gaoler liable to the penalties of this act.

(*e*) Bac. Abr. Habeas Corpus (B) 8. It is said that no action will lie until the return be filed; Salk. 352.

(*f*) See Roll. Abr. Escape (D) 9; Cro. Car. 14, 466; Hard. 476; 1 Mod. 116.

term to the sheriff to bring up a prisoner in his custody on the ensuing term, if he let him go at large in the meantime it is an escape (*g*). But it is laid down by Lord Coke, that if the officer of the sheriff, in taking a prisoner in execution from the county gaol to Westminster on a *habeas corpus*, lodge him in an inn on the direct road, and the defendant of his own head goes at large, but the sheriff has him at Westminster on the return day of the *habeas corpus*, this is no escape (*h*). The sheriff is allowed a reasonable time in which he must bring up a prisoner on a *habeas corpus ;* of the reasonableness thereof the court will judge (*i*). It was said by Hale, C. J., that, "if, on a *habeas corpus ad testificandum*, the sheriff let the defendant go into the country, it is an escape. Though he be not bound to bring him back the direct way, because he may be rescued, yet he ought not to carry him round about a great way for the accommodation of the party; if he doth, it is an escape; but by the evidence you let him go back threescore miles, to which there can be no answer. A *habeas corpus* returnable *immediatè* is not fixed to an hour, but to a convenient time (*k*)." The sheriff is to convey the defendant *sub salvo et securo conductu*, and therefore if the defendant be rescued from the officer whilst in his county, the sheriff is liable to an action for an escape (*l*).

Fees. As to the sheriff's fees on a *habeas corpus*, see the Table of Fees, *ante*, 103.

(*g*) Hard. 476; Roll Abr. Escape (D) 9; 1 Lord Raym. 241; 1 Mod. 116.

(*h*) In Boyton's case, 3 Rep. 44; Moore, 257. See *ante*, 203, 204.

(*i*) Holdroid *v.* Liddell, 1 Lord Raym. 241; Balden *v.* Temple, Hob. 202.

(*k*) Mosedell's case, 1 Mod. 116; S. C. 3 Keb. 305; Bull. N. P. 67.

(*l*) Crompton *v.* Ward, Stra. 429. If the rescue had been in another county, through which the officer was conveying the defendant, would that have altered the case, for there the sheriff has no power to raise the *posse ?*

CHAPTER X.

THE SHERIFF'S DUTIES AND LIABILITIES IN THE EXECUTION AND RETURN OF A FIERI FACIAS.

CHAP. X.
SECT. I.

Section I.

Fieri Facias; when, where, and how executed.

Of the writ.

The writ of *fieri facias* is a writ judicial, that lieth for him who hath recovered any debt or damages in the queen's courts, which writ is directed to the sheriff of the county where the venue is laid, and thereby the sheriff is commanded to levy the debt or damages, together with interest from the time when the judgment was entered up, of the goods and chattels of the person against whom the recovery is had, and to have that money and interest, and the writ itself, before the queen at Westminster, or wheresoever, &c., on the return day (if made returnable on a particular day), or immediately after the execution thereof (*a*).

How executed.

When the writ is delivered to the sheriff, a warrant is made to one or more bailiffs, commanding them to execute the writ (*b*). The officer, in making a levy on the goods of the defendant, should make an actual seizure; but seizing *part* of the goods in the name of the whole on the premises is a good seizure of the whole (*c*). The officer should, from the time of the seizure, either by himself or by some other person, keep possession of the goods, otherwise it might happen that they would be liable to be taken on a second execution (*d*). If the outer door of a

(*a*) Reg. Gen. Hil. 2 Vict. See the form, Append. chap. 10, s. 1. This writ lies within a year and a day after judgment, but if a party should after the year and day sue a writ without a *sci. fa.* yet the sheriff is bound to execute it. The writ should regularly follow the judgment, and therefore a special execution is not warranted by a general judgment, 1 T. R. 82; 7 T. R. 27; so execution against one is not warranted by a judgment against two, 6 T. R. 525; see also 7 B. & C. 486; 1 Ad. & E. 331; 3 Dowl. 464; 5 Dowl. 374. If a *sci. fa.* be issued unnecessarily, the *fi. fa.* must issue on such *sci. fa.*; 1 Bing. 133. Regularly a *fi. fa.* should issue to the sheriff of the county where the venue is laid, before a *testatum fi. fa.* issue to any other county; but if a *testatum fi fa.* or even a *fi. fa.* issue in the first instance to a different county from that in which the venue is laid, the Court will allow the plaintiff to sue out a *fi. fa.* to warrant a *testatum*, by entering the writ, return and award of *testatum* on the roll; or if the first writ were not a *testatum* writ, they will allow that to be amended; 3 T. R. 657; 5 T. R. 272; 6 T. R. 450; see also 3 T. R. 388; 4 Dowl. 119; 9 Dowl. 961. Although the writ be irregular, the sheriff is bound to execute it, and of course is justified in executing it.

(*b*) See form Append. chap. 10, s. 1. As to warrants in general, see *ante*, 71.

(*c*) Cole *v.* Davies, 1 Ld. Raym. 725.

(*d*) See Blades *v.* Arundale, 1 M. & S. 711; Ackland *v.* Paynter, 8 Price, 95; see also Burr *v.* Fruthy, 1 Bing. 71, S. C. *nomine* Burr *v.* Creethy, 7 Moore, 368.

house in which the defendant's goods are placed be locked, such outer door, we have seen, cannot be broken open to seize them (*e*). It has been said that this protection only applies to the house of the defendant himself, but that the sheriff or his officers may, after request to open it, break open the outer door of the house of a third person, to which the defendant's goods have been *clandestinely* removed (*f*). But this by no means must be construed to mean that the house of a stranger can be broken open to execute a *fi. fa.* under any circumstances; for the same principle that protects the house of the defendant from a forcible breaking, equally applies to make the house of every man a sanctuary. If however the officer gain admittance at the outer door, he may break it to release himself from the house (*g*), or he may break open inner doors, or chests, in the house, that are locked, to seize the goods of the defendant, without any request to open them (*h*). So he may break open the outer door of a barn detached from the dwelling-house, even without first demanding that such door should be opened (*i*). However, although the sheriff should break open an outer door, or otherwise become a trespasser in executing a *fieri facias*, the execution is good notwithstanding, and the plaintiff is entitled to the fruits of such levy (*k*), the remedy for the defendant being by action (*l*). It seems that goods may be taken through the window of a house if open (*m*).

At what time.

The officer may seize the goods of the defendant at any time before or on the return day of the writ, if made returnable on a particular day, or if, as is now the usual form, it be made returnable immediately on the execution thereof (in which case it continues in force until it is executed (*n*)), he may execute it within a reasonable or convenient time; and he is bound to sell the goods within a convenient time, without a writ of *venditioni exponas* or *distringas* (*o*). A *fi. fa.* cannot be executed on a

(*e*) *Ante*, 75; Semayne's case, 5 Rep. 92. Nor can a window be broken open in such case; Cooke's case, W. Jones, 429.

(*f*) Semayne's case, 5 Rep. 93.

(*g*) White *v.* Wiltshire, Cro. Jac. 555; 2 Roll. Rep. 137, S. C.; Palm. 52; Pugh *v.* Griffith, 7 Ad. & E. 827; 3 N. & P. 189, S. C.

(*h*) Hutchinson *v.* Birch, 4 Taunt. 619; Ratcliff *v.* Burton, 3 Bos. & Pul. 223; Lee *v.* Gansel, Cowp. 1.

(*i*) Penton *v.* Brown, 1 Sid. 186; 1 Keb. 698, S. C.

(*k*) Brownl. 50; 5 Rep. 92.

(*l*) *Id. ibid.*

(*m*) 1 Roll Abr. 671, pl. 7.

(*n*) Simpson *v.* Heath, 5 M. & W. 31; Greenshields *v.* Harris, 9 M. & W. 774.

(*o*) Clerk *v.* Withers, 6 Mod. 297; Wilbraham *v.* Snow, 2 Saund. 47 e;

CHAP. X. SECT. I.

Sunday (*p*). The officer may, after the death of the defendant, on a *fi. fa.* against him, seize his goods in the hands of his executor or administrator, provided the writ bears teste before his death, although not delivered to the sheriff till after (*q*). So, after the death of the plaintiff, the sheriff may execute a *fi. fa.* tested in his lifetime (*r*), but he should not pay over the proceeds until he is satisfied respecting the person who is personal representative: if there be no executor or administrator, the money should be brought into court, and there deposited until the representative of the plaintiff appear and claim it (*s*). If, while the defendant is in execution, the plaintiff dies, a rule may be made absolute in the first instance for the defendant's discharge, on the production of an affidavit by the next of kin that it is not his intention to prove any will or to take out letters of administration (*t*).

The sheriff may enter the house of the *defendant* when the outer door is open to seize the goods of the defendant (*u*); and if the defendant has goods in the house of a *stranger*, the sheriff may enter it to execute a *fieri facias* (*x*). But the sheriff is not justified in entering the house of a stranger on a *fieri facias*, unless the defendant's goods are *actually in the house*, for it is not a sufficient justification that he entered the house of the stranger on *suspicion* that the goods of the defendant were in the house (*y*). But the house of the defendant himself the sheriff is justified in entering merely on suspicion of his goods being there; so, on a *fieri facias* against the goods of an intestate, in the hands of an administratrix and her husband, the sheriff may legally enter the house of the husband to search for the goods of the intestate, though none be found therein (*z*).

Brown *v.* Jarvis, 1 M. & W. 714; 5 Dowl. 281, S. C; Jacobs *v.* Humphrey, 2 C. & M. 413; Bates *v.* Wingfield, 2 N. & M. 831, S. C.; Mason *v.* Paynter, 6 G. & D. 38.

(*p*) *Ante*, 79.

(*q*) Dalt. 148; Bragner *v.* Langmead, 7 T.R. 20; Waghorne *v* Langmead, 1 Bos. & Pul. 571. But a *fi. fa.* cannot be issued or executed on his goods, if tested after his death; Heapy *v.* Parris, 6 T. R. 368; see also 7 East, 297.

(*r*) Cleve *v.* Veer, Cro. Car. 459; Clerk *v.* Withers, Salk. 322; 6 Mod. 290, S. C.; 11 Mod 35; Ld. Raym. 1072.

(*s*) Thoroughgood's case, Noy, 73; Dyer, 76 b.; Ld. Raym. 1073; Clerk *v.* Withers, 6 Mod. 297; Ellis *v.* Griffith, 16 M. & W. 106.

(*t*) Gore *v.* Wright, 1 Dowl. N.S. 864.

(*u*) Semayne's case, 5 Rep. 92.

(*x*) *Ibid.*

(*y*) Johnson *v.* Leigh, 1 Marsh. 565; Morrish *v.* Murrey, 13 M. & W. 52; Com. Dig. Execution (C 5).

(*z*) Cooke *v.* Birt, 5 Taunt. 765; 1 Marsh. 333, S. C.

The sheriff cannot stay on the premises for more than a reasonable time to remove the goods, without the consent of the defendant (*a*).

CHAP. X. SECT. I.

Privilege.

There are few privileges which extend to protect goods from being taken on a *fi. fa.* A royal palace, wherein either her *majesty*, her *family*, or her servants reside, is such a privileged place, that the sheriff or his officer cannot lawfully execute a *fieri facias* in such palace (*b*). There are no *personal* privileges that protect the goods from being taken in execution, excepting that the goods of ambassadors and of their servants are privileged; for by the statute of 7 Anne, c. 12, s. 2, all writs whereby the goods or chattels of any ambassador or other public minister or his servants may be distrained, seized or detached, are declared to be void (*c*). In a late case it was determined that the goods of the servant of an ambassador, not residing in the ambassador's house, but renting and living in another house, part of which he let in lodgings, were liable to a distress for poor's rates, such goods not being necessary for the discharge of his duty to the ambassador (*d*). The goods of a certificated bankrupt, and of a person discharged under the Insolvent Debtors Act, are protected from being taken on a *fi. fa.* (*e*) upon a judgment for a debt from which the defendant was discharged by his certificate, or by the order of the Insolvent Debtors Court. But if a *fi. fa.* be delivered to the sheriff to execute against any such person, the sheriff or his officer is not bound to take notice of such privilege, but may leave the party to apply to the court to be relieved (*f*). No *bona aut catalla ecclesiastica* can be seized under a *fieri facias* (*g*).

Poundage.

If the sheriff levy the debt and pay the money over to the plaintiff, he is entitled to his poundage, although the execution be set aside (*h*). So also a sheriff, who has seized the defendant's goods, is entitled to poundage, if the parties compromise before

(*a*) *Ante*, 121.

(*b*) Winter *v.* Miles, 10 East, 578; Elderton's case, 2 Ld. Raym. 978; 6 Mod. 73, S. C.; 3 Salk. 91, 284.

(*c*) For the decisions on this statute see *ante*.

(*d*) Novello *v.* Toogood, 1 Barn. & Cress. 554; 2 Dowl. & Ry. 833, S.C.

(*e*) See 5 & 6 Vict. c. 110, s. 37, as to bankrupts; 1 & 2 Vict. c. 110, s. 95, as to insolvent debtors; and see Raynes *v.* Jones, 9 M. & W. 104.

(*f*) Lister *v.* Mundell, 1 Bos. & Pul. 427.

(*g*) Dalt. 219; 2 Inst. 472; Bac. Abr. Execution; 2 Mod. 256.

(*h*) Rawstorne *v.* Wilkinson, 4 M. & Sel. 256; Salk. 332. See Bullen *v.* Ansley, 6 Esp. 111.

CHAP. X. SECT. I.

the sale (*i*). The sheriff is not entitled to poundage upon a sum of money paid over to a landlord for rent on an execution under the 8 Ann. c. 14, s. 1 (*k*).

Poundage and fees may be levied.

Besides his poundage, the sheriff is also empowered, by the stat. 43 Geo. 3, c. 46, s. 5, to levy, under an execution against the goods of a *defendant* (*l*), the fees and expenses of the execution, over and above the sum recovered by the judgment. This statute, as we have seen, does not extend to executions against a *plaintiff* for costs, nor to crown process (*m*). The fees and expenses to be taken by the sheriff are now regulated by the stat. 1 Vict. c. 55, and the table of fees framed by the judges pursuant thereto (*n*). What costs and expenses fall within the terms of the 43 Geo. 3, c. 46, s. 5, and of the 1 Vict. c. 55, has been already fully considered (*o*).

Property of the goods of defendant, how bound by the *fi. fa.*

At common law, the goods of the party against whom a writ of *fieri facias* issued were *bound* from the teste of the writ; by which is meant that the writ bound the property as against the party himself, and all claiming by assignment from or by representation under him (*p*); so that a sale by the defendant of his goods *bonâ fide*, excepting in market overt, did not protect them from a *fieri facias* tested before, although not issued or delivered to the sheriff till after, the sale (*q*); although goods seized on a *fieri facias* were not subject to a second *fieri facias* subsequently issued but tested before (*r*). But by the Statute of Frauds, 29 Car. 2, c. 3, s. 16, it is enacted, "That no writ of *fieri facias*, or other writ of execution, shall bind the property of the goods of the party, against whom such writ of execution is sued forth, but from the time that such writ shall be delivered to the sheriff, under-sheriff or coroners, to be executed; and for the better manifestation of the said time, the sheriff, &c., their deputies or agents, shall upon receipt of any such writ (without fee for doing the same) indorse upon the back thereof the day of the month and year whereon he or they received the same." The *property* in the goods is not altered by the delivery

(*i*) Alchin *v.* Wells, 5 T. R. 470.

(*k*) Gore *v.* Gofton, Stra. 643.

(*l*) *Ante*, 113. See Rumsey *v.* Tuffnell, 2 Bing. 255.

(*m*) *Ante*, 113; 7 Taunt. 179; 2 Chit. Rep. 353.

(*n*) *Ante*, 103.

(*o*) *Ante*, 110, 113.

(*p*) *Per* Lord Ellenborough, C. J., 4 East, 538.

(*q*) Anon. Cro. Eliz. 174; Bailey *v.* Bunning, 1 Sid. 271; Cro. Jac. 451.

(*r*) Payne *v.* Drewe, 4 East, 523.

of the writ to the sheriff, but remains in the defendant until execution executed; but if the defendant make an assignment of his goods after the delivery of a *fieri facias* to the sheriff, excepting by sale in market overt, the sheriff may take them in execution (*s*). This statute was passed solely to protect purchasers, and the goods are bound as against the defendant and his representatives as they were at the common law, and therefore goods of the testator, in the hands of an executor, may be taken on a *fi. fa.* against his testator bearing teste before his death (*t*).

Priority in case of several executions by the subject,

As between two different plaintiffs, if two writs of *fieri facias* are delivered to the sheriff on the same or different days, the sheriff ought first to execute that which was first delivered to him (*u*); unless the first writ was fraudulent, and then he should execute the other (*x*). And if the bailiff, after making a seizure, does not keep possession, but leaves the defendant in possession of the goods, this is strong evidence to show that the first execution was fraudulent (*y*). But if the sheriff levy goods in execution by virtue of the writ last delivered, and make sale of them, the property of the goods is bound by the sale, and the party cannot seize them by virtue of the writ first delivered; but he may have his remedy against the sheriff (*z*). But if the sheriff merely seize but has not sold under the writ last delivered, he may apply that levy to the first writ, although no warrant issued thereon (*a*). Therefore, where two writs of *fieri facias* were in the sheriff's hands at the same time against the same defendant at the suit of different plaintiffs, upon the writ first delivered the officer entered, and whilst he was in possession, the officer under the second writ entered, and remained in possession until the goods were sold, which were not enough to satisfy the first writ; before the sale, the defendant gave

(*s*) Lowthal *v.* Tomkins, 2 Eq. Cas. Abr. 381.

(*t*) Bragner *v.* Langmead, 7 T. R. 20; Waghorne *v.* Langmead, 1 Bos. & Pul. 571.

(*u*) Hutchinson *v.* Johnson, 1 T. R. 729; Sawle *v.* Paynter, 1 Dowl. & Ry. 307.

(*x*) Bailey *v.* Windham, 1 Wils. 44.

(*y*) *Id. ibid.*; Kempland *v.* Macauley, Peake's N. P. C. 66. See also Blades *v.* Arundale, 1 M. & Sel. 711; Toussaint *v.* Hartop, Holt's N. P. C. 335; 7 Moore, 368; 1 Bing. 71, S. C.

(*z*) Smallcomb *v.* Buckingham, 1 Ld. Raym. 251; 1 Salk. 320, S. C.; Carth. 419; Com. Rep. 35. See also 1 T. R. 731, n.; Payne *v.* Drewe, 4 East, 523.

(*a*) Jones *v.* Atherton, 7 Taunt. 56; 2 Marsh. 375, S. C.; Hutchinson *v.* Johnston, 1 T. R. 729.

CHAP. X. SECT. I.

notice to the sheriff that he would move to set aside the first *fi. fa.*, and the judgment whereon it was founded, and upon that writ being set aside by rule of court, the sheriff paid the money over to the defendant, according to the rule: it was held that, on the first writ being set aside, the proceeds of the sale were liable to satisfy the second writ (*b*), and that, under those circumstances, a return of *nulla bona* to the second writ was a false return. So, where the first writ was founded upon a judgment on a warrant of attorney, but the second was in a *bonâ fide* adverse action, and before sale a fiat in bankruptcy issued against the debtor, whereby, under the 6 Geo. 4, c. 16, s. 108, the first writ became void, it was held that the other became in effect the first writ; that the creditor who issued it was entitled to have his execution satisfied out of the proceeds, and that the assignees in bankruptcy could not first claim any part of them under the above section for rateable distribution among the creditors (*c*). Where the first writ is delivered with directions not to execute it till a future day, the sheriff is justified in levying under a second delivered before that day (*d*). Where an attorney, who acted for seven different plaintiffs in different actions, delivered seven writs of *fi. fa.* to the sheriff, in one bundle, at the same time, it was held that the sheriff could not call, by rule of court, upon the plaintiffs or their attorney, to say which writs were to have priority; but it seems that a return to the effect that he had received all the writs at the same time, and had levied under all, would under such circumstances be a good return (*e*).

or by the crown.

As against the crown, as the king is not named in the Statute of Frauds, an extent binds the goods from the teste of that writ. And if the extent be tested before or on the day of the delivery to the sheriff of a writ of *fieri facias*, the extent shall have priority over the subject's execution, although it be not delivered to the sheriff until after the *fieri facias*, provided it be delivered before the goods are actually sold under the *fieri facias*; if the

(*b*) Saunders *v.* Bridges, 3 Bar. & Ald. 95. The court would have allowed the sheriff to have paid the money into court, or to have retained it until indemnified, if he had made application to the court for that purpose.

(*c*) Graham *v.* Witherby, 7 Q. B. 491; see also Goldschmidt *v.* Hamlet, 6 Man. & G. 187; 6 Scott, N. R. 962.

(*d*) Kempland *v.* Macauley, Peake's N. P. C. 66. See Bradley *v.* Wyndham, 1 Wils. 44.

(*e*) Ashworth *v.* Earl of Uxbridge, 2 Dowl. N. S. 337. See Chambers *v.* Coleman, 9 Dowl. 588.

goods are sold under the *fi. fa.* it is otherwise, for by the sale the property is altered (*f*). The Court of Exchequer (*g*) decided in one case, contrary to decisions of the Queen's Bench (*h*) and Common Pleas (*i*), that if a *fieri facias* be delivered to the sheriff, and, after a seizure of goods, but before sale, an extent be delivered to the sheriff, tested after the delivery of the *fieri facias*, the extent shall be preferred; and this is now settled law (*j*). And, in the Queen's Bench, process sued out by the crown against a defendant to recover penalties, upon which judgment for the crown is afterwards obtained, entitles the queen's execution to priority, within the statute 33 Hen. 8, c. 39, s. 74, before the execution of a subject, issued on a judgment recovered against the same defendant prior to the queen's judgment, but subsequent to the commencement of the queen's process, the queen's writ having been delivered to the sheriff before the actual sale of the defendant's goods under the plaintiff's execution (*k*).

SECTION II.

Fieri Facias—What Things may be seized under.

What things may be seized under a *fi. fa.*

The sheriff is commanded by the writ to cause the debt to be levied on the *goods and chattels* of the defendant. Under this writ the wearing apparel of the defendant is not liable to be taken, although "if the defendant have two gowns, the sheriff may sell one (*l*)." But wearing apparel on a man's person, even if it does not extend to goods in the actual possession of the person, cannot be taken under a *fi. fa.*, or under an extent (*m*); and before the statute 1 & 2 Vict. c. 110, nothing could be taken in execution which could not be sold (*n*). Thus, deeds, writings, money, or bank notes, could not be taken in execution

(*f*) Swain *v.* Morland, 1 Brod. & Bing. 370; 3 Moore, 740, S. C.

(*g*) Rex *v.* Wells and Alnutt, 16 East, 278, n.; Rex *v.* Sloper, 6 Price, 114, 144; 8 Price, 293. See also 1 Saund. 219 f, n. (*i*); 1 East, 338. See *post*, chap. 15, s. 2.

(*h*) Rorke *v.* Dayrell, 4 T. R. 402.

(*i*) Uppom *v.* Sumner, 2 Blac. Rep. 1251.

(*j*) Giles *v.* Grover, 1 Clark & Fin. 72; *post*, chap. 15, s. 2.

(*k*) Butler *v.* Butler, 1 East, 338; 8 Price, 364.

(*l*) Comb. 291.

(*m*) Sunbolf *v.* Alford, 3 M. & W. 264, *per* Parke, B.

(*n*) Com. Dig. Execution (C 4).

CHAP. X. SECT. II.

on a *fieri facias* (o); and the courts have refused to allow the defendant's money in the sheriff's hands, whether the produce of an execution at the suit of the defendant himself (p), or even the surplus of a former execution at the suit of the same plaintiff against the same defendant (q), to be stayed in the hands of the sheriff to satisfy the present execution.

By the 12th section of the 1 & 2 Vict. c. 110, however, it is enacted, "that by virtue of any writ of *fieri facias* to be sued out of any superior or inferior court after the time appointed for the commencement of this act, or any precept in pursuance thereof, the sheriff or other officer having the execution thereof may and shall seize and take any money or bank notes, (whether of the Governor and Company of the Bank of England, or of any other bank or bankers,) and any checks, bills of exchange, promissory notes, bonds, specialties, or other securities for money, belonging to the person against whose effects such writ of *fieri facias* shall be sued out; and may and shall pay or deliver to the party suing out such execution any money or bank notes which shall be so seized, or a sufficient part thereof; and may and shall hold any such checks, bills of exchange, promissory notes, bonds, specialties, or other securities for money as a security or securities for the amount by such writ of *fieri facias* directed to be levied, or so much thereof as shall not have been otherwise levied and raised; and may sue in the name of such sheriff or other officer for the recovery of the sum or sums secured thereby, if and when the time of payment thereof shall have arrived; and that the payment to such sheriff or other officer by the party liable on any such check, bill of exchange, promissory note, bond, specialty, or other security, with or without suit, or the recovering and levying execution against the party so liable, shall discharge him to the extent of such payment, or of such recovery and levy in execution, as the case may be, from his liability on any such check, bill of exchange, promissory note, bond, specialty, or other security; and such

(o) Francis *v.* Nash, Rep. Temp. Hard. 53; Staple *v.* Bird, Barnes, 214.

(p) Knight *v.* Criddle, 9 East. 48; Padfield *v.* Brine, 3 Brod. & Bing. 294; Wilkins *v.* Ball, 2 N. R. 376. The case in 1 Doug. 231, *contrà*, passed by consent.

(q) Fieldhouse *v.* Croft, 4 East, 510. If the second writ had been in the office before the goods were sold, the surplus would have been available to the second execution; 3 Bar. & Ald. 95.

sheriff or other officer may and shall pay over to the party suing out such writ the money so to be recovered, or such part thereof as shall be sufficient to discharge the amount by such writ directed to be levied; and if, after satisfaction of the amount so to be levied, together with sheriff's poundage and expenses, any surplus shall remain in the hands of such sheriff or other officer, the same shall be paid to the party against whom such writ shall be so issued; provided that no such sheriff or other officer shall be bound to sue any party liable upon any such check, bill of exchange, promissory note, bond, specialty, or other security, unless the party suing out such execution shall enter into a bond, with two sufficient sureties, for indemnifying him from all costs and expenses to be incurred in the prosecution of such action, or to which he may become liable in consequence thereof, the expense of such bond to be deducted out of any money to be recovered in such action."

Under this section it has been decided that money received by the sheriff in redemption of goods pledged with the defendant, who was a pawnbroker, is seizable under a *fi. fa.* (*r*). A mere *debt* cannot be seized; and therefore, under process of execution, the sheriff cannot seize a debt due from a former sheriff, as the surplus of a former execution, to the defendant (*s*); nor does the section apply to money in the hands of a third party as trustee for the defendant, but only to money in the hands of the debtor himself (*t*); therefore, money deposited in court in one action, pursuant to 43 Geo. 3, c. 46, s. 2, and 7 & 8 Geo. 4, c. 71, s. 2, cannot be paid out to an execution creditor in another action (*u*). So where the sheriff has seized and sold goods under a *fi. fa.*, and holds in his hands the produce of the sale, such produce is not liable to seizure under a *fi. fa.* against the execution creditor, at whose suit the levy was made, unless the sheriff has appropriated and set apart some specific money, as that which is to be paid over under the first *fi. fa.* (*x*). A lease for years, or an annuity for years (*y*), being merely chattel in-

(*r*) Squire *v.* Huetson, 1 Q. B. 308.

(*s*) Harrison *v.* Paynter, 6 M. & W. 387; 8 Dowl. 349, S. C.

(*t*) Robinson *v.* Peace, 7 Dowl. 93.

(*u*) France *v.* Campbell, and Winter *v.* Campbell, 9 Dowl. 914.

(*x*) Wood *v.* Wood, 4 Q. B. 397; see also Masters *v.* Stanley, 8 Dowl. 169.

(*y*) York *v.* Twine, Cro. Jac. 78. *Sed vide* Doct. & Stud. 53; Dalton, 127.

CHAP. X. SECT. II.

terests, like all other chattels, may be taken and sold under a writ of *fieri facias;* and although the sheriff cannot ascertain the length of time that the term has to run, yet he should levy and sell the term notwithstanding; for in the assignment by the sheriff of a term of years, of which the defendant is possessed, it is sufficient to recite that the defendant is possessed of a term of years yet to come and unexpired; for it cannot be intended that the sheriff should know the exact commencement and end of the term (*z*). And it is more prudent for the sheriff so to assign it; for if, instead of stating the defendant's interest thus generally, he attempt to state it particularly, and fail, the vendee will not have a good title (*a*). But the sheriff cannot sell under a *fieri facias* any estate of freehold, as an estate for life, or an estate *pur auter vie* (*b*); but it seems that an outstanding term, vested in a trustee upon trust to attend the inheritance, may be seized under an execution against the *cestui que trust*, the owner of the inheritance (*c*). The sheriff can only give the vendee of a term of years under a *fi. fa.* the right of possession; he has no power to put the defendant forcibly out of possession (*d*); the vendee must bring his ejectment to get into possession (*e*): if, indeed, he can peaceably obtain possession, he may enter and possess himself of the premises without bringing ejectment (*f*). Until actual execution of an assignment by the sheriff, the vendee has no legal title, but the legal interest remains in the debtor (*g*), even as against the execution creditor.

Fixtures.

Fixtures annexed to the freehold cannot be taken under a *fi. fa.*, for they do not fall within the definition of goods and chattels. Therefore, on a *fi. fa.* against the owner of a house, fixtures put up therein by him, which would go to the heir and not

(*z*) Palmer's case, 4 Rep. 74; Cro. Eliz. 584, S. C.; Taylor *v.* Cole, 3 T. R. 292. See also Eaton *v.* Southby, Willes, 131. If the lease be seized before the writ is returnable, the assignment by him after the return day is valid, and conveys a good title to the purchaser; Doe *v.* Donston, 1 B. & A. 230.

(*a*) Palmer's case, 4 Rep. 74; Cro. Eliz. 584, S. C.

(*b*) Harbert's case, 3 Rep. 13; Johnson *v.* Streete, Comb. 291.

(*c*) Doe *d.* Phillips *v.* Evans, 1 C. & M. 450.

(*d*) Rex *v.* Deane, 2 Show. 85.

(*e*) *Id. ibid.*; 3 T. R. 295.

(*f*) Taylor *v.* Cole, 3 T. R. 295. See also Taunton *v.* Costar, 7 T. R. 431; Turner *v.* Meymott, 1 Bing. 158; 7 Moore, 574, S. C. See also Doe *d.* Stevens *v.* Lord, 6 Dowl. 256.

(*g*) Doe *d.* Hughes *v.* Jones, 9 M. & W. 372; 1 Dowl. N. S. 352, S. C.; Playfair *v.* Musgrove, 14 M. & W. 239.

CHAP. X. SECT. II.

to the executor, cannot be seized and sold by the sheriff (*h*); but fixtures which may be removed by the tenant during his term may be seized and sold on a *fi. fa.* against the tenant (*i*). It often becomes a question what fixtures are and what are not removable by the tenant; it has been determined that buildings of brick and mortar, erected on land for the purposes of agriculture by the tenant during the term, are not removable by him (*k*), although if erected by the tenant for the purposes of trade it would be otherwise (*l*). So a conservatory erected on a brick foundation (*m*), or the machinery of a mill (*n*), or ranges, ovens, or pots (*o*), erected and fixed by the tenant during the term, have been held not to be removable by him. But parts of a machine, which are usually valued between out-going and in-coming tenants, are removable by the tenant (*p*). Fixtures erected by the tenant during the term for the *purposes of trade*, if he covenant to yield up all erections made during the term, are not removable by him (*q*). Even if the tenant sever from the freehold fixtures which he cannot lawfully remove, the sheriff cannot take them on a *fi. fa.* against the tenant, for on being severed they become the property of the landlord (*r*).

Growing crops and agricultural produce, how to be sold.

Corn and other crops, growing or sown on the ground, which go to the executor, may be sold under a *fieri facias* (*s*). Thus, a crop of growing potatoes may be seized (*t*); but clover, rye grass, or artificial grass, growing under corn, cannot be seized on a *fi. fa.* (*u*); nor can a growing crop of meadow grass (*x*);

(*h*) Wynne *v.* Ingelby, 1 Dowl. & Ry. 247; 5 B. & Ald. 625, S. C.

(*i*) Poole's case, Salk. 368; Minshall *v.* Lloyd, 2 M. & W. 459, *per* Parke, B.

(*k*) Elwes *v.* Maw, 3 East, 28. See also Steward *v.* Lombe, 4 Moore, 281; 1 Brod. & Bing. 506, S. C.

(*l*) Penton *v.* Robart, 2 East, 87; Elwes *v.* Maw, 3 East, 44. And as to what fixtures pass to the assignees of a bankrupt tenant, see Horn *v.* Baker, 9 East, 215; Storer *v.* Hunter, 5 Dowl. & Ry. 240; 3 B. & C. 368, S. C.

(*m*) Buckland *v.* Butterfield, 4 Moore, 440; 2 Brod. & Bing. 54, S. C.

(*n*) Farrant *v.* Thompson, 2 Dowl. & Ry. 1; 5 B. & Ald. 826, S. C.

(*o*) Wynne *v.* Ingleby, 1 Dowl. & Ry. 247; 5 B. & Ald. 625, S. C.

(*p*) Davis *v.* Jones, 2 Bar. & Ald. 165.

(*q*) Thresher *v.* The East London Water Works Company, 4 Dowl. & Ry. 62; 2 Bar. & Cres. 608, S. C.; Naylor *v.* Collinge, 1 Taunt. 19. See also 7 Taunt. 188; 2 Marsh. 495, S. C.; 4 Bar. & Ald. 206.

(*r*) Farrant *v.* Thompson, 2 Dowl. & Ry. 1; 5 B. & Ald. 826, S. C.

(*s*) Dalton, 556.

(*t*) Evans *v.* Roberts, 5 B. & C. 832, *per* Bayley, J. See also as to what are emblements, Graves *v.* Weld, 5 B. & Adol. 105; 1 Williams on Executors, 555, *et seq.* (3d edit.)

(*u*) 56 Geo. 3, c. 50, s. 7.

(*x*) See Evans *v.* Roberts, 5 B. & C. 832, *per* Bayley, J.

CHAP. X. SECT. II.

nor can growing fruit (y). Where a *fieri facias* was delivered to the sheriff against the tenant of certain land whereon certain crops were standing, and before the return of that writ a writ of *habere facias possessionem* of the same land was delivered to the sheriff, issued on an ejectment on a demise laid anterior to the teste of the *fieri facias*, it was held that those crops were not liable to be taken on the *fieri facias*, inasmuch as the tenant was a trespasser from the day laid in the declaration in ejectment (z). Where corn sold under a *fi. fa.* is not ripe, the vendee has a reasonable time after it is ripe to cut it and carry it away; and whilst remaining on the land it is not liable to a distress for rent, for during all that time it is considered in *custodiâ legis*, the goods in the vendee's possession being protected, in order to render the execution available, although the sheriff's duty ended on the execution of the bill of sale (a).

Formerly, the duty of the sheriff in the sale and disposition of corn or other crops or manure taken on a farm, under a *fieri facias* against a tenant, was the same as in the sale of any other goods and chattels; but now, where there is any covenant or contract in writing between landlord and tenant, stipulating that such crops, &c. shall be spent on the farm, (which act does not relate to produce which the tenant may consistently with his lease remove from the farm), the sale of such goods is regulated by the statute 56 Geo. 3, c. 50, the first section of which provides that where there is a covenant or contract in writing (and whereof the sheriff has notice) for spending agricultural produce upon the farm, the sheriff shall not remove the crops, &c., from the farm for the purpose of sale. The tenant is required to give notice to the sheriff of such covenants or written agreements, and the sheriff is required to give notice by the post to the landlord or his agent of his possession of such agricultural produce; and in case of the silence of the landlord or agent, the sheriff must delay the sale till the latest period he can do (b). And where there is a covenant or written contract between landlord and tenant, the sheriff is to assign or make an agreement with his vendee that he is to consume the produce according to the

(y) Rodwell *v.* Phillips, 9 M. & W. 505, *per* Lord Abinger, C. B.

(z) Hodgson *v.* Gascoigne, 5 Bar. & Ald. 88.

(a) Peacock *v.* Purvis, 2 Brod. & Bing. 362; 5 Moore, 79, S. C.; Wright *v.* Dewes, 1 Ad. & Ell. 641; 3 N. & M. 790, S. C.

(b) Sect. 2.

terms of such covenant or written agreement. If there be no such covenant or agreement, then the vendee is to stipulate to spend the produce of the farm according to the custom of the country, and the vendee is allowed the use of the barns, &c. on the farm (*c*) for that purpose without the sheriff or vendee being a trespasser (*d*); nor are such crops remaining on the premises liable to a distress for rent (*e*). The sheriff is to allow the landlord to bring actions in his name against the vendee for breaches of the agreement in assigning the crops, &c., the landlord indemnifying the sheriff before commencing his action (*f*).

Section III.

Fieri Facias.—What Interest in Goods may be taken.

Goods pawned or leased.

Respecting the *interest* of a *defendant* in goods which will render them liable to be taken on a *fieri facias;* the sheriff cannot sell *absolutely* goods which are pawned or gaged for a debt *with* the defendant, nor goods demised or let to him for years (*g*).

Where a house and the furniture therein were let to A. for six months, and during that period the landlord and A. entered into a written contract for the sale of the house and furniture to A., the purchase-money to be paid on the completion of a good title, but, before the completion of a good title, the contract was rescinded by consent, it was held that, under this contract, the furniture never vested in A. as his property, and therefore could not be taken in execution under a *fi. fa.* against him (*h*).

The sheriff, however, it seems, is not liable to an action for selling the entire property, unless he is informed of the defendant's having only a special property in the goods (*i*).

The sheriff cannot take in execution goods held by the defendant in right of a lien (*k*). Again, goods pawned or gaged

(*c*) Sect. 3.
(*d*) Sect. 10.
(*e*) Sect. 6.
(*f*) Sect. 4.
(*g*) Dean *v.* Whittaker, 1 C. & P. 347; Duffill *v.* Spottiswoode, 3 C. & P. 435; Izod *v.* Lamb, 1 C. & J. 35.
(*h*) Lanyon *v.* Toogood, 13 M. & W. 27.
(*i*) Dean *v.* Whittaker, 1 C. & P. 347; *sed quære,* see Chit. Archb. 432, 7th edit.
(*k*) Legg *v.* Evans, 6 M. & W. 36; 8 Dowl. 177, S. C.

CHAP. X. SECT. III.

for a debt, or leased for years, cannot be taken in execution against the *pawnor* or *lessor* (*l*); subject, however, to the right of the lessee or pawnee, the sheriff may sell the goods so pawned or leased (*m*). Such goods, however, cannot be seized till the expiration of the right of the pawnee or lessee, for the pawnor or lessor has no present right of possession (*n*); but if fixtures or trees demised with land for a term are severed by the tenant, they immediately vest in the lessor, and would be liable to be taken on an execution against the lessor (*o*). Goods distrained or taken in execution are not liable to be taken on a subsequent execution (*p*), unless such former execution was a fraudulent one (*q*).

Equitable interest cannot be taken.

A mere *equitable* interest in a term of years cannot be taken in execution under a writ of *fieri facias* (*r*), and for that reason, on a *fi. fa.* against a mortgagor, an equity of redemption cannot be taken in execution (*s*). But if the legal interest be in the defendant, the term may be taken: thus, where the defendant had agreed to sell the remainder of his term, it was held that before any actual assignment the term might be sold by the sheriff under the *fieri facias* (*t*).

It seems that an outstanding term vested in a trustee upon trust to attend the inheritance, is liable (by stat. 29 Car. 2, c. 3,) to be seized under a *fi. fa.* against the *cestui que trust*, the owner of the inheritance (*u*).

Partnership property.

On a writ of *fieri facias* against one of two partners, the sheriff must seize all the joint property, because the moieties are undivided; for if he seize but a moiety, and sell that, the other partner has a right to a moiety of that moiety; but he must

(*l*) Bro. Pledges, pl. 28; Execution, pl. 107; Dalt. 146; Rogers *v.* Kennay, 15 Law J. (Q. B.) 381.

(*m*) See Tidd's Prac. 1042, 8th edit.

(*n*) See Scott *v.* Scholey, 8 East, 476, 479. If the lease of goods were void, it would be otherwise; see Smith *v.* Plomer, 15 East, 607.

(*o*) See Farrant *v.* Thompson, 2 Dowl. & Ry. 1; 5 B. & A. 826, S. C.

(*p*) Bro. Pledges, 28; see Cro. Car. 149.

(*q*) See as to priority of writs, *ante*, p. 247.

(*r*) Scott *v.* Scholey, 8 East, 467; Metcalf *v.* Scholey, 2 N. R. 461; Moore *v.* Blake, 4 Dow, 230.

(*s*) Shirley *v.* Wright, 3 Atk. 200; Burdon *v.* Kennedy, 3 Atk. 739; Lyster *v.* Dolland, 3 Bro. Chan. Ca. 480; 1 Ves. jun. 431. The proper remedy for the plaintiff, in that case, is by filing a bill in equity to redeem the estate, by paying off the principal and interest due on the mortgage; but before he is entitled to redeem, he must first take out a writ of execution against the defendant, see 3 Atk. 200; though it does not seem to be necessary to have it returned, Redesd. Eq. Pl. 102, 3rd edit.

(*t*) Sparrow *v.* Earl of Bristol, 1 Marsh. 10.

(*u*) Doe *d.* Phillips *v.* Evans, 1 C. & M. 450; 3 Tyr. 339, S. C.

seize the whole, and sell a moiety thereof undivided, and the vendee will be tenant in common with the other partner (*x*). The duty of the sheriff is to sell the share of the defendant in the partnership property, even though he may not be able to ascertain the actual amount of his interest (*y*). If the execution creditor disputes the fact of the partnership, the court will interfere to protect the sheriff under the Interpleader Act (*z*). But where the goods of two partners are taken in execution against one of two partners, on a subsequent execution against the other partner, the sheriff must hold the goods as seized; one moiety for the execution against one partner, the other moiety for the execution against the other; for if to the writ against the second partner he return *nulla bona*, it is a false return (*a*). But in such a case he must make an actual seizure of such other moiety, for the purpose of satisfying the execution against such second partner; for where a *fi. fa.* had issued against one of two partners, under which partnership property was seized, and afterwards a *fi. fa.* was issued against both the partners jointly, which was lodged with the same sheriff who had seized under the first writ, but the warrant was granted to a different officer, and no actual seizure was ever made under the second writ, a fiat in bankruptcy issuing afterwards, it was held that the seizure and possession under the writ against the single partner, and the lodging of the writ against the two partners, did not amount to a seizure within the 108th section of the Bankrupt Act, 6 Geo. 4, c. 16, and therefore the sheriff was not justified in satisfying the second writ out of the proceeds of the goods (*b*).

In one case, where the sheriff had sold the whole of the partnership property, on an execution against one partner, the Court of King's Bench granted a rule for the master to take an account of the partnership property belonging to the other partner,

(*x*) Heydon *v.* Heydon, Salk. 392; Morley *v.* Strombon, 3 Bos. & Pul. 254; Pope *v.* Hanan, Comb. 217; Holmes *v.* Mentze, 4 Ad. & E. 127; Johnson *v.* Evans, 7 Man. & G. 240; 7 Scott, N. R. 1035, S. C. This rule applies as well where the shares are unequal as where they are equal. But see Burton *v.* Green, 3 Car. & P. 306, from which it seems that there is some doubt as to the interest in partnership property, which can be sold by the sheriff; see also Johnson *v.* Evans, *supra*.

(*y*) Holmes *v.* Mentze, 4 Ad. & E. 127.

(*z*) *Ibid.*

(*a*) Buckhirst *v.* Clinkard, 1 Show. 174.

(*b*) Johnson *v.* Evans, 7 Man. & G. 240; 7 Scott, N. R. 1035, S. C.

CHAP. X. SECT. III.

and that the sheriff should pay over to the assignees of such partner the sum found due to them (*c*). But where the sheriff seized, on a *fi. fa.* against one of several partners, his undivided share of the partnership effects, the Court of Common Pleas refused to refer it to the master to inquire what share the defendant had in the partnership effects seized (*d*). And the same court, under similar circumstances, on application by the partnership creditors, refused to enlarge the time for the sheriff to return the writ until an account might be taken of the several claims upon the property (*e*). So where an execution creditor seized partnership property under a *fi. fa.* against one of the partners, afterwards a joint fiat issued against the firm, and the property was then sold "without prejudice" to the rights of the execution creditor, and the proceeds received by the assignees of the bankrupts; it was held that, as the interest applicable to the execution creditor could only be in the surplus coming to the execution debtor, after payment of the partnership debts, and must depend on the settlement of accounts, which a court of law is not competent to take, the execution creditor could not maintain an action for money had and received against the assignees (*f*).

Goods in the hands of *executor, administrator,* or *trustee.*

On a *fieri facias* against an *executor* for his own debt, the goods of the testator in the hands of the defendant cannot be taken in execution (*g*). And the law is the same where goods are in the hands of a defendant as trustee (*h*); unless perhaps where the goods have been for a long time possessed by the defendant under circumstances inconsistent with the trust (*i*). But if an executrix use the goods of her testator as her own, and afterwards marry, and then treat them as the goods of her husband, she shall not be allowed to object to their being taken in execution for her husband's debt (*k*).

(*c*) Eddie *v.* Davidson, 2 Doug. 650.

(*d*) Chapman *v.* Koops, 3 Bos. & Pul. 289.

(*e*) Parker *v.* Pistor, 3 Bos. & Pul. 288.

(*f*) Garbett *v.* Veale, 5 Q. B. 408; 1 Dav. & M. 458, S. C.

(*g*) Farr *v.* Newman, 4 T. R. 621; Whaler *v.* Booth, 4 Dougl. 36; note (*a*) to Farr *v.* Newman, 4 T. R. 625, S. C.; see also Fenwick *v.* Laycock, 2 Q. B. 108.

(*h*) See Fenwick *v.* Laycock, 2 Q. B. 108.

(*i*) See Gaskell *v.* Marshall, 1 Moo. & Rob. 132; 5 C. & P. 31, S. C., *per* Lord Tenterden, C. J.; see also Fenwick *v.* Laycock, *supra*, *per* Lord Denman, C. J.

(*k*) Quick *v.* Staines, 1 Bos. & Pul. 293.

CHAP. X. SECT. III.

Goods vested in trustees for the benefit of the wife.

On a *fieri facias* against a husband, it would appear that the sheriff may sell a term vested in the husband in right of his wife (*l*). On a *fieri facias* against a wife on a judgment obtained against her before coverture, the goods that she had before marriage cannot be taken, for they vest in the husband by the marriage (*m*). And goods *bonâ fide* vested in trustees under a settlement made before marriage for the benefit of the *wife*, and in the possession of the husband, cannot be taken in execution on a *fi. fa.* against the *husband* (*n*), although there has been no inventory of the goods (*o*), and although they are of a fluctuating nature (*p*). And it seems that a settlement after marriage would have the same effect, if made for a good and valuable consideration, and without fraud (*q*); or if made in pursuance of an agreement entered into before marriage (*r*). But whether goods, vested in trustees for the benefit of the wife by settlement made either before or after marriage, be or be not liable to be taken in execution against the husband, always depends upon the fact whether the settlement be *bonâ fide* or not: the cases of settlements made before marriage are *primâ facie* free from fraud (*s*), but the amount of the consideration, and other circumstances in the case, are questions for a jury to say whether the settlement be fraudulent or not (*t*). If, however, the husband carry on trade with the goods settled on the wife (*u*), or his possession be inconsistent with the deed, the goods may be taken on a *fi. fa.* against him (*x*). If a claim be set up by trustees of the wife, on an execution against the husband, the sheriff should apply to the court under the Interpleader Act (*y*). Wearing apparel, purchased by a wife living with her husband, out of money vested in trustees for her sole and separate use

(*l*) See 4 T. R. 638.

(*m*) See Doe *d.* Taggart *v.* Butcher, 3 M. & S. 558.

(*n*) Cadogan *v.* Kennett, Cowp. 432; see also Foley *v.* Burnell, *id.* 435, n.; Simmons *v.* Edwards, 16 M. & W. 838.

(*o*) Jarman *v.* Woolloton, 3 T. R. 618.

(*p*) *Id. ibid.*

(*q*) Nun *v.* Wilsmore, 8 T. R. 521; see also Dewey *v.* Bayntun, 6 East, 257; Earl of Shaftesbury *v.* Russel, 3 Dowl. & Ry. 84; 1 Bar. & Cress. 666, S. C.

(*r*) 1 Eq. Ca. Abr. 148.

(*s*) See Cowp. 432; 3 T. R. 618.

(*t*) Dewey *v.* Bayntun, 6 East, 257.

(*u*) See Jarman *v.* Woolloton, 3 T. R. 618.

(*x*) Derby *v.* Smith, 8 T. R. 82.

(*y*) *Post*, s. 6.

CHAP. X. SECT. III.

before marriage, is liable to be taken under a *fi. fa.* against the husband (*y*).

If the goods in fact are not the property of the defendant.

The sheriff is bound at all events to levy whatever goods the defendant has in his county; and thus he would be, but for the protection of the court, often placed in an awkward dilemma; for if he fail to levy goods of the defendant in his bailiwick, he is responsible to the plaintiff in an action for a false return; if, on the other hand, he seize goods which belong to a stranger, although they apparently are the property of the defendant, he is liable to an action of trespass (*z*). The court however will, whenever the property in the goods is disputed, allow the sheriff, under the stat. 1 Will. 4, c. 58, to *interplead*, and obtain an issue to try who is the real owner of the goods (*a*); and therefore the sheriff should not return the writ when there is a dispute as to the property. Thus, where the defendant has obtained possession of goods by fraud, they cannot be taken in execution against him, for he can have no property in goods obtained by fraud (*b*). And where a woman, having assumed the name and passed for the wife of B., and permitted him to appear to be the owner of the furniture of the house in which they both lived, it was held that such furniture could not be taken in execution against B. (*c*). But where the real owner of goods suffered them, while in the possession of a debtor, to be seized and sold without making any claim to them, it was held that he could not afterwards maintain trover for them against a person who purchased them under the execution with his knowledge and sufferance (*d*). Whether the goods belong to the defendant or to a stranger, the sheriff should apply to the court for protection, whenever there is a reasonable doubt as to the property in the goods; for in Dalton, 146, it is laid down, that if the sheriff take the goods of a stranger on a *fieri facias*, and return the levy, he is concluded by it. However, it has been decided that a sheriff is not in all cases concluded by his return; for where

(*y*) Carne *v.* Brice, 7 M. & W. 183; 8 Dowl. 884, S. C.

(*z*) Dalt. Sheriff, 145, 146; Gilbert on Execution, 21; see also Oughton *v.* Seppings, 1 B. & Adol. 241.

(*a*) See *post*, s. 6.

(*b*) Earl of Bristol *v.* Wilsmore, 2 Dowl. & Ry. 755; 1 Bar. & Cress. 514.

(*c*) Edwards *v.* Bridges, 2 Stark. N. P. C. 396; Glasspoole *v.* Young, 9 B. & C. 696; 4 Man. & Ry. 553.

(*d*) Pickard *v.* Sears, 6 Ad. & E. 469; see also Gregg *v.* Wells, 10 Ad. & E. 90.

the sheriff returned to a *fieri facias* goods in hands for want of buyers, and a commission having issued against the defendant, on an act of bankruptcy committed before the delivery of the writ to the sheriff, it was held, in an action for not selling those goods on a *venditioni exponas*, that the sheriff was not concluded by his return, for the defendant had a defeasible title, which had in fact been defeated (*e*).

Goods assigned by defendant when *bonâ fide*.

Goods sold by the person against whom a *fi. fa.* issues after the delivery of the writ to the sheriff, unless in market overt, are liable to be taken and sold by virtue of the execution (*f*); for the goods are bound by the delivery of the writ to the sheriff (*g*). The *property*, however, in the goods is not changed by the delivery of the writ to the sheriff; and the defendant may, notwithstanding, transfer such property, subject however to the claims of the execution creditor (*h*).

But if the defendant sell his goods *bonâ fide*, and for a valuable consideration, *before the delivery* of the writ to the sheriff, they cannot be taken in execution (*i*); and though he sell them fraudulently, yet if they be afterwards sold *bonâ fide* to another, as where a donee lends the donor money to buy goods, and at the same time takes a bill of sale of them for securing the money, they are not liable to be taken in the hands of a second vendee (*k*). But if the defendant's goods be sold fraudulently, before the delivery of the writ to the sheriff, they may be taken in execution. A principal badge of fraud is the defendant's continuing in possession (*l*). In the old cases it seems to have been considered, that if a man sell goods and continue in possession as visible owner of them, such sale was void and fraudulent against creditors (*m*). But later cases have qualified this position; for although the vendor's continuing in possession is generally a badge of fraud, yet it is not necessarily so; for where

(*e*) Brydges *v.* Walford, 6 M. & S. 42; see also Porter *v.* Viner, 1 Chitty's Rep. 613, n.

(*f*) See Samuel *v.* Duke, 3 M. & W. 622; 6 Dowl. 538, S. C.; 3 Atk. 739. A mere agreement by the defendant to sell his goods will not prevent them from being taken in execution; Sparrow *v.* Earl of Bristol, 1 Marsh. 10.

(*g*) See *ante*, 246; 3 Atk. 739.

(*h*) Samuel *v.* Duke, 3 M. & W. 622; 6 Dowl. 538, S. C.

(*i*) Bull. N. P. 258, *recog.* in Kidd *v.* Rawlinson, 2 Bos. & Pul. 60. See also 10 Ves. 145.

(*k*) Godb. 161; and see 1 M. & Sel. 251, *quære*.

(*l*) Twyne's case, 3 Rep. 81.

(*m*) *Id. ibid.*; Stone *v.* Grubbam, 2 Bulstr. 225; Edwards *v.* Harben, 2 T. R. 587.

CHAP. X. SECT. III.

goods are assigned, and the assignor remains in possession of them on terms consistent with the deed of assignment, the assignment is not considered fraudulent (*n*); as where goods are publicly sold, and are afterwards let by the vendee to the vendor for a rent, who continues in possession (*o*), or where the defendant remains in possession for the purpose of disposing of them for the vendee (*p*), although the defendant is ostensibly the owner, yet they are not liable to be taken on an execution against the defendant. In questions of this kind, possession is to be much regarded, with a view to ascertain the good faith or bad faith of the transaction; but although the defendant continue in possession of goods after a bill of sale executed by him, yet if it appear that the vendee actually paid the consideration for them, and that the sale was notorious in the neighbourhood, as being made under an execution, the question is proper for a jury to say upon the whole case whether the transaction be *bonâ fide* or not (*q*). And where A. put B. into possession of a public-house, and allowed B. to continue the ostensible owner of the goods in the house, it was held that the goods could not be taken in execution against B. (*r*); for it has never been held that a person may not give the possession of his goods to another, without subjecting them to an execution for his debt. Thus, where a creditor, having taken goods of a defendant in execution upon a judgment confessed on a warrant of attorney, bought them by public auction, and took a bill of sale of them from the sheriff for a valuable consideration; after which he let the goods to the defendant for a rent which was actually paid; the Court of Common Pleas held that the creditor had a title which could not be impeached as fraudulent by other creditors having executions against the same defendant (*s*). And where a testator devised goods to trustees, to allow the persons to enjoy

(*n*) Woodham *v.* Baldock, 3 Moore, 11; Martindale *v.* Booth, 3 B. & Ad. 498; Carr *v.* Burdiss, 1 C. M. & R. 782; 5 Tyrw. 309, S. C.; Minshall *v.* Lloyd, 2 M. & W. 450; Reeves *v.* Capper, 5 Bing. N. C. 136, *per* Tindal, C. J.

(*o*) Watkins *v.* Birch, 4 Taunt. 823; Steward *v.* Lomb, 1 Brod. & Bing. 506. See also Leonard *v.* Baker, 1 M. & S. 251; Kidd *v.* Rawlinson, 2 B. & Pul. 60.

(*p*) Jezeph *v.* Ingram, 1 Moore, 189. See Hindle *v.* Bell, 4 Campb. 383.

(*q*) Latimer *v.* Batson, 4 Bar. & Cress. 652; 7 Dow. & Ry. 108, S. C.

(*r*) Dawson *v.* Wood, 3 Taunt. 256.

(*s*) Watkins *v.* Birch, 4 Taunt. 823. And see the other cases cited in note (*o*).

them who should be possessed of a certain mansion-house under the will, it was held that such goods could not be taken in execution against a tenant for life of the mansion-house, who was in possession of the goods under the will (*t*). And where A. cohabited with B., assumed his name, and passed for his wife, and permitted him to appear to be the owner of the furniture of the house in which they lived, it was held that the furniture, being her property, was not liable to be taken in an execution against B. (*u*).

Where the defendant has become a bankrupt.

As the sheriff cannot take the goods of a stranger, if the defendant become bankrupt before the seizure, the goods of the bankrupt cannot be taken on a *fi. fa.* against him; for by the bankruptcy the property in them vests in the assignees (*x*). And where the sheriff, having seized the goods of a defendant on a *fi. fa.* delivered to him before the defendant's bankruptcy, afterwards sold goods enough to satisfy that execution and also another writ delivered to him after the bankruptcy of the defendant, it was held that the sheriff was liable to the assignees, in an action of trover, for the amount of the goods sold to satisfy the second writ (*y*). If the seizure of the goods and the act of bankruptcy happen on the same day, it is open to inquire at what time of the day the goods were seized; for if the goods were seized at an earlier period of the day than the act of bankruptcy, the execution is good (*z*). And if the seizure were made two months before the issuing of the fiat, it is valid, although the act of bankruptcy was before the seizure (*a*). If the sheriff seize and sell the goods before he has notice of an act of bankruptcy, he is excused (*b*); and if he sell them after notice, but before a fiat sued out, although he may be suable in trover (*c*), or for money had and received, yet he is not liable in trespass, for an officer shall never be a trespasser by rela-

(*t*) Earl of Shaftesbury *v.* Russell, 3 Dowl. & Ry. 84; 1 Bar. & Cress. 666, S. C.

(*u*) Edwards *v.* Bridges, 2 Stark. N. P. C. 396; Glasspoole *v.* Young, 9 B. & C. 696; 4 Man. & R. 553, S. C.

(*x*) Smalcomb *v.* Cross, 1 Lord Raym. 252; Phillips *v.* Thomson, 3 Lev. 69, 191.

(*y*) Stead *v.* Gascoigne, 8 Taunt. 527.

(*z*) Thomas *v.* Desanges, 2 Bar. & Ald. 586; Ex parte Dobree, 8 Ves. 82; Saddler *v.* Leigh, 4 Camp. 197; Woodland *v.* Fuller, 11 Ad. & E. 859.

(*a*) 6 Geo. 4, c. 16, s. 81.

(*b*) Cooper *v.* Chitty, 1 Bla. Rep. 65; 1 Burr. 20, S. C.

(*c*) *Id. ibid.* And it lies upon the sheriff to show that he paid over the money to the execution creditor before notice of the act of bankruptcy; Lee *v.* Lopes, 15 East, 230.

CHAP. X. SECT. III.

tion (*d*). If the writ be executed on goods which the bankrupt has acquired since the bankruptcy, the execution will be good, if the bankrupt's certificate be not then signed and allowed (*e*). Yet if the certificate be allowed at any time before the goods are sold, the court will order them to be restored on motion (*f*).

The 2 & 3 Vict. c. 29, s. 1, enacts, "that all contracts, dealings and transactions by and with any bankrupt really and *bonâ fide* made and entered into before the date and issuing of the fiat against him, and all executions and attachments against the lands and tenements or goods and chattels of such bankrupt, *bonâ fide* executed or levied before the date and issuing of the fiat, shall be deemed to be valid, notwithstanding any prior act of bankruptcy by such bankrupt committed; provided the person or persons so dealing with such bankrupt, or at whose suit or on whose account such execution or attachment shall have issued, had not at the time of such contract, dealing or transaction, or at the time of executing or levying such execution or attachment, notice of any prior act of bankruptcy by him committed; provided also, that nothing herein contained shall be deemed or taken to give validity to any payment made by any bankrupt, being a fraudulent preference of any creditor or creditors of such bankrupt, or to any execution founded on a judgment on a warrant of attorney or cognovit given by any bankrupt by way of such fraudulent preference."

If a writ of *fi. fa.* is lodged with the sheriff after the defendant has been declared a bankrupt and assignees appointed, the sheriff should return *nulla bona* (*g*); and this return will not be vitiated by the fiat being afterwards, and after the return, annulled (*h*). The words "*executed and levied*," in the 2 & 3 Vict. c. 29, are satisfied by a *seizure* under the writ; all executions, therefore (except such as are hereafter particularly mentioned, being such as are founded on judgments entered up on warrants of attorney, or on cognovits executed before declaration, and judgments by default, confession, or *nil dicit*, in actions commenced not adversely, or by collusion, or for the

(*d*) Smith *v.* Miller, 1 T. R. 475.

(*e*) Cullen *v.* Meyrick, 1 T. R. 361; Neateley *v.* Engleton, 2 Tidd's Prac. 1049, 8th edit.

(*f*) Lister *v.* Mundell, 1 Bos. & Pul. 427. See also Dimsdale *v.* Eames, 4 Moore, 350; 2 Brod. & Bing. 8, S. C. See also Davis *v.* Shapley, 1 B. & Ad. 54.

(*g*) See Smallcombe *v.* Olivier, 13 M. & W. 77; 2 Dowl. & L. 217.

(*h*) *Ibid.*

purpose of fraudulent preference), are rendered valid by the statute, notwithstanding a prior act of bankruptcy, provided that there has been a *seizure* under the writ before the date and issuing of the fiat, and provided also that the *execution creditor* had not, at the time of such seizure, notice of such prior act of bankruptcy (*i*).

The notice of a prior act of bankruptcy, required by the statute to invalidate an execution *bonâ fide* executed and levied before the date and issuing of the fiat, must be given to *the person at whose suit* the execution has issued, *i. e.* to the creditor himself; and the execution would not be invalidated by notice to the sheriff or his bailiff only (*k*). But notice to the attorney of the execution creditor, given before the issuing of the *fi. fa.*, has been held to be notice to the creditor himself (*l*). No particular form of notice is necessary; and it seems that it would be sufficient to give notice generally that an act of bankruptcy has been committed, without stating the nature of the act (*m*). If the notice contain information of an act done, which may or may not turn out to be an act of bankruptcy, according to circumstances, it is sufficient (*n*). Notice of a docket having been struck has been held not to be notice of an act of bankruptcy (*o*). The time of delivering out the fiat as an operative instrument is the "date and issuing" within the meaning of the statute; and *primâ facie* the delivery of it out of the bankrupt office is the time from which it becomes an operative instrument (*p*). It is not necessary, in order to render an execution valid by virtue of this statute, that there should be *bona fides* on the part of the debtor; for it has been held that the words "*bonâ fide*" in the statute have reference only to the *bona fides* of the creditor who caused the execution to issue, and of the sheriff, who is his minister (*q*).

The stat. 2 & 3 Vict. c. 29, does not, however, protect transactions which are of themselves acts of bankruptcy, and conse-

(*i*) See Giles *v.* Grover, 9 Bing. 267; Cheston *v.* Gibbs, 12 M. & W. 111.

(*k*) Ramsey *v.* Eaton, 10 M. & W. 22.

(*l*) Rothwell *v.* Timbrell, 1 Dowl. N. S. 778.

(*m*) See Ramsey *v.* Eaton, 10 M. & W. 27, *per* Parke, B.

(*n*) Rothwell *v.* Timbrell, 1 Dowl. N. S. 778.

(*o*) Hocking *v.* Acraman, 1 Dowl. & L. 434; 12 M. & W. 170, S. C.

(*p*) Pewtress *v.* Annan, 9 Dowl. 828.

(*q*) Belcher *v.* Magnay, 12 M. & W. 102.

CHAP. X. SECT. III.

quently invalid; and therefore, where the seizure under the execution is itself an act of bankruptcy, by reason of its having been procured by the trader himself, in order to defeat or delay his creditors, the statute will not protect it, although it may have been *bonâ fide* levied so far as regards the execution creditor and the sheriff (*r*). But in order to complete the assignee's right of action under such circumstances, it is necessary that there should be a conversion, *e. g.* by sale of the goods seized after the accrual of their title, that is, after the act of bankruptcy (*s*). Therefore, in an action of trover at the suit of assignees, to a plea framed under the stat. 2 & 3 Vict. c. 29, showing an execution *bonâ fide* executed before the date and issuing of the fiat, and alleging the conversion to be by seizure of the goods under the *fi. fa.*, it may be replied that the debtor procured the *fi. fa.* to be issued with intent to delay his creditors, and thereby then committed an act of bankruptcy, and new assigning that afterwards, and after the seizure of the said goods, the defendant converted them *modo et formâ*, which is the conversion in the declaration mentioned. And such a replication will not be open to the objection that it is an argumentative traverse that the execution was *bonâ fide* executed; and it is not necessary in the new assignment to point out in what the conversion new assigned consists (*t*). Neither does the 2 & 3 Vict. c. 29, protect executions founded on judgments entered up on warrants of attorney, unless such executions are perfected both by *seizure and sale* before the date and issuing of the fiat, for the 2 & 3 Vict. c. 29, does not operate as a repeal of the 108th section of the 6 Geo. 4, c. 16 (*u*). It is not, however, essential to the validity of an execution founded on a judgment entered up on a warrant of attorney, that the proceeds of the sale should be paid over to the creditor before the issuing of the fiat; it is sufficient if the sale has taken place before that time, because immediately on the sale of the goods levied the judgment creditor ceases to be a creditor of the bankrupt within the mean-

(*r*) Hall *v.* Wallace, 7 M. & W. 353; Belcher *v.* Magnay, 12 M. & W. 102.

(*s*) *Ibid.*

(*t*) Belcher *v.* Magnay, 12 M. & W. 102.

(*u*) Whitmore *v.* Robertson, 8 M. & W. 463; Skey *v.* Carter, 11 M. & W. 571; 2 Dowl. N. S. 831, S. C.; see also Rawdon *v.* Wentworth, 10 M. & W. 36; Godson *v.* Sanctuary, 4 B. & Ad. 262.

ing of the 6 Geo. 4, c. 16, s. 108 (*x*). If an execution founded on a judgment on a warrant of attorney is completed by seizure and sale prior to the issuing of the fiat, it is protected by the statute, although the creditor had notice of the act of bankruptcy before the sale (*y*). To a plea to an action of trover at the suit of assignees framed on this statute, justifying a conversion by seizure under a *fi. fa.* against the bankrupt, and alleging that the defendants executed and levied their execution against the goods before the fiat, it may be replied that the judgment on which the writ has issued was entered up on a warrant of attorney, and that *after the fiat* the defendants sold the goods, which is the conversion complained of, and such a replication will not amount to an argumentative traverse that the execution was executed and levied before the fiat, but will be good by way of confession and avoidance, as admitting that the execution was executed and levied (for it has been shown that those words are satisfied by a *seizure* alone under the writ) before the fiat, and avoiding the effect of such execution and levy, by showing circumstances to bring it within the 108th section of the 6 Geo. 4, c. 16 (*z*).

An execution founded on a judgment entered up on a cognovit, executed before declaration filed or delivered, or on a judgment by default, confession, or *nil dicit*, in an action commenced not adversely or by collusion, or for the purpose of fraudulent preference, requires also to be perfected by seizure and sale before fiat, precisely in the same way as executions founded on judgments on warrants of attorney; the 108th section of 6 Geo. 4, c. 16, applying in terms to all judgments by default, confession, or *nil dicit*, and the 1 Will. 4, c. 7, s. 7, having only excepted from the operation of that section judgments on cognovits signed after declaration filed or delivered, and judgments by default, confession, or *nil dicit*, according to the practice of the court, in actions commenced adversely, and not by collusion, or for the purpose of fraudulent preference.

Insolvency of defendant.

In the case of an execution against an insolvent debtor, issued on a judgment founded on a warrant of attorney or cognovit,

(*x*) Ramsey *v.* Eaton, 10 M. & W. 22; Morland *v.* Pellatt, 8 B. & C. 722.

(*y*) Whitmore *v.* Greene, 13 M. & W. 104; 2 Dowl. & L. 174.

(*z*) Cheston *v.* Gibbs, 12 M. & W. 111.

CHAP. X. SECT. III.

the stat. 1 & 2 Vict. c. 110, s. 61, enacts, "that in all cases where any prisoner whose estate shall have been vested in the said provisional assignee under this act shall have executed any warrant of attorney to confess judgment, or shall have given any cognovit actionem, or bill of sale, whether for a valuable consideration or otherwise, no person shall, after the commencement of the imprisonment of such prisoner, avail himself or herself of any execution issued or to be issued upon any judgment obtained or to be obtained upon such warrant of attorney or cognovit actionem, or of such bill of sale, either by seizure and sale of the property of such prisoner, or any part thereof, or by sale of such property theretofore seized, or any part thereof, but that any person or persons to whom any sum or sums of money shall be due in respect of any such warrant of attorney or cognovit actionem, or of such bill of sale, shall and may be a creditor or creditors for the same under this act."

The old Insolvent Act (7 Geo. 4, c. 57) contained a clause (s. 34) in almost the same words, and under that act it was held, that a sheriff who had seized the goods of an insolvent debtor under a *fi. fa.* issued upon a judgment founded on a cognovit, and who sold after notice of the assignment to the provisional assignee, was liable for so selling to an action of trover at the suit of the assignees (*a*), even though the goods were seized by the sheriff under the writ before the commencement of the insolvent's imprisonment (*b*). But the execution creditor is entitled to the amount of all monies actually realized by sale of goods seized under a *fi. fa.* before the commencement of the insolvent's imprisonment, although at that time other part of the goods may remain unsold in the sheriff's hands (*c*).

Section IV.

Fieri Facias.—Goods seized, when and how to be sold.

Goods when and how to be sold.

It seems that if the sheriff seize the goods of the defendant on premises belonging to the defendant or a stranger, he is allowed to remain on the premises a reasonable time in order to remove

(*a*) Groves *v.* Cowham, 10 Bing. 5.
(*b*) Kelcey *v.* Minter, 1 Bing. N.C. 721.
(*c*) Squire *v.* Huetson, 1 Q.B. 308.

the goods. After the sheriff has seized the goods, it is his duty to remove them to a place of safe custody until they can be sold, for if they be rescued the sheriff is liable to the plaintiff for their value (*d*); and it is said, if the sheriff take cattle, and return that he has taken cattle to the value of 100*l.*, and afterwards the cattle die for want of meat, the sheriff is answerable for the value returned (*e*). The court will not interfere to restrain a sheriff from selling goods seized under a *fi, fa.* on an offer of indemnity from a claimant of them (*f*). In selling the goods, the sheriff or his officer is not obliged to sell them by public auction, but the expense of any other mode of sale will fall upon himself (*g*). In the case of a lease for years taken by the sheriff on a *fi. fa.*, the sheriff should assign it by deed, under the seal of office, without specifying the particular time that the lease has then to run (*h*). Although goods are put up to sale by public auction, yet if they are sold for much below their real value, the sheriff is liable to an action; for in such case he should return that he has goods which remain in hands for want of buyers, and wait for a *venditioni exponas* (*i*). But where a broker sold a lease, taken on a *fi. fa.*, for a sum much below its value, which sale the sheriff refused to complete, and returned that the goods remained in his hands for want of buyers, it was ruled at Nisi Prius that the sheriff was liable in an action for a false return (*j*). The sheriff may sell the goods after the return of the writ, even after he is out of office, without a *venditioni exponas* (*k*). The sale or assignment by the sheriff of goods or chattels of the defendant taken on a *fi. fa.*, conveys an indefeasible title to the vendee; so much so, that if the writ be afterwards vacated, the defendant shall not be restored to his goods (*l*). But if the writ were void, as issuing from a court

(*d*) Sly *v.* Finch, Cro. Jac. 514.

(*e*) *Ibid.* 515; 2 Lord Raym. 1075.

(*f*) Harrison *v.* Foster, 4 Dowl. 558.

(*g*) Phillips *v.* Viscount Canterbury, 11 M. & W. 619; 1 Dowl. & L. 283, S. C.

(*h*) *Ante*, 252; Taylor *v.* Cole, 3 T. R. 294; Palmer's case, 4 Rep. 74; Cro. Eliz. 584, S. C.; and see form of a deed of assignment by the sheriff of goods seized by him on a *fi. fa.*, *post*, Append.

(*i*) Keightley *v.* Birch, 3 Camp. 520.

(*j*) Barnard *v.* Leigh, 1 Stark. 43.

(*k*) Doe *d.* Stevens *v.* Donston, 1 Bar. & Ald. 230; Ayre *v.* Aden, Cro. Jac. 73; 1 Roll. Abr. 893, 894; *per* Holt, C. J., 6 Mod. 295; Jeans *v.* Wilkins, 1 Ves. 195; *sed vide* Yelv. 44; 1 Lutw. 589. If the sheriff seize goods, and a *supersedeas* be afterwards delivered to him, a *venditioni exponas* may still issue to him to sell them; Cro. Eliz. 597.

(*l*) Doe *v.* Thorn, 1 M. & S. 425; Doe *d.* Batten *v.* Murless, 6 M. & S. 110; Dyer, 363, pl. 24; 5 Rep. 90 b.

CHAP. X. SECT. IV.

not having jurisdiction, or if the goods were the goods of a stranger and not of the defendant, of course the sale by the sheriff would convey no property (*m*). But the sheriff cannot retain the goods to his own use, on satisfying the plaintiff out of his own money (*n*); so neither can he deliver them to the plaintiff in satisfaction of his debt (*o*). But they may be sold to the plaintiff, though they cannot be delivered to him without a sale (*p*).

Venditioni exponas.

In order to compel a sale of the goods, where the same sheriff continues in office, it is usual to issue a writ of *venditioni exponas.* This writ is not a process distinct from the *fi. fa.*, but is a part of it, and therefore a judge has power to order the sheriff to return it in vacation, under 2 Will. 4, c. 39, s. 15 (*q*). This writ should be sued out without delay; for if, after the sheriff makes his return to a *fi. fa.*, the plaintiff lies by without proceeding against the sheriff, and the goods should in the mean time be taken on an extent, or the defendant become bankrupt, and the sheriff deliver them to the assignees, the court will quash a writ of *distringas* obtained against the sheriff (*r*). After the delivery of the *venditioni exponas* to the sheriff, it is his duty to sell the goods at all events for the best price that can be got for them (*s*). But the Court of Common Pleas refused in one case to grant an attachment against the sheriff for returning to a *venditioni exponas* that the goods remained in hands for want of buyers (*t*). The proper mode of proceeding, if the sheriff do not sell on or before the return of the *venditioni exponas,* is to sue out a *distringas* against him, directed to the coroner, and if he do not sell the goods, and pay over the money before the return of that writ, he shall forfeit issues to the amount of the debt (*u*).

(*m*) See Farrant *v.* Thompson, 2 Dowl. & R. 1; see also Lock *v.* Selwood, 1 Q. B. 736.

(*n*) Noy, 107; Langdon *v.* Wallis, 1 Lutw. 589.

(*o*) Bealey *v.* Sampson, 2 Vent 93; Thomson *v.* Clerk, Cro. Eliz. 504.

(*p*) See Leader *v.* Danvers, 1 Bos. & Pul. 360; Petit *v.* Benson, Comb. 452; Stratford *v.* Twynam, Jacob, 418.

(*q*) Hughes *v.* Rees, 4 M. & W. 468; 7 Dowl. 56, S. C.; Reg. *v.* Sheriff of Berks, 8 Dowl. 97.

(*r*) Ruston *v.* Hatfield, 3 Bar. & Ald. 204; Clutterbuck *v.* Jones, 15 East, 78. And if the act of bankruptcy was prior to the seizure on the *fieri facias*, the sheriff is not concluded by his return of goods in hands for want of buyers; Brydges *v.* Walford, 6 M. & Sel. 42.

(*s*) See Keightley *v.* Birch, 3 Camp. 524; Cowp. 405.

(*t*) Leader *v.* Danvers, 1 Bos. & Pul. 359.

(*u*) Clerk *v.* Withers, 6 Mod. 300; see also Chit. Arch. 437, 7th edit. Where the sheriff has returned to a *fi.*

But where four writs of *fi. fa.* at the suit of different plaintiffs against the same defendant were successively delivered to the sheriff, to the last of which he returned that he had seized goods, value unknown, which remained in his hands for want of buyers, upon which a *venditioni exponas* issued, the court stayed an attachment for not returning the *venditioni exponas*, on the sheriff's paying over the balance in his hands, after satisfying the former writs (*x*).

If the sheriff neglects to sell for an unreasonable time, and the plaintiff thereby sustains any damage, an action on the case may be supported against him for his breach of duty (*y*). In making sale of goods under a *venditioni exponas*, the sheriff is not bound by the value set upon the goods in the return to the *fi. fa.* (*z*). The sheriff ought to stop the sale of the goods as soon as a sufficient sum has been raised to cover the amount of the levy, expenses, &c. (*a*); and after selling enough in fact for that purpose, he is not justified in selling more, on the supposition that by accident, for which he is not answerable, the amount levied may become insufficient (*b*).

Distringas nuper vicecomitem.

If the sheriff return that he has seized goods on a *fi. fa.*, which remain unsold for want of buyers, and go out of office, the plaintiff may sue out a *distringas nuper vicecomitem*, by which writ the new sheriff is commanded to distrain the old sheriff to sell the goods, and have the money in court at the return (*c*). The sheriff's authority to sell the goods, we have seen, is not derived from the *distringas*, for the sheriff, who has seized goods, *may* sell them after he is out of office; but this writ is compulsory upon him (*d*). If there has been laches on the part

fa. that he has levied, he cannot to the *venditioni exponas* return that he has sold the goods, but detains the money for another party, who is a plaintiff under a prior writ; Rowe *v.* Tapp, 9 Price, 317.

(*x*) Reg. *v.* Sheriff of Herts, 9 Dowl. 916.

(*y*) Jacobs *v.* Humphrey, 2 C. & M. 413; Bates *v.* Wingfield, 2 N. & M. 831; 4 Q. B. 580. n. (*a*), S. C.

(*z*) Charter *v.* Peter, Cro. Eliz. 598; Sly *v.* Finch, Cro. Jac. 515; Godb. 276; Wintle *v.* Lord Chetwynd, 7 Dowl. 554; Chambers *v.* Coleman, 9 Dowl. 588; Barton *v.* Gill, 11 M. & W. 315; 1 Dowl. & L. 593, S. C.

(*a*) See Cook *v.* Palmer, 6 B. & C. 739; Bayley, J., Batchelor *v.* Vyse, 4 M. & Sc. 552.

(*b*) Aldred *v.* Constable, 6 Q. B. 370.

(*c*) See the form of the writ, 2 Saund. 47 q, note. The old form of writ was, that the new sheriff should have the money in court; see 6 Mod. 299.

(*d*) Clerk *v.* Withers, 6 Mod. 299; 1 Salk. 323; 2 Lord Raym. 1074, 1075, S. C.; 2 Saund. 47 q.

CHAP. X. SECT. IV.

of the plaintiff, or collusion between him and the officer, the court will not grant the *distringas* (*e*). And if a fiat in bankruptcy issue against the defendant, on an act of bankruptcy committed before the seizure of his goods under a *fi. fa.*, the court will not grant a *distringas* after a return of goods in his hands unsold, for in such case the sheriff is not concluded by his return as to the property in the goods being in the defendant (*f*). Where, to the *distringas*, the new sheriff returned that he had distrained issues to the value of 40*s.*, and in consequence of the delay further costs had been incurred, the court increased the issues to the amount of 100*l.* to meet the costs incurred (*g*).

Payment of debt and costs, or bond or other security to the sheriff, is good.

The sheriff, on a *fieri facias*, may release the goods, or omit to levy them, on payment of the debt and costs to himself, for the sheriff is ordered to levy the debt; and his duty on a *fi. fa.* in this respect differs from his duty on a *ca. sa.* (*h*), for on the former writ payment to the sheriff is a bar to any future execution. Indeed, it has been said that if the sheriff seize the goods after a tender of the debt and costs, he is a trespasser (*i*). And the sheriff may, if he please, take a bond conditioned to pay the money into court on the return of the *fi. fa.* (*k*), or to save him harmless against a false return to a *fi. fa.* (*l*), such bonds not being void under the stat. 23 Hen. 6, c. 9, that statute extending only to bonds given by or for prisoners in custody on *mesne process* (*m*). But the sheriff, for releasing the defendant's goods on taking a bond, would be liable to the plaintiff in an action for a false return, and must seek his remedy over upon the bond.

Sheriff's property in goods seized. Actions by him for injury thereto.

When the sheriff has duly seized goods under a writ of *fieri facias*, he has such a special property in them as to enable him to maintain trespass or trover against any person who may take them out of his possession (*n*), for he is answerable to the plaintiff to the value of the goods; but he acquires no general pro-

(*e*) Ruston *v.* Hatfield, 3 Bar. & Ald. 204; 1 Chitty's Rep. 613, S. C.

(*f*) Clutterbuck *v.* Jones, 15 East, 78; Brydges *v.* Walford, 6 M. & S. 42.

(*g*) Phillips *v.* Morgan, 4 Bar. & Ald. 652; Nowell *v.* Underwood, 5 Dowl. 229.

(*h*) Taylor *v.* Bekon, or Baker, 2 Lev. 203; T. Jones, 97, S. C.

(*i*) *Per* Twysden, J., in Lefans *v.* Moregreen, 1 Keb. 655.

(*k*) Beawfage's case, 10 Rep. 99 b.

(*l*) Knipe *v.* Hobart, 1 Lutw. 596.

(*m*) See Rogers *v.* Reeves, 1 T. R. 421; 1 Saund. 161.

(*n*) Wilbraham *v.* Snow, 2 Saund. 47; 1 Vent. 52, S. C.; 1 Lev. 282; 1 Sid. 438; S. P. Clerk *v.* Withers, 6 Mod. 292.

perty in them (*o*). Where a *fi. fa.* was delivered to the sheriff, and, before it was executed, the attorney of another creditor obtained a warrant from the sheriff, and sold the goods on a second *fi. fa.*, it was held that the sheriff, who returned a levy on the first writ, might recover the amount of the levy from the attorney in an action for money had and received; for the clerk of the attorney must be considered the agent of the sheriff in making the levy, the proceeds of which were liable to satisfy the writ first delivered (*p*). But the sheriff, in order to maintain any action against a person for taking goods seized by him on a *fi. fa.*, must continue in actual possession of them; for where a sheriff's officer seized a table in the name of all the goods in a house, and locked up his warrant in the table-drawer, and left the house, it was held that the sheriff could not maintain an action against the landlord who afterwards distrained them for rent (*q*). And where the sheriff seizes goods in the possession of the defendant, which he obtained by fraud, the sheriff cannot maintain an action against the real owner for rescuing them out of his custody (*r*).

Defendant when discharged by a levy.

The defendant is discharged from the judgment and all further execution, if the sheriff has taken goods to the amount of the debt, although he does not satisfy the plaintiff (*s*); or if the sheriff has levied goods to the amount of part of the debt, no further execution can issue until the writ is returned (*t*); but one obligor cannot plead that the goods of his co-obligor were seized under a *fi. fa.*, for it is no actual satisfaction of the debt; the plea is confined to the party whose goods are taken (*u*).

Restitution, how made.

If, after goods are seized and sold under a writ of *fieri facias*, the judgment be afterwards reversed or set aside, the party against whom the execution was sued out shall have restitution of the money levied, that is, of the money *properly* levied by

(*o*) Doe *d.* Hughes *v.* Jones, 9 M. & W. 372; Playfair *v.* Musgrove, 14 M. & W. 239.

(*p*) Sawle *v.* Paynter, 1 Dowl. & Ry. 307.

(*q*) Blades *v.* Arundale, 1 M. & Sel. 711.

(*r*) Earl of Bristol *v.* Wilsmore, 2 Dowl. & Ry. 755; 1 B. & C. 514, S. C.

(*s*) Slie *v.* Finch, 2 Roll. Rep. 57; Cro. Jac. 514, S. C.; Taylor *v.* Baker, 2 Mod. 214; Clerk *v.* Withers, 6 Mod. 292, 299; 1 Salk. 323, S. C.

(*t*) Miller *v.* Parnell, 2 Marsh. 78; 6 Taunt. 370, S. C.; Chapman *v.* Boulby, 8 M. & W. 249; 1 Dowl. N. S. 83, S. C.; Thomas *v.* Newnam, 2 Dowl. N. S. 34.

(*u*) Dyke *v.* Mercer, 2 Show. 394; 2 Lord Raym. 1072, Gould, J.

CHAP. X. SECT. IV.

the officer (x), but not of the goods themselves. Thus, if a term be sold under a *fi. fa.*, and the judgment be reversed, it is only the money for which it was sold, and not the term itself, which shall be restored (y). But if the judgment be reversed before a term or goods be sold, the term or goods of course must be restored to the party (z). Where the judgment is set aside for irregularity, &c., restitution (when necessary) forms part of the rule; and if the goods or money be not restored, the court will of course grant an attachment (a).

Section V.

Fieri Facias.—Landlord's Claim for Rent.

Landlord's claim for rent.

Where the sheriff has seized goods under a writ of *fieri facias*, they are not liable to be distrained for rent. In order to give a preference to the landlord over all other creditors, it was enacted by stat. 8 Anne, c. 14, s. 1, "that no goods upon any tenements leased for life or lives, term of years, at will or otherwise, shall be liable to be taken by virtue of any execution, on any pretence whatever, unless the party at whose suit the execution is sued out shall, before the removal of such goods from off the said premises by virtue of such execution, pay to the landlord of such premises, or his bailiff, all such sums of money as are or shall be due for rent of the premises at the time of taking such goods by virtue of such execution, provided the arrears do not amount to more than *one year's rent;* and in case the arrears shall exceed one year's rent, then the party at whose suit, &c., paying the landlord or his bailiff one year's rent, may

(x) Whalley *v.* Barnett, 2 Dowl. 33.

(y) Doe *v.* Thorn, 1 M. & Sel. 425; Roll. Abr. Error (I) 1; Cro. Eliz. 278; 5 Rep. 90 b; Dyer, 363, pl. 24.

(z) See 2 Roll. Abr. 491, l. 4. If the judgment be reversed on a writ of error, the plaintiff in error shall have a writ of restitution, in order that he may be restored to all he has lost by the judgment. If execution on the judgment have been executed, and the money paid over, the plaintiff in error shall have restitution without a *scire facias*, because it appears on the record that the money had been paid, and there is a certainty what has been lost; but if the money have not been paid over, a *scire facias quare restitutionem non*, suggesting the matter of fact, viz. the sum levied, &c., must first previously issue; see Chit. Archb. 418, 7th edit.; 2 Tidd's Prac. 8th edit.

(a) Anon. 2 Salk. 588; and see Chit. Archb. Prac. 418, 7th edit.; 2 Tidd's Prac. 8th edit.

proceed to execute his judgment; and the sheriff is required to levy and pay to the plaintiff as well the money paid for rent as the execution money." And by s. 8, it is "provided that nothing in that act contained shall extend to hinder her majesty, her heirs, &c., but that it shall and may be lawful for her majesty, her heirs, &c., to levy, recover, and seize such debts, fines, penalties, and forfeitures, in the same manner as if that act had never been made."

The 7 & 8 Vict. c. 96, s. 67, enacts, "that no landlord of any tenement let at a weekly rent shall have any claim or lien upon any goods taken in execution under the process of any court of law for more than four weeks' arrears of rent; and if such tenement shall be let for any other term less than a year, the landlord shall not have any claim or lien on such goods for more than the arrears of rent accruing during four such terms or times of payment (*a*)."

The statute of 8 Anne applies to any goods upon the premises, to whomsoever those goods belong (*b*). The landlord, under this act, is only entitled, in preference to an execution, to rent due at the time of taking the goods, and not to rent which accrues due during the time that the sheriff is in possession (*c*). To entitle the landlord to a year's rent under the statute, the premises must be held by the tenant at a rent certain; and therefore where the tenant entered into possession in January, 1829, under an agreement made in October, 1828, whereby a lease was to be granted to him from the 20th November, 1828, but no lease was granted, and the tenant continued to occupy until the time of the execution in February, 1842, but it was not shown that any payment of rent had been made; it was held that it did not sufficiently appear that the tenant occupied as tenant at a rent certain to entitle the landlord to a year's rent before the removal of the goods (*d*). But where, in an agreement for the sale of certain premises, there was a stipulation that "in the meantime, and until the assignment was made, the purchaser should pay and allow to the vendor at the rate of

(*a*) See also, as to the right of the landlord in the case of executions out of the county courts established by 9 & 10 Vict. c. 95, the 107th section of that act.

(*b*) Foster *v.* Cookson, 1 Q. B. 419.

(*c*) Hoskins *v.* Knight, 1 M. & Sel. 245.

(*d*) Riseley *v.* Ryle, 11 M. & W. 16.

CHAP. X. SECT. V.

100*l.* per annum from the time of taking possession of the premises until the completion of the purchase, in equal half-yearly payments," the purchaser having taken possession, and one half-yearly payment being due, it was held that it was due as *rent*, and that the vendor was entitled to it under the statute of Anne before the removal of any of the goods which had been seized under an execution after it became due (*e*). The sheriff must pay the landlord his rent under this statute, if he has notice of the rent being due at any time whilst the goods or the proceeds are in his hands, although after the removal of them from the premises (*f*). If the landlord have a year's rent paid to him on one execution, and more rent remains due, he shall not be entitled to receive another year's rent on a subsequent execution (*g*). A ground landlord is not a landlord entitled to a year's rent within this statute (*h*); but the statute applies to a case of lessee and undertenant, and to goods in an apartment, part of a messuage (*i*); and it was held that the trustees of an outstanding term, assigned to attend the inheritance, might sue the sheriff for not paying over a year's rent in levying goods on a *fi. fa.* under this statute (*k*). Where the goods on a farm and premises were seized on a *fi. fa.* against the tenant, and a *habere facias possessionem* in an ejectment at the suit of the landlord, on a demise prior to the issuing of the *fi. fa.*, was afterwards, and before any sale under the *fi. fa.*, delivered to the sheriff; it was holden that the landlord was not entitled to a year's rent, for the tenant was a trespasser from the day laid in the declaration in ejectment, and consequently the defendant was not a tenant within the meaning of the statute at the time the sheriff seized the goods on the premises (*l*).

The statute does not apply where the landlord himself is the execution creditor (*m*); and therefore where the landlord, having seized his tenant's goods under an execution, was afterwards compelled to refund to the assignees of the tenant, who had become an insolvent, it was held that he could not as against them retain a year's rent (*n*). This statute applies to all manner

(*e*) Saunders *v.* Musgrave, 6 B. & C. 524.

(*f*) Arnitt *v.* Garnett, 3 Bar. & Ald. 440; Andrews *v.* Dixon, 3 Bar. & Ald. 645.

(*g*) Dodd *v.* Saxby, Stra. 1024.

(*h*) Bennett's case, Stra. 787.

(*i*) Thurgood *v.* Richardson, 7 Bing. 428; 5 M. & P. 270, S. C.

(*k*) Collyer *v.* Speer, 2 Brod. & Bing. 67.

(*l*) Hodgson *v.* Gascoigne, 5 Bar. & Ald. 88; Riseley *v.* Ryle, 10 M. & W. 101.

(*m*) Taylor *v.* Lanyon, 6 Bing. 536.

(*n*) *Ibid.*

of executions for the subject, upon judgments for the *defendant* as well as for the plaintiff (o). If the sheriff take goods on a *capias utlagatum*, he must satisfy the landlord his year's rent, because that writ is to be considered only as a private execution (p); but a seizure of goods under a power *per vadios* out of the Court of Common Pleas at Durham was held not to be a seizure under an execution within the meaning of the statute, although such a seizure had the effect of a seizure under an execution (q). A commission of bankruptcy is not an execution within this statute; and although the landlord has a right to distrain goods on the premises for a year's rent, notwithstanding the bankruptcy of the tenant (r), yet it was held that where the sheriff executed a *fi. fa.*, and paid the landlord a year's rent after an act of bankruptcy committed by the defendant, that the sheriff was answerable for the amount of that rent to the assignees in an action for money had and received (s).

The landlord is entitled to a full year's rent, although he may have been used generally to remit some portion of it to the tenant (t). The sheriff is not bound to remove the goods in execution, unless the *party at whose suit the execution is sued out* shall, before the removal of such goods, pay the landlord a year's rent (u). Nor is he bound to levy at all, whatever be the value of the goods, unless the execution creditor, having notice, first satisfies the landlord's rent (x). If the goods are not sufficient to satisfy the year's rent of which he has notice, he ought to withdraw from possession (y). If the sheriff do not pay over to the landlord his rent under this statute, an action on the case may be maintained against the sheriff (z), which action will lie, after the death of the landlord, for his executor or administrator (a); but the landlord cannot, to recover under this

(o) Henchett v. Kimpson, 2 Wils. 140.

(p) Rex v. Southerby, Bunb. 5; Greaves v. d'Acastro, Bunb. 194; Rex v. Pritchard, Bunb. 269; St. John's College v. Murcott, 7 T. R. 264.

(q) Brandling v. Barrington, 6 B. & C. 467.

(r) See 6 Geo. 4, c. 16, s. 74.

(s) Lee v. Lopes, 15 East, 230; Ex parte Desharmes, 1 Atk. 103; see also Gethin v. Wilks, 2 Dowl. 189.

(t) Williams v. Lewsey, 8 Bing. 28; 1 M. & Sc. 92, S. C.

(u) Calvert v. Joliffe, 2 B. & Ad. 421, Lord Tenterden, C.J. See also Riseley v. Ryle, 11 M. & W. 21, Parke, B.

(x) Cocker v. Musgrove, 15 Law J., Q. B. 365.

(y) *Ibid.*, and see Foster v. Hilton, 1 Dowl. 35.

(z) Riseley v. Ryle, 11 M. & W. 16.

(a) Palgrave v. Windham, Stra. 212.

CHAP. X. SECT. V.

statute, maintain an action for money had and received (*b*). The sheriff must have notice of the rent being due whilst the proceeds are in his hands, to make him liable to an action (*c*): but no specific form of notice is prescribed by the statute; it is sufficient that knowledge of the rent being due is brought home to the sheriff (*d*). A declaration under the statute of Anne against the sheriff must distinctly allege that the tenancy in the premises was subsisting at the time of the seizure (*e*); but it need not allege that the goods taken were distrainable goods (*f*), nor need it aver any notice to the execution creditor (*g*). The sheriff is not liable to an action unless there has been an actual removal of the goods from the premises, and the execution of a bill of sale of them is not equivalent to such removal (*h*). If the landlord declares against the sheriff in two counts, one on the statute of Anne and the other in trover, claiming, so far as regards the second count, under a fraudulent bill of sale, he is not thereby prevented from recovering on the first count, for that is distinct from the second (*i*). If an action is brought against the sheriff on the statute of Anne, the court will not stay proceedings on payment by him of the proceeds of the sale of the goods removed (*k*). Instead of bringing an action, the landlord may move the court that he may be paid what is due to him out of the money levied, if sufficient for that purpose, or otherwise so much as the sheriff has levied (*l*). The landlord is entitled to his rent without any deduction for poundage (*m*); but where he takes the security of a third person for the rent at the time of the execution, the sheriff is discharged as to the landlord's claim for rent (*n*). If the plaintiff bring an action against the sheriff for the money levied, the sheriff must prove that the rent was

(*b*) Green *v.* Austin, 3 Camp. 260.

(*c*) Smith *v.* Russell, 3 Taunt. 400; Waring *v.* Dewberry, Stra. 97.

(*d*) Collyer *v.* Spear, 2 Brod. & Bing. 67; Andrews *v.* Dixon, 3 Bar. & Ald. 645; Arnitt *v.* Garnett, 3 Bar. & Ald. 440; Riseley *v.* Ryle, 11 M. & W. 20, Parke, B.

(*e*) Riseley *v.* Ryle, 10 M. & W. 101.

(*f*) Riseley *v.* Ryle, 11 M. & W. 16.

(*g*) *Ibid.*

(*h*) Smallman *v.* Pollard, 1 Dowl. & L. 901.

(*i*) Reed *v.* Thoyts, 6 M. & W. 410.

(*k*) Foster *v.* Hilton, 1 Dowl. 30; Calvert *v.* Joliffe, 2 B. & Ad. 418.

(*l*) Henchett *v.* Kimpson, 2 Wils. 140; Darling *v.* Hill, Rep. Temp. Hardw. 255; West *v.* Hedges, Barnes, 211; and see Haun *v.* Capell, Barnes, 199.

(*m*) Gore *v.* Gofton, Stra. 643.

(*n*) Rotheray *v.* Wood, 3 Camp. 24.

due, in order to discharge himself as to a payment for a year's rent made by him to the landlord (o).

And by the statute of the 43 Geo. 3, c. 99, s. 37, it is enacted, that "no goods or chattels whatever belonging to any person at the time any of the said duties" (which are all the duties under the management of the commissioners for the affairs of taxes) "to be assessed under the regulations of this act became in arrear, shall be liable to be taken by virtue of any execution or other process, warrant, or authority, or by virtue of any assignment, on any account or pretence whatever, except at the suit of the landlord for rent, unless the party at whose suit the said execution or seizure shall be sued out or made, or to whom such assignment shall be made, shall, before the sale or removal of such goods or chattels, pay or cause to be paid to the collector or collectors of the said duties so due all arrears of the said duties which shall be due at the time of seizing such goods or chattels, or which shall be payable for the year in which such seizure shall be made, provided the duties shall not be claimed for more than one year; and in case the said duties shall be claimed for more than one year, then the said party at whose instance such seizure shall have been made, paying the collector or collectors the aforesaid duties due for one whole year, may proceed in his seizure as he might have done if no duties had been so claimed; but in case of refusal to pay the said duties, the said collector or collectors are hereby authorized and required to distrain such goods and chattels notwithstanding such seizure or assignment, and proceed to sale thereof according to this act, in order to obtain payment of the whole of the said duties so assessed, together with the reasonable costs and charges attending such distress and sale."

Section VI.

The Sheriff's Duty in Case of adverse Claims.—Interpleader.

As the sheriff is bound to execute the writ at his peril, where the defendant becomes bankrupt, and his assignees claim the goods, or there be any doubt whether or not the goods are liable

(o) Keightley *v.* Birch, 3 Camp. 521.

CHAP. X. SECT. VI.

to be taken on a *fi. fa.*, the sheriff should immediately apply to the court from which the writ issues for protection, if one party will not give him a sufficient indemnity; otherwise, by seizing the goods, or by returning *nulla bona*, the sheriff may subject himself to an action (*p*). Before the passing of the statutes relating to interpleader, wherever the property in goods seized on a *fi. fa.* was disputed, the courts were accustomed, on the suggestion of a reasonable doubt, to enlarge the time for the sheriff to make his return until the right was tried between the contending parties, or until one of them had given a sufficient indemnity to the sheriff or to his officer (*q*). Thus, where the sheriff had seized goods by virtue of a *fi. fa.*, but by the direction of the plaintiff the officer abandoned the execution, the warrant on that writ was placed again in the hands of an officer who was in possession under another writ; the defendant having become bankrupt, the officer, after satisfying the plaintiff in the second writ, delivered the remainder of the goods up to the assignees of the defendant; the sheriff being ruled to return the first writ, the Court of Common Pleas enlarged the time for the sheriff to make his return until he was indemnified (*r*). So the Court of King's Bench, upon the application of the sheriff, enlarged the time for his making a return to a *fieri facias*, (upon the suggestion of a reasonable doubt whether the goods seized under the writ were not covered by an extent, issued at the suit of the crown for malt duties), for the purpose of inducing the plaintiff to go into the Court of Exchequer, and there contest the question of right with the crown in a more eligible manner than in that court (*s*). And where the defendant had become bankrupt after the seizure, but before the goods were sold, and the assignees claimed the goods, the Court of Common Pleas stayed proceedings in an action commenced against the sheriff on his selling the goods and bringing the money into court (*t*). It was, however, quite discretionary in the courts, as well

(*p*) See Keightley *v.* Birch, 3 Camp. 520; Saunders *v.* Bridges, 3 Bar. & Ald. 95.

(*q*) Venables *v.* Wilks, 4 Moore, 339; Thurston *v.* Thurston, 1 Taunt. 120; Ledbury *v.* Smith, 1 Chitty's Rep. 294; Rex *v.* Sheriff of Devon, 1 Chitty's Rep. 643; Shaw *v.* Tunbridge, 2 Blac. Rep. 1064.

(*r*) Burr *v.* Freethey, 1 Bing. 71; 7 Moore, 368, S. C.

(*s*) Wells *v.* Pickman, 7 T. R. 174.

(*t*) MacGeorge *v.* Birch, 4 Taunt. 585; King *v.* Bridges, 1 Moore, 43; 7 Taunt. 294, S. C.; Ledbury *v.* Smith, 1 Chitty's Rep. 294.

whether or not they would interpose to protect the sheriff (*u*), as upon what terms they would protect him. In one case, the court granted a rule for enlarging the time for the sheriff to make his return from term to term until the sheriff should be indemnified (*x*); in another case, the time was enlarged for a certain number of days, in order that the sheriff might satisfy himself as to the property (*y*); in another case, the time was enlarged until the right should be settled in another court (*z*). If the sheriff or his officer had favoured one party by throwing obstacles in the way of or by delaying the other party, the courts would not protect him (*a*); or the sheriff, by not applying to the court in time, might lose its protection. Thus, where the sheriff, under a *fi. fa.* and a writ of extent, seized not only the defendant's goods, but also goods belonging to a stranger which were on the premises, and the sheriff returned to both writs that he had seized goods to the amount, but that they remained in hands for want of buyers, the sheriff being obliged afterwards, by order of the Court of Exchequer, to levy the amount of the extent upon the defendant's goods, and not upon the goods of the stranger, and having no longer goods of the defendant to satisfy the *fi. fa.*, he applied to the court for leave to amend his return to the latter writ. The court, however, refused to allow the amendment, saying, that as he had seized sufficient property of the defendant under this writ, he must be accountable to the plaintiff for it: had he, as soon as he received the order of the Court of Exchequer, stated the facts of the case to that court, they would have relieved him from his embarrassment. Again, where the law was clear on the subject, the courts would not interfere to protect the sheriff. Thus, where the sheriff had seized partnership property on a *fi. fa.* against one of several partners, the Court of Common Pleas refused to enlarge the time for the sheriff to make his return till the partnership creditors had taken an account of the claims on the property, because the law on the case was clear, intimating that the safest course for the sheriff to pursue was for him to put some

(*u*) See cases cited *ante*, notes (*q*), (*r*), (*s*), and (*t*), and *post*, note (*x*).

(*x*) Venables *v.* Wilks, 4 Moore, 339. See also Probinier *v.* Roberts, 1 Chitty's Rep. 577; Thurston *v.* Thurston, 1 Taunt. 120.

(*y*) Etchells *v.* Lovatt, 9 Price, 54.

(*z*) Wells *v.* Pickman, 7 T. R. 174.

(*a*) Timbrell *v.* Mills, 1 Blac. Rep. 205.

CHAP. X. SECT. VI.

person into possession of the defendant's share as vendee, leaving him and the parties to litigate their respective rights in a court of equity (*c*).

Of impanelling a jury to inquire into the right to the goods.

Where the sheriff had a doubt to whom the property in goods seized by him on a *fi. fa.* belongs, he might impanel a jury to inquire as to that fact; and it was formerly supposed that this would justify the sheriff in returning that the defendant had no goods within his bailiwick (*d*), and mitigate the damages in an action of trespass, if the goods seized should happen not to be the defendant's (*e*). But it was afterwards determined that such an inquisition, finding the goods in a third person, was not admissible in evidence in an action against the sheriff for a false return of *nulla bona* to a *fi. fa.* (*f*). In the same case Lord Ellenborough, C. J., said that he should think it might perhaps be evidence if the question were whether the sheriff had acted maliciously, but beyond that he could not see how it could be evidence (*g*). It would therefore seem that there was not any real benefit to be derived by holding such an inquest; and that proceeding has now become altogether obsolete by reason of the statutory provisions which are now to be noticed, enabling the sheriff, in case of adverse claims, to apply to the courts for relief by way of interpleader.

Interpleader.

The stat. 1 & 2 Will. 4, c. 58, s. 6, after reciting that difficulties sometimes arise in the execution of process against goods and chattels, issued by or under the authority of the said courts, by reason of claims made to such goods and chattels by assignees of bankrupts and other persons not being the parties against whom such process has issued, whereby sheriffs and other officers are exposed to the hazard and expense of actions, and it is reasonable to afford relief and protection in such cases to such sheriffs and other officers; it enacts, "that when any such claim shall be made to any goods or chattels taken or intended to be taken in execution under any such process, or to the proceeds or value thereof, it shall and may be lawful to and for the court from which such process issued, upon application

(*c*) Parker *v.* Pistor, 3 Bos. & Pul. 288. See also Chapman *v.* Koops, 3 Bos. & Pul. 289.

(*d*) Gilb. Execution, 21; Dalton, 146; see also Latkow *v.* Eamer, 2 H. Blac. 437; 6 T. R. 88.

(*e*) Bro. Abr. Trespass, 99; Keilw. 119; 4 T. R. 633; Dalton, 146; 1 Doug. 40.

(*f*) Glossop *v.* Pole, 3 M. & Sel. 175.

(*g*) *Ibid.* 177.

of such sheriff or other officer made before or after the return of such process, and as well before as after any action brought against such sheriff or other officer, to call before them, by rule of court, as well the party issuing such process as the party making such claim, and thereupon to exercise, for the adjustment of such claims and the relief and protection of the sheriff or other officer, all or any of the powers and authorities hereinbefore contained, and make such rules and decisions as shall appear to be just, according to the circumstances of the case; and the costs of all such proceedings shall be in the discretion of the court." CHAP. X. SECT. VI.

The reference in this section to the "powers and authorities hereinbefore contained" renders it necessary to state the other sections of the act, the direct application of which is to cases in which a bill of interpleader in equity might before have been brought.

The 1st section enacts, "that upon application made by or on the behalf of any defendant sued in any of his majesty's courts of law at Westminster, or in the Court of Common Pleas of the county palatine of Lancaster, or the Court of Pleas of the county palatine of Durham, in any action of assumpsit, debt, detinue, or trover, such application being made after declaration, and before plea, by affidavit or otherwise, showing that such defendant does not claim any interest in the subject-matter of the suit, but that the right thereto is claimed or supposed to belong to some third party who has sued or is expected to sue for the same, and that such defendant does not in any manner collude with such third party, but is ready to bring into court or to pay or dispose of the subject-matter of the action in such manner as the court (or any judge thereof) may order or direct, it shall be lawful for the court, or any judge thereof, to make rules and orders calling upon such third party to appear and to state the nature and particulars of his claim, and maintain or relinquish his claim, and upon such rule or order to hear the allegations as well as of such third party as of the plaintiff, and in the meantime to stay the proceedings in such action, and finally to order such third party to make himself defendant in the same or some other action, or to proceed to trial on one or more feigned issue or issues, and also to direct which of the parties shall be plaintiff or defendant on such trial, or, with the consent of the plaintiff

CHAP. X. SECT. VI. and such third party, their counsel or attornies, to dispose of the merits of their claims and determine the same in a summary manner, and to make such other rules and orders therein as to costs and all other matters as may appear to be just and reasonable."

The 2nd section provides, "that the judgment in any such action or issue as may be directed by the court or judge, and the decision of the court or judge in a summary manner, shall be final and conclusive against the parties, and all persons claiming by, from, or under them."

By section 3 it is enacted, "that if such party shall not appear upon such rule or order to maintain or relinquish his claim, being duly served therewith, or shall neglect or refuse to comply with any rule or order to be made after appearance, it shall be lawful for the court or judge to declare such third party, and all persons claiming by, from, or under him, to be for ever barred from prosecuting his claim against the original defendant, his executors or administrators, saving nevertheless the right or claim of such third party against the plaintiff; and thereupon to make such order between such defendant and the plaintiff, as to costs and other matters, as may appear just and reasonable."

Section 5 provides, "that if, upon application to a judge in the first instance, or in any later stage of the proceedings, he shall think the matter more fit for the decision of the court, it shall be lawful for him to refer the matter to the court; and thereupon the court shall and may hear and dispose of the same in the same manner as if the proceeding had originally commenced by rule of court, instead of the order of a judge."

The 7th section enacts, "that all rules, orders, matters and decisions to be made and done in pursuance of this act, except only the affidavits to be filed, may, together with the declaration in the cause (if any), be entered of record, with a note in the margin expressing the true date of such entry, to the end that the same may be evidence in future times, if required, and to secure and enforce the payment of costs directed by any such rule or order; and every such rule or order so entered shall have the force and effect of a judgment, except only as to becoming a charge on any lands, tenements, or hereditaments; and in case any costs shall not be paid within fifteen days after notice of the taxation and amount thereof given to the party ordered to pay the same, his agent or attorney, execution may issue for the same by *fieri facias* or *capias ad satisfaciendum*, adapted to the case, together with the costs of such entry, and of the execution if by *fieri facias;* and such writ and writs may bear teste on the day of issuing the same, whether in term or vacation; and the sheriff or other officer executing any such writ shall be entitled to the same fees, and no more, as upon any similar writ grounded upon a judgment of the court."

It will be observed, that although by the other sections of this statute the power of adjudication is given either to the court or a judge thereof, the 6th section, by enacting that it shall be lawful for "the court from which the process issued" to call the parties before them "by rule of court," expressly reserved the jurisdiction, in the case of an application by the sheriff, to the court in banc (*h*). But this being found inconvenient, by a subsequent statute, 1 & 2 Vict. c. 45, s. 2, after reciting the 6th section of the 1 & 2 Will. 4, c. 58, it is provided that it shall be lawful for any judge of the Courts of Queen's Bench, Common Pleas, or Exchequer, with respect to any process issued out of any of those courts, or for any judge of the Court of Common Pleas of the county palatine of Lancaster, or Court of Pleas of the county palatine of Durham (being also a judge of one of the three superior courts), with respect to process issued out of the courts of Lancaster or Durham respectively, to exercise such powers or authorities for the relief and protection of the sheriff or other officer, as may, by virtue of the said act, be exercised by the said several courts respectively, and to make such order thereon as shall appear to be just; and the costs of such proceeding shall be in the discretion of such judge. The application may now, therefore, be made at chambers, and, by reason of the common jurisdiction of the judges of the superior courts of common law under the 1st section of the same statute (1 & 2 Vict. c. 45), to any judge of any of those courts, from whatever court the process issued. If made in court, it can only be to the court in which the action is pending; and if there be two actions in different courts, an application must be made in each (*i*). In the Exchequer and

(*h*) See Bragg *v.* Hopkins, 2 Dowl. 151.

(*i*) Allen *v.* Gylby, 3 Dowl. 143.

CHAP. X. SECT. VI.

Common Pleas, the rule *nisi* will not operate as a stay of proceedings without previous notice (*l*). The decision of the judge is in general subject to review by the court; but where, by consent of the parties, the judge disposes summarily of an interpleader order, the court has no authority to review his decision (*m*). In the exercise of this jurisdiction, it will be seen that most of the principles upon which the courts previously acted, in giving relief to the sheriff in the case of adverse claims (*n*), are still applied.

No action need be pending against the sheriff, to entitle him to apply for relief; but there must be a *bonâ fide* claim actually made, to warrant the application (*o*). Notice of a lien will justify the application (*p*). But a distress for rent (*q*), or a claim arising out of proceedings in equity (*r*), will not suffice. Notice of other writs will not entitle the sheriff to relief (*s*); but the court may relieve him where it is doubtful which writ is entitled to precedence (*t*). The court will not interfere against a naked claim by the defendant's partner; but if the whole property in the goods be claimed, it will (*u*). So mere notice of a fiat in bankruptcy, without a claim by the assignees, will not entitle the sheriff to relief (*x*). The sheriff is not entitled to relief, unless he has actually seized or is in possession of the goods (*y*); but it is immaterial in whose possession the goods were when seized by the sheriff (*z*).

The sheriff must come promptly to the court after he has notice of the claim (*a*), unless the delay can be satisfactorily

(*l*) Smith *v.* Wheeler, 3 Dowl. 431.

(*m*) Shortridge *v.* Young, 12 M. & W. 5; see Harrison *v.* Wright, 13 M. & W. 816.

(*n*) *Ante*, 280.

(*o*) Isaac *v.* Spilsbury, 10 Bing. 3; 3 M. & Scott, 341; 2 Dowl. 211; Slowman *v.* Back, 3 B. & Ad. 103; Fenwick *v.* Laycock, 2 Q. B. 111.

(*p*) Ford *v.* Bayntun, 1 Dowl. 357.

(*q*) Haythorn *v.* Bush, 2 Dowl. 641.

(*r*) Sturgess *v.* Claude, 1 Dowl. 505; see Putney *v.* Tring, 5 M. & W. 425; Roach *v.* Wright, 8 M. & W. 155.

(*s*) Salmon *v.* James, 1 Dowl. 369.

(*t*) Day *v.* Waldock, 1 Dowl. 523; *sed quære.*

(*u*) Holmes *v.* Mentze, 4 Ad. & Ell. 127; 5 N. & M. 563; 4 Dowl. 300.

(*x*) Bentley *v.* Hook, 2 C. & M. 426; 2 Dowl. 339; see Barker *v.* Phipson, 3 Dowl. 590.

(*y*) Holton *v.* Guntrip, 3 M. & W. 145; 6 Dowl. 130.

(*z*) Allen *v.* Gibson, 2 Dowl. 292.

(*a*) Devereux *v.* John, 1 Dowl. 548; Cook *v.* Allen, 1 C. & M. 542; 2 Dowl. 11; Dixon *v.* Ensell, 2 Dowl. 621; Skipper *v.* Lane, 4 M. & Scott, 283; 2 Dowl. 784; Ridgway *v.* Fisher, 3 Dowl. 567; Barker *v.* Phipson, 3 Dowl. 590; Brackenbury *v.* Laurie, 3 Dowl. 180; Beale *v.* Overton, 2 M. & W. 534; 5 Dowl. 599.

accounted for. He must apply before the goods are sold, and the produce paid over, whether at that time he knew of the claim or not (*b*); and if he deliver the goods (or, as it seems, any part of them) to the claimant, he thereby precludes himself from relief under the act (*c*). In prudence, the sheriff should inquire into the nature of the claims before he applies to the court (*d*); but he need not ask the parties for an indemnity (*e*), nor, if offered, is he bound to accept it (*f*). Indeed, he must be indifferent between the parties, and therefore if he take an indemnity, or either himself or his under-sheriff be the execution creditor, or the partner of the execution creditor, the court will not relieve him (*g*). It is not however necessary, as it was at one time supposed, for the sheriff to deny collusion (*h*).

No person can appear before the court or judge on the hearing who is not a party to the rule (*i*); but if a new claim be made after the rule nisi is granted, the sheriff may make such claimant a party to the rule (*k*). It seems that a foreigner residing abroad cannot be compelled to come in under this act (*l*), neither can the Crown (*m*). But the sheriff may be relieved, though the claimant is an infant (*n*).

If the sheriff does not appear to support his rule, it will be discharged with costs. If the claimant does not appear, he will be barred (*o*) from proceeding against the sheriff, and must pay the costs of the execution creditor, but not of the sheriff (*p*). If the execution creditor does not appear, he likewise will be

(*b*) Anderson *v.* Calloway, 1 C. & M. 182; 1 Dowl. 636; 3 Tyr. 237; Scott *v.* Lewis, 2 C. M. & R. 289; 4 Dowl. 259; Ireland *v.* Bushell, 5 Dowl. 147.

(*c*) Braine *v.* Hunt, 2 C. & M. 418; 2 Dowl. 391.

(*d*) Bishop *v.* Hinxman, 2 Dowl. 166; In re Sheriff of Oxfordshire, 6 Dowl. 136.

(*e*) Cropley *v.* Ebers, 1 Harr. & W. 216.

(*f*) Levy *v.* Champneys, 2 Dowl. 454.

(*g*) Dudden *v.* Long, 1 Scott, 281; 1 Bing. N. C. 299; 3 Dowl. 139; Ostler *v.* Bower, 4 Dowl. 605; Patorni *v.* Campbell, 12 M. & W. 277; Cox *v.* Balne, 2 Dowl. & L. 719.

(*h*) Donniger *v.* Hinxman, 2 Dowl. 424; Dobbins *v.* Green, 2 Dowl. 509; Boond *v.* Woodhall, 2 C. M. & R. 604; 4 Dowl. 351.

(*i*) Clarke *v.* Lord, 2 Dowl. 55; but see Ibbotson *v.* Chandler, 9 Dowl. 250.

(*k*) Kirk *v.* Clarke, 4 Dowl. 363.

(*l*) Patorni *v.* Campbell, 12 M. & W. 277.

(*m*) Candy *v.* Maugham, 7 Scott, N. R. 402.

(*n*) Claridge *v.* Collins, 7 Dowl. 698.

(*o*) 1 & 2 Will. 4, c. 58, s. 3.

(*p*) Bowdler *v.* Smith, 1 Dowl. 417; Lewis *v.* Eicke, 2 C. & M. 321; 2 Dowl. 337; Jones *v.* Lewis, 2 M. & W. 204; see Perkins *v.* Burton, 2 Dowl. 108; 3 Tyr. 51; Philby *v.* Eicke, 2 Dowl. 222; Oram *v.* Sheldon, 1 Scott, 697; 3 Dowl. 640.

CHAP. X. SECT. VI.

barred (*q*), and must pay to the adverse claimant the costs of the application (*r*); but not to the sheriff (*s*). If the sheriff has sold, he will in that case have to pay the proceeds to the claimant (*t*); if he has not sold, he must withdraw from the possession (*u*). In this case the sheriff will not be entitled to his poundage, for the execution should not have been levied; but if neither party appears, each, as against the sheriff, will be barred, and the sheriff may levy his poundage and expenses before abandoning the remainder of the levy (*x*). If all the parties appear (and for this purpose it is not necessary to take office copies of the affidavit on which this rule nisi was obtained (*y*)), the court or a judge cannot, without consent of the parties, determine the right, but must direct one or more issues for that purpose (*z*). Although no order can be finally made, the claimant must state the nature and particulars of his claim (*a*); but the execution creditor may rely upon his judgment without more (*b*). The court or judge has power to make such order as to costs as may appear to them or him to be just and reasonable (*c*); if the application be made to a judge at chambers, a judge at chambers only has original jurisdiction as to the costs (*d*), his order being subject to review by the court in *banc* (*e*).

If, after it has been directed, the claimant abandons the issue, the court will compel him to pay the costs of the execution creditor up to the time of his abandoning it (*f*); and also the costs incurred in enforcing such payment (*g*). He will also be liable to the sheriff's costs incurred subsequently to the order for the issue. So, if the execution creditor decline to proceed, he will be liable to the costs of the claimant, and the sheriff's costs subsequent to the rule (*h*). If the issue is tried, the successful

(*q*) Ford *v*. Dilly, 5 B. & Ad. 885; 2 N. & M. 662.

(*r*) Tomlinson *v*. Done, 1 Harr. & W. 123.

(*s*) *Ibid.*; Beswick *v*. Thomas, 5 Dowl. 458.

(*t*) Gethin *v*. Wilks, 2 Dowl. 189.

(*u*) Field *v*. Cope, 2 C. & J. 480; 1 Dowl. 567.

(*x*) Eveleigh *v*. Salsbury, 3 Scott, 674; 5 Dowl. 369; 3 Bing. N. C. 298.

(*y*) Mason *v*. Redshaw, 2 Dowl. 595.

(*z*) 1 & 2 Will. 4, c. 58, s. 1; Curlewis *v*. Pocock, 5 Dowl. 381. As to the extent of the issue, see Abbott *v*. Richards, 15 M. & W. 194.

(*a*) Powell *v*. Lock, 4 N. & M. 852.

(*b*) Angus *v*. Wootton, 3 M. & W. 310.

(*c*) 1 & 2 Will. 4, c. 58, s. 1.

(*d*) Burgh *v*. Schofield, 9 M. & W. 478.

(*e*) Teggin *v*. Langford, 10 M. & W. 556.

(*f*) Wells *v*. Hopkins, 3 Dowl. 346.

(*g*) Scales *v*. Sargeson, 3 Dowl. 707.

(*h*) Dobbs *v*. Humphreys, 1 Scott, 325; 3 Dowl. 377; 1 Bing. N. C. 412.

party will be entitled to the costs of the trial and also of the rule. If, by order of the court, the sheriff has kept possession of the goods, or sold them, or done any other act for the benefit of the parties, he will be entitled to the costs so incurred from the unsuccessful party (*i*). If the execution creditor succeed, the sheriff is entitled to poundage, otherwise he is not (*k*).

SECTION VII.

Fieri Facias, Sheriff's Return to.

Sheriff, when obliged to return a *fi. fa.*

The sheriff is not obliged, unless ruled so to do, to make a return to a writ of *fieri facias*, for it is a sufficient justification to the sheriff, in an action of trespass for taking the defendant's goods, to plead that he took them by virtue of a *fi. fa.* directed to him, without showing it returned (*l*). But either the plaintiff or the defendant may rule the sheriff to return the writ (*m*), and if he neglect to make his return before the expiration of the rule, the court will grant an attachment against him (*n*). Either party may rule the sheriff to return the writ, although there has been no sale, but the defendant has paid the money (*o*). But where there has been a compromise between the parties, neither the plaintiff nor the defendant can rule the sheriff to return the writ (*p*). Where the plaintiff has appointed a special bailiff (*q*), or where there is any collusion between the sheriff's officer and the plaintiff, or his attorney (*r*), the plaintiff cannot rule the sheriff to return the writ; and if the sheriff be ruled to return the writ under such circumstances, he should move to set aside the rule (*s*).

(*i*) Armitage *v.* Forster, 1 Harr. & W. 208; Bland *v.* Delano, 6 Dowl. 293.

(*k*) Barker *v.* Dynes, 1 Dowl. 169.

(*l*) Cheaseley *v.* Barnes, 10 East, 73.

(*m*) France *v.* Clarkson, 2 Dowl. 532; but in the case of a *ca. sa.* see Williams *v.* Webb, 2 Dowl. N. S. 904; *ante*, 81.

(*n*) As to the rule, and at what time the attachment may be moved for, see *ante*, 81 *et seq.*

(*o*) Edmunds *v.* Watson, 2 Marsh. 330; 7 Taunt. 5, S. C.

(*p*) Alchin *v.* Wells, 5 T. R. 470; Hedges *v.* Jordan, 5 Dowl. 6.

(*q*) Pallister *v.* Pallister, 1 Chit. Rep. 614, n.; Porter *v.* Viner, 1 Chit. Rep. 613, n.

(*r*) Ruston *v.* Hatfield, 3 Bar. & Ald. 204; 1 Chit. Rep. 613, S. C.

(*s*) De Moranda *v.* Dunkin, 4 T. R. 119; see also Hamilton *v.* Dalziel, 2 Black. Rep. 952; Alchin *v.* Wells, 5 T. R. 470.

CHAP. X. SECT. VII.

The Court of Common Pleas, however, refused to set aside such a rule, where the object was to have a return of *nulla bona*, in order to issue a *ca. sa.*, the plaintiff undertaking to pay the costs and to bring no action for a false return (*t*). The sheriff must either return *nulla bona* or *bona*, and it is not a good return to say that the defendant's premises are so barricaded and fastened up as to be inaccessible, by reason of which the sheriff is unable to say whether the defendant has any goods whereon a levy can be made (*u*).

In making a return to a *fi. fa.*, a reasonable degree of certainty is sufficient, and therefore a return, "I have caused to be made of the goods of A. B. 22*l.* 2*s.*, out of which I have paid 11*l.* 5*s.* for rent due for the premises wherein the said goods and chattels were taken in execution," &c. was held good, inasmuch as the return as against the sheriff must be understood to be that the rent was due *at the time of the seizure* (*v*).

Where several writs are delivered to the sheriff at the same moment, the court will not compel the plaintiffs, or their attorney, to direct in what priority they are to be executed, so as to enable the sheriff to make his return with certainty (*x*).

Nulla bona.

If the defendant has no goods in the county into which the writ is directed, or if the sheriff is not informed of any that he has, he should return *nulla bona* (*y*); and where there is a dispute whether the goods belong to the defendant or to a third person, the proper course is for the sheriff to apply to the court under the Interpleader Act (*z*). *Nulla bona* means no goods liable to the plaintiff's execution, and therefore it is the proper return to make where goods seized under a warrant are insufficient to satisfy a *fi. fa.* previously lodged (*a*), or where the goods seized are swallowed up by payment of a year's rent to the landlord, under the statute of Anne (*b*). If goods seized under a *fi. fa.* are claimed by a third party, upon

(*t*) Harding *v.* Holder, 9 Dowl. 659; 2 Man. & G. 914, S. C.

(*u*) Munk *v.* Cass, 9 Dowl. 333.

(*v*) Reynolds *v.* Barford, 2 Dowl. & L. 327; 7 Man. & G. 449; see also Wintle *v.* Freeman, 11 Ad. & E. 547, *per* Patteson, J., "the sheriff, in making his return, is not bound by the rules of special pleading."

(*x*) Ashworth *v.* Earl of Uxbridge, 2 Dowl. N. S. 377.

(*y*) See forms, *post*, Appendix.

(*z*) *Ante*, 282 *et seq.*

(*a*) Heenan *v.* Evans, 3 Man. & G. 398; 4 Scott, N. R. 2; 1 Dowl. N. S. 204, S. C.; Drewe *v.* Lainson, 11 Ad. & E. 529.

(*b*) Wintle *v.* Freeman, 11 Ad & E. 539.

which an interpleader order is made directing an issue to be tried, and afterwards the plaintiff directs the sheriff to deliver up the goods to the claimant, it is not sufficient to return those facts, without also returning that the defendant had no other goods out of which the execution could be satisfied (*c*).

Fieri feci.

If the sheriff has seized and sold goods to the amount of the debt, he must make his return, that he has levied, &c., and that he has the money ready; if the goods sold are not sufficient to satisfy the whole debt, he should return *fieri feci* as to so much, and *nulla bona* as to the residue (*d*). It is sufficient to make the return in general terms, for the courts will not compel the sheriff to specify in his return to a *fieri facias* the particular goods taken, and the sum for which each article is sold (*e*). It is the duty of the sheriff, in executing a writ of *fi. fa.*, to seize all the goods of the debtor within his bailiwick, or at least sufficient to satisfy the writ; therefore to a declaration against the sheriff for neglecting to levy, and falsely returning goods in hand for want of buyers, a plea that the plaintiff had directed him to withdraw from the possession of certain goods, and that he had seized certain others, which remained in his hands unsold for want of buyers, was held bad, because both those propositions might be true, and yet there might have been other goods out of which the sheriff might have levied (*f*). If the sheriff, having a full opportunity of ascertaining the facts which would enable him to make such a return as would protect him, returns *fieri feci*, he is bound by his return (*g*). The sheriff cannot return generally that he has seized under two writs, *e. g.* "by virtue of this writ, and of another writ of *fi. fa.* &c. I have seized, &c. (*h*)," but he may return that he has seized by virtue of several previous writs, *according to the priority thereof* (*i*). And he ought to show the amount due on each of the earlier writs, and the value of the goods seized (*k*).

Goods in hand for want of buyers.

If the sheriff take goods, but cannot sell them, he should re-

(*c*) Cleaver *v.* Fisher, 2 Dowl. N. S. 293.

(*d*) See forms, Appendix. ch. 10, s. 7.

(*e*) Willett *v.* Sparrow, 6 Taunt. 576; 2 Marsh. 293, S. C.

(*f*) Pitcher *v.* King, 5 Q. B. 162.

(*g*) Field *v.* Smith, 2 M. & W. 388; 5 Dowl. 735, S. C.

(*h*) Wintle *v.* Lord Chetwynd, 7 Dowl. 554, explained *per* Patteson, J., in Wintle *v.* Freeman, 11 A. & E. 548.

(*i*) Chambers *v.* Coleman, 9 Dowl. 588; and see a form of such a return same case.

(*k*) Wintle *v.* Freeman, 11 Ad. & E. 548, Patteson, J.

CHAP. X. SECT. VII.

turn that he has taken goods of the defendant, which remain in his hands unsold for want of buyers. This return is proper where the sheriff cannot get a fair price for the goods (*l*), for in such case he should wait for a *venditioni exponas*. The return to a writ of *fieri facias*, that the sheriff has seized goods, which remain unsold for want of buyers, must state the goods to be of a certain value (*m*); the value stated is not material, for he may sell them on a *venditioni exponas* for less, and the judgment is only satisfied to the amount for which they are sold, if less than the value returned by the sheriff (*n*). But it is otherwise if the goods, after such a return, are rescued from or lost by the sheriff; in such case he is answerable to the plaintiff for the value returned (*o*). After such a return, the plaintiff may sue out a writ of *venditioni exponas*, reciting the former writ and return, and commanding the sheriff to expose the goods to sale, and have the monies arising therefrom in the court at the return of it; or if the goods are not taken to the value of the whole, the plaintiff may have a *venditioni exponas* for part, and a *fieri facias* for the residue, in the same writ. In a recent case, the Court of Common Pleas would not grant an attachment against the sheriff for returning to a writ of *venditioni exponas* that the goods remained unsold for want of buyers (*p*).

Supersedeas.

If a writ of error be delivered to the sheriff after he has seized goods, he must still proceed, but if a writ of error be allowed before he has taken the goods of the defendant, he should make his return accordingly; for in a recent case, in an action against a sheriff for a false return of *nulla bona*, it appeared that a writ of error was allowed on the same day that the *fi. fa.* had issued: the court held that the plaintiff was entitled to a verdict and nominal damages, for he should have returned the *supersedeas* and not *nulla bona*, and the court would have relieved him (*q*).

(*l*) Keightley *v.* Birch, 3 Camp. 521. But see 1 Starkie, N. P. C. 41.

(*m*) Wintle *v.* Lord Chetwynd, *sup.*; Chambers *v.* Coleman, *sup.*; Barton *v.* Gill, 12 M. & W. 315; 1 Dowl. & L. 593.

(*n*) Cro. Jac. 515; Godb. 276; but in Rex *v.* Bird, 2 Show. 87, it is said that if the sheriff value them too high, if nobody will buy them at that rate, the sheriff must.

(*o*) *Per* Holt, C. J., in Clerk *v.* Withers, 6 Mod. 293; 2 Lord Raym. 107, S. C.

(*p*) Leader *v.* Davis, 1 Bos. & Pul. 359; Anon. 2 Chitt. Rep. 390. *Sed vide* 6 Mod. 299; Cowp. 406.

(*q*) Cleghorn *v.* Desanges, 3 Moore, 83. If a sheriff execute a *fi. fa.* after a writ of error is allowed, but before notice, it is not a contempt; Cotton *v.* Dainty, 1 Vent. 29; 2 Keb. 506, 508, S. C. If the sheriff execute a *fi. fa.* after notice of the allowance of

To a *fi. fa.* without a *non omittas* clause, if the defendant's goods are entirely in a liberty, the bailiff whereof hath the return of writs, *mandavi ballivo*, together with the answer of the bailiff, if he has made any, or that he has made no answer, according to the fact, is a good return (*r*). If the sheriff returns *mandavi ballivo et nullum dedit responsum*, the bailiff should be then ruled to return the writ (*s*).

Mandavi ballivo.

Rescue is not a good return to a *fi. fa.*, for the sheriff is bound to raise the *posse comitatus* (*t*). Indeed, if a sheriff return that he has levied goods to a certain amount, and that they were rescued from him, he will be liable to the whole amount of the value returned, although above their real value (*u*).

Rescue.

To a *fieri facias* against an executor *de bonis testatoris*, if the sheriff cannot find any goods of the testator in the hands of the executor, he may return *nulla bona;* and upon that, the plaintiff may proceed by *scire fieri* inquiry: this writ, after reciting the *fieri facias*, and the sheriff's return of *nulla bona*, suggests that the executor had sold and converted the goods of the testator to the value of the debt and damages recovered, and commands the sheriff to levy the debt and damages of the goods of the testator in the hands of the executor, if they could be levied thereof; but if it should appear to him, by inquisition of a jury, that the executor had wasted the goods of the testator, then the sheriff is to warn the executor to appear, &c. Or, on the sheriff's return of *nulla bona*, the plaintiff may bring an action of debt on the judgment, suggesting a *devastavit* (*x*).

Return to a *fi. fa.* against an executor.

But if the sheriff cannot find assets, he may, if he please, return a *devastavit* as well as *nulla bona* to the writ of *fieri facias de bonis testatoris*, for the *fieri* inquiry is only for his security (*y*). And the sheriff seems to run no great risk by so doing; for the judgment, and no assets to be found, will be sufficient evidence of a *devastavit*, in an action against him for a false re-

a writ of error, he is liable in trespass; Belshaw *v.* Marshall, 4 B. & Adol. 336; 1 N. & M. 689, S. C. Goods seized before a *supersedeas* may be sold afterwards; Cro. Eliz. 597.

(*r*) See *ante*, 98.

(*s*) See Boothman *v.* Earl of Surrey, 2 T. R. 10; 27 Hen. 8, c. 24.

(*t*) Midmay *v.* Smith, 2 Saund. 343; 2 Keb. 789, 821, S. C. See also May *v.* Proby, Cro. Jac. 419; 3 Bulstr. 198, S. C.; 1 Roll. Rep. 388, 440.

(*u*) *Per* Holt, C. J. in Clerk *v.* Withers, 6 Mod. 293; 2 Ld. Raym. 1075, S. C.

(*x*) See note, 1 Saund. 219 a. See also Ward *v.* Thomas, 2 Dowl. 87; 1 C. & M. 537, S. C.

(*y*) Rock *v.* Leighton, 1 Salk. 310; 1 Ld. Raym. 590, S. C.; Com. Rep. 87, cited in 3 T. R. 692.

CHAP. X. SECT. VII.

turn (z). And whether the *devastavit* be returned by the sheriff to the *fieri facias*, or found by the inquisition on the *fieri* inquiry, the return is not conclusive, but the executor may taverse the *devastavit* (a).

Against a clergyman.

On a *fi. fa.* against a beneficed clergyman, if he have no goods, the sheriff, in addition to a return of *nulla bona*, should return that the defendant is a beneficed clerk, and has no lay fee in his bailiwick (b), upon which a *fieri* or *levari facias* goes to the bishop of the diocese where the benefice is, commanding him to levy the sum recovered, of the ecclesiastical goods of the defendant (c). The *levari facias* does not begin to operate until the writ of sequestration is published (d). As against the defendant, the property is bound from the time when the sequestrator is appointed (e). It is not necessary to publish the writ of sequestration before the return day of the *levari facias* (f). The bishop is liable to be ruled to return this writ (g), or to an action for a false return thereto (h). This writ is a continuing execution; and the bishop should take all the profits of the benefice up to the time when the writ is actually returned, although after the return-day of the writ (i). To this writ the bishop must return *fieri* or *levari feci*, and not *sequestrari feci* (k). The bishop may be ruled from time to time to return what he has levied (l); but he cannot be ruled to make a return of what has been levied before he came into office (m): and when a bishop grants a sequestration against the effects of a clergyman within his diocese, he stands in the same situation as a sheriff, and the court has the same power over him as over the sheriff (n). A defendant has no right to have the *levari facias*

(z) Rock *v.* Leighton, 1 Salk. 310; 1 Ld. Raym. 590, S. C.; Com. Rep. 87, cited in 3 T. R. 692; 1 Saund. 219 c.

(a) Gibson *v.* Brook, Cro. Eliz. 859; Mounson *v.* Bourne, Sir W. Jones, 418.

(b) See this return, Append. c. 10, s. 7.

(c) Bac. Abr. Execution (G) 6. See form, Tidd's Forms, 436; Archbold's Forms, 514.

(d) Wait *v.* Bishop, 3 Dowl. 234; 1 C. M. & R. 507, S. C.

(e) Bennett *v.* Apperley, 6 B & C. 630, *per* Bayley, J.

(f) *Ibid.*

(g) Lanquil *v.* Jones, Stra. 87; Rex *v.* Bishop of London, 1 Dowl. & Ry. 486.

(h) Pickard *v.* Paiton, 1 Sid. 276; Moseley *v.* Warburton, 1 Salk. 320; 1 Ld. Raym. 265, S. C.

(i) Marsh *v.* Fawcett, 2 H. Blac. 582.

(k) See 1 Mod. 257; 2 Mod. 259, and Tidd's Prac. 1063, 1064, 8th ed. for the mode in which the bishop is to execute this writ.

(l) See 2 H. Blac. 583.

(m) Phillips *v.* Berkeley, 5 Dowl. 279.

(n) Rex *v.* Bishop of London, 1 Dowl. & Ry. 486.

returned, but he may have a return of the amount of profits received by the sequestrator (*r*). The bishop's return should, it seems, be verified, and it will not be sufficient merely to set forth the debtor and creditor account of the sequestrator (*s*). The bishop should not return the writ of sequestration until after the execution is fully satisfied; if he returns it previously, the court will direct it to be taken off the file and sent back to the bishop in order that he may *certify* what he has done under it, and take the *return* off the writ (*t*). The sequestrator of a benefice is the mere agent of the bishop, and has not himself any such interest as will enable him to maintain an action at law against a person who wrongfully receives the profits of the benefice (*u*).

SECTION VIII.

Actions against the Sheriff for Breach of Duty.

Remedy for the amount levied.

If the sheriff return *fieri feci*, the plaintiff may proceed for the money against the sheriff, either by action of debt, founded on the return (*x*), or by action for money had and received (*y*), or by rule of court (*z*). Although no return be made, an action for money had and received will lie against the sheriff for the amount levied (*a*). In bringing an action for money had and received, to recover money levied on a *fi. fa.*, it is not necessary to prove a demand of the money before action brought (*b*). Although if the plaintiff commence an action against the sheriff for money levied by him, without previously demanding the same, the court will stay proceedings on payment of that sum

(*r*) Hart *v.* Vollans, 1 Dowl. 434.

(*s*) Elchin *v.* Hopkins, 7 Dowl. 146.

(*t*) Alderton *v.* St. Aubyn, 6 M. & W. 150.

(*u*) Harding *v.* Hall, 10 M. & W. 42.

(*x*) Parkinson *v.* Gifford, Cro. Car. 539; Speake *v.* Richards, Hob. 206. In an action of debt founded on the sheriff's return to a *fieri facias*, *nil debet* is not a good plea, for the return is parcel of the record; 2 Saund. 344, n. (2). So, for the same reason, the Statute of Limitations is not a good plea to that action; Cockram *v.* Welby, 2 Mod. 212; 2 Show. 79, S. C.; 1 Mod. 245; Freem. 236.

(*y*) Dale *v.* Birch, 3 Camp. 347. If the sheriff claim by his return to retain money, to which he is not entitled, the plaintiff may recover that money from the sheriff in such an action; Longvile *v.* Jones, 1 Stark. 345.

(*z*) See Stockdale *v.* Hansard, 11 Ad. & E. 253.

(*a*) Parkinson *v.* Gifford, Cro. Car. 539; Sir W. Jones, 430, S. C.; Morland *v.* Pellatt, 8 B. & C. 722.

(*b*) Dale *v.* Birch, 3 Camp. 347.

without costs; for the court will always protect the sheriff where he acts with good faith (*c*). If the assignees of the defendant, who has become a bankrupt, claim the money of the sheriff, it is competent for him, in an action brought by the plaintiff for the money, to show that the assignees are entitled to it (*d*); and he may, in an action of trover, set up such defence under a plea of not possessed (*e*).

It seems that the application for a rule calling on the sheriff to pay over the amount levied should be made to the court, and not to a judge at chambers (*f*).

It would not, it seems, in any case be an answer to a rule nisi, for paying over the money levied, to say that a superior force had prevented the sheriff from bringing into court money which he had levied (*g*); and it has been held that it is no answer to such a rule to say that the House of Commons, by resolutions subsequent to the granting of the rule nisi, declared the levy to be a contempt of the privilege of the House, and ordered the sheriff to refund the money levied to the defendant, and committed the sheriff for contempt (*h*). Nor would the pendency of a conflicting rule in another court, whereby the sheriff was ordered to retain the money, and to show cause why he should not pay it over to a third party, *e. g.* to the provisional assignee of an insolvent, afford any answer to such a rule, because the court, in directing the sheriff to pay the amount of the levy over to the plaintiff, would take care to protect the interests of the parties who might prove to be really interested (*i*).

Where money was in the hands of the accountant-general in bankruptcy, and the sheriffs of London returned to an extent that they had seized the amount directed to be levied into the hands of the queen, the court made absolute a rule for paying over the money, and refused to make the accountant-general a party to the rule (*k*); but the court afterwards discharged the rule and allowed the sheriffs to amend their return, it appearing

(*c*) Jefferies *v.* Sheppard, 2 Bar. & Ald. 696. See also 3 Camp. 347.

(*d*) See 6 M. & Sel. 42; 2 Camp. 452; 6 Taunt. 490; 2 Marsh. 186, S. C.

(*e*) Leake *v.* Loveday, 4 M. & G. 972.

(*f*) See *per* Patteson, J., Stockdale *v.* Hansard, 11 Ad. & E. 263.

(*g*) Stockdale *v.* Hansard, 11 Ad. & E. 253.

(*h*) *Ibid.*

(*i*) *Ibid.*

(*k*) Reg. *v.* Austin, 1 Dowl. N. S. 666.

that the Court of Review had refused to order the accountant-general to pay over the money to the sheriffs (*l*). If the sheriff disobeys the rule for paying over the money, an attachment will lie against him, but the rule for such attachment will be *nisi* only in the first instance (*m*).

It will be no answer to a rule nisi for an attachment to show that the sheriff is in personal confinement, and cannot obey the rule, except by directing his officers to do so, who, if they obeyed him, would probably incur imprisonment themselves (*n*). But although the sheriff has returned that he has levied the debt, yet the courts will not grant a rule for the sheriff to pay over the money levied, if it appear there has been any collusion between the plaintiff and the officer (*o*). In a recent case, where the money had been paid to the assignees of the defendant, who had become bankrupt, and the plaintiff, knowing of such payment, had lain by for some time, without making any objection to it, the Court of Common Pleas refused to grant a rule on the sheriff to pay over the money to the plaintiff (*p*). And the court will not grant a rule to pay over the proceeds of a levy to a *bonâ fide* execution creditor, upon the ground that the levy was made under a *fi. fa.* issued for the fraudulent purpose of defeating the execution of such *bonâ fide* creditor (*q*).

False return: evidence in such action, &c.

If the return of the sheriff be false, an action on the case may be maintained against him at the suit of the person damnified by such false return (*r*). But this action will not lie unless actual damage occurs to the plaintiff (*s*). Or the sheriff may be amerced for such false return, according to an ordinance against sheriffs (*t*). But he is not liable to an action until he has made his return (*u*). Nor is he liable to an action for a false return to a *fi. fa.* issued out of his county court (*x*). The court will not try the truth or falsity of a return upon affida-

(*l*) Reg. *v.* Austin, 10 M. & W. 188; 2 Dowl. N. S. 468.

(*m*) Hatfield *v.* Hatherfield, 1 Dowl. & L. 809.

(*n*) Stockdale *v.* Hansard, 11 Ad. & E. 269.

(*o*) Ruston *v.* Hatfield, 3 Bar. & Ald. 204; 1 Chit. Rep. 613, S. C. See also Porter *v.* Viner, *ib.* n.; Pallister *v.* Pallister, *ib.* 614, n.

(*p*) Tomlinson *v.* Shynn, 2 Brod. & Bing. 77.

(*q*) Barber *v.* Mitchell, 2 Dowl. 574.

(*r*) Com. Dig. Retorn (F 2).

(*s*) Wylie *v.* Birch, 4 Q. B. 566.

(*t*) Com. Dig. Retorn (F 2), citing East, 272 a. By stat. 28 Edw. 1, c. 16.

(*u*) Moreland *v.* Leigh, 1 Stark. N. P. C. 388.

(*x*) Pitcher *v.* King, 9 Ad. & E. 288.

vit (*y*). Thus if the sheriff return that he has seized goods which remain in his hands for want of buyers, where a price has been offered for the goods, although not equal to their full value, he is liable to an action for a false return (*z*). But if, after such a return, the defendant become bankrupt on an act of bankruptcy committed before the seizure, it is competent for the sheriff to show this as an answer to an action for not selling the goods on a *venditioni exponas* (*a*); but where the sheriff returned *fieri feci*, after having received notice that the defendant had petitioned the Insolvent Court, he was held bound by his return (*b*). If the sheriff returns that he has levied part of the debt, and that the defendant has no goods whereof the residue can be levied, the creditor, by accepting the amount levied on account of his debt, does not preclude himself from bringing an action for a false return (*c*). The declaration in an action for a false return must either show special damage to the plaintiff, or must disclose facts from which the law would necessarily infer such damage (*d*). It is no answer to an action for a false return to say that, after the return, the plaintiff brought an action of debt and obtained a judgment on the original judgment (*e*).

In an action for a false return of *nulla bona* to a writ of *fieri facias*, the sheriff cannot give in evidence, even in mitigation of damages, an inquisition held by him to inquire whether the property in the goods be in the defendant or not (*f*). If the sheriff make a return of *nulla bona*, after having taken goods as the goods of the defendant in execution, a person who claims property in the goods, and who has taken them out of the hands of the sheriff, is a competent witness, in an action against the sheriff for a false return, to prove his property in the goods; for the sheriff, after his return of *nulla bona*, cannot maintain an action against him, having disclaimed all interest in the goods, and being precluded by his return (*g*). If the sheriff return to

(*y*) Goubot *v.* De Crouy, 2 Dowl. 86.

(*z*) Barnard *v.* Leigh, 1 Stark. 43. *Sed quære, et vide* Keightley *v.* Birch, 3 Camp. 521.

(*a*) Bridges *v.* Walford, 6 M. & Sel. 42.

(*b*) Field *v.* Smith, 2 M. & W. 388.

(*c*) Holmes *v.* Clifton, 10 A. & E. 673, overruling Beynon *v.* Garrat, 1 C. & P. 154.

(*d*) Wylie *v.* Birch, 4 Q. B. 566.

(*e*) Pitcher *v.* King, 9 Ad. & E. 288.

(*f*) Glossop *v.* Pole, 3 M. & Sel. 175.

(*g*) Thomas *v.* Pearse, 5 Price, 547

a writ of *fieri facias*, that he has levied a certain sum, out of which he has paid a part to the landlord of the premises for arrears of rent, it will be incumbent upon him, in an action against him for a false return, to prove the fact of the rent being in arrear (*h*). When the sheriff defends his return of *nulla bona* on the ground that the person against whom the writ issued was the domestic servant of an ambassador of a foreign state, it is competent for the plaintiff to prove the appointment colourable and fraudulent (*i*). In the declaration in an action for a false return, the judgment and the writ must be stated and proved in evidence, if denied by the pleas. A variance in a material point between the allegation and proof, in either of those particulars, will be fatal. What is held to be a fatal variance in such case has already been considered in treating of the action for an escape (*k*). Where the declaration bore date after the accession of Queen Victoria, and alleged the recovery of a judgment in the reign of the late king, as appeared by the record "still remaining in the said court of our said lord the king, &c." it was held no variance on motion for judgment on production of the record (*l*).

The plea of not guilty, since the rule of H. T. 4 Will. 4, puts in issue merely the breach of duty, admitting the matters stated in the inducement to be true, and therefore under such a plea it will not be competent for the defendant to go into evidence to prove the truth of the return. Thus, in an action against the sheriff for a false return of *nulla bona* to a writ of *fi. fa.*, after having levied under it, the plea of not guilty puts in issue only the fact of the sheriff having made the levy, and the making the return stated in the declaration; and under such a plea the defendant is not at liberty to show that the goods levied were not the goods of the original

See also Ward *v.* Wilkinson, 4 Bar. & Ald. 410; Bland *v.* Ansley, 2 N. R. 331.

(*h*) Keightley *v.* Birch, 3 Camp. 521. Slight evidence of this fact would be sufficient in such case on the part of the sheriff; the landlord himself in such case is not a competent witness; *Id. ibid.*

(*i*) Delvalle *v.* Plomer, 3 Camp. 47. "This is one among many other questions which sheriffs in the execution of process must determine at their own peril. In cases of real difficulty they may call for an indemnity, and the court will enlarge the time for their making their return till an indemnity be given." *Per* Lord Ellenborough, C. J. *Id. ibid.*

(*k*) See *ante*, 209.

(*l*) Lewis *v.* Alcock, 6 Dowl. 78.

CHAP. X. SECT. VIII. defendant, because he had become a bankrupt (*m*). So where a declaration against the sheriff for a false return stated the delivery of the *fi. fa.* to the defendant, and alleged that though there were goods within his bailiwick which he ought to have levied, yet he neglected to levy, and afterwards falsely returned *nulla bona*, it was held that, under the plea of not guilty, it could not be shown that the execution debtor had assigned over his goods to a third party, because the plea of not guilty only puts in issue *the breach of duty*; and the statement of the delivery of the writ to the sheriff, and that there were goods of the debtor within his bailiwick, were mere matters of inducement (*n*).

In an action for a false return of *nulla bona*, alleging a seizure of the debtor's goods under the writ, under a plea denying that the defendant seized the debtor's goods under the writ, it may be shown that the goods were not the goods of the debtor, but of his assignees (*o*). To a declaration alleging that the sheriff (the defendant) seized goods of the debtor under a *fi. fa.* to the value of the amount indorsed thereon, "and then levied the same thereout," but falsely returned *nulla bona*, a plea traversing the allegation that the sheriff had levied the amount indorsed on the plaintiff's writ, raises the whole question whether the defendant has raised by sale of the goods seized monies *applicable to the plaintiff's writ*, involving three issues:—1st, whether the goods were sold at all; 2nd, whether they were sold under the plaintiff's writ; and, 3rd, whether the proceeds were applicable to the plaintiff's writ. And therefore, under such a traverse, the defendant may show that the proceeds of the sale of the goods were all applicable to, and were swallowed up by, other writs of execution which had priority over the plaintiff's; and a plea setting forth such facts specially was held bad, as being argumentative (*p*). To a similar declaration, under a plea denying that the debtor had any goods within the defendant's bailiwick whereof he could cause to be levied the amount indorsed on the writ, it was held that the defendant was at liberty to show that the proceeds of the

(*m*) Wright *v.* Lainson, 2 M. & W. 739.

(*n*) Lewis *v.* Alcock, 3 M. & W. 188; 6 Dowl. 389, S.C.

(*o*) Wright *v.* Lainson, 3 M. & W. 44; Rowe *v.* Ames, 6 M. & W. 747.

(*p*) Drewe *v.* Lainson, 11 Ad. & E. 529.

goods which were seized under the plaintiff's writ were exhausted by payment of a year's rent to the landlord under the statute of Anne, and in part satisfaction of another execution which was entitled to priority over the plaintiff's (*q*). So where to a similar declaration the defendant pleaded that the defendant did not seize or take in execution any goods of the debtor, or levy thereout the money indorsed *modo et forma*, it appearing on the trial that the goods seized under the plaintiff's writ were insufficient to satisfy a prior execution delivered to the sheriff, the defendant was held to be entitled to a verdict, notwithstanding the plaintiff proved that the goods were *seized* under a warrant granted upon his writ (*r*). In answer to such a defence, the plaintiff may show that such prior execution was founded on a fraudulent judgment, without showing the sheriff to be a party to such fraud (*s*).

In an action for *neglecting to seize* goods under a *fi. fa.*, and returning *nulla bona* under a plea denying that there were any goods of the debtor within the sheriff's bailiwick *modo et forma*, it may be shown, that although there were goods of the debtor within the bailiwick, yet that such goods were not applicable to the plaintiff's writ (*t*). The defendant cannot plead that he did not seize *and* levy, for such a plea would raise too large an issue, because either a seizure *or* levy would be sufficient to support the plaintiff's action (*u*). Where to a *fi. fa.* the sheriff returned that he had seized goods which remained in his hands for want of buyers, upon which an action was brought as for a false return, the court refused to allow the return to be amended to *nulla bona* after the sheriff had obtained an order for time to plead on the usual terms (*x*).

Where the declaration discloses a state of facts from which the law would presume damage to the plaintiff, the defendant is at liberty to plead pleas showing that in *fact* no damage accrued to him. Thus where the declaration alleged a seizure and sale under a *fi. fa.*, and a false return that the goods remained in defendant's hands for want of buyers, it was held

(*q*) Wintle *v.* Freeman, 11 A. & E. 539.

(*r*) Heenan *v.* Evans, 3 Man. & G. 398.

(*s*) Imray *v.* Magnay, 11 M. & W. 267; 2 Dowl. N. S. 531.

(*t*) Heenan *v.* Evans, 3 Man. & G. 398.

(*u*) Stubbs *v.* Lainson, 1 M. & W. 728; 5 Dowl. 162, S. C.

(*x*) Wylie *v.* Pearson, 1 Dowl. N. S. 807.

CHAP. X. SECT. VIII.

that pleas showing that the *fi. fa.* was issued on a judgment on a warrant of attorney, and that the debtor had become bankrupt, and alleging such facts as would render the execution invalid as against his assignees, were good as negativing any damage to the plaintiff from the false return; and it was also held that such pleas did not amount to the general issue (*y*).

Wrongful seizure.

Where the sheriff or his officer, on a *fi. fa.* against the goods of A., takes the goods of B., the sheriff is subject to an action of trespass (*z*). To such an action, under a plea of not possessed, the sheriff may show that the plaintiff took the goods under an assignment by the debtor, fraudulent as against the execution (*a*). Or if the officer seize the goods of the defendant after the return day of the writ (*b*), or after a supersedeas has been delivered to the undersheriff (*c*), or after the sheriff has received orders from the plaintiff not to execute the writ (*d*), or if he take them at any place out of his county (*e*), the sheriff and his officers are liable to an action of trespass. If the sheriff break open the outer door of a house to take the defendant's goods, he is a trespasser (*f*). For the requisites of a plea of justification by a sheriff, for any thing done by him in executing a writ of *fi. fa.*, it is sufficient to refer the reader to a former part of this work (*g*). In an action of trespass against the sheriff for a wrongful seizure of goods, the jury may give what damages they please, and are not bound to the amount for which the goods were afterwards sold (*h*).

Actions by the sheriff.

The sheriff, we have seen, has such a special property in goods taken by him upon a *fi. fa.* as to enable him to maintain trespass or trover against a wrong-doer (*i*). So, if goods lawfully taken by the sheriff be rescued out of his possession, he

(*y*) Wylie *v.* Birch, 4 Q. B. 566. *Quære*, whether these pleas did not amount to an argumentative traverse that the sheriff had sold the goods of the debtor.

(*z*) Saunderson *v.* Baker, 2 Bla. R. 832; 3 Wils. 309, S. C. See also Laicock's case, Latch, 187.

(*a*) Ashby *v.* Minett, 8 Ad. & E. 121.

(*b*) Ellis *v.* Jackson, 1 Lev. 143; 1 Sid. 229, S. C.; 1 Keb. 718, 805; 2 Roll. Abr. 278.

(*c*) Prine *v.* Allington, Moor, 677, pl. 921.

(*d*) Barker *v.* St. Quintin, 12 M. & W. 441; 1 Dowl. & L. 542, S. C.; Hunt *v.* Hooper, 12 M. & W. 672; 1 Dowl. & L. 628, S. C. *per* Parke, B.

(*e*) Tyler *v.* Johnson, cited by Nares, J. in 3 Wils. 317, and in 2 Bla. Rep. 834.

(*f*) See *ante*, 75.

(*g*) See *ante*, 122.

(*h*) Lockley *v.* Pye, 8 M. & W. 133.

(*i*) Wilbraham *v.* Snow, 2 Saund. 47; 1 Vent. 52, S.C.; 1 Lev. 282; 1 Sid. 438, S. P.; Clerk *v.* Withers, 6 Mod. 292.

may bring an action on the case against the rescuers; but it is a good defence to such action, that the goods had been fraudulently obtained by the defendant (*k*). If the sheriff seize and sell the goods of the defendant, and pay the proceeds over to the plaintiff, and the sheriff be afterwards sued in trover by the assignees of the defendant, who had committed an act of bankruptcy before the seizure, and a verdict pass against the sheriff, he may maintain an action for money paid against the plaintiff to recover the proceeds of the sale; but there is no implied contract for the plaintiff to indemnify the sheriff against the costs of that action (*l*). If in such case the sheriff, after having called upon the plaintiff to defend an action of trover commenced by the assignees, allow judgment to go by default, it is still open, in an action by the sheriff against the plaintiff, brought to recover back the money paid to him, for the plaintiff to show that the defendant had not become bankrupt (*m*). If the sheriff took any indemnity on releasing the goods, or on paying the money to the plaintiff, the sheriff, if he have been damnified, may put such security in suit for his indemnity.

Where, goods having been seized by the sheriff under a *fi. fa.*, the officer, by arrangement between the debtor and the creditor, and without the knowledge of the sheriff, quitted possession upon the understanding that he might return at any time and sell; and he accordingly, after the lapse of some time, did return, and notice of sale was given; but before the sale, another *fi. fa.* at the suit of another creditor was lodged, to which the sheriff returned *nulla bona*, and paid over the proceeds of the sale to the first execution creditor: it was held that the sheriff, having been compelled to answer in damages for a false return to the second writ, to the amount of the money levied, upon the ground of the officer having quitted possession, as above mentioned, might, in an action for money had and received, recover back from the first execution creditor the amount

(*k*) Wilsmore *v.* Earl of Bristol, 1 Barn. & Cress. 514; 2 Dowl. & Ry. 755, S. C.

(*l*) Wilson *v.* Milner, 2 Campb. 452.

(*m*) Austin, *v.* Ward, 1 Car. & P. 370, 507; 1 Ry. & Mo. 116, S. C. It does not appear to be clear whether or not there is an implied promise by the sheriff to indemnify a person employed by him to conduct the sale of goods seized, where it turns out that the goods were not the goods of the defendant; Farebrother *v.* Simons, 1 Campb. 345.

CHAP. X. SECT. VIII.

which, in ignorance of the facts, he had so paid over to him (*n*). Where a sheriff's officer, in consequence of a false representation made to him, settled, out of his own money, an action against the sheriff, it was held that the sheriff might, on behalf of the officer, sue the party who made such representation (*o*).

(*n*) Crowder *v.* Long, 8 Barn. & Cress. 598.

(*o*) Evans *v.* Collins, 5 Q. B. 804, 820.

CHAPTER XI.

ELEGIT.

Of the nature of the Writ.—What may be taken under it.—How executed.—Lands and Goods how delivered.—Return.—Poundage.—Sheriff's Liability.—Restitution.

At the common law, the only writ of execution against the lands of the defendant was a writ of *levari facias*, but this writ, excepting in case of outlawry, is entirely superseded by the writ of elegit (*a*). The writ of *elegit* is a writ of execution (*b*), founded on the statute of Westm. 2 (13 Edw. 1, c. 18), by which it is enacted, that "when a debt is recovered or acknowledged in the king's court, or damages awarded, it shall be in the election of him who sues for such debt or damages to have a writ of *fieri facias* to the sheriff, for levying the debt upon the

(*a*) See *ante*, 232, as to the writ of *levari facias* and what may be taken under it.

(*b*) This writ is called an *elegit*, because the plaintiff or conusee has made his election to sue out execution of the land itself, which is given by the above-mentioned statute, instead of the common law executions; and the words in the entry of the award of this writ are, "*chose to be delivered to him all the goods, &c.*" After lands are extended on an elegit, the plaintiff cannot sue out any other writ of execution, for this is deemed satisfaction; Crawley *v.* Lidgent, Cro. Jac. 338. Indeed, it was formerly considered that the mere entry of an award of an *elegit* on the roll barred the plaintiff from resorting to any other writ of execution; but now only the sheriff's return, that he had delivered land according to the exigence of the writ, is a bar to a *ca. sa.* or a *fi. fa.*; Foster *v.* Jackson, Hob. 57, 58; Glasscock *v.* Morgan, 1 Lev. 92; 2 Lord Raym. 1451; 12 Mod. 356, 357. And now either of those writs may issue, if the sheriff returns *nihil* to an *elegit*; Knowles *v.* Palmer, Cro. Eliz. 160: or if lands be extended, but cannot be made available to the purposes of the writ; Palmer *v.* Knowles, 1 Leon. 176; 1 Rol. Abr. 905, pl. 6. So if part of the debt be levied on an *elegit on the goods* of the defendant, the plaintiff may have a fresh execution, or debt on judgment for the residue; Hesse *v.* Stevenson, 1 N. R. 133; Bacon *v.* Peck, 1 Str. 226. It is said that an *elegit* may be issued after a year, without a *scire facias*, merely upon entering an award of *elegit* upon the roll within the year, and continuing it by *vicecomes non misit breve* to the time of suing out the writ; Seymour *v.* Greenvill, Carth. 283; *sed quære*, and see 2 Saund. 68 c; Tidd's Pract. 1136.

lands and chattels, or that the sheriff deliver to him all the chattels of the debtor (saving only his oxen and beasts of the plough), and a moiety of his land, until the debt be levied, by a reasonable price or extent; and if he be evicted, he shall recover by writ of *novel disseisin*, and afterwards by writ of *re-disseisin*, if there be occasion."

By statute 1 & 2 Vict. c. 110, s. 11, it is enacted, "that it shall be lawful for the sheriff or other officer to whom any writ of elegit, or any precept in pursuance thereof, shall be directed, at the suit of any person, upon any judgment which, at the time appointed for the commencement of this act, shall have been recovered, or shall be thereafter recovered, in any action in any of her majesty's superior courts at Westminster, to make and deliver execution unto the party in that behalf suing of *all* such lands, tenements, rectories, tithes, rents and hereditaments, including lands and hereditaments of copyhold or customary tenure, as the person against whom execution is so sued, or any person in trust for him, shall have been seised or possessed of at the time of entering up the said judgment, or at any time afterwards, or over which such person shall at the time of entering up such judgment, or at any time afterwards, have any disposing power which he might, without the assent of any other person, exercise for his own benefit, in like manner as the sheriff or other officer may now make and deliver execution of one moiety of the lands and tenements of any person against whom a writ of elegit is sued out; which lands, tenements, rectories, tithes, rents and hereditaments, by force and virtue of such execution, shall accordingly be held and enjoyed by the party to whom such execution shall be so made and delivered, subject to such account in the court out of which such execution shall have been sued out as a tenant by elegit is now subject to in a court of equity: provided always, that such party suing out execution, and to whom any copyhold or customary lands shall be so delivered in execution, shall be liable and is hereby required to make, perform, and render to the lord of the manor, or other person entitled, all such and the like payments and services as the person against whom such execution shall be issued would have been bound to make, perform, and render in case such execution had not issued; and that the party so suing out such execution, and to whom any such copyhold or customary lands shall have been so delivered in execution, shall be entitled to hold the same until the amount of such payments, and the value of such services, as well as the amount of the judgment, shall have been levied; provided also, that as against purchasers, mortgagees or creditors, who shall have become such before the time appointed for the commencement of this act, such writ of elegit shall have no greater or other effect than a writ of elegit would have had in case this act had not passed."

By the writ of elegit the sheriff is commanded (*c*) "that without delay he cause to be delivered to the plaintiff, by a reasonable price and extent (*d*), all the goods and chattels of the said defendant in his bailiwick (except his oxen and beasts of the plough), and also all such lands and tenements, rectories, tithes, rents and hereditaments, including lands and hereditaments of copyhold or customary tenure, in the sheriff's bailiwick, as the defendant, or any person in trust for him, was seised or possessed of on the day the judgment was obtained, or at any time afterwards, or over which the defendant had any disposing power which he might, without the assent of any other person, exercise for his own benefit, to hold the said goods and chattels as his proper goods and chattels, and to hold the said lands, tenements, rectories, tithes, rents and hereditaments respectively, according to the nature and tenure thereof, to him and to his assigns until the debt and damages, together with interest, be thereof levied."

The writ of *elegit* cannot be sued out for *part* only of the sum recovered by the judgment, unless it shows on the face of it that the residue of the judgment has been satisfied or otherwise disposed of (*e*).

What goods may be taken, and how used.

The sheriff's duty on an *elegit* is, in the first instance, to take the goods of the defendant (excepting oxen and beasts of the plough), and deliver them to the plaintiff at the price found by a jury, to be summoned as hereafter mentioned. Whatever

(*c*) See form of writ framed by the judges pursuant to 1 & 2 Vict. c. 110, H. T. 2 Vict. Append.

(*d*) The word "*price*," mentioned in the statute, is referrable to the defendant's goods and chattels; and "*extent*," to the defendant's lands; Palmer's case, 4 Rep. 74 b; 2 Inst. 396.

(*e*) Sherwood *v.* Clark, 15 M. & W. 764; see Webber *v.* Hutchins, 8 M. & W. 319.

may be taken as goods and chattels under a *fieri facias* may be taken under this part of the writ of *elegit*, and no more (*f*). A term of years may either be extended at an extended annual value, as part of the lands of the defendant; or it may be delivered to the plaintiff, as part of the defendant's chattel property, the jury having first appraised it at the gross sum (*g*). The landlord is entitled to a year's rent under the statute of Anne, where goods are taken on an *elegit*, in like manner as where goods are taken on a *fi. fa.* (*h*). But in one respect this writ differs from a *fi. fa.*, for instead of selling the goods as on a *fi. fa.*, and bringing the money into court, it is the duty of the sheriff to deliver the goods to the plaintiff at the value found by the jury (*i*).

What lands may be taken and what not.

If the chattels taken be sufficient to satisfy the debt, then the sheriff ought not to extend the land (*k*). But if the goods be not sufficient, the lands, after being valued by the jury, must be set out by metes and bounds, and delivered to the plaintiff. Whatever land the defendant had at the time the judgment was entered up is liable to be extended on an *elegit* (*l*). All lands of the defendant are liable to be extended, whether he has an estate in fee, in tail, for life, or for years; but formerly, before the stat. 1 & 2 Vict., c. 110, copyhold lands (*m*), or a lease of copyhold lands, were not extendible on an *elegit* (*n*), as part of the realty. But lands held in ancient demesne might be extended and delivered over on an *elegit* (*o*). Although the word "lands" is used in the statute, yet whatever comes under the legal definition of a tenement was always extendible on an *elegit*, as a reversion (*p*), or a rent charge (*q*). But a rent seck (*r*), or an

(*f*) See *ante*, 249.

(*g*) 2 Inst. 395; Fleetwood's case, 8 Rep. 171; Dalt. 137.

(*h*) See *ante*, 274.

(*i*) *Per* Holt, C. J., 1 Ld. Raym. 346. And therefore if a term be taken upon an *elegit*, and judgment be afterwards reversed, the termor shall be restored to his term, and not to the value of it; Goodyere *v.* Ince, Cro. Jac. 246; Bathurst's case, Dyer, 363, in marg.

(*k*) 2 Inst. 395.

(*l*) 2 Inst. 395; stat. 29 Car. 2, c. 3, ss. 14, 15, 18.

(*m*) Morris *v.* Jones, 3 Dowl. & Ry. 603; 1 Roll. Abr. 888; 3 Rep. 9.

(*n*) 1 Roll. Abr. 888.

(*o*) Cox *v.* Barnsley, Hob. 47; Moore, 211; 2 Inst. 397; 1 Roll. Abr. 888, l. 5.

(*p*) Gilb. Execution, 38; Bishop of Bristol's case, 2 Leon. 113; 1 Roll. Abr. 894, l. 5; Mayor of Poole *v.* Whitt, 15 M. & W. 571.

(*q*) Bro. Elegit, 13; Moore, 32; Wotton *v.* Shirt, Cro. Eliz. 742.

(*r*) Walsal *v.* Heath, Cro. Eliz. 656; 3 Rep. 9.

office, as that of filazer, were not extendible on an *elegit* (*s*); an office is not extendible, because it cannot be granted over. Lands which the defendant hath by extent upon a statute are liable to be taken upon an *elegit* (*t*). But lands of which the defendant is disseised, in the hands of the deissor, are not liable to be taken on an *elegit* (*u*). Neither is an advowson in gross (*x*), because a moiety of it could not be set out, nor can it be valued at any certain rent towards payment of the debts; nor the glebe of a parsonage or vicarage; nor can a church-yard be extended upon an elegit (*y*), although it is said that the lands of a bishop may be extended (*z*). So may the lands which a husband has in right of his wife (*a*).

Before the passing of the statute of 29 Car. 2, c. 3, lands held in trust for the defendant could not be extended upon an *elegit*, issued on a judgment, statute, or recognizance of the *cestui que trust*. But by the 10th section of that act it is enacted, that "it shall be lawful for every sheriff or other officer, to whom any writ or precept is directed, at the suit of any person or persons, of, for and upon any judgment, statute, or recognizance, thereafter to be made or had, to do, make and deliver execution unto the party in that behalf suing of all such lands, tenements, rectories, tithes, rents, hereditaments, as any other person or persons are in any manner seised or possessed in trust for him against whom execution is so sued, like as the sheriff or other officer might or ought to have done if the said party against whom execution is so sued had been seised of such lands, &c., of such estate as they are seised of in trust for him *at the time of the said execution sued;* which lands, &c., by force and virtue of such execution, shall accordingly be held and enjoyed freed and discharged from all incumbrances of such person or persons as shall be so seised or possessed in trust for the person against whom such execution shall be sued; and if any *cestui que trust* shall die, leaving a trust in fee simple to descend to his heir, then and in every such case such trust shall be deemed and taken, and is thereby declared to be, assets

(*s*) Dyer, 7 b.
(*t*) Com. Dig. Execution (C 14).
(*u*) Roll. Abr. Execution (M 5).
(*x*) Gilb. Execution, 39; but see 3 P. Wms. 401.
(*y*) Gilb. Execution, 40; Jenk. 407; *per cur.* 3 Bos. & Pul. 327.
(*z*) Dalt. 136.
(*a*) *Id ibid.*

CHAP. XI.

by descent; and the heir shall be liable to and chargeable with the obligation of his ancestor, for and by reason of such assets, as fully and amply as he might and ought to have been, if the estate in law had descended to him in possession in like manner as the trust descended." The estate liable to be taken by virtue of this statute must be a simple trust estate for the benefit of the debtor solely; and therefore where land was vested for a long term of years in a trustee, in trust to permit E. G. to receive the rents and profits until default of payment of a rent-charge, or until E. G. should insure the premises; and in case of such default, in trust to pay to M. G. out of the rents and profits a certain rent charge, it was held that this was not such a trust as could be extended upon an *elegit* against E. G. (*b*). It was, under the stat. of 29 Car. 2, held, that if a man be *cestui que trust* of a term, it is not assets within the statute, for it extends only to a trust of land in fee (*c*). An equity of redemption cannot be taken in execution under this statute, whether it be of a freehold estate (*d*), or of a term of years (*e*). The words in the act, "at the time of the said execution sued," were held to refer to the seisin of the trustee; and therefore, if he has conveyed the lands by the direction of the *cestui que trust* before execution, though seised in trust at the time of the judgment, the lands cannot be taken in execution (*f*); but since the passing of 1 & 2 Vict. c. 110, a conveyance of the lands *after judgment* would not defeat an elegit.

Before the passing of the late statute, where an estate was limited as A. should appoint, and in default of appointment to A. in fee, it was held that A. might defeat the effect of a judgment, by an execution of the power of appointment (*g*). The execution creditor is not entitled to rent which becomes due after the delivery to the sheriff of an *elegit*, but before inqui-

(*b*) Doe *d*. Hull *v*. Greenhill, 4 Bar. & Ald. 684.

(*c*) King *v*. Ballett, 2 Vern. 248; and see 2 Saund. 11.

(*d*) Plunket *v*. Penson, 2 Atk. 290.

(*e*) Lyster *v*. Dolland, 1 Ves. jun., 431; 4 Bro. Chan. Ca. 478, S. C.; and see Scott *v*. Scholey, 8 East, 467, 486; Harris *v*. Booker, 4 Bing. 96; 12 Moore, 283, S. C.; Mayor of Poole *v*. Whitt, 15 M. & W. 571. The plaintiff may, where the land of the defendant is mortgaged, file a bill in equity to redeem, which he is entitled to do on payment of principal money and costs, as the equity of redemption is considered assets to satisfy the judgment.

(*f*) Hunt *v*. Coles, Com. Rep. 226; Com. Dig. Execution (C) 14.

(*g*) Doe *d*. Wigan *v*. Jones, 10 B. & C. 459; 5 Man. & R. 563, S. C.

sition taken (*h*). It has been questioned whether the lands of a borough corporation, held only for the purposes of the borough under the Municipal Corporation Act (5 & 6 Will. 4, c. 76, s. 92), are liable to an *elegit*, but the question as yet has not been determined (*i*).

Inquisition how held.

All the authorities agree that the sheriff, in executing a writ of *elegit*, must take an inquisition, although the writ does not particularly require the sheriff to hold an inquisition; for he cannot appraise the goods, or value the lands himself, but the same must be done by a jury (*k*); therefore, on receiving the writ, the sheriff should forthwith proceed to impanel a jury (*l*). The sheriff and jurors may go into the house or ground of the defendant if the doors and gates be open, but they must not break open the gates or doors for the purpose of executing the writ (*m*). No notice is necessary to be given of executing the *elegit*. The sheriff should charge the jury "to inquire what goods and chattels, (except the oxen and beasts of the plough), and also what lands, tenements, rectories, tithes, rents, and hereditaments, including lands and hereditaments of copyhold or customary tenure, the defendant, or any person in trust for him, hath or had, or was seised or possessed of, in the bailiwick of the sheriff of N., on the —— day of ——, in the —— year of the reign of our sovereign lady Victoria, or at any time since, or over which the defendant had any disposing power, which he might without the assent of any other person exercise for his own benefit, that the same may, at a reasonable price and extent to be made, be delivered to the plaintiff to hold as his own proper goods and chattels, and also to hold the said lands, tenements, rectories, tithes, rents, and hereditaments respectively, according to the nature and terms thereof, to him the plaintiff and his assigns, according to the form of the statute, &c.

(*h*) Sharpe *v.* Key, 8 M. & W. 379; 9 Dowl. 770, S. C.

(*i*) Doe *d.* Parr *v.* Roe, 1 Q. B. 700. *Semble*, that they are liable; see *per* Lord Denman, C. J., *ib.* 706.

(*k*) Co. Litt. 289 b; 2 Inst. 396; Com. Dig. Execution (C) 14; Bac. Abr. tit. Execution (H) 2; Dyer, 100 b; Palmer *v.* Humphrey, Cro. Eliz. 584; 4 Rep. 74. But see Stonehouse *v.* Ewen, Stra. 874, where it is laid down to have been held *per Curiam*: "If it be returned to an *elegit* that there are no lands, the sheriff need not return an inquisition, for the use of that is only to deliver a moiety of the lands by, if there are any." This has been cited to show that where there are only goods the sheriff need not hold an inquest, but this does not prove any such thing.

(*l*) As to the manner of summoning a jury, see the directions for so doing on a writ of inquiry, *post*, chap. 13.

(*m*) Dalt. 134.

CHAP. XI.

Of the finding of the jury.

The inquisition ought to find the lands with convenient certainty; for want of finding some particular estate the inquisition would be insufficient. If the defendant be joint tenant, or tenant in common, it ought to be specially mentioned in the inquisition (*n*). Thus it is said in Palmer's case (*o*), that where an inquisition found that the queen's debtor was possessed of certain lands *for the term of divers years yet to come*, it is insufficient, for a term cannot be extended without showing the beginning and certainty of the term; and also, before the late statute, the jury should find a moiety of the lands by metes and bounds, in order that the sheriff should deliver the same to the plaintiff (*p*). But since the stat. 1 & 2 Vict. c. 110, it is not necessary to set out the premises by metes and bounds: it is sufficient to describe them with such a degree of accuracy that they may be readily identified (*q*). The sheriff was not bound to deliver a moiety of each particular tenement and farm, but it was sufficient if he delivered particular tenements as a moiety in value of the whole (*r*). Thus, it is laid down in Brooke's Abridgment (*s*), "that if an *elegit* issue against one that hath two manors, the sheriff may deliver one of the manors to the plaintiff in the name of a moiety of the whole, and is not bound to deliver a moiety of each manor, and so of two acres, and this seems to be when they are of equal value." Where the defendant had merely a house, if the sheriff upon an *elegit* delivered a moiety of the house without metes and bounds, such return was ill (*t*); but the jury should set out such and such rooms as

(*n*) Hutt. 16; 1 Brownl. 38.

(*o*) 4 Rep. 74; Dalt. Sher. 139. In the report of this case by Croke, it is said that such a finding would be sufficient; Palmer *v.* Humphrey, Cro. Eliz. 584; see also 2 Leon. 121; 3 Leon. 204. "The two reports may perhaps be reconciled by this distinction, that when the whole term is appraised and sold for a gross sum, as part of the debtor's personal estate, then, as the *elegit* is considered in the nature of a *fieri facias*, the sheriff may sell such an uncertain interest under it as well as under a *fieri facias*; but when a moiety is extended *at an annual value*, so general a finding by the inquest may perhaps be insufficient;" but see Lane, 50, 51; 2 Saund. 68 c, n. (1).

(*p*) It would appear to be the province of the jury to ascertain and set out the moiety of the lands by metes and bounds: Sparrow *v.* Mattersock, Cro. Car. 319; Doug. 473. And it would not be sufficient for the sheriff himself to set out the moiety of the lands.

(*q*) Doe *d.* Roberts *v.* Parry, 13 M. & W. 356; Sherwood *v.* Clark, 15 M. & W. 764.

(*r*) Denn *v.* Lord Abingdon, Doug. 473.

(*s*) *Elegit*, 14, cit. 12 Edw. 4, 2.

(*t*) *Per* Holt, C. J., Pullen *v.* Purbeck, Carth. 453; 12 Mod. 356, S. C.

a moiety in value of the house, and the sheriff should deliver those rooms to the plaintiff (*u*).

Before the stat. 1 & 2 Vict. c. 110, if the sheriff did not set out and deliver the *moiety* of the lands by metes and bounds, the return was void (*x*). If the inquisition be void for uncertainty, or for any other defect, the court will set aside the return, and will order the writ to be vacated and grant another, and amerce the sheriff (*y*); but after the return has been filed, the courts formerly would not set aside a writ of *elegit* (*z*); and in a recent case (*a*), on a motion to set aside two writs of *elegit*, the court refused to set aside the second writ, because the sheriff had delivered the whole of the land remaining after the first *elegit* on the second, inasmuch as such return was a mere nullity.

But if lands which cannot be extended on an *elegit* be found on the inquisition together with lands which can properly be extended, and the sheriff sets out each, it would appear that the extent is not bad in toto, but only for the part that is not extendible (*b*). Where fraud, deceit, or partiality has been practised, if the writ be not filed, the court will stay the filing of it and grant another writ (*c*); so if it appear that the lands are extended at an undue value, the court will stop the filing of the return (*d*).

If lands which cannot be extended are notwithstanding extended, the objection may be taken in an action of ejectment (*e*). But if the return be void, the defendant may take the objection on an action of ejectment being brought to obtain possession of the land. Thus, in an action of ejectment (*f*), where the lessor of the plaintiff claimed as tenant by *elegit*, the sheriff's return stated that the jury found that the defendant had certain lands, &c., describing them and finding their value, " one equal moiety of which messuage, &c., the sheriff had caused to be delivered to the lessor of the plaintiff to hold, &c.;" it was ob-

(*u*) *Per* Bayley, J., in Fenny *v.* Durant, 1 Bar. & Ald. 42.

(*x*) *Per* Holt, C. J., Carth. 453; 1 Bar. & Ald. 40.

(*y*) 1 Sid. 91, 239; Pullen *v.* Purbeck, Salk. 563; 12 Mod. 368, S. C.

(*z*) Com. Dig. Execution (C) 14; 2 Inst. 396; *sed vide* 1 Vent. 259; 1 Lord Raym. 718; 12 Mod. 355; Salk. 563.

(*a*) Morris *v.* Jones, 3 Dowl. & Ry. 603; 2 Bar. & Cress. 242, S. C.

(*b*) Morris *v.* Jones, 3 D. & R. 603.

(*c*) 2 Inst. 396.

(*d*) 2 Ca. Ch. 183; Com. Dig. Execution (C) 14.

(*e*) See Doe *d.* Parr *v.* Roe, 1 Q. B. 700.

(*f*) Fenny *d.* Masters *v.* Durant, 1 Bar. & Ald. 40; see Denn *v.* Lord Abingdon, Doug. 473.

CHAP. XI.

jected that the return was void for not setting out the moiety by metes and bounds, which the Court of King's Bench, after argument, held to be fatal, and ordered a nonsuit to be entered; and Bayley, J., said, "In this case the jury might have found that the debtor was seised of such a house, and that such and such rooms constituted a moiety in value, and then the sheriff might have delivered those rooms to the lessor of the plaintiff. If the return is bad, the defendant has a right to say it is bad. The objection was raised the same way as here at Nisi Prius in Denn *v.* Lord Abingdon.

The court will not try the truth of an inquisition on motion (*g*). The words of the old writ of *elegit* were, "to hold as his freehold," because the statute, in case of eviction, gives a remedy by assize; still, however, a tenant by *elegit* has no freehold, but only a chattel interest, which will devolve upon his executors (*h*).

When there are several writs of *elegit*.

If two persons had judgments against a defendant, and one of them had a moiety of the defendant's lands delivered to him upon an *elegit*, the other, upon suing out an *elegit* afterwards, could only have a moiety of the moiety which remained to the defendant (*i*). But if one person had the two judgments, and sued two *elegits* during the same term: on one *elegit* he should have a moiety of the defendant's lands, and the entire of the other moiety on the other *elegit*, and not merely a moiety of a moiety (*k*).

How the sheriff is to deliver the goods and lands.

The sheriff is to deliver the whole of the goods found by the inquisition into the hands of the defendant; and it was formerly usual for the sheriff to deliver *actual* possession of a moiety of the lands; but now he only delivers legal possession, and in order to obtain actual possession, the plaintiff must proceed by ejectment (*l*).

Return.

The writ of *elegit* must in all cases be returned, if the sheriff has done any thing under it; and it is essential that the *elegit*

(*g*) Cooper *v.* Gardner, 3 A. & E. 211.

(*h*) 2 Inst. 396.

(*i*) Huit *v.* Coggan, Cro. Eliz. 483.

(*k*) The Attorney-General *v.* Andrew, Hardr. 23; see also Doe *d.* Davies *v.* Creed, 5 Bing. 327; 2 M. & P. 648, S. C., nom. Doe *d.* Cheese *v.* Creed; *sed vide* Morris *v.* Jones, 3 Dowl. & Ry. 603; 2 Bar. & Cress. 242, S. C.

(*l*) Taylor *v.* Cole, 3 T. R. 295; 2 Saund. 69 a; *sed vide* the judgment of Gibbs, C. J., in Rogers *v.* Pitcher, 6 Taunt. 207, where he expressed himself to be of opinion that there is no necessity for tenant by *elegit* to bring ejectment to obtain possession, but that he might enter at once, excepting where the person in possession held under a lease prior to the plaintiff's judgment.

and the inquisition taken by the sheriff should be returned and filed, when land is extended by the writ (*m*). But if the defendant has no land, the sheriff need not return the inquisition at all (*n*); in such case the proper return is *nihil. Mandavi ballivo* is a good return to a writ of *elegit* (*o*). And it is a good return, that the sheriff has extended the lands of the defendant, but could not deliver them to the plaintiff, for another had them in extent before (*p*). The court will not, at the instance of the sheriff, enlarge the return of an *elegit* by altering it to a later day (*q*).

Poundage.

The sheriff is entitled under the stat. 28 Eliz. c. 4, to poundage on an *elegit*, that is to say, 1*s*. in the pound on the first 100*l*.; and 6*d*. in the pound for the sum above 100*l*. (*r*). But it seems to be questionable whether he be entitled to poundage for executing an *elegit* on the whole debt, or only on the annual value of lands extended (*s*).

If the inquisition be void, it is said that the court will set it aside and amerce the sheriff (*t*). And if the sheriff return that he has delivered land upon inquisition taken, when he refused to deliver it, an action on the case lies for a false return, though the plaintiff may enter without it, yet that is only in mitigation of damages (*u*).

Restitution.

The tenant by *elegit* has only the land until his debt be levied; and whensoever the party pay or satisfy the debt of record, he shall enter into his land; and so it is when the tenant by *elegit* is satisfied by the ordinary extent, the tenant of the land may enter. But if it be of any casual profit, to avoid the extent, he must have a *scire facias* in respect of the uncertainty (*x*). But the Court of King's Bench recently, on motion, referred it to the master to take an account of the rents and profits of an estate, of which the plaintiff was in possession by virtue of a writ of *elegit*; and that the plaintiff should give up

(*m*) Hoe's case, 5 Rep. 90 a; Fulwood's case, 4 Rep. 67; Dyer, 100, in marg.; see Forms of Returns, Append.

(*n*) Stonehouse *v*. Owen, 2 Stra. 874.

(*o*) Sparrow *v*. Mattersock, Cro. Car. 319.

(*p*) Dalt. Sheriff, 232.

(*q*) Hildyard *v*. Baker, 1 C. & M. 611; 2 Dowl. 16, S. C.

(*r*) Tyson *v*. Paske, 2 Lord Raym. 1212; Salk. 333, S. C.; Jayson *v*. Rash, Salk. 209.

(*s*) See *ante*, 112; Price *v*. Hollis, 1 M. & Sel. 105; Peacock *v*. Harris, Salk. 331.

(*t*) See *ante*, 313.

(*u*) Lister *v*. Bromley, 1 Roll. Abr. 738, l. 15.

(*x*) 2 Inst. 395; and see Underhill *v*. Devereux, 2 Saund. 68, 71.

possession, if it appeared that all the monies due to him had been received (*y*). In a court of equity, in taking the account of the profits of the land, the plaintiff is entitled to interest upon his judgment beyond the sum recovered by the judgment (*z*). If judgment be reversed where goods have been taken and delivered upon an *elegit*, the defendant shall be restored to the goods themselves, and not to the value of them as on restitution of goods taken on a *fieri facias* (*a*).

(*y*) Price *v.* Varney, 5 Dowl. & Ry. 612; 3 Bar. & Cress. 733, S. C.

(*z*) Godfrey *v.* Watson, 3 Atk. 517; Earl Bath *v.* Earl Bradford, 2 Ves. sen. 589.

(*a*) Goodyere *v.* Ince, Cro. Jac. 246; Bathurst's case, Dyer, 363, in marg.; Bathurst *v.* Mayo, 1 Roll. Abr. 778, l. 32, 55.

CHAPTER XII.

HABERE FACIAS POSSESSIONEM.

Of the Writ.—How executed.—Sheriff's Duty in Case of Disturbance.—Return.—Fees thereon.—Actions against the Sheriff in respect of.

After a recovery in ejectment, it has been said that the plaintiff may enter upon the land without issuing any writ of possession (*a*); but this doctrine cannot now be considered as law (*b*); and even if it were so, this mode of proceeding is open to very serious objections, as likely to lead to a breach of the peace; and moreover it is highly inconvenient that any other person, except the known responsible officer of the court, should execute its judgments.

The writ of *habere facias possessionem* is the writ of execution in the action of ejectment; by which writ the sheriff is commanded, that without delay he cause the plaintiff to have possession of his term (or, if there be more than one demise, "his several terms yet to come of and in the tenements recovered"); a *fi. fa.* or *ca. sa.* for costs may be included in the writ of *habere facias possessionem.* The duty of the sheriff, in the execution and return of that part of the writ, is the same as on a common *fi. fa.* or *ca. sa.* In such case the sheriff should make his return of both parts of the writ. Of the writ.

On the delivery of the writ to the sheriff, he makes out his warrant to one or more bailiffs to execute it (*c*). He is bound to execute the writ within a reasonable time; and if after a writ is delivered to him, and he has an opportunity to execute it, and refuses or neglects to do so, he is liable to an action at the suit of the lessor of the plaintiff, who may recover against him all damage which he has sustained by reason of his neglect, even though the judgment be afterwards set aside by a judge's order, How executed.

(*a*) Badger *v.* Floid, 12 Mod. 398; Anon. 2 Tid. 156; 1 Burr. 88, arg.

(*b*) See Doe *d.* Stevens *v.* Lord, 6 Dowl. 218; 7 A. & E. 611, S. C.

(*c*) See form, Append. The fee usually charged for the warrant is 2*s.* 6*d.*; as to the legality of which charge, see *ante*, 112.

CHAP. XII. in order to let the landlord in to plead (*d*). It is usual for the lessor of the plaintiff to give the sheriff an indemnity for executing the writ (*e*); and it seems he may demand an indemnity before he executes the writ (*f*). And in executing the writ, the sheriff and officer act under the immediate direction of the lessor of the plaintiff or his attorney, to whom the sheriff is to deliver a full and actual possession of the premises. The officer, if necessary, may break open either the outer or the inner doors of the house, in order to execute a writ of *habere facias possessionem* (*g*); and if violence be apprehended, he should raise the *posse comitatûs* (*h*). And as the sheriff is to give actual possession of the premises recovered, he should remove all persons and their goods from off the premises; for if persons be left on the premises, the execution is not complete (*i*). If there be several tenements in the possession of one person, it is said to be sufficient for the sheriff to deliver possession of part to the plaintiff in the name of the whole (*k*); and this is said to be the safer way for the sheriff, because he executes the writ at his peril (*l*), and if he give possession of any land not included in the writ, he is a trespasser (*m*); but it is recommended as the surest and most effectual way of executing the writ, for the sheriff to remove all the tenants entirely out of each house or parcel of land, and when the possession is quitted, to deliver it to the plaintiff; and this course is absolutely necessary where the land is in the possession of several tenants (*n*). The execution is not complete until the bailiffs have yielded possession to the plaintiff (*o*); and if the tenant, immediately after the sheriff has given possession, ejects the plaintiff, the sheriff may restore him to the possession, for the writ was not executed until the plaintiff has obtained full and *quiet* possession (*p*). As to the quantity of land which the sheriff is to deliver possession of to the plaintiff, as the writ

(*d*) Mason *v.* Paynter, 1 Q. B. 974.

(*e*) Tidd's Prac. 1080, 8th edit.; Com. Dig. Execution (A) 3; Run. Eject. 432; see form of such indemnity, *post*, Append.

(*f*) Adams' Eject. 342, 3rd edit.

(*g*) Semayne's case, 5 Rep. 91 b; see *ante*, 75.

(*h*) See *ante*, 73.

(*i*) Upton *v.* Wils, 1 Leon. 145; Tidd's Prac. 1081, 8th edit.; 2 Archbold's Prac. 767, 7th edit.

(*k*) *Per* Haughton, J., Floyd *v.* Bethell, 1 Rol. Rep. 421; Roll. Abr. Execution (H) 1.

(*l*) Dalt. 256; 10 Vin. 539; Run. Eject. 432, 433; Tidd's Prac. 1081, 8th edit.

(*m*) *Sed vide* Keilway, 119, 120.

(*n*) Roll. Abr. Execution (H) 2.

(*o*) *Per* Holt, C. J., 6 Mod. 115.

(*p*) Molineux *v.* Fulgam, Palm. 289.

does not describe either the quantity or locality with minute certainty, the party is bound to point out to the sheriff, at his peril, the precise lands he is entitled to (*q*); if he take more, the court will order it to be restored (*r*). As where the plaintiff in ejectment, as tenant in common, recovered possession of five-eighths of a cottage, with the appurtenances, it appeared by affidavit that a writ of possession was executed by the sheriff, who turned the tenant out of possession of the whole, and locked up the door; the court granted a rule upon the sheriff and the lessor of the plaintiff to restore the tenant to the possession of three-eighth parts of the premises (*s*). On recovery of land being part of a highway, the sheriff should deliver possession, subject to the right of passage over it (*t*). If the sheriff is to deliver possession of a certain number of acres, it seems that he must give so many acres in quantity, according to the common estimation of the country where the land lies (*u*).

In case of the death of either party.

In ejectment, the plaintiff and defendant being merely nominal, even if real persons, execution might issue, notwithstanding their death, without a *sci. fa.* (*x*). And it seems that after the death of the lessor of the plaintiff, a writ might be issued and executed (*y*); at all events, if it bear teste in his lifetime (*z*). When the real defendant dies after judgment and before execution, it is said that a *hab. fac. poss.* may be issued and executed, because execution is of the land only, and there is no new person to be charged (*a*).

Disturbance of the sheriff. Attachment.

If the officer be disturbed in the execution of the writ, the court, on affidavit, will grant an attachment against the person disturbing him, whether he be defendant or a stranger; for it

(*q*) See Doe *d.* Davenport *v.* Rhodes, 11 M. & W. 608; 1 D. & L. 297, S. C., *per* Lord Abinger, C. B.; Roe *v.* Street, 2 A. & E. 329; 4 N. & M. 42, S. C.

(*r*) Cottingham *v.* King, 1 Burr. 627, 629; Conner *v.* West, 5 Burr. 2673; indeed the sheriff is not bound to execute the writ, unless the lessor of the plaintiff, or some person authorized by him, comes to receive possession; Dalt. 255.

(*s*) Roe *dem.* Saul *v.* Dawson, 3 Wils. 49. In a recent case, where crops were standing on the land, when possession was taken under a *hab. fac. poss.*, the court refused to grant a rule against the lessors of the plaintiff to pay over to the late tenant (defendant), the value of the crops after deducting the rent; Doe *v.* Witherwick, 3 Bing. 11; 10 Moore, 267, S. C.

(*t*) 1 Burr. 133.

(*u*) Floyd *v.* Bethell, 1 Rol. Rep. 420.

(*x*) Tidd's Prac. 1171, 8th edit.

(*y*) Tidd's Prac. 1172, 8th edit.

(*z*) Doe *d.* Boyer *v.* Roe, 4 Burr. 1970.

(*a*) *Per* Holt, C. J., in Withers *v.* Harris, 2 Ld. Raym. 808. But the surer method is said to be to sue out a *sci. fa.*; Adams's Eject. 307, 2d edit.

CHAP. XII.

is a contempt in any person to obstruct the execution of the process of the court: and it seems that even if the execution be complete by the officer leaving the plaintiff in possession, and the defendant *presently* eject him from such possession, the court will grant an attachment against the defendant (*b*). Where a defendant in ejectment, having been dispossessed under a writ of restitution, afterwards, on the night of the same day, came to the premises and took forcible possession of them, Wightman, J., refused to grant an attachment against him, but made absolute a rule for a fresh writ of restitution to be executed within a week, and ordered the defendant to pay the costs of the application (*c*).

New writ when granted.

If the sheriff do not execute the writ, the courts will in general award an alias (*d*). And if the sheriff give possession of part only, the lessor of the plaintiff may have a new *habere facias possessionem* for the rest (*e*). But if the sheriff put the lessor of the plaintiff in possession, and make his return accordingly, and the defendant eject the lessor of the plaintiff, the courts will not grant another *habere facias possessionem* (*f*). And it would appear that if immediately, or soon after the sheriff has given possession, *the defendant* forcibly turn him out, the plaintiff may have a new *habere facias possessionem* before the former writ is returned (*g*). But it is necessary that the defendant should be connected with the dispossession of the lessor of the plaintiff (*h*). But where the lessor of the plaintiff was turned out by the *defendant* after a month's possession, the court held it too long a time to grant a new writ of possession (*i*). And in a recent case, where the lessor of the plaintiff had been put in possession by virtue of a writ of *habere facias possessionem* on the 22nd of February, 1806, which writ had never been returned by the

(*b*) Kingsdale *v.* Mann, 6 Mod. 27; Salk. 321, S. C. In this case the plaintiff was left in possession at nine o'clock in the morning, and he was ousted at six in the evening; but the court doubted whether or not it was too late to grant an attachment.

(*c*) Doe *d.* Pitcher *v.* Roe, 9 Dowl. 971.

(*d*) Molineux *v.* Fulgam, Palm. 289.

(*e*) 2 Keb. 245.

(*f*) 2 Brownl. 216, 253; Devereux *v.* Underhill, 2 Keb. 245.

(*g*) Kingsdale *v.* Mann, 1 Salk. 321; 6 Mod. 27, 115, 298, S. C.; 2 Brownl. 216, 253; Pierson *v.* Tavernor, 1 Rol. Rep. 353. See also Doe *d.* Pitcher *v.* Roe, 9 Dowl. 971; Doe *d.* Thompson *v.* Mirehouse, 2 Dowl. 200; Doe *d.* Lloyd *v.* Roe, 2 Dowl. N. S. 407.

(*h*) Doe *d.* Thompson *v.* Mirehouse, 2 Dowl. 200.

(*i*) Goodright *v.* Hart and ux. Stra. 830.

sheriff, and on the 10th of October, 1807, the person against whom he had recovered entered into the house by force, and resisted with violence all attempts to regain possession; the court refused to grant a new *habere facias*, or an attachment against the party in possession, and held that, possession having been given under the first writ, the sheriff ought to have returned that he had given possession, and that the plaintiff could not afterwards have had another writ. An *alias*, it was said, cannot issue after a writ is executed (*k*); if it could, the plaintiff, by omitting to call on the sheriff to return the writ, might retain the right of suing out a new writ of *habere facias possessionem* as a remedy for any trespass which the same tenant might commit within twenty years after the judgment. Where a *stranger* turns the plaintiff out of possession after execution fully executed, the plaintiff is put to another action, or to an indictment for a forcible entry (*l*). For the title never was tried between the plaintiff and a stranger; and he may claim the land by title paramount to the plaintiff, or he may come in under him, and then the recovery and execution in the former action ought not to hinder the stranger from keeping that possession which he may have a right to. If the law were otherwise, the plaintiff might, by virtue of a new *habere facias*, turn out even his own tenants, who came in after the execution executed; whereas the possession was given to him only against the defendant in the action, and not against others not parties to the suit (*m*).

Return. Strictly speaking, the sheriff should return a writ of *habere facias possessionem;* but it is not essential to the validity of the execution that the sheriff should make his return, nor is it usual, unless called on so to do, for him to return the writ. If the sheriff do make a return, the usual return is, "by virtue of this writ to me directed, I have given full and peaceable possession unto the within-named John Doe of the messuages, lands and premises, with the appurtenances within-mentioned, as within I am commanded;" and if there be a *fi. fa.* or *ca. sa.* in addition thereto, the sheriff adds, that he has levied goods, &c., or *nulla bona* to the former writ, or *cepi corpus* or *non est inventus* to the latter writ, according to the fact (*n*). The sheriff, in excuse,

(*k*) Doe *d.* Pate *v.* Roe, 1 Taunt. 55. The case of Ratcliffe *v.* Tate, 1 Keb. 779, was denied to be law.

(*l*) Fortune *v.* Johnson, Styles, 318; and see *id.* 408; 1 Keb. 779.

(*m*) Bac. Abr. Eject. (G) 3.

(*n*) See forms, Append. ch. 12.

may return that he was always ready to deliver possession to the plaintiff, and that no person on his behalf came to receive possession (*o*), or that no person on behalf of the plaintiff came to show the premises to the sheriff (*p*); but it would not be a good return for the sheriff to say that he was ready on *a certain day* to give possession to the plaintiff, and he gave notice thereof to the plaintiff, but that the plaintiff failed to come (*q*). It would appear that *tarde* is not a good return to a writ of *hab. fac. poss.* (*r*), nor that the sheriff could not execute the writ, being opposed by force, for he should have raised the *posse comitatus* (*s*). *Mandavi ballivo* to a *hab. fac. poss.* without a *non omittas*, is a good return (*t*).

Poundage.

By the stat. 3 Geo. 1, c. 15, s. 16, the sheriff is prohibited from taking, for executing a *hab. fac. poss.*, more (which sums the sheriff is thereby empowered to take) than 12*d.* in every 20*s.*, if the yearly value of the premises do not exceed 100*l.*; but if it exceed 100*l.*, then 6*d.* for every 20*s.* above that sum. But where the sheriff, at the instance of the plaintiff, had been put to extra trouble and expense, the Court of Common Pleas confirmed the prothonotary's taxation of costs, where he had allowed one guinea for the journey of the sheriff's officer; 5*s.* for poundage; 6*s.* 8*d.* for the warrant; and 10*s.* 6*d.* on the delivery of possession. The court indeed said that the statute of the 3 Geo. 1, c. 15, s. 16, which regulates the poundage the sheriff is entitled to on a writ of *hab. fac. poss.*, applied only to cases between party and party, and not as between attorney and client (*u*).

Actions against the sheriff.

If the sheriff make a false return to this writ, there is no doubt that he would be liable to an action for a false return. It would seem that if the lessor of the plaintiff show the sheriff a stranger's land, by force whereof the sheriff enters, yet he is no trespasser (*x*).

We have also seen that an action will lie against the sheriff for negligence in executing the writ (*y*).

(*o*) Floyd *v.* Bethell, Rol. Abr. Retorn (H).

(*p*) Saville, 28.

(*q*) Roll. Abr. Retorn (1).

(*r*) See *ante*, 95. But see such a return, Retorna Brevium, 352.

(*s*) See *ante*, 97. But see Upton *v.* Wells, 1 Leon. 142.

(*t*) See *ante*, 98.

(*u*) Capp *v.* Johnson, 7 Moore, 518.

(*x*) Dalt. 257; Keil. 119, 120. *Sed quære.*

(*y*) Mason *v.* Paynter, 1 Q. B. 974; *ante*, 117.

CHAPTER XIII.

WRIT OF INQUIRY.

Of the Writ.—Inquest, at what Time and before whom to be held.—Inquest, Proceedings before.—Evidence.—Damages, how assessed.—Return.—Fees.—Sheriff's Liability.

THERE are various writs of inquiry, such as writs of *ad quod damnum* (a), inquiry of damages, or of waste; but the sheriff's duty is in all cases to make the inquiry as prescribed by the writ: the manner of holding the inquisition, &c. will be found detailed at large in this chapter. Of the writ.

The writ of inquiry of damages, which is the only writ of inquiry much in use at the present day, is a judicial writ, directed to the sheriff of the county where the venue is laid (b), commanding him, "because it is unknown to the court what damages the plaintiff has sustained," that by the oath of twelve good and lawful men of his bailiwick he diligently inquire what damages the plaintiff in the action has sustained by reason of the premises as for his costs and charges by him about his suit in that behalf expended; and that the sheriff send the inquisition which he shall take therein to the court on the return day (c), "under his seal and the seals of those by whose oath he should take the inquisition." This writ issues only in case of a judgment for the plaintiff by default or on demurrer against all the defendants, and in those actions only where *damages* are recoverable. The writ of inquiry issues merely to inform the conscience of the court of the amount of the damages; but the court, if they please, may themselves assess the damages. And

(a) See inquisition and warrant on a writ of *ad quod damnum*, *post*, Appendix, c. 13. As to the writ of inquiry in replevin, see *post*, chap. 18, s. 3.

(b) But by the stat. 3 & 4 Will. 4, c. 42, s. 22, in local actions, the writ may be executed, by order of the court in which the action shall be depending, or any judge of any of the superior courts of law at Westminster, in any other county or place than that in which the venue is laid, and the court may order a suggestion to be entered on the record to that effect.

(c) See writ, Tidd's Forms, 231, 232, 5th edit.; Archbold's Forms, 342.

CHAP. XIII.

therefore, if in such case final judgment be signed without a writ of inquiry, it is not error (*e*). Indeed, it is now the practice of the courts to refer actions upon bills of exchange and promissory notes, on mortgage deeds, for rent where the lease is in writing, and other demands for a sum certain upon written instruments, to the master, to compute what is due thereon, and in such cases the plaintiff is allowed to sign final judgment without the intervention of a writ of inquiry (*f*). The writ is now tested on the day on which it is issued, in actions within the Uniformity of Process Act, 2 Will. 4, c. 39, and is made returnable on any day certain, in term or in vacation (*g*).

Inquest at what time, and before whom, to be held.

The inquest may be held at any time after the delivery of the writ to the sheriff, and before or on the return day (*h*). But a writ of inquiry would not be well executed after the return day, or even (when the proceedings were by original) between the return day and the *quarto die post* (*i*). Where the sheriff held an inquest on the return day of the writ, but the jury did not give their verdict for two or three days afterwards, the writ was held to be well executed (*k*). Eight days' notice should be given of executing the writ (*l*), and the notice should be given for executing it between some two hours of the day, as between twelve and two o'clock; if notice be given for executing it between a longer period, as between ten and two o'clock, the court would set aside the inquest for irregularity, provided the defendant did not attend (*m*). If the defendant do not attend punctually at the time mentioned in the notice, and the writ be executed in his absence, the court will not relieve him (*n*). On the other hand, if the defendant attend at the hour, he will not be warranted in

(*e*) 2 Saund. 107, n. (2); Gould *v.* Hammersley, 4 Taunt. 148; Bridport *v.* Jones, 3 Man. & G. 627, n. (*a*).

(*f*) Chit. Archb. Prac. 709, 7th edit.; Tidd's Prac. 589, 8th edit.; 2 Saund. 107 a.

(*g*) 1 Will. 4, c. 7, s. 1. So also when issued out of the Court of Pleas at Durham; 2 & 3 Vict. c. 11, s 17.

(*h*) See *ante*, 78.

(*i*) *Ibid.*

(*k*) Rol. Abr. Process (G) 5. See also Dyke *v.* Blakston, 2 Lord Raym. 1449.

(*l*) Unless when it is to be executed in London or Middlesex, and the defendant lives at a greater distance from London than forty miles, in which case fourteen days' notice is necessary; Blaaw *v.* Chater, 6 Taunt. 445; Stevens *v.* Pell, 2 Dowl. 355. The time is computed exclusively of the first and inclusively of the last day, unless the last be a Sunday, Christmas-day, Good Friday, or a public fast day; Reg. Gen. H. 2 Will. 4, r. 8.

(*m*) Foster *v.* Smales, Barnes, 295; Robinson *v.* Philips, Barnes, 296; Le Marque *v.* Newman, Com. 551; Ison *v.* Fowen, Stra. 1142; and see 1 Bos. & Pul. 363.

(*n*) 1 Barnard. 233.

leaving the court at the expiration of the time mentioned in the notice, for the sheriff may have prior business, which may detain him beyond that time (*o*). The inquest is generally held before the under-sheriff himself, but he may appoint a deputy for the purpose of executing it; such deputy should be regularly appointed by a written authority under the seal of office (*p*). The sheriff cannot send his mandate to the bailiff of a liberty to execute a writ of inquiry (*q*). But the sheriff can only make one deputy to hold the inquest; therefore, where two under-sheriffs extraordinary were deputed to take and did take an inquest, the court set aside the inquisition, saying, "if the high sheriff may appoint two, he may appoint twenty or more; if he can exceed one, no line can be drawn to limit the number (*r*)." Indeed, where the under-sheriff lives in the town where the inquest is held, it is irregular to appoint a deputy; in such case the under-sheriff should execute it himself (*s*). Nor can the writ in any case be executed by a deputy of the *under*-sheriff (*t*).

Jurors, who qualified to be, and how punished for non-attendance.

By the statute 6 Geo. 4, c. 50, s. 52, it is enacted, that no person shall be liable to be summoned or impannelled to serve as a juror, in any county in England and Wales, or in London, upon an inquest or inquiry, to be taken or made by or before any sheriff or "coroner, by virtue of any writ of inquiry, or by or before any commissioner appointed under the great seal, and seals of Exchequer, or courts of a county Palatine, or of Wales, who shall not be duly qualified according to that act to serve as a juror on trials at *nisi prius* (*u*). Coroners holding inquests, by virtue of their office, without writ, and sheriff's officers for liberties, &c., or of cities and towns corporate, are excepted out of this act. By section 53 of the same act, "if any man, duly summoned and returned as a juror to serve on such inquest, and shall not, after being three times openly called, appear and serve as such juror, every such sheriff, or in his absence the under-sheriff or secondary, are authorized and required (unless

(*o*) Williams *v*. Frith, Doug. 198.

(*p*) Davis *v*. Skyllins, Barnes 232.

(*q*) Com. Dig. Retorne (D) 3; Wisely *v*. Gunstone, 2 Rol. Abr. 461; Hob. 83, S. C.

(*r*) Denny *v*. Trapnell, 2 Wils. 378.

(*s*) 2 Wils. 379.

(*t*) Jones *v*. Williams, 2 Dowl. N. S. 938.

(*u*) For the qualifications of jurors, see *post*, chap. 17. When it appears that a common jury is an improper one to assess the damages on a writ of inquiry, the court will direct the sheriff to summon a *good* jury, from the special jury book; Price *v*. Williams, 5 Dowl. 160.

CHAP. XIII. some reasonable excuse shall be proved on oath or affidavit) to impose such fine upon every man so making default as they shall respectively think fit, not exceeding five pounds:" the sheriff or under-sheriff shall make out and sign a certificate, containing the christian and surname, the residence and trade or calling of every man so making default, together with the amount imposed and the cause of such fine; and shall transmit such certificate to the clerk of the peace for the county, &c., in which every such defaulter shall reside, on or before the first day of the quarter sessions next ensuing;" and such fines are to be entered on the roll of the fines imposed at the quarter sessions, and levied and applied in the same manner (*u*).

How executed.

The under-sheriff, on the receipt of the writ, should verbally or by writing order a bailiff to summon a jury to attend at the time and place appointed for holding the inquest; when a jury is assembled, the under-sheriff, (or his deputy), after naming the title of the cause, administers the proper oath to the jury (*x*). It is said to have been ruled that jurors on a writ of inquiry cannot be challenged, but it is in the discretion of the sheriff to admit such challenge if it appear to be a good cause of challenge (*y*). The plaintiff's attorney or counsel then opens his client's case, stating the evidence he will adduce in support of his case; and then he proceeds to call his witnesses, whom, after being sworn, he proceeds to examine in support of his case; or, if the case admits it, he may address the jury without offering any evidence. The defendant's attorney or counsel then address the jury, and calls his evidence in mitigation of damages, upon which evidence the plaintiff's attorney has a right to reply. If it be necessary for the ends of justice, as to enable one of the parties to adduce evidence, the sheriff may adjourn the inquest to another day (*z*). The under-sheriff, or his deputy, then sums

(*u*) As to such fines, see *post*, chap. 17, and stat. 3 Geo. 4, c. 46.

(*x*) The oath is usually to each juryman—"You shall well and truly try all such matters and things as shall be given in charge touching this writ of inquiry, and a true verdict give. *So help you God.*" The following form is given in Skirrow, p. 319:—To the foreman—"You, as foreman of this jury, shall well and truly inquire and assess the damages between the parties, and a true verdict give, according to the evidence. *So help you God.*" To the others of the jury—"The same oath which your foreman hath taken on his part, you and each of you shall well and truly observe and keep on your parts. *So help you God.*"

(*y*) Anon. 3 Salk, 81, *per* Holt, C. J.; Anon. 6 Mod. 43.

(*z*) Colman *v.* Mawby, Stra. 853; Markham *v.* Middleton, Stra. 1259.

up the whole case, stating the nature of the injury set out in the pleadings and the evidence. If the direction by the under-sheriff as to the criterion by which the jury are to assess the damages be wrong (*a*), or the jury find a verdict against evidence (*b*), the court out of which the record issues will set aside the inquisition, and grant a new writ of inquiry.

Evidence.

The under-sheriff or his deputy should only admit such persons as witnesses as are competent witnesses in a trial at *nisi prius*. The witnesses, before giving their evidence, should be sworn by the under-sheriff or by the crier (*c*). As the judgment by default admits that the plaintiff has a cause of action as stated in the declaration, all the plaintiff has to prove, or the defendant is allowed to controvert, is the amount of the damages (*d*); therefore it was holden that a lease mentioned in the condition of a bond, set out by the defendant upon *oyer*, need not be proved (*e*). So a bill of exchange or promissory note, if declared upon, need not be proved or even produced (*f*). And if a bill of exchange or promissory note, being produced, appear to be upon a wrong stamp, the defendant cannot take advantage of it (*g*): if, however, it be necessary to prove the instrument in order to show the amount of damages, (as where, in setting it out, the sum is laid under a videlicet,) it must be properly stamped, or it cannot be admitted (*h*). So the defendant, in an action on a contract, will not be allowed, even in mitigation of damages, to give evidence of fraud, or of any other matter which would render the contract void; for by allowing judgment to go by default he has admitted the validity of the contract (*i*). Neither will the defendant be allowed to

(*a*) See Gainsford *v.* Carroll, 2 Bar. & Cress. 624; 4 Dowl. & Ry. 161, S. C.

(*b*) Woodford *v.* Eades, Stra. 425.

(*c*) The following is submitted as the proper oath: "The evidence that you shall give to this inquest in the cause wherein A. B. is plaintiff and C. D. defendant, shall be the truth, the whole truth, and nothing but the truth. *So help you God.*"

(*d*) De Gaillon *v.* L'Aigle, 1 Bos. & Pul. 368; East India Company *v.* Glover, Stra. 612; Thelluson *v.* Fletcher, Doug. 315; Williams *v.* Cooper, 3 Dowl. 204.

(*e*) Collins *v.* Rybot, 1 Esp. 157.

(*f*) Lane *v.* Mullins, 2 Q. B. 254; Lawrence *v.* Clark, 14 M. & W. 250; 3 Dowl. & L. 87, S. C.; overruling Green *v.* Hearne, 3 T. R. 301; Anon., 3 Wils. 155.

(*g*) De la Courtier *v.* Bellamy, 2 Show. 422.

(*h*) King *v.* Beck, 8 Dowl. 735; Cooper *v.* Blick, 2 Q. B. 924; Banbury Union *v.* Robinson, 1 Dav. & M. 96.

(*i*) East India Company *v.* Glover, Stra. 612; De Gaillon *v.* L'Aigle, 1 Bos. & Pul. 368.

CHAP. XIII. give in evidence, in mitigation of damages, any matter which might have been made the subject of a set-off (*k*); or any fact which would be a bar to the action if pleaded (*l*).

Damages, how assessed.

In trespass, or any other action, where the damage actually sustained by the plaintiff is the measure of the damages to be given by the jury, if the plaintiff do not prove the nature of the injury and the amount of the damage sustained by him, the jury should give nominal damages merely; but where the jury are to imply the amount of the damages from the nature of the injury, the jury may give more than nominal damages, without any evidence of the damage being given. Thus, in an action for words imputing subornation of perjury to the plaintiff at the execution of the writ of inquiry, the counsel for the plaintiff offered no evidence, but merely addressed the jury, who gave 50*l*. damages; the court held that they had not estimated damages upon erroneous grounds (*m*). If there be two or more defendants who suffer judgment to go by default, the inquest cannot, even in trespass, sever the damages (*n*); but where there is judgment by default against one defendant, and judgment upon demurrer against the other, the inquest may sever the damages, because the defendants have severed in pleading (*o*).

Return.

When the jury have agreed upon the damages, the under-sheriff fills up the inquisition, and reads it to the jury, which the under-sheriff, in the name of the high-sheriff and the jury, sign opposite to their seals; which inquisition (*p*) the sheriff keeps, and he makes out another upon parchment, sealed with the seal of office, and signed with the sheriff's name, and to this the seals of the jury are affixed, but they do not sign it. The inquisition on parchment is then annexed to the writ of inquiry, and the return is indorsed on the back of the writ in these words: "The execution of this writ appears in a certain inquisition hereunto annexed."

Judgment and execution thereon.

At the return of the writ of inquiry, a rule for judgment may

(*k*) Carruthers *v*. Graham, 14 East, 578.

(*l*) Leicester *v*. Walton, 2 Campb. 251; Speck *v*. Phillips, 5 M. & W. 279.

(*m*) Tripp *v*. Thomas, 5 Dowl. & Ry. 276; 3 B. & C. 427, S. C.

(*n*) Sir John Heydon's case, 11 Rep. 5; Onslow *v*. Orchard, Stra. 422.

(*o*) Chapman *v*. House, Stra. 1140; but see 11 Rep. 5, 7.

(*p*) See form, Appendix, ch. 13.

be given, costs taxed, final judgment signed, and execution issued forthwith, unless the sheriff or other officer, before whom the same may be executed, shall certify under his hand upon such writ that judgment ought not to be signed until the defendant shall have had an opportunity to apply to the court to set aside the execution of such writ, or one of the judges of the said court shall think fit to order the judgment to be stayed until a day to be named in such order: provided always, that in case the signing of judgment on such writ shall be postponed by reason of such certificate or order, or by the choice of the plaintiff or otherwise, and judgment shall be afterwards signed thereon, such judgment shall be entered of record as of the day of the return of such writ, unless the court shall otherwise direct (*q*).

Writ of inquiry under 8 & 9 Will. 3, c. 11.

Before the stat. 3 & 4 Will. 4, c. 42, all assessments of damages in actions upon bonds, or for any penal sum for non-performance of any covenants or agreements in any deed or writing, under the stat. 8 & 9 Will. 3, c. 11, in case where there was judgment for the plaintiff on default or by demurrer, could be made only before the justices of assize or nisi prius for the county in which the venue was laid, for which purpose a writ issued to the sheriff of that county to summon a jury to appear before the justices of assize or nisi prius of that county to inquire into the truth of the several breaches suggested on the roll, and to assess the damages that the plaintiff should have sustained thereby. But by the stat. 3 & 4 Will. 4, c. 42, s. 16, after reciting that it would lessen the expenses of trials and prevent delay if such writs of inquiry were executed before the sheriff of the county where the venue is laid, it is enacted, that all writs issued under and by virtue of the statute 8 & 9 Will. 3, c. 11, shall, unless the court where such action is pending, or a judge of one of the superior courts, shall otherwise order, direct the sheriff of the county where the action shall be brought to summon a jury to appear before the said sheriff, instead of the justices or justice of assize or nisi prius of that county, to inquire of the truth of the breaches suggested, and assess the damages that the plaintiff shall have sustained thereby, and shall command the said sheriff to make return thereof to the court from whence the same shall issue, at a day certain in term or vacation in such

(*q*) 1 Will. 4, c. 7, s. 1. See Reg. Gen. H. 2 Will. 4, r. 67.

CHAP. XIII.

writ to be mentioned; and such proceedings shall be had after the return of such writ as are in the said statute in that behalf mentioned, in like manner as if such writ had been executed before a justice of assize or nisi prius.

By the 19th section of the same statute, the provisions of the 1 Will. 4, c. 7, s. 1 (*r*), are extended to these writs of inquiry.

Fees.

As to the fees chargeable by the sheriff and his officers on a writ of inquiry, see *ante*, p. 103.

Liability of the sheriff.

The liability of a sheriff to an attachment or an action for any misfeasance is the same on a writ of inquiry of damages as on any other writ. It is laid down, that if the sheriff return that the inquest or jury found no damages, he shall not be amerced for this default of the jury; for the sheriff shall not be amerced but where he returns the writ falsely or insufficiently of himself, whereas here he returned it as he presented it (*s*).

(*r*) *Ante*, 329.
(*s*) Bro. Retorne, 20; Fitz. Retorne, 66; 5 Rep. 32, 33.

CHAPTER XIV.

WRIT OF TRIAL.

Of the Writ.—When and how executed.—Return.—New Trial, &c.—Judgment and Execution.—Sheriff's Fees.

By the statute 3 & 4 Will. 4, c. 42, s. 17, it is enacted, that in any action depending in any of the superior courts for any debt or demand in which the sum sought to be recovered, and indorsed on the writ of summons, shall not exceed twenty pounds, it shall be lawful for the court in which such suit shall be depending, or any judge of any of the said courts, if such court or judge shall be satisfied that the trial will not involve any difficult question of fact or law, and such court or judge shall think fit so to do, to order and direct that the issue or issues joined shall be tried before the sheriff of the county where the action is brought, or any judge of any court of record for the recovery of debt in such county, and for that purpose a writ shall issue directed to such sheriff or judge, commanding him to try such issue or issues by a jury to be summoned by him, and to return such writ, with the finding of the jury thereon indorsed, at a day certain in term or in vacation, to be named in such writ; and thereupon such sheriff or judge shall summon a jury, and shall proceed to try such issue or issues. Writ of trial.

The 18th section enacts, that at the return of any writ for the trial of such issue or issues as aforesaid, costs shall be taxed, judgment signed, and execution issued forthwith, unless such sheriff, deputy, or judge before whom such trial shall be had, shall certify under his hand upon such writ that judgment ought not to be signed until the defendant shall have had an opportunity to apply to the court for a new inquiry or trial, or a judge of any of the said courts shall think fit to order that judgment or execution shall be stayed till a day to be named in such order; and the verdict of such jury, on the trial of such issue or issues, shall be as valid and of the like force as a verdict of a jury at

CHAP. XIV. nisi prius; and the sheriff or his deputy, or judge presiding at the trial of such issue or issues, shall have the like powers with respect to amendment on such trial, as are hereinafter given to judges at nisi prius (*a*).

In what cases.

These enactments apply only to actions for debts or pecuniary demands, where both the sum really sought to be recovered, and the sum indorsed on the writ, do not exceed 20*l.* An order for a trial before the sheriff cannot be obtained, therefore, in an action of tort (*b*), nor in an action for unliquidated damages for breach of contract (*c*). If the action is brought substantially, although not directly, for a debt limited to an amount not exceeding 20*l.*, it is sufficient (*d*). If the writ be sued out and indorsed for an amount above 20*l.*, although less is really due, the judge has no power to make the order, even though the plaintiff be willing to waive the excess (*e*). It appears at one time to have been considered, that by consenting to the order and appearing at the trial, the defendant waived any objection to the jurisdiction of the sheriff (*f*); but it seems now to be agreed that the parties cannot, by their consent, give him jurisdiction in a case not triable by him under the statute (*g*). Where the issue is not according to the form given by the rule of H. T. 4 Will. 4 (*h*), the court will give the plaintiff leave to amend on payment of costs (*i*); and such amendment may be made by the court or a judge at any stage of the proceedings, even at or after the trial (*j*). If, however, such amendment be not made, the variance from the form is a ground for arresting the judgment (*k*). But the defendant will not be entitled to set aside the proceedings after verdict, on the ground that irrelevant matter is introduced into the issue which is not in the writ, the

(*a*) Sections 23, 24. On this subject see Chit. Archb. Prac. 7th ed. 281; Jervis's Rules, 202 *et seq.*

(*b*) Watson *v.* Abbot, 2 C. & M. 150; 2 Dowl. 215; Smith *v.* Brown, 2 M. & W. 851; 5 Dowl. 736, S. C.

(*c*) Jacquot *v.* Boura, 5 M. & W. 155; 7 Dowl. 331, S. C.

(*d*) Price *v.* Morgan, 2 M. & W. 53; Allen *v.* Pink, 4 M. & W. 140; 6 Dowl. 668, S. C.

(*e*) Trotter *v.* Bass, 1 Hodg. 23; see Burleigh *v.* Kingdom, 2 Dowl. 351.

(*f*) See Price *v.* Morgan, 2 M. & W. 55.

(*g*) See Smith *v.* Brown, 2 M. & W. 851; Allen *v.* Pink, 4 M. & W. 140.

(*h*) Append. ch. 14.

(*i*) Attwill *v.* Baker, 2 M. & W. 272; 3 Dowl. 462.

(*j*) Cox *v.* Painter, 1 N. & P. 581; Percival *v.* Connell, 3 Bing. N. C. 877; 5 Scott, 191; 6 Dowl. 68, S. C.

(*k*) Handford *v.* Handford, 6 Dowl. 473; see Lycett *v.* Tenant, 4 Bing. N. C. 168; 5 Scott, 479; 6 Dowl. 436, S. C.

plaintiff having given notice before the trial that he does not intend to proceed with such irrelevant matter at the trial (*k*). Where the date of the writ of summons is untruly stated in the writ of trial, it is a ground for setting aside the verdict, at least, if the defendant have not appeared at the trial (*l*). CHAP. XIV.

To whom directed.

The writ is to be directed to the judge of the court of record in those places in which there is a court of record, and to the sheriff where there is no such court (*m*). It seems it cannot go to the coroner (*n*). It is engrossed on parchment and sealed, but not signed (*o*), and then left, together with the rule or order annexed to it, at the sheriff's office a reasonable time (two days at least) before the day of trial. It must be resealed as in other cases (*p*). If it be to assess damages on demurrer (as it may be), it must be framed accordingly (*q*). Blanks must not be left in it (*r*). Form, &c.

When executed

If the cause be tried, even by adjournment, on a day subsequent to the return day of the writ of trial, it seems that it is a mis-trial (*s*). In one case, however, it was held that the defendant waived the objection by appearing at the trial (*t*). An alteration of the record, by the insertion of a different day of trial, will not render a resealing of the writ necessary, except where the alteration is to a day subsequent to the return of the writ (*u*).

The same notice of trial must be given as in a cause at Nisi Prius (*x*).

How executed.

The writ may be executed by the under-sheriff, or other deputy of the sheriff, but not by the *deputy of the under-sheriff* (*y*). The sheriff, &c., has the same power as to the

(*k*) Hiam *v.* Smith, 6 Dowl. 710.

(*l*) White *v.* Farrer, 2 M. & W. 288; S. C. nom. Wight *v.* Perrers, 3 Dowl. 463; Whipple *v.* Manley, 3 M. & W. 432; 5 Dowl. 100; Farwig *v.* Cockerton, 3 M. & W. 169; Ashburton *v.* Sykes, 1 Dowl. & L. 133.

(*m*) Clarke *v.* Marner, 4 M. & Scott, 171.

(*n*) Levy *v.* Magnay, 10 M. & W. 664.

(*o*) Reg. Gen. H. 4 Will. 4, r. 19.

(*p*) Ashburton *v.* Sykes, 1 Dowl. & L. 133.

(*q*) Fryer *v.* Smith, 1 Dowl. & L. 80.

(*r*) Dennett *v.* Harding, 2 Dowl. & L. 488.

(*s*) Mortimer *v.* Preedy, 3 M. & W. 602; 6 Dowl. 544.

(*t*) Sherman *v.* Tinsley, 4 Scott, 286; see Pinkney *v.* Booth, 1 Dowl. N. S. 421; *ante*, 78.

(*u*) Chandler *v.* Bezward, 2 M. & W. 205; 5 Dowl. 311.

(*x*) Charnock *v.* Smith, 3 Dowl. 607; see Dignam *v.* Ibbotson, 3 M. & W. 431.

(*y*) Jones *v.* Williams, 2 Dowl. N. S. 938; see *ante*, 325.

CHAP. XIV. general conduct of the trial as a judge: thus, he may postpone the trial if he see cause (*z*); he may nonsuit the plaintiff (*a*); he may lay down a rule that no person but a barrister or attorney shall appear as the advocate (*b*). But he cannot certify under any statute, or under a Court of Requests Act, to deprive the plaintiff of costs (*c*); but it seems that it would be a sufficient answer to an application for the judge's order for a writ of trial, that the amount in dispute is within the limit of a Court of Requests Act (*d*). He has no power to refer the cause to arbitration (*e*). Where a bill of exceptions was tendered to the direction of an under-sheriff, which he would not receive, the court refused to interfere to stay judgment and execution (*f*).

Jury. The jury to try the issue must be such as are designated in the writ. Thus, where the writ was directed to the recorder of the borough of N., directing him to summon twelve lawful men of his *county* to try, &c., and the cause was tried by juries resident within the *borough* and not on the county list, the trial was held irregular (*g*). But such an irregularity is waived by the consent of the parties to the jury impannelled (*h*). And it is not essential that the jury should come from the *county;* they may be taken from a borough or other limited jurisdiction, where the writ is directed to a judge of an inferior court of record there (*i*).

Return. The statute directs the return to be on "a day certain in term or vacation, to be named in such writ," the time not being further specified. In practice, it is usually made returnable in the term in which the trial is had, where there is sufficient of the term remaining; and when the trial is had in vacation, on the same or the following day (*k*).

New trial, &c. The courts have laid down a rule that a new trial shall not be

(*z*) Fouraker *v.* Jackson, 2 Jurist, 329.

(*a*) Watson *v.* Abbott, 2 Dowl. 215.

(*b*) Tribe *v.* Wingfield, 2 M. & W. 128.

(*c*) Wardroper *v.* Richardson, 3 Nev. & M. 839; 1 Ad. & E. 75; Pritchard *v.* M'Gill, 2 M. & W. 380.

(*d*) Jones *v.* Barnes, 2 M. & W. 313; 3 Dowl. 455; Pritchard *v.* M'Gill, *supra*.

(*e*) Wilson *v.* Thorpe, 6 M. & W. 721; Harrison *v.* Greenwood, 3 Dowl. & L. 353.

(*f*) White *v.* Hislop, 4 M. & W. 73; 6 Dowl. 693.

(*g*) Farmer *v.* Mountfort, 8 M. & W. 266.

(*h*) Pryme *v.* Titchmarsh, 10 M. & W. 605.

(*i*) Farmer *v.* Mountfort, 9 M. & W. 100.

(*k*) Billing *v.* Railton, 2 Dowl. & L. 771.

granted in cases tried under a writ of trial, on the ground of the verdict being against the evidence, where the damages do not exceed 5*l.* (*l*). On motion for a new trial, the notes of the sheriff or his deputy are not conclusive on the parties like those of a judge, but may be supplied or varied by affidavits of what took place at the trial (*m*). Although no application have been made to the sheriff, &c., to stay the signing of judgment, and judgment have been signed and execution issued in vacation, the defendant may apply to the court in the following term to have a suggestion entered on the roll to deprive the plaintiff of costs under a Court of Requests Act (*n*): and the circumstance of the sheriff's having refused to certify does not preclude a party from applying for a new trial within the proper time; and upon such application the court will judicially notice the record (*o*). The plaintiff may tax his costs, sign judgment, and sue out execution *immediately* on the return of the writ, unless prevented by certificate or order under sect. 18 (*p*). And by sect. 19, all the provisions of the 1 Will. 4, c. 7, s. 1 (*q*), are extended to judgments and executions upon writs for the trial of issues under this act, so far as they are applicable thereto. CHAP. XIV.

As to the sheriff's fees on writs of trial, see *ante*, p. 105. Fees.

(*l*) Williams *v.* Evans, 2 M. & W. 220; Lyddons *v.* Combes, 5 Dowl. 560.

(*m*) Lilley *v.* Johnson, 2 M. & W. 386.

(*n*) Johnson *v.* Beale, 5 M. & W. 276; see Baddley *v.* Oliver, 1 C. & M. 219.

(*o*) Angel *v.* Ihler, 8 M. & W. 600.

(*p*) Nicholls *v.* Chambers, 2 Dowl. 693.

(*q*) *Ante*, 329.

CHAPTER XV.

OF THE EXECUTION OF PROCESS IN REAL ACTIONS (*a*).

SECT. I.—*Of Mesne Process.—Summons, Proclamation.—Attachment and Distress Infinite.—Grand Cape.*

II.—*Of the Writ of View.—Trial: Grand Assize.*

III.—*Execution.—Habere facias seisinam.*

Summons.

THE process in real actions, to compel the tenant to appear, is of various kinds, according to the nature of the particular action. It is either—1. Summons and grand cape, as generally in every *præcipe quod reddat;* 2. Summons, attachment, and distress infinite, as generally in every *præcipe quod faciat,* or action in the realty; 3. Summons and resummons, as in assize of *mort d'ancestor, juris utrum,* and *darrein presentment;* or 4. Attachment, as in an assize of *novel disseisin* and nuisance (*b*).

The original writ in all real actions, with one or two exceptions, as in assize of *novel disseisin,* or in a writ of *deceit,* is a writ of summons, by which the sheriff is commanded to summon by good summoners the tenants to appear in court according to the requisition of the writ, and that the sheriff shall have the names of the summoners at the return of the writ.

How executed.

Upon the receipt of the writ, as in other cases, the sheriff must make his warrant to two bailiffs at least; and the sum-

(*a*) Although, by the statute 3 & 4 Will. 4, c. 27, s. 36, all real and mixed actions were abolished from the 31st December, 1834, (with the exception of writs of right of dower, writs of dower *unde nihil habet, quare impedit,* and ejectment,) yet, inasmuch as by the provisions of the 38th section, whenever, on the 1st June, 1835, any person whose right of entry to any land was taken away by descent cast, discontinuance, or warranty, might maintain a real action in respect of such land, the same may still be brought within the period during which, by virtue of the provisions of that act, an entry might have been made upon the land, if the right of entry had not been so taken away, it follows that cases still remain in which, for nearly twenty years to come, a real action *may* be brought for the recovery of land or rent. This chapter has therefore been retained.

(*b*) Roscoe on Real Actions, 146; Finch's Law, 343, 4, 5; Booth, 7; Com. Dig. Process.

moners should be *liberi* and *legales homines*, so that they may give evidence of the fact of summons, if it be desired (*c*). The warrant repeats the mandatory part of the writ, viz. it directs the bailiff to command the tenant to render the land (*d*); and unless he shall do so, to summon him to appear at the return of the writ, and it further directs the bailiffs, after summons made, to make proclamation according to the form of the statute (*e*). On receiving the warrant, the bailiffs must prepare a summons, which pursues the form of the warrant, and must serve it on the tenant on the land (*f*).

It has been said that in practice no summons is now actually made in any real action, though the names of summoners are of course returned by the sheriff upon the writ (*g*). But this practice has been shown to be open to so many objections, that it appears to be essentially necessary that the summons should be actually and formally served (*h*). As to the time when the summons should be made, it ought to be served before sunset (*i*). And the summons must be made fifteen days before the return-day of the writ, and not merely fifteen days before the *quarto die post* (*k*). This is provided by the stat. 18 Edw. 1, c. 15, which, in affirmance of the common law, declares that in summons and attachment in pleas of land, the summons and attachment shall contain the term of fifteen days (*l*). As to the place where the summons should be made, it is said that in all actions for the recovery of land, the summons ought to be *in terrâ petitâ* (*m*); if, however, the tenant appear, it is immaterial where he was summoned (*n*). Summons upon the land in demand

(*c*) Roscoe, 147; Dalt. 153; Booth, 4. For the due service of the summons must be proved by the summoners; and when a trial is by witnesses, the affirmative must be proved by two or three witnesses; Co. Litt. 6.

(*d*) By this is meant a render in court, and not in *pais;* Beecher's case, 8 Rep. 61 b; Keilw. 116 b; Booth, 7.

(*e*) See Form, *post*, Append. chap. 14, s. 1.

(*f*) *Id. ibid.*

(*g*) Booth, 5; note to 2 Saund. 45 c.

(*h*) Roscoe, 147.

(*i*) Green *v.* Arderne, Cro. Eliz. 42; Dalt. 151.

(*k*) Brooke's Abr. Ley Gager, 57; Booth, 24; Roscoe, 147.

(*l*) Fifteen days, according to Sir Edward Coke, were accounted a reasonable time, because a *dieta*, or day's journey, being twenty miles, that space of time was sufficient to enable the person summoned to make his appearance in court on the day given, in whatever part of England he might reside; 2 Inst. 567.

(*m*) Com. Dig. Process (D 3); Vin. Ab. Sommons (B); Finch's Law, 344; Dalt, 152.

(*n*) Dalt. 152; Bro. Sommons, 7; Roscoe, 148.

CHAP. XV. SECT. I.

seems to be sufficient, whether the tenant, or any one for him, be there or not (*o*); and a prayer in aid may be summoned in the land demanded, although it is not his freehold (*p*). But the sheriff cannot summon the party by a rent service, rent charge, common, reversion, or the like, for the soil is another man's freehold (*q*). Where the lands lie in several towns in one county, it seems that summons in one town is sufficient (*r*),

Proclamation.

It has been suggested, that, to avoid all objections, the most prudent mode of serving the summons upon a tenant in a real action is to serve him personally with the summons on the land demanded, or if he be not met with on the land, to summon him personally, and also to make a summons upon the land, by erecting a stick or wand, and affixing to it a copy of the summons (*s*); and it will be proper to read over the summons to the tenant on serving him with the copy, for the summoners ought properly to name the demandant, the land in demand, and the day of the return (*t*). In summoning a defendant on a writ of *quare impedit*, it is said that the summons may be either at the church door, or on the person of the defendant (*u*).

For the purpose of avoiding secret summonses, and in order to give convenient notice to the tenants of the lands, by the 31 Eliz. c. 3, s. 2, it is enacted, "That after every summons upon the land, in any real action, fourteen days, at the least, before the day of the return thereof, proclamation of the summons shall be made on a Sunday, immediately after divine service and sermon, if any sermon there be, and if no sermon there be, then forthwith after divine service, at or near to the most usual door of the church or chapel of that town or parish where the land whereupon the summons was made doth lie, and proclamation so made as aforesaid shall be returned together with the names of the summoners, and if such summons shall not be proclaimed according to the tenor and meaning of this act, then no *grand cape* to be awarded, but *alias* and *pluries* summons as the case shall require, until a summons and proclamation shall be duly made and returned according to the tenor and meaning

(*o*) 2 Saund. 43, n.; 2 Inst. 253.

(*p*) Dalt. 152; Bro. Abr. Sommons in terra, 16; Rol. Abr. Sommons (B) 8.

(*q*) Dalt. 151; Bro. Retorne, 124; *Ibid.* Sommons, 14.

(*r*) Allen *v.* Walter, Hob. 133.

(*s*) Roscoe, 148.

(*t*) Dalt. 151. See also 3 Chitty's Pl. 624, 5.

(*u*) 1 Brownl. 158; Booth, 226; but see Roll. Abr. Summons (A) 1.

of this." If there be no church, it is said that the summons at the common law is sufficient (*x*); and so also when there is no sermon or prayers between the delivery of the writ to the sheriff and the return, the summons at common law is sufficient (*y*). And if a parish extend into two counties, and the land is in one county and the church in the other, the proclamation should be made in that church by the sheriff of the county in which the land lies (*z*). If the lands lie in several parishes, it seems that a proclamation made at the door of the church of one parish is sufficient within the act (*a*).

Return to the summons.

When the summons has been served, which, as we have seen, must be at least fifteen days before the return-day of the writ, the sheriff should return the writ, with the names of the pledges and summoner indorsed. The summoners are the persons who have actually made the summons, but the pledges are John Doe and Richard Roe (*b*). Any matter of excuse, of course, may be returned; thus formerly it was a good return to the summons, that the sheriff did not summon the tenant on account of the demandant or plaintiff not having pledges (*c*); or he may return *tardè* (*d*): or that no one came to show the land to the sheriff (*e*). But it is not a good return to say that the tenant has yielded the lands (*f*).

Return that proclamation has been made.

The sheriff should also return that he has made proclamation of the summons "*according to the form of the statute*" (*g*), without more; but a return that the sheriff has proclaimed "the contents of the writ" is insufficient, because he must proclaim that he made summons of the land (*h*). If the proclamation of the summons be particularly set out in the return, it must appear then that the land lies in the parish in which the proclamation has been made, and that the proclamation was made after the summons (*i*). If the sheriff return that the proclamation of the summons was made at the church door, when

(*x*) Roscoe, 149.
(*y*) Anon. Anders. 278; Vin. Abr. Summons (C 3).
(*z*) *Ibid.*; Ragister's case, Cro. Eliz. 472; Roscoe, 149.
(*a*) Allen *v.* Walter, Hob. 133; 1 Brownl. 126, S. C.
(*b*) See Return, *post*, Append. c. 14, s. 1.
(*c*) Roscoe, 150; Booth, 6; Off. Brev. 357.
(*d*) Roscoe, 150.
(*e*) *Ibid.*
(*f*) Bro. Abr. Retorne, 84; Roscoe, 150.
(*g*) See Form, *post*, Append. c. 14, s. 1; 2 Saund. 43 a, note.
(*h*) Allen *v.* Walter, Hob. 133; 1 Brownl. 126, S. C.
(*i*) Furnis *v.* Waterhouse, 1 Mod. 197.

CHAP. XV. SECT. I.

in fact it was not so made, it is not error (*k*). The mode of taking advantage of such irregularity is by moving to set aside the *grand cape*, or the judgment by default (*l*). If the sheriff return the tenant summoned, when in fact he was not summoned, the party has several remedies:—First, by waging his law of non-summons, by which, if he succeed, the writ abates: secondly, the court, under such circumstances, would set aside a judgment by default; thirdly, the tenant may have a writ of deceit to recover the land; fourthly, an action against the sheriff for a false return; as the law will not suffer the tenant to lose his lands, unless he has received legal and formal notice of the demandant's claim (*m*).

Writ of attachment, when it lies.

In many writs in the realty which are not properly for the demand of land, as in waste, *quod permittat, secta ad molendinum*, &c., the process is by summons, attachment, and distress infinite (*n*). The attachment issues on the default of appearance of the tenant either on the summons, or on his default on the day of the adjournment of the essoign (*o*). The writ of attachment commands the sheriff that he attach the defendant by gages and safe pledges that he be, &c.

How executed.

The mode of executing the attachment is for the sheriff, on the receipt of the writ, to proceed and attach the defendant, which he ought either to do by attaching his goods (*p*), or by compelling him to find pledges for his appearance (*q*); or, as it seems, by merely summoning him to appear, without attaching him either by pledges or goods (*r*). If the sheriff attached goods, he did not return pledges (*s*). Under the writ of attachment, the sheriff could only take the moveable goods of the defendant, and not a chattel real, or a thing fixed to the freehold, nor the horse upon which he was riding, nor the apparel with which he was clothed (*t*). And the sheriff ought to have returned the particular goods seized, and not chattels to the value of 10*l.*; for if the defendant does not appear, the goods attached are forfeited (*u*), and he ought not to have taken goods

(*k*) Collett *v.* Marsh, Cro. Eliz. 371, 397; Moor, 197, 349, S. C.
(*l*) Roscoe, 149.
(*m*) Roscoe, 147.
(*n*) Roscoe, 151.
(*o*) *Ibid.*
(*p*) Dalt. 155; Roscoe, 151.
(*q*) Dalt. 155.
(*r*) *Ibid.*
(*s*) Com. Dig. Process (D) 6.
(*t*) Roscoe, 151; Vin. Abr. Attachment (B); 2 Inst. 254.
(*u*) Lawrence *v.* Netheral, Cro. Eliz. 13; Dyer, 199 a, S. C.; Wells *v.* Wigon, Carter, 224; and see Kitch. on Courts, 157.

of great value, but a single thing sufficient to make the defendant appear (*x*). After taking the goods, the sheriff is bound to keep them safely, and not use them, for they are to be restored to the tenant if he appear (*y*). Or the sheriff may leave the goods with the owner, taking an obligation of the owner of the goods for the delivery thereof, if the owner shall make default of appearance (*z*). The attachment should be made fifteen days before the return day (*a*). If the party be not summoned and attached, it is error, and the officer shall be amerced (*b*).

Distringas.

On default of appearance on the attachment at the common law, a writ of distringas may issue, which commands the sheriff to distrain the goods of the tenant or defendant until he appears (*c*); and by the statute of Westm. 2, c. 45, it was enacted, that if the tenant, after the first attachment returned, make default, the grand distress shall be awarded. By the statute of Marlbridge, c. 7, in a writ of award, in which the process was summons, attachment and distress infinite, a proclamation is directed to be made; and if the defendant do not appear, judgment may be given against him. And by the statute Westm. 2, c. 14, in a writ of waste, if the tenant make default at the return of the distringas, a writ of inquiry of waste done may issue, upon the return of which, judgment may be given.

The sheriff may distrain either the moveable goods of the defendant or the issues of his land; and for this purpose he issues his warrant to two bailiffs, who are to execute the distringas. The sheriff may either keep the goods so distrained, or take money or an obligation for the appearance of the defendant or tenant, according to the exigency of the writ. The return of the sheriff is, that he has distrained the defendant by his lands and chattels, to which he adds the amount of the issues and the names of the manucaptors (*d*). The issues returned must be reasonable (*e*). Where the sheriff returned *mandavi ballivo*, without also returning that the defendant had no issues in his bailiwick, the return was held bad, and the sheriff was amerced (*f*).

(*x*) 2 Lutw. 1457.
(*y*) Dalt. 156.
(*z*) *Ibid.*
(*a*) Dalt. 157; Co. Litt. 134 b; Bro. Attach. 1, 5, 6.
(*b*) Dalt. 157.
(*c*) Fitz. 59 b; Dalt. 160.
(*d*) Dalt. 223.
(*e*) *Ibid.*
(*f*) Bro. Retorn, 23. By the statute 51 Geo. 3, c. 124, continued by the statute of 57 Geo. 3, c. 101, but which act has expired, and has not been renewed, as far as I am aware,

CHAP. XV. SECT. I.

Grand cape.

If the tenant, having been duly summoned, neglects to appear on the return of the writ to cast an essoign, or in case of an essoign being cast, neglects to appear on the adjournment day of the essoign, the next process for the demandant is a judicial writ of grand cape *in manum nostram;* by which writ the sheriff is commanded that he take into the king's hands, by the view of good and lawful men in his county, the lands, &c., for the default of the tenant, and make known the day of the taking to the justices of Westminster; and also that he summon by good summoners the tenant, that he be before the justices on the return day, to answer to the principal plea, and to show wherefore he was not before the justices according to the former summons; or if the default be for not appearing on the adjournment day of the essoign, "To show wherefore he did not keep the day given him by reason of his essoign, before the

the method of procuring an appearance in which the proceedings were summons, attachment and distress, was, for the period it was in force, completely altered. By that act it was provided, that when the proceeding was by summons and attachment in any action against any person not having privilege of parliament, no writ of distringas should issue for default of appearance; but the defendant should be served personally with the summons or attachment, at the foot of which should be written a notice, informing the defendant of the intent and meaning of such service, as follows: "To C. D. You are served with this process at the suit of A. B., to the intent that you may appear by your attorney in his Majesty's court of —— at Westminster, at the return hereof, being the —— day of ——, in order to your defence in this action: and take notice, that in default of your appearance, the said A. B. will cause an appearance to be entered for you, and proceed thereon, as if you had yourself appeared by your attorney." In cases where it was shown to the court, or to a judge in vacation, that this could not be served, the court or judge may allow the plaintiff to sue out a writ of distringas to compel an appearance; at the time of serving such writ of distringas, the officer shall serve on the defendant, or if he be not to be found, leave at the place of his abode a written notice in the following form:

"In the court of ——, between A. B. plaintiff, and C. D. defendant. Take notice, that I have this day distrained upon your goods and chattels for the sum of forty shillings, in consequence of your not having appeared by your attorney in the said court at the return of a writ of ——, returnable there on the —— day of ——; and that in default of your appearing to the present writ of distringas at the return thereof, being the —— day of ——, the said A. B. will cause an appearance to be entered for you, and proceed thereon as if you had yourself appeared by your attorney."

E. F.

(the name of the sheriff's officer.)

To C. D., the above named defendant.

Upon an affidavit of the personal service of such summons or attachment, and notice written on the foot thereof as aforesaid, or of the due execution of such distringas, it may be lawful for the plaintiff to enter a common appearance for the defendant, and to proceed thereon as if the defendant himself had entered an appearance for himself. See Tidd's Prac. 111, 8th edit.

justices at Westminster, &c., and that the sheriff have there the names of those by whose view he shall do this, the names of the summoners, and the writ (*g*)."

How executed.

The sheriff's duty in executing the grand cape is, first, by the view of honest and lawful men of his county, to seize the tenements into the king's hands; secondly, to summons the tenant. For this purpose, the sheriff should make his warrant to the bailiff (*h*) to execute the writ; in the execution thereof the bailiff should take with him four inhabitants of the county, two as viewers, and two as summoners. The process of taking the tenements into the king's hands is a mere formal proceeding; the sheriff in the presence of the viewers verbally seizing them into the king's hands (*i*). As early as the time of Bracton, the seizure of the land on the grand cape was merely formal, and the tenant was left in possession (*k*); and where in dower, upon a writ of grand cape, *cape in manum nostram tertiam partem rectoriæ*, the sheriff took the tithes, and carried them away, the court said that this was not such a seisin as was intended by the writ, and that the sheriff ought to seize generally, but to leave them where he found them (*l*). The summoners should then proceed to summon the tenant in the same manner as upon the first summons (*m*). The grand cape must be served at least fifteen days before the return day; it is not sufficient to serve it fifteen days before the *quarto die post* (*n*).

Return.

The sheriff's return is, that he has taken into the king's hands by the view of A. B. and C. D., good and lawful men, &c., the lands mentioned in the writ, and that he has by E. F. and G. H. given notice to the tenant to be before the justices at Westminster at the time and place in the writ mentioned (*o*). The names of the viewers and summoners ought to be returned by the sheriff, but if the tenant appears and pleads, the omission is not error (*p*).

(*g*) Roscoe, 165.

(*h*) See form, *post*, Append. chap. 14, s. 1.

(*i*) Dalt. 151, 153; Roscoe, 166. It is said by Lord Coke that the *pernors* were the *persons* who seized the land; Co. Litt. 259 b.

(*k*) Bract. 365 b.

(*l*) Roscoe, 166; Michell *v.* Hyde, 1 Leon. 92; and see Jenk. Cent. 122; Atkins *v.* Gage, Noy, 152; Keilw. 117 a.

(*m*) See *ante*, 337.

(*n*) Roscoe, 165; Bro. Ab. Grand cape, 29, 36; Booth, 22.

(*o*) See form, *post*, Append. c. 14, s. 1; and 2 Saund. 43, note.

(*p*) Bro. Abr. Retorn de Br. 86.

CHAP. XV.
SECT. II.

Section II.

Writ of View—Trial.

Writ of view.

By the writ of view the sheriff is commanded that he cause the tenant to have a view of the lands, &c. demanded, and that he appoint four knights of those present at the view to be before the justices at Westminster on the return day to testify such view, and that he have there the names of those knights and the writ, &c. (*q*). In what real actions a view may be demanded and will be granted, and when the demandant can counterplead the view, may be seen in Mr. Roscoe's Treatise on Actions relating to Real Property, page 247 to 253. When a view is demanded and granted, the demandant, to facilitate the proceedings, as the view is generally demanded for delay, may sue out the writ (*r*).

How executed.

The sheriff must give notice to the viewers (who need not really be knights) and to the tenant, of the time when the view will be given, which may be at any time before the return of the writ of view. It is the duty of the demandant to point out the lands to the sheriff, in order that the latter may show them to the party (*s*). It is recommended that the demandant's agent should serve the tenant or his attorney immediately with an appointment corresponding with the one made by the sheriff. The sheriff's summons should be served upon the tenant himself, if resident within the county, but if not, it can only be left upon the premises demanded, in which case the notice to the attorney will be requisite. The demandant must be able to point out with accuracy the land, &c., demanded, and in exact conformity with the writ (*t*).

In an action for rent, the land out of which it issues may be put in view (*u*). So in *quod permittat* of common appendant, a view may be had of the land in which the common is, and also of the land to which it is appendant (*x*); and so in a *quod permittat* of a way, a view may be had of a wall which obstructs the way, and of the way and of the land which is appendant (*y*); so also in a *curia claudenda* for not inclosing a house adjoining

(*q*) Roscoe, 253.
(*r*) *Ibid.*
(*s*) *Ibid.*
(*t*) 3 Chit. Plead. 643.
(*u*) Rol. Abr. View (Z), 2.
(*x*) Bro. Abr. View, 10.
(*y*) *Ibid.*; Brook *v.* Groves, Hutt. 28.

to the house of the plaintiff, the defendant shall have a view of both the houses (z). If land is demanded, and the view is granted, every part of the land shall be put in view; and so when the demand is of a house, every parcel of the house shall be viewed (a); but in making the view it is not necessary to show every acre, for the demandant may show the field, and say that he claims so many acres therein, and then another field, and so on (b). If the demand be of a moiety of a manor, the tenant shall have view of all the manor; but in making view of a manor, the site, with the appurtenances, shall be put in view, and not every parcel of the manor (c). In assize of an office, the place where it is exercised shall be put in view of the jury. Thus in assize of the office of one of the filacers of the Common Pleas, the place where the plaintiff sat when he was first admitted was put in view (d).

Return.

If the tenant or his agent attends, and the sheriff makes a view, the sheriff should return that he has caused the tenant to have a view of the lands, &c. demanded. If neither the tenant nor his agent attended to take the view, the sheriff should make his return accordingly (e). If the demandant did not come to show the lands, this will be a good return (f).

View by the jury.

In certain actions the jurors and not the tenant shall have the view. In such action the sheriff is by the writ commanded that he summon a jury to view the premises and to make recognition, &c. The sheriff accordingly issues his summons to the jurors, six of whom at least ought to view the land (g). The land is then shown to the jurors that attend.

The trial and jury process are the same in real actions as in personal actions in the Common Pleas, excepting in the writs of right.

Trial by the grand assize.

In a writ of right, when the mise is joined on the mere right, the trial must be by the grand assize, and not by a common jury.

(z) Rol. Abr. View (K).

(a) Rol. Abr. View (Z) 14; but see 1 Leon. 267.

(b) Roscoe, 254; Bro. Abr. View, 111.

(c) Roscoe, 254.

(d) Roscoe, 254; Dyer, 114 b; 2 Rol. Abr. 731, l. 14; Bro. Abr. Assize, 2.

(e) *Quære* whether it is sufficient to say that he did not attend at the time appointed. *Semble*, it is not sufficient. *Ante*, 343.

(f) By not attending, the tenant loses his view; if the demandant do not attend, an alias writ of view may be sued out; Roscoe, 254.

(g) Roscoe, 254, 255. The granting a view in waste is now regulated by 4 Anne, c. 16, s. 8, and 3 Geo. 2, c. 25, s. 14.

CHAP. XV. SECT. II.

Indeed in such case, even by consent, the court will not allow the right to be tried by a common jury (*h*). But when the mise is joined on any collateral point, the trial is by a common jury (*i*). The writ of right in either case may be tried at *nisi prius* (*k*). By the writ to summons the grand assize, the sheriff is commanded to assemble four good and lawful knights of his bailiwick, girt with swords, to be in court on a general return day; or if the trial is to be at *nisi prius*, in the alternative, that the knights should be before the justices, on, &c., or before the justices of assize, &c., if they shall first come to N., &c., to choose the grand assize (*l*).

The duty of the sheriff consists merely in summoning the four knights; nor is he obliged to do this before the commission day of the assizes, but may summon the knights from the grand jury at the assizes; having done this, his duty is at an end, for it is not part of the sheriff's duty to procure the knights to be sworn (*m*). If there be not four knights in the county, the sheriff may return others (*n*).

If the four knights, after being summoned, do not appear, the demandant may have a *habeas corpora quatuor militum* in the alternative (*o*). If the sheriff have not returned the writ, an alias may be issued (*p*). When the four knights appear, they are sworn lawfully and truly to choose twenty knights girt with swords, who best know and will declare and say the truth between the parties; these recognitors need not in fact be knights. It seems (*q*) that the four knights may be challenged; if one or two only be challenged, then the residue may proceed to name the recognitors; if these be challenged, a new writ must issue to choose four other knights. Out of themselves and the recognitors the four knights choose a jury, upon which a *venire facias* issues as in other actions (*r*).

(*h*) Galton *v.* Harvey, 1 Bos. & Pul. 192.

(*i*) Roscoe, 297.

(*k*) *Id. ibid.*; Penrose *v.* Maynard, 1 Taunt. 415; 2 Saund. 45, note.

(*l*) As to the form of the writ of summons where the trial is at *nisi prius*, see Roscoe, 297, 298.

(*m*) Windle *v.* Ricardo, 3 Moore, 249; 1 Brod. & Bing. 17, S. C.

(*n*) Co. Litt. 294 a. See 2 Saund. 45 i, note. Dyer, 247 b, margin. In a recent case of Angell *v.* Angell, Hil. 1826, it was objected that the four persons returned as knights were not in fact knights, and the qualification of persons to be returned was discussed.

(*o*) Dyer, 79 b, 104 a; 2 Saund. 45 k.

(*p*) Tyssen *v.* Clarke, 3 Wils. 562.

(*q*) Per Coke and Littleton, Js., 15 Edw. 4, 1; Co. Litt. 294 a, *contrà*; Roscoe, 299.

(*r*) See Roscoe, 298, 299. See as to the number of recognitors, *ibid.* 298, note (*g*).

Section III.

Execution.—Habere facias seisinam.

Execution in real actions.

The execution in most real actions is done by writ of *habere facias seisinam* (*s*), by which writ the sheriff is directed that he cause the demandant to have seisin of the lands which he has recovered. When the writ shows the certainty of the thing recovered, the demandant may, without executing a *hab. fac. seis.*, make an entry upon the lands recovered; and this entry will execute the judgment and vest the freehold in the demandant (*t*). So where the action is for the recovery of a rent or common, &c. in certainty, the demandant after judgment may distrain without issuing any writ of execution (*u*). Either within or after the year after judgment, the demandant may enter on the tenant (*x*), or his heir (*y*). If a stranger enters and dies seised, the demandant may enter within a year after judgment (*z*).

Hab. fac. seis. when necessary.

But where the certainty of the lands demanded does not appear, as in dower, the demandant cannot enter, but must sue out a *habere facias seisinam* (*a*). This writ may be taken out at any time within a year and a day after judgment; if the tenant die after judgment, execution may be sued against his heir, or against the issue in tail, whether the recovery be upon a real title (*b*), or by common recovery (*c*). So if the demandant die, his heir shall have execution (*d*).

The writ of *habere facias seisinam* is executed nearly in the same manner as the writ of *haberc facias possessionem:* in like manner as on a *hab. fac. poss.* the officer may break open the outer door of a house to deliver seisin to the demandant (*e*). Upon a *hab. fac. seis.*, the sheriff should give actual possession of the land to the tenant by turning the tenants off the premises (*f*). Where the writ requires the sheriff to deliver seisin

(*s*) Roscoe, 341; Co. Litt. 34 b; Com. Dig. Execution (A 1).

(*t*) Co. Litt. 34 b; Roscoe, 341.

(*u*) *Id. ibid.*; Com. Dig. Execution (A 1).

(*x*) Roll. Abr. Execution (B).

(*y*) *Id. ibid.* Although several descents have been cast in the blood of the tenant; *id. ibid*

(*z*) Rol. Abr. Execution (B); Com. Dig. Execution (A 1).

(*a*) Even where the delivery of seisin by the sheriff will not reduce the demand to a certainty, as where in dower a woman recovers against one of two tenants in common the third part of a moiety; Roscoe, 341.

(*b*) Roscoe, 342.

(*c*) *Id. ibid.*; Shelly's case, 1 Rep. 106 a; Co. Litt. 361 b; Dyer, 376 b.

(*d*) Com. Dig. Execution (E).

(*e*) Semayne's case, 5 Rep. 91 b.

(*f*) Gilb. Eject. 108, 2nd edit.; Upton *v.* Wells, 1 Leon. 145.

CHAP. XV. SECT. III.

of several messuages in the possession of the same person, it is sufficient if the sheriff delivers seisin of one in the name of all (*g*); but where the houses, &c. recovered are in the possession of several, it is not sufficient to deliver seisin of one in the name of all, but the sheriff ought to go to each in particular (*h*). It is in delivering seisin as in delivering possession, where the sheriff is to deliver seisin of so many acres, they shall be computed by the custom of the county and not by statute measure (*i*). Upon a *habere facias seisinam* in dower, if the sheriff offer to deliver seisin and show in certainty the parcels which make the third part by metes and bounds in severalty, the demandant, though she refuse such seisin, may afterwards enter (*k*). In dower, on a *hab. fac. seis.* against several purchasers, the court will order the sheriff to charge the purchasers proportionably (*l*).

Poundage return.

For executing a writ of *habere facias seisinam*, the sheriff we have seen (*m*), by the stat. 3 Geo. 1, c. 15, s. 16, is entitled to 1*s.* in the pound of the annual value of lands where the whole does not exceed 100*l.*; and 6*d.* in the pound for every 1*l. per annum* over and above the yearly value of 100*l.*

If the demandant has once had execution, he cannot afterwards have execution again; and therefore where the sheriff returns upon *hab. fac. seis.* execution done, an *alias hab. fac. seis.* cannot issue (*n*). So if the fee be executed in the ancestor, it shall never be executed again by the heir (*o*), or a fee tail by the issue in tail (*p*).

(*g*) Rol. Abr. Execution (H 1); Com. Dig. Execution (A 3); Floyd *v.* Bethel, 1 Rol. Rep. 421.

(*h*) Rol. Abr. Execution (H 2).

(*i*) Roll. Abr. Execution (H 7); 1 Rol. Rep. 421. *Sed vide* Dyer, 47 b, margin, *contrà*.

(*k*) Dyer, 278 b.

(*l*) 1 Freem. 227.

(*m*) *Ante*, .

(*n*) Com. Dig. Execution (A 3); Dyer, 278 b.

(*o*) Roll. Abr. Execution (F), 3, 4.

(*p*) *Id. Ibid.*

CHAPTER XVI.

OF THE EXCHEQUER WRITS.

Of the nature of the sheriff's office as collector of the revenue of the crown.

WE have seen that the sheriff, by virtue of his office, is the queen's bailiff, and receiver of the rents and debts of the crown within his bailiwick. By his oath of office, the sheriff swears "that he will promote her majesty's profit in all things that belong to the crown; that he will not assent to decrease, lessen, or conceal the queen's right, or the rights of her franchises; and whensoever he shall have knowledge that the rights of the crown be concealed or withdrawn, be it in lands, rents, franchises, suits, or services, or in any other matter or thing, he will do his utmost to make them be restored to the crown again; and if he

CHAP. XVI. SECT. I.

may not do it of himself, he will certify and inform some of her majesty's judges thereof."

Formerly the sheriff *ex officio* had the power to levy all the revenues of the crown without writ. This revenue is divided into fixed and casual (*a*); the former of these were called "viscontiels," and for the amount of these the sheriff was accountable to the exchequer, whether received by him or not (*b*); and by the statute of 1 Hen. 4, c. 11, it appears that the sheriffs were charged with the ancient farms of the counties, and that they fermed the counties; to this Dalton (*c*) attaches a *quære*, "what these farms of the counties were." It would seem that they were the fixed revenue of the crown, which the sheriff farmed for a certain sum, or accounted for as bailiff; but whether he accounted as bailiff or farmed, he was charged in the exchequer a sum certain for the viscontiels (*d*). These fixed revenues of the crown, or farms, or viscontiels were, 1st. The rents of the tenants of the demesnes of the king. 2nd. Gross ferms of lands, not parcel of the county, let to farm to cities, boroughs, or particular persons, or reserved after the ferm of the county was ascertained. 3rd. Common fines upon towns for *beaupleader*, for suit, ward, not attending the torn, &c., reduced to a certainty. 4th. *Arrentations* of *assarts* in wastes and forests, ascertained by justices in *Eyre*. 5th. *Crementum comitatûs*, or improvements of the king's rents, or other small rents thrown into the *corpus comitatûs* (*e*). The *casual* revenue, called *proficuum comitatûs*, consists of the fines, forfeited recognizances, and other debts due to the crown (*f*). And by the statute of 4 Hen. 5, c. 2, it was enacted, "that all sheriffs of England shall have allowance upon their accompts, by their oaths, of things casual, as of estreats that be not in ferm, nor in demand; but of all such things that be or run in yearly ferms, or yearly demands, they shall be charged to the king (*envers le roi*), as the sheriffs have been charged in that case in times past."

By the statute of the 27 Edw. 1, c. 2, it was ordained "that sheriffs shall not be charged of any issues to be levied, nor shall

(*a*) Hale's Sher. Acc. 34; Dalt. 48, 49.

(*b*) Dalt. 49, 59.

(*c*) Dalt. 48.

(*d*) See Gilb. Exch. 76 *et seq.*; Hale's Sher. Acc.; stat. 4 Hen. 5, c. 2; Dalt. 49.

(*e*) Com. Dig. Viscount (G 1); Gilb. Exch. 86; Dalt. c. 8 and 9.

(*f*) Gilb. Exch. 98; Com. Dig. Viscount (G 1).

levy any before they pass out of the exchequer, there to be delivered by the estreats of the justices." Fines, debts due on estreated recognizances, or otherwise due to the crown, could not be levied by the sheriff without a writ from the Court of Exchequer for that purpose(*g*). In a recent case(*h*), the propriety of the sheriff's levying fines by obtaining a writ of *levari facias*, without the prior sanction of the law officers of the crown, was discussed, and it was decided that the solicitor-general having subsequently adopted the acts of the sheriff, the issuing of, and the levy by virtue of, the *levari facias* were not irregular; and Holroyd, J., there said, "The sheriff is the king's officer, and it is his particular duty to take care of the king's revenue, and amongst other sources of it, the fines due to the crown. The sheriff in this case was justified in suing out the process of the court, in order to enable him to levy the fine upon the property of the person convicted." Sufficient has been here stated to show the nature of the sheriff's duty as collector of the king's revenue. To the historian or the antiquarian, the authorities in the margin (*i*) will yield the only information to be met with on this subject; from these the author of this work has collated the short account thereof above given.

It is to be observed, however, that by the statute referred to in a former part of this work (*j*), the 3 & 4 Will. 4, c. 99, s. 12, it has been enacted, (after reciting "that the present mode of managing and collecting certain quit rents and vicecomital or viscontiel rents due to his majesty, and the present mode of accounting for and paying post fines on alienation of lands and other hereditaments, have been found disadvantageous to the public service, and inconvenient and troublesome to sheriffs"), that after the 10th October, 1833, no sheriff shall receive or be chargeable with the collection and receipt of quit rents, vicecomital or viscontiel rents, and other rents or payments issuing out of or payable to his majesty, in respect of any honours, manors, lands, tenements, or hereditaments in England or Wales; but the same (except such as shall be released pursuant to the provision next hereinafter contained) shall hereafter be considered as part and parcel of the land revenue of the crown, and shall be under the care,

(*g*) Dalt. 58.

(*h*) Rex *v.* Woolfe, 1 Chit. Rep. 583.

(*i*) Dalt. Sher. c. 5 to c. 19; Hale's Sher. Acc.; Gilb. Exch. 76 *et seq.*; Madd. Exch.

(*j*) *Ante*, p. 15.

CHAP. XVI. SECT. I.

management, and direction of his majesty's Commissioners of Woods, Forests, and Land Revenues, who shall have and exercise the same powers and authorities for collecting and enforcing the payment thereof as are given to or vested in them for collecting and enforcing the payment of any other part of his majesty's land revenue by any act or acts now in force concerning the same. The 13th section then, after reciting that many of the said rents are very ancient, and have become obsolete, and it is not known out of or from what hereditaments and premises the same are issuing and payable, so that payment thereof cannot be enforced, empowers the Commissioners of the Treasury, by warrant under their hands, to remit, release, and discharge all or any of the same rents, and the arrears thereof, or any part thereof.

The common process issuing out of the Exchequer.

There are certain crown processes, which have issued for ages, and still issue twice a year to the sheriff of each county, to collect the crown debts; there also issue the summons of the pipe, and also the summons of the green wax, to the sheriff to appear in the Exchequer before the chancellor and barons on a day prefixed, to have the monies collected.

The different writs.

These crown processes, which issue to the sheriff immediately on his entrance into office, are, 1st. The great roll of the pipe. 2ndly. The summons of the pipe. 3rdly. The summons of the green wax. 4thly. A process to levy on clergymen by name for arrears of tenths or first fruits. 5thly. A process, called the *mortuus* process, against the executors and administrators of deceased clergymen. It may be necessary to describe the nature of these several writs, and the manner in which they are to be executed.

The great roll.

The great roll, or long writ, is in the nature of an extent, to levy various sums from the persons mentioned in the schedule. These are sums due on estreated recognizances (*k*), for fines set on jurors, and various other sums particularly specified. A great proportion of the sums in the long writ have been due, and

(*k*) By stat. 3 Geo. 4, c. 46, and 4 Geo. 4, c. 37, it is enacted, that after forfeited recognizances taken before justices of the peace or sessions and fines there taken have been testified to the clerk of the peace, the quarter sessions may issue process to levy the same. The Court of Exchequer, when such recognizances are estreated there, has lost its jurisdiction by those statutes; Rex *v.* Hankin, 1 M'Clel. & Younge, 27; but see Ex parte Pellow, 1 M'Clel. 111.

inserted in the great roll to each succeeding sheriff, for many years, although regularly year after year *nihilled*. On this the sheriff is to levy as much as he can, and therefore on all the rolls for a few years back he should send warrants to bailiffs, directing them at the same time to make every exertion to levy what they can. The sheriff should likewise keep an account of all the warrants that he has issued, to be prepared to answer on his apposals according to the bailiff's return: and therefore he should issue warrants on the rolls as far back as he is likely to be examined. The under-sheriff summons a jury to inquire whether any of the persons in the schedule of the great roll have any goods, chattels, lands, and tenements, whereof the debts charged could be levied. This inquisition (*l*) is a mere matter of form, as no evidence whatsoever is produced before it; indeed, it is said that the under-sheriff sometimes returns the inquisition without calling the jury together. And this inquisition, together with the return, will be a discharge to the sheriff on the great roll.

The summons of the pipe.

The summons of the pipe contains merely an account of the fee-farm rents due to the crown within the sheriff's bailiwick, and for which he is answerable. For all the rents in this roll the sheriff is answerable in his accounts to the crown, whether he can levy them or not; the sheriff cannot *nihil* any of these rents, although in many instances there is no such rent due to the crown. The sheriff sends his warrants (*m*) to bailiffs to levy these rents. The process is sent back with the other processes, but the sheriff makes no return to it. In his accounts he answers for all these rents. The under-sheriff should, in his book of accounts on the crown process, enter all the sums in the summons of the pipe.

Summons of the green wax.

The summons of the green wax is a process to levy estreats and other debts of late date (*n*), also *post* fines, or fines in the Common Pleas. The sheriff made his warrant hereon as on the last process, but he made no return thereto. He kept a copy in his book of accounts, and either totted or *nihilled* the estreats, &c.; but he totted the *post* fines, although never received by him; however, they were allowed him in some way in the ex-

(*l*) See Return and Inquisition, *post*, Append. c. 15, s. 1.

(*m*) See Warrant, *post*, Appendix, c. 15, s. 1.

(*n*) These, if not levied, are afterwards put upon the great roll.

CHAP. XVI. SECT. I.

chequer. All the sums *nihilled* on the summons of the green wax were generally carried in the succeeding year upon the great roll (*o*). However, since the 3 & 4 Will. 4, c. 99, s. 15, the sheriffs of England and Wales (excepting in the county palatine of Lancaster) are no longer chargeable with any fines called *pre* fines or *post* fines, which are to be received by the receiver-general of alienation fines at the alienation office, and paid and applied by him as therein mentioned.

Fieri facias against clergymen for tenths.

This process is executed in the same manner as any other writ of *fieri facias;* but the parties, for the most part, pay the sum on demand.

Process against the representatives of deceased clergymen.

This is executed in the same manner as the last; but on this process there are debts against clergymen who have been dead a hundred years and more. The sheriff holds an inquisition as on the long writ (*p*), for the purpose of his discharge on his accounts as to the charges that are hopeless.

Distringas against collectors, &c.

The above are the *ordinary* exchequer processes, which are invariably sent to the sheriff of each county; besides these, there are processes which the sheriff generally receives against collectors and receivers of the revenue, and against parishes, and also writs of *scire facias* on port bonds. These are, 1st, *Distringas* against collectors for arrears of taxes; 2ndly, *Distringas* against inhabitants of parishes for arrears of taxes; 3rdly, *Distringas* against persons who are accountants of the crown, or against their executors, for taxes or money imprest, viz. receivers-general, agents, paymasters, &c.; 4thly, In the coast counties, writs of *scire facias* against persons who have entered into bonds, generally called port bonds.

Distringas against collectors.

If the collector is to be found, and has received the *insuper*, or is likely to receive it before the time fixed for the sheriff's apposal, he should be called upon to pay it; and if he pay it, or be a responsible person, it is usual to return that he has received the money; but if the solvency of the collector be doubtful, and he has received the *insuper*, strictly speaking, the sheriff should distrain, and return large issues. Although the sheriff on all these writs is ordered that "he should distrain all and every the goods and chattels, &c., so that nobody intermeddle, &c.," yet it is his duty to levy, indeed by his oath he can only levy, reasonable issues: one shilling in the pound is com-

(*o*) Gilb. Exch. 108.

(*p*) See form, *post*, Appendix, c. 15, s. 1.

monly the amount of the issues distrained for. But if the sheriff is not informed that the *insuper* has been received by the collector, or the collector is not to be found, he should return *nihil* (*q*); indeed, this writ is used as the first process against parishes; as they are answerable for collectors, the *distringas* against the parish only issues on a return of the *nihil* against the collector; and as long as the sheriff returns issues on the *distringas* against the collector, the process cannot issue against the parish.

Distringas against parishes.

If the parishes pay the *insuper* to the sheriff, which, generally speaking, they do, the sheriff should make his return accordingly, and thereupon a record of payment is made and drawn down on the pipe to be set against the sheriff. If the sheriff cannot obtain payment from the parish, he should distrain, and return issues to the value of one shilling in the pound (*r*).

Distringas against accountants, &c.

Issues to the amount of one shilling in the pound, that is to say, *reasonable* issues, should be distrained and returned on this writ. If the person mentioned in the schedule, after due diligence, cannot be found, the sheriff should return *nihil*, at the same time he should use due diligence in trying to discover all persons named in the schedule (*s*).

Scire facias on port bonds.

The sheriff should direct his warrant to two bailiffs to give notice to the parties to appear to show cause, &c., according to the terms of the writ. The bailiffs should make a regular return to the sheriff either that they have given notice to the defendant, or that they could not do it. In conformity to the answer of his bailiffs the sheriff makes his return to the court (*t*).

Having now treated of these regular processes to the sheriff from the exchequer, the execution of which is well known to the professional men in all counties, we proceed to a more detailed notice of the writ of extent.

SECTION II.

Of Extents.

Of the nature of the writ.

The writ of extent is a writ of execution against the *body*, *lands*, *and goods*, or the *lands and goods*, of the crown debtor.

(*q*) See Return, *post*, Appendix, c. 15, s. 1.

(*r*) *Id. ibid.*

(*s*) See Return, *post*, Appendix, c. 15, s. 1.

(*t*) *Id. ibid.*

CHAP. XVI. SECT. II.

It is an ancient prerogative writ for obtaining satisfaction of debts originally due or assigned to the queen, or found due to the queen on an inquisition (*a*). Until the statute 33 Hen. 8, c. 39, ss. 50, 55, the extent could not have issued to take the lands in the first instance, but only upon the contingency of there not being sufficient chattels of the defendant to satisfy the debt; for by *Magna Charta* (*b*), the king and his bailiffs were restrained from seizing any land or rent for any debt, as long as the present chattels were sufficient to pay the debt. It was formerly usual to issue an extent to levy on the lands of the debtor, provided the chattels were not sufficient: this writ is said by Lord Coke (*c*) to have been introduced after the statute of Hen. 8; but it is the opinion of Chief Baron Gilbert that it was used before that statute (*d*); which would seem to be the better opinion, as the writ in that form seems to have been framed precisely to meet the prohibition in *Magna Charta*. However, since the statute of Hen. 8, the practice has been to issue the writ of extent, to levy the debt on the body, lands, and chattels of the crown debtor absolutely, without any previous inquisition touching the goods (*e*). But it would appear that a writ of extent against the *land only* of the crown debtor, before it appears by record that there are no chattels to satisfy the debt, is irregular (*f*).

Of the different kinds of extents.

In what cases the courts will, and in what they will not, grant a writ of extent, and the practice of the Court of Exchequer in granting the writ, are matters which do not belong to a treatise on the duty of the sheriff in executing it; for if the writ be

(*a*) The writ against the lands of an heir, on a judgment obtained against him on the bond of his ancestor, and the writs of execution on a statute staple or merchant, are also called extents. The word extent strictly refers to land only; Palmer's case, 4 Rep. 74. The first mention of it to be found is in the statute of *elegit*, 13 Edw. 1, (Westm. 2), c. 18, and the stat. 13 Edw. 1, stat. de Merc. (Westm. 1). The crown cannot recover a debt of record by an information in the nature of a popular action of debt, but only by extent, *scire facias*, or by filing an information on the record itself; Att.-Gen. *v.* Sewell, 4 M. & W. 77.

(*b*) At common law, before *Magna Charta*, the body, lands, and goods of the king's debtor were *liable* to the king's execution; but see West on Extents, chap. 1.

(*c*) 2 Inst. 19; West, 76.

(*d*) Gilb. Exchequer, 127, 128; West, 79.

(*e*) West, 73, 80.

(*f*) Rex *v.* Lambe, M'Clel. 402, 416. On an extent against both lands and goods, where the goods seized are sufficient to satisfy the debt, the court will not make an order for the sale of the lands; Rex *v.* Hopper, 3 Price, 40; West, 187, 225, S. C. Indeed in such case the lands should not be seized by the sheriff; West, 79.

issued to the sheriff, he is bound to obey it, provided the court from which it issued had jurisdiction, without questioning the regularity of the proceedings (*g*); it may suffice, therefore, to notice shortly the different kinds of extent.

Writs of extent are of two kinds: extents in *chief*, or in *aid*. An extent in chief is an adverse proceeding by the queen for the recovery of her own debt; an extent in aid is sued out at the instance and for the benefit of the debtor to the crown, or his surety, for the recovery of a debt due to himself (*h*). A crown debtor is not entitled to use the prerogative process against his own debtor after he has paid his debt to the crown, or after his debtor has become discharged by the insolvent act, or the like (*i*). In case of the death of the crown debtor, whenever an extent might have issued against the queen's debtor in his lifetime, a writ of *diem clausit extremum*, which is an extent against his lands and chattels, may issue after his death (*j*). But no *diem clausit extremum* can regularly issue against the estate of any person who was not a debtor to the crown, or found in his lifetime to be a debtor to the queen's debtor (*k*). An extent may issue for the queen as well for debts of record as debts not of record. Debts of record are founded on judgments, or recognizances, or inquisitions, taken and returned on commission issuing out of the Court of Exchequer (*l*): debts not of record are on bonds, or simple contracts; which latter are either due from the known officers and accountants to the queen, or from third persons (*m*).

(*g*) See Rex *v.* Shackell and others, M'Clel. & Younge, 514.

(*h*) Rex *v.* Shackle, 11 Price, 772. See 57 Geo. 3, c. 117, for regulating the granting of extents in aid; and see Tidd's Prac. 8th edit. 110 *et seq.* This statute does not apply to extents in chief in the second degree; Rex *v.* Shackle, *supra*. The crown, therefore, may proceed by extent to recover a debt due from a person indebted to a crown debtor who has received and misapplied the crown money, although he be not a debtor to the crown within the 4th section of that statute; *ibid.*

(*i*) Rex *v.* Bingham, 1 C. & J. 131; 1 C. & M. 862.

(*j*) Bunb. 119.

(*k*) Rex *v.* The Estate of H. Boon, Parker, 16. But a *diem clausit extremum* may issue if the debt were really due on simple contract, although not found by commission till after the death of the debtor; Rex *v.* Estate of Curtis, Parker, 95.

(*l*) As to which, see Reg. *v.* Ryle, 9 M. & W. 227; Dean *v.* Reg., 15 M. & W. 475.

(*m*) When by the inquisition on an extent debts are found and seized into the queen's hands, the crown, on an affidavit of danger, and a baron's fiat, may proceed by an immediate extent for their recovery, which is called an extent in the *second degree*. So where debts are found on an extent in the second degree, on an affidavit of dan-

CHAP. XVI. SECT. II.

Of the form of the extent.

The writ of extent issues out of the equity side of the Court of Exchequer, (which for the purposes of its revenue jurisdiction still subsists, notwithstanding stat. 5 Vict. c. 5) (*n*), and after particularly reciting the debt due to the crown, commands the sheriff, to whom it is directed, to omit not by reason of any liberty, but to enter the same and take the defendant; and to inquire by a jury what lands and tenements, and of what yearly value, the defendant had on the day when he first became debtor to the crown, or at any time since, (or in the case of a simple contract debt, what lands, &c., he now hath), and what goods and chattels, and of what sorts and prices, and what debts, credits, specialties, and sums of money, the defendant, or any *person in trust for him or to his use*, hath in his bailiwick, and to appraise and extend all and singular the said goods and chattels, lands, tenements, debts, &c., and to take and seize the same into the queen's hands. The sheriff is also thereby directed to summon before him such persons as he shall think proper, to examine them in the premises, and to return the writ to the court, with a proviso that he do not sell the goods and chattels till he shall be otherwise commanded. The writ of extent cannot be antedated (*o*), but should bear teste on the day it issues, though in vacation; for it issues out of the equity side of the Exchequer, which is always open (*p*). The writ is returnable on a general return day. The writ of extent is granted upon the fiat of a baron, and is tested by the chief baron, signed by the queen's remembrancer, and sealed with the exchequer seal (*q*). And to prevent *extents in aid* being issued for larger or greater sums of money than are really due, by the 57 Geo. 3, c. 117, s. 1, 2, it is enacted, " that upon the issuing of every extent in aid on behalf of any debtor to his majesty, his majesty's Court of Exchequer at Westminster, or the chancellor of his majesty's exchequer, or lord chief baron or other baron of the said court,

ger, and a baron's *fiat*, the crown may have an extent in the *third degree* for their recovery. It seems that on an extent in *chief*, the crown may seize debts found to be due to its debtor, &c., *in infinitum*; Bunb. 303; and see Gilb. Excheq. 177. But on an *extent in aid* debts cannot be seized beyond the third degree, counting the queen's debtor as one of the degrees; Ewins's case, Parker, 259, 260; West, 303.

(*n*) Attorney-General *v.* Halling, 15 M. & W.

(*o*) Rex *v.* Rawlings, 2 C. M. & R. 471; 4 Dowl. 407.

(*p*) Rex *v.* Mann, 2 Stra. 749; Bunb. 164, S. C.; Gilb. Rep. 222; Rex *v.* Maberley, 3 Dowl. 383.

(*q*) West, 56.

granting the fiat for the issuing of such extent in aid, shall cause the amount of the debt or sum of money due or claimed to be due to his majesty, to be stated and specified in the said *fiat;* and that in all cases in which the debt or debts found due to the debtor to his majesty shall be equal to or exceed the debt stated and specified in the said *fiat* as aforesaid, *the amount of the debt so stated and specified in the said fiat* shall be indorsed upon the writ; and the writ so indorsed shall be deemed to be and be the authority and direction to the sheriff or other officer who shall execute such writ in making his levy and executing the same as to the amount to be levied and to be taken under the said writ: and that in all cases in which the debt or debts found due to the debtor to his majesty shall be of less amount than the debt stated and specified in the said *fiat* as aforesaid, the amount of such debt or debts found due to such debtor to his majesty shall be indorsed upon the writ, and the writ so indorsed shall be deemed to be and be the authority and direction to the sheriff or other officer who shall execute the said writ in making his levy and executing the same as to the amount to be levied and taken under the said writ."

Warrant.

A warrant should be made under the seal of the sheriff to an officer, to take the defendant and seize his goods according to the exigency of the writ (*r*); the usual fee allowed for such warrant is five shillings.

An outer door may be broken open to execute an extent.

The officer may break open the outer door of a dwelling house if not opened on request, for the purpose of arresting the defendant or of seizing his goods, by virtue of a writ of extent at the suit of the crown (*s*); and, of course, admittance being obtained at the outer door, for the like purposes an inner door may be broken open, even without a previous request of admittance (*t*). As the writ of extent contains a *non omittas* clause, the sheriff may enter a liberty to execute it (*u*), consequently he should not direct a mandate to the bailiff of the liberty to execute it, although the defendant, his lands and goods be entirely within a liberty.

Sheriff's duty on taking the body of the defendant.

With respect to the duty of the sheriff in taking the body of the defendant on an extent, he should be taken if found, although

(*r*) See form, *post*, Append. c. 15, s. 2.

(*s*) Semayne's case, 5 Rep. 92; Godb. 297.

(*t*) Hutchinson *v.* Birch, 4 Taunt. 619.

(*u*) See *ante*, 58.

CHAP. XVI. SECT. II.

there may be goods and lands sufficient to satisfy the crown debt. A defendant taken on an extent cannot be admitted to bail by the sheriff, the extent being an execution and not mesne process, and the statute 23 Hen. 6, c. 9, does not extend to the crown. It is clear that a person who has become bankrupt and obtained his certificate, or been discharged under an insolvent act, subsequent to the accruing of the crown debt, is not privileged from arrest even on an extent in aid; for the crown is not bound by the Bankrupt Act, not being specially mentioned therein (*x*). So it has been held that a bankrupt may be arrested on an extent during his privilege (*y*). But where a bankrupt was arrested on a writ of extent, while actually attending to give evidence before commissioners of bankrupt, the chancellor discharged him, as being privileged from arrest at common law (*z*). It seems to have been doubted whether the defendant could be in custody at the suit of a subject at the same time that he was in custody at the suit of the crown, as it is said by Dyer, C. J., "The queen hath not an equal in her kingdom to have interest in the body of her prisoner together with her (*a*)." But it is now clear that if a defendant be in execution at the suit of a subject, and he be afterwards charged in execution with an extent, he is in custody as well at the suit of the subject as at the suit of the crown (*b*).

In seizing the defendant's goods.

The duty of the sheriff on the extent is to seize all the goods and chattels of the defendant, and therefore he must issue his

(*x*) Rex *v.* Pixley, Bunb. 202; Anon. 1 Atk. 262; and see 8 Price, 671.

(*y*) Ex parte Temple, 2 Rose, 22.

(*z*) Ex parte Russel, 1 Rose, 273; see also West, 95.

(*a*) Dyer, 297, pl. 24.

(*b*) Stevenson's case, Cro. Car. 389; Savile, 29; Lord Dacre *v.* Lassels, Dyer, 197, pl. 44. When the crown is concerned, the courts will not in general change the custody of a defendant, in order that he may be charged with a civil suit, or rendered in discharge of his bail, without the consent of the Attorney-General; Tidd's Prac. 289, 8th edit.; West, 90, 91, 92, 95. In Hodgson *v.* Temple, 5 Taunt. 503; 1 Marsh. 166, S. C., where a defendant was held to bail in a civil action, after which he was taken into custody by the sheriff on an extent: on an application on behalf of the bail for relief, it was held, 1st, That the bail were not entitled to have an *exoneretur* entered on the bail piece; 2d, That the crown having refused its consent to the defendant's being surrendered, unless he should immediately be remanded to the custody of the marshal, that court had no authority so to remand him, after he had been rendered to the warden of the Fleet: And 3d, That the bail could not surrender the defendant by *habeas corpus* as a matter of right without the consent of the crown; but the court offered to give the bail time for rendering the defendant. See observations on this decision, West, 91, 92 *et seq.*

warrant to an officer to execute this part of the writ; the seizure of the goods by virtue of an extent is a seizure in *fact*, and not a mere seizure in *law*, as in seizing the debts of the defendant by virtue of an extent. The writ of extent only authorizes the sheriff to *seize* the goods of the defendant into his hands, but expressly directs him *not to sell* them until further commanded. Whatever, therefore, under the denomination of goods and chattels, may be taken under a writ of *fieri facias*, may be taken under an extent (*c*). Money also, even before the statute 1 & 2 Vict. c. 110, might be taken on an extent (*d*). A term of years may be either appraised as a chattel, or extended as land under the extent (*e*). Goods held by another in trust for the defendant may be taken on the extent (*f*); but goods pawned or pledged, or demised or letten, prior to the teste of the extent, for a term certain, during the term, or whereon a third person has a lien, cannot be taken on an extent, although it seems on satisfaction of the pledge or lien they may be taken (*g*). Upon an extent against one partner, the crown may *seize* the property of the partnership, but the crown can only *sell* the interest of the partner against whom the extent issues, which is his share of the surplus after payment of the partnership debts (*h*). The goods which the crown debtor has in *autre droit*, as executor or administrator, cannot be taken on an extent against him in his own right (*i*). It is said that cattle *levant and couchant*, or other goods of a third person on the lands of a defendant, may be taken for the queen's debt, but it is apprehended that this is not correct, if it be meant that they can be taken on an extent as goods and chattels; it is however true, that cattle of a stranger *levant and couchant* on the land of the defendant may be taken on a *levari facias*, for such cattle are considered to be the profits of the land (*k*).

(*c*) See *ante*, c. 10, s. 2 and 3. In 2 Roll. Abr. 160, l. 5, it is said that all the goods and chattels of the defendant may be taken, *excepting necessary victuals for the defendant and his family, and oxen and beasts of the plough.*

(*d*) West, 172.

(*e*) Sir Gerard Fleetwood's case, 8 Rep. 171.

(*f*) This clause was first inserted by order of the court, 1712; West, 116.

(*g*) Bro. Abr. Pledges, 28; King *v.* Humphreys, 1 M'Clel. & Yo. 173; see West, 116.

(*h*) Rex *v.* Sanderson, 1 Wightwick, 51.

(*i*) 2 Roll. Abr. 159, l. 49.

(*k*) Stafford *v.* Bateman, Roll. Abr. 159; Cro. Eliz. 431, S. C.; Britton *v.* Cole, 1 Lord Raym. 305; Salk. 395, S. C.; Carth. 441; 5 Mod. 112.

CHAP. XVI. SECT. II.

Goods from what time bound on a writ of extent.

As executions at the suit of the crown are not particularly mentioned in the Statute of Frauds, the goods of the defendant, as upon executions at the suit of the subject at the common law, are bound from the *teste* of the writ of extent (*l*). That is, notwithstanding any sale or assignment by the defendant of his goods, even in market overt (*m*), after the *teste* of the writ of extent, such goods may be taken by the sheriff on an extent. But goods *bonâ fide* assigned, sold, or pawned, *before the teste of* the extent, cannot be seized by virtue of such extent (*n*).

Priority in favour of execution at the suit of the crown.

When the crown had commenced proceedings first.

By the statute 33 Hen. 8, c. 39, s. 74, it is enacted, that "if any suit be commenced or taken, or any process be hereafter awarded for the king, for the recovery of any of the king's debts, then the same suit and process shall be preferred before the suit of any person or persons. And that our said sovereign lord, his heirs and successors, shall have first execution against any defendant or defendants of and for his said debts before any other person or persons; *so always that the king's said suit be taken and commenced, or process awarded* for the said debt, at the suit of our said sovereign lord the king, his heirs or successors, *before judgment* given *for the said other person or persons*." On this clause of the statute it has long been settled law, that if the crown suit be commenced, or the fiat for the extent be made, before the judgment be given for the subject, the execution for the crown is to be preferred (*o*).

When the *fi. fa.* is delivered before the teste of the extent.

As between the crown and a subject, when the judgment of the subject is prior to the commencement of the crown suit, the law was not so clearly settled. Where goods are taken on a *fi. fa.* and remain in the hands of the sheriff unsold at the time when a writ of extent, bearing teste prior to the delivery of the *fi. fa.*, is delivered to him, the extent shall be preferred; so where the extent is tested on the same day that the *fi. fa.* was delivered to the sheriff, the extent shall be preferred, although the extent was tested on a later period of the day than the issuing of the *fi. fa.* (*p*), for as between the crown and the subject the law does not take notice of the fraction of a day. But it long remained

(*l*) Reg. *v.* Arnold, 7 Viner, 105. See also Sir Gerard Fleetwood's case, 8 Rep. 171 a; Parker, 103.

(*m*) Property in goods is not altered as against the crown by sale in market overt; 2 Inst. 713; 35 Hen. 6, p. 29; West, 96.

(*n*) West, 97.

(*o*) Butler *v.* Butler, 1 East, 340; Rex *v.* Aldersey, cit. 1 East, 341.

(*p*) Rex *v.* Crump and Hanbury, Parker, 126; Rex *v.* Earl, Bunb. 33.

a doubtful point whether, when a sheriff had seized goods on a *fi. fa.*, which remained in his hands unsold, and an extent tested subsequently to the delivery of the *fi. fa.* was delivered to the sheriff, the crown or the execution creditor should have the preference. It was decided both in K. B. (*q*) and C. P (*r*) that in such case the subject should be preferred. In the case of Rex *v.* Wells and Allnutt (*s*), and the subsequent one of Rex *v.* Sloper and Allen (*t*), the Court of Exchequer came to a different determination, *viz.* that in such case the crown was to be preferred. The same question was agitated in an action for money had and received, brought by the party at whose suit the *fi. fa.* issued against the sheriff, who had paid over the money to the crown, and was then much argued in the Court of King's Bench, but the case ultimately turned upon the form of the action being incorrect (*u*). At length, however, it was solemnly decided by the House of Lords, in affirmance of the successive judgments of the Court of Common Pleas and of the Exchequer Chamber, that where the sheriff seized the goods of a debtor under a *fi. fa.*, and whilst they remained in his hands unsold an extent in chief, tested *after the seizure*, was delivered to the sheriff, the goods might be seized and sold under the extent, without regard to the writ of *fi. fa.*; and further, that it made no difference in this respect whether the extent was in chief or in aid (*x*). The effect of the stat. 33 Hen. 8, c. 39, is thus stated in that case by Lord Tenterden:—"I am of opinion that the true effect of that statute is to allow the subject to obtain judgment, and even to sue out execution, without first rendering satisfaction to the king; but nevertheless to leave the law in all other respects as it stood before, namely, if the king's execution comes while the goods remain *the property of the debtor* (*y*), the king's execution shall prevail." The course to be pursued by the sheriff is

(*q*) Rorke *v.* Dayrell, 4 T. R. 413. Lord Kenyon's ground taken there, that the *property* in the goods is altered by the seizure under the *fi. fa.*, is now abandoned. See Giles *v.* Grover, *infra*, n. (*x*).

(*r*) Uppon *v.* Sumner, 2 Bla. Rep. 1251.

(*s*) 16 East, 278, in notes.

(*t*) 6 Price, 114. See also Rex *v.* Osbourne, 6 Price, 94; Rex. *v.* Giles, 8 Price, 293.

(*u*) Thurston *v.* Mills, 16 East, 254.

(*x*) Giles *v.* Grover, 1 Clark & Finnelly, 72; 9 Bing. 128, S. C.; 2 M. & Scott, 197. See also Stringefellow *v.* Brownesoppe, Dyer, 67 b; Rex *v.* Beck, Bunb. 8; and dicta in Attorney-General *v.* Capel, 2 Show. 480; Smallcomb *v.* Buckingham, 5 Mod. 376; Rex *v.* Cotton, Parker, 112.

(*y*) See *ante*, 246.

CHAP. XVI. SECT. II.

clear; for where an extent is delivered to the sheriff whilst he has goods in his hands taken by him on a *fi. fa.*, which has been delivered to him prior to the teste of the extent, he should refuse to proceed to sale without an indemnity from the plaintiff; if that be refused, the sheriff, when ruled to return the writ, should apply for further time to make his return, which the court will grant on an affidavit of the circumstances (*z*). But if the goods have been sold under the *fi. fa.* before the teste of the extent, the proceeds in the sheriff's hands shall be applicable to the *fi. fa.*, and not to the extent (*a*).

Goods distrained for rent, &c.

Goods which have been distrained for rent before the teste of the extent, but not sold, may be seized under the extent (*b*). Nor is the landlord in such case entitled to a year's rent under the statute 8 Anne, c. 14, s. 1. For by the eighth section of that act it is provided, that "nothing in that act contained shall extend or be construed to extend to let, hinder or prejudice her majesty, her heirs or successors, in the levying, recovering or seizing any debts, fines, penalties or forfeitures that are or shall be due, payable or answerable to her majesty, her heirs or successors; but that it shall and may be lawful for her majesty, her heirs and successors, to levy, recover, and seize such debts, fines, penalties and forfeitures in the same manner as if that act had never been made; any thing in the act contained to the contrary thereof in anywise notwithstanding (*c*)."

When the defendant has become bankrupt.

Goods of a bankrupt may be taken under an extent, the teste of which is previous to the appointment of assignees; for the queen is not bound by the acts relating to bankrupts, (not being named therein,) and before the appointment of assignees, the commissioners have but a power (*d*). But if the goods are vested in the assignees previous to the teste of the writ, they cannot be taken on the extent, because then the property is

(*z*) Wells *v.* Pickman, 7 T. R. 174; Thurston *v.* Thurston, 1 Taunt. 120; In cases like these, the sheriff should get the jury to find the fact specially, as was done in Rex *v.* Cotton, Parker, 112; and Rex. *v.* Wells and Allnutt, 16 East, 281. But the facts must be found so that some certain traverse may be taken on the inquisition; Rex *v.* Sherwood, West, 114.

(*a*) Swain *v.* Morland, 1 Brod. & Bing. 370; 3 Moore, 740, S. C. See also Payne *v.* Drewe, 4 East, 540; Rex *v.* Sloper, 6 Price, 114.

(*b*) Rex *v.* Cotton, Parker, 112; and see West, 101.

(*c*) See Rex *v.* Pritchard, Bunb. 269.

(*d*) Awdley *v.* Halsey, Sir W, Jones, 202; Parker, 127; Brassey *v.* Dawson, 2 Stra. 978.

absolutely transferred (*e*). If the appointment of assignees and the teste of the extent be on the same day, the queen's prerogative shall prevail (*f*).

Goods assigned to creditors.

Goods assigned by the defendant before the teste of the extent, in trust for creditors, if the assignment be not fraudulent, cannot be taken on an extent, even though the defendant were a trader within the bankrupt laws, and the assignment be an act of bankruptcy, and void as against his assignees (*g*). But goods fraudulently conveyed away before the teste of the extent to defeat the execution, may be taken as well under an extent as under a *fi. fa.* (*h*). The lien of an agent or factor of the crown debtor on goods of his in the factor's hands, for bills of exchange accepted by him to the amount of the value of the goods, will prevail against the right of the crown on an extent tested after the goods came into the factor's hands (*i*).

Priority between several writs of extent.

As to *priority between several writs of extent.* Extents in chief take place *inter se* according to their teste. An extent in chief, finding the same goods found upon a former extent in aid, shall be preferred and paid before it (*k*). So after the sale of goods on an extent in aid, and before the payment over of the money, if an extent in chief come, and the same goods be found in the inquisition, the extent in chief shall be preferred (*l*). If goods are found on an extent in aid, and then an extent in chief comes, on which goods are found, but not the same that were found on the extent in aid, as to which no evidence is offered, nor is it insisted that they should be found; and then another extent in chief comes, and the party prosecuting it offers to find what was seized in aid, and is refused: the court will order a new extent of the like teste as the second extent in chief, and refuse it to the first extent in chief (*m*).

(*e*) Rex *v.* Marsh, M'Clel. & Younge, 250; Rex *v.* Crump and Hanbury, Parker, 126; 1 Atk. 95.

(*f*) Rex *v.* Earl, Bunb. 33.

(*g*) Rex *v.* Watson, West, 115.

(*h*) West, 115.

(*i*) Rex *v.* Lee, 6 Price, 369. See Rex *v.* Cuther, Parker, 118.

(*k*) Reg. *v.* Quash, Parker, 281; Rex *v.* Larking, 8 Price, 683.

(*l*) Parker, 282.

(*m*) Rex *v.* Bowdage, Parker, 283. Where the same goods are found under a subsequent extent which have been found under a prior extent, it should be mentioned in the second inquisition that these goods are subject to the first extent. And where the two extents are executed at the same time, as the sheriff may have some doubt about their priority, it would seem to be the safest way to mention in the inquisition under each extent that the goods are seized under the other extent; West, 118.

CHAP. XVI. SECT. II.

Materials used in manufacturing exciseable articles.

Under an extent for duties or penalties incurred under the excise laws, the utensils, goods, materials, preparations, and vessels, employed in the particular manufactory in which such duties and penalties have arisen, may be taken, although the property in such utensils does not, nor ever did, belong to the defendant; for by the stat. 28 Geo. 3, c. 37, s. 21, a specific lien on such materials, &c. has been given to the crown for the duties and penalties arising from such manufacture. So also if the utensils have been seized and sold under a *fi. fa.* prior to the teste of the extent, yet they are liable to be taken under a crown extent in the hands of such purchaser (*n*). And in the case of Rex *v.* Wells and Allnutt (*o*), it was argued that the crown, under the several excise laws, had a specific lien upon all the goods and materials used by the defendant in his excise manufactory, and that no subsequent act of the defendant could divest such lien. The point was not then determined.

It has been decided, on this statute, that the crown has a lien upon malt for malt duties unpaid at the time of the bankruptcy; and the malt of the bankrupt is liable, although seized by the assignees under the assignment (*p*). And if after the assignment under a commission of bankrupt against a candle-maker, an information be exhibited against him for not having paid the single duties then due and payable for candles made by him for some time before he was a bankrupt; and upon such information he be convicted in the penalty of double duties; all his candles, and all his materials and utensils for making candles, in the possession of the assignees, are liable to the payment of the double duties (*q*). Under this statute, malt held by a maltster as a pledge for the payment of bills of exchange accepted by him for

(*n*) The Attorney-General *v.* Fort, Sittings at Serjeants' Inn, after Trinity Term, 1804, on a special case; which was an information against the sheriff of Wilts, for a false return of *nulla bona* to an exchequer execution against a paper-maker for penalties incurred under the 34 Geo. 3, c. 2, s. 1, 9, 14, and 15. The sheriff had a few days anterior to the teste of the crown's execution seized the paper-making utensils of defendant's mill under a *fi. fa.* and sold them; but they remained in the sheriff's bailiwick at the time of the teste of the crown's execution, and it was adjudged that the return of *nulla bona* was false, for which reason the sheriff was responsible to the crown for damages to the amount of the value of these paper-making utensils; 8 Price, 364.

(*o*) 16 East, 278, n.

(*p*) Attorney-General *v.* Senior, Dougl. 416; Rex *v.* Fowler, *ib.*

(*q*) Stracy *v.* Halse, Doug. 412. *Sed vide* Austin *v.* Whitehead, 6 T. R. 437.

the maker of the malt, with liberty to sell it in case the bills are not paid, are seizable in the hands of the maltster for duties for which he was liable in respect of other goods (*q*).

Lands of the crown debtor.

On an extent, the freehold lands of a crown debtor were liable, at the common law, to be taken for the crown debt, and may be taken as well as his body and goods (*r*). The sheriff may seize into the king's hands, not only the legal estate of the defendant, but also trust estates (*s*), or an equity of redemption (*t*), or lands over which the crown debtor has a power of revocation (*u*). But copyhold lands cannot be taken under an extent (*x*). Leasehold property may be either taken as goods or chattels, or as the land of the defendant (*y*). And the interest of the crown debtor in leaseholds renewable on lives may be taken under the statute 25 Geo. 3, c. 35, s. 1 (*z*). In one case it was held that a term for years created out of an estate, prior to the right of the crown attaching on the estate, and assigned to a trustee in trust for a purchaser, would not protect such purchaser against crown debts, though he purchased *bonâ fide* and without notice (*a*). But in a more recent case it was held, that a term of years originally created out of an estate purchased by a person who afterwards became a debtor to the crown, to secure a sum of money due from him to one of the vendors, and vested in a trustee for that purpose, and afterwards assigned to a trustee for a subsequent purchaser of the estate to attend the inheritance, is not liable to an extent for a crown debt, for the last purchaser claims directly under the first incumbrancer, by a title paramount to the crown debt (*b*). An equitable mortgage by deposit of title deeds by an accountant of the crown in the hands of a person who has an opportunity of knowing that the depositor is, or is likely to become, a debtor of the crown, is not available against an extent (*c*). So an assignment, in a voluntary settlement, of a term

(*q*) Attorney-General *v*. Trueman, 11 M. & W. 694. See now the stat. 4 & 5 Vict. c. 20.

(*r*) See Wilde *v*. Fort, 4 Taunt. 334.

(*s*) Harbert's case, 3 Rep. 12.

(*t*) Rex *v*. Delamotte, Forest's Rep. 162; Rex *v*. Coombes, 1 Price, 207; Hard. 488.

(*u*) Godbolt, 289; Attorney-General *v*. Sands, Hard. 488.

(*x*) Rex *v*. Lord Viscount Lisle, Parker, 195.

(*y*) Fleetwood's case, 8 Rep. 179; but it is only bound from the teste of the extent, and not from the time of the crown debt being recorded.

(*z*) Reg. *v*. Lane, 6 M. & W. 489.

(*a*) Rex *v*. Smith, Sugd. Vend. and Purchas. Append. 24, 5th edit. See Pleadings, M'Cleland's Rep. 417.

(*b*) Rex *v*. Lamb, M'Cleland, 402.

(*c*) Broughton *v*. Davis, 1 Price, 216. See Casberd *v*. Attorney-General, 1 Daniel, 238.

CHAP. XVI. SECT. II.

to a trustee to attend the inheritance as limited by the settlement, will not protect the inheritance in fee against a crown debt due from the settlor (*d*). But a *bonâ fide* agreement, on the borrowing of money, that real property of the borrower shall stand pledged for repayment of it, and a delivery of the title deeds to the lender, creates a lien binding as against the prerogative lien of the crown in respect of a debt subsequently accruing due to the crown from the borrower; and the equitable mortgagee is therefore entitled to be first paid his principal and interest out of the produce of the sale of the lands, when seized under an extent for the crown debt (*e*).

Lands from what time bound.

The lands are bound, as to time, according to the nature of the debt. Debts of record seem always to have bound the lands from the date of the record (*f*). Specialties do not bind the lands otherwise than simple contract debts, which only bind the lands from the time they are recorded (*g*). Bonds, which are taken in the form prescribed by the 33 Hen. 8, and which are thereby put on the footing of statutes staple, bind the land from the time they are entered into (*h*). Simple contract debts due to the crown from any of the officers, collectors, receivers, &c. described in 13 Eliz. c. 4, s. 2, bind the lands (if incurred at any time during the continuance in office) from the time of entering into the office (*i*). By the 33 Hen. 8, c. 39, s. 74, where the process of the crown is awarded, even on a simple contract debt, before the subject's judgment, the crown is entitled to a preference (*k*). But judgment and execution executed on an *elegit*, before the commencement of the crown process, shall be preferred to the extent (*l*). And it is said if the subject's debt be by statute staple, or judgment, prior to the queen's debt, and the queen extend the lands first, the subject shall not by any after-execution take them out of the hands of the crown (*m*). So if after an extent on such judgment, and before the *liberate*, a crown extent comes to the sheriff, the subject's execution shall be postponed to the crown extent (*n*). Lands bargained and sold

(*d*) Rex *v.* St. John, 2 Price, 317.

(*e*) Fector *v.* Philpott, 12 Price, 197.

(*f*) Gilb. Exch. 88; Dyer, 224; 8 Rep. 171.

(*g*) Rex *v.* Smith, 1 Wightw. 34.

(*h*) *Ibid.*

(*i*) West, 127, 128; Wilde *v.* Fort, 4 Taunt. 334.

(*k*) West, 102.

(*l*) Attorney-General *v.* Andrew, Hard. 23; West, 160.

(*m*) Gilb. Exch. 91; but see West, 151.

(*n*) Gilb. Exch. 91; but see West, 156.

by the commissioners of bankrupt to the assignees may be taken under an extent, the teste of which is subsequent to the bargain and sale, but prior to the inrolment (*o*).

Debts, what may be taken on an extent.

The debts due to the defendant are liable to a crown extent; even on extents in aid, debts to the third degree are so liable, that is to say, those of the defendant's debtor's debtor, whether such debts be by simple contract or by specialty (*p*). The defendant, as well as his debtors to the third degree, are bound to disclose the nature and particulars of such debts before the inquisition (*q*). Debts, like goods and chattels, are bound from the teste of the writ of extent; that is, a mere assignment of the debt to the assignees of a bankrupt, or any other assignment thereof, between the teste of the extent and the caption of the inquisition, will not discharge the debtor as against the crown (*r*). But the payment of a debt to the crown debtor, after the teste of the extent, and before the caption of the inquisition, will discharge the party paying without notice of the crown process; for an inquisition upon an extent finding a debt due to the crown debtor must find it to be due *on the day of the taking of the inquisition, as well as on the issuing of the extent* (*s*). Specialties, although not then due (*t*); money in the defendant's possession (*u*); or bills of exchange in the hands of the crown debtor, although not due, should be found in the inquisition (*x*), stating the liabilities of the several parties on the bill to the crown debtor; although it would appear that if the bill were due at the taking of the inquisition, the crown could not have a *scire facias* against the drawer without finding a default by the acceptor (*y*). If the crown debtor has indorsed over a bill, which is not due at the time of the inquisition, such debt should not be found (*z*). So if the debtor of the crown debtor have accepted a bill drawn on him by the crown debtor in favour of a third person (*a*); or if the

(*o*) West, 149.

(*p*) Parker, 259.

(*q*) Reg. *v.* Newell, Parker, 269.

(*r*) West, 164; Reg. *v.* Arnold, 7 Vin. 104; S. C. West, 327.

(*s*) Rex *v.* Green, Bunb. 265; S. C. West, 329; Rex in aid of Cox *v.* Gleny, West, 163, 164.

(*t*) Hughes, 118, 119; West, 172, 173.

(*u*) West, 172; but money is not bound from the teste of the extent.

(*x*) West, 165. The regular proof of the handwriting of the acceptor, &c., requisite in an action on such an instrument, is necessary to enable the jury to find such liability; if such evidence be not produced, the inquisition should find that the bill *purported to be made, &c.*

(*y*) West, 167.

(*z*) Rex *v.* Dawson, Wightw. 32.

(*a*) Hughes, 186; West, 169.

CHAP. XVI. SECT. II.

debtor to the crown debtor have drawn a bill on a third person for the debt in favour of the crown debtor, which has been accepted by the drawee, and is not due at the time of the inquisition, such debts cannot be found on the inquisition (*b*). Under an extent against one, the debts due to that one and others jointly may be seized (*c*); but in such cases the partner of the crown debtor may have account against the crown in equity (*d*). The sheriff has no power by virtue of the extent to levy or receive the debts found on the inquisition; he is merely to seize the debts, which is a mere seizure in law; upon the return of the inquisition the Court of Exchequer will issue a *scire facias*, or immediate extent, to the sheriff, to levy the debt from the debtor of the crown debtor.

Of the holding and form of the inquisition.

If any goods are seized, or if information be given (which is generally done by the officers of the revenue) that the defendant has any lands or goods, or debts due to him, or has any other property, it is the duty of the sheriff to hold an inquisition, in order to find whether or not the defendant is possessed of any property. A summons should be issued by the sheriff to the defendant, and to all other persons who can give any evidence as to the defendant's property, to attend before the inquisition (*e*); if either the defendant or the witnesses summoned do not attend, or refuse to answer any questions put to them (excepting only questions the answers to which would subject them to punishment), the Court of Exchequer will grant an attachment against them (*f*). It often happens that the defendant, or other persons set up *bonâ fide* sales or mortgages of the defendant's property; in case of such claim, it is apprehended that the evidence necessary in the Court of Exchequer in a similar case should be required before the inquisition, viz. the actual payment of the money by the vendee or mortgagee (*g*). The under-sheriff may either adjourn the inquisition, or hold another

(*b*) West, 169; Hughes, 155.

(*c*) West, 170.

(*d*) West, 171.

(*e*) See form, Append. chap. 16, sect. 2.

(*f*) Reg. *v.* Newell, Parker, 269.

(*g*) Rex *v.* Ward and others, executors of Ralph Kittle, Excheq. 1803. The defendants claimed property in certain leasehold houses seized under an extent against William Forge, for penalties for which the crown had obtained a verdict against him for carrying on a private candle manufactory. To this extent the defendants pleaded, that before the recovery of the king's judgment, Forge, in consideration of a certain sum of money, by indenture assigned the houses to defendant's testator for the residue of

before the return-day of the writ, to find the property not found by the first, and return both inquisitions to the court. The form of the inquisition, and of the various findings, as well as in what manner it is to be executed, will be found in the Appendix to this work (*h*). The sheriff, on hearing the evidence, should allow all competent witnesses to be examined; for where he refuses to permit a witness to be examined to prove the property taken under the extent, or a question to be put in the nature of a cross-examination, the court will quash the inquisition (*i*), as the inquisition on an extent is an office of entitling, and not of instruction.

In the findings, every fact should be stated with precision, and the lands particularly described; if the facts are not found with sufficient precision, so as to enable the party to traverse them, the return is bad, and the court will set it aside, and issue a new writ (*k*).

The return.

The sheriff makes his return to the extent according to the fact; if there be no lands or goods, the sheriff should return that at once; if lands or goods be extended, the sheriff should return that the execution of the writ will appear by the inquisition annexed, which inquisition, engrossed on parchment, under the seal of the sheriff and of each of the jurymen, is annexed to the writ. The sheriff returns *cepi corpus* or *non est inventus*,

the terms; to which the attorney-general replied that this indenture was made by fraud and covin; issue thereon. At the trial, the defendants proved the execution of the deed, and of Forge's signature to the receipt indorsed, but the attorney-general insisted that the crown was entitled to a verdict, for want of proof of the testator having actually paid Forge the consideration money. The lord chief baron ruled for the crown, and the jury gave a verdict accordingly; the Court of Exchequer refused to grant a new trial, on a motion to that effect made on this ground. The same point arose in Rex *v.* George Wilson, who, on an extent issued against one Sawyer, was returned in the sheriff's inquisition as being a debtor to Sawyer; but Wilson refusing to pay this debt to the crown, an exchequer *sci fa.* was issued against him: to the *sci. fa.* Wilson put in a plea denying the debt, and the issue thereon was tried at the sittings after Hilary term, 1806, when Wilson's witnesses produced Sawyer's receipts for the money, and proved the signatures thereto to be Sawyer's handwriting. The attorney-general contended that the receipts were of no validity against the crown; and that nothing but proof of the money having been actually paid by Wilson to Sawyer would bar the crown. The lord chief baron, after hearing the point argued by the counsel on behalf of Wilson, ruled in favour of the crown. The point was very fully argued on a motion for a new trial in the Exchequer, in Trinity term, 1806, when the court refused a new trial.

(*h*) Append. to chap. 16, sect. 2. See also West, 330.

(*i*) Rex *v.* Bickley, 3 Price, 454.

(*k*) Rex *v.* Sherwood, 3 Price, 269.

CHAP. XVI. SECT. II.

according to the fact. Upon an extent on a statute staple, the sheriff returned the extent of the lands, and not of the goods, yet it was held good (*l*). It is a good return by the sheriff that he hath extended the land of the defendant, but that he cannot deliver the same, for that another had the same in extent before (*m*). So, as it seems, it would be a good return, that the sheriff has extended goods or money of the debtor, but that he cannot deliver it because it is in the possession of a third party (*n*).

Venditioni exponas.

The Court of Exchequer, after the return of the writ and inquisition, will issue a writ of *venditioni exponas,* to sell the goods, an order to sell the land, or a *scire facias* to collect the debts. The court refused, at the instance of the crown, to direct a sale by private contract instead of by auction, but referred it to the remembrancer to certify which was the most advantageous mode of selling the property (*o*). The duty of the sheriff is only to issue his warrant to the bailiffs in possession, to proceed according to the exigency of such writs or order (*p*).

Sheriff's liabilities.

The sheriff is liable in an information at the suit of her majesty's attorney-general for damages, if he has made a false return (*q*), or has allowed the defendant, arrested by him by virtue of an extent, to escape.

(*l*) Bro. Trav. 438.

(*m*) Dalt. 125, and see forms, *post*, Append. c. 16, s. 2.

(*n*) Reg. *v.* Austin, 10 M. & W. 691.

(*o*) Reg. *v.* Lane, 6 M. & W. 489.

(*p*) See form, *post*, Append. c. 16, s. 2.

(*q*) Attorney-General *v.* Fort, Esq. sheriff of Wilts, *ante*, p. 366, n. (*n*).

Section III.

Poundage on Crown Process (*r*).

The poundage to be allowed on an extent, &c.

By the statute 3 Geo. 1, c. 15, s. 3, it is enacted, that all sheriffs who shall levy any debts, duties, or sums whatsoever, except *post* fines due to the king's majesty, his heirs or successors, by process to them directed upon the summons of the pipe or green wax, or by *levari facias* out of the Court of Exchequer, shall have an allowance of 12*d.* out of every 20*s.* for any sum not exceeding 100*l.* levied or collected, and 6*d.* only for every 20*s.* above the first 100*l.*; and for all debts (except *post* fines) due to his majesty, &c., by process of *fieri facias* and extent, issuing out of the Court of Exchequer, 1*s.* 6*d.* out of every 20*s.* for any sum not exceeding 100*l.* levied, and 12*d.* only for every 20*s.* over and above the first 100*l.*; provided that such sheriff shall answer the same upon his account by the general sealing day of such term in which he ought to be dismissed the court, or in such time to which he shall have a day granted to finish his accounts by warrant signed by the lord chief baron, or one of the barons of the coif of the said court for the time being.

Apportionment betwee the late and the present sheriff.

Sect. 9 enacts, that when any sheriff shall, by process out of the Exchequer, seize or extend any goods, &c. into the hands of his majesty for any debts due to the crown, and shall die or be superseded before a writ of *venditioni exponas* be awarded to him for sale, or before such sheriff hath made actual sale, and a writ shall afterwards be awarded to a subsequent sheriff, who shall make sale, &c. of such goods, &c. so seized by such preceding sheriff, in such case the Exchequer, if then sitting, and if not sitting the said barons, or any one of them, being of the degree of the coif, shall order and apportion poundage due for such seizure and sale betwixt such preceding and subsequent sheriffs, as to him or them shall seem meet, with regard to the expense and trouble each sheriff hath had or shall have in the execution of the said process.

Penalties for extortion.

Sect. 13. No sheriff, &c. in levying debts due to the crown by process out of the Exchequer, shall take any fee on pretence

(*r*) Which is not affected by the 1 Vict. c. 55 (*ante*, p. 103), the crown not being expressly named therein.

CHAP. XVI. SECT. III.

of such levying, &c. (except 4*d.* for an acquittance of such sum as shall be levied), which acquittance such officer is to give to the person on whom such debt, &c. is levied, and the bailiff, &c. receiving such debt, &c., shall account for the same to the sheriff, and may require an acquittance from such sheriff without a fee; from which debts the sheriffs shall discharge the debtors by totting and answering the same on their accounts in the Exchequer.

Penalties for not duly answering, &c.

And in case any sheriff, &c. shall *nihil* or not duly answer to the crown any debt or sum so levied, collected, or received, such sheriff, &c. for every such offence shall forfeit treble damages to the party grieved, and double the sum so *nihilled* or not duly answered as aforesaid; which damages and penalty shall be ordered, decreed, and given to the person grieved by the Court of Exchequer, upon complaint and proof of such abuse as aforesaid, made and exhibited before the barons of the said court, in such short and summary method as to them shall seem meet. And in case any sheriff, &c. shall presume to demand, take, or receive any sum of money of any person whatsoever, from whom any debt is or shall be due and payable to the crown by process out of the Court of Exchequer, for or in respect or upon pretence of fees for collecting or receiving the same, contrary to this act; or if any of the officers, &c. shall demand, take and receive any sum for not levying, or forbearing to levy any debts, &c., which are or shall be due to his majesty, and written out to them, or any of them, by the process aforesaid, in every such case every person so offending and convicted shall be adjudged guilty of extortion; and all persons, being thereof lawfully convicted, shall forfeit for every such offence treble damages and costs to the party grieved, and double the sum so extorted, which shall be ordered, decreed and given by the barons of the Exchequer, on complaint and proof made and exhibited before them, in such short and summary method as to them shall seem meet; provided such conviction be had and made within two years after such offence committed.

Sect. 14. Provided, that nothing shall be construed to deprive any sheriff of such poundage or allowance as is allowed and given to them by this act; or of such poundage, allowance, or reward, as may thereafter be made, allowed, and given by warrant or order from the lord high treasurer or commissioners of the treasury, chancellor of the exchequer, or barons of the Court of Exchequer for the time being, for or in respect of any extraordinary service to the crown that may happen to be performed by them: but that the said sheriffs shall and may enjoy the full benefit and advantage of such poundage, allowance and reward, without any impeachment or molestation whatsoever.

Orders for penalties how enforced.

Sect. 16. That whatsoever order or decree shall be made by the barons for costs, damages, and penalties, in the cases aforementioned, or any of them, or in any other case in that act hereafter mentioned, by virtue of that act, in such short and summary way and method as is before directed and prescribed, shall have the same effect as any other order or decree of the same court; and the same costs, damages, and penalties shall be raised, levied, and obtained by such process, ways, and methods as are used in the said court to enforce a compliance with any other orders or decrees of the same court.

Sheriff's poundage, how levied or obtained.

The sheriff, under this statute, is entitled to his poundage, not from the defendant, but from the crown, or the prosecutor of the extent. The sheriff cannot levy his poundage over and above the debt by virtue of an extent upon a simple contract debt (*s*). But where the debt is secured by a penalty, then poundage may be levied in addition to the debt, so that the levy do not exceed the penalty (*t*). Where the crown is entitled to its costs and charges, poundage may be levied as an item thereof, as in suits on obligations or specialties made to the queen, or to her use, under the 33 Hen. 8, c. 39; or under the 43 Geo. 3, c. 99, in extents against the collectors of taxes, by which act the crown is entitled to costs and charges, so in either of those cases or the like the crown may levy poundage where the sheriff is entitled to poundage against the crown (*u*). Where the sheriff seizes land only on the extent, and the crown proceeds for the debt by sale of such land, under the statute 25 Geo. 3, and not by *levari facias*, the sheriff is not entitled to poundage (*v*). The sheriff is entitled to his poundage on a levy, under the 3 Geo 1, c. 15, on an *extent in aid:* and if the sheriff seize under an extent in aid, and before a *venditioni exponas* the

(*s*) Rex *v.* Tidmarsh, 5 Price, 189.
(*t*) Rex *v.* Dean, 2 Anst. 369.
(*u*) West, 237.
(*v*) *Ibid.*

CHAP XVI. SECT. III.

debt be paid to him, and he pay it over to the prosecutor of the extent, he is entitled to his poundage (*x*); so if the debt be paid by compulsion of the levy to the prosecutor of the extent (*y*). But though the whole debt be paid to the extent holder, it seems that the sheriff shall have poundage only on the amount levied (*z*). The sheriff may deduct his poundage out of the sum levied on the extent, and need not wait for the allowance of it in his accounts (*a*): or if the whole money be paid over to the prosecutor, the sheriff may obtain his poundage by motion in court (*b*).

The sheriff cannot deduct any extra expense he has been put to out of the sum levied, but must apply to the court for the allowance of his extra charges (*c*), who will refer it to the master to ascertain what the sheriff is fairly entitled to (*d*). He cannot retain against the crown a sum of money deposited by an agent of the crown to cover the expenses of the sale under the *venditioni exponas* (*e*). As to the apportionment of poundage between the sheriffs of two counties into which two extents have been issued, it has been determined that if both sheriffs seize goods, and the debt is paid to one of the sheriffs before a *venditioni exponas* to either, that the sheriff to whom the money is paid shall have full poundage (*f*). But in such case, where the debt is paid to the officers of the crown immediately, the poundage shall be apportioned between the sheriffs (*g*).

Section IV.

Sheriff's Accounts.

Sheriff's charge as to debts, &c., due to the crown.

It will be recollected, that by the sheriff's oath of office, he swears that "he will promote her majesty's profit in all things that belong to his office as far as he legally can or may," and

(*x*) Rex *v.* Jetherell, Parker, 180.
(*y*) Rex *v.* Fry, 3 Anstr. 718, n.; 3 T. R. 470.
(*z*) West, 239.
(*a*) Parker, 177; Bunb. 305; and see Rex *v.* Jones, 1 Price, 205.
(*b*) Rex *v.* Jetherell, Parker, 180.
(*c*) Rex *v.* Jones, 1 Price, 206.
(*d*) Rex *v.* Fereday, 4 Price, 131.
(*e*) Rex *v.* Jones, 1 C. & J. 140.
(*f*) Rex *v.* Caldwell, 1 Anstr. 279; Rex *v.* Barcher, 3 Anstr. 717; Rex *v.* Bowles, 1 Wightwick, 117.
(*g*) Rex *v.* Fry, 3 Anstr. 718, n.

"that whensoever he shall have knowledge that the rights of the crown are concealed or withdrawn, be it in lands, rents, franchises, suits or services, or in any other matter or thing, he will do his utmost to make them to be restored to the crown again; and if he may not do it himself, he will certify and inform the queen thereof." This duty, says Dalton, is "1st, truly to keep the king's rights of his crown within his county, to wit, the king's lands, franchises, suits, rents, and all other things that belong to the crown. 2ndly, truly to gather (and bring into the Exchequer) the profits and monies due to the king within his bailiwick, to wit, the king's rents, farms, debts, issues, amerciaments, fines and forfeitures." It will be seen by reference to Dalton, that the sheriff might, within his own county, *ex officio* seize into the hands of the crown all lands which descended or belonged to the crown (*h*), and it was his duty to keep the king's franchises (*i*), to keep the king's suits (*k*), to collect the king's rents (*l*), to be accountable for the ordinary issues and profits of his county, (but not for other issues) (*m*), amerciaments (*n*), and fines (*o*). So also he might seize *ex officio* to the king's use the profits of the lands and the goods of persons attainted, outlawed, &c. (*p*); or goods forfeited to the king as *bona waivata*, estrays, and *bona confiscata* (*q*); so he may take treasure trove, wrecks of the sea (*r*), &c. Although the same power still remains to the sheriff (*s*), yet he never acts in the collection of the crown *ex officio*, but only when he is particularly ordered so to do by process out of the Court of Exchequer, or other courts having jurisdiction to enforce the payment of fines, &c.

Of the apposal, and how made.

The sheriff, by his office, is the queen's bailiff to gather her rents; and, before the passing of the statute 3 & 4 Will. 4, c. 99, the first thing, after his constitution, was to prefix him a day to account; and there were two other days prefixed, one after the *utas* of Easter, and the other after the *utas* of Michaelmas; and these were called his *proffers*, because he then did *proffer*

(*h*) Dalt. c. 6.
(*i*) Dalt. c. 7.
(*k*) Dalt. c. 8.
(*l*) Dalt. c. 9.
(*m*) Dalt. c. 11.
(*n*) Dalt. c. 12.
(*o*) Dalt. c. 13.
(*p*) Dalt. c. 44.
(*q*) Dalt. c. 15.
(*r*) Dalt. cc. 16, 17, &c.
(*s*) Rex *v.* Moseley Woolfe, 1 Chit. Rep. 587.

CHAP. XVI. SECT. IV.

the king's rents (*t*). The sheriff paid in *proffers* to the value of the county rents, because these he must *tot* or *o'ni'* before the curzitor baron; he could not *nihil* these, because the lands might be seized into the king's hands, and out of the profits and issues the rents might be answered, as the sheriff was looked upon to farm the rents, and therefore was obliged to pay them to the crown; but he might *o'ni'* (*oneratur nisi habeat sufficientem exonerationem*) these rents; for if the king granted any of them, he might show the record in his discharge (*u*). When the sheriff, or rather the under-sheriff (for the sheriff used not to attend), kept his day of prefixion, he was to be *apposed* (*x*) before the barons upon the great roll, before the cursitor baron on the summons of the pipe, and before the foreign apposer upon the summons of the green wax; which is, that the sheriff was put to account on the different processes which he had received from the Exchequer, and which was done either by charging himself with the receipt of certain sums, or *totting*, as it was termed; where he had not been able to levy any thing, he answered *nihil*, excepting as to the crown rents with which he was chargeable (*y*) whether he had received them or not. The rents charged against the sheriff were generally some gross sum, as 100*l.* or 50*l.*; in Norfolk they were greater (*z*); but afterwards, by the statute 3 Geo. 1, c. 15, s. 2, it was enacted, "that the lord treasurer, commissioner of the treasury, and the barons of the exchequer, or two or any more of them, should and might from time to time, at request of any sheriff or sheriffs, or as often as they should think fit, call before them the remembrancer in the Court of Exchequer, commonly called the treasurer's remembrancer, and the clerk of the pipe, or their deputies, secondaries, and such other officers as they should think fit, and should cause the said officers, or some of them, to bring before them an account or particular of all the rents and certainties written out yearly in processes to the sheriff in each respective county in England to levy for the crown; and, upon

(*t*) Gilb. Exch. 147. For not coming in at those days, the sheriff was considered as an accountant in default, and therefore a fine of 5*l.* per diem was set upon his head for four days together to bring him in; which was levied by *fi. fa.*, or a distress to make him account.

(*u*) Gilb. Exch. 150.

(*x*) This word is said to be derived from the Latin verb, *apponere*.

(*y*) See *ante*, 353.

(*z*) Gilb. Exch. 149, 150.

due examination and consideration thereof had, were thereby empowered and required from time to time to alter, diminish, reduce or establish the several sums wherewith the said sheriffs stood chargeable on the rolls or *proffers* in the said Court of Exchequer, to such reasonable and moderate sums as to them should seem just and reasonable, with regard to the amount or value of the rents in each county respectively, and that the orders of the Court of Exchequer be drawn up pursuant thereto, and entered upon record in the several offices of his majesty's remembrancer, the lord treasurer, or the commissioners of the treasurer's remembrancer, and the clerk of the pipe, some time before the last day of Michaelmas term then next following; and that from time to time the sum and sums of money so reduced, ascertained and settled, should be deemed and taken to be the *proffers* of each respective county, and the rolls of *proffers* from time to time shall be made conformable thereto; and the said sum and sums so reduced, ascertained and settled as aforesaid, and no other, should be paid by the said respective sheriffs for their *proffers*, at the days and times and in the manner formerly used for *proffers*."

The fees payable by the under-sheriff on passing the accounts, for their apposals, and for making out their *quietus* to the officers in the exchequer, were regulated by the statute of 3 Geo. 1, c. 15, s. 1.

Sheriffs of England and Wales, before *whom* to account.

The sheriff's accounts of the English counties (excepting the counties palatine) were (before the 3 & 4 Will. 4, c. 99) passed before the clerk of the pipe. By the 22d section of the statute 3 Geo. 1, c. 15, it was enacted that the sheriffs of Wales should not be compelled to appear to be apposed in his majesty's Court of Exchequer, but might account before his majesty's auditor or auditors of the principality of Wales, and not elsewhere, any law, statute, custom or usage to the contrary notwithstanding; and the *quietus* of the said sheriffs, under the auditor's hand, or that of his deputy, was to be a sufficient discharge to the said sheriffs in that behalf (*a*). And by the same act, section 23, as to the passing of the accounts of the sheriffs of Chester, Lancaster and Durham, it was enacted that the respective auditors of the said counties or their deputies, by virtue of their respective

(*a*) See also 11 Geo. 4 & 1 Will. 4, c. 70, s. 33.

CHAP. XVI. SECT. IV.

offices, should take, state, and allow the accounts of the sheriffs of the said respective counties, and appose the said sheriffs respectively touching the execution of the process to them respectively directed, called the king's process; and that the said respective sheriffs, upon such their accounts touching the premises, should have, sue forth, and obtain their respective *quietus est* and discharge from the said respective auditors or their deputies, according to the ancient course and usage of the sheriffs of the said counties palatine only. And by the same statute, section 24, the sheriffs of the *city and county of the city of Chester*, and their successors, were enabled to account, as formerly, before the mayor of the same city and his successors for the time being, for and touching all such matters and things as had been theretofore granted from the crown to the same city in and by their several and respective charters. And by the 25th section of the same statute, the *sheriffs of the said city of Chester*, and their successors, might at all times thereafter account for and concerning the same before, and be apposed by, and obtain their *quietus est* and discharge from, the auditor of the county of Chester or his deputy, in like manner as the sheriffs of the said county of Chester were by that act appointed to do, and not elsewhere, or in any other manner whatsoever.

3 & 4 Will. 4, c. 99.

Such was the complicated form of accounting to which sheriffs were subjected before the passing of the statute 3 & 4 Will. 4, c. 99; but by the 1st section of that act (after reciting that the appointment of sheriffs, and the audits and passing of their accounts in the Court of Exchequer, are attended with unnecessary expense, delay, and trouble), it is enacted that so much of the 3 Geo. 1, c. 15, as entitles and authorizes certain officers therein and in the schedule thereto mentioned to demand and receive the fees named in that schedule, and also the statute 3 Geo. 1, c. 16 (for better enabling sheriffs to sue out their patents and pass their accounts), shall be repealed. The 2nd section then proceeds to enact, "that, from and after the passing of this act, it shall not be necessary for any sheriff or sheriffs of any county, city, or town in England or Wales, to sue out any patent or writ of assistance, or to make or pay proffers, nor shall any bailiff or bailiffs of liberties in England or Wales be required to make or pay any proffers, nor shall he or they have any day of prefixion, or be apposed, or take any oath or oaths before the cursitor baron to account, or account, or be cast out of court, as now or heretofore in use in his majesty's Court of Exchquer, any law, statute, or usage to the contrary notwithstanding."

The 8th section then enacts, that the accounts of the present and future sheriffs of counties, cities, and towns within England (except the counties palatine of Chester, Lancaster and Durham) shall thenceforth be examined and audited by the commissioners for auditing public accounts, appointed under the statutes 25 Geo. 3, c. 52, 46 Geo. 3, c. 141, and 1 & 2 Geo. 4, c. 121.

The 9th section provides, "that every person and persons who now are or who hereafter shall be sheriff or sheriffs of any county, city or town within England (except the said counties palatine of Chester, Lancaster and Durham) shall within two calendar months next after the expiration of his or their office, or in case of the death of any sheriff or sheriffs, the under-sheriff by him or them appointed, shall within two calendar months next after the death of such sheriff or sheriffs, transmit to the said commissioners for auditing public accounts a just and true account, under his or their hand or hands, of all sums received by such sheriff or sheriffs to or for the use of his majesty, and of all sums paid or claimed by him or them, or on his or their behalf (save such sums as are or have been usually inserted and allowed in the bill of cravings), with all such particulars as shall be needful to explain the same: provided always, that such under-sheriff shall not be personally responsible for any sum or sums received by such deceased sheriff, but that the same shall be answered by the representatives of the said deceased sheriff, or otherwise in due course of law: provided always, that the sheriff of Westmorland shall yearly, within two calendar months next after the first day of January in every year, transmit or cause to be transmitted to the said commissioners for auditing the public accounts a like account under his hand, or the hand of his under-sheriff, of all sums paid by him to or for the use of his majesty within or during the year of our Lord next preceding, and of all sums paid or claimed by him or on his behalf during the same period (save such sums as are or have been usually inserted in the bill of cravings), with all such particulars as shall be needful to explain the same."

By the 10th section, "in case it shall be necessary for any

CHAP. XVI. SECT. IV.

such sheriff or sheriffs, or his or their under-sheriff, to make oath or affidavit to any such account, or any article, matter, or thing relating thereto, such oath or affidavit, except when the said commissioners shall require his or their personal examination before them, shall and may be sworn before any of the judges of his majesty's superior courts of record at Westminster, or before any commissioner for taking affidavits in any of the same courts, or before any master or master extraordinary in the High Court of Chancery, or before any of his majesty's justices of the peace."

The 11th section provides, that the claim of every sheriff for certain allowances usually called the *bill of cravings* (that is, the bill of charges paid by the sheriff for the judges' lodgings, &c. at the assizes, for crown calendars, for the execution of criminals, &c.), shall, after the passing of that act, be preferred to the lord high treasurer or commissioners of the treasury, who, or any three or more of whom, shall grant a warrant for the allowance of the same in the account of such sheriff, or for the payment of such sum or sums of money in respect thereof as they shall think reasonable in that behalf.

The 39th section saves the rights, liberties, and privileges of the crown in right of the duchy and county palatine of Lancaster and duchy of Cornwall, of the Bishop of Durham and the county palatine of Durham (*a*), and the rights, customs, &c. of the city of London; and the 40th section provides, that nothing in the act contained shall prejudice the rights, liberties and privileges of the city and county of the city of Chester, but that the sheriffs thereof shall and may account and obtain their *quietus* in like manner as had theretofore been accustomed.

The mode of making up, transmitting, and passing the accounts of the sheriffs in England and Wales is now as follows: The sheriffs of all counties, cities, and towns in England (excepting those above referred to) receive, about the period of the expiration of their term of office, three copies of the printed form of account given in the Appendix (*b*): within two calendar months next after the expiration of office or death of the sheriff (as the case may be), or, in the case of Westmorland, within

(*a*) As to which see 6 & 7 Will. 4, c. 19, whereby the palatinate rights are transferred to the crown; and *ante*, p. 11.

(*b*) Chap. XVI. sect. 4.

two calendar months after the 1st of January in every year, the blank forms so received are filled up, signed by the high sheriff, and, with the bill of cravings, are transmitted either directly or through the agent employed to pass the accounts, one to the treasury, one to the audit office, and one to the office of the queen's remembrancer. The bill of cravings is also at the same time transmitted to the treasury, and from thence sent to the secretary of the chancellor of the exchequer, who reviews or *taxes* it, and gives his *allocatur;* it is then signed by three or more lords of the treasury. The person passing the accounts then prepares a receipt, to be signed by the sheriff, of the amount allowed on the bill of cravings, and upon the production of that receipt receives a cheque at the treasury upon the Bank of England for that amount. After acceptance thereof, the person passing the accounts attends before the inspector and receiver-general of fines and penalties, who examines the account transmitted to and received by him from the treasury with the quarterly returns received from the different clerks of the peace, and the copies of the process issued from the Court of Exchequer, from the superior courts and courts of assize, and then forwards it with his certificate to the commissioners of audit, by whom it is then passed. The inspector and receiver-general of fines and penalties also receives from the sheriff the amount due from him on the balance of the account, if any.

Surplusage, how obtained.

Formerly, if the sheriff disbursed more money for the crown than he had received, the remedy was by record of surplusage, which proceeding was both dilatory and expensive: to remedy which inconvenience, by the statute 3 Geo. 1, c. 15, s. 7, it was enacted, "that from the first day of Michaelmas Term, 1717, if any sheriff of any county in England (except the counties palatine of Chester, Durham, and Lancaster, and the several counties of Wales, which do not pass their accounts before the clerk of the pipe) shall happen to be in surplusage upon his account, by reason of any disbursements whatsoever by him made for the service of his majesty, his heirs or successors (other than for the rewards of 40*l.* severally and respectively allowed and given by virtue of the several acts thereinbefore mentioned to such persons as shall apprehend a clipper, coiner, highwayman, or housebreaker), such sheriff shall not be obliged to take out a

CHAP. XVI. SECT. IV.

record of surplusage for the same, but shall and may apply to the lord high treasurer of Great Britain, or to the commissioners of the treasury for the time being, for the payment of such surplusage, who are hereby required and authorized to pay the same upon the sheriff's producing a certificate of such surplusage from the clerk of the pipe or his deputy."

CHAPTER XVII.

OF JURIES, AND OF THE SHERIFF'S DUTY AT SESSIONS AND ASSIZES.

SECT. I.—*Of Juries; who are qualified to serve on.—List of Persons qualified, how made out.—Venire facias, Sheriff's Duty thereon.—Special Juries, how struck and summoned.—Penalty on Sheriff for breach of Duty.*

II.—*Sheriff's Duty at Assizes.*

III.—*Sheriff's Duty at Sessions.*

SECTION I.

Of Juries.

Venire facias, to whom directed.

WE come now to treat of the sheriff's duty respecting the returning and summoning of juries. The sheriff is the officer of all the superior courts to return and summon juries; when causes are at issue, the courts issue their writs of *venire facias* directed to the sheriff, commanding him to cause a jury to come according to the exigency of the writ. If the sheriff (*a*) be interested in the suit, or of kin to the parties, the *venire* suggesting such fact should be directed to the coroners of the county. If the coroners also be interested, the *venire* should be directed to two persons named by the court for that purpose, and sworn, who are called *elisors*.

Of the jurors' book.

The qualifications of jurors, and the exemptions and disqualifications of persons from serving on juries, are now regulated by the statute of the 6 Geo. 4, c. 50, s. 1, 2, 3, 48, 49, 50, and by the 5 & 6 Will. 4, c. 76, ss. 122, 123, and 2 & 3 Vict. c. 71, s. 4, which statutes will be found at large in the Appendix to this work. By reference to the 4th, 5th, 6th, 7th, 8th, 9th, 10th and

(*a*) If the sheriff be a party, or akin to the parties, or his under-sheriff or the person who summoned the jury be of relation to the parties, or interested, this is a cause of challenge to the array.

CHAP. XVII. SECT. I.

11th sections of the 6 Geo. 4, c. 50, will be found the manner in which an annual jurors' book is to be formed, which book is to be kept by the sheriff, and from which he is to select the jurors. By the 12th section of the same act it is provided, "that the clerk of the peace shall keep lists returned (as in the act directed), arranged with every hundred in alphabetical order, and every parish and township within such hundred likewise in alphabetical order, and shall cause the same to be fairly and truly copied in the same order in a book to be by him provided for that purpose, at the expense of the county, &c., with proper columns for making the register thereinafter mentioned, and shall deliver the same book to the sheriff of the county, or his under-sheriff, within six weeks next after the close of such sessions, which book shall be called 'The Jurors' Book for the year ——,' (inserting the calendar year for which such book is to be in use); and that every sheriff, on quitting his office, shall deliver the same to the succeeding sheriff; and that every jurors' book so prepared shall be brought into use on the 1st day of January after it shall be delivered by the clerk of the peace to his sheriff, or under-sheriff, and shall be used for one year then next following.

Juries, how selected.

The sheriff, coroners, or elisors, upon the receipt of every writ of *venire facias* and precept for the return of jurors, are to return the names of men contained in the jurors' book for the then current year, and no others, unless there be no jurors' book for that year, then from the jurors' book for the year preceding (*b*): and by the 39th section of the above-mentioned act, the sheriff is indemnified for impannelling and returning any man named in the jurors' book, although he may not be qualified or liable to serve on juries; but if the sheriff shall wilfully return any man to serve on any jury (excepting the grand jury at assizes), whose name is not in the jurors' book for the current year, the court may set such fine upon the sheriff as the court shall think fit. The sheriff is to keep an alphabetical register in the jurors' book of all persons who have been summoned and have attended as jurors on trials at assizes, and to give every such person a certificate of his attendance and service (*c*). And the clerk of the peace is to make out, and transmit to the sheriff, a list of all persons who have served either on the grand or petty jury

(*b*) 6 Geo. 4, c. 50, s. 14.

(*c*) 6 Geo. 4, c. 50. s. 40.

at sessions, and those persons' names are to be included in the register in the sheriff's book as having so served (*d*).

Persons having served, how long exempted.

In Middlesex, no person shall be returned as a juror, who has served at any session of *nisi prius*, or gaol delivery, in either of the two terms or vacations preceding; and no man shall be returned as a juror to serve on trials before any court of assize, gaol delivery, &c., who has served as a juror at any of the courts within one year before in Wales, or in the counties of Hereford, Cambridge, Huntingdon, or Rutland; or four years before in the county of York; or two years before in any other county (*e*).

Summons of jurors, when and how made.

By the 25th section of this act, it is required that the officer shall summon every person to serve on juries (not being special juries), by leaving a note in writing at the dwelling of such person ten days at least before the day on which the juror is to attend. And the summons of special juries is, in like manner, to be three days before the day of attendance (excepting in London and Middlesex, where no longer time is required for the summoning of juries than heretofore); but where there shall not be ten days between the awarding of such writ and the return thereof, every person may be summoned, attached, or distrained, to appear at the day or time therein mentioned, as he might theretofore have been.

At the assizes the jury process should therefore, in the case of common jurors, be sent to the sheriff ten days, and in the case of special jurors three days, at least, before the commission day (*f*).

Punishment on officers taking rewards for not summoning persons to serve on juries.

By the 43d section of the 6 Geo. 4, c. 50, it is enacted, that no sheriff, under-sheriff, coroner, elisor, bailiff, or other officer or person whatsoever, shall, directly or indirectly, take or receive any money or other reward, or promise of money or reward, to excuse any man from serving or from being summoned to serve on juries, or under any such colour or pretence; and that no bailiff or other officer appointed by any sheriff, under-sheriff, coroner, or elisor, to summon juries, shall summon any man to serve thereon other than those whose names are specified in a warrant or mandate signed by such sheriff, under-sheriff, coroner, or elisor, and directed to such bailiff or other

(*d*) 6 Geo. 4, c. 50, s. 41.

(*e*) *Ibid.* s. 42.

(*f*) Charlton *v.* Burfit, 1 M. & Scott, 450.

CHAP. XVII. SECT. I.

officer; and if he shall wilfully transgress in any of the cases aforesaid, or shall summon any juror, not being a special juror, less than ten days before the day on which he is to attend, except the cases thereinbefore excepted," the court under whose jurisdiction it falls is empowered to set such a fine upon every person so offending as the court shall think meet.

Panels, how made.

When the sheriff receives the *venire facias*, we have seen that he is to select the persons to serve on the jury from the jurors' book. The panel which he annexes as his return must contain the names of the jury alphabetically arranged, with their places of abode and their addition; the same panel is affixed to every *venire facias* at the same assizes. The number of jurors for any county is not to be less than forty-eight, nor more than seventy-two, unless by order of one of the justices of assize. In practice, the *venire* issues at the same time as the *distringas*, or *habeas corpora juratorum*, although these latter writs presume a default in the appearance of the jurors on the *venire* (*g*). In court, at the assizes, the sheriff returns the several writs of *habeas corpora*, or *distringas*, in each cause, with the same panel annexed to each (*h*).

Lists of jurors to be kept for inspection.

By section 19, the sheriff is to make out an alphabetical list of the names of the persons contained in the panels to the several writs of *venire facias*, and shall keep the same in the under-sheriff's office at least seven days before the assizes, and the parties in the suits or their attornies, without fee, are to be at full liberty to inspect such list.

Names to be put in a box.

And by the 26th section of that act, the under-sheriff (or secondary in London) is to write the name of each juror, with his addition, on a separate card or piece of parchment, and deliver the same to the associate. And twelve names are to be drawn indiscriminately from a box in which these pieces of parchment or card are placed (*i*).

Special juries.

The sheriff has also to summon special juries. The panel affixed to the *venire facias* is made in the same manner as in common juries; but the qualifications of special jurors, and the

(*g*) See s. 16, 6 Geo. 4, c. 50, by which a plaintiff is allowed to sue out a new writ of *venire facias*, where a *venire facias* and *distringas* had already issued, but not been proceeded on.

(*h*) See Rogers *v.* Smith, 1 Ad. & E. 772; 3 N. & M. 772, S. C.

(*i*) See this section at length in the Appendix, for the detailed provisions therein contained.

manner in which they are to be selected, will be found by reference to section 30, 31, 32, 33, 34 and 35, of the Jury Act, which will be found in the Appendix to this chapter; and as to the mode of granting views, see s. 23.

Good jury.

If a judge's order is made for the return of a "good jury" upon a writ of inquiry (*i*), that means a jury taken from the special jury book (*k*).

Juries in criminal cases, &c.

The statute of 6 Geo. 4, c. 50, has left the power of judges of gaol delivery to make any award or order, orally or otherwise, for the return of a jury for the trial of any issue in any criminal court, as it formerly stood; this is expressly provided for by section 20 of that act. And by section 22 it is enacted, that where the justices of assize shall so direct, the sheriff may summon and impanel such number of jurors, not exceeding 144, as such justices shall direct, to serve indiscriminately on the criminal and civil side, to be divided into two lots, one set to attend at the commencement, the second at the end of the assizes.

Punishment of sheriff for misbehaviour.

By section 46 of that act it is enacted, "that if any sheriff or under-sheriff shall neglect or refuse to provide or prepare a list of special jurors in the manner or within the time prescribed, or shall wilfully write or cause to be written therein the name of a person not qualified, or shall wilfully omit thereout the name of any person duly qualified as a special juror, or shall neglect or refuse to write, or cause to be written, the several numbers contained in such list upon distinct pieces of parchment or card in the manner and within the time prescribed, or shall subtract or destroy, or by any default or neglect lose, any of the said pieces of parchment or card, or shall neglect or refuse, upon discovery of such loss, to supply the same within five days; or shall neglect or refuse to prepare, or keep for inspection as aforesaid, a copy of the panel in the case provided for, or to register the service of any juror as by the act directed, or to deliver to any man who shall have been summoned and have duly attended and served as a juror at any court of assize, &c., a certificate of such man's service, on his application and payment as aforesaid, or shall refuse or neglect, within ten days after the next succeeding sheriff shall be sworn into or have

(*i*) R. G., H. T. 2 Will. 4.

(*k*) Price *v.* Williams, 5 Dowl. 160.

entered upon office, to deliver over to him, as well all the jurors' books and lists that shall be made or prepared in the year of his shrievalty, as also all such other like books and lists as were prepared in the shrievalty of any of his predecessors, within four years then next preceding, and which were delivered over to him by any of his predecessors:" such sheriff or under-sheriff offending in any of the said cases shall for every such offence forfeit the sum of *50l.*, one half to the crown, the other half to the informer.

Section II.

The Sheriff's Duty before and at the Assizes.

Assize precepts.

A sufficient time before the circuit, the sheriff will receive the assize precepts, and also precepts to summon special juries; the forms of these precepts will be found in the appendix to this chapter.

The sheriff's duty before and at the assizes consists in—1st, proclaiming the assize; 2ndly, the summoning of the different juries, viz., the grand jury, the *nisi prius* jury, the crown jury, and also the special juries, if any, and granting views; 3dly, making his returns to the assize precepts; 4thly, making and delivering a list of the prisoners to the judges, and attending the judges, providing lodgings, &c.

Warrants to bailiffs.

On the receipt of the assize precepts, warrants should forthwith be made out and delivered to the bailiffs of each hundred, commanding them to summon the grand jury, to make proclamation of the assize, to give notice to coroners, constables, &c. to attend, and to summon the jurors named in the margin to attend The sheriff, where there are any special juries, should direct his warrant to the bailiff to summon them. The sheriff makes the proclamation required himself, by inserting an advertisement in the county newspapers; in some counties this is done by placarding printed proclamations in the principal towns and villages throughout the county.

Summoning the grand jury.

There is no statutable regulation respecting the persons to be summoned on the grand jury; and as in all counties it is considered an honour, the sheriff should summon the gentlemen of fortune in his county below the rank of peer. A list of persons who are usually summoned on grand juries at assizes may be obtained from the former under-sheriff, and these are to be inserted in the warrants: the number summoned is always much greater than the number of grand jurors sworn.

Return to the assize precepts.

The sheriff's return to the assize precept consists of four panels. On the back of the precept the sheriff indorses the reference to the panels, viz. "*the return of this precept appears in certain panels hereunto annexed,*" and that he has *made proclamation* (*l*); those panels are:—

1st. The names of the magistrates, mayors, bailiffs of liberties, constables of hundreds, and sheriff's officers of the different hundreds.

2nd. The names of the persons summoned to serve on the grand jury.

3rd. The names of persons summoned to serve on the petty jury.

4th. The calendar of the prisoners.

These panels are written on parchment, and should be tied to the precept, and delivered by the sheriff himself to the judge. Copies of the calendar of the prisoners should be printed and circulated.

If there be any *capiases*, they must be returned according to the fact at the same time.

Copies of the *nisi prius* jury must be printed on parchment, and one copy annexed to each (*m*) *distringas*, or *habeas corpora juratorum*, returnable at the assizes; besides this, the under-sheriff should write the name and addition of each juryman on paper, or a piece of parchment or card, and put them into the balloting box, which, with the key of the box, is delivered to the clerk of assize, that he may draw the jury from it (*n*).

Copies of the petty jury should be made on parchment, to annex to traverses.

If there be a view, or special jury, the sheriff strikes the same, and issues his warrant (*o*) to summon the special jurors, accord-

(*l*) See form of return and panels, Append. The list of the magistrates is obtained from the clerk of the peace: the other lists will be found in the under-sheriff's office.

(*m*) See form, Append.

(*n*) See 6 Geo. 4, c. 50, s. 26.

(*o*) See form of warrant, *post*, Appendix.

CHAP. XVII. SECT. II.

ing to the provisions of the statute 6 Geo. 4, c. 50, s. 30, 31; and as to a sheriff's duty on a view, it will be seen in a former part of this work, excepting that the jury and not the parties are to have the view. The sheriff then annexes the special jury panel to the record with issues, and if there has been a view, the sheriff adds this to his return (*p*).

The sheriff, as well as his under-sheriff, must be in constant attendance on the judges during the whole of the assizes, and should provide the judges with lodgings, according to the custom of the particular county. The sheriff should also go in state to meet the judges at the accustomed place before they enter the town. This and the other ceremonies vary in different counties; the under-sheriff will always easily inform himself of what attention he should pay to the judges. The under-sheriff has a great many payments to make to the cryers, to the attendants of the judges, to his javelin-men, &c. &c.; these are also regulated by custom. For payments for the lodgings of the judges, and for other payments, as rewards directed by act of parliament to be paid by the sheriff, he should take receipts, and these will be allowed him on passing his accounts (*q*).

The fees taken for returning *venires*, &c., and otherwise in relation to the striking and summoning of juries, are regulated by the table of fees prepared by the judges pursuant to the stat. 1 Vict. c. 55 (*r*).

Section III.

The Sheriff's Duty before and at the Quarter Sessions.

Of the precept to summon the sessions.

We next come to notice the sheriff's duty at the sessions. The sheriff receives from the clerk of the peace a precept, under

(*p*) See form, *post*, Appendix.

(*q*) In case of any person being condemned to death and left for execution, the under-sheriff should attend, and should also collect his constables, bailiffs, and all the disposable civil force he can command, to attend the execution. See Rex *v.* Antrobus, 2 Ad. & E. 788.

(*r*) *Ante*, p. 107.

the hands and seals of justices of the peace, for summoning the sessions; by which the sheriff is commanded that he cause to come before the justices, at the time and place which the sessions are appointed to be held, "twenty-four good and lawful men of the body of the county, then and there to inquire, present, do, and perform, all and singular such things, which on the behalf of our sovereign lady the queen shall be enjoined them; also that he make known to all coroners, keepers of gaols and houses of correction, high constables and bailiffs of liberties, within the county, that they may be then there to do and fulfil those things which, by reason of their offices, shall be to be done; moreover, that he cause to be proclaimed through the county, in proper places, the aforesaid sessions of the peace to be held at the day and place aforesaid; and that he should be there to do and execute those things which belong to his office; and that he have then there as well the names of the jurors, coroners, keepers of gaols and houses of correction, high constables, and bailiffs aforesaid, as that precept."

Sheriff's duty thereon.

Although the precept requires the sheriff to proclaim the sessions, yet this is never done by him, but the sessions are proclaimed by the clerk of the peace, who does it by advertising the day and time in one or more of the provincial newspapers. Neither does the sheriff attend in person at the sessions, but the under-sheriff usually attends.

Summoning jurors, &c.

A warrant should be made out and delivered to one or more bailiffs, to summon the grand and petit juries to serve at sessions; and also to the bailiffs of liberties and constables of hundreds to attend the sessions (*s*). The jurors to serve on the grand or petit jury at sessions must be qualified according to the provisions of the statute 6 Geo. 4, c. 50 (*t*). By section 42 of that act, "no man shall be returned to serve upon any grand jury or petit jury at any sessions of the peace to be holden for any county, riding, or division in England or Wales, who has served as a juror at any such session within one year before in Wales, or in the counties of Hereford, Cambridge, Huntingdon or Rutland, or two years before in any other county, and has the certificate of the clerk of the peace of having so served (*u*)."

(*s*) See forms, *post*, Append.

(*t*) See sect. 20.

(*u*) By sect. 41, the clerk of the peace is to make out a list of all per-

And by section 48 of the same act, "no justice of the peace shall be summoned or impannelled to serve as a juror at any sessions of the peace for the jurisdiction of which he is justice." The jurors should be summoned at least ten days before the day on which they have to attend, by serving on each person, either personally or by leaving at his place of abode, a note in writing, under the hand of the sheriff, containing the substance of such summons (*x*). By section 20 of that act, the courts of session of the peace in England shall have and exercise the same power and authority as they have heretofore had and exercised in issuing any writ or precept, or making any award or order, orally or otherwise, for the return of a jury for the trial of any issue before any such courts respectively.

Sheriff's return to sessions' precept.

The sheriff makes his return to the precept by affixing three pieces of parchment thereto, in the same manner as the return to the precept at the assizes, by writing on the back, "the execution of this precept appears in certain panels hereunto annexed." The first panel contains the names of the coroners, bailiffs of liberties and of hundreds, and constables of hundreds. The second is the grand jury panel, and the third the petty jury panel, which contain the names of all the persons summoned to serve on those juries (*y*).

To receive all fines, and to pay the wages of justices.

The under-sheriff, at the sessions, receives all the fines paid there; and he is also to pay the justices of the peace their wages, viz., four shillings *per diem*, and two shillings to the clerk of the peace, which the sheriff will be allowed in his accounts.

Of levying recognizances estreated at sessions.

The sheriff's duty respecting the *levying* fines and recognizances imposed and taken by justices of peace, and by the court

sons who have been summoned and have attended on any grand or petit jury at sessions, with the place of abode and date of services, within twenty days after the end of each session, and transmit it to the sheriff. And the party himself, on application, may demand from the clerk of the peace a certificate of having served as a juror at sessions.

(*x*) 6 Geo. 4, c. 50, s. 25. See form of note of summons, *post*, Append.

(*y*) See forms, *post*, Append.; and as to the power in the court to fine jurors for non-attendance, &c., see stat. 6 Geo. 4, c. 50, Append. As to juries at the quarter sessions in boroughs and towns corporate, see 5 & 6 Will. 4, c. 76, ss. 122, 123; and 2 & 3 Vict. c. 71, s. 4, *post*, Append. As to the formation of lists of jurors in the new county courts, see 9 & 10 Vict. c. 95, s. 72, *post*, Append.

of quarter sessions, is now regulated by two recent statutes (3 Geo. 4, c. 46, and 4 Geo. 4, c. 37); which statutes have taken away the jurisdiction of the Court of Exchequer, both under Geo. 3 and under the standing writ of privy seal, to mitigate or discharge recognizances forfeited at sessions, although a duplicate or certificate thereof has been delivered into that court (z). By the statute 3 Geo. 4, c. 46, all fines, issues, amerciaments, forfeited recognizances, &c., set, imposed, lost, or forfeited by or before any justice of the peace, are to be certified by such justice before the next quarter sessions after the fine, &c. is imposed, to the clerk of the peace; and the clerk of the peace is to copy on a roll such fines, &c., and all fines, issues, amerciaments, forfeited recognizances, &c. imposed or forfeited at the quarter sessions; and shall, within the time fixed by the court of quarter sessions (not exceeding twenty-one days) after the adjournment of the court, send a copy of such roll, with a writ of *distringas* and *capias*, or *fieri facias* and *capias* (a), to the sheriff of the county (or the person in a borough, &c. having execution of process), which is to be the authority to the sheriff for proceeding to the immediate levying and recovering such fines, issues, amerciaments, forfeited recognizances, &c. on the goods and chattels of such persons, *in case sufficient goods and chattels shall not be found whereon distress can be made for the recovery thereof;* and every person so taken shall be lodged in the common gaol until the next general or quarter sessions, there to abide the judgment of the court. And all fines, &c., not levied or otherwise discharged, are to be continued upon the subsequent rolls until it has been ascertained, to the satisfaction of the commissioners of the treasury, that the fines, &c. cannot be levied on the person taken; and it is provided that the sheriff shall keep and detain the original writs and rolls delivered to him, delivering to the quarter sessions a copy of the roll and also of the old rolls; and the original writ and roll shall continue in force without any further writ or roll: and the sheriff is, on quitting his office, required to deliver to his successor all the writs and rolls in his possession, particularly the sums paid,

(z) Rex *v.* Hankin, 1 M'Clel. & Younge, 27, overruling Ex parte Pellow, M'Clel. Rep. 111.

(a) According to the form given in the schedule of the act. See form, *post*, Append.

CHAP. XVII. SECT. III.

so that the new sheriff may use every means in his power for recovering sums unpaid: the officer or officers entrusted with the execution of the process in any courts, &c. being first duly and diligently examined on oath by the court on the delivery of the roll, or on some subsequent day (*b*). The clerk of the peace is required (*c*) to make oath as to the sums due on the roll, such oath to be indorsed on the writ.

Sheriff may take bond for appearance.

The sheriff, instead of proceeding to seize the goods or take the body of the person mentioned on the roll whose recognizance is forfeited, may (*d*) discharge such person on his giving security to the sheriff, bailiff, or officer for his appearance at the next general or quarter sessions of the peace, then and there to abide the decision of the court, and also to pay such forfeited recognizance, together with all such expenses as shall be ordered and adjudged by the court.

Where the defendant resides out of the jurisdiction.

Where the person shall reside or shall have fled or removed out of the jurisdiction where the recognizance was forfeited, the sheriff should issue his warrant, together with a copy of the writ, directed to the sheriff, &c. of the county, riding, &c. where that person or his goods may be, and the sheriff to whom the warrant is directed has as full power in executing it in his county, as the sheriff to whom the writ was directed had in his county; and the sheriff, within thirty days after the receipt of the warrant, must return to the sheriff from whom he received the warrant what he shall have done in the execution of such process, and whether the party shall have given good security to appeal at sessions; and in case a levy shall have been made, to pay over all monies received in pursuance of the warrant to the sheriff from whom he shall have received the same (*e*).

Return.

The sheriff is to make his return on the first day of each session, stating what fines he has levied and what not; he should make his return on a copy of the writ and roll, and keep the original by him (*f*).

Copy of rolls to be delivered into the Exchequer.

The clerk of the peace of each county is required, on or before the second Monday after the morrow of All Souls in every

(*b*) 4 Geo. 4, c. 37, s. 1, that the sheriff may be chargeable with all sums not satisfactorily accounted for on the final passing of his accounts.

(*c*) 3 Geo. 4, c. 46, s. 3.

(*d*) 3 Geo. 4, c. 46, s. 5.

(*e*) 4 Geo. 4, c. 37, s, 3.

(*f*) 3 Geo. 4, c. 46, s. 8; 4 Geo. 4, c. 37, s. 1.

year, to make and deliver into the Court of Exchequer a true and perfect duplicate or certificate of all fines, amerciaments, recognizances and other forfeitures contained in the rolls and copies delivered to the sheriff for the purpose of levying, and which shall have been set, imposed, or forfeited in any of the sessions of the peace, before Michaelmas in each year, to the intent that the sheriffs, on their apposals in the said Court of Exchequer, may be charged in their accounts with the monies levied and received by him or them respectively upon such writs or otherwise, and that all persons entitled to the fines, &c. may be at liberty to claim the same before the foreign apposer, according to the ancient practice of the court (*g*).

And by the 4 Geo. 4, c, 37, s. 4, "every sheriff shall and he is thereby required to make up, or cause to be made up, annually and immediately after the expiration of the year for which he shall act (or after the usual period for making up his account, in case he shall act under any grant for a longer period than one year), an account in writing containing the names and residences of all persons incurring fines, issues, amerciaments, forfeited recognizances, sum or sums of money paid or to be paid in lieu or satisfaction of them or any of them, which he has been authorized or required to levy by virtue of any writ or writs issued to him or to any predecessor in office; and in case any fine, issue, amerciament, forfeited recognizance, sum or sums of money paid or to be paid in lieu or satisfaction of them or any of them, shall not have been levied or paid, the causes of non-payment shall be fully and particularly stated; and such account such sheriff is thereby required to transmit within thirty days from the expiration of the year for which such account ought to be made up to the commissioners of his majesty's treasury or any three or more of them, in order that such account may be duly examined, checked and inspected under the direction of the said commissioners or any three of them." When the quarter sessions make an order for the discharge of any recognizance, or any person taken thereon from

(*g*) 3 Geo. 4, c. 46, s. 14; and by 4 Geo. 4, c. 37, s. 5, clerks of the peace are to send to the treasury, within twenty days from the opening of quarter sessions, a copy of the rolls delivered to the sheriff, and of the sheriff's return thereto. See *ante*, p. 376.

prison, that order will be a discharge as to the sheriff in the passing of his accounts (*h*).

Any sheriff, bailiff, or officer, for refusing or neglecting to perform his duty as to levying any fine, is subject to a forfeiture of 50*l.*, to be recovered by a common informer by action (*i*).

(*h*) 3 Geo. 4, c. 46, s. 6.

(*i*) 3 Geo. 4, c. 46, s. 10. This act does not affect the rights of the crown in respect of the duchy or county of Lancaster; nor does it affect bodies politic, or the rights of the city of London.

CHAPTER XVIII.

OF THE SHERIFF'S COURTS, AND PROCEEDINGS THEREIN.

SECTION I.

Of the Sheriff's Torne.

WHEN this kingdom was divided into counties, the sheriff had the power committed to him of holding courts both of criminal and civil jurisdiction; these courts were, 1st, The sheriff's torne, into which all the county, to wit, every man of a certain age, should come, there to hear the articles or things given in charge, so that they might not be ignorant of the laws whereby they were to be governed, and where also they were sworn to their allegiance to the king. In this court the sheriff was to inquire of criminal matters, and to reform common nuisances, &c., throughout the whole shire. 2d, The county, or shire court, wherein the sheriff held and still holds plea of causes of action, hereafter specified, under 40*s*., and grants replevin of goods or cattle distrained(*a*). Likewise by writ of justicies the sheriff may hold plea in his county court to any amount. The business of this court was, however, much lessened by the establishment of hundred courts; but they were again, by the statutes of 2 Edw. 3, c. 12; 14 Edw. 3, c. 9, rejoined to the county court.

Jurisdiction of the torne. The sheriff's torne, in ancient times, had jurisdiction (and therein the sheriff might inquire and hold plea) of all criminal offences whatsoever, as well treasons as felonies and misdemeanours; he might there inquire of wayfes, estrays, the king's

(*a*) Dalt. 184.

CHAP. XVIII. SECT. I.

franchises, and of all encroachments thereon. The sheriff's torne was a court of record, and therefore the sheriff might fine and imprison all those who were guilty of offences punishable therein, or who should have failed to do suit there (*b*). But the power of the sheriff in his torne, and the importance of the court, received their death blow by Magna Charta, c. 17, by which it is ordained that "no sheriff, constable, escheator, coroner or other bailiff of the king shall hold pleas of the crown." Ever since, the sheriff's power to hold plea in any criminal offence has ceased; but indictments and inquests were still found in the torne, and process granted thereon; and this was found to be so great a source of oppression and extortion, that to obviate this evil, by the statute 1 Edw. 4 it was ordained "that upon all presentments and indictments which shall be taken before any sheriffs in their counties (except in London), their under-sheriff or officers in their torne or law days, they shall have no power to make or grant out any process against any person so indicted; nor to attach, arrest, or put in prison; nor to assess, levy or take any fines or amerciaments of any person so indicted or presented before them by reason or colour of any such indictment or presentment; nor to take of any person so indicted or presented any fine or ransom; but that the said sheriff, &c., shall bring and deliver all such indictments and presentments taken before them in their tornes to the justices of the peace at their next sessions of the peace that shall be holden in the county where such indictments or presentments shall be taken, upon pain that every sheriff, under-sheriff, &c., failing to deliver or present any such indictments to the justices of the peace at such sessions of the peace shall forfeit 40*l*." "And if any sheriff, under-sheriff, &c., do arrest, attach or put in prison, or cause any fine or ransom to be taken, or levy any amerciament of any person or persons so indicted or presented, by reason or colour of any such indictment or presentment taken before them at their tornes or law days, before that they have process from the justices of the peace, or estreats delivered out of the said indictments or presentments so brought, delivered and presented to them, that then the sheriffs that so do shall

(*b*) As to the power which the sheriff had in his torne, see Dalton's Sheriff, cap. 106.

forfeit 100*l.*;" and if the sheriff levy an amerciament imposed at the torne before it has been certified and enrolled at sessions, and process therefrom, he is a trespasser (*c*). So that even at this day an indictment might be found at the torne, but the sheriff has no power to grant process thereon (*d*). The sheriff's torne, however, has for centuries back fallen completely into disuse; indeed its existence and power are now merely matters of history. The reasons of the disuse of the torne assigned by Dalton are fivefold—1st, that all matters inquired at the leet are now inquired of before the judges of gaol delivery and at quarter sessions; 2d, by the increase of leets the suitors at the torne have been diminished; 3d, the travelling from all parts of the county to attend the torne, and therefore they rather attend the leet; 4th, the trouble and expense to the sheriff in keeping the torne twice in every year (*e*); 5th, that the profits, emoluments and advantages arising to the sheriff from the torne are now taken away (*f*).

(*c*) Griffith *v.* Biddle, Cro. Car. 275; Sir W. Jones, 301, S. C.

(*d*) Formerly it would appear that the sheriff made inquiries, and found indictments of felony by commission; but this power is taken away by the stat. 28 Edw. 1, c. 9.

(*e*) By magna charta, the sheriff should hold his torne in the accustomed place; and by the stat. 31 Edw. 3, the sheriff should hold his torne within a month of Easter and Michaelmas; if taken at any other time, all proceedings were *coram non judice;* and the sheriff was to lose the profits thereof; Dalt. 390.

(*f*) Dalton (page 403) complains "for the trouble and charge of the sheriffs in keeping this their court, as also for the profits thereof, which be now taken away from them, perhaps some sheriffs may regard more their private gain than the common good and weal of the country, (which also is now grown to be the common cause almost in all other men, as well officers as others.) But yet it cannot be denied, that of reward and punishment (as one saith) all commonwealths do consist, and that the care of equity and justice waxeth cold, unless there be reward ready for virtue. And therefore though all sheriffs be, or ought to be, men of the best sufficiency in their county, and such as need no reward for their care, diligence, travel, and charges in that behalf, yet oftentimes (now of late years) the charge and burthen thereof lieth upon men of no great estate; yea, upon such as find it over burthensome to them in regard of the charge. And besides, be they of the best and ablest sort, yet they must of necessity employ under them inferior officers and ministers, to aid their under-sheriffs and others, who with more cheerfulness and care (yea with more honesty and conscience) would, in all likelihood, proceed in their affairs, when they shall find due recompence or reward yielded them for their travel and pains."

CHAP. XVIII. SECT. II.

Section II.

Of the County Court(g).

Ancient jurisdiction of the county court.

The civil court, which is or may be held in every county, is called the sheriff's or county court. In the time of the Saxons nearly all suits were viscontiel, and determined in the county court (*h*); and it would also appear that the bishop and sheriff sat jointly in the county court, and had jurisdiction of all causes, both secular and ecclesiastic; but the power of the bishop and the holding of ecclesiastical pleas in the county court were done away at the Norman Conquest (*i*).

Of its jurisdiction in general.

This court is not a court of record, and holds plea either *by plaint* (*loquela*) or *by writ of justicies*, which is a commission out of chancery, empowering the sheriff to hold plea in a particular cause. There are divers personal actions suable in the county court, which shall be noticed hereafter in this section; there are also two proceedings which are peculiar to the county court; viz. proceedings in outlawry, which have been already noticed (*j*), and suits in replevin, which will be treated hereinafter in the next section (*k*).

(*g*) By the statute 9 & 10 Vict. c. 95 (which has since been carried into effect throughout the country), her majesty was empowered to divide the counties, &c., of England and Wales into districts, and to order that the "County Court" should be holden for the recovery of debts and demands (not exceeding 20*l.*) under that act in each of such districts; the courts so holden to have all the jurisdiction and powers of the County Court for the recovery of debts and demands throughout each district, and to be courts of record; and the lord chancellor is empowered to appoint a judge for each district, whose jurisdiction and duties are defined by the act. The judge so appointed is also to appoint a clerk or clerks of the court, a high bailiff to execute its process, &c. But it is expressly enacted by the 4th section, that for all purposes, except those which shall be within the jurisdiction of the courts holden under that act, the County Court shall be holden as if that act had not been passed; and that all proceedings commenced in the County Court of any county, before the time when any court shall be holden under that act in such county, may be continued, executed, and enforced against all persons liable thereunto, in the same manner as if they had been commenced under the authority of that act. By section 72, the sheriff of every county is directed to cause to be delivered to the clerk of the court established under that act, a list of persons qualified and liable to serve as jurors in the courts of assize and nisi prius for his county, within fourteen days from the receipt of the jury book from the clerk of the peace (see *ante*, p. 386), containing the names of persons within the jurisdiction of the court, for which list the sheriff is to receive out of the general fund of the court a fee after the rate of twopence for every folio of seventy-two words.

(*h*) Selden, 412; Greenwood, 3.

(*i*) *Id. ibid.*

(*j*) *Ante*, p. 215.

(*k*) *Post*, p. 413.

By the 9 Hen. 3, c. 35, and 2 Edw. 6, c. 25, it is ordained, that the holding of the county court shall be no longer deferred but one month from court to court, and the court is to be kept every month on a day certain, and not otherwise; and by 27 Hen. 8, c. 26, in Wales, (and in Chester, by 33 Hen. 8, c. 13,) the sheriffs shall keep their courts monthly, which months are lunar and not calendar months (*l*). And by the 7 & 8 Will. 3, c. 25, s. 9, it is enacted, "that the county courts held for the county of York, or any other county courts which theretofore used to be held on a Monday, shall be called and begun on a Wednesday, and not otherwise."

At what time to be holden.

At the common law, and still, with a few exceptions introduced by statute, the sheriff may keep or hold his court at any place within his county that he pleases. By the stat 2 Edw. 6, c. 25, the sheriff of Northumberland is to hold the county court of that shire in the town or castle of Alnwick, and none other place. The sheriff of Sussex is to hold his county court alternately at Chichester and at Lewes (*m*). The sheriff of Chester is to hold his county court in the shire hall of the said county (*n*). In the counties of Wales, by stat. 27 Hen. 8, c. 26, the county courts are to be held as follows:—of Brecknockshire, at Brecknock; of Radnor, at New Radnor and Presteign; of Montgomery, at Montgomery and Machynlleth; of Denbigh, at Wrexham; of Monmouth, at Monmouth and Newport, *alternis vicibus*.

At what place.

In the county court, whether in suit by plaint or by justicies, the sheriff is not a judge, but only minister, although the court is called the sheriff's court; but the freeholders of the county are judges there in all suits (*o*). In outlawries, the coroners are only judges there to give judgment upon the writs of exigent, that if the defendant do not come in on the fifth proclamation, then the coroners give judgment that he be out of the queen's protection (*p*). Although the suitors be judges in the county court, the judgments and writs, and all other acts in that court, are in the name of the sheriff. And if the sheriff give judgment, or do any act in the county court, without the assent of the freeholders or suitors, an action on the case may be maintained

Of the judge of the court.

(*l*) 2 Inst. 71; Greenwood, 4.

(*m*) 19 Hen. 7, c. 24; Dyer, 135, pl. 14.

(*n*) 33 Hen. 8, c. 13.

(*o*) 4 Rep. 32; 6 Rep. 11; Bro. Judges, 15; *id.* Justicies, 6; Dalt. 409; Jones *v.* Jones, 5 M. & W. 523.

(*p*) Dalt. 406.

CHAP. XVIII. SECT. II.

against the sheriff; but a writ of false judgment does not lie (*q*). The sheriff cannot appoint a deputy for the purpose of holding the county court (*r*); that is to say, that if the proceedings be alleged to have been before a deputy, the proceedings are void. Therefore, on a justicies, he cannot direct his warrant to the bailiff of a liberty to be executed (*s*). But the sheriff always appoints a person to preside in the county court, generally his under-sheriff; and if the proceedings be alleged to be before the sheriff, although they were held before the under-sheriff, it is good (*t*).

County clerk. Besides deputing some person to hold and preside in the county court, the sheriff appoints a clerk of the county court, who is styled the county clerk; it is, however, optional in the sheriff whether or not he will appoint such officer, and the appointment is entirely in the sheriff. In Mitton's case (*u*), it was resolved that a grant by Queen Elizabeth of the office of county clerk, during the vacancy of the office of sheriff, was void; for the appointment belongs and is incident to the office of sheriff. The appointment of the county clerk is made by entry or minute on the proceedings of the county court (*x*).

Attornies. Plaintiffs and defendants may sue or defend suits brought by or against them in the county court by attorney (*y*). By 6 & 7 Vict. c. 73, s. 2, no person can act as an attorney or solicitor in any county court unless he is duly qualified to act as an attorney or solicitor, and has been duly admitted; and by section 36 of that act it is enacted, "that in case any person shall commence or defend any action, or sue out any writ, process, or summons, or carry on any proceedings in the court commonly called the county court, holden in any county in that part of Great Britain called England and Wales, who is not or shall not then be legally admitted an attorney or solicitor according to this act, or shall not himself be plaintiff or defendant in such

(*q*) Fitz. Bill, 12; Dalt. 405, 407.

(*r*) 2 Leon. 34, 210; Com. Dig. County (C) 2; Bro. Officer, 13; Deputy, 29.

(*s*) Bro. Justicies, 2; Fitz. Bar. 161.

(*t*) 21 Hen. 6, 24.

(*u*) 4 Rep. 33. As to the appointment of replevin clerks, see *post*, next section, and *ante*, p. 29.

(*x*) It is said that the county clerk should be imbued with the following qualities (all of which seldom concur in one mortal): *Provideat sibi vicecomes de clerico circumspecto et fideli, viro provido et discreto, gratioso, humili, pudico, pacifico et modesto, qui in legibus consuetudinibusque provinciæ et officio comit. clerici se cognoscat, et jura in omnibus tenere affectet, quique subbalivos in suis erroribus et ambiguis sciat instruere et docere, &c.*

(*y*) West. 2, c. 10; 6 Edw. 1, c. 8; 20 Hen. 3, c. 10.

proceeding respectively, such person shall and is hereby made incapable to maintain or prosecute any action or suit in any court of law or equity for any fee, reward, or disbursement on account of prosecuting, carrying on, or defending any such action, suit, or proceeding, or otherwise in relation thereto; and such offence shall be deemed a contempt of the court in which such action, suit, or proceeding shall have been prosecuted, carried on, or defended, and shall and may be punished accordingly." In an action by an attorney for his charges for suits carried on by him in the county court, he must deliver his bill one month before action commenced, according to the provisions of the 37th section of the same statute.

Bailiffs.

The officers of the county courts for the execution of their processes are styled bailiffs; these must be some persons recommended for their steadiness and good character. These bailiffs are always bound to the sheriff with sureties for the strict performance of their duties (*z*).

What pleas may be held in the county court by *plaint*.

The county court has jurisdiction to hold plea by *plaint* in debt, detinue, or other personal actions (not being *vi et armis*) under the value of 40*s*.(*a*). So, if the debt were originally above 40*s*., and if the plaintiff acknowledge by his declaration that the debt has been reduced below 40*s*., he may sue in the county court (*b*); but it has been ruled that he cannot falsely acknowledge satisfaction of part, to reduce the debt under 40*s*. (*c*). But the county court has no jurisdiction by *plaint* in any personal action where the debt or damage amounts to 40*s*. or upwards. If the debt exceed 40*s*., the plaintiff cannot sue in the county court by *plaint*, even by dividing his demand into several sums below 40*s*. each (*d*); but if he has two debts, separate and distinct, each under 40*s*., he may bring two actions in the county court (*e*); and it must appear affirmatively by the declaration that the cause of action is under 40*s*., otherwise the proceedings would be entirely erroneous (*f*). Where, therefore, the declaration stated that the defendant was indebted to the plaintiff in 1*l*. 9*s*. 6*d*. for goods sold and delivered, *and* in 1*l*. 9*s*. 6*d*. upon an account

(*z*) See stat. 7 & 8 Vict. c. 19, as to the protection of bailiffs of inferior courts from actions.

(*a*) 2 Inst. 312; 4 Inst. 266; 6 Edw. 1, c. 8; Dalt. c. 110.

(*b*) See form of such admission, *post*, Append.

(*c*) Palm. 564; Com. Dig. County (C) 8.

(*d*) *Id. ibid.*; 2 Inst. 312. See Grimbly *v.* Aykroyd, 1 Exch. Rep. 479.

(*e*) Rex *v.* Sheriff of Herefordshire, 1 B. & Adol. 672.

(*f*) *Id. ibid.*; 2 Mod. 206.

CHAP. XVIII. SECT. II.

stated, it was held that, a demand of more than 40*s*. appearing upon the face of the declaration, the county court had no jurisdiction, and that the particulars of demand, which really claimed less than 40*s*., could not be looked at to aid the defect (*g*). This court cannot hold plea in the action of account, though the demand be under 40*s*., for the sheriff cannot assign auditors who are judges of record (*h*). Nor can the county court hold plea in any action of trespass *vi et armis;* the reason whereof is, that a fine is due to the king in such action, and the county court, not being a court of record, cannot impose or assess a fine (*i*). Mayhem, deceit, or maintenance, or the forging of a false deed, cannot be sued in the county court (*k*). Nor can the county court hold plea by *plaint* of debt upon a record or specialty, nor of plea concerning freehold (*l*), nor in detinue of charters concerning freehold or inheritance (*m*); and although the county court may have jurisdiction in a cause, yet if a question of freehold be pleaded, the court is ousted of its jurisdiction; as if a man in a plaint in replevin justifies, avows, or makes cognizance as in the freehold of B., the jurisdiction of the county court is gone (*n*).

Jurisdiction by *justicies*.

In the county court, pleas are also holden by the queen's writ out of chancery, called a *justicies* or viscontiel writ, by which the sheriff is commanded and empowered to hold plea in the particular case. This writ is not returnable. If the sheriff do not proceed thereon, an *alias* and *pluries* may issue: if he cannot show cause for not executing those writs, an attachment will be granted against him (*o*). By justicies the county court may hold plea in assumpsit, debt, detinue, and other personal actions (excepting in trespass *vi et armis*), to any amount (*p*). In actions for torts, although the damages be laid to any amount, the county court may hold plea by justicies, but not when the cause of action is laid to be *vi et armis* (*q*); and although freehold

(*g*) Dempster *v*. Purnell, 3 Man. & G. 375; 1 Dowl. N. S. 172, S. C.

(*h*) 2 Inst. 380; Com. Dig. County (C) 8.

(*i*) 2 Inst. 311; 4 Inst. 266.

(*k*) Com. Dig. County (C) 8.

(*l*) Com. Dig. County (S) 8; but it is otherwise of debt on record in the same court, Dalt. 412.

(*m*) Fitz. Nat. Brev. 138; 2 Inst. 311.

(*n*) 3 Lev. 196, 203.

(*o*) Dalt. 421; Fitz. N. B. 125 e.

(*p*) Com. Dig. County (C) 5.

(*q*) Dalt. 423; Fitz. N. B. 85, 86, 87; Reg. Brev. 92. But see 2 Inst. 312; Com. Dig. County (C) 5, *contrà;* but the reason given above why the county court cannot hold plea in trespass *vi et armis*, viz. because, not being a court of record, the court cannot impose a fine, is equally applicable to proceedings by justicies.

come in question, the county court may hold plea by justicies (*r*). So in annuity (*s*), or in debt for tithes (*t*), plea may be holden in the county court by justicies; also in divers real actions the county court may hold plea by justicies, as in dower *unde nihil habet*, in admeasurement of pasture, in a *quod permittat*, nuisance, &c., *in rationabile divisis*, *curiâ claudendâ*, in *secta ad molendinum*, in right patent or right of ward, in *nativo habendo*, or in *plegiis acquietandis* (*u*).

The cause of action must have arisen within the jurisdiction.

The county court, whether in suit by plaint or justicies, has only jurisdiction in cases where the defendant resides, and the cause of action arises, within its jurisdiction, viz. within the precincts of the county. The rule in the superior courts, which supposes debts and contracts to be of a transitory nature, and to have arisen wherever the venue is laid, does not apply to suits in inferior courts; for in such courts it must be distinctly alleged and proved, that not only the promise, but the cause of action itself, arose within the jurisdiction of the court (*x*). If the cause of action, however, arose within the jurisdiction of the county court, any matter merely in aggravation of damages is triable there, although arising out of the jurisdiction (*y*).

Process.

A *capias* does not lie in the county court, either in proceedings by plaint or by justicies (*z*). The process is by summons, attachment, and distress infinite; or by attachment and distress infinite, as in actions of trespass on the case (*a*). Those writs run in the name of the sheriff, directed to his bailiffs (*b*). The summons may issue two or three days before the court day; the practice respecting the issuing of summonses varies in different counties (*c*). The under-sheriff should, on his entrance into office, get a sufficient number of county court summonses printed, and keep a regular account with the bailiffs respecting the number used. If the defendant do not appear upon the summons, thereupon an attachment issues, by virtue of which

(*r*) 14 Hen. 8, 15 b; Bro. Jurisdiction, 98; Finch, 320.

(*s*) 4 Inst. 266.

(*t*) 1 Lev. 253.

(*u*) Dalt. 421—423; Com. Dig. County (C) 5.

(*x*) 1 Saund. 74 a, note (1).

(*y*) Peacock *v.* Bell, 1 Saund. 74 a, n. (1); see also Dunn *v.* Crump, 3 Brod. & Bing. 309.

(*z*) Com. Dig. County (C) 9.

(*a*) *Id. ibid.*

(*b*) 3 Lev. 203; Lutw. 1413.

(*c*) In a pamphlet published on the practice of the Yorkshire County Court, it is stated that in that court it had been a practice to serve summonses before they were issued, and frequently before the plaint had been entered; in consequence of so many abuses arising therefrom, a rule had been made not to issue any summons, or enter a plaint, after Monday previous to the court day.

CHAP. XVIII. SECT. II.

the bailiff should seize and detain, but not sell, some chattel of moderate value, that is to say, of the value of 40*s.*, to compel an appearance; or it is sufficient to warn the defendant to appear, if it is returned that he has been warned (*d*). If the defendant do not appear on the attachment, a *distringas* issues, whereon the bailiff should take and detain goods of the defendant of the value of 40*s.* until the defendant appear. Goods taken on the attachment or *distringas* are forfeited, if the defendant do not appear at the next county court (*e*).

Declaration. The plaint must be entered in writing *sedente curiâ,* and is the first proceeding in the suit. When the defendant appears, the plaintiff files his declaration, giving a rule to plead, according to the practice of the court, which is generally eight days. The declaration is the same as in the courts above, with this addition, that every material fact must be laid to have arisen within the jurisdiction; but matter merely in aggravation of damages need not be laid to have arisen within the jurisdiction (*f*). In a writ of false judgment, where the declaration alleged that the defendant was indebted to the plaintiff for work and labour in curing horses, &c. within the jurisdiction, and for *potions* administered *on those occasions,* it was held that the whole cause of action was sufficiently alleged to have arisen within the jurisdiction (*g*). So where the declaration stated that the defendant was indebted to the plaintiff within the jurisdiction, &c., for the wages of and due and owing to the plaintiff within the jurisdiction, &c., as the servant of the defendant, it was conceded that the jurisdiction was sufficiently laid (*h*).

The defendant can only plead one plea to a declaration in the county court, for the statute 4 & 5 Ann. c. 16, which allows defendants to plead several pleas, is confined to courts of record; and if the defendant pleads two distinct pleas, the plaintiff may reply to the first and take no notice of the other (*i*). In case of a plea of freehold, in a suit by plaint, the suit cannot proceed further; it is, however, otherwise in a suit by justicies in the county court (*k*). Upon a plea in the nature of a demurrer to

(*d*) Com. Dig. County (C) 9.
(*e*) Com. Dig. Process (D) 6, 7.
(*f*) See note (1), 1 Saund. 74 a.
(*g*) Dunn *v.* Crump, 3 Brod. & Bing. 309.
(*h*) Chitty *v.* Lusford, 3 Ad. & E. 319.
(*i*) See Chitty *v.* Dendy, 3 Ad. & E. 319.
(*k*) Bro. Jurisd. 98.

the jurisdiction, the county court, in giving judgment for the defendant, cannot award him costs (*l*).

Trial.

In a suit in the county court by justicies, the trial is by jury; also in a suit by plaint, the trial there by prescription may be by jury; otherwise, in suits by plaint in the county court, the trial is by wager of law, or by examination of witnesses (*m*).

Execution.

The execution in the county court is by distress, to compel the defendant to satisfy the judgment (*n*); although the officer may seize the defendant's goods, yet, without a custom, he cannot sell, but must detain them (*o*). Execution on a judgment in the county court, by custom, may be by *levari facias* against the goods and chattels, but not against the lands (*p*). A *capias ad satisfaciendum* cannot issue on the judgment in the county court (*q*); but by the statute 34 Hen. 8, c. 26, the sheriffs of Wales are enabled, upon every judgment had before them in their counties or hundred courts, in every plaint under 40*s*., to award a *capias ad satisfaciendum* against the body, or a *fieri facias*, at the plaintiff's choice. If the sheriff delay execution, a writ *de executione judicii* may be directed to him out of chancery, to do execution; and thereupon, if execution be not done, an *alias* and *pluries*, and attachment, may go against the sheriff (*r*).

The different writs for removing causes from the county court.

Causes in the county court may be removed into the superior courts by writ of *pone*, or writ of *recordari facias loquelam*, before judgment; or after judgment, by a writ of false judgment; and also, if the court hold plea where it has not jurisdiction, the superior courts will grant prohibition.

Writ of *pone*.

The writ of *pone* only lies where the suit is in the county court by original writ out of Chancery, as replevin by writ, or in a suit by justicies (*s*): this writ is an original writ issuing out of chancery, commanding the sheriff to *put* before the queen, on a general return day, wheresoever, &c., the proceedings in the suit, and the sheriff is also to summon the plaintiff or defendant, as the case may be, &c., to be in the court above on the return day, so that the parties may proceed in the plea.

(*l*) See Dempster *v*. Purnell, 3 Man. & G. 372; 1 Dowl. & L. 172, S. C.

(*m*) Com. Dig. County (C) 11. See form of *venire* in the county court, *post*, Append.

(*n*) Com. Dig. County (C) 13; Dalt. 419.

(*o*) *Id. ibid.*

(*p*) Com. Dig. County (C) 10.

(*q*) Dalt. 419; Com. Dig. County (C) 13.

(*r*) *Id. ibid.*

(*s*) Fitz. N. B. 69; Gilb. Repl. 102.

CHAP. XVIII. SECT. II.

The sheriff makes his return to this writ, that he has *put*, &c., and annexes a schedule containing a copy of the proceedings to his return (*t*); and if, after the cause be removed, the parties proceed in the court below, an attachment shall go against the sheriff for contempt (*u*). The cause assigned at the end of the writ of *pone* for removing the plaint is mere form, and is not traversable (*x*).

Re. fa. lo.

The writ of *recordari facias loquelam* is also an original writ issuing out of chancery, and lies for the removal of causes before judgment in the county court by *plaint* without writ. This writ may be obtained either by the plaintiff or the defendant as a matter of course. It is only calculated for the removal of actions of replevin from the county court, for it is beneath the dignity of a superior court to proceed in other actions where the damages are under 40*s*., and therefore in such case, if the cause were removed, the court would award a *procedendo*. By the writ of *re. fa. lo.* the sheriff is commanded that in his full county he cause to be recorded the plaint which is in the same court without the queen's writ; and that he have the record in the court above on a general return day, under his seal and the seals of four lawful knights of his county, who were present at that recording; and that he prefix the same day to the parties that they be then there to proceed in the action (*y*). The sheriff should also direct his warrant to two or more bailiffs to summon the plaintiff or defendant (*z*). The sheriff makes his return to this writ according to the terms of it, and annexes all the proceedings in a schedule to his return (*a*). The *re. fa. lo.* will remove the plaint, although it may have been discontinued, or although the *re. fa. lo.* may have issued before the plaint was entered (*b*). The sheriff should make a positive and not an argumentative return to the *re. fa. lo.;* he should either return the plaint, or that no plaint is pending, and it is bad to return the plaint and all subsequent proceedings, leaving it for the court to judge if there is a plaint pending or not (*c*).

(*t*) See return, *post*, Append. But the original minute of the proceeding is not removed. *Per* Holroyd, J., Dyson *v*. Wood, 3 Bar. & Cress. 453.

(*u*) Greenwood, 58.

(*x*) Parkes *v*. Renton, 3 B. & Ad. 105; see also Grimshaw *v*. Emerson, 1 Dowl. 337.

(*y*) Fitz. Nat. Brev. 70.

(*z*) See form, *post*, Append.

(*a*) See return, *post*, Append.

(*b*) Greenwood, 57, 58.

(*c*) Wright *v*. Lewis, 8 Dowl. 514.

Accedas ad curiam.

The writ of *accedas ad curiam* lies for the removal of plaints out of the court of the lord; it is a writ issuing out of Chancery, directed to the sheriff of the county, commanding him that, taking with him four discreet and lawful knights of his county, he go in his proper person to the court of the lord, and in that full court he cause to be recorded the plaint, and that he have that record in the court above, on a general return day, under his seal and the seals of four lawful men who were present at that recording, and to prefix the same day to the parties aforesaid, that they be then there to proceed, &c., and that the sheriff should have the writ with the names of the suitors on the return day (*d*). This writ is executed by directing a precept to the steward and suitors of the court, ordering them to return the plaint to the sheriff, and to prefix a day to the parties to appear, and thereupon the sheriff returns the *accedas ad curiam*, with a return in compliance with the terms of the writ, with the plaint annexed in a schedule thereto (*e*). The persons who are alleged to have gone with him need not in fact be knights, it is sufficient if they be stated to be so (*f*). It is a good return for the sheriff to state that after the receipt of the writ, and before the return thereof, no court was holden, and that he also required the lord to hold his court, which he refused to do (*g*). It seems to be a good return for the sheriff, that the suitors refused to record the plea (*h*), or denied that there was any such plea (*i*), or that the suitors would not deliver him the record (*j*). In such cases the court above would award a writ of *distringas*, directed to the sheriff, against the suitors, with a summons against the party (*k*).

Writ of false judgment.

The writ of false judgment is a writ issuing out of Chancery, directed to the sheriff for the removal of a suit after judgment, out of the county or other inferior court, *not of record*. The writ of false judgment is exactly the same as the writ of *recordari facias loquelam*, excepting that it alleges that the defendant complains that false judgment hath been given against him in

(*d*) Greenwood, 61. The writ always alleges some special cause; but this is mere surmise, and never inquired into at this day.

(*e*) See return, *post*, Append.

(*f*) Fitz Nat. Brev. 10.

(*g*) Greenwood, 63; Dalt. 201, 243; Fitz. Retorn, 21; thereupon the court will grant a *distringas* to compel the lord to hold his court; *Id. ibid.*

(*h*) Fitz. Faux Judgment, 6, 8, 21; Process, 167; Dyer, 262; Dalt. 243.

(*i*) Fitz. Faux Judgment, 13; Fitz. Nat. Brev. 16; Dalt. 243.

(*j*) Fitz. Process, 128; Dalt. 243.

(*k*) Dalt. 243, 244.

CHAP. XVIII. SECT. II.

the said county court. To the writ of false judgment the sheriff makes this return, and summons the parties in the same manner as on a *re. fa. lo.* To the writ of false judgment it is not necessary to return the original minute of the proceedings, but merely a statement of the proceedings, for it is not necessary to the validity of the proceedings in a suit in the county court that any memorandum thereof should be made (*l*), although regular entries of all the proceedings there should be kept; and if on a return to a writ of false judgment the sheriff merely returns minutes of the proceedings, the court will compel him to complete the entries of those proceedings, and to certify the practice of the court (*m*). If the proceedings be erroneous, as if the cause of action be not laid to have arisen within the jurisdiction of the court, or the like, the court above will reverse the judgment (*n*).

Bill of exceptions.

A bill of exceptions will lie to the direction of the judge of a county court (*o*).

Prohibition.

Also if a suit is brought in the county court over which it has not jurisdiction, the superior courts will grant a prohibition to the inferior court from proceeding further in the suit (*p*).

Actions against the sheriff, &c. in respect of process issuing out of the county court.

It is said, that if the sheriff pronounce judgment, or do any other act without the assent of the suitors, an action on the case lies against him (*q*). But if the bailiff, to whom the process of the county court is directed to distrain on the goods of A., seize the goods of B., an action of trespass cannot be maintained by B. against the sheriff; for the sheriff is a constituent and essential part of the county court, although the suitors are judges: the bailiff, and not the sheriff, is the minister of the court for the execution of its process, consequently the bailiff is solely responsible for any trespass committed in the execution of such process (*r*). No action will lie, therefore, against the

(*l*) Dyson *v.* Wood, 5 Dowl. & Ry. 295; 3 Bar. & Cress. 449, S. C.

(*m*) Overton *v.* Swettenham, 5 Dowl. 641.

(*n*) See Bishop *v.* Kaye, 3 Bar. & Ald. 610; Dempster *v.* Purnell, 3 Man. & G. 375; 1 Dowl. N. S. 172, S. C.

(*o*) Strother *v.* Hutchinson, 4 Bing. N. C. 83.

(*p*) Dalt. 426.

(*q*) Dalt. 405, 407.

(*r*) Holroyd *v.* Breare, 2 Bar. & Ald. 473; see also Carratt *v.* Morley, 1 Q. B. 18; Bradley *v.* Carr, 3 Man. & G. 221; Tunno *v.* Morris, 2 C. M. & R. 298; Tinsley *v.* Nassau, Moo. & M. 52; Brown *v.* Copley, 13 Law J., N. S., C. P. 164; Cresswell, J., 2 Dowl. & L. 332, S. C. *Quære*, as to the law, supposing the sheriff received the poundage on such writ?

sheriff for a false return to an execution out of the county court (*s*). CHAP. XVIII. SECT. II.

Fees. See a table of fees generally charged for proceedings in the county court in the appendix to this chapter.

Section III.

Replevin.

In what cases replevin lies. Replevin lies for the unlawful taking of *any goods and chattels*, whether living animals or inanimate chattels (*t*), and for the young of cattle born after the distress taken (*u*); but for fixtures, or things affixed to the freehold, replevin is not grantable (*x*). Replevin does not lie for chattels relating to the inheritance, for they are not esteemed personal chattels in law (*y*). As the landlord is empowered to distrain sheaves or cocks of corn, or loose corn (*z*) lying upon any part of the demised premises, or corn growing on the demised premises (*a*), where corn is distrained, replevin will lie. It lies at common law in all cases where goods are improperly taken, or taken under a pretended authority (*b*); thus it lies for goods taken under a distress warrant of justices, issued on an order which on the face of it shows that they had no authority to make it (*c*). It lies also for goods distrained for a poor rate (*d*).

It has been held that replevin does not lie for goods taken in execution (*e*), nor for goods distrained under a conviction for deer-stealing (*f*), nor for goods seized for duties due to the crown (*g*). And formerly it was held that in general, where goods were taken by virtue of a statute, by which distress and

(*s*) Pitcher *v.* King, 9 A. & E. 288.

(*t*) Com. Dig. Replevin (A); and see Dore *v.* Wilkinson, 2 Stark. N. P. C. 288; Wilk. Replevin, 2, 3.

(*u*) Gilb. Replevin, 170.

(*x*) Bac. Abr. Replevin (F); Roscoe, 621; see Niblett *v.* Smith, 4 T. R. 504.

(*y*) Gilb. Replevin, 170.

(*z*) 2 Will. & M. c. 5, s. 3.

(*a*) 11 Geo. 2, c. 19, s. 8.

(*b*) George *v.* Chambers, 11 M. & W. 149; 2 Dowl. N. S. 783, S. C.

(*c*) *Ibid.*; see also Morrell *v.* Martin, 3 Man. & G. 581.

(*d*) Sabourin *v.* Marshall, 3 B. & Adol. 440; Selby *v.* Bardons, 3 B. & Adol. 2.

(*e*) Com. Dig. Replevin (D); but replevin lies for goods taken by virtue of an execution issuing out of an inferior court; Gilb. Replevin, 167.

(*f*) Rex *v.* Monkhouse, Stra. 1184; and for so doing, the court granted an attachment against the sheriff. And see Wilson *v.* Weller, 1 Brod. & Bing. 57.

(*g*) Rex *v.* Oliver, Bunb. 14.

CHAP. XVIII. SECT. III.

sale was given, inasmuch as this was considered in the nature of an execution, replevin did not lie (*h*), unless the statute by implication empowered the party whose goods were seized to replevy them (*i*). But the Court of Common Pleas refused to set aside proceedings in an action of replevin brought for goods taken on a distress for an assessment under the Highway Act, 13 Geo. 3, c. 78, s. 47 (*k*); indeed, it seems that the court will not enter into the question whether replevin lies or not, on a motion to set aside proceedings (*l*). Replevin, however, does not lie where goods are simply *detained* by a party to whom they have been delivered *upon a contract*, as where they are unjustly detained by a carrier (*m*); but only where they are unlawfully *taken*. But replevin lies for a wrongful detention of goods taken under a lawful distress, for such detention amounts to a new taking (*n*).

By whom.

A person, in order to obtain replevin, must have either an absolute or a special property in the goods distrained (*o*). If the goods of a *feme sole* are distrained, and she afterwards marries, her husband alone may bring replevin, or the two may join (*p*). Executors may have replevin for a taking in the lifetime of their testator (*q*).

Against whom.

The action of replevin may be brought against the bailiff who makes, or against the landlord who authorizes the distress, or against both.

Of the different kinds of replevin.

The proceeding in the action of replevin at the common law was by original writ, issuing out of Chancery, by which the sheriff was commanded to grant replevin of the goods distrained, and to determine the matter in his county court (*r*). The mode of proceeding in replevin by plaint was introduced by the Sta-

(*h*) Bradshaw's case, Bac. Abr. Replevin (C); 1 Barnard, B. R. 110; Wilson *v.* Weller, 1 Brod. & Bing. 63; Willes, 672, note (*b*); but see Anon., T. Jones, 25; Hutchins *v.* Chambers, 1 Burr. 588.

(*i*) Fletcher *v.* Williams, 6 East, 287. As in a distress for poor rates, under 43 Eliz. c. 2, where the party "making avowry" is allowed to plead, &c., Milward *v.* Coffin, 2 Bla. Rep. 1330; Hurrell *v.* Wink, 8 Taunt. 369.

(*k*) Fenton *v.* Boyce, 2 N. R. 392.

(*l*) Pritchard *v.* Stephens, 6 T. R. 522.

(*m*) Galloway *v.* Bird, 12 Moore, 547; 4 Bing. 299, S. C.

(*n*) Evans *v.* Elliott, 5 Ad. & E 142; 6 Nev. & Man. 606, S. C.

(*o*) Co. Litt. 145 b.

(*p*) Burn *v.* Maltaire, Cas. Temp. Hard. 120; Blackburn *v.* Greaves, 2 Lev. 107; Milner *v.* Milner, 3 T. R. 627; and see Serres *v.* Dodds, 2 N. R. 405.

(*q*) Arundell *v.* Turvil, 1 Sid. 82; Bull. N. P. 53.

(*r*) 2 Inst. 240.

tute of Marlbridge, c. 21, by which the sheriff was authorized to deliver the goods and to hold the plea in replevin by plaint, as he might at common law, on a writ of replevin (*s*). The action of replevin by writ has long been obsolete. And by the recent statute, 9 & 10 Vict. c. 95, s. 119, it is declared and enacted, that all actions of replevin, in cases of distress for rent in arrear or damage faisant, which shall be brought in the county court, shall be brought without writ in a court held under that act. Sect. 120 enacts, that in every such action of replevin, the plaint shall be entered in the court holden under that act for the district wherein the distress was taken. And by sect. 121 it is enacted, that in case either party to any such action of replevin shall declare to the court in which such action shall be brought, that the title to any corporeal or incorporeal hereditament, or to any toll, market, fair, or franchise is in question, or that the rent or damage in respect of which the distress shall have been taken is more than the sum of twenty pounds, and shall become bound with two sufficient sureties, to be approved by the clerk of the court, in such sums as to the judge shall seem reasonable, regard being had to the nature of the claim, and the alleged value or amount of the property in dispute, or of the rent or damage, to prosecute the suit with effect and without delay, and to prove before the court by which such suit shall be tried, that such title as aforesaid is in dispute between the parties, or that there was ground for believing that the said rent or damage was more than twenty pounds, then and not otherwise the action may be removed before any court competent to try the same, in such manner as hath been accustomed. Sect. 127 enacts, that every bond given on the removal of any action out of the county court shall be made to the other party to the action, at the costs of such other party, and shall be approved by the judge, and attested under the seal of the court; and if the bond so taken be forfeited, or if, upon the proceeding for securing which such bond was given, the judge before whom such proceeding shall be had shall not certify upon the record in court that the condition of the bond hath been fulfilled, the party to whom the bond shall have been so made may bring an action of debt, and recover there-

(*s*) 2 Inst. 240; Wilson *v.* Hobday, 4 M. & Sel. 128. The word "beasts" only is mentioned in this statute, but it has been construed to extend to all goods and chattels; Wilk. Replevin, 8.

on: provided always, that the court in which such action as last aforesaid shall be brought, may by a rule of court give such relief to the parties liable upon such bond as may be agreeable to justice and reason, and such rule shall have the nature and effect of a defeasance to such bond.

Replevin clerks.

We have already seen, that by the statute 1 & 2 Philip & Mary, c. 12, s. 3, the sheriff, at his first county day, or within two months after he has received his patent, is required to appoint at least four clerks for granting replevins in his county. The mode of appointing, and the liability of, such replevin clerks have already been pointed out in a former part of this work (*t*).

The 9 & 10 Vict. c. 95, has not pointed out any fresh mode of proceeding for obtaining replevin, in the cases to which the above-mentioned provisions of that statute apply; it is conceived, therefore, that all the proceedings antecedent to the entering of the plaint must still be according to the former practice, which therefore we proceed to state.

Replevin, how granted.

If a person whose goods are distrained, having found the requisite sureties, make application to the sheriff or his deputies, a precept will be granted, in the name of the sheriff, to two or more bailiffs, to replevy the goods taken, and to summon the defendant to appear at the next county court (*u*). Strictly speaking, the plaint should be levied in the county court before the goods are replevied (*x*); but the precept may be granted, and the goods delivered thereon, between one county court and another, and the plaint entered at the next court (*y*). In one case the Court of King's Bench refused to grant a motion to compel the sheriff to enter a plaint in replevin (*z*). Where the lord of the franchise has the prescriptive right to grant replevins in the same manner as the sheriff had before the Statute of Marlbridge, the sheriff has not a concurrent jurisdiction with him (*a*).

Pledges in replevin.

By the Statute of Westm. 2, (13 Edw. 1, c. 2), the sheriff is required, before he makes his deliverance of the distress, to take from the plaintiff the usual pledges to prosecute, and also

(*t*) *Ante*, p. 29. In Trevanion's case, 11 Mod. 32, the court granted an information against an attorney for granting a replevin in his own cause without any deputation.

(*u*) See form of precept, and summons thereon, Append.

(*x*) Seal *v*. Philips, 3 Price, 18; Wilk. Replevin, 9.

(*y*) 2 Inst. 139; Co. Litt. 145 b.

(*z*) Ex parte Boyle, 2 Dowl. & Ry. 13.

(*a*) Mounsey *v*. Dawson, 6 Ad. & E. 752; 1 N. & P. 763, S. C.

to make a return of the beasts, if a return be awarded: otherwise he shall answer for the price of the beasts, and he who distrains shall have his recovery by writ, that the sheriff shall render to him so many cattle or goods; and if the bailiff have not wherewith he may render, his superiors shall answer. Under this statute, the sheriff may take a bond, either from the plaintiff himself (*b*), or from one (*c*) or more pledges (*d*), conditioned to prosecute the suit with effect, and to make a return, if a return should be adjudged; but the sheriff cannot take money in lieu of pledges, in granting replevin (*e*). It is usual to insert in the replevin bond a condition to save the sheriff harmless, and it has been determined that a bond with such condition is not therefore void (*f*). Bonds taken under this statute are not assignable (*g*).

Of the taking and the assigning of a replevin bond under the 11 Geo. 2, c. 19.

In granting replevins in cases of distress for rent, the sheriff's duty in taking replevin bonds is regulated by the statute 11 Geo. 2, c. 19, s. 23, which has been holden to extend to a replevin granted of a distress for a rent-charge (*h*). By that statute it is enacted, "that all sheriffs and other officers having any authority to grant replevin (*i*) may and shall, in every replevin of a distress for rent, take, in their own names, from the plaintiff and two responsible persons as sureties, a bond in the double value of the goods distrained (*k*), (such value to be ascertained by the oath of one or more credible witness or witnesses (*l*) not interested in the goods or distress, which oath the person granting such replevin is thereby authorized and required to administer), and conditioned for prosecuting the suit with effect and without delay, and for duly returning the goods and chattels distrained, in case a return shall be awarded, before any deliverance be made of the distress; and that such sheriff

(*b*) Blackett *v.* Crissop, 1 Lord Raym. 278.

(*c*) In a replevin for a distress damage feasant, it is sufficient if the sheriff take one pledge; Hucker *v.* Gordon, 1 C. & M. 58.

(*d*) Moyser *v.* Gray, Cro. Car. 446.

(*e*) *Id. ibid.*

(*f*) Short *v.* Hubbard, 2 Bing. 357; Blackett *v.* Crissop, 1 Lord Raym. 278; see also Miers *v.* Lockwood, 9 Dowl. 975.

(*g*) Wilk. Replevin, 12.

(*h*) Short *v.* Hubbard, 2 Bing. 349.

(*i*) A replevin bond may be taken and assigned by any officer who has power to grant replevins; and it has been held that one of the sheriffs of London has such power without his companion; Thompson *v.* Farden, 1 Man. & G. 585.

(*k*) *Semble*, if the bond be taken in a greater amount, the court would, if speedy application were made, set it aside; Miers *v.* Lockwood, 9 Dowl. 975.

(*l*) See Middleton *v.* Bryan, 3 M. & Sel. 157.

CHAP. XVIII. SECT. III.

or other officer as aforesaid taking any such bond shall, at the request and costs of the avowant, or person making conuzance, assign such bond to the avowant or person aforesaid, by indorsing the same, and attesting it under his hand and seal, in the presence of two or more credible witnesses; which may be done without any stamp, provided the assignment so indorsed be duly stamped before any action brought thereupon (*m*); and if the bond so taken and assigned be forfeited, the avowant or person making conuzance may bring an action and recover thereupon in his own name; and the court where such action shall be brought may, by a rule of the same court, give such relief to the parties upon such bond as may be agreeable to justice and reason; and such rule shall have the nature and effect of a defeasance to such bond (*n*)."

The sheriff, under this statute, takes a bond either from the plaintiff and two responsible persons, or from the latter alone; and where the bond had been executed by one of the sureties only, it was held that the sheriff was entitled to sue upon such bond (*o*). The bond must, by the statute, be in double the value of the goods distrained (*p*), and conditioned for prosecuting the suit *with effect* and *without delay* (*q*), with all due diligence (*r*), and for duly returning the goods and chattels distrained, in case a return shall be awarded. A bond conditioned for appearance at the next county court, for prosecuting the plaint with effect, making a return if adjudged, *and indemnifying the sheriff from all charges and damages by reason of the replevin*, is authorized by the statute (*s*); but a condition that the party shall appear at the next county court, and *then* and *there* prosecute his suit *with effect*, is not warranted by the statute (*t*); for it is sufficient if the party at the next court *begins* to prosecute his suit. If a surety in the replevin bond is a material witness in the cause, the court will grant a rule for substituting another

(*m*) A stamp is no longer required on the bond or assignment: 5 Geo. 4, c. 41.

(*n*) See form of replevin bonds and assignment, Append.

(*o*) Austin *v.* Haward, 2 Marsh. 352; 7 Taunt. 28, 327, S. C.

(*p*) But it ought not to be in a greater amount; see Miers *v.* Lockwood, 9 Dowl. 975.

(*q*) This means that the suit is to be prosecuted to a not unsuccessful termination; Jackson *v.* Hanson, 8 M. & W. 477; 1 Dowl. N. S. 69, S. C.; Perreau *v.* Beavan, 5 B. & C. 284; Harrison *v.* Wardle, 5 B. & Ad. 146; 2 N. & M. 703, S. C.

(*r*) *Id. ibid.*

(*s*) Short *v.* Hubbard, 2 Bing. 349.

(*t*) Jackson *v.* Hanson, *supra.*

surety in his place, upon giving the defendant's attorney notice of such rule (*u*). CHAP. XVIII. SECT. III.

The mode in which deliverance is made of goods distrained is by the sheriff's precept above noticed. If the cattle were taken and impounded within a liberty, the sheriff should issue his warrant to the bailiff of the liberty to make deliverance (*x*); and if he make no answer nor replevy the cattle, the sheriff, by the statute of Marlbridge, 52 Hen. 3, c. 21, and statute Westm. 2, c. 17, may enter the franchise and grant replevin (*y*); but the sheriff has no concurrent jurisdiction with the lord of a franchise, who has a prescriptive right to grant replevins, in the same manner as the sheriff had before the statute of Marlbridge (*z*).

By the statute of Westminster 1, c. 17, the sheriff, after demand made, may break open the house of the person who has made the distress, in order to deliver the cattle or goods distrained. The officer may also raise the *posse comitatûs*, if necessary, to make deliverance of goods distrained (*a*). If the goods cannot be taken on the first precept, the sheriff should issue another precept in nature of an *alias*, and then a *pluries*; and if the cattle, by inquest of office, are found to be eloigned, a precept issues, in the nature of a writ of withernam, to take other cattle in lieu of those eloigned (*b*). The goods or cattle taken in withernam cannot be replevied until the original distress is forthcoming; if the cattle are withheld, the plaintiff may nevertheless proceed in the cause, and recover damages to the full value of the cattle, as well as for the detention (*c*).

Writ *de proprietate probandâ.*

If a defendant claim property in the goods distrained, the sheriff cannot proceed to replevy them; for he is not authorized to determine questions of property in his court, without the queen's writ (*d*). In case of a claim of property by the defendant, the proceeding to obtain deliverance is by writ *de proprietate probandâ*, by which the sheriff is commanded to inquire by a jury to whom the property belongs; the sheriff thereupon is to

(*u*) Bailey *v.* Bailey, 1 Bing. 92; 7 Moore, 439, S. C.

(*x*) See Mounsey *v.* Dawson, 6 A. & E. 752; 1 N. & P. 763, S. C.

(*y*) 2 Inst. 140, 194.

(*z*) Mounsey *v.* Dawson, 6 A. & E. 752; 1 N. & P. 763, S. C.

(*a*) Dalt. 435; 2 Inst. 193.

(*b*) Gilb. Repl. 98—108; Bac. Abr. Replevin (E. 7).

(*c*) Wilk. Replev. 20.

(*d*) Co. Litt. 145, 146; Leonard *v.* Stacy, 6 Mod. 140; Wilk. Repl. 16, 17. See *ante*, 406, 415.

CHAP. XVIII. SECT. III.

hold an inquest of office. If the property be found in the plaintiff, the sheriff is then to make deliverance; if in the defendant, the proceedings are at an end (*e*). The sheriff should give notice to the parties of the time and place appointed for holding the inquest (*f*).

Proceedings in the county court.

The proceedings in the county court in the action of replevin are the same as in any other suit by plaint; the process, properly speaking, is by attachment to compel an appearance, but in practice it is generally a summons (*g*). If the defendant pleads any plea by which the freehold may come in question, the jurisdiction of the county court is at an end (*h*); the defendant, also, can plead only one plea in the action of replevin in the county court (*i*). A replevin suit may be removed from the county court by the same process, and in the same manner, as before pointed out respecting the removal of suits in general from the county court (*k*).

Of the *retorno habendo*, and the sheriff's duty in executing it.

The execution in the action of replevin at the common law (and still, where the avowant cannot or does not proceed under the 17 Car. 2, or 7 Hen. 8, c. 4, or 21 Hen. 8, c. 19) is by writ of *retorno habendo*, by which writ the sheriff is commanded that he make a return of the goods to the defendant. Under this writ he should take from the plaintiff the goods that were replevied; this is seldom, if ever, done. To this writ the sheriff generally returns *elongata*, that the goods were eloigned and removed to places unknown (*l*). Upon this return being filed, the defendant may have a *capias in withernam*, by which writ the sheriff is commanded to take *in withernam* the cattle, goods and chattels of the plaintiff, to the value of the cattle, goods and chattels before taken, to be delivered to the defendant; to be kept by him till the sheriff can cause to be returned the cattle, goods and chattels before taken; and to put, by gages and safe pledges, the plaintiff to answer, as well for his contempt as to the defendant, for the damages and injury to him done (*m*). The writ of *retorno habendo* has been generally sued out for the purpose of founding proceedings on the bail-

(*e*) Co. Litt. 145 b. It is there said that the claim of property must be made by the defendant in person, and not by bailiff.

(*f*) Dalt. 274.

(*g*) Wilk. Repl. 20. As to the proceedings in the courts established under 9 & 10 Vict. c. 95, see the 59th and following sections of that act; and *ante*, 415.

(*h*) See *ante*, 406, 415.

(*i*) See *ante*, 408.

(*k*) See *ante*, 409, 415.

(*l*) See form, Append.

(*m*) Wilk. Repl. 110.

bond, or against the sheriff; but this is unnecessary, for as the replevin-bond is conditioned to prosecute the suit with effect, and also to make a return, if return be awarded, the bond is forfeited by the plaintiff not prosecuting his suit *with success* (*n*).

Proceedings against the sheriff.

Formerly, when the sheriff returned to the writ *de retorno habendo* that the goods were eloigned, the defendant thereupon sued out a *scire facias* against the pledges to show cause why their cattle and goods, to the value of the cattle and goods eloigned, should not be delivered to the defendant; and if no cause was shown, a writ issued to take their cattle (*o*). If the sheriff returned *nihil* upon that writ, a *scire facias* was awarded against the sheriff that he should render to the defendant as many cattle (*p*). But now these proceedings have fallen entirely into disuse; and if the defendant in replevin obtain judgment, but is not able to obtain satisfaction either against the principal or against the sureties, an action on the case may be maintained against the sheriff for taking insufficient pledges (*q*); or if the sheriff has lost the replevin-bond, an action may be maintained against the sheriff for thereby depriving the defendant of his remedy against the sureties (*r*). But the courts will not grant an attachment against the sheriff, even where he has neglected to take a replevin-bond (*s*). The person who would be entitled to the assignment of the replevin-bond is the proper person to bring the action against the sheriff for taking insufficient pledges (*t*). And although the defendant in replevin had elected to proceed under the statute 17 Car. 2, c. 7, it was held that he might still proceed against the sheriff (*u*). And although the defendant in replevin had never issued a writ of *retorn. habend.*, this action for losing the bond lies against the sheriff (*x*); for the replevin-bond is forfeited by the plaintiff in replevin not prosecuting his suit with effect, and consequently in default of the sureties an action lies against the sheriff (*y*). This action

(*n*) Perreau *v.* Bevan, 5 Bar. & Cress. 584; see *ante*, 418, n. (*q*).

(*o*) 1 Saund. 195 a, n.; Dorington *v.* Edwin, 3 Mod. 56.

(*p*) 1 Saund. 195 a, n.; Nevors *v.* Michelbourne, Hutt. 77.

(*q*) Moyser *v.* Clarke, Cro. Car. 456; 16 Vin. Abr. 399; 1 Saund. 195 a, n. It seems that the sheriff may recover against his replevin clerk for taking insufficient sureties; see Bowden *v.* Hall, 1 Dav. & M. 54.

(*r*) Perreau *v.* Bevan, 5 Bar. & Cress. 284.

(*s*) Rex *v.* Lewis, 2 T. R. 617; Yea *v.* Lethbridge, 4 T. R. 435; Tessyman *v.* Gilbert, 1 N. R. 292.

(*t*) Page *v.* Eamer, 1 Bos. & Pul. 378.

(*u*) Perreau *v.* Bevan, 5 Bar. & Cress. 284.

(*x*) See Hucker *v.* Gordon, 1 C. & M. 58.

(*y*) *Id. ibid.*

CHAP. XVIII. SECT. III.

may be maintained after the defendant in replevin has taken an assignment of the replevin-bond, and sued both principal and sureties thereon; for the sheriff is not discharged by the defendant in replevin proceeding on the bond (*z*). In support of an action for taking insufficient pledges in replevin, it must appear that the pledges were insufficient at the time they executed the bond. If the pledges were apparently responsible, and the sheriff did not omit any means in his power to ascertain to the contrary, this action cannot be maintained against the sheriff (*a*). The sheriff is not bound to go out of the office to make inquiries respecting the sufficiency of the sureties; but he ought to have reasonable grounds for believing them to be sufficient, and whether in accepting them he exercises a reasonable discretion, is a question for the jury (*b*).

Sheriff, to what extent liable.

As to the extent of the liability of the sheriff for taking insufficient pledges in replevin, there were formerly conflicting decisions (*c*). But it seems to be now settled, that the sheriff is not liable beyond the extent to which the sureties themselves would have been liable, viz., to the extent of the penalty of the bond (*d*). In the case of Scott *v.* Waithman, Abbott, C. J. (*e*), is reported to have said, "as the verdict in the replevin suit was *merely for a return of the goods*, the jury could not in their verdict exceed the value of the goods." Nor can the assignee of a replevin bond recover from the sheriff, as special damage, the costs of suing the sureties without effect, unless he gave notice to the sheriff of his intention to sue them, previous to his doing so (*f*).

Writ of inquiry under stat. 17 Car. 2, c. 7.

In cases of distress for *rent*, by the 2nd section of the statute 17 Car. 2, c. 7, it is enacted, that whensoever any plaintiff in replevin in any suit in the courts at Westminster, shall be nonsuited before issue joined, the defendant making a suggestion

(*z*) 1 Saund. 195, n.

(*a*) Hindle *v.* Blades, 5 Taunt. 225; Sutton *v.* Waite, 8 Moore, 27; Scott *v.* Waithman, 3 Stark. N. P. C. 170; Jeffery *v.* Bastard, 4 A. & E. 823. The sureties themselves are competent witnesses to prove their sufficiency or insufficiency; 5 Taunt. 225; 2 Phil. Evid. 274.

(*b*) Jeffery *v.* Bastard, 4 A. & E. 823.

(*c*) See Yea *v.* Lethbridge, 4 T. R. 433; Concanon *v.* Lethbridge, 2 H. Bl. 36.

(*d*) Jeffery *v.* Bastard, 4 A. & E. 823; Paul *v.* Goodluck, 2 Bing. N. C. 220; Evans *v.* Branden, 2 H. Bl. 547; Perreau *v.* Bevan, 5 Bar. & Cress. 290; Hofford *v.* Alger, 1 Taunt. 218.

(*e*) Scott *v.* Waithman, 3 Stark. N. P. C. 171.

(*f*) Baker *v.* Garratt, 10 Moore, 324; 3 Bing. 56, S. C.

in the nature of an avowry or cognizance for rent, to ascertain the court of the cause of such distress, the court, upon his prayer, shall award a writ to the sheriff of the county, to inquire by oath of twelve good and lawful men of his bailiwick, *touching the sum in arrear at the time of such distress taken, and the value of the goods or cattle distrained.* Fifteen days' notice of such inquiry is to be given to the plaintiff or to his attorney, and the sheriff is to inquire of the truth of the matters in the writ, by the oaths of twelve good and lawful men; and on the return of the writ, the court is to give judgment for the defendant for the arrears of rent, if the value of the cattle amounts thereto; if not, to the value of the cattle, and full costs: and by section 3 of the same statute, in case of judgment upon demurrer for the defendant, the court at his prayer may award a writ to inquire the value of such distress. These writs are to be executed in the same manner as other writs of inquiry (*g*), forms of the inquisition and return thereto will be found in the Appendix to this work (*h*).

(*g*) See *ante*, p. 323.

(*h*) Append. c. 18, s. 3.

CHAPTER XIX.

OF THE SHERIFF'S DUTY IN THE ELECTION OF MEMBERS OF PARLIAMENT.

SECT. I.—*Of the Writ for the Election of Members.—Proclamation.—Polling Districts.—Erection of Poll-Booths.—Poll-Clerks, &c.—Time and manner of Election.*

II.—*Election by View.—Poll, how taken.—Inquiry to be made of Voters.—Poll, how closed.—Scrutiny.—Sheriff's Return.*

III.—*Liabilities of Sheriff for Misbehaviour.—Action by Sheriff for Expenses.*

SECTION I.

Of the Writ for the Election of Members.—Proclamation.—Polling Districts.—Erection of Poll-Booths.—Poll-Clerks, &c.—Time and manner of Election.

WE have seen that it is one of the duties of the office of sheriff to decide the elections of knights of the shire (subject to the control of the House of Commons); and to return such as he shall determine to be elected (*a*).

Of the writ. The writ to the sheriff for the election of members of parliament commands him that (proclamation being made of the day and place aforesaid) two knights, of the most fit and discreet of the said county, girt with swords, and of the borough of —— two burgesses (*b*), of the most sufficient and discreet, freely and indifferently, by those who at his county court to be holden for the purpose of the election shall be present, according to the form of the statutes, &c., he cause to be elected; and the names of those knights, &c., so to be elected (whether they be present

(*a*) *Ante*, p. 3.

(*b*) *Mutatis mutandis*, according to circumstances. See 2 Will. 4, c. 45, s. 77.

or absent), he cause to be inserted in certain indentures, to be thereupon made between him and those who shall be present at such election: "willing, nevertheless, that neither he nor any other sheriff of this kingdom be in anywise elected, and that the election in his full county so made, distinctly and openly, under his seal, and the seals of those who shall be present at such election, he do certify to us in our Chancery, at the day and place aforesaid, without delay, remitting to us one part of the aforesaid indenture annexed to these presents, together with this writ." The messenger attending the great seal is the officer whose duty it formerly was to deliver the writs for the election of members of parliament to the sheriff; this, of course, he did by deputy, and the only restriction imposed on him for appointing a deputy was, that he should not transmit the writ by a candidate. The legislative provisions on this subject are contained in 7 & 8 Will. 3, c. 25, s. 1, by which it is enacted, "that, as well upon the calling or summoning any new parliament, as also in case of any vacancy during the then present or any future parliament, the several writs shall be delivered to the proper officer to whom the execution thereof shall properly belong or appertain, and to no other person whatsoever;" and in 53 Geo. 3, c. 89, which allows the transmitting of the writs through the post-office, except in the cases of the sheriffs of London and Middlesex, and sheriffs holding their offices in London, Westminster, or Southwark, or within five miles thereof. Section 2 of the same act requires sheriffs to transmit to the post-office, in manner therein mentioned, an account of the places where they hold their offices. If the person intrusted with the writ, or any other person, delay or obstruct the delivery of the writ, he is considered guilty of a contempt of the privileges of the House of Commons (*c*).

Sheriff to indorse the time of receiving the writ.

By stat. 7 & 8 Will. 3, c. 25, s. 1, the sheriff is required, without any fee, gratuity, or reward, "upon receipt of the writ, upon the back thereof to indorse the day he receives the same."

To send precepts to the returning officers of boroughs, &c.

The duty of the sheriff, as to sending his precept to the returning officers (*d*) of cities and boroughs, is pointed out by

(*c*) See cases cited in 1 Heyw. from p. 4 to 28.

(*d*) As to who are the returning officers of certain cities and boroughs, see 2 Will. 4, c. 45, s. 11, and scheds. (C) and (D).

CHAP. XIX. SECT. I.

23 Hen. 6, c. 14, viz., to "make and deliver, without fraud, a sufficient precept, under seal, to every mayor and bailiff, or to the bailiffs where no mayor is of the cities, &c., in his county, reciting the said writ, commanding them by the same precept, if it be a city, to choose by citizens of the same city citizens; if a borough, to choose by the burgesses of the same borough burgesses, to come to parliament;" which precept or precepts, by the before-mentioned statute, 7 & 8 Will. 3, c. 25, the sheriff, without any fee or reward (*e*), "*within three days after the receipt of the said writ of election*, shall by himself or his proper agent, deliver or cause to be delivered to the proper officer of every such borough, town corporate, port, or place within his jurisdiction, to whom the execution of such precept doth belong or appertain, and to no other person whatsoever (*f*)."

In cities, towns, &c. the sheriff or other officer shall proceed to election within eight days after receiving the writ, giving three clear days' notice.

By 3 & 4 Vict. c. 81, s. 1, it is enacted, "that in every city or town in England being a county of itself, and in every borough, town corporate, port, or place in England returning or contributing to return a member or members to serve in parliament, the sheriff, or other officer to whom the duty of giving such notice belongs, shall proceed to election within eight days after the receipt of the writ or precept, giving three clear days' notice at least of the day appointed for the election, exclusive of both the day of proclamation and the day appointed for the election."

Where no returning officer in cities or boroughs, sheriff may act as returning officer.

And by 6 & 7 Vict. c. 18, s. 99, it is enacted, that in cities and boroughs where there is no other returning officer, "it shall be lawful for the sheriff or sheriffs whose business it may be to direct the precept for the return of a member or members to serve in parliament for any such city or borough, by himself or themselves, or by his or their deputy, to act as returning officer for such city or borough."

Of the time for making proclamation, and for holding the election.

As the election of knights of the shire was formerly required to be made in the *full* county (*in pleno comitatu*), at the next county court, the election often took place on the day or the day after the receipt of the writ, which being inconvenient, it was afterwards provided (*g*) that the election was to take place at

(*e*) Sect. 2. See form of sheriff's precept, Append.

(*f*) Sect. 1. By 10 & 11 Will. 3, c. 7, s. 2, the officer receiving the writ for the election of members for the Cinque Ports, is allowed *six days* for making his precepts.

(*g*) 7 & 8 Will. 3, c. 25, s. 3.

the next county court, unless such court took place more than six days after the receipt of the writ, but in such case it should be adjourned to some other time, whereof ten days' notice should be given; thus leaving it in the power of the sheriff to make long adjournments; by another statute (*h*), such adjournment was not to be for a longer period of time than sixteen days. The time for holding the election for counties was afterwards regulated by 25 Geo. 3, c. 84, s. 4; by which statute the sheriff was required "within two days after the receipt of the writ of election, to cause proclamation to be made at the place where the ensuing election ought to be holden, of a special county court to be there holden for the purpose of such election only on any day, Sunday excepted, not later from the day of making such proclamation than the sixteenth day, nor sooner than the tenth day; and that he shall proceed in such election at such special county court, in the same manner as if the said election was to be held at a county court or at an adjourned county court, according to the laws then in being (*i*)."

Notice of the election.

By 33 Geo. 3, c. 64, it is required that all notices of the time and place of election shall be given at the usual place or places of election, within the hours of eight o'clock in the forenoon and four o'clock in the afternoon, from the 25th of October to the 25th of March inclusive; and within the hours of eight o'clock in the forenoon and six o'clock in the afternoon, from the 25th day of March to the 25th day of October inclusive, and not otherwise; and no notice of election otherwise given shall be deemed or taken to be a good or valid notice for any purpose whatsoever. It appears that if the notice be not given within the time prescribed, the officer cannot proceed to an election (*k*). The expense of making the proclamation must be defrayed by the sheriff, and cannot be charged to the candidates (*l*).

Sheriffs to proclaim time of elections, and to preside at them.

The 61st section of the 2 Will. 4, c. 45, enacts, "that the sheriffs of Yorkshire and Lincolnshire, and the sheriffs of the counties divided by that act, shall duly cause proclamation to be made of the several days fixed for the election of a knight or knights of the shire for the several ridings, parts, and divisions

(*h*) 18 Geo. 2, c. 18, s. 10.

(*i*) It is also thereby provided, that such special county court shall not interrupt the holding or adjournment of the regular county court.

(*k*) See 1 Peck. 289; 1 Heyw. 395.

(*l*) By the 43 Geo. 3, c. 62, the bribery oath is to be taken at the poll.

of their respective counties, and shall preside at the election by themselves or their lawful deputies."

Of erecting booths.

The sheriff's duty in erecting booths and in appointing poll-clerks, where a contest is expected, is pointed out and prescribed by the statute 2 Will. 4, c. 45.

Counties divided into polling districts.

By sect. 63 of that act it is provided, that the several counties, &c., shall be divided into different districts for polling, as therein mentioned.

Polling booths to be erected.

By sect. 64 it is enacted, "that at every contested election for any county or riding, parts or division of a county, the sheriff, under-sheriff, or sheriff's deputy, shall, if required thereto by or on behalf of any candidate, on the day fixed for the election, and, if not so required, may, if it shall appear to him expedient, cause to be erected a reasonable number of booths for taking the poll at the principal place of election, and also at each of the polling places so to be appointed as aforesaid, and shall cause to be affixed on the most conspicuous part of each of the said booths the names of the several parishes, townships, and places for which such booth is respectively allotted; and no person shall be admitted to vote at any such election in respect of any property situate in any parish, township, or place, except at the booth so allotted for such parish, township, or place; and if no booth shall be so allotted for the same, then at any of the booths for the same district; and in case any parish, township, or place shall happen not to be included in any of the districts to be appointed, the votes in respect of property situate in any parish, township, or place so omitted shall be taken at the principal place of election for the county or riding, parts or division of the county, as the case may be."

Poll-clerks.

By sect. 65 it is enacted, "that the sheriff shall have power to appoint deputies to preside and clerks to take the poll at the principal place of election, and also at the several places appointed for taking the poll for any county, or any riding, parts or division of a county; and that the poll-clerks employed at those several places shall at the close of each day's poll enclose and seal their several books, and shall publicly deliver them, so enclosed and sealed, to the sheriff, under-sheriff, or sheriff's deputy presiding at such poll, who shall give a receipt for the same, and shall, on the commencement of the poll on the second day, deliver them back, so enclosed and sealed, to the persons from whom he shall have received them; and on the final close of the poll, every such deputy who shall have received any such poll-books shall forthwith deliver or transmit the same, so enclosed and sealed, to the sheriff or his under-sheriff, who shall receive and keep all the poll-books unopened until the re-assembling of the court on the day next but one after the close of the poll, unless such next day but one shall be Sunday, and then on the Monday following, when he shall openly break the seals thereon, and cast up the number of votes as they appear on the the said several books, and shall openly declare the state of the poll, and shall make proclamation of the member or members chosen, not later than two o'clock in the afternoon of the said day."

Sheriff may act in places of exclusive jurisdiction.

Sect. 66 enacts, "that in all matters relative to the election of knights or a knight of a shire to serve in any future parliament for any county, or for any riding, parts or division of a county, the sheriff of the county, his under-sheriff, or any lawful deputy of such sheriff, shall have power to act in all places having any exclusive jurisdiction or privilege whatsoever, in the same manner as such sheriff, under-sheriff, or deputy, may act within any part of such sheriff's ordinary jurisdiction."

Lists of voters to be forwarded every year to the sheriff.

Copies to be provided for each polling booth.

By 2 Will. 4, c. 45, s. 54, provision is made for the supply to the sheriff in every year of a list of the voters of the county; and sect. 72 enacts, "that the sheriff or other returning officer shall, before the day fixed for the election, cause to be made, for the use of each booth or other polling place at such election, a true copy of the register of voters, and shall under his hand certify every such copy to be true."

Oath to be taken by the poll-clerks.

By the 7 & 8 Will. 3, c. 25, s. 3 (which first provided for the appointment of poll-clerks), it is required that every clerk shall take an oath (to be administered by the sheriff, under-sheriff or deputy-sheriff), truly and indifferently to take the poll, and to set down the names of each freeholder, and the place of his freehold, and for whom he shall vote; and to poll no freeholder who is not sworn, if so required by the candidates, or any of them.

Inspectors.

The sheriff, or his under-sheriff (by the last-mentioned statute), shall appoint for each candidate such one person as shall be nominated by each candidate, to be inspectors of every clerk

CHAP. XIX. SECT. I.

who shall be appointed for taking the poll; and further, by the 18 Geo. 2, c. 18, s. 9, "the sheriff, under-sheriff, or his deputies, shall, at every such election, allow a cheque-book for every poll-book for each candidate to be kept by their respective inspectors at every place where the poll for such election shall be taken or carried on."

Deputy sheriffs.

Besides the poll-clerks, the sheriff should appoint a deputy or subsheriff for taking the votes in each of the booths. It is usual to pay such deputy-sheriffs five guineas *per* day and their expenses (*m*).

Hour and mode of proceeding at the election.

By the 23 Hen. 6, c. 14, s. 2, the sheriff is directed to proceed to the election, "in his full county," betwixt the hour of eight and of eleven before noon, without collusion (*n*). After making proclamation for silence, the election commences by the sheriff reading, or causing to be read, the writ of election; *immediately after which*, by the 2 Geo. 2, c. 24, s. 3, the sheriff is required to take and subscribe the following oath (which oath may be administered by a justice of the peace of the county, or, if none present, by any three electors), viz. "*I, A. B., do solemnly swear, that I have not directly or indirectly received any sum or sums of money, office, place, or employment, gratuity or reward, or any bond, bill or note, or any promise or gratuity whatsoever, either by myself or any other person, to my use or benefit, or advantage, for making any return at the present election of members to serve in parliament; and that I will return such person or persons as shall, to the best of my judgment, appear to me to have the majority of votes.*" After which the sheriff should read or cause to be read the Bribery Act.

Of the candidates, their qualification, oath, &c.

These preliminaries having been gone through, the sheriff then calls upon the electors to name the candidates, upon which the candidates are put in nomination by their respective friends. It is generally the case that all the candidates are proposed at the place of election, but a candidate may be proposed at any time before the close of the poll (*o*). If any person is objected to as a person disabled from sitting in parliament, although the sheriff may offer his opinion as to the disability of the candi-

(*m*) See 1 Peck. 289; 1 Heyw. 395.

(*n*) Under a penalty of 100*l*., to be sued for by a common informer, within three months.

(*o*) 1 Doug. 246; and see 1 Heyw. 377, 378.

date, and although the votes given for him after such objection may be thrown away, yet the sheriff should not judge of the disability of the candidate, but receive all the votes tendered for such person, and leave the party objecting to petition (*p*). Nor is the sheriff to judge of the qualification of the candidates; but it is his duty to take the votes for any candidate, although objected to as ineligible. The election of such person would be void if he did not take the oath prescribed (*q*) by the 9 Anne, c. 5, s. 5, which provides that every candidate for a county (except the eldest son or heir apparent of any peer, or of any person qualified to serve as knight of the shire,) is required, upon reasonable request to him to be made, (at the time of such election, or before the day prefixed in the writ of summons for the meeting of parliament,) by any other person who shall stand candidate at such election, or by any two or more persons having right to vote at such election, to take a corporal oath in the form and to the effect following:

"*I, A. B., do swear that I truly and bonâ fide have such an estate, in law or equity, to and for my own use and benefit, of or in lands, tenements or hereditaments (over and above what will satisfy and clear all incumbrances that may affect the same), of the annual value of* 600*l., above reprises, as doth qualify me to be elected and returned to serve as a member for the county of N., according to the tenor and true meaning of the act of parliament in that behalf; and that my said lands, tenements or hereditaments, are lying or being within the parish, township or precincts of or in the several parishes, townships or precincts of* ——, *in the county of* ——, *or in the several counties of* —— [as the case may be](*r*)."

And if any of the candidates or persons proposed to be elected as aforesaid shall wilfully refuse, upon reasonable request to be made at the time of election, or at any time before the day upon which such parliament, by the writ of summons, is to meet, to take the oath thereby required, the election and return of such

(*p*) See cases cited in 1 Heyw. from page 526 to 547.

(*q*) 1 Heyw. 548; 1 Peck. 496, n., 526; 1 Lud. 72, 455.

(*r*) The sheriff, or two justices of the peace of the county, are empowered to administer this oath, who are required within three months after the taking the same, to certify them into the Courts of Queen's Bench or Chancery, under a penalty of 100*l.* on failing so to do. The fee for administering the oath is 1*s.*; for making the certificate 2*s.*; for filing the certificate 2*s.*; subject to a penalty of 20*l.* for taking more.

CHAP. XIX. SECT. I.

candidate or person shall be void. But it would appear from the decision of the House of Commons, in the case of Serjeant Comyns, that the sheriff would not be justified in refusing votes tendered for a candidate who refuses to take the oath on the hustings (*s*), for it would be sufficient if he took the oath before the meeting of the parliament, as would appear from the following entry of the resolution of the committee of the House (18 Journ. 129, Maldon, 20 May, 1715), "John Comyns, Esq., Serjeant-at-Law, having at the late election for the borough of Maldon, in the county of Essex, wilfully refused to take the oath of qualification, as is directed by the 9 Anne, c. 5, though duly required so to do, *and not having at any time before the meeting of this parliament* taken the said oath, the election is thereby avoided."

Section II.

Election by View.—Poll, how taken.

Election by view or poll.

If there be no more candidates proposed than there are members to be returned, the sheriff is bound to return the candidates proposed; and in opening the poll in such case, either for the purpose of giving the voters an opportunity of polling, or for the purpose of giving time for another candidate to come forward, he would be acting contrary to his duty (*t*). If there be more candidates proposed than persons to be returned, the election may be made either by *view* or by poll; that is, when the candidates are proposed, the sheriff calls upon the freeholders to hold up their hands for such of the candidates as they think fit to represent the county; he then declares in whose favour the show of hands is, and if a poll be not properly demanded, such person is elected on the *view*. If a poll be demanded, the sheriff is bound o grant it: and this is provided for by the 7 & 8 Will. 3, c. 25, s. 3, by which it is enacted, that "in case the election of knights of the shire be not determined upon the view with the consent of the freeholders there present, but *that a poll shall be required for the determination thereof*, then the said sheriff, or in his absence his under-sheriff, with *such others as shall be deputed by him*, shall forthwith there proceed to take the said poll in

(*s*) 2 Heyw. 551.

(*t*) Nottingham case, 1 Peck. 85.

some open and public place or places, by the same sheriff or his under-sheriff, as aforesaid, in his absence, or others appointed for taking thereof as aforesaid (*u*)."

By 2 Will. 4, c. 45, s. 62, it is enacted, "that at every contested election of a knight or knights to serve in any future parliament for any county, or for any riding, parts, or division of a county, the polling shall commence at nine o'clock in the forenoon of the next day but two after the day fixed for the election, unless such next day but two shall be Saturday or Sunday, and then on the Monday following, at the principal place of election, and also at the several places to be appointed as hereinafter directed for taking polls; and such polling shall continue for two days only, such two days being successive days; (that is to say,) for seven hours on the first day of polling, and for eight hours on the second day of polling; and no poll shall be kept open later than four o'clock in the afternoon of the second day; any statute to the contrary notwithstanding."

Poll, during what hours to be open, and when to be finally closed.

By the 25 Geo. 3, c. 84, s. 1, the parties, it seems, may consent that the poll should be closed before the end of the last polling day (*x*), but without such consent it would appear that the sheriff has power to close the poll before that time, after proclamation, if there be no voters coming to the poll (*y*).

Of the inquiry to be made of voters at the election.

By 6 & 7 Vict. c. 18, ss. 81 and 82, it is enacted, "that in all elections whatever of a member or members to serve in parliament for any county, riding, parts, or divisions of a county, or for any city or borough in England or Wales, or the town of Berwick-upon-Tweed, no inquiry shall be permitted at the time of polling as to the right of any person to vote, except only as follows; (that is to say,) that the returning officer or his respective deputy shall, if required on behalf of any candidate, put to any voter, at the time of his tendering his vote, and not afterwards, the following questions, or either of them:

"1. *Are you the same person whose name appears as A. B. on the register of voters now in force for the county of* —— [or '*for the* —— *riding*,' '*parts*,' or '—— *division of the county of* ——,' or '*for the city* [or '*borough*'] *of* ——' as the case may be]?

(*u*) See 1 Heyw. 367, 368.
(*x*) See 1 Lud. 351.
(*y*) See 2 Will. 4, c. 45, s. 70.

CHAP. XIX. SECT. II.

"2. *Have you already voted, either here or elsewhere, at this election for the county of* —— [or '*for the* —— *riding,*' '*parts,*' or '—— *division of the county of* ——,' or '*for the city* [or '*borough*'] *of* ——' as the case may be]?

"And if any person shall wilfully make a false answer to either of the questions aforesaid he shall be deemed guilty of a misdemeanor, and shall and may be indicted and punished accordingly; and the returning officer or his deputy, or a commissioner or commissioners to be for that purpose by law appointed, shall, if required on behalf of any candidate at the time aforesaid, administer an oath to any voter in the following form:

"*You do swear* [or '*affirm,*' as the case may be], *that you are the same person whose name appears as A. B. on the register of voters now in force for the county of* —— [or '*for the* —— *riding,*' '*parts,*' or '—— *division for the county of* ——' or '*for the city*' or '*borough of* ——' as the case may be], *and that you have not before voted, either here or elsewhere, at the present election for the county of* —— [or '*for the* —— *riding,*' '*parts,*' or '—— *division of the county of* ——, or '*for the city* [or '*borough*'] *of* ——' as the case may be]. *So help you God.*"

Sect. 82 enacts, "that, save as aforesaid, it shall not be lawful to require any voter at any election whatever of a member or members to serve in parliament to take any oath or affirmation, either in proof of his freehold, or of his residence, age, or other qualification or right to vote, any law or statute, local or general, to the contrary notwithstanding; nor to reject any vote tendered at such election by any person whose name shall be upon the register of voters in force for the time being, except by reason of its appearing to the returning officer or his deputy, upon putting such questions as aforesaid, or either of them, that the person so claiming to vote is not the same person whose name appears on such register as aforesaid, or that he had previously voted at the same election, or except by reason of such person refusing to answer the said questions or either of them, or to take the said oath or make the said affirmation, or to take or make the oath or affirmation against bribery; and no scrutiny shall hereafter be allowed by or before any returning officer with regard to any vote given or tendered at any such election; any law, statute, or usage to the contrary notwithstanding."

No scrutiny before returning officer.

In case of a riot at the election, it is by 2 Will. 4, c. 45, s. 70, enacted, "that where the proceedings at any election shall be interrupted or obstructed by any riot or open violence, the sheriff or other returning officer, or the lawful deputy of any returning officer, shall not for such cause finally close the poll, but, in case the proceedings shall be so interrupted or obstructed at any particular polling place or places, shall adjourn the poll at such place or places only until the following day, and if necessary shall further adjourn the same until such interruption or obstruction shall have ceased, when the returning officer or his deputy shall again proceed to take the poll at such place or places."

In case of riot.

When the voter offers himself at the booth, he is asked by the deputy-sheriff his name and for whom he votes, and his answer is recorded on the poll-book.

Voter, how examined.

Stat. 6 & 7 Vict. c. 18, s. 86, enacts, "that if at the time any person tenders his vote at such election, or after he has voted and before he leaves the polling booth, any such agent so appointed as aforesaid shall declare to the returning officer or his respective deputy presiding therein, that he verily believes and undertakes to prove that the said person so voting is not in fact the person in whose name he assumes to vote, or to the like effect, then and in every such case it shall be lawful for the returning officer or his deputy, and he is hereby required, immediately after such person shall have voted, by word of mouth to order any constable or other peace officer to take the said person so voting into his custody, which said order shall be a sufficient warrant and authority to the said constable or peace officer for so doing: provided always, that nothing herein contained shall be construed or taken to authorize any returning officer or his deputy to reject the vote of any person who shall answer in the affirmative the questions authorized by this act to be put to him at the time of polling, and shall take the oaths or make the affirmations authorized and required of him; but the said returning officer or his deputy shall cause the words, 'protested against for personation,' to be placed against the vote of the person so charged with personation when entered in the poll-book."

Personating voters.

A voter cannot poll twice at the same election, nor can he retract or alter his vote after it is entered on the poll. It often happens, at contested elections, that an ignorant voter gives in

Voter cannot vote twice.

CHAP. XIX. SECT. II.

the name of only one candidate for whom he intends to vote, thinking that he will be allowed to give the other vote afterwards; when such persons poll, they should be cautioned that they have not a right to vote for any other person (z).

Where a vote has been received and another party tenders in respect of the same qualification.

The stat. 6 & 7 Vict. c. 18, s. 91, enacts, "that in case the vote of any person shall have been received, and any other person shall afterwards tender his vote as being registered in respect of the same qualification, stating at the time the name or names of the candidate or candidates for whom he tenders such vote, the returning officer or his deputy shall enter upon the poll-book every vote so tendered, distinguishing the same from the votes admitted and allowed at such election; provided such person shall duly answer the questions hereinbefore authorized to be put to any voter at the time of tendering his vote."

Mistake in the poll.

If there be any mistake in the poll, it is competent for the sheriff to correct it; and it is his duty, if any of the candidates allege that there is a mistake in taking the poll, for the sheriff to produce the poll and rectify it by the cheque-book, if wrong (a).

Tendered votes.

Until the passing of the Reform Act, 2 Will. 4, c. 45, it was the duty of the sheriff or other returning officer not only to receive the votes at the poll, but to judge of the qualification of the voters. Since that statute, this inquiry takes place annually before the revising barristers nominated by the judges of assize, and the sheriff has no longer any judicial duty to perform in this respect. It is provided, however, by the 59th section of that act, that persons whose claims to be upon the register have been rejected by the revising barrister may, with the view of appealing to the Court of Common Pleas against the decision of the barrister, or of petitioning the House of Commons against the return, tender their votes at the poll; in such case the returning officer or his deputy must enter the same upon the poll-book, distinguishing the same from the votes admitted and allowed at such election.

Closing the poll.

If there be no voters to poll, or none come forward for that purpose, the sheriff, after proclamation made, may close the poll when he deems it expedient (b); but this is a power which a sheriff should be very cautious in exercising.

(z) See 1 Heyw. 683.
(a) 1 Lud. 350.
(b) 1 Lud. 551; 1 Heyw. 590.

If the votes be equal, the sheriff must make his return accordingly, for he has no casting voice (*e*).

Equality of votes.

By 2 Will. 4, c. 45, s. 68, the mode is prescribed for adding up and declaring the result of the election.

Declaring the persons elected.

Custody of poll-books after election declared.

By 6 & 7 Vict. c. 18, s. 93, it is enacted, "that at every contested election of a member or members to serve in parliament for any county, riding, parts, or division of a county, or for any city or borough in England or Wales, or for the town of Berwick-upon-Tweed, the sheriff, under-sheriff, or returning officer, after having declared the state of the poll, and made proclamation of the member or members chosen to serve in parliament, in the manner provided for by the said hereinbefore in part recited act (2 Will. 4, c. 45,) shall forthwith enclose and seal up the several poll-books, and tender the same to each of the candidates, to be sealed by them respectively; and in case any candidate shall neglect or refuse to seal the same, the sheriff, under-sheriff or returning officer shall thereupon indorse on one of the said poll-books the fact of such neglect or refusal; and every such sheriff, under-sheriff, or other returning officer shall, by himself or his agent, as soon as possible after such proclamation as aforesaid, deliver the same poll-books, so sealed as aforesaid, to the clerk of the crown in the High Court of Chancery or his deputy, or deliver the same, directed to the said clerk of the crown, to the postmaster or deputy postmaster of the city, town, or place wherein such proclamation shall have been made as aforesaid, who on receipt thereof shall give an acknowledgment in writing of such receipt to such sheriff, under-sheriff, or returning officer, expressing therein the time of such delivery, and shall keep a duplicate of such acknowledgment, signed by such sheriff, under-sheriff, or returning officer; and the said postmaster or deputy postmaster shall dispach all such poll-books, so sealed and directed as aforesaid, by the first post or mail after the receipt thereof, to the General Post Office in London; and the postmaster or postmasters general are hereby directed, immediately on receipt of such poll-books, to convey the same to the Crown Office, and to deliver the same there, so sealed as aforesaid, to the said clerk of the crown or his dequty; and the said clerk of the crown or his deputy is hereby required to give to such postmaster or postmasters general, sheriff, under-sheriff, returning

(*e*) 1 Heyw. 601.

officer, or agent delivering the same, a memorandum in writing, acknowledging the receipt of such poll-books, and setting forth the day and hour when the same were delivered to the Crown Office; and the said clerk of the crown or his deputy is hereby required, immediately on receipt of such poll-books, to register the same in the books of the said Crown Office, and to indorse thereon the day and hour upon which he received the same; and every such sheriff, under-sheriff, or returning officer is hereby required, at the time of transmitting such poll-books as aforesaid through the post office, to address and forward a letter by the same post or mail to the said clerk of the crown, informing him of such transmission and giving the number and description of such poll-books so transmitted."

Copy of the poll to be delivered to person demanding it.

By 7 & 8 Will. 3, c. 25, s. 6, every returning officer shall forthwith deliver to such person or persons as shall desire the same, a copy of the poll taken at such election, paying only a reasonable charge for writing the same, subject to the penalty of 500*l.*

Section III.

Of the Liabilities of the Sheriff for Misbehaviour in the Election of Members, and of Actions by him for Expenses incurred therein.

Punishment by the House.

If the sheriff, in the discharge of his duty in the election of members to serve in parliament, act wilfully and corruptly, it is considered a contempt of the House, for which the House will commit him to custody. Thus, in the Middlesex case, the committee resolved that the sheriffs, on certain days of the poll, wilfully, knowingly and corruptly did admit to poll 300 persons claiming under a fictitious right, whereby one of the candidates obtained a colourable majority in his favour:—"Resolved, that it appears to this committee that the sheriffs at the poll acted in a judicial capacity, by allowing counsel to argue the validity of votes, and by deciding, in some instances, on the validity of such votes; that in other instances they refused to decide on the validity of votes which were objected to, and stated that they would admit any persons to poll who would take the oaths, declaring themselves to be only ministerial officers, thereby acting in a manner contradictory to their practice in other cases, and in flagrant violation of their duty:—Resolved, that it appears to the committee that the obvious tendency of their conduct was to admit persons having no right to poll, and to afford the greatest encouragement to perjury." After hearing counsel, the House of Commons agreed to the resolutions of the committee, and resolved, "that the sheriffs, by their conduct and practices at the said election, as stated in the foregoing resolutions, as well as by refusing to refer to the assessments for the land tax, acted in violation of their duty, contrary to law, and in breach of the privilege of this House." And it was ordered that they should be committed to Newgate (*e*).

False return.

By the stat. 7 & 8 Will. 3, c. 7, if the sheriff or returning officer "wilfully" make a false return of any member to serve in parliament (returning members contrary to the last determination of the House of Commons is to be considered a false return), or if any officer shall "wilfully, falsely, and maliciously" make a return of more persons than are required, he is liable to an action at the suit of the party grieved. In the great case of Ashby *v.* White, where the declaration alleged that a returning officer maliciously refused the vote of a person having a right to vote, it was determined by the House of Lords that an action lay against the returning officer for such refusal (*f*). But it would appear that *malice* is a necessary ingredient in such action (*g*). And if the party had in fact no right to vote, although his name was on the register, he cannot maintain any action at all against the returning officer for refusing to receive his vote (*h*). By 2 Will. 4, c. 45, s. 76, it is enacted, "that if any sheriff, returning officer, barrister, overseer, or any person whatsoever, shall wilfully contravene or disobey the provisions of this act or any of them, with respect to any matter or thing which such sheriff, returning officer, barrister, overseer, or other person is hereby required to do, he shall for such his offence be liable to be sued in an action of debt in any of his majesty's courts of record at Westminster for the penal sum of five hundred pounds, and the jury before whom such action shall be tried may find their verdict for the full sum of five hundred pounds, or for any less

(*e*) 1 Peck. 28, 29.

(*f*) 2 Lord Raym. 938, 958; Salk. 19, S. C.; 6 Mod. 45.

(*g*) Drewe *v.* Cotton, note, 1 East, 563.

(*h*) Pryce *v.* Belcher, 16 Law J. 264, C. B.

CHAP. XIX. SECT. III.

sum which the said jury shall think it just that he should pay for such his offence; and the defendant in such action, being convicted, shall pay such penal sum so awarded, with full costs of suit, to the party who may sue for the same: provided always, that no such action shall be brought except by a person being an elector or claiming to be an elector, or a candidate or a member actually returned, or other party aggrieved: provided also, that the remedy hereby given against the returning officer shall not be construed to supersede any remedy or action against him according to the law now in force." By 6 & 7 Vict. c. 18, s. 97, it is enacted, "that every sheriff, under-sheriff, clerk of the peace, town clerk, secondary, returning officer, clerk of the crown, postmaster, overseer, or other person or public officer required by this act to do any matter or thing, shall for every wilful misfeasance or wilful act of commission or omission contrary to this act forfeit to any party aggrieved the penal sum of one hundred pounds, or such less sum as the jury before whom may be tried any action to be brought for the recovery of the before-mentioned sum shall consider just to be paid to such party, to be recovered by such party, with full costs of suit, by action for debt in any of her majesty's superior courts at Westminster: provided always, that nothing herein contained shall be construed to supersede any remedy or action against any returning officer according to any law now in force." And by various other acts of parliament, the sheriff or returning officer is subjected to penalties for not discharging his duty; these will be found by reference to the particular subjects.

Sheriff may commit persons disturbing the election.

If any person make a riot or otherwise disturb the proceedings at the election, the sheriff may commit such person to prison (*i*).

Actions by sheriff for expenses.

A candidate at an election for members of parliament is liable to no expense except such as the *statute law casts upon him, or he takes upon himself by his express or implied consent* (*k*). Thus, by the 18 Geo. 2, c. 18, s. 7 (*l*), the sheriff is to erect booths, &c. at the *expense of the candidates;* and by 2 Will. 4, c. 45, s. 71, it is enacted, "that from and after the end of this present parliament, all booths erected for the convenience of taking polls

(*i*) Spilsbury *v.* Micklethwaite, 1 Taunt. 146.

(*k*) *Per* Lord Ellenborough, C.J., 1 Camp. 222.

(*l*) This act is extended to the elections for Westminster, by the stat. 51 Geo. 3, c. 126.

shall be erected at the joint and equal expense of the several candidates, and the same shall be erected by contract with the candidates, if they shall think fit to make such contract, or if they shall not make such contract, then the same shall be erected by the sheriff or other returning officer at the expense of the several candidates as aforesaid, subject to such limitation as is hereinafter next mentioned; that is to say, that the expense to be incurred for the booth or booths to be erected at the principal place of election for any county, riding, parts, or division of a county, or at any of the polling places so to be appointed as aforesaid, shall not exceed the sum of forty pounds in respect of any one such principal place of election or any one such polling place; and that the expense to be incurred for any booth or booths to be erected for any parish, district, or part of any city or borough, shall not exceed the sum of twenty-five pounds in respect of any one such parish, district, or part; and that all deputies appointed by the sheriff or other returning officer shall be paid each two guineas by the day, and all clerks employed in taking the poll shall be paid each one guinea by the day, at the expense of the candidates at such election: provided always, that if any person shall be proposed without his consent, then the person so proposing him shall be liable to defray his share of the said expenses, in like manner as if he had been a candidate; provided also, that the sheriff or returning officer may, if he shall think fit, instead of erecting such booth or booths as aforesaid, procure or hire and use any houses or other buildings for the purpose of taking the poll therein, subject always to the same regulations, provisions, liabilities, and limitations of expense as are hereinbefore mentioned with regard to booths for taking the poll." The contested election mentioned in section 68 means the poll, and the candidates mentioned in section 71 mean those who go to or demand a poll. A candidate who declines to go to the poll after having been nominated, is not liable to any part of the expenses (*m*). And by 34 Geo. 3, c. 73, the expense of administering oaths is to be borne by the candidates. A person who is returned to parliament by certain electors, without showing himself or otherwise offering himself for the suffrages of the electors, or assuming, by himself or his agents, the character of a candidate, although afterwards elected,

(*m*) Muntz *v.* Sturge, 8 M. & W. 302.

is not a candidate within the meaning of this act (*n*). But if the committee of the candidate ask for places and tickets for the hustings, to which the candidate assents, although he protests against being charged with the expenses, yet he will be liable (*o*). The candidates, without a joint undertaking to the sheriff to pay the expense, are not jointly liable (*p*); but if they jointly request the sheriff to erect booths, &c., they will be jointly liable (*q*). In two *nisi prius* cases, the charges that the sheriff might make against the candidates were canvassed by the respective judges who tried the causes (Lord Ellenborough and Lawrence, J.) In one case, Wathen *v.* Sandys (*r*), a joint action was brought against two candidates for the expenses incurred during the election; two objections were taken,—1st, that the action should not have been joint but separate; 2nd, that the action should have been on the statute, and not an action of *indebitatus assumpsit.* And several of the items were also objected to as not being chargeable against the candidates. Lawrence, J., is reported to have said, "Both objections admit of the same answer. The plaintiff does not proceed upon the statute. If the sheriff had merely been desired to erect booths in pursuance of the statute, then we should have had to consider what remedy the statute gives him. But there is an express undertaking on the part of both to pay for the hustings, the assessor, and the poll-clerks, on which the two are jointly liable. However, although the action is certainly maintainable, there are several parts of the plaintiff's demand with which he has no right to charge the defendants. The first eight items, amounting to 40*l.* 5*s.* for the indentures, &c., only concern the execution of his office of sheriff, and there is no pretence for throwing them upon the candidates. The same thing may be said of the charge for constables. The sheriff is bound to preserve the peace of the county: if he is put to any extraordinary expense in this way, let him represent the matter when he passes his accounts in the Exchequer, or directly to his majesty's government. Any claims he may have for remuneration will thus be attended to; but he has no more right to recover such charges from a candidate at the election than from any other

(*n*) Morris *v.* Burdett, 2 M. & S. 13.

(*o*) Morris *v.* Burdett, 1 Camp. 225.

(*p*) Morris *v.* Lord Cochrane, 1 M. & Sel. 283.

(*q*) Wathen *v.* Sandys, 2 Camp. 640.

(*r*) 2 Camp. 640.

individual in his bailiwick." There were several other items that his lordship advised the jury to disallow entirely; such as the surveyors, and printing the poll-books. Another class he advised them considerably to reduce. The plaintiff could only recover the original expense of erecting the hustings, not the costs of any action brought against him by the person who had erected them. For the assessor his lordship thought the defendants liable, although this was an expense not mentioned in the statute, which was meant for the protection of the sheriff, not of the candidates; but the accompanying charges for agent's fees, &c. in retaining the assessor, he considered as exorbitant. Advantage, he observed, was often taken of the situation of candidates to sit in parliament, who were afraid to resist any demand, however unreasonable, lest they should render themselves unpopular; and thus a sort of custom was set up for the imposition practised upon them; but such charges as twenty-five guineas for leaving a retainer with a gentleman at the bar, and paying him his fee, could not be supported in a court of justice, however long established.

In the other case, Morris *v.* Burdett (*s*), Lord Ellenborough, C. J., is reported to have said, "A candidate at an election for members of parliament is liable to no expenses except such as the statute law casts upon him, or he takes upon himself by his express or implied consent. A great number of the items in this case may therefore be entirely laid out of consideration, as arising from acts which the plaintiff was bound to do by reason of his office, or as of such a nature that no promise to contribute to them can possibly be inferred. *To proclaim the election* is a duty which the law imposes upon the high bailiff; and there is the less pretence for charging the candidates with it, as they had not then been nominated. It does not seem necessary that he should have been attended on the occasion with six under-bailiffs, the crier on horseback, &c.; but if it was, he must consider the consequent expense a burthen he took upon himself along with his office. So the law requires him to do whatever is necessary to making the return. For a share of the expense incurred in administering the oaths to the Roman Catholic electors the defendant appears to be liable, if he shall be considered as having conceded to the character of a candidate."

(*s*) 1 Camp. 222.

CHAPTER XX.

OF THE SHERIFF'S DUTY IN THE ELECTION OF CORONERS.

Writ *de coronatore eligendo.*

WHEN the office of coroner becomes vacant, a writ, styled a writ *de coronatore eligendo*, issues out of Chancery, directed to the sheriff of the county, by which, after reciting the death of the late coroner, the sheriff is commanded "that in his full county he cause one other to be chosen in the place of the deceased coroner, who, having taken his oath in the usual manner, may do all things which belong to the office of coroner, and cause such an one to be chosen as best knoweth and can attend that office; and that the sheriff certify to the court the name of the person chosen."

Qualifications for the office.

By stat. Westm. 1 (3 Edw. 1), c. 10, it is enacted, "that through all shires sufficient men shall be chosen, of the most loyal and wise knights, which know, will and may best attend upon such offices, and which lawfully shall attach and present pleas of the crown." And by 14 Edw. 3, stat. 1, c. 8, it is enacted, "that no coroner be chosen unless he have land in fee sufficient in the same county whereof he may answer to all manner of people." In ancient times it appears that no person under the degree of knight was chosen for this office, and it was deemed a sufficient cause for discharging a person from the office of coroner that he was not a knight (*a*). But the object of the above statutes was merely to prevent persons of mean ability from being chosen coroners; the qualification of the person for the office of coroner is sufficient, provided he is a person of property; and for ages past it has been the usage to elect persons below the degree of knights to be coroners (*b*).

How elected.

By 28 Edw. 3, c. 6, it is enacted, "that all coroners of counties shall be chosen in the full counties by the commons of the said counties, of the most meet and lawful people that shall be

(*a*) 2 Inst. 32, 176; 4 Inst. 271; Fitz. Nat. Brev. 164; Reg. 177.

(*b*) 2 Hawk. P. C. c. 9, s. 3; 2 Leon. 260.

found in the same counties to execute the said offices; saving always to the king and other lords, who ought to make such coroners, their seignories and franchises (*c*)."

The election of county coroners is to be by the freeholders of the county, and it is regulated by the statute 7 & 8 Vict. c. 92. The first section of that act recites, that the regulations for the elections of coroners for counties are insufficient, and that such elections are made with much inconvenience and are attended with great and unnecessary expense, and then proceeds to repeal the 58 Geo. 3, c. 95, under which such elections were previously conducted.

Sect. 2 enacts, "that when and so often as it shall seem expedient to the justices of any county that such county should be divided into two or more districts for the purposes of this act, or that any alteration should be made of any division theretofore made under this act, it shall be lawful for the said justices, in general or quarter sessions assembled, to resolve that a petition shall be presented to her majesty, praying that such division or alteration be made, and thereupon to adjourn the further consideration of such petition until notice thereof shall be given to the coroner or coroners of such county as herein-after provided."

Sect. 3 enacts, "that the clerk of the peace shall give notice of any such resolution to every coroner for such county, and of the time when the petition will be taken by the said justices into consideration, and the justices shall confer with every such coroner, who shall attend the meeting of the justices for that purpose, touching such petition, having due regard to the size and nature of each proposed district, the number of the inhabitants, the nature of their employments, and such other circumstances as shall appear to the justices fit to be considered in carrying into execution the provisions of this act; and such

(*c*) The queen may claim this franchise by prescription; but the privilege is of so high a nature, that no subject can claim it otherwise than by grant from the crown; Co. Litt. 114 a; 2 Hawk. P. C. c. 9, s. 11. The mayor of London is by charter coroner of that city. By charter (Hen. 7) the Bishop of Ely has the power to appoint the coroners for that isle. Queen Catherine had the hundred of Colridge granted to her by Hen. 8, in the thirty-fifth year of his reign, with power to nominate coroners. The coroner of the admiralty is appointed by the Lord High Admiral. The appointment of coroner of the Verge is settled in perpetuity in the Lord High Steward, or Lord Great Master of the King's House, for the time being; Bac. Abr., Coroners.

CHAP. XX. petition, with a description of the several proposed districts, and of the boundaries thereof, with the reasons upon which the petition is founded, shall be certified to her majesty under the hands and seals of two or more of the justices present when such petition shall be agreed to, and the clerk of the peace for such county shall forthwith give or send a true copy of such petition, certified under his hand, to every coroner for such county."

Sect. 4 enacts, "that it shall be lawful for her majesty, if she shall think fit, with the advice of her privy council, after taking into consideration any such petition, and also any petition which may be presented to her by any coroner of the same county concerning such proposed division or alteration, or whenever it shall seem fit to her majesty to direct the issue of a writ *de coronatore eligendo*, for the purpose of authorizing the election of an additional coroner above the number of those who have been theretofore customarily elected in such county, to order that such county shall be divided into such and so many districts, for the purposes of this act, as to her majesty, with the advice aforesaid, shall seem expedient, and to give a name to each of such districts, and to determine at what place within each district the court for the election of coroner for such district shall be holden as hereinafter provided, and every such order shall be published in the London Gazette."

Sect. 5 enacts, "that the justices in general or quarter session assembled shall assign one of such districts to each of the persons holding the office of coroner in such county, and upon the death, resignation, or removal of any such person, each of his successors, and also every other person thereafter elected into the office of coroner in such county, shall be elected to and shall exercise the office of coroner, according to the provisions of this act, and shall reside within the district in and for which he shall be so elected, or in some place wholly or partly surrounded by such district, or not more than two miles beyond the outer boundary of such district."

Sect. 6 enacts, "that whenever it shall appear to her majesty, with the advice aforesaid, and shall be set forth in the said order in council, that any such county has been customarily divided into districts for the purpose of holding inquests during the space of seven years before the passing of this act, and it shall seem expedient to her majesty, with the advice aforesaid, that the same division of the county be made under this act, each of such districts shall be assigned to the coroner usually acting in and for the same district before the passing of this act; but if it shall appear expedient to her majesty, with the advice aforesaid, that a different division of such county be made, and any such coroner shall present a petition to her majesty, praying for compensation to him for the loss of his emoluments arising out of such change, it shall be lawful for her majesty, with the advice aforesaid, to order the lord high treasurer or commissioners of her majesty's treasury to assess the amount of compensation which it shall appear to him or them ought to be awarded to such coroner, and the amount of such compensation shall be paid by the treasurer of the county to such coroner, his executors or administrators, out of the county rate."

Sect. 7 enacts, "that such justices so assembled as aforesaid shall order a list to be prepared by the clerk of the peace for their respective counties of the several parishes, townships, or hundreds, as the case may be, in each and every of the several districts into which the respective counties shall be divided under the authority of this act, specifying in such list the place within each district at which the court for the election of coroner is to be holden, and also the place or places at which the poll shall be taken, inserting the parishes, townships, and places for each of such polling places, and shall cause such order to be enrolled among the records of the county."

Sect. 8 enacts, "that all isolated or detached parts of counties shall be considered, for the purposes of this act, as forming a part of that county, riding, or division respectively, whereby such isolated or detached parts shall or may be wholly surrounded, but if any such isolated or detached part shall be surrounded by two or more counties, ridings, or divisions, then as forming part of that county, riding, or division, with which such isolated or detached part shall have the longest common boundary."

Sect. 9 enacts, "that from and after the time when any county shall have been so as aforesaid divided, every election of a coroner for any such district shall be held at some place within the district in which he shall be elected to serve the office of coroner; and that every person to be so elected shall be chosen

CHAP. XX. by a majority of such persons residing within such district as shall at the time of such election be duly qualified to vote at the elections of coroners for the said county.

Sect. 10 enacts, "that from and after the division of any counties as aforesaid into coroners' districts, upon every election to be made of any coroner or coroners for any county, the sheriff of the county where such election shall be made shall hold a court for the same election at some convenient place within the district for which the election of coroner shall take place, on some day to be by him appointed, which day shall not be less than seven days nor more than fourteen days after the receipt of the writ *de coronatore eligendo;* and in case the said election be not then determined upon the view, with the consent of the electors there present, but that a poll shall be demanded for determination thereof, then the said sheriff, or in his absence his under-sheriff, shall adjourn the same court to eight of the clock in the forenoon of the next day but one, unless such next day but one shall be Saturday or Sunday, and then of the Monday following; and the said sheriff, or in his absence the under-sheriff, with such others as shall be deputed by him, shall then and there proceed to take the said poll in some public place or places by the same sheriff, or his under-sheriff as aforesaid in his absence, or others appointed for the taking thereof as aforesaid; and such polling shall continue for two days only, for eight hours in each day; and no poll shall be kept open later than four of the clock in the afternoon of either of the said days."

Sect. 11 enacts, "that for more conveniently taking the poll at all elections of coroners under the authority of this act, the poll for the election of the coroner in each district shall be taken at the place to be appointed for holding the court for such election, and at such other places within the same district as may for the time being be appointed by the quarter sessions."

Sect. 12 enacts, "that at every contested election of coroner for any district of the said county, the sheriff, under-sheriff, or sheriff's deputy, shall, if required by or on the behalf of any candidate on the day fixed for the election, and, if not so required, may, if it shall appear to him expedient, cause a booth or booths to be erected for taking the poll at the court or principal place of election, and also at each of the polling places within the district hereinbefore directed to be used for the purposes of such election, and shall cause to be affixed on the most conspicuous part of each of the said booths the names of the several parishes, townships, and places, for which such booth is respectively allotted; and no person shall be admitted to vote at any such election in respect of any property situate in any parish, township or place, except at the booth so allotted for such parish, township, or place, and if no booth shall be allotted for the same, then at any of the booths for the same districts; and in case any parish, township, or place, or part of any parish, township, or place, shall happen not to be included in any of the districts, the votes in respect of property situate in any parish, township or place, or any part of any parish, township, or place, so omitted, shall be taken at the court or principal place of election for such district of the said county."

Sect. 13 enacts, "that the said sheriff, or in his absence the under-sheriff, or such as he shall depute, shall appoint such number of clerks as to him shall seem meet and convenient for the taking thereof, which clerks shall take the said poll in the presence of the said sheriff or his under-sheriff, or such as he shall depute; and before they begin to take the said poll, every clerk so appointed shall by the said sheriff or his under-sheriff, or such as he shall depute as aforesaid, be sworn truly and indifferently to take the same poll, and to set down the names of each elector, and the place of his residence, and for whom he shall poll, and to poll no elector who is not sworn, if required to be sworn by the candidates or either of them; and which oaths of the said clerks the said sheriff or his under-sheriff, or such as he shall depute, shall have authority to administer; and the sheriff, or in his absence his under-sheriff as aforesaid, shall appoint for each candidate such one person as shall be nominated to him by each candidate, to be inspector of every clerk who shall be appointed for taking the poll; and every elector, before he is admitted to poll at the same election, shall, if required by or on behalf of any candidate, first take the oath hereinafter mentioned; which oath the said sheriff, by himself or his under-sheriff, or such sworn clerk by him appointed for taking the said poll as aforesaid, shall have authority to administer; that is to say,

"*I swear* [or, being one of the people called Quakers, or entitled by law to make affirmation, '*solemnly affirm*'], *That I am*

CHAP. XX. *a freeholder of the county of —— and have a freehold estate, consisting of —— lying at —— within the said county; and that such freehold estate has not been granted to me fraudulently or colourably on purpose to qualify me to give my vote at this election; and that the place of my abode is at ——* [and, if it be a place consisting of more streets or places than one, specifying what street or place]; *that I am twenty-one years of age, as I believe; and that I have not been before polled at this election* [adding, except in cases of solemn affirmations] *So help me God.*"

Sect. 14 enacts, "that every elector or other person who shall wilfully and falsely take the said oath or affirmation hereby appointed to be taken by the electors as aforesaid, shall for every such offence incur the penalties by law inflicted on persons guilty of perjury; and every person who shall unlawfully and corruptly procure or suborn any freeholder or other person wilfully and falsely to take the said oath or affirmation in order to be polled, shall for every such offence incur such pains and penalties as are by law inflicted on persons guilty of subornation of perjury."

Sect. 15 enacts, "that the poll clerks shall, at the close of the poll, enclose and seal their several books, and shall publicly deliver them, so enclosed and sealed, to the sheriff, under-sheriff, or sheriff's deputy, presiding at such poll, who shall give a receipt for the same; and every such deputy who shall have received any such poll books shall forthwith deliver or transmit the same, so enclosed and sealed, to the sheriff or his under-sheriff, who shall receive and keep all the poll books unopened until the reassembling of the court on the day next but one after the close of the poll, unless such next day but one shall be Sunday, and then on the Monday following, when he shall openly break the seals thereon, and cast up the number of votes as they appear on the said several books; and shall openly declare the state of the poll, and shall make proclamation of the person chosen, not later than two of the clock in the afternoon of the said day."

Sect. 16 enacts, "that all the reasonable costs, charges, and expenses, which the said sheriff, or his under-sheriff or other deputy, shall expend or be liable to in and about the providing of poll books, booths, and clerks (such clerks to be paid not more than one guinea each for each day), for the purpose of taking the poll at any such election, shall be borne and paid by the several candidates at such election in equal proportions."

Sect. 19 enacts, "that every coroner elected under the authority of this act, although such coroner may be designated as the coroner for any particular district of a county, and may be elected by the electors of such district, and not by the freeholders of the county at large, shall for all purposes whatsoever, except as hereinafter mentioned, be considered as a coroner for the whole county, and shall have the same jurisdiction, rights, powers and authorities throughout the said county, as if he had been elected one of the coroners of the said county by the freeholders of the county at large."

Sect. 27 enacts, "that nothing in this act contained touching the divisions of counties into districts, or the appointment or election of coroners, shall extend to the county of Chester, or any county palatine, city, borough, town, liberty, franchise, part, or place, the appointment or election of coroner whereof takes place by law otherwise than under the writ *de coronatore eligendo*."

Sect. 28 enacts, "that in construing this act, the word "county" shall be taken to mean county, riding, or division of a county in and for which a separate coroner hath been customarily elected; and that in the counties of York and Lincoln, all things hereinbefore directed to be done by and with respect to the justices in general or quarter sessions assembled and by their clerk, shall be done by and with respect to the justices of the said counties of York and Lincoln in general gaol session assembled and by their clerk."

Sect. 29 enacts, "that nothing herein contained shall be construed to abridge or affect the royal prerogative, or the authority of the lord chancellor, for issuing a writ *de coronatore eligendo*, as fully as if this act had not been passed."

The election is to be by the freeholders at large in the county court; and therefore, in counties where the county court is not required by statute to be held in any particular place, the sheriff may, if he please, hold the election in any place in his county. A sufficient time before the day of election, the sheriff should make a proclamation of the day and place of election(*d*).

(*d*) See form of proclamation, Append.

CHAP. XX. At that day, after the candidates are proposed, the sheriff is to say, by show of hands, on whom the election has fallen. If a poll be demanded, it is the sheriff's (*e*) duty to grant it, to take down the names of the freeholders who poll, and to examine into and judge of the right of voting of the persons tendering their votes. At the close of the poll (when there are no more freeholders to poll) the sheriff is to declare on whom the election has fallen. If a scrutiny be demanded, the sheriff may (for scrutiny is incident to every election by vote) grant it; but it would appear to be discretionary whether he grant it or not.

Oath. As soon as the new coroner is elected, the sheriff should administer to him in open court the oath of office here-under mentioned (*f*). In addition to this oath, the coroner should take the oath of allegiance, supremacy and abjuration; and within six months after his election he should take the sacrament.

Return. The sheriff makes his return conformable to the election (*g*).

If the sheriff refuse to return a person elected coroner, it appears that an action on the case would lie against him (*h*).

(*e*) The sheriff rarely attends, but the under-sheriff performs this part of the office.

(*f*) "You shall swear that you will well and truly serve our Sovereign Lady the Queen's Majesty and her liege people in the office of coroner, and as one of her Majesty's coroners of the county of N., and therein you shall diligently and truly do and accomplish all and every thing and things appertaining to your office, after the best of your cunning, wit, and power, both for the queen's profit and for the good of the inhabitants within the said county, taking such fees as you ought to take by the laws and statutes of this realm, and not otherwise. So help you God."

(*g*) See return, *post*, Append.

(*h*) Per Archer, J., in Turner *v.* Stirling, 2 Vent. 27.

CHAPTER XXI.

SCIRE FACIAS, ATTACHMENTS, ETC.

THE duty of a sheriff, on a writ of *scire facias*, is to indorse on it the day of the month on which it was left with him (*a*), and if he know that the defendant can be served, to issue his warrant thereon (*b*) to two or more bailiffs, to warn the defendant; the bailiffs make an indorsement on this warrant either that they have or have not served the process, and return it to the sheriff; conformably thereto the sheriff returns either *nihil* or *scire feci* (*c*). In proceeding against bail by *scire facias*, the defendant may be summoned at any time *before* the rising of the court on the return day of the *scire facias* (*d*); if made on that day after the rising of the court, the summons is bad (*e*). Whether *nihil* or *scire feci* be returned, it is said that the alias *sci. fa.* in the first case, or the *scire facias* in the latter, must lie in the sheriff's office the last four days, exclusive of the day of lodging the writ and the return, in order to fix the bail (*f*). *Scire facias.*

Attachments for contempt are so far considered in the nature of civil process, that they cannot be executed on a Sunday (*g*). Nor will such process lie against a peer (*h*) or member of parliament (*i*). **Attachment for contempt.**

The sheriff's duty on such an attachment is to take the defendant, and keep him in custody if he does not give bail, so that he may have him in court at the return of the writ, to answer interrogatories; for that reason an attachment is con- **Sheriff's duty on attachment.**

(*a*) R. E. 5 Geo. 2, r. 3.

(*b*) See form, Append.

(*c*) See form, *id. ibid.*

(*d*) Clarke *v.* Bradshaw, 1 East, 88; see also Lewis *v.* Pyne, 1 C. & M. 771; 2 Dowl. 133, S. C.

(*e*) Webb *v.* Harvey, 2 T. R. 757, explained in 1 East, 88.

(*f*) Williams *v.* Mason, note, 1 East, 89; Wilson *v.* Far, 4 B. & Ald. 537; Bell *v.* Jackson, 4 T. R. 663. An intervening Sunday is not reckoned one of the four days, Howard *v.* Smith, 1 Bar. & Ald. 528; Dicas *v.* Perry, 2 D. & R. 869. But Whit Monday, Tuesday, and Wednesday, being days on which search might be made, are to be reckoned, Armitage *v.* Rigbye, 5 A. & E. 76.

(*g*) Rex *v.* Myers, 1 T. R. 266; Watson on Awards, 183.

(*h*) Walker *v.* Earl Grosvenor, 7 T. R. 171.

(*i*) Catmur *v.* Sir E. Knatchbull, *ib.* 448.

sidered in the nature of mesne process, so that if the sheriff arrest the defendant, and afterwards allow him to go at large, but has him at the return of the writ, the sheriff is not liable for an escape (*k*). On an attachment issuing out of chancery for contempt, it has frequently been decided that the sheriff may, if he please, take bail, and such security, although not within the stat. 23 Hen. 6, c. 4, is good at common law (*l*). So on an attachment issuing out of a court of law, notwithstanding conflicting decisions, it would appear that bail might be taken (*m*); and such has been the practice for some time back (*n*). But although a bail bond taken on an attachment is good, yet it is perfectly optional with a sheriff whether he will take bail in such case or not (*o*). And such a bond is not assignable as a bail bond under the stat. 4 Ann. c. 16, s. 20 (*p*).

Poundage on attachment.

It would appear that the sheriff is not entitled to poundage on money received by him in executing an attachment (*q*).

The sheriff cannot be compelled summarily to pay into court money received by him under an attachment for non-payment of money (*r*).

If a person committed for contempt become afterwards entitled to his discharge, notice of his being so entitled must be given to the sheriff before the sheriff will be answerable for his detention (*s*).

(*k*) Lewis *v.* Morland, 2 Bar. & Ald. 56.

(*l*) Morris *v.* Hayward, 6 Taunt. 569, S. C.; 2 Marsh. 280; Danby *v.* Lawson, Prec. in Chan. 110, S. C.; 1 Eq. Cas. Abr. 350, pl. 4; Anon. 2 Atk. 107.

(*m*) Rex *v.* Dawes, 1 Ld. Raym. 722; Salk. 608, S. C.; 2 Bar. & Ald. 63; but see Field *v.* Workhouse, Com. Rep. 264; Phelps *v.* Barrett, 4 Price, 23; *contra.*

(*n*) Per Lens, Serjt. arg., 6 Taunt. 571.

(*o*) Studd *v.* Acton, 1 H. Bl. 468; per Bayley, J., 2 Bar. & Ald. 63.

(*p*) Miller *v.* Palfreyman, 4 B. & Adol. 146.

(*q*) Rex *v.* Palmer, 2 East, 411; Rex *v.* Sheriff of Devon, 3 Dowl. 10.

(*r*) Rex *v.* Sheriff of Devon, 3 Dowl. 10.

(*s*) Smith *v.* Egginton, 7 A. & E. 167.

APPENDIX.

CHAP. II.—Sect. 2.

Schedule of the Oaths to be taken by the Sheriff, and which Schedule is annexed to the Return of the Dedimus.

I, A. B., do sincerely promise and swear, that I will be faithful, and bear true allegiance to her Majesty Queen Victoria.

So help me God.

I, A. B., do swear, that I do, from my heart, abhor, detest and abjure, as impious and heretical, that damnable doctrine and position, that princes excommunicated or deprived by the Pope, or any authority from the See of Rome, may be deposed or murthered by their subjects, or any other whatsoever. And I do declare, that no foreign prince, person, prelate, state or potentate hath or ought to have any jurisdiction, power, superiority, pre-eminence or authority, ecclesiastical or spiritual, within this realm. So help me God.

Oath of Office of the Sheriffs of Wales.

Ye shall swear that well and truly ye will serve the queen's majesty in the office of sheriff of the county of M., in Wales, and do the queen's profits in all things that belong to you to do by way of your office, as far forth as you can or may. Ye shall truly keep the queen's rights, and all that belong to the crown. Ye shall not assent to decrease, to lessen or to concealment of the queen's rights or of her franchises. And whensoever ye shall have knowledge that the queen's rights, or the rights of her crown, be concealed or withdrawn, be it in lands, rents, franchises, suits or any other thing, ye shall do your power to make them to be restored to the queen again; and if ye may not do it yourself, ye shall certify the queen, or some of her council, thereof, such as ye hold for certain, will say it unto the queen. Ye shall not respite the queen's debts for any gift or favour, when ye may raise the same without great grievance to the debtors. Ye shall truly and righteously treat the people of your sheriffwick, and do right as well to poor as to rich, in all things that belongeth to your office. Ye shall do no wrong to any man for any gift or other behest, or promise of goods, for favour or hate. Ye shall disturb no man's right. Ye shall truly acquit all those of whom ye shall any thing receive of the queen's debts. Ye shall nothing take whereby the queen may lose, or whereby that right may be disturbed, letted, or the queen's debts delayed. Ye shall truly return and truly serve all the queen's writs, as far forth as it is in your cunning. Ye shall none have to be your under-sheriff of any of the sheriff's clerks of the last year past. Ye shall take no bailiff into your service but such as ye will answer for. Ye shall make each of your bailiffs to make such oath as ye make

CHAP. II. SECT. II.

yourself, in that that belongeth to their occupation. Ye shall receive no writ, by you or any of yours, unsealed, or any sealed under the seal of any justice saving justice in eyre, of justice assigned in the same shire where ye be sheriff in, or other justices having power and authority to make any writs unto you by the laws of the land, or of justice of Newgate. Ye shall make your bailiffs of the true and sufficient men of the county. Ye shall not let your sheriffwick, nor any bailiwick thereof, to farm to any man. Ye shall truly set and return reasonable and due issues of them that be within your bailiwick, after their estate and their haviour; and make your panels yourself of such persons as be most meet, most sufficient, and not suspected nor procured, as is ordained by the statutes; and over this, in eschewing and restraint of the manslaughters, robberies and other manifold grievous offences that be done daily, namely, by such as name themselves soldiers, and other vagrant persons, which increase in number and multiply, so that the queen's subjects may not surely ride nor go to do such things as they have to do, to their intolerable hurt and hindrance. Ye shall truly and effectually, with all diligence possible to your power, execute the statutes as the statutes of Winchester and of vagabonds. These things ye shall well and truly observe and keep.

So help you God.

Recognizance of Sheriffs of Wales.

2s. stamp.

The condition of this recognizance is such, that whereas the above bound A. B. is appointed sheriff of the county of N.; If the said A. B., or he being dead, his heirs, executors or administrators do personally appear before the queen's majesty's auditors for her revenue of her highness's crown there, or her deputy for the time being, at such time and place as the next audit shall be holden and kept for the said revenue, and then and there make and yield a true and lawful account to the queen's majesty, her heirs or successors, before the said auditor or his deputy, of the issues and profits of the said office, and of all things belonging to the queen's majesty which shall come to his hands, or to the hands of the under-sheriff or any of his bailiffs, ministers or servants, or which he may or ought lawfully to levy or receive before the time of his said account, or which he may reasonably be charged with, to the queen's use, by reason of the said office, or of any process to him directed, before his said account, without any manner of concealment or delay. And do also, immediately upon determination of the same accounts, and before his or their departure from the same audit, pay or cause to be paid to the hands of the queen's majesty's receiver-general of the said revenue or his deputy for the time being, to her highness's use, her heirs and successors, all and every such sum and sums of money as shall be due to her majesty by him or them, by reason of and upon the same account. And also do and shall observe, perform and fulfil all and every such articles and ordinances concerning the sheriffs of the counties of Wales, as were taken the twenty-fifth day of November, *anno Domini* one thousand five hundred and fifty-nine, and remain of record in her majesty's Court of Exchequer; which, on the part of him, his executors, administrators or assigns, are or ought to be observed, performed and done according to the full and true intent and meaning of the same. And also if the said sheriff do assign and appoint, by his sufficient warrant, his able or sufficient attorney or deputy in every of her majesty's Courts of Chancery, the Queen's Bench, the Common Pleas and Exchequer at Westminster and elsewhere, wheresoever the said courts shall happen to be kept; which shall attend the said courts so long as they shall be open and sitting, and receive, open and return all writs, process and commandments which shall be directed to the same sheriff or his deputy, in any and every of the said courts, so long as he shall be sheriff of the said county, according to the statute in that behalf made, and as the sheriff of England use and ought to do. And further, if the said A. B., so long as he shall be sheriff of the said county of N., do or shall, by himself or his sufficient deputy in that behalf, to be allowed by her majesty's justices of assize for the said county, not only well and sufficiently serve and execute all processes, mandates and commandments which to him shall be directed, awarded or commanded by the said court; and make full and perfect returns of the same, according to the tenor and true purport of the same processes, mandates and commandments; but also do and shall give their personal and ready attendance at and before the said court, for the better service of her majesty, her heirs or successors, by the said sheriff or his deputy, to be had and done as often and when as he the said sheriff or his deputy shall be required or commanded thereunto by the said court. And lastly, if the said A. B. do and shall, during all the time of the said shrievalty, by himself or his sufficient deputy, obey and observe, make, do and perform all such attendances, offices, services, acts and things for and concerning the said office of shrievalty, as other sheriffs of the said counties of England do or ought, by reason of the like offices of shrievalty, to do and perform, and as in that behalf shall appertain: That then this present recognizance to be void and of no effect; else to remain in full force and virtue.

CHAP. II.—SECT. 3.

Letter of Attorney to receive the Gaol, &c.

To all to whom these presents shall come, I, A. B., of ——, in the county of N., esquire, present sheriff of the said county, do by these presents appoint, depute, authorize and empower C. D., of the town of —— , gent., E. F., of —— and G. H., of ——, gent., or any one of them, for me, and in my stead and place, to receive and take the gaol of the said county of N., with all the prisoners therein, and the rolls, writs, memorandums and all other matters and things to the office of sheriff of the said county of N. belonging, to and from D. P., esq., late sheriff of the said county of N., or of or from his late under-sheriff, or such other person or persons as he shall lawfully authorize and empower to deliver the same. And I do hereby authorize and empower C. D., E. F. and G. H., or any of them, to receive from the said late sheriff or his late under-sheriff, or such other person or persons as he shall for that purpose lawfully authorize and appoint, an indenture made or to be made between the said late sheriff and me in that behalf; and likewise for me and in my place and stead to set my name to the counterpart of the said indenture, and to seal and as my act and deed to deliver the same, and to do and execute whatsoever else may be necessary to be done and executed for me in this behalf. In witness whereof I have hereunto set my hand and seal this —— day of ——, in the year of our Lord ——.

Sealed and delivered, &c. A. B. (*Seal of office.*)

CHAP. II.
SECT. III.

Letter of Attorney to deliver the Gaol.

To all to whom these presents shall come, I, D. P., of ——, in the county of N., esquire, late sheriff of the said county, do by these presents appoint, depute, authorize and empower ——, of ——, gent., (*naming three or four*) or any of them, for me, and in my stead and place, to deliver the gaol of the said county of N., with all the prisoners therein, and all writs, memorandums, and other matters and things to the office of sheriff of the said county belonging, to A. B., of ——, in the said county of N., esq., present sheriff of the said county, or to such person or persons as he hath authorized or shall authorize to receive the same; And I do hereby authorize and empower the said —— and ——, or any of them, to set my name to an indenture between me and the said present sheriff, and to seal and as my act and deed deliver the same, and likewise to receive for me an indenture from the said present sheriff, or such person or persons as he hath appointed or shall appoint for that purpose. In witness whereof I have hereunto set my hand and seal this —— day of ——, 18—.

Signed and delivered, &c. D. P. (*Seal of office.*)

CHAP. III.—Sect. 1.

Letter of Attorney appointing Replevin Clerks (*a*).

N. (*to wit*). Know all men by these presents, that I, A. B., esq., sheriff of the county of N., have constituted and appointed, and by these presents do constitute and appoint W. H. of , in the county of N., gent., one of my deputies for making or granting Replevins within the said county of N., pursuant to the statute in such case made and provided. In witness whereof I have hereunto set my hand and seal this —— day of ——, in the year ——.

A. B., esq., sheriff. (*Seal of office.*)

Sealed and delivered
in the presence of ——.

Letter of Attorney appointing Deputies to hold the County Court.

To all to whom these presents shall come, I, A. B. of ——, in the county of N., esq., send greeting: Whereas I, the said A. B., by virtue of her Majesty's letters patent bearing date the 29th day of April last past, was appointed and took upon me the office of sheriff, of and for the said county of N. Now know ye, that I, the said A. B., upon the special trust and confidence I have and repose in G. H. of A., in the said county, gent., and T. K. of the same place, gent., have (and at the special instance and request of C. D. of the town of ——, gent., whom I have constituted and appointed my under-sheriff) nominated, constituted, and appointed, and by these presents do nominate, constitute, and appoint the said G. H. and T. K. and either of them severally and respectively assistants to and under me the said A. B. and the said C. D. my under-sheriff, to

(*a*) The appointment may be made by entry in the county court book, according to the form, *ante*, p. 29, note (*i*).

sit, preside, and hold my county courts, and to do and execute what to the said office of holding the said courts shall appertain, when they or either of them shall hold the said courts in the absence of the said C. D.; and I do hereby ratify and confirm what they the said G. H. and T. K., and either of them, shall lawfully do or cause to be done in and about the premises by virtue of these presents. In witness whereof I have hereunto set my hand and seal the 3rd day of June, in the year of our Lord, 1848.

A. B., esq., sheriff. (*Seal of office.*)

Sealed and delivered, &c.

SECT. 2.

Appointment of Under-sheriff.

To all to whom these presents shall come, I, A. B of ——, in the county of N., esq., send greeting: Whereas I, the said A B., have been appointed during her majesty's will and pleasure high sheriff of the county of N., by her majesty's warrant of appointment bearing date the —— day of —— A. D. ——. Now know ye, that I have nominated, constituted and appointed, and by these presents do nominate, constitute and appoint, C. D. of ——, in the said county, gentleman, my under-sheriff of and for the said county, and do depute and authorize him to act, do, and execute for me and in my stead all things to the said office of under-sheriff in anywise belonging or appertaining. Dated this —— day of ——, in the year of our Lord ——. A. B.

Form of Covenants between Under-Sheriff and Sheriff.

This indenture, made the second day of February, in the —— year of the reign of her Majesty, Queen Victoria, and in the year of our Lord ——, between A. B. of G., in the county of M., esq., of the one part; and C. D., &c., gentleman, of the other part; witnesseth, that the said A. B., being elected, and having this day taken upon himself the office of sheriff of the county of M.; in consequence of the trust and confidence which he hath in the said C. D., and that he will take care that the office of under-sheriff of the said county be honestly, uprightly, and duly discharged; and for other the considerations hereinafter mentioned, he, the said A. B , hath deputed and ordained, and by these presents doth depute and ordain the C. D. to be his under-sheriff of the said county of M.: And doth authorize, appoint, and empower him to sign, seal, and execute, and as the act and deed of the said sheriff to deliver, all assignments of bail-bonds, bills of sale, assignments of goods and chattels taken in execution: And also to take inquisitions upon process directed to the said sheriff; to make out precepts for the election of members to serve in parliament; to preside or to assist in the county courts, and upon the hustings, at the election of knights of the shire; to appoint county clerks, replevin clerks, and bailiffs; to receive rules for the returning of writs; and give receipts and discharges for all monies whatever, to be received or collected in the office of sheriff of the said county; to sign the name of the said sheriff to all certificates, and other instruments and writings requiring the same; and to do all other acts in the name of the said A. B., as sheriff of the

Deed Stamp.

CHAP. III. SECT. II.

county of M., necessary and requisite in the due execution of the said office. In consideration whereof the said C. D., and the said E. F., as surety for the said C. D., for themselves, their heirs, executors, and administrators, do hereby covenant, promise, and agree to and with the said A. B., his executors and administrators, in manner following, that is to say: that he, the said C. D., shall and will well and sufficiently perform the office of under-sheriff during the shrievalty of the said A. B.; and in that capacity summon and return all juries and inquests to be impanelled before her majesty's justices of assize or of the peace, or upon any issue whatsoever to be tried, or inquisition to be taken, within the said county; and also grant warrants on, and execute, or cause to be executed, all writs, process, precepts, mandates, and warrants, to be directed to the said sheriff from the several courts of law or equity, or other competent authority; and make due and sufficient inquisitions and returns thereon, as by law is required; and shall and will save harmless, and keep indemnified, the said sheriff, his heirs, executors, and administrators, and his and their goods and chattels, lands and tenements, of and from all and all manner of action and actions, cause and causes of actions, suits, fines, and amerciaments, contempts and forfeitures, and all other charges and incumbrances whatsoever, which shall or may happen to be assessed or imposed upon the said A. B. as sheriff, by reason of the executing or not executing, returning or not returning, or the misreturning any such writs, process, precept, mandate, or warrant, or touching or concerning the same, or the summoning or impanelling the juries as aforesaid; and also of and from any escapes, rescues, or the letting any prisoner voluntarily or negligently go at large; or the taking of insufficient bail, or the refusing to take bail, or for the making or not making any assignments of a bail bond or bonds; or the not filing any warrant of attorney in any of the courts of record at Westminster or elsewhere; or for or by reason of any negligence, misfeasance, nonfeasance, abuse, omission, delay, or contempt, or any other cause or thing whatsoever, that should or ought to be done by the said under-sheriff or agent, or by the clerks, bailiffs, or servants to be employed, concerning the said office: And also shall and will upon demand produce and show, or deliver to the said sheriff, a true inventory or account of the different writs in the office of the said sheriff, and what has been done thereon respectively; and that it shall be in the power of the said sheriff, upon complaint, to discharge any bailiff or other person in the service of the said sheriff, and to appoint another in his stead for the remainder of the shrievalty: And further, that the said under-sheriff shall, from time to time, give due notice to the said sheriff of such personal attendance as shall be requisite to be made by him; and shall attend on, and assist him thereat, and be aiding and assisting in raising and levying such force within the said county as the sheriff shall be enjoined to raise; and from time to time give his personal attendance on the said sheriff when required, and collect and levy the post fines, forfeitures, profits, services, fee farm rents, pipe silver, exchequer silver, goods of traitors, felons, and outlaws, and all taxes, levies, charges, or impositions, to the use of her majesty, by virtue of any writ or process whatsoever, lawfully issued for that purpose, and directed to the said sheriff; and shall duly account for and pay the same to her said majesty's use, and obtain acquitances from the proper offices, and deliver the same to the sheriff when thereunto required: And shall duly pass the sheriff's accounts before the barons and officers of the Exchequer, (or before her majesty's auditor in Wales); and obtain a quietus for the same, so that the lands and tenements, goods and chattels of the said sheriff may stand fully acquitted: And shall and will bear and pay such costs, charges, and expenses, as shall attend the execution of the duties of the said office (except the costs and charges of the recognizance and patent), the assignment of prisoners, and appointment of the under-sheriff; the seal of office and deed of covenant; the advertising the assizes; the expenses attending the trumpeters and javelin men, and their clothes, and the clothes of the officers and bailiffs; the fees to the chaplain and inferior officers; the calendar of prisoners, the executing prisoners, the judges' lodgings, court-keepers and tavern expenses at the assizes; and the expenses of the under-sheriff, deputy, and agent, to, at, and from the assizes; also the convicts' bread money, and all the expenses of an election of members or coroners; also the charges of passing the sheriff's accounts at the Exchequer (or before her majesty's auditor in Wales); and obtaining the *quietus* and the fee-farm rents, if any, charged to the sheriffs, and not recoverable; and the personal expenses of the under-sheriff and deputy in attending any public meeting within the county (which are to be paid by the sheriff); and cause to be executed and punished all such persons as shall be convicted or attainted, according to his or her sentence; and well and faithfully do, execute and perform all and every act, matter and thing belonging to the said office of under-sheriff. And the said A. B. doth hereby, for himself, his heirs, executors, and administrators, covenant, promise, and agree to and with the said C. D., his respective executors and administrators, in manner following, that is to say: that the bonds or obligations to be entered into or given to the said sheriff by the gaoler and bailiffs, or by any person or persons to be arrested during the said shrievalty, shall be considered as well for the indemnity of the said under-sheriff or agent, as of the said sheriff: and that the said under-sheriff, performing the aforesaid covenants, shall have and enjoy the said office of under-sheriff during the shrievalty of the said A. B.; and keep, by himself or deputy, the courts by law established in the said county; and have and take all lawful fees, dues, profits, and emoluments whatsoever, belonging to the said office of sheriff. Provided, nevertheless, that nothing herein contained shall preclude the said sheriff from receiving the allowances for judges' lodgings, and patent money, and also for bread money and the execution of convicts, allowed in the bill of cravings to his own use. In witness whereof the said parties to these presents have hereunto set their hands and seals, the day and year first above written.

Signed, sealed, &c.

Bond of Indemnity from Under-Sheriff's Deputy or Agent to the Under-Sheriff, where the Under-Sheriff appoints a Deputy.

Know all men by these presents, that I, E. F., am held and firmly bound to C. D., under-sheriff to A. B., esq., high sheriff of the county of N., in the penal sum of —— pounds of good and lawful money of Great Britain, to be paid to the said C. D., or his certain attorney, executors, administrators or assigns, for which payment to be well and faithfully made, I bind myself and my heirs, executors and administrators, firmly by these presents, sealed with my seal. Dated this —— day of —— in the year of our Lord one thousand eight hundred and ——.

Whereas the above-named C. D., under-sheriff of the county of N., hath constituted and appointed the above-named E. F. to be his deputy

CHAP. III. SECT. II.

and agent in the said office; and in such appointment it was agreed that the said E. F. should enter into the indemnity hereinafter mentioned. Now the condition of the above-written obligation is such, that if the said E. F., his heirs, executors and administrators, and every or any of them, do and shall, from time to time, and at all times hereafter, save harmless, and keep indemnified, A. B. esq., sheriff of the said county of N., and also the said C. D., his under-sheriff, and each of them, their and each of their heirs, executors and administrators, goods and chattels, lands and tenements, touching and concerning the return and execution of all process, writs and mandates, of what nature soever they be, as shall or may be directed to the sheriff of the county aforesaid, and shall be brought and delivered to the said E. F. during the time the said A. B. shall be sheriff of the said county; and of, from and against all and all manner of fines, issues and amerciaments, actions, suits and prosecutions, costs, charges, damages and expenses, which the said sheriff, or the said C. D., or either of them, their or either of their executors or administrators, shall or may pay, bear, sustain or be put unto, or which shall or may be brought, commenced, or prosecuted against them, either or any of them, for or by reason of the not returning, wrongfully executing, or misreturning, or detaining in their hands, any writ or writs, process or processes, or mandates whatsoever: And also if he, the said E. F., his executors or administrators, shall and do, in due time, and from time to time, make a true and just account, and due satisfaction and payment of all and singular the sum and sums of money, which shall be received by the said E. F., by virtue of any writ, process, or other mandate, directed to the said sheriff; or for fees, dues, perquisites or emoluments, or otherwise, as such deputy or agent as aforesaid, during the time the said A. B. shall continue sheriff, or the said C. D. under-sheriff of the said county: And also if the said E. F. shall and do, upon demand, produce and show, or deliver to the said sheriff or under-sheriff, a true inventory or account of the different writs and processes in the office of the said sheriff, and what has been done thereon respectively: And also if the said E. F., his heirs, executors or administrators, or any of them, shall and do save harmless, and keep indemnified, the said sheriff and under-sheriff, and each of them, their and each of their heirs, executors and administrators goods and chattels, lands and tenements, of, from and against all actions, suits, prosecutions, costs, charges, damages, and expenses, which they or either of them, their or either of their heirs, executors, or administrators, shall or may bear, sustain, or be put unto, of or concerning all or any such monies which shall be received by the said E. F., and not paid or accounted for as aforesaid: then the above-written obligation to be void, but otherwise, and on failure of performance of all and every, or any of the said conditions, stipulations, and agreements, the same is to be and remain in full force and virtue.

Signed, sealed, and delivered,
by the above-named E. F.,
in the presence of

SECT. 3.

Bond of Indemnity from Bailiffs and their Sureties.

STAMP. (*h*)

Know all men by these presents, that we C. D. of —— and E. F. of —— are held and firmly bound to A. B. Esq., High Sheriff of the county of C., in the sum of £—— to be paid to the said A. B., or to his certain attorney, executors, administrators, or assigns, for which payment to be well and truly made we bind ourselves and each of us, our and each of our heirs, executors, and administrators, and every of them, jointly and severally by these presents. Dated, &c.

Whereas the said sheriff, at the request of the said C. D. and of his surety the said E. F., hath nominated and appointed the said C. D. to be one of the bailiffs of the said sheriff during the pleasure of the said sheriff, permitting him to receive to his own use all lawful fees usually received by sheriff's bailiffs in the said county of ——, save and except the poundage and such other fees and profits on writs of execution and extent as have been usually received by the sheriff of the said county of ——, and all other fees and emoluments to the said sheriff or his under-sheriff belonging: and whereas the said E. F., in consideration of the nomination and appointment of the said C. D. as aforesaid, hath consented and agreed to execute such bond or obligation as is above written, with such condition as is hereinafter expressed and contained: Now therefore the condition of the above-written obligation is such, that if the said bailiff shall duly execute all warrants or mandates to him directed by the said sheriff, under-sheriff, or deputies, or any of them, in the name of the said sheriff, and shall duly make a true and sufficient return in writing to all warrants which shall come to his hands as such bailiff for execution: and also if the said bailiff shall and will take sufficient pledges and sureties in replevin, and shall and will deliver up to the said sheriff or under-sheriff all bonds and other securities belonging to the said sheriff within two days after the same shall be taken; and also if the said bailiff shall not suffer any escape, or permit any prisoner in his custody as bailiff aforesaid to go at large without a lawful authority, nor permit any prisoner to go at large who shall be left with him or at his house for safe custody by the said sheriff or any other bailiff, without the said sheriff or his order in writing first had and obtained; and also if the said bailiff shall give day by day instructions in writing for the sheriff's return to each and every writ and process upon which any warrant shall have been granted to him, or under or in respect of or by colour of which he shall in any way act or assume to act as bailiff to the said sheriff, whether such writ or writs shall have been executed or not; and also if the said bailiff shall duly execute all writs delivered to him for execution, whether from a court of law or equity; and also if the said bailiff shall make a true return and inventory of all goods and chattels seized in execution by him as bailiff to the said sheriff, and if he shall before removal thereof pay to the landlord the rent in arrear, not exceeding one year, and all taxes due in respect thereof, pursuant to the statute, and shall indemnify the said sheriff on account of any mistake or default relating thereto; and also if the said bailiff shall pay to the said sheriff or under-sheriff the consideration or purchase-money mentioned in every bill of sale or assignment

(*b*) The stamp will depend on the sum mentioned in the bond.

CHAP. III. SECT. III.

executed by the said sheriff or under-sheriff at the request of the said bailiff, notwithstanding the acknowledgment of the receipt thereof by the said sheriff contained in any such bill of sale or assignment; and also if the said bailiff shall and will forthwith pay to the said sheriff or under-sheriff all monies received by the said bailiff on any arrest or levy by him made, or with which he shall be entrusted for the said sheriff, without deduction; and also if the said bailiff shall in all things truly and honestly demean and behave himself as bailiff aforesaid, and faithfully and diligently serve and attend the said sheriff, his under-sheriff and their deputies, and in due and lawful manner all their and every of their lawful commands or directions touching any manner of service incident or belonging to the said office of sheriff shall and will execute and perform; and also if the said bailiff and his sureties, some or one of them, shall indemnify and save harmless the said sheriff and his under-sheriff from all damages, loss, costs, and charges which they or either of them shall or may suffer, sustain, or be put unto, or be liable to suffer, sustain, or be put unto, for or by reason of the nonfeazance, malfeazance, or misfeazance of the said bailiff, or for or by reason of the payment of any money by the said sheriff, under-sheriff, or deputies to any person or persons, or by reason of any return to any writ or process made by the said sheriff, under-sheriff, or deputies, at the request of the said bailiff; and also if the said bailiff and his said sureties, some or one of them, their or some one of their heirs, executors, or administrators, shall and will save harmless and indemnified the said sheriff and under-sheriff, their and each of their executors and administrators, from and against all actions, suits, fines, and amerciaments, penalties, contempts, forfeitures, loss, costs, charges, damages, and expenses which may be commenced, prosecuted, imposed, or set upon them or either of them, or which they or any or either of them may suffer, pay, or be liable unto, for or by reason of any extortion or escape happening by the act or default of the said bailiff, or for or by reason of the executing, not executing, returning, not returning, or mis-return of any writ, process, mandate, precept, or warrant, the not taking bail or pledges, taking insufficient bail or pledges, the not bringing into court the body of any defendant, or any other cause whatsoever, happening by or arising from the act or omission of the said bailiff; then the above-written obligation shall be void, otherwise to be and remain in full force and virtue.

Bailiff's Oath.

I, A. B., shall not use or exercise the office of bailiff corruptly during the time that I shall remain therein, neither shall or will accept, receive, or take by any colour, means, or device whatsoever, or consent to the taking of, any manner of fee or reward of any person or persons for the impanelling or returning of any inquest, jury, or tales in any court of record for the queen, or betwixt party and party, above two shillings or the value thereof, or such fees as are allowed and appointed for the same by the laws and statutes of this realm, but will according to my power truly and indifferently with convenient speed impanel all jurors, and return all such writ or writs touching the same as shall appertain to be done by my duty or office, during the time that I shall remain in the said office. So help me God.

Indorsement on a Writ, when a Bailiff is specially appointed. Such Indorsement should be signed by the Plaintiff's Attorney.

Whereas the sheriff of N. hath, at our request, directed the warrant upon the within writ to J. S. and I. M., as special bailiffs for executing the same; in consideration thereof, we do hereby promise to save harmless and keep indemnified the said sheriff, his under-sheriff, and clerk, of and from all costs, troubles, and charges, that shall or may happen by reason of his or their directing the said warrant to the said special bailiffs. As witness our hands, the ——— day of ———.

A. and B., plaintiff's attornies.

The same, in another form.

Mr. Sheriff,—Please grant your warrant on this writ, directed to ———, as special bailiff, at the instance and peril of the plaintiff; and for so doing this shall be your indemnity.

Yours,
A. and B., attornies for the plaintiff.

Form of Warrant to a Special Bailiff.

[Commencement the same as other warrants.]

"To A. B., my bailiff for this time only, at the instance and peril of the plaintiff, and not otherwise, specially appointed, greeting," &c.

Sect. 4.

Security from Gaoler.—Form of Bond.

Know all men by these presents, that we, J. K., gentleman, keeper of the county gaol of N. (being in the ——— of ——— in the said county), C. D. of, &c., upholsterer, and E. F. of, &c., farmer, are held and firmly bound unto A. B. of, &c., esquire, sheriff of the county of N. aforesaid, in 3,000*l.* (c), of good and lawful money of Great Britain, to be paid to the said sheriff, or his certain attorney, executors, administrators or assigns: for the true payment whereof we bind ourselves, jointly and severally, our and each of our heirs, executors and administrators, firmly by these presents. Sealed with our seals. Dated this ——— day of ———, in the ——— year of the reign, &c., and in the year of our Lord, &c.

Whereas the above-named A. B. being by the queen's most excellent majesty appointed high sheriff for the county of N. aforesaid, hath, at the instance and request of the above-bounden J. K., authorized, nominated and appointed the said J. K. to be his gaoler, or keeper of the gaol in and for the said county of N., for and during all such time as

(c) This, as well as the penalty of the bailiff's bonds, must depend upon circumstances, as the size of the county, &c.

CHAP. III. SECT. IV.

the said A. B. shall be and continue high sheriff of the county of N. aforesaid, with full power and authority to execute the said office, in as large and ample a manner as any former gaoler or gaol-keeper have or hath heretofore lawfully executed the same: Now the condition of this obligation is such, that if the said J. K. do and shall from time to time, and at all times so long as the said A. B. shall continue high sheriff of the said county, and until the next succeeding sheriff shall take delivery of the said gaol, keep in safe custody, as well all such prisoner and prisoners as are now in the said county gaol, or in the custody of the keeper of the said gaol for I. M., esquire, the last preceding high sheriff of the said county, and delivered, or which shall be delivered over by the said I. M. or his deputy, by indenture under his or his deputy's hand and seal, to him the said A. B.; and by him the said A. B. delivered, or which shall be delivered, into the custody and keeping of the said J. K., as keeper of the said gaol, for him the said A. B.; as also all and every prisoner or prisoners, which at any time or times hereafter shall be committed, sent, or delivered to the said J. K., his servants, agents, deputy or deputies, upon or by virtue of any warrant or warrants, precept or precepts, or commandment whatsoever, or by or from the said sheriff, his under-sheriff, deputy or deputies, or other person employed and entrusted by him to manage or execute the office of sheriff for the county of N. for the time being, or from or by any of her majesty's justices of the peace, justice or justices of assize, of *nisi prius*, gaol delivery, or *oyer* and *terminer*, or of or from any other person or persons having lawful power and authority in that behalf: And also, if the said J. K. do give his attendance upon the said sheriff at the assizes and general gaol delivery, and general quarter sessions of the peace, to be holden in and for the said county; and safely convey and conduct to the assizes, general gaol delivery, general quarter sessions of the peace, or any other lawful court of judicature to be holden in and for the said county, all such persons then in his custody as shall be required by any lawful authority and command, and also shall convey such prisoners to the common gaol again, upon the like command of any magistrate or magistrates, or courts of judicature; (but the said J. K. to be at no expense for horses or other carriages, for the necessary conveying such prisoners to any court or courts of judicature, which shall be holden out of the county of N.; nor for the maintenance of such prisoners, upon their going or returning to or from such court of judicature): And also if the said J. K. be attending, aiding and assisting upon the said high sheriff at all and every the time and times when any execution shall be done within the said county, upon any person or persons attainted or to be attainted of or for high treason, murder, felony, or for any other capital crime, (but not to be compelled to do or execute any corporal punishment of any kind upon the person or persons of any prisoner who shall be condemned to undergo the same or other punishment whatsoever): And also if the said J. K. do and shall, as often as he is required and desired, and at his own costs and charges, make and deliver to the said A. B. or his under-sheriff, a true and perfect calendar, containing all the prisoners' names within the said gaol, or in his custody, containing and mentioning also the several causes of their and every of their respective imprisonments, and in all things well and truly execute the office of gaoler of and for the said county of N., during all the term aforesaid: And lastly, if the said J. K., his heirs, executors and administrators, and every of them, do and shall at all and every the time and times hereafter save, defend, and keep harmless and indemnified the said A. B., his heirs, executors and administrators, and every of them, and his and their goods and chattels, lands and tenements, of, from, and against all and every escape or escapes of any prisoner or prisoners, delivered or to be delivered over to him the said A. B., his servants, agents, deputy or deputies, or any of them, by any warrant or warrants, precept or precepts, or commandments whatsoever, as aforesaid, or for or by reason of any neglect or default or abuse of the said J. K., his servants, agents, deputy or deputies, in his said office, during such time as he shall continue gaoler and keeper of the said county gaol as aforesaid; and likewise from and against all and all manner of action and actions, suits, troubles, judgments, executions, fines, issues, amerciaments, forfeitures, and all other costs and damages whatsoever, which at any time or times hereafter shall or may arise, grow or happen to be brought upon the said sheriff, for or by reason of any such escapes, neglect, or default as aforesaid, or for any other cause aforesaid, relating to the said office of gaoler and keeper of the said county gaol as aforesaid; then this obligation, &c.

A Charge to the Gaoler against a Prisoner.

N. (*to wit.*) A. B., esquire, sheriff of the said county, to J. K., my gaoler, greeting: Whereas you have in your custody the body of G. H., these are to give you notice, that there is an execution, or *capias ad satisfaciendum*, delivered into the office against the said G. H., issuing out of her majesty's court of ——, at the suit of C. D. for ——, returnable immediately after the execution thereof; of which you are to take notice, and charge him therewith accordingly. Given under the seal of my office, this —— day of —— in the year of our Lord ——.

(*Seal of office.*) By the sheriff.

Gaoler's Receipt upon the same.

Received this —— day of ——, into my hands and custody, the body of G. H., upon an execution, or *capias ad satisfaciendum*, issued out of her majesty's court of ——, at Westminster, at the suit of ——, for ——, returnable immediately after the execution thereof. I say, received by me, J. K. gaoler.

Witness, E. F.

Liberate in pursuance of an Authority from the Plaintiff or his Attorney.

N. (*to wit.*) A. B., esquire, sheriff of the said county, to Mr. J. K., my gaoler, greeting: If you have in your custody the body of R. N., upon a writ of —— issued forth of her majesty's court of *Queen's Bench*, at Westminster, at the suit of E. F., bearing date the —— day of ——, for 76*l.*, indorsed for bail for 36*l.* 18*s.*, you are, in pursuance of an authority under the hands *of the said plaintiff*, (*or* "of Mr. A. B., attorney for the said plaintiff,") *to the said sheriff directed, and delivered into the office of the said sheriff*, to deliver and discharge the said R. N. from his imprisonment, if for no other cause you detain him, on

CHAP. III. SECT. IV.

payment of your fees. Given under the seal of my office, this ——— day of ———, 18—.

(*Seal of office.*) By the sheriff.

A Discharge to a Gaoler upon a Supersedeas.

N. (*to wit.*) A. B., esquire, sheriff of the county aforesaid, to Mr. J. K., my gaoler, greeting: If you have in your custody the body of R. N., upon a writ of ———, issued out of her majesty's court of ———, at Westminster, at the suit of ———, for ———, you are, according to a *supersedeas* issued out of the said court, and delivered into my office, to deliver and discharge the said R. N. from his imprisonment, if for no other cause you detain him. Given under the seal of my office, this ——— day of ———, 18—.

(*Seal of office.*) By the sheriff.

CHAP. IV.

Form of a Sheriff's Mandate to the Bailiff of a Liberty.

N. (*to wit.*) A. B., esquire, sheriff of the county aforesaid, to the Right Honourable A., earl of B., high bailiff of the liberty of L., in the county aforesaid, or to his deputy there, greeting: By virtue of a certain writ of our lady the queen, to me directed, I command you, and every of you, that you take the said C. D., if he be found in your liberty of L., and him safely keep, so that you may have, &c. (*the same as a common warrant.*)

Return of the Bailiff of a Liberty (*d*).

By virtue of the same mandate, to me directed and delivered, I have (*the matter of the return the same as in ordinary cases*).

"The answer of the Right Honourable A., earl of B., high bailiff of the liberty of L., in the county of N."

CHAP. V.—Sect. 2.

Warrant to raise the Posse Comitatus (*e*).

A. B., esquire, sheriff of N., to J. S., my bailiff, greeting: By virtue of the common law of this realm, and by virtue of my office, I do hereby command you, that you summon the *posse comitatus* of the county of N., to attend you in the execution of your office in executing a warrant upon a writ of *fi. fa.* issued out of the Common Pleas at Westminster, against C. D., late of, &c., farmer, at the suit of E. F.; and all knights, gentlemen, and yeomen, labourers, servants, and apprentices, and other young men above the age of fifteen years, are to attend you herein, as they will answer the contrary, upon pain of fine and imprisonment. Given under the seal of my office, this —— day of ——, 18—.

(*Seal of office.*) By the sheriff.

(*d*) As to return of bailiff of liberty, see *ante*, 60.

(*e*) This seems unnecessary. See *ante*, 73.

CHAP. VI.—Sect. 1.

Warrant on a Bailable Capias.

N. (*to wit.*) A. B., esquire, sheriff of the county aforesaid, to —— and ——, my bailiffs, greeting: By virtue of the queen's writ of *capias* to me directed, I command each and every of you jointly and severally that you omit not by reason of any liberty in my bailiwick, but that you enter the same and take ——, if he shall be found in my bailiwick, and him safely keep until he shall have given me bail or made deposit with me according to law, in an action *on promises*, at the suit of ——, or until the said —— shall by other lawful means be discharged from my custody; and I do further command each and every of you, jointly and severally, that on execution hereof you do deliver to him a copy of the said writ herewith delivered to you; and I do further command you, that immediately after the execution hereof you do certify to me the manner in which you shall have executed the same, and the day of the execution thereof, so that I may return the same to her majesty's said court, or that, if the same shall remain unexecuted, then you do so return this my warrant at the expiration of one calendar month from the date of the said writ, or sooner if thereto required. Dated the —— day of ——, 18—.

(*Seal of office.*) ——, High Sheriff.

Mandate to Sheriff of Lancashire.

A. B., Chancellor of the Duchy of Lancaster, to the Sheriff of Lancashire, greeting: We command you that you omit not by reason of any liberty in your bailiwick, but that you enter the same, and take C. W. of ——, if he shall be found in your bailiwick, and him safely keep (*&c. as in the writ of capias, to the teste*). Witness ourself at Lancaster the —— day of ——, in the —— year of our reign.

By the same Chancellor.

Sect. 2.

Bail Bond.

Know all men by these presents, that we —— are held and firmly bound to ——, sheriff of the county of ——, in the penal sum of £——, of good and lawful money of Great Britain, to be paid to the said sheriff, or his certain attorney, executors, administrators or assigns; for which payment to be well and faithfully made, we bind ourselves and every one of us by himself for the whole and every part thereof, and the heirs, executors, and administrators of us and every of us, firmly by these presents sealed with our seals. Dated this, &c. Whereas the above bounden —— was, on the —— day of ——, taken by the said sheriff in the bailiwick of the said sheriff, by virtue of the queen's writ of *capias* issued out of her majesty's court of ——, bearing date at Westminster the —— day of ——, to the said sheriff directed and delivered, against the said ——, in an action on ——, at the suit of ——: And whereas a copy of the said writ, together with every memorandum or notice subscribed thereto, and all indorsements thereon, was on execution thereof duly delivered to the said ——: And whereas the said —— is by the said writ required to cause special bail to be put in to the said action in the said court within eight days after execution thereof on him, inclusive of the day of such

CHAP. VI. SECT. II.

execution: Now the condition of this obligation is such, that if the said —— do cause special bail to be put in for him to the said action in her majesty's said court, as required by the said writ, then this present obligation to be void and of no force, otherwise to stand and remain in full force, vigour, and effect.

Sealed and delivered in the presence of ——.

Assignment of Bail Bond, indorsed thereon.

I, the within-named sheriff, at the request of the within-named plaintiff, assign over to —— this bail bond, pursuant to the statute. In witness whereof I have hereto set my hand and seal this —— day of ——, 18—.

G. A., esquire, sheriff.

Sealed and delivered in the presence of A. M., S. B.

Sect. 3.

RETURNS TO BAILABLE WRITS OF CAPIAS.

Non est inventus.

The within named C. D. is not found in my bailiwick.

The answer of A. B., esquire, sheriff.

Cepi Corpus et Paratum habeo.

On the —— day of ——, A.D. 18—, I took the within named C. D. in my bailiwick, and forthwith delivered to him a copy of this writ, and him safely kept until he gave me bail (*or* "made deposit with me") according to law.

The answer of A. B., esquire, sheriff.

On the —— day of ——, A.D. 18—, I took the within named C. D. and forthwith delivered to him a copy of this writ, and whose body I have ready as within I am commanded.

The answer of A. B., esquire, sheriff.

On the —— day of ——, A.D. 18—, I took the within named C. D. and forthwith delivered to him a copy of this writ, and whose body is now under my custody in the county gaol at A.

The answer of A. B., esquire, sheriff.

Return of prior removal by Habeas Corpus.

By virtue of this writ to me directed, I did, on the —— day of ——, take the within named C. D. and did safely keep him in her majesty's prison in and for the county of W., until afterwards, to wit, on &c., I received her said majesty's writ of *habeas corpus cum causâ*, commanding me to have the body of the said C. D. before the Right Hon. ——, at his chambers in Rolls Yard, Chancery Lane, London, immediately after the receipt of that writ: By virtue of which said writ, on the day and at the place therein mentioned, I had the body of the said C. D. before, &c., who then received of me the body of the said C. D., and then committed him to the queen's prison (*or as the case may be*), and then wholly discharged me from further keeping him under my custody:

Wherefore I cannot have the body of the said C. D. before our said lady the queen at the day and place within contained, as within I am commanded.

The answer of A. B., esquire, sheriff.

Rescue.

By virtue of this writ to me directed, I made my certain warrant in writing, under my seal of office, to E. F. and G. H., my bailiffs, jointly and severally, to take and arrest the within named C. D.; by virtue of which warrant the said E. F. and G. H. afterwards, to wit, on the —— day of —— last, at ——, in my county, and within my bailiwick, took and arrested the within named C. D. according to the exigency of the said writ, and safely kept him in their custody until J. K., of ——, and divers other persons to my said bailiffs unknown, on ——, at —— aforesaid, with force and arms assaulted and illtreated my said bailiffs, and the said C. D. out of the custody of my said bailiffs then and there rescued, and the said C. D. then and there with force and arms rescued himself, and escaped out of the custody of my said bailiffs, against the peace of our lady the now queen, and afterwards the said C. D. is not found in my bailiwick.

The answer of A. B., esquire, sheriff.

Discharge on Supersedeas.

By virtue of this writ to me directed, I took the within named C. D. and safely kept him in her majesty's prison in and for the county of ——, until afterwards, to wit, on ——, by virtue of another certain writ of our said lady the now queen to me directed, and to this writ annexed, I caused the said C. D. to be delivered out of the said prison, wherefore I cannot have the body of the said C. D. before our said lady the queen (*or, in C. P.*, "before the justices of our said lady the queen") at the day and place within contained, as within I am commanded.

The answer of A. B., esquire, sheriff.

Languidus in Prisoná.

By virtue of this writ to me directed, I have taken the within named C. D., who remains in her majesty's prison of —— under my custody, so weak and infirm, that without great peril and danger of his life I cannot have his body before our said lady the queen at the day and place within contained, as within I am commanded.

The answer of A. B., esquire, sheriff.

Return, Cepi Corpus and Languidus in Prisoná, as to one Defendant; and Non est Inventus as to another.

By virtue of this writ to me directed, I have taken the body of the within named C. D., late of, &c., whose body remains so sick, weak and infirm, in prison in my custody, that, for fear of the death of the said C. D., I cannot have his body before the justices within mentioned at the day and place within contained, as the within writ commands me. And I further certify the same justices, that G. H., of, &c., the other defendant within named, is not found in my bailiwick.

The answer of A. B., esquire, sheriff.

Return of Languidus.

By virtue of this writ to me directed, I made my certain warrant in writing to E. K. and G. H , my bailiffs, jointly and severally, to take and arrest the within named C. D.; by virtue of which said warrant the said E. K. and G. H. proceeded to an asylum for lunatics, where the said defendant then was, in order to arrest him; and then there found the said C. D. insane, and in a desperate and raving state, so that he could not be taken or removed without danger to the life of the officer. And the within named C. D. then was and still remains so sick, weak and infirm, that, without peril and danger of his life, I cannot have his body before our said lady the queen at the day and place within contained, as I am within commanded.

The answer of A. B., esquire, Sheriff.

Return of Mandavi Ballivo.

By virtue of this writ to me directed and delivered, I have made my mandate to the bailiff of the liberty of L., in my county, to take and arrest the within named C. D.; which said bailiff hath the full return of all writs and process, and the execution of the same within the liberty aforesaid, so that no execution of this writ can be made by me within the said liberty; which said bailiff has not yet given me any answer thereto (*or*, "hath answered that the within named C. D. is not found in his bailiwick;" *or*, "that he hath taken the within named C. D., whose body he hath ready," &c.)

Defendant privileged as Servant of an Ambassador.

I certify to the said justices within-mentioned, that the within-named C. D., at the time of the delivery of this writ to me, and from thence hitherto continually hath been, and still is, a domestic servant of the Duc de M., ambassador extraordinary and minister plenipotentiary from the queen of Spain at the British court. Therefore I cannot have the body of the said C. D. before the said justices, at the day and place within-mentioned, as I am commanded.

The answer of A. B., esquire, sheriff.

Defendant privileged as a Member of Parliament.

I certify to our said lady the queen, that the within-named C. D., at the time of the delivery of this writ to me, and from thence hitherto continually hath been, and still is, knight of the shire for the —— division of the county of ——, returned to serve in the present parliament of Great Britain: and as such knight of the shire hath, during all that time, served in the said parliament. And I further certify that the said parliament was, during all that time, sitting at Westminster, in the county of Middlesex. Therefore I cannot have the body of the said C. D. before our said lady the queen, at the day and place within mentioned, as I am within commanded. A. B., esquire, sheriff.

CHAP. VII.—Sect. 1.

Warrant on a Ca. Sa.

N. (*to wit*). A. B., esq., sheriff of the said county, to J. S., my bailiff, greeting: By virtue of her majesty's writ of *capias ad satisfaciendum*, to me directed and delivered, I command you, that you omit not by reason of any liberty in my county, but that you enter the same, and take C. D., wheresoever he shall be found in my bailiwick, and him safely keep, so that I may have his body before the barons of her majesty's Exchequer, (*or*, *in Q. B.*, " before our lady the queen;" *or*, *in C. P.* " before the said justices,") at Westminster, immediately after the execution hereof, as in the said writ I am commanded, and in what manner you shall have executed this warrant certify to me immediately after the execution thereof. Given under the seal of my office, this —— day of ——, 18—.

(*Seal of office.*) By the sheriff.

RETURN TO CA. SA.

Non est inventus.

The within-named C. D. is not found in my bailiwick.

The answer of A. B. esquire, sheriff.

Withdrawal or Suspension of Writ.

I do hereby certify and return, that after the coming of this writ to me directed, that is to say, on the —— day of ——, A. D. 18—, I was commanded by the within-named A. B. (*or* " by one E. F. the attorney of the within-named A. B.") to forbear (*or* " suspend") the execution thereof, and have forborne (*or* " suspended") accordingly.

The answer, &c.

Cepi Corpus, and Discharge out of Custody.

I have taken the within-named C. D., and committed him to the common gaol of our lady the queen of her castle of C., there to be kept in safe custody, so that I might have his body before our lady the queen, (" before the justices of our lady the queen," *or* " barons of her Exchequer") at Westminster, as within I am commanded; and I do hereby further certify and return, that afterwards, that is to say, on the —— day of ——, A. D. 18—, by command of a certain other writ of our lady the queen to me directed and delivered, a transcript whereof is annexed to this writ, (*or*, " by the direction and command of the within-named A. B." *or*, " of one E. F. the attorney of the within-named A. B.") I caused the said A. B. to be delivered from that prison, and therefore the body of the said C. D. before, &c., at the day and place within contained, I cannot have, as within I am commanded. The answer, &c.

That the Defendant had become Bankrupt and obtained his Certificate, wherefore the Sheriff forbore to take him.

I do hereby certify and return, that, before the coming of the annexed writ to me directed, the said C. D. in the said writ named, then being a trader within the meaning of the laws relating to bankrupts, and being

CHAP. VII. SECT. I.

then indebted to E. F., a subject of this realm, in the sum of 50*l.* and upwards, and being also then indebted to divers other subjects of this realm in divers other large sums of money, became and was a bankrupt within the true intent and meaning of the said statute, and thereupon a certain fiat in bankruptcy was upon the petition of the said E. F. duly issued, and the said C. D. was thereupon duly found and declared to be a bankrupt. And I do hereby further certify and return, that such proceedings were thereupon had, that the said C. D. afterwards, and after the recovery of the damages and interest (*or*, " debt, damages, and interest,") in the said writ mentioned, and before the coming of the said writ to me directed, to wit, on the —— day of ——, in the said year of our Lord 18—, duly obtained his certificate of conformity to the statute aforesaid, and which certificate afterwards, and before the coming of the said writ to me directed, was duly allowed and confirmed according to the form of the statute in such case made and provided. And I hereby further certify and return, that the cause of action, upon which the recovery in the said writ mentioned was had and obtained, accrued to A. B. in the said writ named against the said C. D., before such time as the said C. D. so became a bankrupt. Wherefore I, the said sheriff, having notice of all and singular the premises aforesaid, did forbear to take the body of the said C. D., as within I am commanded. The answer, &c.

That the Defendant is a privileged Person.

Before and at the time of the coming of this writ to me directed, the within-named C. D. was and still is a peer of the realm, having privilege of parliament (" a menial servant of her majesty the queen," *or the like*,) wherefore the body of the said C. D. before our lady the queen, on the day and at the place within contained, I cannot have as within I am commanded. The answer, &c.

CHAP. VIII.—Sect. 1.

Return to the Exigent, Quinto Exactus, and Outlawed.

By virtue of this writ to me directed, at my county court (*f*) at A., in and for the county of N., on the —— day of ——, in the —— year of the reign of our sovereign lady Queen Victoria, the within-named C. D. was a first time demanded, and did not appear: And at my county court, held at A. aforesaid, in and for the said county of N., on ——, the —— day of ——, in the year aforesaid, the said C. D. was a second time demanded, and did not appear: And at my county court, held at A. aforesaid, in and for the said county of N., on the —— day of ——, in the year aforesaid, the said C. D. was a third time demanded, and did not appear: And at my county court, held at A. aforesaid, in and for the said county of N., on the —— day of ——, in the year aforesaid, the said C. D. was a fourth time demanded, and did not appear: And at my county court, held at A. aforesaid, in and for the said county of N., on the —— day of ——, in the year aforesaid, the said C. D. was a fifth time demanded, and did not appear: Therefore, upon the judgment of

(*f*) If the outlawry is in London, instead of " county court," say, " at the husting of pleas of land, holden in the Guildhall of the city of London."

G. H., esq., and J. K., esq., coroners of our sovereign lady the queen for the county aforesaid, the said C. D., according to the law and custom of England, is outlawed.

The answer of A. B., esquire, sheriff.

Return to Exigent, where there are not five County Courts.

By virtue of this writ to me directed, at my county court, held at A., in and for the county of N., on the —— day of ——, in the —— year of the reign of our sovereign lady Queen Victoria, the within-named C. D. was a first time demanded.

Answer of A. B., esquire, sheriff.

Where the Sheriff goes out of office, and the new Sheriff exacts the Defendant.

[In addition to the last precedent.]

This writ, as above indorsed, was delivered to me, the under-named present sheriff, by the above-named late sheriff, at his going out of office. At my county court, held at A. (*as above.*)

Where the Defendant appears.

By virtue of this writ to me directed, at my county court, held at A., in and for the said county of N., on the —— day of ——, in the —— year of the reign of our sovereign lady Queen Victoria, the within-named C. D. was a first time demanded, and then and there appeared, and then rendered himself into my custody; whose body I have ready before our lady the queen, at the day and place within-mentioned, as within I am commanded.

The answer of A. B., esquire, sheriff.

Return to the Writ of Proclamations.

By virtue of this writ to me directed, I have caused the within-named C. D. to be proclaimed at my county court, held at A., within my bailiwick, the —— day of ——, in the year within-mentioned: I also caused him to be proclaimed at the general quarter sessions of the peace, held at M., within my bailiwick, the —— day of ——, in the same year: And I likewise caused him to be proclaimed at the usual door of the parish church of H., within my bailiwick (in which said parish the said C. D. lived), on Sunday, the —— day of ——, in the same year; that he may render himself unto me, (*or, if a foreign proclamation,* "to the sheriff of ——, so that they,") so that I may have his body before her majesty's justices at Westminster, at the time within-mentioned, to answer the within-named J. W., of the plea within-mentioned.

The answer of A. B., esquire, sheriff.

Sect. 2.

Return to Special Capias Utlagatum.

The execution of this writ appears in a certain schedule hereunto annexed The answer of A. B., esquire, sheriff.

Inquisition.

N. (*to wit.*) An inquisition indented, taken at A., in the county of N., the —— day of ——, in the —— year of the reign of our sovereign lady Queen Victoria, before me, A. B., esq., sheriff of the said county of N., by virtue of her said majesty's writ to me directed in this behalf, and to this inquisition annexed, by the oath of (*here name the jurors who were upon the inquest*) twelve honest and lawful men of the county aforesaid, who say upon their oath, that C. D. named in the writ hereunto annexed, on the —— day of —— last past (on which day he was outlawed, as in the said writ is mentioned), was possessed of the goods and chattels following: that is to say, (*here describe the goods*) of the value of £——, of his own proper goods and chattels; (*or, if he had no goods, say,* "had no goods nor chattels in my bailiwick to the knowledge of the said jurors"): and the jurors aforesaid, upon their oath aforesaid, do further say, that the said C. D., on —— last past (on which day he was outlawed as aforesaid), was seised in his demesne as of fee of and in (*g*) ——, with the appurtenances, now in the tenure and occupation of P. M., the same being of the yearly value of £——, in all issues beyond reprize; all and singular which said goods and chattels, lands and tenements, I the said sheriff, by virtue of the said writ, on the day of the taking of this inquisition, have taken and caused to be seized into the hands of our said lady the queen, as by the said writ I am commanded. And the jurors aforesaid, upon their oath aforesaid, do further say, that the said C. D., on —— last past (on which day he was outlawed as aforesaid), or at any time afterwards, had not, nor hath he any other or more (goods or chattels, lands or tenements) in my bailiwick, to the knowledge of the said jurors. In witness whereof, as well as I the said sheriff, as the jurors aforesaid, have set our respective seals.

(*Seal of office.*) (*Twelve seals.*)

CHAP. IX.

Return to a Writ of Habeas Corpus.

N. (*to wit.*) I. A. B., esquire, sheriff of the said county, do humbly certify and return to the Right Honourable Thomas Lord Denman, her majesty's chief justice, mentioned in the writ to this schedule annexed, that the said C. D., in the said writ named, was taken on the —— day of ——; and in her majesty's gaol in and for the said county at M. is detained under my custody, by virtue of a writ of *capias ad satisfaciendum;* the tenor of which said writ follows in these words: "Victoria," &c. (*setting forth the writ and all indorsements thereon verbatim*). And this is the cause (*or* "causes") (*h*) of taking the said C. D., which, together with his body, I have ready, as by the said writ I am commanded.

The answer of A. B., esquire, sheriff.

(*g*) See different findings of property, *post*, Append. chap. 16, s. 2.

(*h*) In case of the prisoner being detained by several writs, all the writs should be set out in the return, in like manner. If the prisoner was taken in the late sheriff's time, the above form would do, but it is better to state that the prisoner was taken by the late sheriff, and, after setting out the writ, "which said writ, and the custody of the body of the said C. D. was duly assigned, transferred and delivered over to me by the said late sheriff, at his going out of office,"

Warrant to Gaoler and Bailiff to convey Prisoner on a Habeas Corpus.

N. (*to wit.*) A. B., esquire, sheriff of the said county of N., to E. F., keeper of the gaol of M., in this county, and to W. W., my bailiff (for this time specially appointed): By virtue of her majesty's writ, to me directed, I command you that you safely and securely convey the body of C. D., immediately after the receipt of this warrant, to and before Thomas Lord Denman, chief justice of our lady the queen, before the queen herself, at his chambers in Rolls' Gardens, Chancery Lane, London; to do, submit, and receive what the said chief justice shall then and there consider of him in this behalf. Hereof fail not at your peril. Given under my hand and seal of office, this —— day of ——, 18—.

(*Seal of office.*) By the sheriff.

CHAP. X.—Sect. 1.

Warrant on a Fieri Facias.

N. (*to wit.*) A. B., esquire, sheriff of the county aforesaid, to —— and —— my bailiffs, greeting: By virtue of her majesty's writ of *fi. fa.* to me directed and delivered, I do hereby command you and each of you jointly and severally, that of the goods and chattels of C. D. in my bailiwick you or one of you cause to be made £——; that I may have that money before our lady the queen (*in C. B.* "before the justices of our lady the queen," *in Exch.* "before the barons of her majesty's Exchequer,") at Westminster, as required by the said writ, and that you do all such things, &c., and in what manner you shall have executed this warrant certify to me immediately after the execution thereof. Given under the seal of my office, this —— day of ——, 18—. By the sheriff.

Levy £—— (*as indorsed on the writ*). (*Seal of office.*)

Sect. 4.

Bill of Sale from the Sheriff, of Goods taken under a Fieri Facias.

To all to whom these presents shall come, I, A. B., esquire, sheriff of N., send greeting: Whereas by virtue of her majesty's writ of *fi. fa.* issued out of her majesty's Court of Queen's Bench at Westminster, to me directed and delivered, for levying 20*l.*, and 60*s.* damages or costs of suit, on the goods and chattels of C. D., which E. F. in the said court had recovered against him, as by the said writ in —— may more at large appear, I have taken into my hands the several goods and chattels of the said C. D. hereafter mentioned (*i*), that is to say, (*here insert the particulars,*) which by good and lawful men have been valued and appraised at £——. Now know ye, that I, the said A. B., by virtue of the said warrant and my office, and for and in consideration of the sum of £—— of lawful money of Great Britain, to me in hand paid by the said E. F., do hereby, as much as in me lieth, by virtue of my said office, fully and absolutely bargain, sell, and deliver to the said E. F., his executors, administrators, and assigns, the said goods and chattels, to have, hold, and enjoy the same as his, her and their own proper goods and chattels for ever, in part satisfaction of his debt and damages aforesaid. In witness, &c.

Signed, sealed, &c.

(*i*) Or "in a certain schedule hereto annexed."

SECT. 6.

Condition of a Bond indemnifying the Sheriff for selling Goods on a Fi. Fa.

Whereas the above-named A. B. as sheriff of the county of N., by virtue of her majesty's writ of fieri facias to him directed, issued at the suit of E. F., out of the Court of Queen's Bench, and returnable on ——, to levy on the goods and chattels of C. D. the sum of £——, hath seized and taken divers goods and chattels, as the proper goods and chattels of C. D. in execution: And whereas, since the seizing and taking of the said goods and chattels in execution as aforesaid, the said goods and chattels have been claimed by one X. Y., who hath given notice to the said sheriff not to proceed to a sale of the said goods and chattels, or to pay over the money arising from the sale thereof to the said E. F.: And whereas the said E. F. hath applied to the said sheriff, and requested him to sell the said goods and chattels so seized as aforesaid, under and by virtue of the said writ of fieri facias, notwithstanding such claim and notice, and to pay to him the said E. F., the money arising from the sale thereof, in satisfaction of the said sum of money directed to be levied by the said writ of fieri facias, which the said A. B. hath consented to do upon being indemnified for so doing: Now the condition of the above-written obligation is such, that if the above-bounden E. F., his heirs, executors, and administrators, do and shall from time to time and at all times hereafter well and sufficiently save harmless and keep indemnified the said sheriff, his under-sheriff, deputy, and officers, and each and every of them, of, from, and against all losses, costs, charges, damages and expenses, which he or they shall or may sustain, suffer, bear, pay, expend or be put unto, for, or by reason or means of seizing or selling the said goods and chattels so seized and taken in execution as aforesaid, or paying unto the said E. F. the money arising from the sale thereof, in satisfaction of the said sum of £—— so directed to be levied by the said writ of fieri facias; and also of, from, and against all action and actions, suit and suits, or any proceeding or proceedings at law or equity, which now are, or shall or may at any time or times hereafter be brought, commenced or prosecuted, rightfully or wrongfully, against the said A. B., his under-sheriff, deputy, or officers, or any or either of them, for or on account or by reason or by means of the seizing or selling the said goods and chattels under and by virtue of the said writ of fieri facias, or paying unto the said E. F. the money arising from the sale thereof, as aforesaid, or for or by reason or means of any other act, matter, cause, or thing whatsoever relating thereto, or to the execution of the said writ of fieri facias, then the above-written obligation to be void, otherwise to stand and remain in full force, vigour, and effect.

Sealed, &c.

Condition of a Bond of Indemnity for abandoning Goods, and returning Nulla Bona.

Whereas the above-named sheriff, by virtue of her majesty's writ of fieri facias to him directed, against the goods and chattels of C. D., issued out of her majesty's Court of Queen's Bench at Westminster, and there returnable on ——, at the suit of one E. F., hath seized and taken divers goods and chattels as the proper goods and chattels of the said C. D. in execution: And whereas the above-bounden I. K. hath given notice to the said sheriff, and claimed the said goods and chattels, and hath requested the said sheriff to quit possession of, and abandon and deliver to the said I. K., the said goods and chattels so seized as aforesaid, and to make his return to the court when called on so to do, that the said C. D. had not any goods in his bailiwick, [*or if there were other goods, this should be stated according to the fact,*] which the said sheriff had consented to do, on the said I. K. indemnifying him the said sheriff for so doing: Now the condition of the above-written obligation is such, that if the above-bounden I. K., his heirs, executors, and administrators, do and shall from time to time, and at all times hereafter, well and sufficiently save harmless and keep indemnified the same sheriff, his under-sheriff, deputy, or officers, and each and every of them, of, from, and against all losses, costs, charges, damages, and expenses, which he or they shall or may sustain, suffer, bear, pay, expend, or be put unto, for or by reason or means of quitting possession of, abandoning, and delivering to the said I. K., the said goods and chattels so seized as aforesaid, and returning that the said C. D. had no goods in his bailiwick: And also of, from, and against all action and actions, suit and suits, proceeding or proceedings, either in law or equity, which now are, or shall or may at any time or times hereafter be brought, commenced, or prosecuted, rightfully or wrongfully, by the said E. F., or by any person or persons whomsoever, against the said sheriff, his under-sheriff, deputy and officers, or any or either of them, for or on account, or by reason or by means of the quitting possession of, abandoning, and delivering to the said I. K. the said goods and chattels, and returning that the said C. D. had not any goods in his bailiwick, or for or by reason or means of any other act, matters, cause, or thing whatsoever, relating thereto, or to the execution or return of the said writ of fieri facias, then the said obligation to be void, otherwise to stand and remain in full force, vigour and effect.

Sealed, &c.

Sect. 7.

RETURNS TO WRIT OF FI. FA.

Nulla Bona.

The within-named C. D. hath not any goods or chattels in my bailiwick, whereof I can cause to be made the debt, damages and interest [*or* "damages and interest,"] as the within writ commands me.

The answer of A. B., esquire, sheriff.

Fieri Feci.

By virtue of this writ to me directed, I have caused to be made of the goods and chattels of the within-named C. D., the debt, damages and interest [*or* "damages and interest"] within written, which I have ready at the time and place within mentioned, to be rendered to the within-named E. F. as within I am commanded.

A. B., esquire, sheriff.

CHAP. X.
SECT. VII.

Fieri Feci as to part, and Nulla Bona as to the remainder.

By virtue of this writ to me directed, I have caused to be made of the goods and chattels of the within-named C. D., to the value of £——, [*If in hands for want of buyers, insert the words in italics in next precedent, instead of the words in italics in this,*] *which said monies I have ready at the time and place within contained, to render to the within-named* G. H. *in part satisfaction of his debt, damages, and interest within specified.* And I further certify and return that the said C. D. hath no more goods or chattels in my bailiwick, whereof I may cause to be made the residue of the said debt, damages, and interest, or any part thereof, as the within writ commands me.

A. B., esquire, sheriff.

Fieri Feci, and that the Goods remain in the Sheriff's hands for want of buyers.

By virtue of this writ to me directed, I have caused to be made of the goods and chattels of the within-named C. D. to the value of the damages and interest within written, *which said goods and chattels remain with me unsold for want of buyers; therefore I cannot have that money, or any part thereof, at the time and place within mentioned, as the said writ commands me.*

A. B., esquire, sheriff.

Return that Goods to the amount of part of the Debt and Damages have been sold; the rest unsold.

By virtue of this writ to me directed, I have caused to be made of the goods and chattels of the within-named C. D., to the value of £——, and have thereof sold to the value of £——, which money I have ready at the time and place within contained, to be rendered to the within-named E. F., as the within writ commands me, but the residue of the said goods and chattels remain in *my hands for want of buyers.*

The answer of A. B., esquire, sheriff.

Fieri Feci as to part, and that the Sheriff has paid part of the Sum levied to the Landlord for Rent.

By virtue of this writ to me directed, I have caused to be made of the goods and chattels of the within named C. D., to the value of £——, *part of which said sum of £—— I have paid to* H. Y., *the landlord of the premises on which the said goods and chattels were taken, for half a year's rent due to him for the said premises, at —— last,* and I have retained in my hands the sum of £—— for poundage and expenses; and £——, the residue of the said sum of £——, I have ready at the time and place within mentioned, to render to the said E. F. in part satisfaction of his damages and interest. And the said C. D. hath not any more goods and chattels in my bailiwick, whereof I can cause to be made the residue of the said damages and interest, as within I am commanded.

The answer of A. B., esquire, sheriff.

Fieri Feci as to part, and payment of Queen's Taxes.

[*The same as the last precedent, excepting, instead of the words in italics:*] £ —, part of which said sum of £——, I have paid for queen's taxes, due and owing to her majesty for and in respect of the said premises at the time of taking the said goods and chattels.

Mandavi Ballivo.

By virtue of this writ to me directed, I made my mandate to ——, bailiff of the liberty of L., in my county, to whom belongeth the execution and return of all writs and processes within the said liberty, and without whom no execution of this writ could be made by me within the same; which said bailiff hath returned to me, that by virtue of my mandate, to him thereupon directed as aforesaid, he hath caused to be made of the goods and chattels of the within-named C. D. the damages within mentioned, and that he hath the money ready before our said lady the queen, at the time and place within mentioned, as by the said mandate he was commanded.

A. B. esquire, sheriff.

Nulla Bona to a Fi. Fa. de bonis testatoris.

The within-named C. D. has no goods or chattels which were of the within-named X. Y. at the time of his death in the hands of the said C. D. to be administered, in my bailiwick, whereof I can cause to be levied the damages within mentioned, or any part thereof.

A. B. esquire, sheriff.

The same, with a Devastavit.

[*The same as the last precedent, to the end, then proceed:*] but divers goods and chattels which were of the said X. Y., at the time of his death, to the value of the damages within mentioned, after the death of the said X. Y. came to the hands of the said C. D. to be administered, which said goods and chattels the said C. D. hath, before the coming of this writ to me, eloigned, wasted, and converted to his own use.

The answer of A. B. esquire, sheriff.

Nulla Bona to a Fi. Fa. de bonis testatoris, si non, de bonis propriis.

[*The same as the last precedent but one to the end, then proceed:*] nor hath he the said C. D. any of his own proper goods and chattels in my bailiwick, whereof I can cause to be made the within-mentioned sum of £——, &c. (*as the case may be*) or any part thereof, as the said writ commands me.

The answer of A. B. esquire, sheriff.

Sheriff's Return to Scire Fieri Inquiry.

The within-named C. D. has no goods or chattels which were of the within-named X. Y., deceased, at the time of his death, in the hands of the said C. D. to be administered, in my bailiwick, whereof I can cause

CHAP. X. SECT. VII.

to be made the damages within-written, or any part thereof; but the said C. D., after the death of the said X. Y., had divers goods and chattels, which were of the said X. Y. at the time of his death, in the hands of him the said C. D. to be administered, to the value of the damages and interest within-written; which said goods and chattels the said C. D. afterwards, and before the coming of this writ to me, sold, wasted, eloigned, and converted to his own use, as appears by a certain inquisition taken before me in this behalf, on the oath of honest and lawful men of my said bailiwick, and to this writ annexed: and I further certify and return, that the said C. D. hath nothing in my bailiwick, where or by which I can make known to him, as by the said writ I am commanded; nor is he found in the same. The residue of the execution of this writ appears in a certain inquisition hereunto annexed.

The answer of A. B. esquire, sheriff.

An inquisition indented, taken at —— on the day of —— in the —— year of the reign of our sovereign lady Victoria, queen of the united kingdom of Great Britain and Ireland, &c., before A. B. esquire, sheriff of the county aforesaid, by virtue of a writ of our said lady the queen, directed to the said sheriff, and to this inquisition annexed, to inquire of and upon certain matters in the said writ contained and specified, by the oath of G. H., &c., honest and lawful men of the bailiwick of the said sheriff, who, upon their oath aforesaid, say, that C. D., in the said writ named, after the death of the said X. Y., in the said writ also named, had divers goods and chattels, which were of the said C. D. at the time of his death, in the hands of him the said C. D. to be administered, to the value of the damages and interest, (*or* " debt, damages and interest,") in the said writ specified, which said goods and chattels the said C. D. hath sold, wasted, eloigned, and converted to his own use. In witness whereof, as well the said sheriff as the jurors aforesaid have caused their seals to be affixed to this inquisition, the day and year above mentioned.

Return that the Defendant is a beneficed Clerk.

The within-named C. D. has no goods or chattels, nor any lay fee, in my bailiwick, whereof I can cause to be made the damages within-mentioned, or any part thereof, as within I am commanded; but I do hereby certify and return, that the said C. D. is a beneficed clerk, to wit, rector of the rectory (*or* " vicar of the vicarage") and parish church of ——, in my county, which said rectory (*or* " vicarage") and parish church are within the diocese of the Right Reverend Father in God, John, by divine permission, bishop of ——. The answer of A. B., esquire, sheriff.

CHAP. XI.

Warrant to take the Defendant's Goods on Elegit.

N. (*to wit*). A. B., esquire, sheriff of the said county of N., to E. F., &c., my bailiffs, greeting: By virtue of her majesty's writ of *elegit* to me directed, I command you and each of you, that without fail you jointly or severally seize and take all the goods and chattels of C. D. (except his oxen and beasts of the plough) in my bailiwick; so that I may, by reasonable price, cause the same to be delivered to I. K., to hold to the said I. K. as his proper goods and chattels, and forthwith certify the same to me. Given under my hand and seal of office.

(*Seal of office.*) By the sheriff.

Charge to the Jury.

Your charge is to inquire what goods and chattels (except oxen and beasts of the plough) C. D. was possessed of on the —— day of ——, A.D. 18— (*k*), or at any time afterwards in my bailiwick, and the value thereof; your charge also is to inquire what lands, tenements, rectories, tithes, rents and hereditaments, including lands and hereditaments of copyhold or customary tenure, C. D. or any one in trust for him was seised or possessed of on the —— day of ——, A. D —— (*l*), or at any time afterwards, or over which the said C. D. on the —— day of ——, A. D. ——, or at any time afterwards, had any disposing power which he might, without the assent of any other person, exercise for his own benefit, and also to inquire and say what is the yearly value thereof, that the same may at a reasonable price and extent be made to be delivered to A. B. to hold as his own proper goods and chattels, and also to hold the said lands, tenements, rectories, tithes, rents and hereditaments respectively, according to the nature and tenure thereof, to him and his assigns until the said sum of £——, together with interest as aforesaid, shall have been levied.

Juryman's Oath and Affirmation.

You shall well and truly try what goods and chattels (except his oxen and beasts of the plough) C. D. was possessed of on the —— day of —— A. D. 18— (*m*), or at any time afterwards in my bailiwick, and the value thereof. You shall also well and truly try what lands, tenements, rectories, tithes, rents and hereditaments, including lands and hereditaments of copyhold or customary tenure, C. D., or any one in trust for him, was seised or possessed of on the —— day of ——, A. D. 18— (*n*), or at any time afterwards, or over which the said C. D. on the —— day of, A. D. 18—, or at any time afterwards, had any disposing power which he might, without the assent of any other person, exercise for his own benefit in my bailiwick, and the yearly value thereof, and a true verdict give according to the evidence. So help you God.

Return to Elegit.

The return of this writ appears in the inquisition hereunto annexed.

A. B. esquire, sheriff.

Inquisition.

N. (*to wit.*) An inquisition indented, taken at A., in the county of N., the —— day of —— in the —— year of the reign of our sovereign lady

(*k*) The day when the writ was delivered to the sheriff or his deputy for execution.

(*l*) The day of entry of judgment or date of order, decree, &c.

(*m*) The day when the writ was delivered for execution.

(*n*) The day of the entry of the judgment.

CHAP. XI. Queen Victoria, before me, A. B., esquire, sheriff of the said county, by virtue of her said majesty's writ to me directed in this behalf, and to this inquisition annexed, by the oath of (*here name the jurors who were upon the inquest*) twelve honest and lawful men of the county aforesaid, who being sworn and charged, upon their oath say, that C. D., named in the writ hereunto annexed, on the day of the taking of this inquisition, was possessed in his own right of the goods and chattels following, that is to say (*here describe the goods*), of the price of £——, as of his own proper goods and chattels; which said goods and chattels I, the said sheriff, have caused to be delivered to the said I. K., to hold the said goods and chattels as his own proper goods and chattels, in part satisfaction of his debt, damages and interest, (*or* " damages and interest,") in the said writ mentioned, as by the said writ I am commanded; (or *if there be no goods or chattels, say,* " had no goods or chattels in my bailiwick, to the knowledge of the said jurors;") and the jurors aforesaid, upon their oath aforesaid, do further say that the said C. D., on the —— day of —— in the —— year of the reign, &c., (on which day the judgment, in the said writ mentioned, was obtained,) was seised in his demesne as of fee of and in (*here describe the lands in such a manner as they would be described in a conveyance, stating the place and county in which they lie, the estate the defendant had in them, and whether seised in severalty, or as joint tenant, or tenant in common. See the next form, and post, appendix, chap.* 15, *s.* 2; *adding after each messuage or parcel of land the value of it, thus:* " the same being of the clear yearly value of £——, in all issues beyond reprises,") which said lands and tenements I, the said sheriff, on the day of the taking of this inquisition, have caused to be delivered to the said I. K., by a reasonable price and extent, to hold as his freehold to him and his assigns, according to the force of the statute in such case made and provided, until the debt, damages and interest (*or* " damages and interest") in the said writ mentioned, shall be thereof levied; as by the said writ I am commanded. And the jurors aforesaid, upon their oath aforesaid, do further say that the said C. D. (*o*), *on the day of the taking of this inquisition aforesaid, had no other or more goods and chattels in my bailiwick;* nor had he, or any person or persons in trust for him, on the —— day of (the day on which the judgment aforesaid was obtained), or at any time afterwards, any other or more lands and tenements in my bailiwick, to the knowledge of the said jurors. In witness whereof, as well I, the said sheriff, as the jurors aforesaid, have severally set our respective seals to this inquisition, on the day and year and at the place aforesaid.

The like, where Lands holden in joint Tenancy are extended.

[*Same as the last precedent, to the words*] who being sworn and charged, upon their oath say, that C. D., named in the said writ hereunto annexed, on the day of the taking of this inquisition, had no goods or chattels in my bailiwick, to the knowledge of the said jurors; and the jurors aforesaid, upon their oath aforesaid, do further say, that the said C. D., on the —— day of —— in the —— year of the reign, &c., (on which day the said judgment, in the said writ mentioned, was obtained)

(*o*) If there are no goods found, omit the words in italics; this has been stated in a former part of this form.

was seised in his demesne as of fee of and in one undivided moiety (the whole in two equal moieties to be divided) of and in one messuage or tenement, with the appurtenances, situate, lying and being in the parish of ——, in the county aforesaid, now in the tenure and occupation of X. Y., abutting towards the east on, &c., towards the north on, &c., towards the west on, &c., and towards the south on, &c; and being of the clear yearly value of twenty pounds, in all issues beyond reprises; and also of and in one undivided moiety (the whole into equal moieties to be divided) of and in one other messuage, &c.; which said undivided moieties of the said several messuages with the appurtenances, so in the tenure and occupation of the said X. Y. as aforesaid, I, the said sheriff, on the day of the taking of this inquisition, have caused to be delivered to to the said I. K., by a reasonable price and extent, to hold as his freehold, [*concluding as in the last form*].

CHAP. XII.

Warrant on a Hab. Fac. Poss.

N. (*to wit.*) A. B., esquire, sheriff of the county aforesaid, to J. S., my bailiff, greeting: By virtue of her majesty's writ of *habere facias possessionem* to me directed and delivered, I command you that you deliver to John Doe possession of his term yet to come and unexpired of and in the tenements in the said writ specified, with the appurtenances, and forthwith certify the same to me. Given under the seal of my office this —— day of ——, 18—.

(*Seal of office.*) By the sheriff.

Return to a writ of Hab. Fac. Poss.

By virtue of this writ to me directed, on the —— day of ——, in the year within mentioned, I delivered to the within named John Doe possession of the within mentioned term of and in the tenements with the appurtenances within mentioned, as I am within commanded.

A. B., esquire, sheriff.

Return to a Writ of Hab. Fac. Poss. where the Recovery was of a Moiety of the Premises.

By virtue of this writ to me directed, on the —— day of ——, in the year within mentioned, I delivered to the within named A. B. possession of the within term of and in one moiety or half part of the tenements, with the appurtenances, within mentioned, as I am within commanded.

A. B., esquire, sheriff.

The like, with a Return to a Fi. Fa. for Costs.

By virtue of this writ to me directed, on the —— day of ——, in the year within mentioned, I delivered full possession to the within named John Doe of the within mentioned term of and in the tenements, with the appurtenances, within mentioned, as within I am commanded; and I further certify and return, *that the said C. D. hath not any goods or chattels whereof I can cause to be made the damages within mentioned, or any part thereof* (n).

The answer of A. B., esquire, sheriff.

Return that no Person came to point out the Lands.

I certify our said lady the queen (*or* " the justices within mentioned") that this writ was delivered to me on the —— day of ——, since which time I have always been ready and willing to execute the same, as within I am commanded; but no person on behalf, or on the part of the said John Doe, ever came to me to show me the tenements within mentioned, or any part thereof, or to receive possession of the same, or any part thereof, from me. The answer of A. B., esquire, sheriff.

CHAP. XIII.

Deputation to take an Inquisition (o).

N. (*to wit.*) A. B., esquire, sheriff of the county aforesaid, to I. S., gentleman, greeting: By virtue of a writ of inquiry issued out of her majesty's court of Queen's Bench, at Westminster, to me directed, I do hereby authorize and empower you to summon a jury, and take an inquisition in my name, in a cause wherein J. H. is plaintiff, and E. A., widow, is the defendant; and render me an account of what you shall do therein, so that I may certify the same to our sovereign lady the queen, at Westminster, on the —— day of —— next coming; hereof fail not. Given under the seal of my office the —— day of ——, 18—.

(*Seal of office.*) By the sheriff.

Oath to be administered to the Jury.

You shall well and truly try all such matters and things *as shall be given you in charge* touching this writ of inquiry, and a true verdict give, according to the evidence. So help you God.

(*From the nature of the oath, it is necessary that the sheriff should give a short charge to the jury, which need be little more than reading the writ.*)

Oath to be administered to the Witnesses.

The evidence you shall give to this court and jury, touching the matters in question in the cause wherein A. B. is plaintiff and C. D. defendant, shall be the truth, the whole truth, and nothing but the truth.

So help you God.

(n) Or, instead of the words in italics, return *fieri feci*, as *ante*, p. 479; or if a *ca. sa.* was issued for costs, insert a return *cepi corpus*, or *non est inventus*, as *ante*, instead of the words in italics.

(o) If a deputy is appointed to execute a writ of inquiry, the appointment must be under seal of office; Barnes, 232; a verbal appointment is bad, *ante*, p. 325.

Sheriff's Return to a Writ of Inquiry.

The execution of this writ appears in the inquisition hereunto annexed.
The answer of A. B., esquire, sheriff.

Inquisition on a Writ of Inquiry.

N. (*to wit.*) An inquisition indented, taken at ——, in the county aforesaid, the —— day of ——, between the hours of —— and —— in the forenoon of the same day, in the —— year of the reign of our sovereign lady Queen Victoria, before me, A. B., esquire, sheriff of the said county, by virtue of her majesty's writ to me directed, and to this inquisition annexed, upon the oaths of (*here name the twelve jurors*) good and lawful men of the said county of N., who being chosen, tried and sworn, upon their oaths say, that E. F., in the said writ named, hath sustained damages by reason of not performing the *promises and undertakings* (*or as the case may be*) of C. D., in the said writ also named, to the value of £——, and also forty shillings for his costs and charges by him in his suit in this behalf occasioned. In witness whereof, as well the said sheriff as the jurors aforesaid to this inquisition have severally put their seals the day and year aforesaid.

(*Seal of office.*) A. B., esquire, sheriff (*p*).
E. F. (*Seal.*)
G. H. (*Seal.*)

(*And so the remainder of the twelve jurors.*)

Warrant on a Writ of ad quod damnum.

N. (*to wit.*) A. B., esquire, sheriff of the said county, to E. F. and C. D., my bailiffs, greeting: By virtue of her majesty's writ of *ad quod damnum* to me directed and delivered, I command you that you or the one of you personally summon (*name twenty-four persons living in the neighbourhood*) to be and appear at ——, in the said county, on ——, the —— day of ——, between the hours of —— and —— in the —— of the same day, then and there to inquire upon their oaths whether it will be to the prejudice of her majesty or of any other (*take a full abstract of the writ*). Given under the seal of my office this —— day of ——, &c.

(*Seal of office.*) By the sheriff.

Return to be indorsed on a Writ ad quod damnum.

The execution of this writ appears in a certain inquisition hereunto annexed.
A. B., esquire, sheriff.

Inquisition.

N. (*to wit.*) An inquisition taken at the house of ——, situate in ——, in the county of N. aforesaid, the —— day of ——, in the —— year of the reign of our sovereign lady Queen Victoria, and in the year

(*p*) One part on paper, signed and sealed by the sheriff and jurors, the sheriff keeps; a duplicate of the inquisition must be written on parchment, and signed by the sheriff only, opposite to the seal of office, and twelve seals must also be affixed, but the inquisition need not be signed by the jury.—N.B. Indent both parts of the engrossment.

CHAP. XIII. of our lord ——, before me, A. B., esquire, sheriff of the said county, by virtue of a writ of our sovereign lady the queen to me directed, and to this inquisition annexed, upon the oaths of (*name the jury*) good and lawful men of my county, who being sworn and charged upon their oath aforesaid to inquire into the matters in the said writ specified, say, that it will not be to the damage or prejudice of our lady the queen or any other if our lady the queen should grant to —— licence to inclose such part of the common highway, leading from the village of ——, which lies (*describe particularly the part and the exact length*). And the jurors aforesaid, upon their oath aforesaid, do also say, that it will not be to the damage or prejudice of our said lady the queen or any other if our said lady the queen should grant to the said —— licence to inclose such part of another common highway, leading from the town of —— to ——, &c. To hold the said two several parts of the said two common highways so to be inclosed to the said —— and his heirs for ever. And the jurors aforesaid, upon their oath aforesaid, further say, that the said ——, in lieu of the first above-mentioned parts of the common highway to be inclosed, hath in his own lands and grounds set out to be held and used a highway leading from (*describe it very particularly, with the exact length and breadth*); and which is as convenient for the liege subjects of our said lady the queen passing and repassing along the same. And the jurors aforesaid, upon their oath aforesaid, further say, that the said ——, in lieu of the last-mentioned part of the said highway to be inclosed, hath in his own lands and grounds set out to be held and used a highway, beginning in certain other lands and grounds of the said ——, &c., and which is as convenient, &c. In witness whereof, as well I the said sheriff, as the jurors aforesaid, have hereunto interchangeably set our hands and seals the day, year, and place above written.

A. B., esquire, sheriff.

(*Seal of office.*) (*Twelve seals.*)

CHAP. XIV.

Sheriff's Precept to summon Jury on a Writ of Trial.

N. (*to wit.*) I, A. B., esquire, sheriff of the said county, to G. and B., my bailiffs, greeting: These are to require you, or one of you, that you cause to come twelve good and lawful men of the said county, and to be and appear at ——, on ——, by —— o'clock in the forenoon, to try the issues joined between C. D., plaintiff, and E. F. defendant, in a plea of debt (*or according to the case*), and herein fail not at your peril. Given under the seal of my office this —— day of ——, 18—.

(*Seal of office.*) A. B. sheriff.

Oath to Jurymen.

You shall well and truly try the issues joined between the parties, and a true verdict give according to the evidence. So help you God.

Oath to Witnesses.

The evidence you shall give to the court and jury, touching the matters in question, shall be the truth, the whole truth, and nothing but the truth. So help you God.

Certificate to stay Judgment.

I hereby certify, that judgment ought not to be signed herein until the —— day of ——, in order that the within named defendant (*or* " plaintiff") may have an opportunity to apply to the court for a new trial herein.

A. B. under-sheriff.

Postea (*a*).

Afterwards, on the —— day of ——, in the year of our Lord 18—, before me, A. B. esquire, sheriff of the county of N., came as well the within named plaintiff as the within named defendant, by their respective attorneys within named, and the jurors of the jury, by me duly summoned as within commanded, also came, and being duly sworn to try the said issue within mentioned, on their oath said that, &c.

The answer of A. B. sheriff.

The like, in case of Nonsuit (*a*).

[*As above, to the words* " the said issue within mentioned," *and proceed:*] And were ready to give their verdict in that behalf, but the said C. D., being solemnly called, came not, nor did he further prosecute his said suit against the said E. F.

CHAP. XV.—Sect. 1.

Writ of Quare Impedit.

Victoria, by the grace of God of the united kingdom of Great Britain and Ireland queen, defender of the faith, &c., to the sheriff of N. greeting: Command John, bishop of Chester, Mary D. widow, F. T. esq., and M. H. clerk, that justly and without delay they permit L. D., to present a fit person to the church of C., which is void, and in the gift of the said L., as he saith, and whereof he complaineth that the aforesaid bishop, Mary, F. and M., unjustly hinder him, and unless they shall so do, and if the said L. shall give you security to prosecute his suit, then summon by good summoners the said bishop, Mary, F. and M., that they be before our justices at Westminster, on the morrow of the Holy Trinity, to show why they will not do it, and have you there the summoners and this writ. Witness ourself at Westminster, the —— day of ——, in the —— year of our reign.

Quare impedit for L. D.

Warrant upon a Writ of Quare Impedit.

N. (*to wit.*) A. B., esquire, sheriff of the county aforesaid, to H. B., the younger, and G. C., my bailiffs, greeting: By virtue of her majesty's writ of *quare impedit*, under the great seal of Great Britain, to me

(*a*) See Reg. Gen. H. T. 4 Will. 4.

CHAP. XV. SECT. I.

directed and delivered, I command you that you command John, bishop of Chester, Mary D. widow, F. T. esquire, and M. H., clerk, that justly and without delay they permit L. D., clerk, to present a fit person to the church of ——, which is void, and in the gift of the said L., as he saith; and whereof he complaineth that the aforesaid bishop, Mary, F., and M., unjustly hinder him: and unless they shall so do, then I command you that you summon, by good summoners, the said bishop, Mary, F., and M., that they be before her Majesty's justices at Westminster, on the morrow of the Holy Trinity, to show why they will not do it. Given under the seal of my office this —— day of ——, 18—.

(*Seal of office.*) By the sheriff.

[*The two bailiffs named in the above warrant* (*or somebody for them*), *must make out as many summonses as there are persons to be summoned. The form is as follows; and the bailiffs must both subscribe their names to each summons; and they must keep by them an examined copy of the summonses, so as to be able to swear to it, if necessary.*]

Summons from the Bailiffs, in pursuance of a Warrant to them directed, issued on a Quare Impedit.

By virtue of her majesty's writ of *quare impedit*, under the great seal of Great Britain, to the sheriff of the county of N. directed, and by virtue of the said sheriff's warrant thereupon, to us directed, we do hereby require and command you, John, bishop of Chester, Mary D., F. T., esq., and M. H., clerk, that ye justly and without delay permit L. D., clerk, to present a fit person to the church of ——, which is void, and in the gift of the said L., as he saith, and whereof he complaineth that ye, the said bishop, Mary, F., and M., unjustly hinder him: and unless ye shall so do, then we do hereby summon you, that ye be before her majesty's justices at Westminster, on the morrow of the Holy Trinity, to show cause why ye will not do it. Given under our hand this —— day of ——, 18—.

To the Right Rev. Father in God, John, Lord Bishop of Chester, Mary D., F. T., esq., and M. H., clerk, and each and every of them. } H. B. jun. G. C. } bailiffs.

Return of Summons on Quare Impedit.

Pledges to prosecute { John Doe, Richard Roe.

Summoners { H. B., the younger, and G. C.

By virtue of this writ to me directed, I have summoned the within named bishop, Mary, F., and M., that justly, and without delay, they permit the within named L. to present a fit person to the church within mentioned: and I have also summoned, by the good summoners above named, the said bishop, Mary, F., and M., that they be before her majesty's justices at Westminster, on the morrow of the Holy Trinity, to show why they will not do it, as by this writ I am commanded.

A. B., esquire, sheriff.

Pone issued after the return of the Quare Impedit.

Victoria, by the grace of God of the united kingdom of Great Britain and Ireland queen, defender of the faith, &c., to the sheriff of N., greeting: We command you that you put, by sureties and safe pledges, Mary D., widow, F. T., esquire, and M. H., clerk, that they be before our justices at Westminster, on the morrow of All Souls, to answer us of a plea, that they permit L. D. to present a fit person to the church of ——, which is void, and in the gift of the said L., and whereof the said Mary, F., and M., together with John, bishop of Chester, unjustly hinder the said L.; and to show wherefore they were not, together with the said bishop, in our court before our justices at Westminster, at a certain day now past, as they have been summoned: and have you there the names of the pledges, and this writ. Witness, Sir Thomas Wilde, knight, at Westminster, the —— day of ——, in the —— year of our reign.

Return indorsed on the Pone.

The answer of A. B., sheriff of the county of N.

Summoners of the within-named Mary D., F. T., and M. H. are { H. B., the elder, H. B., the younger.

Pledges are { John Doe, Richard Roe.

A. B., esquire, sheriff.

Warrant from the Sheriff upon the Pone.

N. (*to wit.*) A. B., esquire, sheriff of the county aforesaid, to H. B., the elder, and H. B., the younger, my bailiffs, greeting: By virtue of her majesty's writ to me directed and delivered, I command you that you put, by sureties and safe pledges, Mary D., widow, F. T., esquire, and M. H., clerk, that they be before her majesty's justices at Westminster, on the morrow of All Souls, to answer her majesty in a plea, that they permit L. D., clerk, to present a fit person to the church of ——, which is void, and in the gift of the said L.; and whereof the said Mary, F., and M., together with John, bishop of Chester, unjustly hinder the said L.; and to show wherefore they were not, together with the said bishop, in her majesty's court, before her majesty's justices at Westminster, at a certain day now past, as they have been summoned, so that I may have there the names of the pledges, and the said writ: and have you this, and so forth. Given under the seal of my office, this —— day of ——, in the year of our Lord 18—.

(*Seal of office.*) By the sheriff.

Distringas issued after the Return of the Pone.

Victoria, by the grace of God of the united kingdom of Great Britain and Ireland queen, defender of the faith, &c., to the sheriff of N., greeting: We command you that you distrain Mary D., widow, of all her lands and chattels in your bailiwick, so that neither she, or any for her, lay hands upon them, until you have from us another precept, so that you answer us of the issues thereof; and that you have her body before our justices at Westminster, in eight days of St. Hilary, to answer us of a plea, that she, together with John, bishop of Chester, F. T., esquire, and M. H., clerk, permit L. D. to present a fit person to the church of ——, which is void, and in the gift of the said L., as he saith, and to hear judgment of her many defaults: and have you there this writ. Witness Sir Thomas Wilde, knight, at Westminster, the —— day of ——, in the —— year of our reign.

Return indorsed on the Distringas.

I humbly certify to the justices within written, that, by virtue of the writ within contained, I have distrained the within-named Mary D., by her lands and chattels in my bailiwick; and that I have issues on them to the value of 40*s*.; and I further certify that the said Mary D. is not found in my bailiwick.

A. B., esquire, sheriff.

If no Distress is made, the following should be the Sheriff's Return.

I humbly certify to the justices within written, that the within-named Mary D. hath no lands or chattels in my bailiwick, whereby I could cause her to be distrained, as I am within commanded; neither is she found within the same.

The answer of A. B., esquire, sheriff.

CHAP. XVI.—Sect. 1.

Warrant to Levy on the Great Roll.

N. (*to wit.*) A. B. esquire, sheriff of the county aforesaid, to I. S., my bailiff, greeting: By virtue of the queen's writ to me directed, I command you that you omit not by reason of any liberty in my bailiwick, but that you enter the same, and levy of the goods and chattels, lands and tenements of the several persons named in the schedule hereunder written, the several sums of money on them respectively charged, so that I may have that money before the barons of the queen's Exchequer at Westminster, from time to time as you shall levy the same; and if the said goods and chattels, lands and tenements, are not sufficient, then take the said several persons by their bodies, and keep them safe until they shall satisfy her majesty the said several debts; and in what manner you shall execute this warrant, make appear to me, so that I may certify the same to the said barons in one month from the day of Easter next ensuing. Hereof fail not. Given under the seal of my office, the —— day of ——, in the year of our Lord 18—.

(*Seal of office.*) By the sheriff.

Of A. B. of, &c., because, &c.
Of C. D. of, &c., because, &c.

Warrant on the Summons of the Pipe.

N. (*to wit.*) A. B., esquire, sheriff of the county aforesaid, to I. S., my bailiff, greeting: By virtue of the queen's writ to me directed, I command you that you omit not by reason of any liberty within my bailiwick, but that of the goods and chattels of the several persons in the schedule hereunder written named, you cause to be made the several sums of money, on them respectively charged, due to her majesty for the rents (*and duties*) therein particularly mentioned, so that I may have those monies before the barons of her majesty's exchequer at Westminster, on —— next to come, there to be paid to her majesty. Hereof fail not. Given under the seal of my office, this —— day of ——, in the year of our Lord 18—.

(*Seal of office.*) By the sheriff.

Of A. B. for the manor of, &c.
Of C. D. for one messuage, &c.

Warrant on the Summons of the Green Wax.

N. (*to wit.*) A. B., esq., sheriff of the county aforesaid, to I. S., my bailiff for this purpose only, greeting: By virtue of her majesty's writ to me directed, I command you that you omit not by reason of any liberty in my bailiwick, but that of the goods and chattels of the several persons hereunder named you cause to be made the several sums of money on them respectively charged, and that you summon them so that they be and appear before the barons of the queen's Exchequer at Westminster, in —— next to come. Hereof fail not. Given under the seal of my office, this —— day of ——, 18—.

(*Seal of office.*) By the same sheriff.

Of A. B., because, &c.
Of C. D., because, &c.

Return to the Great Roll

I humbly certify to the barons within named, that, by virtue of this writ to me directed, I have caused to be levied of the goods and chattels of the several persons following the several sums hereinafter mentioned, that is to say, of A. B., named in the twenty-seventh roll to this writ annexed, the sum of 10*l.*; of C. D., named on the back of the said twenty-seventh roll, the sum of 10*l.*; of E. F., named on the twenty-eighth roll to this writ also annexed, the sum of 5*l.*; and of G. H., named in the twenty-ninth roll to this writ also annexed, the sum of 5*l.*: Which said sums I have ready at the day and place within written, to pay to her majesty, as within I am commanded. And I further certify, that the other persons in the several schedules annexed named have not, nor have nor hath any or either of them, any goods or chattels, lands or tenements, in my bailiwick, whereby I can levy the several sums of money on them respectively charged, as in and by the said writ I am directed and commanded. The said several persons are not found in my bailiwick, nor are there any executors of the last will and testament of them or either of them, neither administrators of the goods, or heirs or possessors of lands of them, or either of them, to whom I can give notice as within I am commanded. The remainder of the execution of this writ appears in and by the inquisition hereunto annexed. A. B., esquire, sheriff.

Inquisition to be annexed.

N. (*to wit.*) An inquisition indented, taken at —— in the county aforesaid, on ——, the —— day of ——, in the —— year of the reign

CHAP. XVI. SECT. I.

of our sovereign lady Queen Victoria, and in the year of our Lord ——, before me, A. B., esq., sheriff of the said county, by virtue of a writ of our lady the queen to me directed, and to this inquisition annexed, by the oaths of T. P., L. L., &c., twelve good and lawful men of my bailiwick, who, being sworn and charged, upon their oaths say, that to the knowledge of the said jurors, the several persons in the several rolls or schedules to this writ annexed named, or any of them, had not, on the several days and times they became indebted to the crown, or at any time since, any goods or chattels, lands or tenements, which can be found to be taken, seized, or extended into the hands of her majesty. And the jurors aforesaid further say, that they know not whether the said several persons be dead, or when or where they or any of them died; nor did the said several persons deceased, or any of them, to the knowledge of the said jurors, die seised of any lands or tenements in the bailiwick of me the said sheriff, so that they cannot appraise, nor can I the said sheriff take or seize any such goods or chattels, lands or tenements as aforesaid, as by the said writ is commanded. In witness whereof as well I the said sheriff, as the said jurors, have to this inquisition set our hands and seals the day and year first above written.

(*Seal of office.*) A. B., esquire, sheriff.
(*Twelve seals.*)

Return of Process for Tenths or First Fruits.

To the barons within written I humbly certify, that I have levied and received of the several persons in the schedule annexed mentioned the several sums of money on them respectively charged, which I have ready to be paid to her majesty's use, as within I am commanded.

A. B., esquire, sheriff.

Part levied and others not found.

I humbly certify to the barons within written, that, by virtue of this writ to me directed, I have received of A. B. and C. D. the several sums of money on them respectively charged in the schedules at the foot of this writ mentioned, which said sums I have ready at the day and place within written, to pay to her majesty, as by the said writ I am commanded. And I further certify, that the within named E. F. and G. H. are not found in my bailiwick (or are departed this life).

A. B., esquire, sheriff.

Nulla Bona on the same.

I humbly certify to the barons within mentioned, that the several persons at the foot of this writ named have not any goods or chattels, lands or tenements, in my bailiwick, whereof I can levy the sums of money upon them respectively charged, nor are they or either of them found in my bailiwick. A. B., esquire, sheriff.

To the Mortuus Process.

I humbly certify that there are no heirs, executors or administrators of the several persons in the schedule to this writ annexed named, nor any of them, in my bailiwick, to whom I can give notice, as within I am commanded. The residue of the execution of this writ appears in the inquisition hereunto annexed.

Inquisition to be annexed.

N. (*to wit*). An inquisition indented, taken at ——, in the county of N. aforesaid, on ——, the —— day of ——, in the —— year of the reign of our sovereign lady Queen Victoria, and in the year of our Lord ——, before me, A. B., esq., sheriff of the said county, by virtue of the writ of our lady the queen to me directed, and to this inquisition annexed, by the oaths of I. L., E. S., &c., twelve good and lawful men of my bailiwick, who being sworn and charged, on their oath say, that the several persons in the schedule to the said writ annexed named, at the time of their respective deaths, had not, nor had any or either of them, any goods or chattels, lands or tenements, in my bailiwick, to the knowledge of the said jurors. In witness whereof as well I the said sheriff as the said jurors have to this inquisition set our hands and seals the day and year first above written. A. B., esquire, sheriff.

RETURN OF DISTRINGAS.

First, against Collectors.—Received and ready.

I humbly certify to the barons within mentioned, that I have received of the within named C. D. the sum of —— charged upon him, which sum I have ready to pay as within I am commanded.

A. B., esquire, sheriff.

Received of one Collector, and Issues as to others.

I humbly certify to the barons within mentioned, that I have received of C. D., collector of S., in the schedule to this writ annexed named, the sum of —— charged upon him, which sum I have ready to pay, as within is commanded. The issues set on the several other persons in the schedule to this writ annexed appear in the margin of the said schedule.

A. B., esquire, sheriff.

Nihil.

The within-named C. D., and the rest of the persons named in the schedule to this writ annexed, have not, nor hath either of them, any thing in my bailiwick, by which I can distrain them or any of them, nor are they, or either of them, found in my bailiwick.

A. B., esquire, sheriff.

Against Parishes.

Received of one Parish, and Issues on others.

By virtue of this writ to me directed, I do certify and return to the barons of her majesty's Court of Exchequer, that I have received of the inhabitants of the parish of W., in one of the schedules to this writ annexed named, the sum of —— charged upon them for, &c., which said sum I have ready to pay, as within I am commanded. The issues set on the inhabitants of the several other parishes in the several schedules to this writ annexed appear in the margin of the said schedules.

A. B., esquire, sheriff.

CHAP. XVI. SECT. I.

Another Form.

Parish and Collectors.

By virtue, &c., I do certify and return, first, issues on the inhabitants of the borough of S., in this writ annexed named, 3*l.* 10*s.*; that I have received the sum of —— charged upon the inhabitants of the parish of H., in the hundred of L., for, &c., and first mentioned in the fourth schedule to this writ annexed. And I return 40*s.* issues upon the inhabitants of the parish of I., afterwards mentioned in the same schedule. And I further certify and return that the several other persons named in the schedule to this writ annexed have not, nor hath either of them, any lands or chattels in my bailiwick whereby I can cause them to be distrained, nor are they or either of them found in the same.

A. B., esquire, sheriff.

Warrant on an Exchequer Writ, in the nature of a Sci. Fa.

N. (*to wit.*) A. B., esq., sheriff of the said county, to J. S. and J. M., my bailiffs, greeting: By virtue of her majesty's writ to me directed and delivered, I command you, that you give notice to T. H., of H., in the county of N. aforesaid, shipowner, to be and appear before the barons of her majesty's Exchequer, at Westminster, on the —— day of —— instant, to show cause, if he can, why her majesty should not have execution against him for the sum of 2000*l.*, upon a bond entered into by G. R., master mariner, of S., in the county of D., and the said T. H., jointly and severally to her majesty, bearing date the —— day of ——, in the —— year of her majesty's reign; and for so doing this shall be your warrant. Given under the seal of my office this —— day of ——, 18—.

(*Seal of office.*) By the sheriff.

Summons upon the above Warrant.

By virtue of her majesty's writ to the sheriff of N. directed, and of the said sheriff's warrant to us thereon, we do hereby give you notice to be and appear before the barons of her majesty's Exchequer, at Westminster, on the —— day of —— instant, to show cause, if you can, why her majesty should not have execution against you for the sum of 2000*l.*, upon a bond entered into by G. R., master-mariner, of S., in the county of D., and you, jointly and severally, to her majesty, bearing date the —— day of —— in the —— year of her said majesty's reign. Dated this —— day of ——, 18—.

To Mr. T. H., of H., in the county of N. } J. S.
J. M.

Return of Scire Feci to the foregoing Writ.

By virtue of this writ to me directed, I have, by I. S. and J. M., good and lawful men of my bailiwick, given notice to the within named T. H., that he be and appear before the barons of her majesty's Exchequer, at Westminster, on the day within mentioned, to show cause, if he can, why her majesty should not have execution against him for the sum within mentioned, as I am within commanded.

A. B., esquire, sheriff.

(*It is prudent to get the summoners to sign the following return, indorsed on the warrant.*)

We do hereby certify, that we have given notice to the within named T. H. to be and appear before the barons of her majesty's Exchequer, at Westminster, on the —— day of —— instant, to show cause, if he can, why her majesty should not have execution against him for the sum within mentioned, as we are commanded by the within warrant. Given under our hands the —— day of ——, 18—.

J. S.
J. M.

Return of Nihil to a Sci. Fa.

The within-named C. D. hath nothing in my bailiwick by which I can cause him to be summoned, neither is he found in the same.

A. B., esquire, sheriff.

(*If it be out of the Exchequer, then say*)

I humbly certify the barons within written, that the within named C. D. (*as above.*)

Sect. 2.

Warrant on an Extent.

N. (*to wit.*) A. B., esquire, sheriff of the county aforesaid, to J. S., my bailiff. By virtue of the queen's writ to me directed, I command you, that without delay you take C. D. by his body, wheresoever he shall be found in my bailiwick, so that I may keep him safely and securely in prison till he shall make satisfaction to her majesty of the sum of £—— due to her majesty for (*this of course follows the writ*) *duties on malt made in Great Britain by the said C. D.;* and that you do forthwith seize and take the goods and chattels of the said C. D. in my bailiwick, and them safely keep, so that I may cause them to be appraised, and taken into her majesty's hands, and an inquisition to be taken, according to the command of the said writ. In what manner you shall execute this warrant forthwith make known to me, so that I may return the same to the barons of her majesty's Exchequer at Westminster. Given under the seal of my office.

Dated the —— day of ——.

(*Seal of office.*) By the sheriff.

Form of a Summons duces tecum, to a Witness to attend the Inquisition.

N. (*to wit.*) To Mr. J. S. By virtue of her majesty's writ of extent against C. D., to me directed, I summon and require you to be and appear before me, or my under-sheriff, at the house of Mr. ——, known by the sign of the Red Lion, in N., in my county, on the —— day of ——, 18—, at —— o'clock in the fore- (*or* "after") noon, precisely, to give evidence on the part of her majesty, touching matters then and there to be inquired of, by a jury of the country, on the said extent; and that you then and there produce and give in evidence before me, or my under-sheriff, and the said jury, on the said extent, all and every mortgage and other deeds, assignments, papers and writings in your custody or power,

CHAP. XVI. SECT. II.

relating to any estate, messuages, lands, tenements or hereditaments wherein the said C. D. hath, or claims to have, or lately had, or claimed to have, any interest, property, claim or demand whatsoever, either at law or in equity: and also every bond and bonds, bill and bills of exchange, promissory note and promissory notes, and all and every security and securities for money, and all papers and writings in your custody or power, belonging to the said C. D., or wherein the said C. D. hath, or claims to have, or lately had, or claimed to have, any interest, property, claim, or demand; and also all and every book and books, letter and letters, invoice and invoices, bill and bills of parcels, bill and bills of lading; and all and every other paper and papers in your custody or power, wherein or whereon is or are written any entry, minute or memorandum, entries, minutes or memorandums, respecting or relating to any goods, wares, merchandize, or commodities whatsoever, sold or delivered by any person or persons to the said C. D., or sold or delivered by the said C. D. to any person or persons whatsoever, or wherein the said C. D. hath, or claims to have, or lately had, or claimed to have, any interest, property, claim or demand whatsoever; or respecting or relating to any sum or sums of money now or lately due or owing, or claimed to be now or lately due or owing from any person or persons whatsoever to the said C. D., or wherein the said C. D. hath, or claims to have, or lately had, or claimed to have, any interest, property, claim or demand whatsoever; and hereof fail not, as you will answer the contrary at your peril. Dated this —— day of ——, 18—.

(*Seal of office.*) A. B. esquire, sheriff.

Return to a Writ of Extent, where Defendant is taken, and Goods levied.

By virtue of this writ to me directed, I have taken the within named C. D., and keep him safely and securely in prison, as within I am commanded. The residue of the execution of this writ appears by the inquisition hereunto annexed.

The answer of A. B. esquire, sheriff.

Return that Goods are taken, and Non est Inventus as to Defendant.

The within named C. D. is not found in my bailiwick. The residue of the execution of this writ appears by the inquisition hereunto annexed.

The answer of A. B. esquire, sheriff.

Return of Non est Inventus, and that Defendant has no Lands or Goods.

The within named C. D. hath not, nor have any persons, nor hath any person, to his use, or in trust for him, any lands or tenements, goods or chattels, debts, credits, specialties or sums of money in my bailiwick, nor is he found in the same.

The answer of A. B. esquire, sheriff.

Return that Defendant is taken, but hath no Lands or Goods.

By virtue of this writ to me directed, I have taken the within named C. D., and keep him safely and securely in prison, as within I am commanded; but the said C. D. hath not, nor have any persons nor hath any person to his use, or in trust for him, any lands or tenements, goods or chattels, debts, credits, specialties, or sums of money in my bailiwick.

The answer of A. B. esquire, sheriff.

Form of Inquisition on an Extent, with various findings of different sorts of Freehold Interest, and Personal Estates and Effects.

N. (*to wit.*) An inquisition indented, taken at the house of J. L., known by the name or sign of the Queen's Head Inn, in the town of M., in the said county, the —— day of ——, in the —— year of the reign of our sovereign lady queen Victoria, and in the year of our Lord 18—, before me, A. B. esquire, sheriff of the said county; by virtue of her majesty's writ of *non omittas capias ad satisfaciendum* and extent, issued out of her majesty's court of exchequer at Westminster, bearing teste the —— day of ——, in the —— year of her said majesty's reign, directed to the sheriff of the county of N., and to this inquisition annexed, on the oaths of (*the names of the twelve jurors*), good and lawful men of my bailiwick; who, being sworn and charged to inquire touching the matters in the said annexed writs mentioned, do upon their oaths say, that the (*t*) said C. D., in the said writ named, was (*u*), *on the day of issuing the said writ*, seised in his demesne as of fee of and in a certain messuage or dwelling house, with the appurtenances, situate and being at ——, in the said county, in the tenure and occupation of ——, esquire, of the clear yearly value of £—— (*x*), in all issues thereof beyond reprizes: And also of and in six acres by estimation of arable land, two acres of meadow, and two acres of pasture, situate, lying and being in the township, fields or places of N., in the said county, and now or late in the tenure or occupation of ——, gent., of the clear yearly value of £—— (*y*), in all issues thereof beyond reprizes: And also of and in all that messuage or tenement, with outhouses, buildings, malting-office, kilns, kiln-houses, yards, gardens and appurtenances, containing by estimation one acre and a half, in N., in the said county, late in the occupation of the said C. D., of the yearly value of 20*l.* (*z*), or thereabouts, in all issues thereof beyond reprizes; *subject* (*a*) to a certain term of 1000 years, created by a certain

1st, Finding defendant seised of a freehold.

2nd, Seised also of land.

3d, Finding defendant seised in fee of a messuage, &c., subject to mortgage.

(*t*) The finding of real estate belonging to the defendant must have the following requisites: 1st, a correct description of the estate (whether farms, lands, houses, &c.) and the parish or place where situated: 2nd, a sum of money, as its *yearly value*, must be found: 3d, a seizure into the king's hands.

(*u*) If the extent issues on a judgment, or on a bond, the day and year of the date of the bond, or other specialty (which day and year will always be found in the body of the writ), followed by the words "on which day the said C. D. became and was first indebted to her majesty," must (in conformity to the mandatory part of the extent issuing on any such specialty), be inserted instead of the words in italics.

(*x*) The exact amount is not material; it is, however, necessary to find something as the yearly value of the lands.

(*y*) See last note.

(*z*) See note (*x*).

(*a*) If it be questionable whether the mortgage can prevail against the

CHAP. XVI. SECT. II.

indenture, bearing date the —— day of —— in the year of our Lord ——, and by assignment now vested in M. D., spinster, as surviving executrix named in the will of M. D., deceased, for securing the sum of 200*l.* and interest; also subject to a certain other mortgage thereon to J. H. of S., in the said county, farmer, for securing the sum of 200*l.* and lawful interest to the said J. H., his executors, administrators and assigns, by a certain indenture, bearing date the —— day of ——, in the year of our Lord ——: And also of the reversion expectant on the death of ——, widow, aged —— years or thereabouts, of and in the tenements following; that is to say, of and in a messuage or dwelling-house, with a garden or orchard thereto belonging, situate, lying and being in the parish of K., in the said county of N., in the occupation of ——, gentleman, of the clear yearly value of £——, in all issues thereof beyond reprizes; and of and in one other messuage or dwelling-house, with a garden and orchard thereto adjoining, situate, lying and being in the parish of N., in the said county of N., in the occupation of ——, gentleman, of the clear yearly value of £——, in all issues thereof beyond reprizes: And also in his demesne as of freehold, for the term of his natural life, of, in and to an undivided moiety of a certain messuage, lands and hereditaments situate at N., in the said county of N., with the appurtenances, containing about fifty acres of pasture land, now on the day of taking this inquisition in the tenure or occupation of ——, the whole of the said estate being of the clear yearly value of £——, in all issues thereof beyond reprizes: And the jurors aforesaid, upon their oath aforesaid, further say, that the said C. D., in the said writ named, had, on the day of issuing the said writ, a freehold farm, consisting of a messuage, a tenement, and fifty acres of freehold land, with the appurtenances called ——, situate, lying and being in the parish of —— in the said county, now or late in the tenure or occupation of ——, of the clear yearly value of £——, in all issues thereof beyond reprizes: And which said several messuages or tenements, lands and undivided moiety respectively, with the appurtenances, I, the said sheriff, have seized into her majesty's hands, as by the said writ is commanded: And the jurors aforesaid, upon their oath aforesaid, further say, that the said C. D., in the said writ named, was on the day of issuing the said writ possessed as of his own proper goods and chattels of and in a (*c*) messuage or dwelling-house, warehouses and shop, situate and being in the parish of ——, in the town of —— aforesaid, late in the occupation of the said C. D., for the remainder then to come and unexpired of a certain term of twenty-one years by one J. H., late of, &c., to the said C. D., granted and demised by indenture of lease, bearing date the —— day of ——, in the year of our Lord ——, and made between the said J. H. of the one part, and the said C. D. of the other part: And the jurors aforesaid do find the said remainder of the said term to be of the value of £—— (*d*), and do appraise the same at the sum of £——: And

[Margin notes: 4th, Finding defendant seised of the reversion in fee expectant on the death of a tenant for life in certain tenements. — Finding defendant seised of the undivided moiety of a farm for life. — Finding that defendant had a freehold farm of a particular name (*b*). — Seizure of freeholds into her majesty's hands. — Finding defendant possessed of a dwelling-house, &c. granted by a lease to himself.]

extent, the sheriff may leave it open to be litigated between the parties in the Court of Exchequer: it should be stated that it was *claimed* to be subject.

(*b*) If the title deeds to defendant's property cannot be got at, so as to allow the finding of the jury to be precise, the finding may be according to the adjudication in Sir Edward Coke's case; Godb. Rep. 289.

(*c*) It is requisite that the finding should particularise the property found as far as possible.

(*d*) The value must be found, although the exact value is not material; in finding freehold property the annual value is to be found; in chattels, the full value.

the jurors aforesaid, on their oath aforesaid, further say, that the said C. D., in the said writ named, was on the day of issuing the said writ possessed as of his own proper goods and chattels of and in the remainder to come and unexpired of a term of sixty-one years, which did commence on the —— day of ——, 18—, granted by indenture of lease, bearing date the —— day of ——, 18—, made between E. P. &c. of the one part, and the said C. D., in the said writ named, of and in, &c. (*describe the premises*), subject to the covenants in the said indenture contained, and the payment of the rent of a pepper corn for the first year, and at the yearly rent of 28*l.* during the remainder of the said term: And the jurors aforesaid do find the said remainder of the said term to be of the value, and do appraise the same at the sum of £——: And the jurors aforesaid, upon their oath aforesaid, further say, that the said C. D., in the said writ named, was on the day of issuing the said writ possessed, as of his own proper goods and chattels, of and in the remainder to come and unexpired of and in a certain term of twelve years or thereabouts of and in a certain malt house, situate at ——, in the said county: And the jurors aforesaid do find the said remainder of the said last mentioned term to be of the value, and do appraise the same at the sum of five shillings: And the jurors aforesaid, on their oath aforesaid, further say, that the said C. D., in the said writ named, was, on the day of issuing the said writ, possessed as of his own proper goods and chattels of and in seven-sixteenth parts or shares, the whole into sixteen equal parts or shares to be divided, of and in the brewing vessels and utensils for brewing, and of the materials and stock in trade of and belonging to a certain brewhouse for the brewing and malting of beer, ale and worts, situate and being in or near —— street, in the parish of ——, in the said county of ——: And the jurors aforesaid do find the said last mentioned parts or shares of the said C. D. to be of the value of, and do appraise the same at the sum of £——: And the jurors aforesaid, on their oath aforesaid, further say, that the said C. D. in the said writ named, was, on the day of issuing the said writ, possessed as of his own proper goods and chattels of and in the goods and chattels following, at and in his the said C. D.'s malthouse, in or near —— street, in the town of ——, in the said county, a large corn screw, fifty sacks (*enumerate the different articles there*), and there being malting vessels and utensils for malting, and having been respectively made use of by him the said C. D. for and in the making of malt in the said malthouse, and also of and in fifty quarters or thereabouts of barley (*here enumerate the barley, malt, &c.*), the said several quantities of malt and barley respectively being on the said —— day of ——, in the said —— year of the reign aforesaid, and on the said day of taking this inquisition, in the custody and possession of the said C. D., then and there being a maker of malt, and the said barley being then and there materials for the making of malt by him the said C. D., then and there being such maker of malt as aforesaid; and also of and in the following quantities of fuel for the drying and making malt, that is to say, about —— bushels or thereabouts of Welch

Finding defendant possessed of a lease of certain premises, subject to a rent and covenants.

Finding defendant possessed of part of the utensils and stock in trade of brewhouse.

Finding malting utensils, &c. (*e*).

(*e*) See 4 & 5 Vict. c. 20, s. 24, enacting that all goods subject to duties of excise, and all materials, machinery, vessels, and implements used in their manufacture, shall be liable to and chargeable with all duties, arrears and penalties chargeable upon or owing by the person carrying on the trade, while in his custody or possession, or that of any person in trust for him. And see *Attorney-General v. Trueman*, 11 M. & W. 694.

CHAP. XVI. SECT. II.

coals, about —— bushels or thereabouts of charred pit coal or cinders, and about twenty cart loads of beech billet wood: And the jurors aforesaid do find the said malting vessels and utensils for malting to be of the value, and do appraise the same at the sum of £——; the said barley in operation for making of malt to be of the value, and do appraise the same at the sum of £——; the said dry barley to be of the value, and do appraise the same at the sum of £——; the said malt dust to be of the value, and do appraise the same at the sum of £——: All which said residues of terms of years, goods and chattels, I the said sheriff have taken and seized into her majesty's hands, as by the said writ is commanded.

Seizure into the queen's hands.

Finding defendant possessed of goods specified in a schedule.

And the jurors aforesaid, on their oath aforesaid, further say, that the said C. D., in the said writ named, was, on the day of issuing the said writ, also possessed as of his own proper goods and chattels of and in the several goods and chattels mentioned in the schedule (*g*) hereunto annexed, marked with the letter A., and the values whereof respectively are severally and respectively mentioned in the said schedule, and do amount in the whole, and the jurors aforesaid do appraise the same at the sum of £——: And the jurors aforesaid, upon their oath aforesaid, further say, that the said C. D. was, on the day of issuing the said writ, possessed of and in one-eighth part or share, the whole into eight equal parts or shares to be divided, of and in a certain ship or vessel called the ——, whereof —— then or lately theretofore was master; and the jurors aforesaid do find the said eighth part or share of the said ship or vessel to be of the value and do appraise the same at the sum of £——: And the jurors aforesaid, upon their oath aforesaid, further say, that J. K. of, &c. in the county of, &c. merchant, on the —— day of ——, in the year of our Lord ——, by his bond (*h*) or writing obligatory bearing date the day and year last aforesaid, sealed with his seal, and as his deed delivered, acknowledged himself to be held and firmly bound to the said C. D. in the sum of £1000 of lawful money of Great Britain, to be paid to the said C. D. whenever he the said J. K. should be thereunto afterwards requested, with a condition thereunder written for the payment by the said J. K. to the said C. D., his executors, administrators or assigns, of the sum of £500, with lawful interest for the same, on the —— day of ——, in the said condition mentioned, and long since past; which said sum of £——, in the said condition mentioned, with lawful interest for the same, was not paid or satisfied according to the said condition, but on the contrary thereof was, on the day of issuing of the said writ, unpaid, and that the said writing obligatory, and the said penalty contained therein, then was forfeited, due and payable to the said C. D.: And the jurors aforesaid, upon their oath aforesaid, further say, that J. K. of, &c. in the county of &c. merchant, on the —— day of ——, in the year of our Lord ——, by his bond or writing obligatory sealed with his seal, bearing date the same day and year last aforesaid, acknowledged himself to be held and firmly bound to the said C. D. in the sum of £1000 of lawful money of Great Britain, payable at a day long since past, and that

Finding of a share in a ship.

Finding of a bond entered into by a third person and become forfeited.

Finding a bond, where it cannot be ascertained what is due for principal and interest.

(*g*) If the goods are numerous, it is as well to refer to a schedule annexed, as is done here.

(*h*) The forms of findings here given, of debts due to defendant, may easily be filled up, if debts in the second or third degree be found, by merely alleging that defendant's debtor's debtor is indebted to defendant's debtor, according to any of the forms here given.

on the day of issuing the said writ, the said sum of £1000 was unpaid: And the jurors aforesaid, upon their oath aforesaid, further say, that J. K. late of, &c. in the said county, merchant, was, on the day of issuing the said writ, indebted to the said C. D. in the sum of £500 upon a certain bill of exchange for that sum, bearing date the —— day of ——, in the year of our Lord ——, drawn by one E. F. upon him the said J. K., and payable to him the said C. D. (*or, if indorser,* "to L. M.") thirty days after the date thereof, and which said bill of exchange was duly accepted by him the said J. K. (*if the defendant was indorser of the bill, say here,* "and was afterwards, and before the issuing of the said writ, duly indorsed and delivered by the said L. M. to the said C. D.") whereby the said J. K. became liable to pay to the said C. D. the sum of £—— mentioned in the said bill of exchange, according to the tenor and effect of the said bill of exchange and his said acceptance thereof, and that the said sum of £—— was, on the day of issuing the said writ, wholly unpaid.

Finding a person indebted as acceptor of a bill of exchange to defendant, as payee.

[*In finding an indorser indebted, the same as the last form, varying only as follows:*] Upon one G. H. and payable to J. K. or order thirty days after sight thereof; which said last mentioned bill of exchange was afterwards and before the issuing of the said writ, seen and duly accepted by the said G. H., and was afterwards and before the issuing of the said writ, duly indorsed and delivered by the said J. K. to the said C. D.; and was afterwards and when the said sum of £500 became due and payable, according to the tenor and effect of the said bill of exchange, and of the said acceptance thereof, and before the issuing of the said writ, shown and presented to the said G. H. for payment of the said sum of £500; but the said G. H. then and hitherto wholly neglected and refused to pay the same, whereof the said J. K. had notice.

Finding a person as indorser of a bill of exchange indebted to defendant.

And the jurors aforesaid, upon their oath aforesaid, further say, that I. K. late of N. in the county of N., merchant, was, on the day of issuing the said writ, indebted to the said C. D. in the sum of £—— upon a certain note in writing, commonly called a promissory note, made by the said I. K. bearing date the —— day of ——, in the year of our Lord ——, by which note the said I. K. promised to pay to the said C. D. or his order the sum of £500, on demand, for value received, and that the said sum of £500 was on the day of issuing the said writ wholly unpaid: And the jurors aforesaid, upon their oath aforesaid, further say, that the said C. D. was, on the day of issuing the said writ, possessed as of his own proper goods and chattels of and in two certain notes in writing, commonly called Bank of England notes, by one of which notes the governor and company of the Bank of England promised to pay to Mr. Matthew Marshall or bearer, on demand, the sum of £20; by the other of which notes the said governor and company promised to pay to Mr. Matthew Marshall or bearer, on demand, the sum of £5; the said notes being in full force and of the value of £20 and £5 respectively: And the jurors aforesaid, upon their oath aforesaid, further say, that the said C. D., on the day of issuing the said writ, was possessed of and in, and entitled to *or* ("the reversion after the death of L. M. of and in") £5000 interest or share in the capital or joint stock three per cent. consolidated annuities, transferable at the Bank of England, and now standing in the name of I. K. in the books of the governor and company of the Bank of England, *and that the said I. K. was, on the day and year last aforesaid, a trustee for the said C. D. with respect to the* (*or* "said reversion of and in the

Finding of a promissory note drawn payable to defendant.

Finding defendant possessed of bank notes.

Finding defendant possessed of stock in the funds, standing in the name of a trustee.

CHAP. XVI. SECT. II.

said interest") *said annuities*, and that (*or* "the said reversion of and in") the said interest or share is worth to be sold the sum of £—— (*i*): And the jurors aforesaid, upon their oath aforesaid, further say, that the said C. D. was, on the day of issuing the said writ, possessed as of his own proper money, goods and chattels of the sum of £500 of lawful money of Great Britain, in monies numbered: And the jurors aforesaid, upon their oath aforesaid, further say, that J. R. and J. L. of —— street, London, malt factors, were, on the day of issuing the said writ, indebted to the said C. D. in the sum of £400 by them the said J. R. and J. L. had and received to and for the use of the said C. D.: And that J. R. of ——, in the said county of ——, gentleman, was, on the day of issuing the said writ, indebted to the said C. D. in the sum of £400 for so much money before that time lent and advanced by the said C. D. to the said J. R. at his special instance and request: And that J. R. was, on the day of issuing the said writ, indebted to the said C. D. in the sum of £400 for so much money before that time paid, laid out, and expended by the said C. D. to and for the use of the said C. D., at his special instance and request: And that J. R. of ——, in the said county of ——, merchant, was, on the day of issuing the said writ, indebted to the said C. D. in the sum of £400 for divers goods, wares and merchandize before that time sold and delivered by the said C. D. to the said J. R.: And that ——, of —— aforesaid, bankers, were, on the day of issuing the said writ, indebted to the said C. D. in the sum of £400, being the balance of cash in their hands as bankers to the said C. D.: And that J. R. of ——, in the county of ——, was, on the day of issuing the said writ, indebted to the said C. D. in the sum of £——, being the balance of an account, before the issuing of the said writ, made up, stated and settled between the said C. D. and J. R.: And the jurors aforesaid, upon their oath aforesaid, further say, that the several persons named in the schedule to this inquisition annexed, marked with the letter B., were, on the day of the issuing of this writ, severally and respectively indebted to the said C. D. in the several sums of money set against their respective names, amounting in the whole to the sum of £500, for goods, wares and merchandize by the said C. D. before that time sold and delivered to the said several persons respectively: All which said goods and chattels, debts, sum and sums of money, I the said sheriff have taken and seized into the hands of her said majesty, as by the said writ commanded: And the jurors aforesaid, upon their oath aforesaid, further say, that the said C. D. in the said writ named, had not, nor hath any person or persons to his use, or in trust for him, on the day of issuing the said writ, or at any time since, any lands or tenements, or any goods, chattels, debts, credits, specialties or sums of money in my bailiwick, save as hereinbefore set forth, to the knowledge of the said jurors, which can be extended, appraised, taken or seized into her majesty's hands, as by the said writ is commanded. In witness whereof, as well I the said sheriff as the said jurors, to this inquisition have set our respective seals the day, year and place above written.

Finding defendant possessed of money. Finding partners indebted to defendant for money had and received to his use. Finding a person indebted to defendant for money lent. Finding a person indebted to defendant for money paid, laid out and expended by defendant. Finding a person indebted for goods sold and delivered. That defendant's bankers are indebted to him for the balance of cash in hand. That another person is indebted for the balance of an account. Finding several persons indebted, the names, &c. particularised in a schedule annexed. Seizure into queen's hands. Conclusion.

A. B., esquire.

(*Seal of office.*) (*twelve seals.*)

(*i*) If the stock is in defendant's own name, it should be so stated, and the words in italics left out.

Warrant on a Venditioni Exponas of Goods taken under an Extent.

N. (to wit.) A. B., esquire, sheriff of the said county, to J. S. and J. M., my bailiffs, greeting: By virtue of her majesty's writ to me directed and delivered, I command you, and each of you, that you forthwith sell, or cause to be sold, the several goods and chattels in the schedule hereunto annexed named (being the proper goods and chattels of C. D.), and every part thereof, for the best price or prices you can get for the same: but at least for the sum of 3,372*l.* 7*s.* 7*d.*, at which the same were appraised, upon the oath of W. B., and others, lawful men of my bailiwick, by an inquisition taken at the house of Mr. G. W., known by the name of, &c., the —— day of —— last, before Sir T. S., baronet, late sheriff of the said county, by virtue of her majesty's writ of immediate extent, issued out and under the seal of her majesty's Court of Exchequer, directed to the said Sir T. S., late sheriff as aforesaid, against the said C. D., his estate and effects, so that I may have the money to arise from the sale thereof before the barons of her majesty's Exchequer at Westminster, on the —— day of —— next, to be then and there paid to her majesty's use; and that you have this, and so forth. Given under the seal of my office, this —— day of ——.

(*Seal of office.*) By the sheriff.

CHAP. XVII.—Sect. I.

6 Geo. IV. c. 50.

An Act for consolidating and amending the Laws relative to Jurors and Juries.

Whereas the laws relative to the qualification and summoning of jurors, and the formation of juries in England and Wales, are very numerous and complicated, and it is expedient to consolidate and simplify the same, and to increase the number of persons qualified to serve on juries, and to alter the mode of striking special juries, and in some other respects to amend the said laws: be it therefore enacted by the king's most excellent majesty, by and with the advice and consent of the lords spiritual and temporal, and commons, in this present parliament assembled, and by the authority of the same, that every man, except as hereinafter excepted, between the ages of twenty-one years and sixty years, residing in any county in England, who shall have in his own name or in trust for him, within the said county, ten pounds for the year above reprizes, in lands or tenements, whether of freehold, copyhold, or customary tenure, or of ancient demesne, or in rents issuing out of any such lands or tenements, or in such lands, tenements, and rents taken together, in fee simple, fee tail, or for the life of himself or some other person; or who shall have within the same county twenty pounds by the year above reprizes, in lands or tenements held by lease or leases for the absolute term of twenty-one years, or some longer term, or for any term of years

Qualification of jurors in England in superior courts, assizes and sessions of the peace. (See 13 Ed. I. c. 38; 27 Eliz. c. 6; 4 & 5 W. & M. c. 25, s. 15; 3 Geo. II. c. 25, s. 15.

CHAP. XVII. SECT. I.

determinable on any life or lives; or who being a householder shall be rated or assessed to the poor rate, or to the inhabited house duty in the county of Middlesex, on a value of not less than thirty pounds, or in any other county on a value of not less than twenty pounds, or who shall occupy a house containing not less than fifteen windows, shall be qualified and shall be liable to serve on juries for the trial of all issues joined in any of the king's courts of record at Westminster, and in the superior courts, both civil and criminal, of the three counties palatine, and in all courts of assize, nisi prius, oyer and terminer, and gaol delivery, such issues being respectively triable in the county in which every man so qualified respectively shall reside, and shall also be qualified and liable to serve on grand juries in courts of sessions of the peace and on petty juries for the trial of all issues joined in such courts of sessions of the peace, and triable in the county, riding, or division in which every man so qualified respectively shall reside; and that every man (except as hereinafter excepted) being between the aforesaid ages, residing in any county of Wales, and being there qualified to the extent of three-fifths of any of the foregoing qualifications, shall be qualified and shall be liable to serve on juries for the trial of all issues joined in the courts of great sessions, and on grand juries in courts of sessions of the peace, and on petty juries for the trial of all issues joined in such courts of sessions of the peace, in every county of Wales, in which every man so qualified as last aforesaid respectively shall reside.

Qualification in Wales. (See 4 & 5 W. & M. c. 25, s. 15.)

Exemptions from serving on juries. (See 1 W. & M. c. 18, s. 11; 19 Geo. 3, c. 44; 31 Geo. 3, c 32, s. 8; 52 Geo. 3, c. 155, s. 9.)

II. Provided always, and be it further enacted, that all peers; all judges of the king's courts of record at Westminster, and of the courts of great session in Wales; all clergymen in holy orders; all priests of the Roman Catholic faith, who shall have duly taken and subscribed the oaths and declarations required by law; all persons who shall teach or preach to any congregation of Protestant dissenters, whose place of meeting is duly registered, and who shall follow no secular occupation except that of a schoolmaster, producing a certificate of some justice of the peace of their having taken the oaths, and subscribed the declaration required by law; all serjeants and barristers at law actually practising; all members of the society of doctors of law, and advocates of civil law actually practising; all attorneys, solicitors, and proctors, duly admitted in any court of law or equity, or of ecclesiastical or admiralty jurisdiction, in which attorneys, solicitors, and proctors have usually been admitted, actually practising, and having duly taken out their annual certificates; all officers of any such courts actually exercising the duties of their respective offices; all coroners, gaolers, and keepers of houses of correction; all members and licentiates of the Royal College of Physicians in London actually practising; all surgeons being members of the Royal Colleges of Surgeons in London, Edinburgh, and Dublin, and actually practising; all officers in his majesty's navy or army on full pay; all pilots licensed by the Trinity House of Deptford Strond, Kingston-upon-Hull, or Newcastle-upon-Tyne, and all masters of vessels in the buoy and light service, employed by either of those corporations, and all pilots licensed by the Lord Warden of the Cinque Ports, or under any act of parliament or charter for the regulation of pilots of any other port; all the household servants of his majesty, his heirs and successors; all officers of customs and excise; all sheriff's officers, high constables, and parish clerks, shall be and are hereby absolutely freed and exempted from being returned, and from serving upon any juries or inquests whatsoever, and shall not

(See 5 Hen. 8, c. 6; 18 Geo. 2, c. 15, s. 10. See 6 & 7 W. & M. c. 4; 55 Geo. 3, c. 164.)

be inserted in the lists to be prepared by virtue of this act as hereinafter mentioned: provided also, that all persons exempt from serving upon juries in any courts aforesaid, by virtue of any prescription, charter, grant, or writ, shall continue to have and enjoy such exemption in as ample a manner as before the passing of this act, and shall not be inserted in the lists hereinafter mentioned.

CHAP. XVII. SECT. I.

See 5 & 6 W. 4, c. 76, ss. 122, 123, and 2 & 3 Vict. c. 71, s. 4.

III. Provided also, and be it enacted and declared, that no man, not being a natural born subject of the king, is or shall be qualified to serve on juries or inquests, except only in the cases hereinafter expressly provided for; and no man who hath been or shall be attainted of any treason or felony, or convicted of any crime that is infamous, unless he shall have obtained a free pardon, nor any man who is under outlawry or excommunication, is or shall be qualified to serve on juries or inquests in any court, or on any occasion whatsoever.

Aliens disqualified, except on juries de medietate.

Convicts or outlaws, &c. disqualified.

IV. And be it further enacted, that the clerk of the peace in every county, riding, and division in England and Wales, shall, within the first week of July in every year, issue and deliver his warrant (in the form set forth in the schedule hereunto annexed, or as near thereto as may be) to the high constables of each hundred, lathe, wapentake, or other like district, by which he shall command them to issue forth their precepts to the churchwardens and overseers of the poor of the several parishes, and to the overseers of the poor of the several townships within their respective constablewicks, requiring them to prepare and make out, on the first day of September then next ensuing, a true list of all men residing within their respective parishes and townships, qualified and liable to serve on juries according to this act as aforesaid, and also to perform and comply with all other the requisitions in the said precepts contained.

Clerks of the peace to issue warrants to the high constables in July. (See 3 & 4 Anne, c. 18, s. 5; 3 Geo. 2, c. 25.)

V. And be it further enacted, that every such clerk of the peace shall cause a sufficient number of warrants, precepts and returns to be printed, according to the several forms set forth in the schedule hereunto annexed, at the expense of the county, riding, or division, and shall annex to every warrant a competent number of precepts and returns, for the use of the respective persons by whom such precepts are to be issued, and such returns to be made.

Clerk of the peace to annex printed forms of precepts and returns to his warrants.

VI. And be it further enacted, that within fourteen days after the receipt of such warrant of the clerk of the peace, every high constable shall issue and deliver his precept (in the form set forth in the schedule hereunto annexed, or as near thereto as may be), together with a competent number of the printed forms of returns, to the churchwardens and overseers of the poor of the several paaishes, and to the overseers of the poor of the several townships within his constablewick, requiring them by such precept to prepare and make out a true list of all men residing within their respective parishes and townships, qualified and liable to serve as jurors as aforesaid, and to perform and comply with all the requisitions in the said precept contained: provided always, that where in any hundred, lathe, wapentake, or other like district, there shall be more than one high constable, in such case the clerk of the peace shall issue and deliver his warrant, together with a competent number of the precepts and returns as aforesaid, to every one of such high constables, each of whom shall be individually liable for the due performance of the several matters commanded in such warrant throughout the whole of such hundred, lathe, wapentake, or other like district, and shall for the non-performance thereof be subject to all and every the penalties by this act imposed upon any high constable: provided also, that where in any parish there shall

High constable to issue precepts to churchwardens and overseers within their constablewicks, commanding them to make out the jury lists.

Where there are several high constables, each to be responsible for the duties required by this act throughout the whole hundred.

CHAP. XVII. SECT. I.

be no overseers of the poor, other than the churchwardens, such churchwardens shall be deemed and taken to be the churchwardens and overseers of the poor of such parish within the meaning of this act, to all intents and purposes: provided also, that where any parish or township shall extend into more than one hundred, lathe, wapentake, or other like district, either in the same or different counties, such parish and township shall be deemed and taken, for all the purposes of this act, to be within that hundred, lathe, wapentake, or other like district, in which the principal church of such parish or township shall be situate.

Parishes, &c. extending into more than one hundred to be treated as entirely within the hundred where the parish church is.

Justices of the division may order any extra-parochial place to be annexed to any adjoining parish or township for the purposes of this act.

VII. And be it further enacted, that it shall be lawful for the justices of the peace of any division in England or Wales, at a special petty sessions to be holden for that purpose before the first day of July in any year, to make an order for annexing any extra-parochial place, whenever they shall think it expedient, to any parish or township adjoining thereto, for the purposes of this act, and a copy of such order shall, within five days from the making thereof, be served upon the churchwardens and overseers of such adjoining parish, or upon the overseers of such adjoining township, and such extra-parochial place shall from thence continually be deemed and taken, for all the purposes of this act, to be within and to form an integral part of such parish or township; and the churchwardens and overseers of such parish, and the overseers of such township, shall be, and they are hereby respectively authorized and required to make out, according to this act, a true list of all men qualified and liable to serve on juries as aforesaid, residing as well in their own respective parish or township as in the extra-parochial place thereto annexed, and shall from time to time perform and execute within such extra-parochial place for the purposes of this act, but for no other purpose, all and every the same acts, duties, powers and authorities, as in their own respective parish or township, and shall be as fully liable to the same penalties for the non-performance thereof within such extra-parochial place, as if they had in every instance been mentioned in this act with reference to such extra-parochial place.

Churchwardens and overseers to make out lists of persons qualified to serve on juries, with their residences, titles, &c. (See 3 & 4 Anne, c. 18, s. 5.)

VIII. And be it further enacted, that the churchwardens and overseers of every parish, and the overseers of every township, within the meaning of this act, shall forthwith, after the receipt of such precept from the high constable, prepare and make out in alphabetical order a true list of every man residing within their respective parishes or townships who shall be qualified and liable to serve on juries as aforesaid, with the christian and surname written at full length, and with the true place of abode, the title, quality, calling, or business, and the nature of the qualification of every such man, in the proper columns of the form of return set forth in the schedule hereunto annexed.

Lists to be fixed on church doors, and also kept by churchwardens for inspection, 3 G. 2, c. 25.

IX. And be it further enacted, that the churchwardens and overseers of each parish, and the overseers of each township, having made out according to this act a list of every man qualified and liable to serve on juries as aforesaid, shall, on the three first Sundays of the month of September, fix a true copy of such list upon the principal door of every church, chapel, or other public places of religious worship within their respective parishes or townships, having first subjoined to every such copy a notice, stating that all objections to the list will be heard by the justices of the peace at a time and place to be mentioned in such notice, and having also signed their names at the foot of such copy, and shall likewise keep the original list, or a true copy thereof, to be perused by any of the inhabitants of their respective parishes or townships, at any reasonable time during the three first weeks of the month of September, without any fee or reward, to the end that notice may be given of men qualified who are omitted, or of men inserted who ought to be omitted out of such list; and the churchwardens and overseers of each parish, and the overseers of each township, are hereby authorized to cause a sufficient number of copies of such lists, for the purposes aforesaid, to be printed at the expense of their respective parishes or townships.

Petty sessions to be held in the last week of September.

X. And be it further enacted, that the justices of the peace in every division in England and Wales shall hold a special petty sessions for the purposes herein mentioned within the last seven days of September in every year, on some day and at some place, of which notice shall be given by their clerk, before the twentieth day of August next preceding, to the high constable and to the churchwardens and overseers of every parish, and to the overseers of every township, within such division; and the churchwardens and overseers of each parish, and the overseers of each township, shall then and there produce the list of men qualified and liable to serve on juries as aforesaid within their respective parishes or townships, by them prepared and made out, as herein before directed, and shall answer upon oath such questions touching the same as shall be put to them, or any of them, by the justices then present; and if any man, not qualified and liable to serve on juries as aforesaid, is inserted in any such list, it shall be lawful for the said justices, upon satisfaction from the oath of the party complaining, or other proof, or upon their own knowledge, that he is not qualified and liable to serve on juries, to strike his name out of such list, and also to strike thereout the names of men disabled by lunacy or imbecility of mind, or by deafness, blindless or other permanent infirmity of body, from serving on juries; and it shall also be lawful for such justices to insert in such list the name of any man omitted therein, and likewise to reform any errors or omissions which shall appear to them to have been committed in respect to the name, place of abode, title, quality, calling, business, or the nature of the qualification of any man included in any such list: provided always, that no man's name, if omitted, shall be inserted in such list, nor shall any error or omission in the description of any man in such list be reformed by the said justices, unless upon the application of such men respectively, or unless such men respectively shall have had notice that an application for such purpose would be made to the justices at such petty sessions, or unless the said justices at such sessions, or any two of them, shall cause notice to be given to such men respectively, requiring them to show cause, at some adjcurnment of such petty sessions to be holden within four days thereafter, why their names should not be inserted in such list, or why any error or omission in the description of such men in such list should not be reformed; and when every such list shall be duly corrected at such sessions, or at any such adjournment thereof, it shall be allowed by the justices present, or two of them, at such sessions or such adjournment, who shall sign the same, with their allowance thereof; and the high constable shall receive every list so allowed, and deliver the same to the court of quarter sessions next holden for the county, riding, or division, on the first day of its sitting, at the same time attesting on oath his receipt of every such list from the petty sessions, and that no alteration hath been made therein since his receipt thereof.

Lists to be there produced, considered, reformed, and allowed, 3 G. 2, c. 25.

Petty sessions not to alter any list without notice to the party to be affected by the alterations.

Power of adjournment. Lists after allowance by petty sessions, to be delivered to high constable, and by him to the next quarter sessions. (See 3 G. 2, c. 25, s. 7.)

XI. And be it further enacted, that the respective churchwardens and overseers of every parish, and the overseers of every township, shall, for their assistance in completing the lists, pursuant to the intent of this act,

Tax assessments and poor rates to be inspected.

CHAP. XVII. SECT. I.

(See 3 G 2, c. 25, s. 1.)

(upon request made by them or any of them at any reasonable time between the first day of July and the first day of October in every year, to any collector or assessor of taxes, or to any other officer having the custody of any duplicate or tax assessment for such parish or township,) have free liberty to inspect any such duplicate or assessment, and take from thence the names of such men qualified to serve on juries, dwelling within their respective parishes or townships, as may appear to them or any of them to be necessary or useful; and every court of petty sessions and justice of the peace shall, upon the like request to any collector or assessor of taxes, or any other officer having the custody of any duplicate or tax assessment, or to any churchwarden or churchwardens, or overseer or overseers, having the custody of any poor rate within their respective divisions, have the like free liberty to inspect and make extracts from any such duplicate, tax assessment, or poor rate, for the purpose of assisting them in the reformation and completion of the jury lists within their respective divisions.

Lists to be kept by clerk of peace, and copied into a book to be delivered to sheriff. (See 7 & 8 W. 3, c. 32, s. 4; 3 G. 2, c. 25, s. 4.)

Book to be called "The Jurors' Book."

Sheriff to deliver it to his successor.

To be used for one year from 1st January.

XII. And be it further enacted, that the clerk of the peace shall keep the lists, so returned by the high constable to the court of quarter sessions, among the records of the session, arranged with every hundred in alphabetical order, and every parish or township within such hundred likewise in alphabetical order, and shall cause the same to be fairly and truly copied in the same order, in a book to be by him provided for that purpose, at the expense of the county, riding, or division, with proper columns for making the register hereinafter directed, and shall deliver the same book to the sheriff of the county or his under-sheriff, within six weeks next after the close of such sessions, which book shall be called "The Jurors' Book for the Year ——" (inserting the calendar year for which such book is to be in use); and that every sheriff on quitting his office shall deliver the same to the succeeding sheriff; and that every jurors' book so prepared shall be brought into use on the first day of January after it shall be so delivered by the clerk of the peace to the sheriff or his under-sheriff, and shall be used for one year then next following.

Form of *venire facias* (see 4 Anne, c. 16, ss. 6, 7; 24 G. 2, c. 18,) and of precept for jurors at gaol deliveries and sessions of the peace.

XIII. And be it further enacted, that every writ of *venire facias juratores* for the trial of any issue whatsoever, whether civil or criminal, or on any penal statute, in any of the courts in England or Wales hereinbefore mentioned, shall direct the sheriff to return twelve good and lawful men of the body of his county, qualified according to law, and the rest of the writ shall proceed in the accustomed form: and that every precept to be issued for the return of jurors before courts of oyer and terminer, gaol delivery, the superior criminal courts of the three counties palatine, and courts of sessions of the peace in England, and before the courts of great sessions and sessions of the peace in Wales, shall in like manner direct the sheriff to return a competent number of good and lawful men of the body of his county, qualified according to law, and shall not require the same to be returned from any hundred or hundreds, or from any particular venue within the county, and that the want of hundredors shall be no cause of challenge; any law, custom, or usage to the contrary notwithstanding.

Juries to be returned from jurors' book, by sheriff, and by coroners and elisors.

XIV. And be it further enacted, that every sheriff upon the receipt of every such writ of *venire facias* and precept for the return of jurors, shall return the names of men contained in the jurors' book for the then current year, and no others; and that where process for retaining a jury for the trial of any of the issues aforesaid shall be directed to any coroner, elisor, or other minister, he shall have free access to the jurors' book for the current year, and shall in like manner return the names of men contained therein, and no others; provided always, that if there shall be no jurors' book in existence for the current year, it shall be lawful to return jurors from the jurors' book for the year preceding.

Sheriff, &c. on return of writs of *venire facias*, to annex a panel of jurors, &c. (See 3 G. 2, c. 25, s. 8.)

XV. And be it further enacted, that every sheriff or other minister, to whom the return of juries for the trial of issues before any court of assize or *nisi prius* in any county of England, except the counties palatine, may belong, shall, upon his return of every writ of *venire facias* (unless the causes intended to be tried at bar, or in cases where a special jury shall be struck by order or rule of court), annex a panel to the said writ, containing the names alphabetically arranged, together with places of abode and additions, of a competent number of jurors named in the jurors' book, and that the names of the same jurors shall be inserted in the panel annexed to every *venire facias* for the trial of all issues at the same assizes or sessions of *nisi prius* in each respective county, which number of jurors shall not in any county be less than forty-eight nor more than seventy-two, unless by the direction of the judges appointed to hold the assizes or sessions of *nisi prius* in the same county, or one of them, who are and is hereby empowered, by order under their or his hands or hand, to direct a greater or lesser number, and then such number as shall be so directed shall be the number to be returned; and that in the writ of *habeas corpora juratorum* or *distringas*, subsequent to such writ of *venire facias*, it shall not be requisite to insert the names of all the jurors contained in such panel, but it shall be sufficient to insert in the mandatory part of such writs respectively, "the bodies of the several persons in the panel to this writ annexed named," or words of the like import; and to annex to such writs respectively panels containing the same names as were returned in the panel to such *venire facias*, with their places of abode and additions; and that for making the returns and panels aforesaid, and annexing the same to the respective writs, the ancient legal fee, and no other, shall be taken; and that the men named in such panels, and no others, shall be summoned to serve on juries at the then next court of assizes or sessions of *nisi prius* for the respective counties named in such writs.

If plaintiff sue forth a *venire*, &c. in order to trial, and not proceed, he may afterwards sue forth another *venire*, &c. and try at any subsequent assizes. (See 7 & 8 W. 3, c. 32, § 1.)

XVI. And be it further enacted, that if any plaintiff or demandant in any cause which shall be at issue in any of his majesty's courts of record at Westminster, or any defendant in any action of *quare impedit* or *replevin* which shall be so at issue, shall sue out any writ of *venire facias*, upon which any writ of *habeas corpora* or *distringas* with a *nisi prius* shall issue, in order to the trial of the said issue at the assizes or sessions of *nisi prius*, and shall not proceed to trial at the first assizes or sessions of *nisi prius* after the teste of such writ of *habeas corpora* or *distringas*, then and in every such case (except when a view by jurors shall be directed, as hereinafter mentioned) such plaintiff, demandant or defendant, whensoever he shall think fit to try the said issue at any other assizes or sessions of *nisi prius*, shall sue forth a new writ of *venire facias*, commanding the sheriff to return anew twelve good and lawful men of the body of his county, qualified according to law, and the rest of the writ shall proceed in the accustomed manner; which writ being duly returned, a writ of *habeas corpora* or *distringas* with a *nisi prius* shall issue thereupon (for which the same fees shall be paid as in the case of the *pluries habeas corpora* or *distringas* with a *nisi prius*), upon which such plaintiff, demandant or defendant shall and may proceed to trial as lawfully and effectually to all intents and purposes as if no former writ of *venire facias* had been prose-

CHAP. XVII. SECT. I.

cuted in that cause, and so *toties quoties*, as the case shall require; and if any defendant or tenant in any action depending in any of the said courts shall be minded to bring to trial any issue joined against him, where by the practice of the court he may do the same by proviso, he shall or may, of the issuable term next preceding such intended trial to be had at the next assizes or sessions of *nisi prius*, sue out a new *venire facias* to the sheriff in the form aforesaid by proviso, and prosecute the same by writ of *habeas corpora* or *distringas* with a *nisi prius*, as lawfully and effectually to all intents and purposes as if no former writ of *venire facias* had been sued out or returned in that cause, and so *toties quoties*, as the matter shall require.

Defendant may do the same.

Returns of jurors in the counties palatine. (See 3 G 2, c. 25, § 10.)

XVII. And be it further enacted, that every sheriff or other minister to whom the return of juries for the trial of causes in the superior courts of the said counties palatine may belong, shall, ten days at least before the said courts shall respectively be held, summon a competent number of men, named in the jurors' book, to serve on juries in the said courts, so as such number be not less than forty-eight, nor more than seventy-two, without the direction of the judge or judges of the courts for such counties palatine respectively; and the sheriff or other minister who shall summon such jurors shall return a list containing the names, alphabetically arranged, and the places of abode and additions of the jurors so summoned, on the first day of the court to be held for the said counties palatine respectively; and the jurors so summoned, or a competent number of them, as the judge or judges of such court respectively shall direct, and no others (unless in cases where a special jury shall be struck), shall be named in every panel to be annexed to every writ of *venire facias juratores, habeas corpora juratorum* and *distringas*, which shall be issued out and returnable for the trial of cases in such courts respectively.

Returns of jurors in Wales. (See 3 G. 2, c. 25, § 9.)

XVIII. And be it further enacted, that every sheriff, or other minister to whom the return of juries for the trial of causes in the court of great sessions in any county of Wales may belong, shall, at least ten days before every great sessions, summon a competent number of men named in the jurors' book, so as such number be not less than forty-eight or more than seventy-two, without the direction of the judge or judges of the great sessions for such county, who is and are hereby empowered, if he or they shall see cause, by rule of court, or by an order of any judge thereof, to be made in vacation, if necessary, to direct a greater or lesser number to be summoned; and that the sheriff or other minister who shall summon such jurors shall return a list containing the names, alphabetically arranged, and the places of abode and additions of the jurors so summoned, at the first court of the second day of every great sessions; and that the jurors so summoned, or a competent number of them, as the judge or judges of such great sessions shall direct, and no others (unless in cases where a special jury shall be struck), shall be named in every panel to be annexed to every writ of *venire facias juratores, habeas corpora juratorum* and *distringas*, which shall be issued out and returnable for the trial of causes at such great sessions.

Copy of the panel to be kept in the sheriff's office, for the inspection of the parties and their attornies.

XIX. And be it further enacted, that the sheriff or minister to whom the return of jurors for the trial of causes in any county in England (except the counties palatine) may belong shall cause to be made out an alphabetical list of the names of all the jurors contained in the panels to the several writs of *venire facias* annexed as aforesaid, with their respective place of abode and additions; and the sheriff or other minister to whom the return of jurors for the trial of causes in any county palatine, or in any county in Wales, may belong, shall cause to be made out in like manner a list of all the jurors so summoned in such respective counties as aforesaid; and every such sheriff or other minister shall keep such list in the office of the under-sheriff or deputy for seven days at least before the sitting of the next court of assize or *nisi prius*, or the next court to be holden for any county palatine, or the next court of great sessions in Wales; and the parties in all causes to be tried at any such court of assize or *nisi prius*, or court of any county palatine or great sessions, and their respective attornies, shall, on demand, have full liberty to inspect such list without any fee or reward to be paid for inspection.

CHAP. XVII. SECT. I.

(See 42 Ed. 3, c. 11, and 6 H. 6, c. 2.)

XX. Provided always, and be it further declared and enacted, the Court of King's Bench and all courts of *oyer* and *terminer*, gaol delivery, the superior criminal courts of the three counties palatine, and courts of sessions of the peace in England, and all courts of great sessions and sessions of the peace in Wales, shall respectively have and exercise the same power and authority as they have heretofore had and exercised in issuing any writ or precept, or making any award or order, orally or otherwise, for the return of a jury for the trial of any issue before any of such courts respectively, or for the amending or enlarging the panel of jurors returned for the trial of any such issue; and the return to every such writ, precept, award, or order, shall be made in the manner heretofore used and accustomed in such courts respectively, save and except that the jurors shall be returned from the body of the county, and not from any hundred or hundreds, or from any particular venue within the county, and shall be qualified according to this act.

Juries in all criminal courts to be returned as before.

(3 H. 8, c. 12.)

XXI. And be it further enacted, that when any person is indicted for high treason or misprision of treason, in any court other than the Court of King's Bench, a list of the petit jury, mentioning the names, profession, and place of abode of the jurors, shall be given at the same time that the copy of the indictment is delivered to the party indicted, which shall be ten days before the arraignment, and in the presence of two or more credible witnesses; and when any person is indicted for high treason or misprision of treason in the Court of King's Bench, a copy of the indictment shall be delivered within the time, and in the manner aforesaid; but the list of the petit jury, made out as aforesaid, may be delivered to the party indicted at any time after the arraignment, so as the same be delivered ten days before the day of trial: provided always, that nothing herein contained shall any ways extend to any indictment for high treason in compassing and imagining the death of the king, or for misprision of such treason, where the overt act, or overt acts of such treason alleged in the indictment shall be assassination or killing of the king, or any direct attempt against his life, or any direct attempt against his person, whereby his life may be endangered, or his person may suffer any bodily harm; or to any indictment of high treason for counterfeiting his majesty's coin, the great seal, or privy seal, his sign manual or privy signet; or to any indictment of high treason, or to any proceedings thereupon, against any offender or offenders who by any act or acts now in force is and are to be indicted, arraigned, tried and convicted by such like evidence, and in such manner as is used and allowed against offenders for counterfeiting his majesty's coin.

Copy of the panel to be delivered to parties indicted for high treason.

7 W. 4, c. 3. (See 7 Anne, c. 21, § 7.)

Exceptions 39 & 40 G. 3, § 23.

G. 3, c. 53, s. 3.

XXII. And be it further enacted, that in any county in which the justices of assize in England, or the justices of the superior courts of the said counties palatine, or the judges of the great sessions in any county of Wales, shall think fit so to direct, the sheriff or other minister to whom

Judge of assize may direct the same panel for the criminal and

CHAP. XVII. SECT. I.

civil sides, and may direct two sets of jurors to be summoned, one to attend at the beginning of each assizes, and the other to attend the residue thereof, to serve indiscriminately on the criminal and civil side. (See 1 & 2 G. 4, c. 46.)

Summons shall be made out either for the first or second set.

In case of view, the judge to appoint trial during the attendance of the viewers.

the return of the *venire facias juratores*, or other process for the trial of causes at *nisi prius*, doth belong, shall summon and impanel such number of jurors, not exceeding one hundred and forty-four, as such judges or justices respectively shall think fit to direct, to serve indiscriminately on the criminal and civil side; and that where such judges or justices respectively shall so direct, the sheriff or other minister shall divide such jurors equally into two sets, the first of which sets shall attend and serve for so many days at the beginning of each assize or great sessions, as such judges or justices respectively shall, within a reasonable time before the commencement of such assize or great sessions, respectively think fit to direct, and the other of which sets shall attend and serve for the residue of such assize or great sessions: provided always, that such sheriff or other minister shall, in the summons to the jurors in each of such sets, specify whether the juror named therein is in the first or second set, and at what time the attendance of such juror will be required; and the sheriff or other minister to whom the return of the *venire facias juratores*, or other process, for the trial of causes at *nisi prius*, doth belong, shall, upon his return of every such writ or process, annex thereto a panel containing the names, alphabetically arranged, together with the additions and places of abode of the jurors in each of such sets; and during the attendance and service of the first of such sets, the jury on the civil side shall be drawn from the names of the persons in that set, and during the attendance and service of the second of such sets, from the names of the persons in such second set: provided always, that in any case wherein an order for a view shall have been obtained as hereinafter mentioned, it shall be lawful for the judge before whom such case is to be tried, and he is hereby required, on the application of the party obtaining such order, to appoint such case to be tried during the attendance and service of that set of jurors in which the viewers, or the major part of them, are included.

Where jurors are to view lands, &c. court may order special writs of *venire facias*, or *distringas*, or *habeas corpora*. (See 4 Anne, c. 16, § 8; 3 G. 2, c. 25, § 14.)

XXIII. And be it further enacted, that where in any case, either civil or criminal, or on any penal statute, depending in any of the said Courts of Record at Westminster, or in the counties palatine or great sessions in Wales, it shall appear to any of the respective courts, or to any judge thereof in vacation, that it will be proper and necessary that some of the jurors who are to try the issues in such case should have the view of the place in question, in order to their better understanding the evidence that may be given upon the trial of such issues, in every such case such court, or any judge thereof in vacation, may order a rule to be drawn up, containing the usual terms, and also requiring, if such court or judge shall so think fit, the party applying for the view to deposit in the hands of the under-sheriff a sum of money to be named in the rule for payment of the expenses of the view, and commanding special writs of *venire facias distringas*, or *habeas corpora* to issue, by which the sheriff or other minister to whom the said writs shall be directed, shall be commanded to have six or more of the jurors named in such writs, or in the panels thereto annexed (who shall be mutually consented to by the parties, or, if they cannot agree, shall be nominated by the sheriff or such other minister as aforesaid), at the place in question, some convenient time before the trial, who then and there shall have the place in question shown to them by two persons in the said writs named, to be appointed by the court or judge; and the said sheriff, or other minister who is to execute any such writ, shall, by a special return upon the same, certify that the view hath been had according to the command of the same, and shall specify the names of the viewers.

CHAP. XVII. SECT. I.

XXIV. And be it further enacted, that where a view shall be allowed in any case, those men who shall have had the view, or such of them as shall appear upon the jury to try the issue, shall be first sworn, and so many only shall be added to the viewers who shall appear, as shall, after all defaulters and challenges allowed, make up a full jury of twelve.

Viewers in case of appearance to be sworn upon the jury first. (See 3 G. 2, c. 25, § 14.)

XXV. And be it further enacted, that the summons of every man to serve on juries, not being special juries, in any of the courts aforesaid, shall be made by the proper officer ten days at the least before the day on which the juror is to attend, by showing to the man to be summoned, or in case he shall be absent from the usual place of his abode, by leaving with some person there inabiting, a note in writing, under the hand of the sheriff, or other proper officer, containing the substance of such summons; and the summons of every man to serve on special juries in any of the courts aforesaid, shall be made by the like persons, and in the like manner as aforesaid, three days at the least before the day on which the special juror is to attend; provided always, that this act shall not require any longer time for summoning any jurors in the city of London or county of Middlesex, than has been heretofore by law required, nor shall give any longer time for the return of any writ of *venire facias, habeas corpora*, or *distringas*, than has been heretofore by law required; but that where there shall not be ten days between the awarding of such writ and the return thereof, every juror may be summoned, attached or distrained to appear at the day and time therein mentioned, as he might heretofore have been.

Jurors to be summoned ten days before the day of attendance. (See W. 3, c. 32, § 5 & 11), and for special jurors three days. Time for summoning jurors for London, &c. as heretofore.

XXVI. And be it further enacted, that the name of each man who shall be summoned and impanelled in any court of assize or *nisi prius*, or for the trial of issues in the civil courts of the counties palatine or great sessions, with the place of his abode and addition, shall be written on a distinct piece of parchment or card, such pieces of parchment or card being all as nearly as may be of equal size, and shall be delivered unto the associate or prothonotary of such court by the under-sheriff of the county, or the secondary of the city of London, and shall, by direction and care of such associate or prothonotary, be put together in a box provided for that purpose, and when any issue shall be brought on to be tried, such associate or prothonotary shall in open court draw out twelve of the said parchments or cards one after another, and if any of the men whose name shall be so drawn shall not appear, or shall be challenged and set aside, then such further number, until twelve men be drawn, who shall appear, and, after all just causes of challenge allowed, shall remain as fair and indifferent; and the said twelve men so first drawn and appearing, and approved as indifferent, their names being marked in the panel, and they being sworn, shall be the jury to try the issue, and the names of the men so drawn and sworn shall be kept apart by themselves until such jury shall have given in their verdict, and the same shall be recorded, or until such jury shall, by consent of the parties or by leave of the court, be discharged, and then the same names shall be returned to the box, there to be kept with the other names remaining at the time undrawn, and so *toties quoties* as long as any issue remains to be tried: provided always, that if any issue shall be brought on to be tried in any of the said courts before the jury in any other issue shall have brought in their verdict or been discharged, it shall be lawful for the court to order twelve of the residue of the said parchments or cards, not containing the names of any of the jurors who shall not have so brought in their verdict, or been discharged, to be drawn in such manner as is aforesaid, for the

Names of jurors to be delivered to the associate, and ballotted for juries in civil courts.

(See 3 G. 2, c. 25, § 11 & 12.)

Where the jury have not brought in their verdict, twelve others to be drawn.

CHAP. XVII. SECT. I.

The same jury, if not objected to, may try several issues in succession without being re-drawn.

trial of the issue which shall be so brought on to be tried: provided also, that where no objection shall be made on behalf of the king or any other party, it shall be lawful for the court to try any issue with the same jury that shall have previously tried or been drawn to try any other issue, without their names being returned to the box and re-drawn, or to order the name or names of any man or men on such jury, whom both parties may consent to withdraw, or who may be justly challenged or excused by the court, to be set aside, and another name or other names to be drawn from the box, and to try the issue with the residue of such original jury, and with such man or men whose name or names shall be so drawn, and who shall appear and be approved as indifferent, and so *toties quoties* as long as any issue remains to be tried.

Want of qualification in common jurors to be cause of challenge. (See 4 & 5 W. & M. c. 24, § 15.)

XXVII. And be it further enacted, that if any man shall be returned as a juror for the trial of any issue in any of the courts hereinbefore mentioned, who shall not be qualified according to this act, the want of such qualification shall be good cause of challenge, and he shall be discharged upon such challenge, if the court shall be satisfied of the fact; and that if any man returned as a juror for the trial of any such issue shall be qualified in other respects according to this act, the want of freehold shall not on such trial in any case, civil or criminal, be accepted as good cause of challenge, either by the crown or by the party, nor as cause for discharging the man so returned upon his own application; any law, custom or usage to the contrary notwithstanding; provided, that nothing herein contained shall extend in anywise to any special juror.

Not to extend to special jurors.

Where challenges not admitted. (See 24 G. 2, c. 18, § 4.)

XXVIII. And be it further enacted, that no challenge shall be taken to any panel of jurors for want of a knight's being returned in such panel, nor any array quashed by reason of any such challenge; any law, custom or usage to the contrary notwithstanding.

The king shall only challenge for cause. 33 Ed. 1, st. 4.

Prisoner allowed 20 peremptory challenges only in felony. (See 22 H. 8, c. 14; 1 & 2 P. & M. c. 10.)

XXIX. And be it further enacted, that in all inquests to be taken before any of the courts hereinbefore mentioned, wherein the king is a party, howsoever it be, notwithstanding it be alleged by them that sue for the king, that the jurors of those inquests, or some of them, be not indifferent for the king, yet such inquests shall not remain untaken for that cause; but if they that sue for the king will challenge any of those jurors, they shall assign of their challenge a cause certain, and the truth of the same challenge shall be inquired of according to the custom of the court; and it shall be proceeded to the taking of the same inquisitions, as it shall be found, if the challenges be true or not, after the discretion of the court; and that no person arraigned for murder or felony shall be admitted to any peremptory challenge above the number of twenty.

Court to have the power of ordering special juries to be struck before the proper officer. (See 3 G. 2, c. 25, § 15; and 6 G. 2, c. 37, as to counties palatine; and 31 G. 3, c. 51, as to Wales.)

XXX. And be it further enacted and declared, that it is and shall be lawful for his majesty's courts of King's Bench, Common Pleas, and Exchequer, at Westminster respectively, and for the judges of the said courts of the three counties palatine, and of the courts of great sessions in Wales, upon motion made on behalf of the king, or upon the motion of any prosecutor, relator, plaintiff, or demandant, or of any defendant or tenant, in any case whatsoever, whether civil or criminal, or on any penal statute, excepting only indictments for treason or felony, depending in any of the said courts, and the said courts and judges respectively are hereby authorized, in any of the cases before mentioned, to order and appoint a special jury to be struck before the proper officer of each respective court, for the trial of any issue joined in any of the said cases, and triable by a jury, in such manner as the said courts respectively have usually ordered the same; and every jury so struck shall be the jury returned for the trial of such issue.

CHAP. XVII. SECT. I.

XXXI. And be it further enacted, that every man who shall be described in the jurors' book for any county in England or Wales, or for the county of the city of London, as an esquire or person of higher degree, or as a banker or merchant, shall be qualified and liable to serve on special juries in every such county in England and Wales, and in London respectively; and the sheriff of every county in England and Wales, or his under-sheriff, and the sheriffs of London or their secondary, shall, within ten days after the delivery of the jurors' book for the current year to either of them, take from such book the names of all men who shall be described therein as esquires or persons of higher, or as bankers or merchants, and shall respectively cause the names of all such men to be fairly and truly copied out in alphabetical order, together with their respective places of abode and additions, in a separate list to be subjoined to the jurors' book, which list shall be called "the Special Jurors' List," and shall prefix to every name in such list its proper number, beginning the numbers from the first name, and continuing them in a regular arithmetical series down to the last name, and shall cause the said several numbers to be written upon distinct pieces of parchment or card, being all as nearly as may be of equal size, and after all the said numbers shall have been so written, shall put the same together in a separate drawer or box, and shall there safely keep the same to be used for the purpose hereinafter mentioned.

Qualifications of special jurors in English and Welsh counties and in London; the sheriff shall extract from the jurors' book the names of all men qualified as special jurors; and shall write them in a separate list, and prefix numbers to all the names in such list; and shall write all the numbers on distinct cards, and put them in a box for safe custody.

XXXII. And be it further enacted, that whenever any of the courts or judges above mentioned shall order a special jury to be struck before the proper officer of such court, such officer shall appoint a time and place for the nomination of such special jury; and a copy of the rule of court, and of such officer's appointment, shall be served on the under-sheriff of the county in England or Wales in which the trial is to be had, or on the secondary of the city of London, if the trial is to be had there, and also on all the parties who have usually been served with the same respectively, in the accustomed manner; and the said officer, at the time and place appointed, being attended by such under-sheriff, or secondary, or his agent, who are hereby respectively required to bring with them the jurors' book and such special jurors' list, and all the numbers so written upon distinct pieces of parchment or card as aforesaid, shall, in the presence of all the parties in any of the cases aforesaid, and of their attornies (if they respectively choose to attend, or if the said parties or their attornies, all or any of them, do not attend, then in their absence), put all the said numbers into a box, to be by him provided for that purpose, and after having shaken them together, shall draw out of the said box forty-eight of the said numbers, one after another, and shall, as each number is drawn, refer to the corresponding number in the special jurors' list, and read aloud the name designated by such number; and if at the time of so reading any name, either party, or his attorney, shall object that the man whose name shall have been so referred to is in any manner incapacitated from serving on the said jury, and shall also then and there prove the same to the satisfaction of the said officer, such name shall be set aside, and the said officer shall instead thereof draw out of the said box another number, and shall in like manner refer to the corresponding number in the said list, and read aloud the name designated thereby, which name may be in like manner set aside, and other numbers and names shall in every such case be resorted to, according to the mode of proceeding hereinbefore described, for the purpose of supplying names in the places of those set aside, until the whole number of forty-eight names not

Officer of court is to appoint the time and place for nominating the special jury. Under-sheriff or his agent to attend the officer with the special jurors' list, and all the numbers; Officer to put all the numbers in a box, and to draw out 48, and to check them with the numbers and names in the list;

CHAP. XVII. SECT. I.

liable to be set aside shall be completed; and if in any case it shall so happen that the whole number of forty-eight names cannot be obtained from the special jurors' list, in such case the said officer shall fairly and indifferently take, according to the mode of nomination heretofore pursued in nominating special juries, such a number of names from the general jurors' book, in addition to those already taken from the special jurors' list, as shall be required to make up the full number of forty-eight names, all and every of which forty-eight names shall in such case be equally deemed and taken to be those of special jurors; and the said officer shall afterwards make out for each party a list of the forty-eight names, together with their respective places of abode and additions, and after having made out such list, shall return all the numbers so drawn out, together with all the numbers remaining undrawn, to such under-sheriff or secondary, or his agent, to be by such under-sheriff or secondary safely and securely kept for future use; and all the subsequent proceedings for reducing the said list, and all other matters whatsoever relating to special juries, shall remain and continue in force as heretofore, except where the same or any part thereof is expressly altered by this act; and all the fees heretofore payable on the striking of special juries shall continue to be paid in the accustomed manner.

and to deliver a list of the 48 names to each party, to be reduced as heretofore.

The parties may, by consent, have a special jury struck according to the ancient mode. The same special jury may, by consent, try any number of causes. The court may discharge any man who has served as a special juror once during the same assizes.

XXXIII. Provided always, and be it further enacted, that nothing herein contained shall be construed to prevent the parties in any cause, or their attornies, from consenting to have a special jury nominated, according to the mode used and accustomed before the passing of this act, and upon a consent to that effect, signed by each party, or his attorney, being communicated to the proper officer, he is thereby authorized and required to nominate a special jury for the trial of every such cause, according to the mode used and accustomed before the passing of this act; provided also, that nothing herein contained shall be construed to prevent the same special jury, however nominated, from trying any number of causes, so as the parties in every such cause, or their attornies, shall have signified their assent in writing to the nomination of such special jury for the trial of their respective causes: provided always, that it shall be lawful for the court, if it shall so think fit, upon the application of any man who shall have served upon one or more special juries at any assizes or sessions of *nisi prius*, to discharge such man from serving upon any other special jury during the same assizes or sessions of *nisi prius*.

Costs of special jury. (See 24 G. 2, c. 18.)

XXXIV. And be it further enacted, that the person or party who shall apply for a special jury, shall pay the fees for striking such jury, and all the expenses occasioned by the trial of the cause by the same, and shall not have any further or other allowance for the same, upon taxation of costs, than such person or party would be entitled unto in case the cause had been tried by a common jury; unless the judge before whom the cause is tried shall, immediately after the verdict, certify, under his hand, upon the back of the record, that the same was a cause proper to be tried by a special jury.

Fees to special jurors. (See 24 G. 2, c. 18.)

XXXV. And be it further enacted, that no juror who shall serve upon any special jury shall be allowed or take for serving on any such jury more than such sum of money as the judge who tries the issue shall think just and reasonable, and which shall not exceed the sum of one pound one shilling, except in causes wherein a view is directed, and shall have been had by such juror.

Mode of striking special juries in

XXXVI. Provided always, and be it further enacted, that where any special jury shall be ordered, by any rule in any of the courts aforesaid, to be struck by the proper officer of such court, in any cause arising in any county of a city or town, except the city of London, the sheriff or sheriffs thereof, or the under-sheriff respectively, shall be commanded by such rule to bring or cause to be brought, before the proper officer of such court, the books or lists of persons qualified to serve on juries within the same county of a city or town; and in every such case the jury shall be taken and struck out of such books or lists respectively, in the manner heretofore used and accustomed; any thing in this act to the contrary notwithstanding.

any county of a city or town (except London) to remain as heretofore. (See 3 G. 2, c. 25, s. 17.)

XXXVII. And be it further enacted, that where a full jury shall not appear before any court of assize or *nisi prius*, or before any of the superior civil courts of the three counties palatine, or before any court of great sessions, or where, after appearance of a full jury, by challenge of any of the parties, the jury is likely to remain untaken for default of jurors, every such court, upon request made for the king by any one thereto authorized or assigned by the court, or on request made by the parties, plaintiff or demandant, defendant or tenant, or their respective attornies, in any action or suit, whether popular or private, shall command the sheriff or other minister, to whom the making of the return shall belong, to name and appoint, as often as need shall require, so many of such other able men of the county then present as shall make up a full jury; and the sheriff or other minister aforesaid shall, at such command of the court, return such men duly qualified as shall be present or can be found to serve on such jury, and shall add and annex their names to the former panel, provided that where a special jury shall have been struck for the trial of any issue, the talesmen shall be such as shall be impanelled upon the common jury panel to serve at the same court, if a sufficient number of such men can be found; and the king, by any one so authorized or assigned as aforesaid, and all and every the parties aforesaid, shall and may, in each of the cases aforesaid, have their respective challenges to the jurors so added and annexed, and the court shall proceed to the trial of every such issue with those jurors who were impanelled, together with the talesmen so newly added and annexed, as if all the said jurors had been returned upon the writ or precept awarded to try the issue.

Tales de circumstantibus. **(See 34 & 35 H. 8, c. 23, s. 103, as to Wales; 35 H. 8, c. 6; 4 & 5 P. & M. c. 7; 5 Eliz. c. 25; 14 Eliz. c. 9; 7 & 8 W. 3, c. 32.)**

XXXVIII. And be it further enacted, that if any man, having been duly summoned to attend on any kind of jury in any of the courts in England or Wales hereinbefore mentioned, shall not attend in pursuance of such summons, or being thrice called shall not answer to his name, or if any such man, or any talesman, after having been called, shall be present but not appear, or after his appearance shall wilfully withdraw himself from the presence of the court, the court shall set such fine upon every such man or talesmen so making default (unless some reasonable excuse shall be proved by oath or affidavit), as the court shall think meet: provided always, that where any viewer, having been duly summoned to attend on any jury, shall make default as aforesaid, the court is hereby authorized and required to set upon such viewer (unless some reasonable excuse shall be proved as aforesaid) a fine to the amount of ten pounds at the least, and as much more as the court under the circumstances of the particular case shall think proper.

Fine on jurors making default. (See 7 & 8 W. 3, c. 32; 3 G. 2, c. 25, s. 13.)

XXXIX. And be it further enacted, that every sheriff and other minister, to whom the return of juries shall belong, shall be and is hereby indemnified for impanelling and returning any man named in the jurors' book, although he may not be qualified or liable to serve on juries: and that if any sheriff or other such minister shall wilfully impanel and return

Sheriff indemnified in returning any person whose name is in the list. (See 7 & 8

CHAP. XVII. SECT. I.

W. 3, c. 32, s. 6.) If he returns one not in the list; (see 3 Geo. 2, c. 25, s. 3); or if clerk of assize records appearances when the party did not appear, to be fined.

any man to serve on any jury before any of the courts in England or Wales hereinbefore mentioned (except on the grand jury at any assizes or great sessions), such man's name not being inserted in the jurors' book for the current year, or, if such book has not been delivered, then in the jurors' book last delivered, or if any clerk of assize, associate, prothonotary, clerk of the peace, or other officer of any of the courts aforesaid, shall wilfully record the appearance of any man so summoned and returned, who did not really appear, in every such case the court shall and may, upon examination in a summary way, set such fine upon such sheriff, minister, clerk of assize, associate, prothonotary, clerk of the peace, or other officer offending, as the court shall think meet.

Sheriff, &c. to register the names of jurors who have served. (See 3 G. 2, c. 25, s. 5.)

XL. And be it further enacted, that the sheriff or his under-sheriff shall from time to time register alphabetically, in proper columns, to be prepared in the jurors' book for that purpose, the services of such men as shall be summoned and shall attend to serve as jurors on trials, before any court of assize or *nisi prius*, oyer and terminer, or gaol delivery, or in the said courts of the said counties palatine or great sessions, and also the times of their services; and every man so summoned, and having duly attended or served until discharged by the court, shall (upon application by him made to such sheriff or under-sheriff, before he shall depart from the place of trial) receive a certificate testifying such his service, which certificate the sheriff or under-sheriff is hereby required to give on payment of one shilling: provided always, that nothing herein contained shall extend to any grand jurors or special jurors.

Clerk of the peace to make out a list of all who serve at sessions on grand or petty juries, and transmit the same to sheriff to register.

Certificates of services to be given by the clerk of the peace.

XLI. And be it further enacted, that the clerk of the peace, at every sessions of the peace to be holden for any county, riding or division in England or Wales, shall make out a list of such men as shall be summoned and shall attend to serve on any grand jury or petty jury at such sessions, together with their respective places of abode and additions, and the date of their services, and shall, within twenty days after the close of every such sessions, transmit such list to the sheriff or under-sheriff of the county, who is hereby required forthwith to register the names of the men included in such list in the proper columns of the jurors' book for that purpose, together with the date of their services; and every man so summoned, and having duly attended or served until discharged by the court of sessions, shall, upon application by him made to such clerk of the peace, before he shall depart from the place where the sessions are holden, receive a certificate testifying such his service, which certificate the said clerk of the peace is hereby required to give, on payment of one shilling.

Jurors not to be summoned again within certain periods to assizes. (See 3 G. 2, c. 25, s. 4; 4 G. 2, c. 7.)

Nor to quarter sessions.

XLII. And be it further enacted, that no man shall be returned as a juror to serve at any session of *nisi prius* or of gaol delivery, in the county of Middlesex, who has served as a juror at either of such sessions in the said county, in either of the two terms or vacations next immediately preceding, and has the sheriff's certificate of having so served; and no man shall be returned as a juror to serve on trials before any court of assize, *nisi prius*, oyer and terminer, or gaol delivery, or any of the said courts of the three counties palatine, or the said great sessions, who has served as a juror at any of such courts within one year before, in Wales, or in the counties of Hereford, Cambridge, Huntingdon or Rutland, or four years before in the county of York, or two years before in any other county, and has the sheriff's certificate of having so served; and no man shall be returned to serve upon any grand jury or petty jury, at any sessions of the peace to be holden for any county, riding or division in England or Wales, who has served as a juror at any such session within one year before, in Wales, or in the counties of Hereford, Cambridge, Huntingdon or Rutland, or two years before in any other county, and has the certificate of the clerk of the peace of having so served; and if any sheriff or other minister shall wilfully transgress in any of the cases aforesaid, the court may and is hereby required, on examination and proof of every such offence in a summary way, to set such fine upon every such offender as the court shall think meet: provided, that nothing herein contained shall extend to grand jurors at the assizes or great sessions, or to special jurors.

No money to be taken to excuse persons serving. (See 3 G. 2, c. 25, s. 6.) None to be summoned but those named in the warrant.

XLIII. And be it further enacted, that no sheriff, under-sheriff, coroner, elisor, bailiff, or other officer or person whatsoever, shall, directly or indirectly, take or receive any money or other reward, or promise of money or reward, to excuse any man from serving or from being summoned to serve on juries, or under any such colour or pretence; and that no bailiff or other officer appointed by any sheriff, under-sheriff, coroner, or elisor, to summon juries, shall summon any man to serve thereon, other than those whose names are specified in a warrant or mandate, signed by such sheriff, under-sheriff, coroner, or elisor, and directed to such bailiff, or other officer; and if any sheriff, under-sheriff, coroner, elisor, bailiff, or other officer, shall wilfully transgress in any of the cases aforesaid, or shall summon any juror, not being a special juror, less than ten days before the day on which he is to attend, or shall summon any special juror less than three days before the day on which he is to attend, except in the cases hereinbefore excepted, the court of assize, nisi prius, oyer and terminer, gaol delivery, great sessions, or superior court of the said counties palatine, or court of sessions of the peace, within whose jurisdiction the offence shall have been committed, may and is hereby required, on examination and proof of such offence, in a summary way, to set such a fine upon every person so offending, as the court shall think meet, according to the nature of the offence.

Penalties on high constables for neglecting to issue precepts, &c.

XLIV. And be it further enacted, that if any high constable within the meaning of this act shall, for fourteen days after the warrant of the clerk of the peace shall be served on him, or left at his usual place of abode, refuse or neglect to issue and deliver his precept as hereinbefore directed, to the churchwardens and overseers of any parish, or to the overseers of any township within his constablewick; or shall in like manner refuse or neglect to issue and deliver his precept to the churchwardens and overseers of any parish, or to the overseers of any township, where such parish or township extends into any other hundred, lathe, wapentake, or other district besides his own, either in the same or a different county, (provided the principal church of such parish or township shall be situate within his own hundred, lathe, wapentake, or other like district,) or shall refuse or neglect in any of the foregoing cases to annex to the respective precepts such a number of the forms of return as he shall *bonâ fide* deem sufficient, or to deliver such additional number as may be demanded of him by any churchwarden or overseer as aforesaid (provided he has such additional number in his possession), or in case of his not so having them, shall refuse or neglect to apply forthwith to the clerk of the peace for such additional number, and to deliver the same to the party so demanding within three days after his receipt thereof; or shall on due notice refuse or neglect to attend at any such petty sessions, or such adjournment thereof as aforesaid, or to receive any list or lists there tendered by the justices present, or to deliver the same to the quarter sessions next holden for the county, riding, or division, at the time and in the manner

CHAP. XVII. SECT. I.

hereinbefore directed, or shall make any alteration in any such list after his receipt thereof; every such high constable offending in any of the foregoing cases, shall for every such offence forfeit a sum not exceeding ten pounds, nor less than forty shillings, at the discretion of the justice before whom he shall be convicted.

Penalties on churchwardens and overseers for neglecting to make out lists, &c.

XLV. And be it further enacted, that if any churchwarden or overseer of any parish, or any overseer of any township within the meaning of this act, shall refuse or neglect (unless prevented by sickness) to assist in making out any list required by this act, so that the same shall not be made out at the time and in the manner hereinbefore directed; or shall wilfully omit out of such list any man whose name ought to be inserted therein, or shall wilfully insert therein the name of any man who ought to be omitted, or shall take any money or other reward for omitting or inserting any man whatsoever, or shall wilfully insert therein a wrong description of the name, place of abode, title, quality, calling, business, or the nature of the qualification of any man; or shall refuse or neglect, in case the number of forms of return delivered by the high constable shall be insufficient, to apply to the high constable for a sufficient number, so that the list may be made out at the time and in the manner hereinbefore directed; or shall refuse or neglect to fix a copy of such list duly signed, or to subjoin thereto such notice as hereinbefore required, on the principal door of any church, chapel, or other public place of religious worship within their respective parishes or townships, on any of the Sundays on which the same ought to be so fixed; or shall refuse to allow any inhabitant of their respective parishes or townships to inspect such list or a true copy thereof gratis, at any reasonable time during the three weeks hereinbefore mentioned; or shall, on due notice, refuse or neglect to produce such list at such petty sessions as aforesaid, or to answer on oath such questions touching the same as shall there be put, or to attend at such petty sessions, or any such adjournment thereof as aforesaid; or shall refuse to allow the said petty sessions, or any justice of the peace, upon due request, to inspect or make any extracts from the poor rate of any parish or township within their respective divisions, for the purposes hereinbefore mentioned, such rate being in the custody of the party so refusing; every such churchwarden or overseer offending in any of the foregoing cases shall, for every such offence, forfeit a sum not exceeding ten pounds nor less than forty shillings, at the discretion of the justice before whom he shall be convicted; and the justice, before whom such offender shall be convicted of any such offence of wrongful insertion or omission, shall forthwith, in writing under his hand, certify the same to the clerk of the peace of the county, riding, or division in which the man or men so wrongfully omitted or inserted shall reside, and the said clerk of the peace shall cause the list in which such wrongful insertion or omission shall have occurred to be corrected according to such certificate, and shall also give notice thereof to the sheriff or under-sheriff, who shall correct the jurors' book accordingly.

Penalties on clerks of peace and sheriffs neglecting their duty.

XLVI. And be it further enacted, that if any clerk of the peace shall refuse or neglect to cause a sufficient number, either of warrants, precepts, or forms of return, to be printed in the manner hereinbefore directed, or shall refuse or neglect to issue and deliver to any high constable within the meaning of this act, the warrant and precepts as hereinbefore directed, or to annex to the same such a number of the forms of return as he shall *boná fide* deem sufficient, or to deliver to any high constable such additional number thereof as he may apply for within three days after such application; or shall refuse or neglect to provide or prepare a jurors' book within the time or in the manner and form hereinbefore prescribed, or to deliver the same to the sheriff or under-sheriff of the county within the time hereinbefore prescribed, or to give notice to the sheriff or under-sheriff of any wrongful insertion or omission, certified to him by any justice of the peace as aforesaid, or to deliver to any man who shall have been summoned and have duly attended or served as a grand juror, or petty juror, at the sessions of the peace, a certificate of such man's service, on his application and payment as aforesaid, or to transmit to the sheriff or under-sheriff a list of the men who shall have been so summoned and have so attended or served, within the time and in the manner hereinbefore directed; or if any clerk of any such petty sessions, to be holden as aforesaid, shall refuse or neglect to give due notice thereof to any high constable, or to the churchwardens and overseers of any parish, or to the overseers of any township within such division: or if any sheriff or under-sheriff of a county shall make or cause to be made any alteration whatsoever in the list of jurors contained in the jurors' book, except in consequence of the conviction of the churchwarden or overseer hereinbefore provided for; or if any sheriff or under-sheriff of a county, or any sheriff or secondary of London, shall neglect or refuse to provide or prepare a list of special jurors in the manner and within the time hereinbefore prescribed, or shall wilfully write or cause to be written therein the name of any person not qualified, or shall wilfully omit thereout the name of any person duly qualified as a special juror, or shall neglect or refuse to write or cause to be written the several numbers contained in such list upon distinct pieces of parchment or card, in the manner and within the time hereinbefore prescribed, or shall subtract or destroy, or by any default or neglect lose, any of the said pieces of parchment or card, or shall neglect or refuse, upon discovery of such loss, to supply the same within five days; or if any sheriff or under-sheriff of a county shall refuse or neglect to prepare, or keep for inspection as aforesaid, a copy of the panel in the cases hereinbefore provided for, or to register the service of any juror, as hereinbefore directed, or to deliver to any man who shall have been summoned, and have duly attended or served as a juror at any court of assize, nisi prius, oyer and terminer, or gaol delivery, or in any of the said courts of the three counties palatine or great sessions, a certificate of such man's service, on his application and payment as aforesaid; or shall refuse or neglect, within ten days after the next succeeding sheriff shall be sworn into or have entered upon office, to deliver over to him, as well all the jurors' books and lists that shall be made or prepared in the year of his sheriffalty, as also all such other like books and lists as were prepared in the sheriffalty of any of his predecessors, within four years then next preceding, and which were delivered over to him by any of his predecessors; every such clerk of the peace, clerk of the petty sessions, sheriff or under-sheriff, sheriff of London or secondary, offending in any of the said cases, shall for every such offence forfeit the sum of fifty pounds, one moiety whereof shall be to the use of his majesty, his heirs and successors, and the other moiety, with full costs, to such person as shall sue for the same, in any of his majesty's courts of record at Westminster, by action of debt, bill, plaint, or information, wherein no essoign, protection, or wager of law, nor more than one imparlance shall be allowed.

Juries de medietate. (See 27 Edw. 3, st. 2, c. 8; 28 Edw. 3, c. 13; 8 H. 6, c. 29.)

XLVII. Provided always, and it is hereby further enacted, that nothing herein contained shall extend or be construed to extend to deprive any alien indicted or impeached of any felony or misdemeanour, of the right

CHAP. XVII. SECT. I.

of being tried by a jury *de medietate linguæ*, but that, on the prayer of every alien so indicted or impeached, the sheriff or other proper minister shall, by command of the court, return for one half of the jury a competent number of aliens, if so many there be in the town or place where the trial is had, and if not, then so many aliens as shall be found in the same town or place, if any; and that no such alien juror shall be liable to be challenged for want of freehold or of any other qualification required by this act; but every such alien may be challenged for any other cause, in like manner as if he were qualified by this act.

Justices not to be summoned as jurors at sessions.

XLVIII. And be it further enacted, that no justice of the peace shall be summoned or impanelled as a juror, to serve at any sessions of the peace for the jurisdiction of which he is a justice.

Inhabitants of Westminster not liable to serve at Middlesex sessions (7 & 8 Will. 3, c. 32, s. 9.)

XLIX. And be it further enacted, that the inhabitants of the city and liberty of Westminster shall be and are hereby exempted from serving on any jury at the sessions of the peace for the county of Middlesex.

Qualification of jurors in liberties, cities, and boroughs, to remain as before.

Qualification in London. (See 3 Geo. 2, c. 25, s. 19.)

Repeals 11 Hen. 7, c. 21.

(3 Geo. 2, c. 25, s. 20.) Persons, unless qualified to serve as jurors in civil causes, not to be returned to serve on trials for capital offences.

L. And be it further enacted, that the qualification hereinbefore required for jurors, and the regulations for procuring lists of persons liable to serve on juries, shall not extend to the jurors or juries in any liberties, franchises, cities, boroughs, or towns corporate not being counties, or in any cities, boroughs, or towns being counties of themselves, which shall respectively possess any jurisdiction, civil or criminal; but that in all such places the sheriffs, bailiffs, or other ministers having the return of juries, shall prepare their panels in the manner heretofore accustomed: provided always, that no man shall be impanelled or returned by the sheriffs of the city of London, as a juror to try any issue joined in his Majesty's Courts of Record at Westminster, or to serve on any jury at the sessions of oyer and terminer, gaol delivery, or sessions of the peace, to be held for the said city, who shall not be a householder, or the occupier of a shop, warehouse, counting-house, chambers, or office, for the purpose of trade or commerce, within the said city, and have lands, tenements, or personal estate of the value of one hundred pounds; and that the lists of men resident in each ward of the city of London, who shall be so qualified as herein mentioned, shall be made out, with the proper quality or addition, and the place of abode of each man, by the parties who have heretofore been used and accustomed in each ward to make out the same respectively; and that such shop, warehouse, counting-house, chambers, or office as aforesaid, shall, for the purposes of this act, be respectively deemed and taken to be the place of abode of every occupier thereof: provided also, that no man shall be impanelled or returned to serve on any jury for the trial of any capital offence in any county, city or place, who shall not be qualified to serve as a juror in civil causes within the same county, city or place; and the same matter and cause being alleged by way of challenge, and so found, shall be admitted and taken as a principal challenge; and the person so challenged shall and may be examined, on oath, of the truth of the said matter.

Courts of nisi prius, &c. in London may fine jurors.

LI. And be it further enacted and declared, that every court of nisi prius, oyer and terminer, gaol delivery, and sessions of the peace held for the city of London, shall and may fine any man duly summoned to attend upon any kind of jury in any of such courts respectively, and making default, or any talesman or viewer making default, in the same manner to all intents and purposes as such respective courts in England and Wales hereinbefore mentioned.

Qualification of jurors on inquests, &c.

LII. And be it further enacted, that no man shall be liable to be summoned or impanelled to serve as a juror in any county in England or

Wales, or in London, upon any inquest or inquiry to be taken or made by or before any sheriff or coroner, by virtue of any writ of inquiry, or by or before any commissioners appointed under the great seal, or the seal of the court of Exchequer, or the seals of the courts of the said counties palatine, or the seals of the courts of great session of Wales, who shall not be duly qualified according to this act to serve as a juror upon trials at nisi prius in such county in England or Wales, or in London respectively: provided always, that nothing herein contained shall extend to any inquest to be taken by or before any coroner of a county by virtue of his office, or to any inquest or inquiry to be taken or made by or before any sheriff or coroner of any liberty, franchise, city, borough or town corporate, not being counties, or of any city, borough, or town, being respectively counties of themselves, but that the coroners in all counties, when acting otherwise than under a writ of inquiry, and the sheriffs and coroners in all such places as are herein mentioned, shall and may respectively take and make all inquests and inquiries by jurors of the same description, as they have been used and accustomed to do before the passing of this act.

Sheriffs, coroners, and commissioners may fine jurors for non-attendance.

LIII. And be it further enacted, that if any man having been duly summoned and returned to serve as a juror in any county in England or Wales, or in London, upon any inquest or inquiry before any sheriff or coroner, or before any of the commissioners aforesaid, shall not, after being opently called three times, appear and serve as such juror, every such sheriff, or in his absence the under-sheriff or secondary, and such coroner and commissioners respectively, are hereby authorized and required (unless some reasonable excuse shall be proved on oath or affidavit), to impose such fine upon every man so making default as they shall respectively think fit, not exceeding five pounds; and every such sheriff, under-sheriff, secondary, coroner and commissioners respectively, shall make out and sign a certificate, containing the christian and surname, the residence and trade or calling of every man so making default, together with the amount of the fine imposed, and the cause of such fine, and shall transmit such certificate to the clerk of the peace for the county, riding or division in which every such defaulter shall reside, on or before the first day of the quarter sessions next ensuing; and every such clerk of the peace is hereby required to copy the fines so certified on the roll on which all fines and forfeitures imposed at such quarter sessions shall be copied; and the same shall be estreated, levied, and applied in like manner, and subject to the like powers, provisions and penalties, in all respects, as if they had been part of the fines imposed at such quarter sessions.

(See 3 Geo. 4, c. 46.)

Persons summoned to serve on juries in inferior courts, not attending, (see 29 Geo. 2, c. 19,) to forfeit not more than 40s. nor less than 20s., unless the court be satisfied with the cause of absence.

LIV. And be it further enacted, that every man duly summoned and returned to serve upon any jury for the trial of any cause or criminal prosecution, to be tried in any court of record holden within the said city of London, other than the courts hereinbefore respectively mentioned, or in any other liberty, franchise, city, borough, or town, who shall not appear and serve on such jury (after being openly called three times, and on proof being made on oath of the man so making default having been duly summoned) shall forfeit and pay for every such his default such fine, not exceeding forty shillings, nor less than twenty shillings, as the court shall deem reasonable to impose, unless some just cause for such defaulter's absence shall be made appear, by oath or affidavit, to the satisfaction of the court; and that if any person on whom such fine shall be imposed shall refuse to pay the same to the person who shall be authorized by the court to receive the same, it shall be lawful for such court

CHAP. XVII. SECT. I.

Fine leviable by distress and sale.

then, or at its next sitting, and the same is hereby authorized and required, by order of the court, signed by the proper officer thereof, to cause every such fine to be levied by distress and sale of the goods and chattels of the person on whom such fine shall have been imposed: and the overplus money, if any, which shall remain after payment of such fine, and deducting the reasonable charges of such distress and sale, shall be rendered to the person whose goods and chattels shall have been so distrained and sold; and that every fine which shall be so imposed, shall, when received or levied, be paid by the person who shall receive or levy the same to the proper officer of the liberty, franchise, city, borough or town in which the court was holden wherein such fine was imposed, to be applied to such uses as issues set on jurors, or other fines set in courts holden within such liberty, franchise, city, borough or town, are by charter, prescription, or usage, applicable.

Fine to be paid to the proper officer of the court, to be disposed of as other fines of court.

How fines and penalties shall be recovered and applied.

LV. And be it further enacted, that all fines to be imposed under this act by any of the king's courts of record at Westminster, or any of the superior courts, civil or criminal, of the three counties palatine, or by any court of assize, nisi prius, oyer and terminer, or gaol delivery, or by any court of sessions of the peace in England, or by any court of great sessions or sessions of the peace in Wales, shall be levied and applied in the same manner as any other fines imposed by the same court; and that all other penalties hereby created (for which no other remedy is given) shall, on conviction of the offender before any one justice of the peace within his jurisdiction, be levied, unless such penalty be forthwith paid, by distress and sale of the offender's goods and chattels, by warrant under the hand and seal of such justice, who is hereby authorized to hear and examine witnesses on oath or affirmation on any complaint, and to determine the same, and to mitigate the penalty, if he shall see fit, to the extent of one moiety thereof; and all penalties, the application whereof is not hereinbefore particularly directed, shall be paid to the complainant; and for want of sufficient distress, the offender shall be committed by warrant under the hand and seal of such justice, to the common gaol or house of correction, for such term not exceeding six calendar months, as such justice shall think proper, unless such penalty be sooner paid.

LVI. And for the more easy and speedy conviction of offenders against this act, be it further enacted, that the justice before whom any person shall be convicted of any offence against this act, shall and may cause the conviction to be drawn up in the following form of words, or in any other form of words to the same effect, as the case shall happen, videlicet:—

Form of conviction.

"Be it remembered, that on —— in the year of our lord ——, at ——, A. B. is convicted before me, C. D., one of his majesty's justices of the peace for the —— of ——, for that he the said A. B. did [*specifying the offence, and the time and place where the same was committed, as the case shall be*], and the said A. B. is for his said offence adjudged by me the said justice to forfeit and pay the sum of ——.

"Given under my hand and seal, the day and year first above-mentioned."

Conviction not to be quashed for want of form.

LVII. And be it further enacted, that no such conviction shall be quashed for want of form, or be removed or removable by certiorari, or by any other writ or process whatsoever, into any of his majesty's courts of record at Westminster; and that where any distress shall be made for any penalty to be levied by virtue of this act, the distress itself shall not be deemed to be unlawful, nor the party making the same be deemed a trespasser, on account of any defect or want of form in the summons, conviction, warrant of distress, or other proceedings relating thereto, nor shall such party be deemed a trespasser ab initio, on account of any irregularity which shall be afterwards done by him; but the person aggrieved by such irregularity shall and may recover full satisfaction for the special damage (if any) in an action upon the case, first giving notice in writing of the cause of action to the opposite party one calendar month before the commencement of such action; but no plaintiff shall recover in any action for such irregularity, if tender of sufficient amends shall have been made before such action brought, or if a sufficient sum of money shall have been paid into court after such action brought, by or on behalf of the party distraining.

Persons sued for any thing done in pursuance of this act may plead the general issue.

LVIII. And be it further enacted, that if any suit or action shall be prosecuted against any person, for any thing done in pursuance of this act, such person may plead the general issue, and give this act and the special matter in evidence at any trial to be had thereupon; and if a verdict should pass for the defendant, or the plaintiff shall become nonsuit, or discontinue his or her action after issue joined, or if, upon demurrer or otherwise, judgment shall be given against the plaintiff, the defendant shall recover double costs, and have the like remedy for the same as any defendant hath by law in other cases; and though a verdict shall be given for the plaintiff in any such action, such plaintiff shall not have costs against the defendant, unless the judge before whom the trial shall be shall certify his approbation of the action, and of the verdict obtained thereupon.

Venue to be laid in the county where the fact is committed.

LIX. And be it further enacted, that all actions, suits and prosecutions to be commenced against any person for any thing done in pursuance of this act, shall be laid and tried in the county where the fact was committed, and shall be commenced within six calendar months after the fact committed, and not otherwise; and that notice in writing of such cause of action shall be given to the defendant or defendants one calendar month at least before the commencement of the action.

Writs of attaint to be abolished; and concealments of inquests.

LX. And be it further enacted, that from and after the passing of this act, it shall not be lawful either for the king, or any one on his behalf, or for any party or parties, in any case whatsoever, to commence or prosecute any writ of attaint against any jury or jurors, for the verdict by them given, or against the party or parties who shall have judgment upon such verdict; and that no inquest shall be taken to inquire of the concealments of other inquests; but that all such attaints and inquests shall henceforth cease, become void, and be utterly abolished; any law, statute or usage to the contrary notwithstanding.

Embracers and corrupt jurors punishable by fine and imprisonment.

LXI. Provided always, and be it further enacted and declared, that, notwithstanding any thing herein contained, every person who shall be guilty of the offence of embracery, and every juror who shall wilfully or corruptly consent thereto, shall and may be respectively proceeded against by indictment or information, and be punished by fine and imprisonment, in like manner as every such person and juror might have been before the passing of this act.

CHAP. XVII.
SECT. I.

5 & 6 Will. IV. c. 76.

An Act to provide for the Regulation of Municipal Corporations in England and Wales.

Who to be jurors.

CXXI. And be it enacted, that every person, being a burgess of any borough wherein there shall be a separate court of sessions of the peace, or a court of record for the trial of civil actions, (unless he shall be exempt or disqualified otherwise than in respect of property from serving on juries by virtue of an act passed in the sixth year of the reign of King George the Fourth, intituled "An Act for consolidating and amending the Laws relative to Jurors and Juries,") shall be qualified and liable to serve on grand juries in such borough, and also upon juries for the trial of all issues joined in any court of quarter sessions of the peace, and in any court of record for the trial of civil actions triable within the borough of which such person shall be a burgess; and the clerk of the peace of every such borough shall give public notice of the time and place of holding every such quarter sessions of the peace, ten days at the least before the holding thereof, and shall, seven days at the least before the holding thereof, cause to be summoned a sufficient number of persons, being qualified and liable as aforesaid, to serve as grand jurors at such sessions; and the clerk of the peace and registrar of the court of record respectively shall also cause to be summoned not less than thirty-six nor more than sixty persons so qualified and liable as aforesaid to serve as jurors at every such sessions, and at the holding of every such court of record for the trial of causes, in case there shall be any cause then to be tried; and such summons shall be made by showing to the person to be summoned, or in case he shall be absent from the usual place of his abode by leaving with some person therein inhabiting, notice under the hand of such clerk of the peace or registrar respectively containing the substance of such summons; and such clerk of the peace shall make out a list of the names of such persons so summoned as grand jurors, and the clerk of the peace and registrar respectively shall also make out a panel of such persons so summoned other than grand jurors, and such list and panel shall respectively contain therein the Christian names and surnames, places of abode, and descriptions of the several persons therein named; and if any person, having been duly summoned to attend on any jury, shall not attend in pursuance of such summons, or, being thrice called, shall not answer to his name, or after his appearance wilfully withdraw himself from the presence of the court, the court shall impose such fine upon every person so making default (unless some reasonable excuse shall be proved to the satisfaction of the court) as the court shall think meet; and if any person on whom such fine shall be imposed shall refuse to pay the same to the person who shall be authorized by the court to receive the same, it shall be lawful for the court, then or at its next sitting, by order of the court, signed by the clerk of the peace or registrar respectively, to cause to be levied, by distress and sale of the goods of the person on whom such fine shall have been imposed, every such fine, and the reasonable charges of such distress and sale; and every fine so received shall be paid to the treasurer of the borough, to be by him carried to the account of the borough fund hereinbefore mentioned: provided nevertheless, that no person shall be summoned to serve as a juror at such sessions or court of record oftener than once in one year.

6 G. 4, c. 50.

Summoning of jurors, &c.

Fine on jurors for non-attendance.

Members of the counsel, &c. exempt from serving on juries; burgesses of boroughs which have quarter sessions exempt from juries of county quarter sessions.

CXXII. And be it enacted, that after the passing of this act every member of the council for the time being of every borough, and every justice assigned to keep the peace therein, and the treasurer and town clerk for the time being of every such borough, shall be exempt and disqualified from serving on any jury summoned within such borough respectively, and exempt from serving on any jury summoned to serve in the county wherein such borough is situate; and all burgesses of every borough in and for which a separate court of quarter sessions of the peace shall be holden shall be exempt from serving on any jury summoned for the trial of issues joined in any court of general or quarter sessions of the peace in the county wherein such borough is situate.

All chartered exemptions from serving on juries abolished.

CXXIII. And be it enacted, that after the passing of this act no person in any borough shall continue to be exempt from serving on juries in any of the king's courts of record at Westminster, or in the superior courts, civil or criminal, of the counties palatine of Lancaster and Durham, or in any court of assize, *nisi prius*, oyer and terminer, gaol delivery, or sessions of the peace, or in any other of the king's courts, by virtue of any writ, grant, charter, prescription or otherwise; and so much of an act made in the sixth year of the reign of his late majesty King George the Fourth, intituled "An Act for consolidating and amending the Laws relative to Jurors," as provides that all persons in any borough exempt from serving upon juries in any of the courts aforesaid, by virtue of any prescription, charter, grant or writ, shall continue to have and enjoy such exemption in as ample a manner as before the passing of that act, and shall not be inserted in the lists thereafter mentioned, shall be and the same is hereby repealed.

6 G. 4, c. 50. in part repealed.

---

2 & 3 Vict. c. 71.

An Act for regulating the Police Courts in the Metropolis.

Magistrates, &c. exempt from serving on juries.

IV. And be it enacted, that the said magistrates (appointed to the police courts of the metropolis), and their clerks, ushers, doorkeepers and messengers, shall be exempt and disqualified from being returned and from serving on any juries or inquests whatsoever, and shall not be inserted in any lists of men qualified and liable to serve as jurors.

---

9 & 10 Vict. c. 95.

An Act for the more easy Recovery of Small Debts and Demands in England.

Actions may be tried by a jury when parties require it.

LXX. And be it enacted, that, in all actions where the amount claimed shall exceed five pounds, it shall be lawful for the plaintiff or defendant to require a jury to be summoned to try the said action; and in all actions where the amount claimed shall not exceed five pounds it shall be lawful for the judge, in his discretion, on the application of either of the parties, to order that such action be tried by a jury; and in every case such jury shall be summoned according to the provisions hereinafter contained: provided always, that the party requiring a jury to be summoned shall give to the clerk of the court, or leave at his office, such notice thereof as shall be directed by the rules made for regulating the practice of the court as hereinafter provided; and the said clerk shall cause notice of such demand of a jury, made either by the plaintiff or defendant, to be communicated to the other party to the said action, either

CHAP. XVII. SECT. I.

by post, or by causing the same to be delivered at his usual place of abode or business; but it shall not be necessary for either party to prove on the trial that such notice was communicated to the other party by the clerk.

Who shall be jurors.

LXXII. And be it enacted, that the sheriff of every county, and the high bailiffs of Westminster and Southwark, shall cause to be delivered to the clerk of the court a list of persons qualified and liable to serve as jurors in the courts of assize and *nisi prius* for their county, city and borough respectively, within fourteen days from the receipt of the jury book from the clerk of the peace of the county or other officer, each list containing only the names of persons residing within the jurisdiction of the court, for which list the said sheriffs and high bailiffs shall be entitled to receive out of the general fund of the court a fee after the rate of twopence for every folio of seventy-two words; and whenever a jury shall be required the clerk of the court shall cause so many of the persons named in the list as shall be needed in the opinion of the judge to be summoned to attend the court at a time and place to be mentioned in the summons, and shall administer or cause to be administered to such of them as shall be impanelled to try any cause or causes an oath to give true verdicts according to the evidence; and the persons so summoned shall attend at the court at the time mentioned in the summons, and in default of attendance shall forfeit such sum of money as the judge shall direct, not being more than five pounds for each default; and the delivery of such summons to the person whose attendance is required on such jury, or delivery thereof to his wife or servant, or any inmate at his usual place of abode, trading or dealing, shall be deemed good service; provided always, that no person shall be summoned or compelled to serve on such jury more than twice within one year, or who shall have been summoned and shall have attended upon any jury at the assizes, or any court of *nisi prius*, or at the central criminal court for the same county, within six calendar months next before the delivery of such summons.

Number of the jury.

LXXIII. And be it enacted, that whenever there are any jury trials five jurymen shall be empanelled and sworn, as occasion shall require, to give their verdicts in the causes which shall be brought before them in the said court, and being once sworn shall not need to be re-sworn in each trial; and either of the parties to any such cause shall be entitled to his lawful challenge against all or any of the said jurors in like manner as he would be entitled in any superior court; and the jurymen so sworn shall be required to give an unanimous verdict.

SECT. 2.

Warrant to summon Nisi Prius Jury at Assizes.

[First copy the jurors' names, places of abode, and descriptions; then proceed as follows:]

N. (*to wit.*) A. B., esquire, sheriff of the said county, to J. S., my bailiff, greeting: You are hereby required to warn and summon the several persons above-named, personally to be and appear upon the jury, at the next assizes or general gaol delivery to be held for this county, at the castle of C., on Saturday, the —— day of —— instant, then and there to try the several issues between the parties, on pain of one hundred shillings a man. Hereof fail not. Given under the seal of my office, this —— day of ——, 18—.

(*Seal of office.*) By the sheriff.

Warrant to summon Crown Jury.

The same as before, only instead of "to try the several issues between the parties," *say* "to try such matters and things as shall be given them in charge."

Warrant to summon a Special Jury on a View.

N. (*to wit.*) A. B., esquire, sheriff of the said county, to ——, my bailiff, greeting: You are hereby required to warn and summon the several persons undernamed, personally to be and appear at the next assizes to be held for this county, on Saturday, the —— day of ——, at the castle of N., to try the said cause (*k*): *and in the meantime the said persons are desired and requested to be and appear at the house of Mr.* ——, *known by the sign of* ——, *in* ——, *at* —— *o'clock in the* —— *noon of the same day, where they will be attended by* —— *and* ——, *persons appointed by the court to show them the premises in question:* and hereof fail not at your peril. Given under the seal of my office, this —— day of ——, 18—.

(*Seal of office.*) By the sheriff.

Return of the Assize Precept.

I have caused to be publicly proclaimed throughout my whole bailiwick, that all who shall prosecute against those prisoners be then and there to prosecute against them, as shall be just. I have also given notice to all justices of the peace, mayors, coroners, escheators, stewards, and also to all chief constables and bailiffs of every hundred and liberty within my county, that they be then and there, in their own person, with their rolls, records, indictments, and other remembrances, to do those things which to their offices in this behalf appertain to be done, as is within commanded me. The residue of the execution of this precept appears in certain schedules to the same annexed.

A. B., esquire, sheriff.

First Panel.

Names of the grand jury to inquire for our lord the king, for the body of the said county.

1. The Right Honourable Lord Viscount R.
2. H. B., of A., esquire.

&c. A. B., esquire, sheriff.

Second Panel.

N. (*to wit.*) Names of the jury to try traverses, and the prisoners at the bar.

1. A. B., of ——.
2. C. D., of ——. } Summoning officer, S. S.

Each of the said jurors is by himself separately attached by pledges.—John Doe and Richard Roe.

A. B., esquire, sheriff.

(*k*) The words in italics not to be inserted, unless there is to be a view.

Third Panel.

N. (*to wit.*) Names of the jury to try the issues joined, &c. &c.

1. A. B., of ——.
2. C. D., of ——. A. B., esquire, sheriff.

Fourth Panel.

N. (*to wit.*) A calendar of the justices of the peace of our lord the king, mayors, coroners, bailiffs of liberties and hundreds, and constables of hundreds, in the county of N., summoned to be at the assizes and general session of oyer and terminer and gaol delivery, to be holden at ——, in the said county, the —— day of ——, in the —— year of the reign, &c. And the names of the prisoners being in the gaol of the said county, together with their attachments.

The names of the justices.
A. B., of, &c.
C. D., &c.

Names of the mayors.
R. J., mayor of, &c.

Names of the coroners.
C. D., of, &c. gent.
E. F., of, &c. gent.

Names of bailiffs of liberties.
C. D., high bailiff of D.

Names of the constables of hundreds.
Hundred of H. C. D., of, &c.
Hundred of O. E. F., of, &c.

Names of the officers.
Hundred of H. J. K., of, &c.
Hundred of O. L. M., of, &c.

Names of prisoners in the gaol.
1. A. B., committed by ——, charged with ——.

A. B., esquire, sheriff.

Return of the Assize Venire, which Venire is under the Hand and Seals of the Judges.

By virtue of this precept to me directed, I have caused to come before the justices within named, and their fellows, justices within mentioned, twenty-four as well knights as other good and lawful men of my bailiwick, to do and receive all things which, on behalf of our lady the now queen, shall be then and there enjoined them, as within I am commanded. The residue of the execution of this precept appears in a certain panel to the same annexed.

A. B., esquire, sheriff.

Return of a Hab. Corp. Jur., where a View was directed, and none of the Jury appeared.

I humbly certify that, by virtue of this writ to me directed, I summoned Sir C. D. &c., being the first twelve jurors within named, personally to be and appear at the time and place within mentioned, and to do as the within writ commands and requires; and I further certify, that I attended at the time and place within mentioned, to cause the place in question to be shown to six or more of the first named twelve jurors, but the above named jurors or any one of them did not appear, so that I could not further proceed on the said view of the place in question, as this writ commands and requires. The residue of the execution of this writ appears in a certain schedule hereunto annexed.

A. B. esquire, sheriff.

Return on a Distringas Juratores, where a View was directed, and none of the Jurors appeared.

I humbly certify, that by virtue of this writ to me directed, I caused to be distrained Sir C. D., &c. &c., being the first twelve jurors within named, personally to be and appear, &c. (*as in the last precedent*).

Return of Distringas Juratores, where a View is directed.

By virtue of this writ to me directed, I have caused the place in question to be shown to (*here name the jury that attend*), in the panel hereunto annexed named, at such time and in such manner and form as the writ commands and requires. The residue of the execution of this writ appears in the said panel hereunto annexed.

A. B. esquire, sheriff.

Where no View is directed.

The execution of this writ appears in a certain panel hereunto annexed.

A. B. esquire, sheriff.

Letter of Attorney to carry the Sentence of the Law into execution.

To all to whom these presents shall come, I, A. B., of ——, in the county of N., esquire, sheriff of the said county, do by these presents appoint, depute, authorise, and empower G. H. of M., in the said county, gentleman, for me, and in my stead and place, to execute the sentence passed at the late assizes held for the said county, upon T. Y., and do hereby delegate to the said G. H. all the power and authority of my office, in anywise necessary or expedient in the premises, as fully and in every respect as if I was personally present and did the same; and I require and command all my officers and ministers to be aiding and assisting the said G. H. in all things tending to the due execution of the said sentence. In witness whereof I have hereunto set my hand and seal of my office this —— day of ——, A. D. 18—.

(Sealed and delivered, &c.) (*Seal of office.*)

SECT. 3.

Warrant to summons a Sessions Jury.

[Copy jurors' names, places of abode, and descriptions.]

N. (*to wit.*) A. B. esquire, sheriff of the said county, to J. S., my bailiff, greeting: You are hereby required to warn and summon the

CHAP. XVII. SECT. III. several gentlemen above named personally to be and appear upon the petit (*or* " grand"] jury, at the next general sessions of the peace to be holden in and for the county, at ——, on the —— day of —— next; then and there to inquire of and concerning such things as shall be given them in charge, on pain of one hundred shillings. Given under the seal of my office this —— day of ——.

(*Seal of office.*) By the sheriff.

Return to Sessions Precept.

The execution of this precept appears in certain schedules hereunto annexed.

First Panel.

Calendar of the names of the coroners, &c. (*the same as the calendar of justices, &c., annexed as a panel to assize precept, ante, p.* 532, *omitting the names of justices and mayors.*)

A. B. esquire, sheriff.

Second Panel.

N. (*to wit.*) The names of the grand jury to inquire for our lady the queen for the body of the said county.

(*Names of persons.*) (*Summoning officers*).
J. L. G. H.

Third Panel.

N. (*to wit.*) The names of the jury to try the traverses and the prisoners at the bar.

A. B., of &c., carpenter }
C. D., of &c., grocer } (*Summoning officer*, J. L.)

Each of the said jurors is attached by pledges.

John Doe }
Richard Roe } A. B. esquire, sheriff.

CHAP. XVIII.—Sect. 2.

Form of Admission in Declaration in the County Court, in order to reduce Damages under 40s.

[*In the counts stating the sum due, at the end, each count concludes thus:*] out of which said sum of 20*l.* the said plaintiff acknowledges to have received of and from the said defendant the sum of 18*l.* 5*s.*, and the said defendant from the same doth freely here in court acquit and discharge.

Warrant upon a Justicies.

N. (*to wit.*) A. B. esquire, sheriff of the county aforesaid, to I. K., my bailiff, greeting: By virtue of her majesty's writ of *justicies*, to me directed and delivered, I command you that you summon E. F. personally to be and appear at my next county court, to be holden at A., on

Thurday next, the —— day of —— instant, to answer C. D. *in a plea of trespass on the case upon promises, to the damage of the said C. D. of* £—— (*or* " in a plea of debt"), as is alleged, and have you there this precept. Given under the seal of my office.

(*Seal of office.*) By the sheriff.

Mr. ——, attorney for the plaintiff.

Summons upon the above Warrant.

By virtue of her majesty's writ of *justicies*, to the sheriff of the county of N. directed and delivered, and by virtue of the said sheriff's precept to me directed, I do hereby summon you that you be and appear personally before the said sheriff, at his usual county court, to be holden at A., on Thursday the —— day of —— instant, to answer C. D. in a plea of trespass on the case upon promises, to the damage of the said C. D. of £——, as is alleged. Dated this —— day of —— 18—.

Mr. ——, attorney for the plaintiff.

To E. F., the defendant.

A County Court Execution.

N. (*to wit.*) A. B. esquire, sheriff of the county aforesaid, to J. S., my bailiff, greeting: You are hereby commanded to levy on the goods and chattels of C. D., within my said county, the sum of £——, which E. F. in my county court recovered against the said C. D. for damages which the said E. F. sustained by occasion of not performing certain promises to the said E. F. by the said C. D., at A., in my county, whereof he is convicted, and have you the said sum at my next county court to be holden in and for my said county, to render to the said E. F. for damages aforesaid. Dated the —— day of ——, in the year of our Lord 18—.

(*Seal of office.*) By the sheriff.

A County Court Subpœna.

N. (*to wit.*) A. B. esquire, sheriff of the county aforesaid, to J. S. and E. K., greeting: I command you, and each of you (all excuses whatsoever being laid aside), that you and every of you be and personally appear at my next county court, to be held at A., on Thursday, the —— day of —— next, to testify the truth according to your knowledge, in a certain action there depending between E. F., plaintiff, and C. D., defendant, in a plea of trespass on the case upon promises, and this by no means you omit, under the penalty of one hundred shillings. Given under the seal of my office this —— day of ——, in the year of our Lord 18—.

(*Subpœna.*) By the sheriff.

Return indorsed on the Re. Fa. Lo. (*l*).

By virtue of this writ to me directed, I have in my full county court of N., held at A., in my said county, caused the plaint to be recorded, which is

(*l*) The return to a writ of *accedas ad curiam, pone,* or writ of false judgment, is made in the same manner as the return to a *re. fa. lo.*, varying of course with the terms of the writ, and annexing the proceedings in a schedule to the writ.

CHAP. XVIII. SECT. II.

in the same court between the parties within written, whereof mention is within made, which said plaint appears to a certain schedule to this writ annexed, and that record I have before the justices within written, at the day and place within mentioned, under my seal, and under the seals of J. B., E. L., T. S., and J. W., four lawful knights of the said county, of those who were present at the said record; and I have prefixed the same day to the said parties, that then they may be there ready to proceed in the said plaint as shall be just, as is within commanded me.

A. B. esquire, sheriff.

Schedule annexed to the Re. Fa. Lo., written on a square piece of unstamped Parchment.

N. (*to wit.*) At my full county court for N. (*if it was a county court of late sheriff, say* "at the county court of A. B. esquire, late sheriff of the county"), held at A., in the said county, on the —— day of ——, in the —— year of the reign of queen Victoria, before T. B., E. L., T. S., and J. W., four suitors of the said court, amongst other things it is contained thus:

N. (*to wit.*) J. P. complains of G. H., in a plea of taking and unjustly detaining his goods and chattels, to his damage of thirty-nine shillings and eleven pence, and so forth, and there are pledges of prosecution, and also of having a return of the said goods and chattels, if a return thereof shall be adjudged.

Pledges of prosecution { John Doe, Richard Roe.

In witness whereof the said T. B., E. L., T. S., and J. W., four lawful knights of those that were present at that record, have in full court severally put their seals the day and year above said.

(*Seal of office.*) A. B. esquire, sheriff.

T. B. (*L. S.*) E. L., &c.

Transfer of County Court Plaint, to be inserted at the bottom of the List made out by the late Sheriff.

I, A. B., esquire, late sheriff of the county of N., do hereby assign and transfer over unto C. D., esquire, present sheriff of the said county, the actions or plaints above mentioned, as witness my hand and the seal of my late office this —— day of ——, 18—.

A. B. esquire, late sheriff. (*Seal.*)

SECT. 3.

Warrant in Replevin.

N. (*to wit.*) A. B., esquire, sheriff of the county aforesaid, G. C. and I. S. my bailiffs, and to each of them, jointly and severally, greeting: because J. P. hath found me sufficient security, as well for prosecuting his suit with effect against C. D. and E. F., for taking his goods and chattels, to wit (*specifying the goods*), and also for making a return thereof, if return thereof shall be adjudged: Therefore, on behalf of the said J. P., by virtue of my office, I command you and every of you, jointly and severally, without delay, to replevy and deliver to the said J. P. his said goods and chattels, &c., which C. D., esquire, and E. F., took and unjustly detained, as is alleged; and also that you summon the aforesaid C. D. and E. F., that they be at my next county court to be held at A., in and for the said county; and in what manner you shall have executed this precept, certify to me at my next said county court, to be held at the time and place aforesaid: fail not at you peril. Given under my seal of office this —— day of ——, 18—.

(*Seal of office.*) By the sheriff.

Summons thereon.

N. (*to wit.*) By virtue of a warrant from the sheriff of the county of N. to me directed, we summon you to appear at the next county court, to be holden at A., in and for the county aforesaid, to answer J. P. in a plea of taking and unjustly detaining his cattle, goods and chattels. Dated the —— day of ——, 18—.

To C. D. esquire. G. C. / J. S. } bailiffs.

Form of Replevin Bond.

Know all men by these presents, that we, J. P. of N., in the county of N., farmer, and C. B. of H., in the same county, gentleman, and J. H. of D, in the same county, yeoman, are held and firmly bound to A. B., esquire, sheriff of the county of N. aforesaid, in the sum of £—— of good and lawful money of Great Britain, to be paid to the said sheriff, or his certain attorney, executors, administrators, or assigns, for which payment well and truly to be made we bind ourselves, and each of us, our and each of our heirs, executors, and administrators, jointly and severally, firmly, by these presents, sealed with our seals, dated this —— day of ——, in the —— year of the reign of our sovereign lady queen Victoria, and so forth, and in the year of our Lord 18—.

The condition of the above written obligation is such, that, whereas the above named sheriff, by virtue of his office, and upon the complaint of the above bounden J. P., hath delivered and replevied to the said J. P. the cattle, goods and chattels following, (*to wit*): two red steer, one branded steer, (*setting out the whole of the articles, according to the inventory*), which C. D. of ——, in the same county, esquire, and E. F. of —— in the same county, yeoman, took and wrongfully withheld, as he the said J. P. alleges; if, therefore, the said J. P. do appear at the next county court to be holden at A., in the said county, and then and there do prosecute his suit with effect against the said C. D. and E. F., for the taking and withholding of the said cattle, goods and chattels, and do make return thereof, if return thereof shall be adjudged by law; and the said sheriff, his heirs, executors, administrators, and assigns, shall acquit, discharge, and save harmless, against our sovereign lady the queen, and the said C. D. and E. F., of, from, and against all and every thing and things concerning the premises: Then this obligation to be void, or otherwise to be and remain in full force and virtue.

Sealed, &c. in the presence of, &c.

J. P. (*Seal.*)
C. B. (*Seal.*)
J. K. (*Seal.*)

Assignment of Replevin Bond, to be indorsed on the Bond.

Know all men by these presents, that I, A. B., esquire, sheriff of the county of N., have, at the request of the above named C. D., esquire, the avowant, (*or* " the person making cognizance") assigned over unto him, the said C. D., the replevin bond, pursuant to the statute in that case made and provided. In witness whereof I have hereunto set my hand and seal of office this —— day of ——, 18—.

(*Seal of office.*) A. B. esquire, sheriff.

Sealed in the presence of (*two witnesses*).

Precept in the nature of Withernam.

N. (*to wit.*) A. B., esquire, high sheriff of the said county, to all and singular my bailiffs of the said county, greeting: Forasmuch as J. P. hath found me sufficient security, as well to prosecute his plaint against C. D., for taking and unjustly detaining his cattle, goods, and chattels, *to wit*, &c. (*setting out the cattle and goods*), as to make return thereof, if return thereof shall be adjudged; and thereupon, by virtue of my office, I have often commanded you and every of you, that you or some or one of you, should cause to be replevied to the said J. P. his aforesaid cattle, goods and chattels, which the said C. D. hath taken and unjustly detains, as it is said. And you, upon my several precepts of replevin, to you directed as aforesaid, have returned to me that the aforesaid cattle, goods, and chattels, are eloigned to places to you unknown, so that you cannot replevy the same to the said J. P.: therefore I now command you, and every one of you, that you or some or one of you, do take in *withernam* the cattle, goods and chattels of the said C. D., to the value of the said cattle, goods and chattels, so eloigned as aforesaid, and deliver the same to the said J. P. for his cattle, goods and chattels last aforesaid; and also that you put by gages and safe pledges the said C. D., so that he be and appear at my next county court, to be holden at ——, in and for the said county, on the —— day of —— next, to answer to the said J. P. of the plea aforesaid; and that you, or one of you, return an answer to this my mandate, at my next county court. Given under the seal of my office this —— day of ——, 18—.

(*Seal of office.*) By the sheriff.

Warrant on the Writ de Retorno Habendo.

N. (*to wit.*) A. B., esquire, sheriff of the said county, to J. S., my bailiff, greeting: By virtue of her majesty's writ *de retorno habendo*, to me directed and delivered, stating that J. M., lately in her majesty's court, before her majesty's justices at Westminster, was summoned to answer T. J. in a plea why he took the goods and chattels of him the said T., *to wit*, nine stacks, &c., and unjustly detained the same against sureties and pledges, as it is said; and the same T., in her majesty's same court, before her majesty's justices at Westminster, made default, wherefore it was considered in her majesty's same court, before her majesty's justices, that he and his pledges to prosecute should be in mercy; and that the said J. should go thereof without day, and that he should have a return of the goods and chattels aforesaid. Therefore I command you, as by the said writ I am commanded, that without delay you cause the goods and chattels aforesaid to be returned to the aforesaid J., and do not deliver them on the complaint of the said T., without her majesty's writ, which shall make express mention of the judgment aforesaid; and in what manner you shall execute this precept render me an account, so that I may make the same appear to her said majesty's justices at Westminster, on the morrow of the Holy Trinity; and have you this, and so forth. Given under the seal of my office the —— day of ——, 18—.

(*Seal of office.*) By the sheriff.

Return of Bona et Catalla Elongata fuerunt, on the Writ de Retorno Habendo.

I humbly certify the within justices, that, before the coming of this writ to me directed, the goods and chattels within mentioned were conveyed away by the within named T. J. to places to me unknown; wherefore the said goods and chattels to the within named J. M. I cannot cause to be returned, as I am within commanded.

The answer of A. B. esquire, sheriff.

Return to the foregoing Writ de Retorno Habendo, where the whole of the Goods are returned.

I humbly certify the within justices, that I have caused the goods and chattels within mentioned to be returned to the within J. M., as I am commanded.

The answer of A. B. esquire, sheriff.

Return to the foregoing Writ de Retorno Habendo, where part of the Goods were returned and part eloigned.

I humbly certify the within justices, that I have caused one stack of oats, &c., part of the goods and chattels within mentioned, to be returned to the within named J. M., as I am within commanded; and I also humbly certify the said justices, that, before the coming of this writ to me directed, the rest of the goods and chattels within mentioned were conveyed away by the within named T. J. to places to me unknown, wherefore I cannot cause the same to be returned to the said J. M., as I am within commanded.

A. B. esquire, sheriff.

Warrant on the Writ of Second Deliverance.

N. (*to wit.*) A. B., esquire, sheriff of the said county, to J. S., my bailiff, greeting: By virtue of her majesty's writ of second deliverance, to me directed and delivered, I command you, as by the said writ I am commanded, that without delay you cause nine stacks, &c., which J. M., lately in her majesty's court, before her majesty's justices at Westminster, were adjudged, by the default of T. J., to be delivered to the said J. M., and that you put by sureties and safe pledges the said J. M., that he be before her majesty's justices at Westminster, on the morrow of All Souls, to answer to the said J. T. of the taking and unjustly detaining the goods and chattels aforesaid; and have you this, and the names of the pledges, and so forth. Given under the seal of my office this —— day of ——, 18—.

(*Seal of office.*) By the sheriff.

Return of the Writ of Second Deliverance, where the Goods are delivered.

By virtue of this writ to me directed, I have caused to be delivered to the within-named T. J. the goods and chattels within mentioned, as I am within commanded to do. The pledges are John Doe and Richard Roe.

The answer of A. B., esquire, sheriff.

Return, when part only of the Goods could be delivered.

By virtue of this writ to me directed, I have caused to be delivered to the within-named T. J. part of one rick of hay, part of the goods and chattels within mentioned, being all of the said goods and chattels which are to be found in my bailiwick. The pledges are John Doe and Richard Roe.

The answer of A. B., esquire, sheriff.

Bond to be taken before issuing Warrant on a Writ of Second Deliverance.

Know all men by these presents, that we, T. J., of ——, in the county of N., and ——, are held and firmly bound to A. B., esquire, sheriff of the county of N. aforesaid, in the sum of £——, of lawful money of Great Britain, to be paid to the said sheriff, or his certain attorney, executors, administrators, and assigns, for which payment, to be well and truly made, we bind ourselves, and each of us, and each and every of our heirs, executors, and administrators, jointly and severally, firmly by these presents. Sealed with our seals. Dated this —— day of ——, in the —— year of the reign of our sovereign lady Queen Victoria, and in the year of our Lord 18—.

The Condition of the above Bond, when part only of the Goods could be delivered.

The condition of the above-written obligation is such, that whereas the above-named sheriff, by virtue of her majesty's writ *de retorno habendo*, did cause one stack of oats, &c., and part of nine stacks, &c. in the said writ mentioned, to be returned to J. M., in the said writ named; the rest of the said goods and chattels being, before the coming of the said writ to the said sheriff, conveyed away by the above-bounden T. J. to places to the said sheriff unknown, wherefore he could not cause the same to be returned to the said J. M., as by the said writ he was commanded: and whereas the above-named sheriff, by virtue of her majesty's writ of second deliverance, hath delivered to the above-bounden T. J. the said one stack, &c.: if, therefore, the above-bounden T. J. shall prosecute his complaint according to the tenor of second deliverance, and shall make return of the said nine stacks, &c., if a return thereof shall be adjudged, and the said sheriff, his heirs, executors, and administrators, shall acquit, &c. &c., as *ante*, 537. (*The same where all the goods are delivered.*)

Return to a Writ of Inquiry under the stat. Car. II. c. 17, sect. 2 (m).

The condition of the above-written obligation is such, that whereas the above-named sheriff, by virtue of her majesty's writ of second deliverance to him directed and delivered, hath delivered to the above-bounden T. J. the goods and chattels following; to wit, nine stacks of oats, &c., which

(*m*) Fifteen days' notice should be given of executing a writ of inquiry.

to J. M., lately in her majesty's court, before her majesty's justices at Westminster, were adjudged by the default of the said T. J. If, therefore, the above-bounden T. J. shall prosecute his complaint according to the tenor of the said writ, and shall make return of the said goods and chattels, if a return thereof shall be adjudged, and the said sheriff, his heirs, executors, and administrators, shall acquit, indemnify, and save harmless, against our sovereign lady the queen, and also against the said J. M., of, from and against all and every thing and things concerning the premises, then the above written obligation to be void, otherwise to remain in full force and virtue. (*Seal.*)

Sealed and delivered, &c. (*Seal.*)

(*Seal.*)

The execution of this writ appears in the inquisition hereunto annexed.

Inquisition.

N. (*to wit.*) An inquisition indented, taken at the house of ——, called or known by the name or sign of ——, in the said county of ——, on the —— day of ——, in the —— year of the reign, &c., before A. B., esquire, sheriff of the county aforesaid, by virtue of a writ of our said lady the queen, to the said sheriff directed, and to this inquisition annexed, to inquire of certain matters in the said writ specified by the oath of (*the names of the jurors*), honest and lawful men of the said county, who upon their oath say, that the sum of £——, of the yearly rent in the said writ mentioned, was in arrear and unpaid from the said J. P. to the said C. D. at the time of the taking and distraining the cattle, goods, and chattels in the said writ also mentioned; and that the cattle, goods and chattels were then worth, according to their true value, the sum of ——. In witness whereof as well I the said sheriff, as the said jurors, have set our seals to this inquisition the day and year and place above mentioned.

CHAP. XIX.—Sect. 1.

Precept to the returning officer of a borough, on a general election.

N. (*to wit.*) A. B., esquire, sheriff of the said county, to the mayor of the borough of S., in the said county, greeting: Know, that I have received a certain writ of our lady the queen, to me directed, the tenor whereof followeth (*here copy the writ verbatim*): therefore, by virtue of the said writ, I require that you forthwith cause two burgesses to be elected for the said borough, according to the command of the said writ; and how this my warrant shall be executed you shall make known to me immediately after the said election made, so that I may certify the same, together with the said writ and this precept, to our lady the queen, in her chancery, forthwith. Hereof fail not. Given under the seal of my office. Dated the —— day of ——, 18—.

A. B., sheriff.

(*To be indorsed when received.*)

Received this —— day of ——, 18—, from the sheriff of N., by the hands of Mr. O. D., at twelve o'clock at noon.

C. D.

(*To be indorsed when returned.*)

The execution of this precept appears in the schedule hereunto annexed.

C. D., mayor.

CHAP. XIX. SECT. 1.

Notice of the election.

Borough of S., ——, 18—.

In pursuance of a precept received from the sheriff of the county of N. for electing two burgesses to serve in the ensuing parliament for this borough, I do hereby give notice, that I shall proceed to election accordingly, on Thursday, the —— day of —— instant, at nine of the clock in the forenoon, in the town-hall of the same borough; when and where all persons concerned are to give their attendance.

A. B., mayor (or bailiff).

SECT. 2.

Bribery oath. (2 Geo. 2, c. 24; 43 Geo. 3, c. 74.)

I, A. B., do swear, that I have not directly or indirectly received any sum or sums of money, office, place, or employment, gratuity, or reward, or any bond, bill, or note, or any promise or gratuity whatsoever, either by myself or any other person to my use or benefit or advantage, for making my return at the present election of members to serve in parliament, and that I will return such person or persons as shall to the best of my judgment appear to have the majority of legal votes.

Declaration of qualification by candidate.(2 Vict. c. 48, s. 3).

I, A. B., do solemnly and sincerely declare, that I am, to the best of my knowledge and belief, duly qualified to be elected as a member of the House of Commons, according to the true intent and meaning of the act passed in the second year of the reign of Queen Victoria, intituled "An Act to amend the Laws relating to the Qualification of Members to serve in Parliament," and that my qualification to be so elected doth arise out of (*here let the party state the nature of his qualification, as the case may be; if the same ariseth out of lands, tenements or hereditaments, let him state the barony or baronies, parish or parishes, township or townships, precinct or precincts, and also county or counties, in which such lands, tenements or hereditaments are situate, and also the estate in the said lands, tenements or hereditaments, or in the rents or profits thereof, of or to which he is seised or entitled; or if the same ariseth out of personal estate or effects, let him state of what nature and where situate such personal estate or effects are, and what interest he hath in such personal estate or effects, and upon what securities and in whose names the same are vested*) as hereunder set forth.

Certificate of declaration. (Id. s. 4.)

I do hereby certify, that C. D., one of the candidates for the Eastern Division of the county of C., being first duly requested in writing in that behalf, such request being made and signed by A. B., one of the candidates at the said election (*or* "by C. and D., being two registered electors having respectively a right to vote at the said election"), did on the —— day of ——, 18—, before me, duly authorized in that behalf, make and subscribe a declaration, that he to the best of his knowledge and belief was duly qualified to be elected as a member of the House of Commons, according to the true intent and meaning of the act passed in the second year of the reign of Queen Victoria, intituled "An Act to amend the Laws relating to the Qualification of Members to serve in Parliament."

Sir G. M., bart., high sheriff.

Questions to be put to

1. Are you the same person whose name appears as A. B. on the register of voters now in force for the county of —— (*or* "for the ——

riding, parts or division of the county of ——," *or* "for the city" *or* "borough of ——," *as the case may be*)? CHAP. XIX. SECT. II.

2. Have you already voted either here or elsewhere at this election for the county of —— (*or* "for the —— riding, parts or division of the county of ——," *or* "for the city" *or* "borough of ——," *as the case may be*)? voter. (6 & 7 Vict. c. 18, s. 81.)

Return for a county.

This indenture (*n*), made in the full county of N., holden at A., in and for the said county, on Wednesday, the —— day of ——, in the —— year of the reign of our sovereign lady Victoria, by the grace of God of the united kingdom of Great Britain and Ireland queen, defender of the faith, and so forth, and in the year of our Lord 18—, between A. B., esquire, sheriff of the said county, of the one part, and C. D., E. F., &c., and many other persons of the county aforesaid, and electors of knights to parliament for the said county, of the other part; witnesseth, that proclamation being made by the said sheriff, by virtue of and according to a writ of our sovereign lady the queen, directed to the said sheriff and hereunto annexed, for the electing of two knights, of the most fit and discreet of the said county, girt with swords, to serve in a certain parliament to be holden at the city of Westminster, on the —— day of —— next ensuing: the said parties to these presents, together with the major part of the electors for the county aforesaid, present in the full county of N., at A. aforesaid, on the day of the date hereof, by virtue of the said writ, and according to the force and effect of divers statutes in that case made and provided, have, in the said full county of N., by unanimous assent and consent, freely and indifferently elected and chosen two knights, of the most fit and discreet of the said county, girt with swords, to wit, Sir G. S., baronet, and H. D., of, &c., esquire, to be knights to the said parliament so to be holden at the day and place in that behalf hereinbefore mentioned, for the commonalty of the county of N.; giving and granting to the aforesaid knights full and sufficient power, for themselves and the commonalty of the same county, to do and consent to those things which, in the said parliament, by the common council of the kingdom of our said lady the queen (by the blessing of God), shall happen to be ordained upon the affairs in the said writ specified. In witness whereof the parties to these presents have interchangeably put their hands and seals, the day, year and place first above written.

Oath of allegiance.

I, A. B., do sincerely promise and swear, that I will be faithful and bear true allegiance to her majesty Queen Victoria.

So help me God.

Oath of supremacy.

I, G. M., do swear that I do from my heart abhor, detest and abjure, as impious and heretical, that damnable doctrine and position, that princes excommunicated or deprived by the Pope, or any authority from the see of Rome, may be deprived or murdered by their subjects or any other whatsoever: And I do declare that no foreign prince, person, prelate, state or potentate hath or ought to have any jurisdiction, power, superiority, pre-eminence, or authority, ecclesiastical or spiritual, within this realm.

So help me God.

(*n*) To be engrossed on the usual stamp for deeds.

CHAP. XIX. SECT. II.

Oath of abjuration. (6 G. 3, c. 53.)

I, A. B., do truly and sincerely acknowledge, profess, testify and declare in my conscience, before God and the world, that our sovereign lady Queen Victoria is lawful and rightful queen of this realm, and all other her majesty's dominions thereunto belonging: And I do solemnly and sincerely declare, that I do believe in my conscience, that not any of the descendants of the person who pretended to be Prince of Wales during the life of the late King James the Second, and since his decease pretended to be and took upon himself the style and title of King of England, by the name of James the Third, or of Scotland by the name of James the Eighth, or the style and title of King of Great Britain, hath any right or title whatsoever to the crown of this realm, or any other the dominions thereunto belonging: and I do renounce, refuse and abjure any allegiance or obedience to any of them. And I do swear, that I will bear faith and true allegiance to her majesty Queen Victoria, and her will defend to the utmost of my power against all traitorous conspiracies and attempts whatsoever which shall be made against her person, crown or dignity. And I will do my utmost endeavour to disclose and make known to her majesty and her successors, all treasons and traitorous conspiracies which I shall know to be against her or any of them. And I do faithfully promise, to the utmost of my power, to support, maintain, and defend the succession of the crown against the descendants of the said James, and against all other persons whatsoever; which succession, by an act, intituled "An Act for the further Limitation of the Crown, and better securing the Rights and Liberties of the Subjects," is and stands limited to the Princess Sophia, Electoress and Duchess dowager of Hanover, and the heirs of her body, being Protestants. And all these things I do plainly and sincerely acknowledge and swear, according to these express words by me spoken, and according to the plain and common sense and understanding of the same words, without any equivocation, mental evasion or secret reservation whatsoever. And I do make this recognition, acknowledgment, abjuration, renunciation and promise, heartily, willingly, and truly, upon the true faith of a Christian.

So help me God.

Declaration or affirmation to be made by Quakers, instead of the oath of abjuration.

(*o*) I, A. B., do most solemnly, sincerely and truly acknowledge, profess, testify and declare, that Queen Victoria is lawful and rightful queen of this realm, and of all other her dominions and countries thereunto belonging; and I do solemnly and sincerely declare, that I do believe that not any of the descendants of the person who pretended to be Prince of Wales during the life of the late King James the Second, and since his decease pretended to be and took upon himself the style and title of King of England, by the name of James the Third, or of Scotland by the name of James the Eighth, or the style and title of King of Great Britain, hath any right or title whatsoever to the crown of this realm, or any other the dominions thereunto belonging; and I do renounce and refuse any allegiance or obedience to any of them. And I do solemnly promise, that I will be true and faithful and bear true allegiance to Queen Victoria, and to her will be faithful against all treacherous conspiracies and attempts

(*o*) By the 8 Geo. 1, c. 6, Quakers were allowed to take the effect of the abjuration oath, according to the form therein prescribed; but when the oath of abjuration was altered by the 6 Geo. 3, c. 53, on the death of the Pretender, no provision was made for altering the Quaker's affirmation or declaration conformable thereto. The form, however, will be as here given.

whatsoever which shall be made against her person, crown or dignity. And I will do my best endeavour to disclose and make known to Queen Victoria and her successors all treasons and traitorous conspiracies which I shall know to be against her or any of them. And I will be true and faithful to the succession of the crown against the descendants of the said James, and against all other persons whatsoever, as the same is and stands settled by an act, intituled "An Act declaring the Rights and Liberties of the Subject, and settling the Succession of the Crown to the late Queen Anne, and the heirs of her body, being Protestants;" and as the same, by one other act, intituled "An Act for the further Limitation of the Crown, and better securing the Rights and Liberties of the Subject," is and stands settled and entailed, after the decease of the said late Queen, and for default of issue of the said late Queen, to the late Princess Sophia, Electoress and Duchess Dowager of Hanover, and the heirs of her body, being Protestants. And all these things I do plainly and sincerely acknowledge, promise and declare, according to these express words by me spoken, and according to the plain and common sense and understanding of the same words, without any equivocation, mental evasion or secret reservation whatsoever. And I do make this recognition, acknowledgment, renunciation, and promise, heartily, willingly and truly.

Roman Catholic's oath. (10 Geo. 4, c. 7.)

I, G. M., do sincerely promise and swear that I will be faithful and bear true allegiance to her majesty Queen Victoria, and will defend her to the utmost of my power against all conspiracies and attempts whatever which shall be made against her person, crown or dignity; and I will do my utmost endeavour to declare and make known to her majesty, her heirs and successors, all treasons and traitorous conspiracies which may be formed against her or them: And I do faithfully promise to maintain, support, and defend, to the utmost of my power, the succession of the crown, which succession, by an act intituled "An Act for the further Limitation of the Crown and better securing the Rights and Liberties of the Subject," is and stands limited to the Princess Sophia, Electress of Hanover, and the heirs of her body, being Protestants; hereby utterly renouncing and abjuring any obedience or allegiance unto any other person claiming or pretending a right to the crown of this realm: And I do further declare that it is not an article of my faith, and that I do renounce, reject and abjure the opinion, that princes excommunicated or deprived by the Pope or any other authority of the see of Rome may be deposed or murdered by their subjects, or any person whatsoever: And I do declare that I do not believe that the Pope of Rome or any other foreign prince, prelate, person, state, or potentate, hath or ought to have any temporal or civil jurisdiction, power, superiority, or pre-eminence, directly or indirectly, within this realm. I do swear that I will defend, to the utmost of my power, the settlement of property within this realm, as established by the laws: And I do hereby disclaim, disavow, and solemnly abjure any intention to subvert the present Church Establishment, as settled by law within this realm: And I do solemnly swear that I never will exercise any privilege to which I am or may become entitled, to disturb or weaken the Protestant religion or Protestant government in the united kingdom: And I do solemnly, in the presence of God, profess, testify and declare, that I do make this declaration, and every part thereof, in the plain and ordinary sense of the words of this oath, without any evasion, equivocation or mental reservation whatsoever. So help me God.

CHAP. XX.

Notice of the time for electing a Coroner.

The sheriff of N. will proceed to the election of a coroner for the said county, in the room of E. F., esquire, deceased, at the county court, to be held at —— by adjournment, on Wednesday the —— day of —— next, at ten o'clock in the forenoon of the same day, at which time and place the freeholders of the said county are desired to attend.

A. B. esquire, sheriff.

Return to a Writ De Coronatore eligendo.

By virtue of this writ to me directed, in my full county court, held (by adjournment) at A., in the county of N., on the —— day —— in the year within written, by the assent of the same county, I have caused E. H., esquire, to be chosen coroner in the place of the within named E. F., deceased, which said E. H., as the manner is, hath taken his corporal oath to do and keep those things which to the office of coroner in the said county doth belong, as I am within commanded.

The answer of A. B. esquire, sheriff.

CHAP. XXI.

Warrant on an Exchequer Attachment.

N. (*to wit.*) A. B., esquire, sheriff of the said county, to J. S., my bailiff, greeting: By virtue of her majesty's writ to me directed and delivered, I command you that you omit not by reason of any liberty in my county, but that you enter the same, and attach C. D., if he shall be found in my bailiwick, and him safely keep, so that I may have his body before the barons of her majesty's exchequer at Westminster, on ——, to answer her majesty concerning divers trespasses, contempts, and offences by him lately done and committed. And have you this, and so forth. Given under the seal of my office this —— day of ——, 18—.

(*Seal of office.*) By the sheriff.

(*Indorsed.*)

Mr. I. K., solicitor for the plaintiff, at the suit of T. P. in the office of pleas: the writ issued on the —— day of ——, 18—.

N. B.—Take no bail-bond whatever, unless the plaintiff or his solicitor desires you to do so, and approves of the sureties, under his hand.

Warrant upon an Attachment out of Chancery, with Proclamations.

N. (*to wit.*) A. B., esquire, sheriff of the said county, to ——, keeper of the gaol of the said county, and also to E. F., my bailiff, greeting: By virtue of her majesty's writ to me directed and delivered, I command you do, in her majesty's behalf, make public proclamation in the town of H., within my bailiwick, that A. M., otherwise S., do, upon his allegiance, within eight days of St. Hilary next ensuing, personally appear before her majesty, in her majesty's Court of Chancery, wheresoever it shall then be, and, nevertheless, in the meantime, if you can find the said A. M., otherwise S., attach him so that I may have him before her majesty, in her majesty's said court, at the time before mentioned, there to answer to her majesty, as well touching a contempt which he, as it is alleged, committed against her majesty, as touching those things which shall be then and there laid to his charge, and to perform and abide such order as her majesty's said court shall make in this behalf; and hereof fail not; and have you this, and so forth. Given under the seal of my office this —— day of ——, 18—.

(*Seal of office.*) By the sheriff.

For not answering at the suit of R. S., esquire, plaintiff. The writ is tested the —— day of ——, 18—. T. Clerk.

Return of Non est Inventus, on an an Attachment out of Chancery.

I humbly certify our sovereign lady the queen within written, that the within named C. D. is not found in my bailiwick.

A. B. esquire, sheriff.

If two Defendants.

That the within named C. D. and G. H. are not, nor is either (*if more than two, for* " either,") *say* " any" of them found in my bailiwick.

Non est Inventus as to one Defendant, and Cepi Corpus as to another.

That the within named C. D. is not found in my bailiwick; and I further certify that the within named C. D. hath been attached, and his body is now in my custody.

Return to an Attachment for non-appearance out of Chancery, where the Defendant is in Gaol at other Suits.

By virtue of this writ to me directed, I humbly certify to our lady the queen within written, that I have taken the body of the within named C. D., and him in the prison of our sovereign lady the queen I have safe in my custody; but because he is charged with divers other actions, I cannot have his body ready before our said lady the queen, at the day and place within contained, without a writ of *habeas corpus cum causâ* to me in that behalf to be directed.

A. B. esquire, sheriff.

Return of an Attachment out of Chancery, with Proclamations, Non est Inventus.

By virtue of this writ to me directed, I humbly certify to our lady the queen within written, that I have caused proclamation to be made in all and singular the places in the said writ contained, according to the form and effect of the said writ, as it is therein to me commanded; and I do further humbly certify to our said lady the queen, that the within C. D. is not found in my bailiwick.

A. B. esquire, sheriff.

Writ of Ne Exeat Regno.

Victoria, &c. To the sheriff of N., greeting: Whereas it is represented unto us, in our Court of Chancery, on the part of R. R., complainant, against C. D., defendant, amongst other things, that he the said defendant is greatly indebted to the said complainant, and designs quickly to go

CHAP. XXI.

into parts beyond the seas, as by oath made in that behalf appears, which tends to the great prejudice and damage of the said complainant. Therefore, in order to prevent this injustice, we do hereby command you that you do, without delay, cause the said C. D. personally to come before you, and give sufficient bail or security in the sum of 300*l.*, that he the said C. D. will not go or attempt to go into parts beyond seas, without leave of our said court. And in case the said C. D. shall refuse to give such bail or security, then you are to commit him the said C. D. to our next prison, there to be kept in safe custody until he shall do it of his own accord; and when you have taken such security, you are forthwith to make and return a certificate thereof to us in our said Court of Chancery, distinctly and plainly, under your seal, together with this writ. Witness ourself at Westminster, the —— day ——, in the year of our reign.

Warrant thereon.

N. (*to wit.*) A. B., esquire, sheriff of the county aforesaid, to the keeper of the gaol of the said county, and also to J. L., my bailiff, greeting: By virtue of her majesty's writ to me directed and delivered, I command you, jointly and severally, that you or either of you forthwith arrest the body of C. D., and him safely keep until he finds sufficient bail or security in the sum of 300*l.*, that he will not go or attempt to go into parts beyond seas, without leave of her majesty's Court of Chancery; and in case he refuses so to do, I command you or the one of you that you commit him to her majesty's next prison within my bailiwick, there to be kept in my custody, until he shall do it of his own accord, and have you this, and so forth. Given under the seal of my office this —— day of ——, 18—.

(*Seal of office.*) By the sheriff.

Take security in the sum of 300*l.*

Fees on a Writ Ne Exeat Regno.

	£	s.	d.
Warrant	0	6	8
Return	0	11	8
	£0	18	4

Three shillings is the fee upon a common warrant; and 6*s*. 8*d*. when the writ is of a special or uncommon nature.

Return to a Writ of Ne Exeat Regno, where a Defendant is not to be found.

I humbly certify that the within named C. D. is not found in my bailiwick.

A. B. esquire, sheriff.

Return to the same Writ, where Defendant has been arrested, and given security.

I humbly certify, that I have caused the within named C. D. personally to come before me, and he hath found bail in the sum of 300*l.*, according to the command of the within named writ. Given under the seal of my office.

(*Seal of office.*) (*a*) A. B. esquire, sheriff.

Return to the same Writ, when the Defendant has been arrested, and on refusing to find bail is committed.

I humbly certify, that I have caused the within named C. D. personally to come before me, and he having refused to give the bail or security within mentioned, I have his body in the prison of our lady the queen under my custody.

A. B. esquire, sheriff.

Warrant on a Writ de Excommunicato Capiendo.

N. (*to wit.*) A. B., esquire, sheriff of the county aforesaid, to J. S. and T. P., my bailiffs, greeting: The right reverend Father in God Edward, by divine providence bishop of Durham, having signified unto our sovereign lady the queen by the said bishop's letters patent, that T. G., master of arts, surrogate, lawfully appointed of William W., doctor of laws, vicar-general, and official principal of the consistorial court of Durham, lawfully constituted, in a certain cause of defamation or slander, and merely spiritual, depending before him, rightly and duly proceeding between W. E. of, &c. in my county and diocese of Durham, gentleman, the party agent and complainant, of the one part, and H. D., of the same parish, county, and diocese, blacksmith, the party defendant, and late of, &c. of the other part, did, at the petition of the proctor of the said W. E., decree the said H. D., for his manifest contempt and contumacy, in not appearing before the said surrogate, at a certain competent day, time, and place to him in this behalf appointed and long since elapsed, to answer the said William E. in the aforesaid cause, being lawfully and peremptorily cited thereto, three times publicly called, long and sufficiently expected, and in no wise appearing, but contumaciously absenting himself, to be excommunicated, and is by the ordinary authority of the same bishop excommunicated, nor will he submit to the justice of ecclesiastical censure; but forasmuch as the royal power ought not to be wanting to the holy church in its complaints, I do, by virtue of her majesty's writ, to me directed and delivered, command you, or the one of you, to attach the said H. D. by his body, according to the custom of England, until he shall have made satisfaction to the holy church, as well for the contempt as for the injury by him done unto it, so that I may notify unto our said lady the queen how the said writ shall be executed on the morrow of the Holy Trinity, wheresoever her majesty shall then be in England, that her majesty may cause further to be done in the premises, what of right and according to the form of the statute in this case made and provided shall be meet to be done: and have you this, and so forth. Given under the seal of my office this —— day of ——, 18—.

(*Seal of office.*) By the sheriff.

(*a*) The writ requires, when bail is taken, that it shall be certified under seal.

INDEX.

A.

B.

I.

L.

M.

O.

P.

Q.

R.

T.

LONDON:
C. ROWORTH AND SONS, PRINTERS,
BELL YARD, TEMPLE BAR.